kôhkominawak otâcimowiniwâwa

ᑰᐦᑯᒥᓇᐘᐠ ᐅᑖᒋᒧᐏᓂᐚᐘ

Our Grandmothers' Lives as Told in Their Own Words

OUR OWN WORDS 3

kôhkominawak otâcimowiniwâwa

ᑰᐦᑯᒥᓇᐘᐠ ᐅᑖᒋᒧᐏᓂᐚᐘ

Our Grandmothers' Lives as Told in Their Own Words

Cree texts edited and translated by

Freda Ahenakew and H.C. Wolfart

New Foreword by Arok Wolvengrey

FIRST NATIONS UNIVERSITY OF CANADA

SIFC

NOTE: All royalties are paid to Rae-ann Wahobin in trust for the Freda Ahenakew Education Fund.

Printed and bound in Canada at Imprimerie Gauvin. The text of this book is printed on 100% post-consumer recycled paper with earth-friendly vegetable-based inks.

COVER AND TEXT DESIGN: Duncan Noel Campbell
PROOFREADERS: Arok Wolvengrey, Kelly Laycock, and Jellyn Ayudan
COVER PHOTO: Courtesy of the Ahenakew-Greyeyes Family

Library and Archives Canada Cataloguing in Publication

TITLE: kôhkominawak otâcimowiniwâwa = Our grandmothers' lives as told in their own words / Cree texts edited and translated by Freda Ahenakew and H.C. Wolfart ; foreword by Arok Wolvengrey.

OTHER TITLES: Our grandmothers' lives as told in their own words

NAMES: Ahenakew, Freda, 1932-2011, editor, translator. | Wolfart, H. Christoph, editor, translator. | Wolvengrey, Arok, 1965- writer of foreword.

SERIES: Our own words ; 3.

DESCRIPTION: Series statement: Our own words ; 3 | Cree syllabics in title not transcribed. | Includes bibliographical references. | Text in original Cree and in English translation. Introductory materials in English.

IDENTIFIERS: Canadiana (print) 20230489796 | Canadiana (ebook) 20230489869 | ISBN 9780889779495 (softcover) | ISBN 9780889779525 (hardcover) | ISBN 9780889779501 (PDF) | ISBN 9780889779518 (EPUB)

SUBJECTS: LCSH: Cree women—Saskatchewan—Interviews. | LCSH: Cree women—Saskatchewan—Biography. | LCSH: Cree women—Alberta—Interviews. | LCSH: Cree women—Alberta—Biography. | LCSH: Cree language— Texts. | LCGFT: Interviews. | LCGFT: Autobiographies.

CLASSIFICATION: LCC E99.C88 K65 2023 | DDC 971.24004/97323—dc23

10 9 8 7 6 5 4 3 2 1

University of Regina Press

University of Regina, Regina, Saskatchewan, Canada, S4S 0A2
TEL: (306) 585-4758 FAX: (306) 585-4699
WEB: www.uofrpress.ca

We acknowledge the support of the Canada Council for the Arts for our publishing program. We acknowledge the financial support of the Government of Canada. / Nous reconnaissons l'appui financier du gouvernement du Canada. This publication was made possible with support from Creative Saskatchewan's Book Publishing Production Grant Program.

Canada Council for the Arts Conseil des arts du Canada
Canada
CREATIVE SASKATCHEWAN

Contents

Foreword

Arok Wolvengrey

It is a great pleasure and an honour to include ***kôhkominawak otâcimowiniwâwa*** in the Our Own Words series, and to introduce it to a new generation. Though it serves as the third volume of our current series, it is in many ways the first, and the inspiration for Our Own Words, in name and content. This new edition also allows us to pay tribute to the late Dr. Freda Ahenakew and the extraordinary work that she did in service to her language, ***nêhiyawêwin***, her cultural identity, ***nêhiyâwiwin***, and her people, the ***nêhiyawak***.

Among the many recordings that Freda made with Cree Elders throughout the 1980s (particularly between 1987 and 1990), those gathered in *kôhkominawak* formed the second major set of texts to reach publication. This was also the first set fully produced by the wonderful and productive partnership between Freda and Dr. H.C. Wolfart, both mentors of mine. As a student, I apprenticed with them, and particularly with Freda, on one part of this volume, the *Reminiscences* text of Chapter 9. I was thus able to observe (and hopefully learn from) the meticulous care that they took with the entire process of recording, transcription, and translation, not to mention the editing, and re-editing, and final editing that is needed to bring a volume of this quality to publication. A glimpse of this can be seen in the Introduction and Notes sections, but we see it most clearly in the presentation of the texts, to which we have strived to do justice in this new edition.

Preceding all of this material, you will find Freda's wonderfully personal introductions to the grandmothers whose stories, narration, and conversation fill this volume with wisdom and humour and history. And yet, there is no introduction to Freda herself; one more thing that this new edition allows us to address. Thus, the daunting responsibility of providing even a beginning of such an introduction falls to her unworthy student. In advance, I beg forgiveness for all I may fail to say about this remarkable woman and her accomplishments.

• • • •

IRENE FREDA AHENAKEW was born on Ahtahkakohp First Nation to Edward and Annie (née Bird) Ahenakew, joining the prodigious Ahenakew family, descendants of Ahenakew himself, brother of Chief Ahtahkakoop (*atâhk-akohp*). Freda was thus also the grandniece – or more appropriately *ôsisima* – to the Reverend Canon Edward Ahenakew who made his own tremendous contribution to Cree language maintenance. This included his own publications, such as *Voices of the Plains Cree*, his long-running series of syllabic newsletters titled the *Cree Monthly Guide* (ᓀᐦᐃᔭᐤ ᐅᑭᐢᑭᓄᐦᑕᐦᐃᑯᐃᐧᐣ / *nêhiyaw okiskinohtahikowin*), and his contribution as editor of the Plains Cree material in Watkins and Faries' revised 1938 edition of *A Dictionary of the Cree Language*. Obviously, *omosôma* Edward was a model and inspiration in many ways for the work that Freda would ultimately take on.

Following her early education, which included high school for a time at the St. Albans Indian Residential School in Prince Albert and Prince Albert Collegiate Institute, she married Harold Greyeyes of Muskeg Lake Cree Nation (*maskêko-sâkahikanihk*) and began raising her own formidable family. This included her twelve children: Dolores Greyeyes Sand, Brenda Ahenakew, Barbara Ahenakew, Harold (Hal) Greyeyes, Judy Greyeyes, Elaine Greyeyes, Lawrence (Boss) Greyeyes, Gloria Greyeyes, (the late) Kevin Greyeyes, Spencer (Duke) Greyeyes, Nancy Greyeyes, and Josephine (Jo)

Greyeyes. Ultimately, it would also include many others adopted in the traditional way, including Linda Fidler, Chief Daryl Watson, and three of her non-Indigenous students and colleagues, Eric Tang, Arden Ogg, and the present writer, Arok Wolvengrey.

Though Freda's eldest children were initially raised with the Cree language, advice from school administrators quickly led to an increased use of English within the family. This was ultimately a source of some regret to Freda, but also an added inspiration in her future work championing *nêhiyawêwin*. Before her youngest children had even begun their formal schooling, she joined her eldest nine on the school bus, returning to classes and completing her own interrupted high school education in 1969. From there, she worked as education liaison for the Federation of Saskatchewan Indian Nations (FSIN, now Federation of Sovereign Indigenous Nations), which in turn led to the University of Saskatchewan for a Bachelor's Degree in Education (1979). Teaching positions in northern Saskatchewan and Saskatoon followed, including some time at the Saskatchewan Indian Cultural Center (SICC), where she was further inspired by Ida Mcleod, another Cree language champion. This led Freda to the Master's program in Linguistics at the University of Manitoba under the supervision of H.C. Wolfart, who would become her colleague in the production of so many of the resources that she would produce in her lifetime, and indeed beyond.

As part of her graduate work, Freda recorded Peter Vandall and Joe Douquette narrating the texts that would be published as *wâskahikaniwiyiniwak otâcimowiniwâwa / Stories of the House People*. The success of this project would set her on her path of creating a written literature for *nêhiyawêwin*, one that continues to bear fruit through the dedication of H.C. Wolfart and many of Freda's children and students (and "grandstudents" and "great-grandstudents," etc.).

Upon completing her M.A., Freda returned to Saskatoon to teach at the University of Saskatchewan and become director of the Saskatchewan Indian Languages Institute (1985–1989). It was at this time and through these two roles that I had the great fortune to take classes with Freda. In pursuit of my own M.A. in

Linguistics, I would eventually follow her to Winnipeg when she returned to teach Cree as a faculty member of the Native Studies Department at the University of Manitoba. There, the partnership of Ahenakew and Wolfart flourished anew and the original version of *kôhkominawak* became the first of an astounding seven volumes of Cree texts. The magnitude of this accomplishment cannot be overstated, as anyone who has attempted even a single such volume will understand.

With additional titles still moving towards publication, Freda retired from teaching in 1996, and from her research in 1997, due to health issues, but she continued to enjoy an exceptionally rich family life, adored by her children, grandchildren, and great-grandchildren who continue to perpetuate reverence for her memory in each new generation. Meanwhile, her work continued to inspire so many of us, and to garner many well-deserved accolades. She was awarded an honorary doctorate from the University of Saskatchewan in 1997 and was named to the Order of Canada in 1998. She received a National Aboriginal Achievement (now Indspire) Award in Education in 2001, was awarded the Saskatchewan Order of Merit in 2005, and a second honorary doctorate, from the University of Manitoba, in 2009. In 2016, a branch of the Saskatoon Public Library was posthumously named in her honour. On April 8, 2011, she passed on to join her ancestors, surrounded by the love of her family.

• • • •

AND THIS RETURNS us to our own attempt to honour the memory of Dr. Freda Ahenakew and the love she had for her family and her language. Although the words in this volume are largely those of other grandmothers, none of them could have been presented in this way without the tireless dedication of this most remarkable Cree woman. To her children and descendants, including those not yet born, to all of those she taught, and to those who continue to pass her inspiration on to future generations, this volume is dedicated.

ninanâskomimâwa kahkiyaw anihi kâ-âhkami-pimitisahamiyit *Freda* otatoskêwin. mitoni ninanâskomimâwa *H.C. Wolfart*a kâ-kî-miyo-wîc-âtoskêmikot *Freda* êkosi ka-kaskihtâyahk ka-âhkami-kiskinwahamâkosiyahk. mitoni mistahi ninanâskomâwak nimisak, *Dolores* êkwa *Arden*, ê-wîcihicik kwayask ôma ka-masinahamân. êkwa wâwîs mîna, nikâwîpan *Freda*: kâkikê kika-nanâskomitin êkwa kâkikê mîna kâkikê kika-sâkihitin.

Arok Wolvengrey
pâskâwêhowi-pîsim, 2023

ANNOTATED BIBLIOGRAPHY OF THE WORKS OF DR. FREDA AHENAKEW

Text Collections

Ahenakew, Freda, ed. 1986. *kiskinahamawâkan-âcimowinisa / Student Stories*. Written by Cree-speaking students. Memoir 2. Winnipeg: Algonquian and Iroquoian Linguistics.

[Collection of short stories written by Freda's fluent students in various courses that she taught, and the inspiration for the current First Nations Language Readers series, University of Regina Press.]

——. 1987. *wâskahikaniwiyiniw-âcimowina / Stories of the House People*. Told by Peter Vandall and Joe Douquette. Winnipeg: University of Manitoba Press.

[Published edition of texts that Freda recorded as part of her Master's degree. Peter Vandall was the father of Freda's mentor, Ida McLeod.]

Ahenakew, Freda, and H.C. Wolfart, ed. 1992. *kôhkominawak otâcimowiniwâwa / Our Grandmothers' Lives, as Told in Their Own Words.* Told by Glecia Bear et al. Saskatoon: Fifth House Publishers.

[Original printing; reprinted in facsimile, 1998 with a new preface, Canadian Plains Reprint Series,

Canadian Plains Research Center, University of Regina. Republished 2023, in the present volume.]

———. 1997. *kwayask ê-kî-pê-kiskinowâpahtihicik / Their Example Showed Me the Way: A Cree Woman's Life Shaped by Two Cultures*. Told by Emma Minde. Edmonton: The University of Alberta Press.

[Autobiograhical texts narrated in 1988 by Emma Minde (née Memnook), born at Saddle Lake, but married into the Ermineskin Reserve at Maskwacîs, Alberta.]

———. 1998. *ana kâ-pimwêwêhahk okakêskihkêmowina / The Counselling Speeches of Jim Kâ-Nîpitêhtêw*. Publications of the Algonquian Text Society. Winnipeg: University of Manitoba Press.

[Lectures delivered by "Old Jim" Kâ-Nîpitêhtêw, a monolingual Cree Elder from Onion Lake, Saskatchewan, to audiences at the Saskatchewan Indian Cultural College and Saskatchewan Indian Languages Institute in 1987 and 1989.]

Wolfart, H.C., and Freda Ahenakew, ed. 1993. *kinêhiyâwiwininaw nêhiyawêwin / The Cree Language is Our Identity: The La Ronge Lectures of Sarah Whitecalf*. Publications of the Algonquian Text Society. Winnipeg: University of Manitoba Press.

[First published collection of texts by Sarah Whitecalf, a monolingual Cree speaker born at Moosomin Reserve and married into Sweetgrass First Nation, Saskatchewan. Recorded as she answered student questions during a course taught by Freda.]

———. 2000. *âh-âyîtaw isi ê-kî-kiskêyihtahkik maskihkiy / They Knew Both Sides of Medicine: Cree Tales of Curing and Cursing Told by Alice Ahenakew*. Publications of the Algonquian Text Society. Winnipeg: The University of Manitoba Press.

[Texts narrated by Alice Ahenakew (née Bush) in 1989 and 1994. Raised by adoptive grandparents at Sturgeon Lake, Saskatchewan, Alice married into Ahtahkakoop First Nation. Her late husband was Reverend Andrew Ahenakew.]

———. 2010. *piko kîkway ê-nakacihtât: kêkêk otâcimowina ê-nêhiyawastêki*. Memoir 21. Winnipeg: Algonquian and Iroquoian Linguistics.

[Monolingual Cree texts, told by Cecilia Masuskapoe, born at Big River Reserve and married into Ahtahkakoop First Nation. Published without English translation.]

———. 2021. *mitoni niya nêhiyaw – nêhiyaw-iskwêw mitoni niya / Cree is who I truly am – me, I am truly a Cree woman: A life told by Sarah Whitecalf*. Winnipeg: University of Manitoba Press.

[Second published collection of Sarah Whitecalf texts, recorded between 1989 and 1990, ultimately completed for publication by H.C. Wolfart.]

Children's Books

Ahenakew, Freda. 1999. *Wisahkecahk Flies to the Moon*. Winnipeg: Pemmican Publications.

[Traditional Cree story retold by Freda and illustrated by Sherry Farrell Racette.]

Ahenakew, Freda, ed. 1988. *nāpēsis ēkwa āpakosīs ācimowinis: ātayōhkēwin*. Saskatoon: Saskatchewan Indian Cultural Centre.

[Originally written by Ray Smith in 1982, this story is excerpted from *kiskinahamawâkan-âcimowinisa*, and illustrated by George Littlechild. The Cree edition is cited here. The separate English edition is titled, *How the Mouse Got Brown Teeth: A Cree Story for Children*.]

———. 1988. *wīsahkēcāhk ēkwa waskwayak: ātayōhkēwin*. Saskatoon: Saskatchewan Indian Cultural Centre.

[Originally written by Dean Whitstone in 1982, this story is excerpted from *kiskinahamawâkan-âcimowinisa*, and illustrated by George Littlechild. The Cree edition is cited here. The separate English edition is titled, *How the Birch Tree Got Its Stripes: A Cree Story for Children*.]

Ahenakew, Freda, and H.C. Wolfart, ed. 1991. *wanisinwak iskwêsisak / Two Little Girls Lost in the Bush*. Told by Nêhiyaw / Glecia Bear. Saskatoon: Fifth House Publishers.

[Excerpted from a story told by Glecia Bear and illustrated by Jerry Whitehead. An additional version of the story can be found in the present volume.]

Pedagogical and Grammatical Materials

Ahenakew, Freda. 1987. *Cree Language Structures: A Cree Approach*. Winnipeg: Pemmican Publications.

[Published form of Freda's 1984 MA thesis: "Text-based Grammar in Cree Language Education," University of Manitoba.]

Ahenakew, Freda, ed. 1987. *A Preliminary Checklist of Plains Cree Medical Terms*. Saskatoon: Saskatchewan Indian Languages Institute.

[Much needed medical terminology, gathered at an Elders' workshop and published to support interactions with monolingual Cree speakers in medical settings.]

Ahenakew, Freda, and Shirley Fredeen, ed. 1987. *Our Languages, Our Survival: Proceedings of the 7th Annual Native American Languages Institute*. Saskatoon: Saskatchewan Indian Languages Institute.

[Published papers from the conference, hosted under Freda's directorship by Saskatchewan Indigenous Languages Institute.]

Ahenakew, Freda, Brenda Gardipy, and Barbara Lafond, ed. 1993. *Native Voices*. The Issues Collection. Toronto: McGraw-Hill Ryerson Limited.

[Indigenous writings in English intended for a high school audience.]

———. 1995. *Voices of the First Nations*. The Senior Issues Collection. Toronto: McGraw-Hill Ryerson Limited.

[Indigenous writings in English, "dedicated to all students who are seeking their identities; may they come to understand themselves and others."]

Ahenakew, Freda, Brenda Gardipy, Barbara Lafond, and Gillda Leitenberg, ed. 1994. *Native Voices: Teacher's Guide*. The Issues Collection. Toronto: McGraw-Hill Ryerson Limited.

[Teacher's guide to *Native Voices*, 1993, cited above.]

Ahenakew, Freda, and H.C. Wolfart. 1983. "Productive Reduplication in Plains Cree." 369–377 in W. Cowan, ed., *Actes du Quatorzième Congrès des Algonquinistes*. Ottawa: Carleton University.

[Published form of a conference presentation.]

——. 1991. "The Reality of Morpheme-boundary Rules." *Algonquian and Iroquoian Linguistics* 16:27-32.

[journal article on Cree morphology]

Wolfart, H.C., and Freda Ahenakew, ed. 1998. *The Student's Dictionary of Literary Plains Cree, based on contemporary texts*. Memoir 15. Winnipeg: Algonquian and Iroquoian Linguistics.

[Bilingual Cree-English glossary of vocabulary from the assembled (pre-1998) text collections of Ahenakew and Wolfart cited above.]

Additional References

Ahenakew, Edward. 1995. *Voices of the Plains Cree*. Regina: Canadian Plains Research Center.

Felice, Michelle. 2015. "Freda Ahenakew." The Canadian Encyclopedia. Accessed online on June 15, 2023, at: https://www.thecanadianencyclopedia.ca/en/article/freda-ahenakew

Ogg, Arden C. 2019. "My 2019 IYIL Cree Literacy Quest." Cree Literacy Network. Accessed online on June 15, 2023 at: https://creeliteracy.org/2019/12/31/my-2019-iyil-cree-literacy-quest/

Ogg, Arden C., and Dolores Greyeyes Sand. 2017. *nicâpân owâskahikan / Câpân's House: a family album from the home of Dr Freda Ahenakew*. Winnipeg: Cree Literacy Network, Inc.

[audio accessible at: https://creeliteracy.org/2017/02/07/capans-house/]

Watkins, E. A, and R. Faries, eds. 1938. *A Dictionary of the Cree Language*. Toronto: Anglican Book Centre.

Wikipedia. "Freda Ahenakew." Accessed online on June 15, 2023, at: https://en.wikipedia.org/wiki/Freda_Ahenakew

*With especial thanks to *nimisak* Dolores Greyeyes Sand and Arden Ogg for personal communication and review of this foreword.

Preface to the 1992 Edition

In this book, the spoken word is written down in the hope that the life experiences of Cree grandmothers will reach a wider audience if printed. In presenting the original Cree texts – in both roman and syllabic orthography and accompanied by a careful translation into English – told by seven women, we want to make sure that they are heard speaking to us in their own words.

The personal reminiscences which make up this book give voice to the daily struggle of Indian women during a century of fundamental changes. They represent the collective experience of a small group of Cree women who have lived their entire lives in or near the places in western Canada where they were born. While far from comprehensive, their recollections range from the practical to the spiritual and from childhood memories to prophetic visions. Their presentation is informal and intimate, spanning simple narratives and sharply focussed stories, detached contemplation and anguished outcry.

We want to thank Glecia Bear, Irene Calliou, Janet Feitz, the late Minnie Fraser, Alpha Lafond, Rosa Longneck, and Mary Wells who gave their texts to Freda Ahenakew to record and publish – above all, but by no means exclusively, for the benefit of their granddaughters, who sometimes seem to live in another world entirely.

The texts were recorded, transcribed, analysed, translated, annotated, and prepared for publication with the support of the

Social Sciences and Humanities Research Council of Canada under the auspices of the Saskatchewan Indian Languages Institute and the Cree Language Project at the University of Manitoba. We are also grateful to our colleagues in both Saskatoon and Winnipeg who encouraged and helped us in many ways during the long process of getting speech into type.

F.A. & H.C.W.

Preface to the 1998 Reprint

In an ironic reversal, the present facsimile is printed on more permanent paper than the first edition (1992). Its publication is due largely to the initiative and insistence of Heather Hodgson and a gratefully acknowledged subsidy from the Peter Ballantyne and Montreal Lake Cree Nations.

Of the many companions who travelled to Winnipeg with Freda Ahenakew over the years, none took a greater interest in the intellectual side of our research than Willy Hodgson (the daughter of her paternal grandfather's sister), to whom Freda – echoing her father's kin term for Minnie Fraser – formally refers as *nisikos*.

To her, in friendship old and new, this book in its restored state is dedicated.

kôhkominawak

ᑰᐦᑯᒥᓇᐊᐧᐠ

Our Grandmothers

Freda Ahenakew

ᐅᓵᒼ ᐱᑯ ᒫᓇ 'Auntie Minnie' ᐁ ᑮ ᐯᐦᑕᒫᐣ ᐁ ᐃᑎᐦᐟ; ᓅᐦᑖᐃᐧᐩ ᐃᐧᔭ ᑮ ᐅᓯᑯᓵᐦᑰᒣᐤ. 'Louis Ahenakew' ᑳ ᑮ ᐃᑎᐦᐟ ᐅᑖᓂᓴ, ᔦᑲᐃᐧᐢᑳᐃᐧᑲᒫᕽ ᐅᐦᒋ.

ᒑᐦ ᒌᑳᐦᑕᐤ ᐁ ᑮ ᐄᐧᑭᔮᕽ ᒫᓇ ᐁ ᒣᑳᐧ ᐅᐦᐱᑭᔮᕽ, ᑖᐢᐹᐧᐤ ᒫᓇ ᐁ ᑮ ᐯ ᑳᐦ ᑳᐧᐱᑫᒋᐠ, ᐁ ᒨᐦᑭᒋᐊᐧᓂᐯᔮᐠ ᐃᑕ ᑳ ᑮ ᐄᐧᑭᔮᕽ, ᐁᑲᐧ ᒥᐢᑕᐦᐃ ᐁ ᐄᐧᐦᑲᓯᐠ ᓂᐱᐩ.

Norman, Minnie ᑳ ᑮ ᐅᓈᐯᒥᐟ, ᐁᑲᐧ ᓅᐦᑖᐃᐧᐩ ᒫᓇ ᐁ ᑮ ᓈᐦ ᓃᓱ ᒫᒌᒋᐠ, ᐋᐧᒌᕽ ᑮ ᐃᑕᒪᐧᐠ ᒫᓇ.

ᒥᐢᑕᐦᐃ ᒫᓇ ᐁ ᑮ ᒥᔪᐦᑖᐧᐟ Minnie, ᐁᑲᐧ ᐁ ᑮ ᓂᐦᑖᐋᐧᒋᒧᐟ ᑳ ᑭᔪᑳᐦᐟ.

ᓂᒥᐦᑖᑌᐣ ᒫᓇ ᐁᑳ ᓇᐊᐧᐨ ᐄᐧᐸᐨ ᐁ ᑮ ᑲᑫᐧ ᓂᑕᐃᐧ ᐋᒋᒨᐦᐊᐠ, ᒥᑐᓂ ᐁ ᑫᐦᑌ ᐊᔨᐃᐧᐟ ᐁᑲᐧ ᐋᓴᐩ ᐁ ᐋᐦᑯᓯᐟ ᑳ ᑮ ᐋᒋᒧᐢᑕᐃᐧᐟ ᐆᒪ.

osâm piko mâna *'Auntie Minnie'* ê-kî-pêhtamân ê-itiht; nôhtâwiy wiya kî-osikosâhkômêw. *'Louis Ahenakew'* kâ-kî-itiht otânisa, yêkawiskâwikamâhk ohci.

câh-cîkâhtaw ê-kî-wîkiyâhk mâna ê-mêkwâ-ohpikiyâhk; tâspwâw mâna ê-kî-pê-kâh-kwâpikêcik, ê-môhkiciwanipêyâk ita kâ-kî-wîkiyâhk, êkwa mistahi ê-wîhkasik nipiy.

Norman, Minnie kâ-kî-onâpêmit, êkwa nôhtâwiy mâna ê-kî-nâh-nîso-mâcîcik, 'wacîhk' kî-itamwak mâna.

mistahi mâna ê-kî-miyohtwât *Minnie,* êkwa ê-ki-nihtâwâcimot kâ-kiyokâht.

nimihtâtên mâna êkâ nawac wîpac ê-kî-kakwê-nitawi-âcimohak; mitoni ê-kêhtê-ayiwit êkwa âsay ê-âhkosit kâ-kî-âcimostawit ôma.

Minnie Fraser

I used to hear everybody call her 'Auntie Minnie'; she was my father's paternal aunt. She was from *yêkâwiskâwikamâhk,* the daughter of Louis Ahenakew.

We used to live quite close together when my siblings and I were growing up; as a matter of fact, they used to come over and get their drinking water at our spring, where we used to live, and the water is very tasty.

Norman, Minnie's husband, and my father used to go hunting together, at a place they used to call *wacîhk*.

Minnie used to be a very good-natured person, and she used to be a great storyteller when you visited her.

I am sorry I did not try to go and record her stories earlier; she was very old and already sick when she told me this story.

ᓀᐦᐃᔭᐤ ᐁ ᐃᓯᔩᐦᑳᓱᐟ ᐊᐘ ᓂᑳᐑᐢ, ᓇᒨᔭ ᐑᐦᑳᐨ ᓂᑑᐦᒋ ᑭᐢᑫᔨᐦᑌᐣ 'Glecia' ᐊᐏᔭ ᑭᑕ ᐊᔨᓯᔩᐦᑳᑎᑯᐟ.

ᑳᑭᑫ ᒫᓇ ᑳ ᐹᐦᐱᕽ ᐃᑕ ᑳ ᐊᔮᐟ, ᐁ ᓂᐦᑖᐚᒋᒧᐟ, ᐊᐦᐴ ᒫᓇ ᐊᔨᐢ ᑳ ᐑ ᐘ ᐏᔮᐦᑵᐏ ᐋᒋᒧᒋᐠ, ᐃᑐᐘᕽ ᐊᐘ. ᒫᑲ ᒫᓇ ᒥᑐᓂ ᐁ ᒨᒋᑲᕽ ᑳ ᑭᔪᑳᐦᐟ ᐊᐦᐴ ᑳ ᑭᔪᑫᐟ.

ᐁ ᑲᒁᐦᔭᑭ ᓂᐦᑖᐏᒁᓱᐟ, ᓇᓈᑐᕽ ᓲᐢᒁᐨ ᑮᒁᕀ ᐸᐦᑫᑭᐣ ᐅᐦᒋ, ᒥᐢᑯᑖᑲᔭ, ᐊᐢᑎᓴ, ᒪᐢᑭᓯᓇ. ᐁ ᓂᐦᑖ ᒦᑭᓯᐢᑕᐦᐃᑫᐟ, ᓲᐢᒁᐨ ᐁ ᓂᐦᑖᐑᐦᒋᑫᐟ.

ᑫᔮᐱᐨ ᑲᑳᔭᐚᑎᓯᐤ, ᐁᒁ ᐁ ᒥᔦᐧᔨᐦᑕᕽ ᐁ ᒣᑕᐍᐟ bingo ᐊᐦᐴ ᐯᔭᑯᐯᐦᐃᑲᓇ. ᐁ ᓇᐦᐄᐟ ᓲᐢᒁᐨ ᐱᑯ ᐃᓯ.

'nêhiyaw' ê-isiyîhkâsot awa nikâwîs, namôya wîhkâc nitôhci-kiskêyihtên *'Glecia'* awiya kita-ay-isiyîhkâtikot.

kâkikê mâna kâ-pâhpihk ita kâ-ayât, ê-nihtâwâcimot; ahpô mâna ayis kâ-wî-wa-wiyâhkwêwi-âcimocik, itowahk awa. mâka mâna mitoni ê-môcikahk kâ-kiyokâht ahpô kâ-kiyokêt.

ê-kakwâhyaki-nihtâwikwâsot; nanâtohk sôskwâc kîkway pahkêkin ohci, miskotâkaya, astisa, maskisina. ê-nihtâ-mîkisistahikêt, sôskwâc ê-nihtâwîhcikêt.

kêyâpic kakâyawâtisiw, êkwa ê-miywêyihtahk ê-mêtawêt *bingo* ahpô pêyakopêhikana. ê-nahît sôskwâc piko isi.

Glecia Bear

Nêhiyaw is the name of this maternal aunt of mine, I have never known anyone to use the name Glecia for her.

Wherever she is there is always laughter, she is a great storyteller; she is even known as one of those who like to tell risqué stories. But it is always great fun to visit her or to have a visit from her.

Her sewing is very beautiful; she makes simply everything that is made from leather, such as jackets, mitts, moccasins. She does beautiful beadwork, she simply makes beautiful things.

She is still very active, and she likes playing bingo or cards. She is good at whatever she does.

ᐁᑫᔮᐨ ᐊᐘ ᓃᓱ ᐊᐢᑭᐩ ᐊᐢᐱᐣ ᐁ ᑮ ᓇᑭᐢᑲᐘᐠ ᐊᐘ ᐃᐢᑵᐤ, ᐆᑌ ᐅᐦᒋ ᑮᐍᑎᓄᕽ, 'La Ronge' ᑳ ᐃᓯᔩᐦᑳᑌᐠ.

ᒥᐢᑕᐦᐃ ᓂᑮ ᑳᐦ ᑯᐢᑯᒥᐠ ᐁ ᐋᐦ ᐋᒋᒧᐢᑕᐏᐟ ᐆᒪ ᒫᓇ ᑳ ᐸ ᐯᔭᑯᐟ ᐅᐘᓂᐦᐃᑫᐢᑲᓈᕽ. ᐱᒥᐦᐋᑲᐣ ᒫᓇ ᐁ ᓂᑕᐏ ᐸᑭᑎᓂᑯᐟ ᐁᑯᑌ ᐃᐢᑯᕽ ᓅᐦᑌ ᐯ ᑮᐍᒋ, ᐁᑿ ᒫᓇ ᐁ ᓈᑕᐦᐅᑯᐟ.

ᓂᑮ ᓂᑐᒥᐠ ᑲ ᓂᑕᐏ ᐑᒋ ᐊᔮᒪᐠ, ᑲᓇᑫ ᐯᔭᐠ ᐁ ᐃᐢᐸᔨᐠ, ᒫᑲ ᓇᒨᔭ ᒉᐢᑿ ᑮ ᒥᔪᐸᔨᐤ ᑕ ᑮ ᐃᑐᐦᑌᔮᐣ. ᓂᑮ ᐋᒋᒧᐢᑖᐠ, «ᓲᐢᑳᐧᐨ ᐁ ᒥᔽᓯᐠ ᐁᑯᑌ, ᒥᑐᓂ ᒫᓇ ᓂᐸᐹ ᒫᐦ ᒥᓯ ᐊᔭᒥᐦᐁᐏ ᓂᑲᒧᐣ ᐁᑯᑌ,» ᑮ ᐃᑘᐤ.

Janet ᒫᓇ ᐁ ᓇᓈᑐᐦᑯᑳᐧᓱᐟ, ᐊᐚᓯᓰᐦᑳᓂᓴ ᐁ ᐘᐍᓰᐦᐋᐟ, ᓇᓈᑐᕽ ᑮᑳᐧᓴ ᒦᓇ ᑲ ᐊᑯᑖᕽ ᐁ ᑲᐢᑭᑳᐧᑕᕽ ᐁ ᒫᐦ ᒥᔽᓯᓂᔨᑭ.

ᑲᑳᔭᐚᑎᓯᐤ ᒥᐢᑕᐦᐃ ᑫᔮᐱᐨ. ᒥᑐᓂ ᐁᑎᑵ ᐊᓂ ᒫᒪᐢᑳᐨ ᐃᔨᑯᕽ ᐁ ᑕᑲᐦᑫᔨᐦᑕᕽ ᐅᑕᐢᑭᐩ, ᑳ ᓴ ᓰᐱᐦᑫᔨᐦᑕᕽ ᐃᔨᑯᕽ ᒫᓇ ᑳ ᐸ ᐯᔭᑯᐟ.

êkwêyâc awa nîso-askiy aspin ê-kî-nakiskawak awa iskwêw, ôtê ohci kîwêtinohk, '*La Ronge*' kâ-isiyîhkâtêk.

mistahi nikî-kâh-koskomik ê-âh-âcimostawit ôma mâna kâ-pa-pêyakot owanihikêskanâhk. pimihâkan mâna ê-nitawi-pakitinikot êkotê iskohk nôhtê-pê-kîwêci; êkwa mâna ê-nâtahokot.

nikî-nitomik ka-nitawi-wîc-âyâmak, kanakê pêyak ê-ispayik, mâka namôya cêskwa kî-miyopayiw ta-kî-itohtêyân. nikî-âcimostâk, "sôskwâc ê-miywâsik êkotê, mitoni mâna nipapâ-mâh-misi-ayamihêwi-nikamon êkotê," kî-itwêw.

Janet mâna ê-nanâtohkokwâsot, awâsisîhkânisa ê-wawêsîhât, nanâtohk kîkwâsa mîna ka-akotâhk ê-kaskikwâtahk ê-mâh-miywâsiniyiki.

kakâyawâtisiw mistahi kêyâpic. mitoni êtikwê ani mâmaskâc iyikohk ê-takahkêyihtahk otaskiy, kâ-sa-sîpihkêyihtahk iyikohk mâna kâ-pa-pêyakot.

Janet Feitz

It was only two years ago that I met this woman, she is from the north, the place they call La Ronge.

She really amazed me with her stories about being on her trapline by herself. A plane takes her there and leaves her until she wants to return home; then the plane comes for her.

She has invited me to go and be with her [on the trapline], even if it were only for a week, but until now things have not worked out so that I could go there. In telling me about the trapline, she said, "It is so peaceful over there that I actually go around singing hymns."

Janet sews all kinds of things; she dresses up dolls and also sews beautiful things to hang on walls.

She is still extremely active. She must love her land enormously to be able to persevere in living there by herself.

Irene ᐁᑲᐧ ᒦᓇ Mary ᓂᐢᑕᒼ ᐁ ᑮ ᓇᑭᐢᑲᐊᐧᑭᐠ ᐆᑌ ᑮᐁᐧᑎᓄᕽ, 'Grouard, Alberta' ᐃᓯᔩᐦᑳᑌᐤ ᐊᓂᒪ ᐋᐱᐦᑕᐃᐧᑯᓯᓵᓅᒉᓈᐢ. ᐁ ᑮ ᓂᑐᒥᑲᐃᐧᔮᐣ ᐊᓂᒪ ᐁᑯᑌ ᑳ ᓂᑕᐃᐧ ᑭᐢᑭᓇᐦᐊᒫᑫᔮᐣ ᑖᓂᑕᐦᑐ ᓃᐱᐣ ᐊᐢᐱᐣ, ᓀᐦᐃᔭᐁᐧᐃᐧᐣ ᑕ ᐃᓯ ᒪᓯᓇᐦᐊᒧᕽ, ᐁᑲᐧ ᒦᓇ ᑖᓂᓯ ᐁ ᐃᓯ ᐃᐧᔭᐢᑌᐠ ᐆᒪ ᓀᐦᐃᔭᐁᐧᐃᐧᐣ, ᐁᑯᑕ ᐆᑭ ᐄᐧᐢᑕᐋᐧᐤ ᐁ ᑮ ᐯ ᑭᐢᑭᓇᐦᐊᒫᑯᓯᒋᐠ. ᒥᐢᑕᐦᐃ ᓂᑮ ᒫᐦ ᒨᒋᑭᐦᑖᓈᐣ ᐁᑯᑌ, ᑲᐦᑭᔭᐤ ᐊᔨᐢ ᐁ ᓀᐦᐃᔭᐁᐧᔮᕽ.

Irene ᐃᐧᔭ ᐊᐊᐧ ᒥᑐᓂ ᐁ ᑭᐦᒋ ᐃᐢᑫᐧᐃᐧᓈᑯᓯᐟ, ᐁᑲᐧ ᒥᑐᓂ ᐃᑐᐊᐧᕽ ᑳ ᐄᐧ ᑲᑳᒫᐧᑎᓯᒋᐠ. ᒫᑲ ᒥᑐᓂ ᒫᓇ ᑳᐦ ᑲᐯ ᐊᔨ ᐁ ᓃᓯᒋᐠ, ᐁ ᑖᐦ ᑕᑲᐦᑭᐦᑕᐋᐧᐟ ᐁᑎᑫᐧ Maryᐊᐧ ᐁ ᑳᐦ ᑮᐢᑫᐧᑐᓈᒧᔨᐟ.

ᒥᑐᓂ ᒫᓇ ᐁ ᑮ ᑭᐢᑭᓱᐦᐃᐟ ᓅᐦᑯᒪ ᐁ ᐊᔨᑎᐢᑫᐧᐦᑫᐟ, ᐊᐦᐴ ᐱᑯ ᐁ ᐃᑕᐁᐧᐦᐃᑫᐟ, ᐁᑯᓯ ᒦᓇ ᒫᓇ ᓅᐦᑯᒼ ᑖᐱᐢᑰᐨ ᐁ ᑮ ᑲᑳᒫᐧᑎᐢᑫᐧᐦᑫᐟ. ᒫᑲ ᑯᓂᑕ ᐃᐧᔭ ᐁᐊᐧᑯ, ᐹᐦᑲᒋ ᑳ ᒫᒋ ᐋᒋᒧᐟ Irene, ᐊᑎ ᒪ ᒥᔦᐧᔨᐦᑕᒼ, ᐋᐧᐄᐧᐢ ᐃᐧᔭ ᐁᑳ ᑳ ᐅᑎᓇᒪᐧᐠ ᐅᐲᑭᐢᑫᐧᐃᐧᐣ. ᒫᑲ ᑳ ᒫᒋ ᐋᒋᒧᐢᑕᐃᐧᐟ ᐁᑲᐧ ᐁ ᐅᑎᓇᒪᐧᐠ ᐅᐲᑭᐢᑫᐧᐃᐧᐣ, ᐋᐧᐦ ᐄᐧᐸᐨ ᐊᓂ ᑳ ᑲᑫᐧ ᐹᐦ ᐴᔪᐟ, ᐱᑯ ᒫᓇ ᐁ ᑳᐦ ᑮᐦᑖᐧᒼ ᑭᐢᑭᓱᒪᐠ ᐊᓂᒪ ᑮᑲᐧᐩ ᑳ ᑮ ᐋᐦ ᐋᒋᒧᐢᑕᐃᐧᐟ ᒪᐧᔦᐢ.

Irene êkwa mîna *Mary* nistam ê-kî-nakiskawakik ôtê kîwêtinohk, *'Grouard, Alberta'* isiyîhkâtêw anima âpihtawikosisânôcênâs. ê-kî-nitomikawiyân anima êkotê kâ-nitawi-kiskinahamâkêyân tânitahto-nîpin aspin, nêhiyawêwin ta-isi-masinahamohk, êkwa mîna tânisi ê-isi-wiyastêk ôma nêhiyawêwin; êkota ôki wîstawâw ê-kî-pê-kiskinahamâkosicik. mistahi nikî-mâh-môcikihtânân êkotê, kahkiyaw ayis ê-nêhiyawêyâhk.

Irene wiya awa mitoni ê-kihc-îskwêwinâkosit, êkwa mitoni itowahk kâ-wî-kakâmwâtisicik. mâka mitoni mâna kâh-kapê-ayi ê-nîsicik, ê-tâh-takahkihtawât êtikwê *Mary*wa ê-kâh-kîskwêtonâmoyit.

mitoni mâna ê-kî-kiskisohit nôhkoma ê-ay-itiskwêhkêt, ahpô piko ê-itawêhikêt, êkosi mîna mâna nôhkom tâpiskôc ê-kî-kakâmwâtiskwêhkêt. mâka konita wiya êwako, pâhkaci kâ-mâci-âcimot *Irene,* ati-ma-miywêyihtam, wâwîs wiya êkâ kâ-otinamwak opîkiskwêwin. mâka kâ-mâci-âcimostawit êkwa ê-otinamwak opîkiskwêwin, wâh-wîpac ani kâ-kakwe-pâh-pôyot, piko mâna ê-kâh-kîhtwâm-kiskisomak anima kîkway kâ-kî-âh-âcimostawit mwayês.

Irene Calliou

I first met Irene and Mary in northern Alberta, at a little Métis settlement called Grouard. I had been asked to go over there a few summers ago, and I taught a class in Cree orthography and also in Cree grammar; and they had come there, too, and taken my class. We had a very good time there for we all spoke Cree.

Irene looked very much a lady and seemed to be one of those who are quiet. But she and Mary were always together, so she must have liked the sound of Mary's lively chatter.

She used to remind me a lot of my grandmother, she looked like her and even wore her hair the same way, and my grandmother also gave the impression of being a quiet woman. But that was misleading for when Irene actually began to tell stories, she became animated, especially when I was not recording what she said. But when I recorded the stories she began to tell, she would at once try to quit, again and again, and I would have to remind her of what she had been telling me before.

Mary ᐊᐘ ᐑᐢᑕ ᐁ ᑮ ᐯ ᑭᐢᑭᓇᐦᐊᒫᑯᓯᐟ Grouard, ᐯᔭᑿᐣ ᐃᐢᐲ ᐊᓂᒪ Irene ᐑᐢᑕ ᐁᑯᑌ ᑳ ᑮ ᐊᔮᐟ. ᑖᐢᑇᐤ ᑖᐱᑕᐏ ᒫᓇ ᑖᐱᐢᑰᐨ ᐁ ᑮ ᐸᐹ ᓈᐦ ᓃᔁᐦᐱᓱᒋᐠ.

ᐁᑯᑌ ᐆᒪ ᑳ ᑲᑵᒋᒪᑭᐠ, ᑮᐢᐱᐣ ᐊᐏᔭᐠ ᑲ ᑌᐯᔨᒧᐟ ᑲ ᐋᒋᒧᐢᑕᐏᐟ ᐁᑿ ᑲ ᐅᑎᓇᒷᐠ ᐅᐲᑭᐢᑵᐏᓂᐚᐤ ᐁᑿ ᑲ ᐊᑎ ᒪᓯᓇᐦᐊᒷᐠ.

ᒥᑐᓂ ᐏᔭ Mary ᓭᒫᐠ ᒌᐦᑫᔨᐦᑕᒼ, ᐊᔨᐢ ᒥᑐᓂ ᐆᑭ ᐃᑐᐘᕽ ᐃᐢᑵᐘᐠ ᑳ ᐏᔮᐦᑎᑯᓯᒋᐠ. ᑳ ᓈᐦ ᓂᑲᒧᔮᕽ ᒫᓇ ᐆᐦᐃ ᓀᐦᐃᔭᐤ ᓂᑲᒧᐏᓂᓴ, ᐑᐢᑕ ᒫᓇ ᒥᑐᓂ ᑖᐦ ᑕᑲᐦᑲᑖᒧᐤ, ᑫᑕᐦᑕᐍ ᒦᓇ ᒫᓇ ᑯᓂᑕ ᑳ ᐱᒥ ᓃᓱᓯᒧᐟ. ᐹᐢᑲᐨ ᑲᒁᐦᔭᑭ ᓂᐦᑖᐏᓯᒧᐤ, ᐃᔨᓂᑐ ᒥᑐᓂ ᑖᐱᐢᑰᐨ ᒋᒋᐸᐦᐚᓂᐢ.

ᐁᑿ ᐏᔭ ᑳ ᒣᒁ ᑭᐢᑭᓇᐦᐊᒪᐘᑭᐠ, ᓇᒨᔭ ᐏᔭ ᑮᑿᐩ ᑲ ᒫᐦ ᒪᒥᐦᑎᓯᐦᑳᓱᐟ. ᒥᑐᓂ ᓲᐢᒁᐨ ᑕᑲᐦᑭ ᑭᐢᑭᓇᐦᐊᒪᐚᑲᓂᐢ. ᐁᑯᓯ ᐆᒪ ᑳ ᐑ ᐋᒋᒧᐢᑖᑯᔭᕽ – ᑿᔭᐢᐠ ᐁᓴ ᐁ ᑮ ᓂᐦᑖᐍᔨᐦᑕᕽ ᐁ ᐊᐚᓯᓰᐏᐟ, ᑫᔮᐱᐨ ᓴᐱᑯ ᐊᓄᐦᐨ.

Mary awa wîsta ê-kî-pê-kiskinahamâkosit *Grouard,* pêyakwan ispî anima *Irene* wîsta êkotê kâ-kî-ayât. tâspwâw tâpitawi mâna tâpiskôc ê-kî-papâ-nâh-nîswahpisocik.

êkotê ôma kâ-kakwêcimakik, kîspin awiyak ka-têpêyimot ka-âcimostawit êkwa ka-otinamwak opîkiskwêwiniwâw êkwa ka-ati-masinahamwak.

mitoni wiya *Mary* sêmâk cîhkêyihtam, ayis mitoni ôki itowahk iskwêwak kâ-wiyâhtikosicik. kâ-nâh-nikamoyâhk mâna ôhi nêhiyaw-nikamowinisa, wîsta mâna mitoni tâh-takahkatâmow, kêtahtawê mîna mâna konita kâ-pimi-nîsosimot. pâskac kakwâhyaki-nihtâwisimow, iyinito mitoni tâpiskôc cicipahwânis.

êkwa wiya kâ-mêkwâ-kiskinahamawakik, namôya wiya kîkway ka-mâh-mamihtisihkâsot. mitoni sôskwâc takahki-kiskinahamawâkanis! êkosi ôma kâ-wî-âcimostâkoyahk – kwayask êsa ê-kî-nihtâwêyihtahk ê-awâsisîwit, kêyâpic sapiko anohc.

Mary Wells

Mary, too, had come to Grouard as a student, she was there at the same time as Irene. As a matter of fact the two of them used to go around at all times as though harnessed together.

It was there that I asked if anyone would be willing to tell me stories and then for me to record what they said and to write it down.

Mary was ready and eager right away, for she is one of those women who have a bubbly personality. When we were singing Cree songs in class, she would sing out beautifully, and at times she would lapse into a jig. And, to cap it all, she was excellent at jigging, just like a top.

And while I was in class with them, she never was one to hesitate with an answer. What a truly good little student! Now she is going to tell us her stories – she was never at a loss what to do when she was a child, and in fact she is still like that today.

Alpha ᑮ ᐯ ᐅᐦᐱᑭᐦᐁᐤ ᐅᑕᐚᓯᒥᓴ ᐆᑕ ᒪᐢᑫᑯ ᓵᑲᐦᐃᑲᓂᕽ, ᐁᑯᑕ ᐑᐢᑕ ᐁ ᑮ ᐅᐦᒌᐟ. ᓂᔮᓇᐣ ᑮ ᐊᔮᐍᐤ, ᒫᑲ ᐯᔭᐠ ᑮ ᒫᔨᐸᔨᐤ ᐅᑖᓂᓴ. ᐁᑯᓯ ᐊ· ᐅᐦᐱᑭᐦᑕᒫᓱᐤ ᐃᐢᑵᓯᓴ, ᐅᓯᓯᒪ.

ᓃᐢᑕᓇᐤ ᐊᐢᑭᕀ ᐁ ᐯ ᓃᑳᓃᐢᑕᒪᐚᐟ ᐆᑕ ᒪᐢᑫᑯᐏᔨᓂᐘ, ᐁ ᑮ ᐅᐏᔭᓯᐍᐏᐟ ᐁᑿ ᓃᓱ ᐊᐢᑭᕀ ᐁ ᑮ ᐅᑭᒫᐦᑳᓂᐏᐟ. ᒥᐦᒉᑣᐤ ᐸᐹᒫᒋᐦᐅᐤ ᐆᒪ, ᒫᒪᐅᐧᐱᐏᓂᕽ ᐁ ᐃᑐᐦᑌᐟ.

ᒥᓴᑳᒣ ᐑᐢᑕ ᐯ ᓲᐦᑲᑐᐢᑫᐤ. ᑕᐦᑐ ᓃᐱᐣ ᒫᓇ ᐁ ᑕᑲᐦᑭᑭᐦᑖᐟ ᐲᓯ ᑭᐢᒋᑳᓂᓴ, ᓇᐸᑖᒁ, ᐁᑯᓯ ᐃᓯ ᑮᑿᕀ.

ᐆᑕ ᑮ ᓃᑳᓇᐱᐤ ᑭᐢᑭᓇᐦᐊᒫᑐᐏᐣ ᐅᐦᒋ, ᐆᑕ ᒪᐢᑫᑯ ᓵᑲᐦᐃᑲᓂᕽ, ᒫᑲ ᐊᓄᐦᒋᐦᑫ ᑮ ᐅᑎᓇᒼ ᐆᒪ ᑫᐦᑌ ᐊᔭᐠ ᑳ ᐊᔨᐍᐱᒋᐠ.

Alpha kî-pê-ohpikihêw otawâsimisa ôta maskêko-sâkahikanihk, êkota wîsta ê-kî-ohcît. niyânan kî-ayâwêw, mâka pêyak kî-mâyipayiw otânisa. êkosi wa-ohpikihtamâsow iskwêsisa, osisima.

nîstanaw-askiy ê-pê-nîkânîstamawât ôta maskêkowiyiniwa, ê-kî-owiyasiwêwit êkwa nîso-askiy ê-kî-okimâhkâniwit. mihcêtwâw papâmâcihow ôma, mâmawopiwinihk ê-itohtêt.

misakâmê wîsta pê-sôhkatoskêw. tahto-nîpin mâna ê-takahkikihtât pîsi-kiscikânisa, napatâkwa, êkos îsi kîkway.

ôta kî-nîkânapiw kiskinahamâtowin ohci, ôta maskêko-sâkahikanihk, mâka anohcihkê kî-otinam ôma kêhtê-ayak kâ-ayiwêpicik.

Alpha Lafond

Alpha has raised her children at *maskêko-sâkahikanihk* and was born there herself. She had five children but tragically lost one daughter. Therefore she is raising her orphaned grandchild, a little girl.

She has been a leader on Muskeg Lake Reserve for twenty years; she used to be a Councillor, and for two years she was Chief. She has travelled around and gone to many meetings.

She, too, has been working hard all along. Every summer she has a nice garden with vegetables, potatoes, and the like.

She was Director of Education at *maskêko-sâkahikanihk* but recently took retirement.

ᑲᔮᐢ ᑳ ᐯ ᐅᐦᒋ ᑭᐢᑫᔨᒪᐠ ᐊᐘ ᐃᐢᑵᐤ; ᐅᓵᒼ ᐱᑯ ᑳᑭᑫ ᐁ ᐯ ᐑᑭᐟ ᒪᐢᑫᑯ ᓵᑲᐦᐃᑲᓂᕽ, ᓂᑮ ᐯ ᐚᐦ ᐑᒋᐦᐃᐠ ᒫᓇ ᑲᔮᐢ, ᐁ ᒣᒁ ᐊᐱᓰᓯᓯᒋᐠ ᓂᑕᐚᓯᒥᓴᐠ, ᐁᑿ ᐁᑯᐢᐲ ᓃᐢᑕ ᐁ ᐑᑭᔮᐣ ᒪᐢᑫᑯ ᓵᑲᐦᐃᑲᓂᕽ.

ᒥᐢᑕᐦᐃ ᐁ ᐯ ᑲᑳᔭᐏᓰᐟ ᑲᐯ ᐊᔨ ᑫᔮᐱᐨ ᐆᒪ ᐊᓄᐦᐨ. ᐚᐚᐨ ᐁ ᑮ ᓈᐯᐘᑐᐢᑫᐟ, ᐁ ᒥᐢᑎᑯ ᓈᐯᐏᐟ, ᐁ ᓂᑯᐦᑌᐟ ᐁᑯᓯ ᐃᓯ ᑮᑿᕀ. ᐁᑿ ᒦᓇ ᐁ ᐊᑐᐢᑫᐟ ᐑᑭᕽ, ᐁ ᐯ ᐸᒥᐦᐋᐟ ᐅᑕᐚᓯᒥᓴ, ᐅᓯᓯᒪ ᑖᓂᑕᐦᑐ ᐁ ᐯ ᐅᐦᐱᑭᐦᐋᐟ.

ᒥᐦᒉᐟ ᐁᑎᑵ ᐊᓂ ᐊᑯᐦᐸ ᐁ ᑮ ᐯ ᐅᓰᐦᑖᐟ, ᐁᑿ ᒦᓇ ᑳ ᐊᓈᐢᑫᕽ ᐆᐦᐃ, ᐁ ᐊᐱᐦᑳᑕᕽ ᐁᑿ ᐁ ᐚᐏᔦᒁᑕᕽ. ᑫᔮᐱᐨ ᐆᒪ ᑳᐦ ᑲᐯ ᐊᔨ ᐁ ᐘᐅᑕᒥᔪᐟ, ᐯᐢᑭᐢ ᒫᓇ ᐁ ᐑ ᓲᓂᔮᐦᑫᓯᐟ ᑲ ᓂᑕᐏ ᒣᑕᐍᐟ bingo.

ᓲᐢᒁᐨ ᑲᒁᐦᔭᑭ ᐃᐢᑵᐤ.

kayâs kâ-pê-ohci-kiskêyimak awa iskwêw; osâm piko kâkikê ê-pê-wîkit maskêko-sâkahikanihk, nikî-pê-wâh-wîcihik mâna kayâs, ê-mêkwâ-apisîsisicik nitawâsimisak, êkwa êkospî nîsta ê-wîkiyân maskêko-sâkahikanihk.

mistahi ê-pê-kakâyawisît kapê-ayi kêyâpic ôma anohc. wâwâc ê-kî-nâpêwatoskêt, ê-mistiko-nâpêwit, ê-nikohtêt êkosi isi kîkway. êkwa mîna ê-atoskêt wîkihk, ê-pê-pamihât otawâsimisa, osisima tânitahto ê-pê-ohpikihât.

mihcêt êtikwê ani akohpa ê-kî-pê-osîhtât, êkwa mîna kâ-anâskêhk ôhi, ê-apihkâtahk êkwa ê-wâwiyêkwâtahk. kêyâpic ôma kâh-kapê-ayi ê-wa-otamiyot, pêskis mâna ê-wî-sôniyâhkêsit ka-nitawi-mêtawêt *bingo*.

sôskwâc kakwâhyaki-iskwêw.

Rosa Longneck

I have known this woman for a long time; as she has more or less always been living at *maskêko-sâkahikanihk,* she sometimes used to come and help me while my children were young, when I, too, lived at *maskêko-sâkahikanihk.*

She has always been working very hard, and still is. She even used to do man's work, as a carpenter and in cutting firewood and doing things like that. And she has always worked in her home, looking after her children and raising a number of her grandchildren.

She must have made many blankets, and she also makes braided rugs, round ones. She still keeps herself busy all the time, making a little money besides so that she can go and play bingo.

She is simply a superwoman.

Introduction to the Texts

H.C. Wolfart

In reading this book, it is essential – especially for the English-speaking reader – to keep in mind at all times that these reminiscences of Cree women were recorded in their own language rather than in English.

Even those of us who are fluent in a second language typically rely on our first to talk about our memories and about what is most important to us; when one tries to deal with such things in another language, it is easy for fine distinctions to be glossed over, nuances and emphases to be lost and the right word to remain elusive. The seven women who recorded these texts were able to use their mother tongue in speaking about their lives.

Theirs is an authentic record: they were not forced to use a foreign language, nor were their texts shaped by an outside interviewer. They told them to Freda Ahenakew, who also speaks Cree as her first language; herself a grandmother many times over, most of the women whose life experiences she collected have known her for a long time. This, above all, makes these reminiscences exceptional: that they were not told to an outsider.

They are also extraordinary in another respect: that they have not been re-written, smoothed over, cut or otherwise re-worked for some particular audience or some further purpose. Instead, they are presented in their narrators' own words, as Cree texts, but made accessible to a wider audience through an English translation which closely follows the original.

OUTSIDE THEIR OWN COMMUNITIES, almost nothing has been heard until now about the life of Indian women. What little most Canadians have been able to read about Indian life concerns an earlier period and is focussed on the activities of men in the buffalo hunt, in intertribal warfare and the like.

Here, for the first time, we have autobiographical narratives which deal with the daily life of Cree women and the division of labour, with household chores and the livelihood provided by snaring and gathering. They are also concerned with childbirth, infant care, and the raising and education of children in a society where practical and spiritual matters rarely seem far apart.

Spanning several generations, these memories reach back at least to the turn of the century, concentrating on life in the bush and on reserves before roads and television admitted the industrial world into the most remote settlement. They illustrate the prominent role which women have always played in exercising social control, but they also tell of the decline in social cohesion which marks the present. Without being didactic, they exemplify a value system quite unlike that held by the larger society.

The texts selected for this book represent a number of literary genres. In addition to plain, almost technical accounts and an extended dialogue, there are autobiographical narratives which make use of a more elevated literary style and several stories which focus on specific incidents. These range from the childhood memories of Mary Wells, who tells tales out of school, and Glecia Bear, lost in the wilderness with her little sister, to Minnie Fraser's story of how her husband killed his first moose at the age of twelve and two recent encounters with bears by Janet Feitz, a grandmother in her seventies who still goes out to the trapline on her own.

Literary Form

The life experiences here recorded differ fundamentally from the vast majority of books about Indian women: the fact that they are spoken texts, told to a friend sharing both the language and the collective experience, is evident in their literary form as in their content.

For the most part, the non-Indian world has based its view of Indian life on the summary depictions of outsiders – be they fur-traders or missionaries, ethnographers or painters, novelists or filmmakers. Even where they have been highly perceptive in their analyses (and paid attention, as some have, to the female condition), their pictures necessarily reflect the perspective of the outside observer.

Inevitably, too, such observations have always been couched in the literary form dictated by the conventions of the observer's society: sober account of an expedition or tale of fiction, sensationalist article or systematic study. In the texts recorded by Freda Ahenakew we hear Cree women speaking to other Cree women. Since the discourse is not directed to an English-speaking public, it has not been filtered through the many layers of review and revision which prepare a work for a particular audience – whether the solitary reader of a scholarly treatise or the crowds flocking to see the latest visual myth.

The style of these reminiscences is casual, familiar, and marked by numerous interruptions and exchanges. These are intimate conversations, not the formal discourses which may be found in the *wâskahikaniwiyiniw-âcimowina / Stories of the House People* (Vandall & Douquette 1987) or in the La Ronge lectures of Sarah Whitecalf (1993); except when the discussion turns to the impact of alcohol or the decline in breastfeeding, there is relatively little of the *kakêskihkêmowin* 'counselling text' which is so typical of formal Cree rhetoric.

Instead, this book consists of unadorned narrative, of technical descriptions, of discussion back and forth (especially, of course, in the dialogue text which forms Part III); only occasionally is there a definite *âcimowin* 'account, report' interspersed amongst these, most commonly either a *wawiyatâcimowin* 'funny story' or an *âcimisowin*, a 'story about oneself' which lets the audience laugh along with the narrator about some misfortune she suffered.

This volume is a record of live performances. The authors used no notes and added no corrections except for those which all of us insert in the course of speaking. Unlike the finely spun memoirs of the European tradition, their memories were presented *viva voce*: impromptu and unrehearsed, full of asides and ad libs.

Where their performances attain poetic power, the rhetorical patterns and devices are those of spoken discourse, not the results of later revision by writer or editor. Where they are mundane, they have not after the fact been abridged or expurgated, titivated or re-shaped.

The texts brought together in this anthology could hardly be more different from the all-too-familiar digests and paraphrases, composed in English, of Indian customs or Indian thought. With the translation always taking second place, the texts themselves are authentic both in their delivery, told in Cree to a Cree-speaking audience, and in their printed presentation, in Cree and as spontaneous, spoken documents.

Topics

In genre and content, these autobiographical accounts reflect a larger context: an effort to have Indigenous women themselves tell about their lives. The general question about 'the old times' has on occasion resulted in a preoccupation with changes in domestic technology; but even where the material circumstances appear to dominate the narrative, they provide a framework for incidental remarks illustrating the underlying system of cultural and personal values.

In Mary Wells's recollections, for example, there are lists of animals eaten and detailed accounts of how blackbirds were entrapped and prairie-chickens snared while dancing; but there are also glimpses of little girls competing with one another in their childish games and of a born leader asserting herself and exercising her role; when social rules are broken, the sanctions are made explicit; some of the conflicts provoked by the alien lifestyle of the

Whites may be mediated by humour; and, above all, there is the figure of the grandmother – an old woman of such vitality that she herself one morning baked the bannock which is eaten at her wake the same night.

The four texts which have been grouped together in Part I of this anthology reflect life in the bush and on the northern prairie during a part of the twentieth century when in many places people led a life that cannot have differed much from that of the previous two centuries: clearly bearing the stamp of the fur-trade but not yet, or at least by no means fully, that of the reserve system.

While the division is not always sharp, the four texts of Part II focus on a life that already shows the pervasive influence of a settled existence, with cows and agricultural implements, teachers and priests. This is also the lifestyle, as it is the period, which is reflected in the dialogue text of Part III.

JANET FEITZ'S REPORT of her 'Encounters with Bears' (Chapter 1) is plain and unaffected; their narrative effect is all the more powerful.

The two brief stories are told in a matter-of-fact tone which makes it an everyday occupation for a woman of seventy years to fish and trap and deal with bears all by herself at a remote cabin only reached by two-way radio and float-plane. Her life under siege is treated as no less ordinary than the practical question of what was achieved on the occasion of her second encounter with a bear: one hide finished and a few small trout.

Despite her use of radio and plane, Janet Feitz clearly lives the traditional bush life, but she by and large restricts her account to material facts: in view of the important position which bears occupy in Cree religious thought, it is remarkable that she makes no reference at all to this aspect of her dealings with them.

In the second story, when the bear escapes despite all attempts by snare and gun, there is a touch of self-mocking detachment, echoing the manner in which, at the juncture between the two parts of the text, she gives herself the nickname *masko-nôcokwêsiw* 'Old Lady Bear'. These light touches balance the bitter end of the first story: Janet Feitz's abhorrence of killing meat that cannot be preserved during summer and the double irony of the bear falling prey to trophy hunters and the blame being put on her.

IN THE OPENING PART of 'Daily Life' (Chapter 2), Glecia Bear's recital of menial jobs in a wage-labour economy contrasts sharply with the seemingly effortless serenity of Janet Feitz's life on the trapline. She goes on to relate her interviews with three very old women about the daily lives of an even earlier generation.

In the first, we learn about the preparation of various types of hides and their use in bedding, the *astinwân* 'loin-sinew' of a moose as a source of thread and the provenance of other sewing implements. The counselling text of the third old woman includes a still earlier prophesy and expresses her own pessimistic view of the future; it culminates in a remarkable personal lament about the fate of her daughters. And it is quite rare for a Cree text to include, as does the second of these interview reports, a relatively technical account (sketchy though it may be) of traditional practices at childbirth.

This is the only text in the collection to contain long sequences of dialogue reported in the form of direct speech (and, in a few rare instances, also as indirect speech). While the quotative pattern is even more obvious in purely narrative texts, where the single third-person verb form *itwêw* 'so she/he said' tends to predominate, Glecia Bear's report offers a classical example of dialogue related in first-and-third-person form.

IN HER BRIEF SURVEY of the old days and the present lifestyle in 'Then and Now' (Chapter 3), Janet Feitz castigates the modern reliance on store-bought – and, more specifically, canned – foods for having left the current generation weaker and more susceptible to disease than the previous ones.

The past she evokes is not a distant mythical age but that of her childhood, marked by Christian discipline at school and at home and flour, tea, sugar, and lard as the main foodstuffs supplementary to those of the land.

Without offering technical details, she points out that the method of snaring she saw her grandmother employ differs from her own, and that her grandfather had told of a time when metal traps had not yet been in use. Comparing the security guaranteed by a trapline with the life insurance arrangements of non-Indians, she makes much of individual providence and hard work.

IN TELLING ABOUT her late husband, then twelve years old, and 'His First Moose' (Chapter 4), Minnie Fraser moves back and forth between reporting the events from her own perspective (letting him appear in the third person) and quoting him directly as he had told his own story.

Killing the first moose is an event of great significance in a hunter's life, and the hero is already the sole provider of meat for his mother and his siblings. Is it the burden of responsibility or boyish nonconformity which makes him reluctant to give away all the meat?

His mother and her parents insist on the traditional Cree custom appropriate to a hunter's first kill; at the same time, she is meticulous in her observance of Easter services. The fact that there is a correlation between the boy's good deed – of trying to provide for his younger siblings by carrying home part of the Easter meal – and his future success as a hunter is made explicit by his mother's prayer, but it is left to the audience to infer whether the boy's action and the man's success are related causally (as a reward in the Roman Catholic sense) or simply by subsequence (a provider who early shows his mettle) – or both at once, given the coexistence of religious doctrines and practices from both Aboriginal and colonial traditions.

The Cree perspective is particularly obvious in the transformation of the boy's grandfather; from a Cree point of view, it is entirely normal for *macôhow*, whose name might be translated as 'Bad-Owl', to turn into an owl in order to reassure himself of his daughter's welfare. That his visit upsets his granddaughter reflects the ambiguous position of owls, often harbingers of evil but occasionally bearers of good will, in Cree thought.

SET AGAINST THE BACKDROP of a much more sedentary life, but to be dated not much more than a decade later, 'Lost and Found' (Chapter 5) is another autobiographical story, this time told at first hand, which combines the devout practice of Roman Catholicism with pre-contact Cree beliefs.

Lost in the bush for several days, Glecia Bear, then eleven, and her eight-year-old sister ultimately come upon an owl but disagree on what to make of its conspicuous behaviour; in the event, Glecia's interpretation turns out to have been right, as the owl leads the two little girls into the hands of the search parties.

At the same time, the story begins with Sunday mass and communion, digresses into theology and the liturgical impact of the Second Vatican Council, describes the priest leading continuous prayers during the search, and concludes with Glecia, after the rescue, once more being given communion.

Glecia Bear's narrative also throws some light on the social position of the Hudson's Bay Company and its post manager in the early twentieth century. The Company post not only provides every kind of equipment and all the supplies required for the search, with the man in charge functioning much as would be expected of a patron or lord of the manor; but he is also a human being who is personally moved by the events. When the children are safely back but in tatters, he calls for new clothes to be brought from his store and, in a charming vignette, the children's grandmother scurries off to take up the offer.

ALTHOUGH IRENE CALLIOU's record of 'Household Chores' (Chapter 6) takes the form of short stretches of recollection, she provides many specific details. She tells of bannock made with fish-roe and of the edible root of cattails, of duck guts and 'the stuff inside a moose'. And she recalls the toys which she had as a child: fish bladders blown up as balloons, fishbones used as combs.

While concentrating on practical matters, she also mentions another point where Cree tradition and colonial exploitation intersect in a remarkable manner: in digging seneca-root, probably the most common form of working for cash income, her grandmother would never fail to place some tobacco into the hole left by the removal of the root.

MARY WELLS'S MEMORIES are by no means limited to 'Fun and Games' (Chapter 7). Hers was one of the first families to settle at the newly established Elizabeth colony, and she recalls how her father built both house and furniture and the pride she and her mother took in keeping the floors spotless. She gives fairly detailed descriptions of her grandmother's techniques of entrapping blackbirds and snaring prairie-chickens while they dance, and also praises the taste of the skunk prepared by her.

Social obligations are shared; a coin is baked into a cake and whoever finds the coin holds the next communal dance – a European lottery for European dances. A dance at her parents' house leaves a deep impression on the little girl, and she gives convincing illustrations of the fascination which the fabled attractions of modern life – such as lipstick or mail-order catalogues – held for her. She provides the fullest sketches of children at play; but at the very end of her account she also gives us a glimpse of traditional competitiveness in games.

Mary Wells's gift for storytelling reveals itself in a series of engaging short stories, ranging from the child's first experience of crime and punishment to social conflicts which arise in playing house and to the sexual overtones introduced into girlish dolls' play by the boys. The limitless imagination and inventiveness of the little girl she once was and her remarkable leadership qualities are at their most impressive when she decides to manufacture cigarettes and, later, lipstick.

Even the death of her beloved grandmother, whose untiring industry makes her a paragon of womanly virtue, turns into a story which is as funny as it is moving.

IN 'A WOMAN'S LIFE' (Chapter 8), Glecia Bear contrasts the poverty of her early years with the easy life provided for today's children, whom she scolds as lazy. She reserves her severest censure – and the most bitter ridicule – for young mothers who neglect their children.

Her discourse moves back and forth between her recollections of practical matters, such as keeping a clean house or storing fresh meat in a cache dug into the muskeg, and the importance of non-material values: respect for one's Elders and generosity in the sharing of food along with bedtime prayers when the entire household would say the rosary after her mother. Although causality is not made explicit, a link is at least suggested between the decline in simplicity, cleanliness, etc., and the more general disintegration of the social fabric.

For Glecia Bear, a lifetime of hard work had begun early, with chores around the house; by the age of eleven she is given responsibility for a cow at calving time (see Chapter 5), and at thirteen she is already hauling fish to town. Later she participates, however marginally, in the cash economy and the wage-labour market while also helping her husband with his commercial efforts, running her own household and raising a large number of children and grandchildren.

Many of the scenes sketched by Glecia Bear – taking her infant daughter along while digging seneca-root, or seeing their sod-roof dissolve in a rainstorm – are memorable indeed. But none is more compelling than the portrait she evokes of herself at the age of sixteen, having to come to terms with an arranged marriage and a husband and mother-in-law who are strangers to her.

PART III CONSISTS of an extended dialogue between Alpha Lafond and Rosa Longneck in which Freda Ahenakew, too, occasionally takes a part.

Ranging widely, their discussions touch on most of the topics dealt with in Parts I and II, but the Muskeg Lake women also go beyond these to talk about medical services and practices and the belief that diabetes is brought on by the consumption of fried food, about language maintenance and the folly of selling land. In reviewing plans for a reunion at Muskeg Lake, they discuss tools and personal ornaments, photographs and priests as well as people they have known and their place in the social network. Two worlds meet in a stew of beaver with onions and pepper.

The dialogue regularly returns to questions of livelihood and the various ways of making a living either by traditional means or in one of the niches left unexploited by the larger economy.

While laundry practices are recalled in various contexts, Rosa Longneck's step-by-step description of soap-making is easily the most detailed of all the technical accounts in this book.

Also included is a story of the kind conventionally told about old women – and often enough, as in this case, also by old women themselves: funny, gently ribald and full of (self-) mockery.

There are glimpses of domestic violence and a cameo scene of peace and quiet as Alpha Lafond recalls her grandmother teaching the children to pray and lousing them while they kneel around her.

Themes

Told by grandmothers, these texts are at their most powerful when they conjure up the time when the narrators were themselves little girls. As they were raised and educated by their own grandmothers, they in turn try to counsel their granddaughters and great-granddaughters.

They stress personal competence, self-reliance, and hard work. They insist on the importance of keeping one's house clean, and they recall admiringly how their grandparents made do with what was readily available. The use of moss is a recurring theme, in the washing of wooden floors as in infant care and personal hygiene. While tobacco is mentioned in a ceremonial context, the ordinary material for smoking is clearly the bark of the 'red willow'.

In the all-pervasive discussion of foodstuffs and their preparation and preservation, they draw attention to the variety of animals eaten, with gophers evidently a significant part of the diet. Rabbits are treated as a uniquely Indian food, spurned by the White neighbours, and there is no better illustration of this view (which seems oblivious to the status of rabbits in French cuisine) than Mary Wells's restaurant joke.

They tell without complaint of the indignities of wage-labour and other, locale-specific ways of working for cash. There is some mention of menial work in restaurants, hospitals, and similar institutions and also of domestic service, and there are still echoes, in Glecia Bear's recollections of her father, of the realm of haulage once dominated by the Métis. But the universal sources of cash income for these marginalised people at the edge of the prairies must have been cutting cordwood and digging seneca-root.

The frequent use of the temporal adverb *kayâs* 'long ago', which reaches from the recent past to time immemorial, should not obscure the fact that many of the reminiscences here collected do not represent a pre-colonial 'golden age' but a much more recent period. The prominence of wooden floors which need to be washed, the weight placed on a registered trapline, and the culinary and social practices which betray deep European influence point to a largely sedentary life. As most of the accounts are, in fact, presented in the form of direct, personal reminiscences by women between the ages of sixty and ninety, it is presumably the time between the two world wars which constitutes the primary period of reference.

THE OVERWHELMING IMPRESSION, however, is not of specific times or endeavours but of overall deprivation, of being caught between two worlds without much control over either. The mud-shacks described so vividly by Glecia Bear and the comparison she draws between them and a properly built log-house are more revealing than any statistical tables of the level of poverty endured by these people.

And yet, there is always laughter – about the childish pranks of a Mary Wells, the old-woman story of Rosa Longneck, or the misfortunes which are told about time and again by the victims themselves; typical examples are Mary Wells's tough-luck story (the stolen dried meat turns out to be a dried moccasin instead) and Rosa Longneck's wistful account of her trip back from town. Finally, there is also the bitter irony of Janet Feitz being blamed for killing the bear which she in fact had protected.

Poverty and lack of control over large areas of their lives notwithstanding, the general sentiment – as if by a dialectic leap – seems to be one of an earlier age which was less dissonant and oppressive, more properly ordered and thus also more appropriate to human existence. Often enough, of course, the picture is tinted with nostalgia, expressed most explicitly in the form of assertions about diseases which were rare then but are common now. (While a general distinction between 'bush food' and 'store-bought food' may well capture the sharp increase in the consumption of carbohydrates and, especially, highly refined sugars during the past half-century, the prevalence of diabetes is attributed specifically to the switch from boiled to fried food, and there is no mention of the possibility that the higher incidence of certain diseases, or indeed of white hair, may simply reflect a higher overall life expectancy.) It is a generally held belief, widely echoed in other Cree texts, that the traditional lifestyle was healthier and that people used to be stronger, less prone to illness and more long-lived.

IN ADDITION TO VALUES which are unambiguously Cree, such as the sharing of meat after a kill, the texts are suffused with admiration for hard work, a virtue which may well enjoy equal esteem in the Aboriginal worldview and in Catholic doctrine.

While ceremonial requirements are specified on one or two occasions, there is no discussion of spiritual matters even where (to the editors at least) it might have seemed appropriate. In her dealings with bears, for example, Janet Feitz makes no mention at all of any spiritual ramifications, and neither do Minnie Fraser or Glecia Bear in the two stories in which owls play a significant part. Similar reticence is shown in the several passages devoted to childbirth and infant care and in Glecia Bear's narrative of her arranged marriage.

Christian values, on the other hand, reverberate through several of the texts. In Minnie Fraser's story as in Glecia Bear's of the two little girls lost in the bush, the church and its institutions are simply part of the background, but Janet Feitz (in Chapter 3) is quite explicit in her approval, and so on several occasions is Glecia Bear.

It is remarkable how intimately the solemn rituals of Catholicism (here mainly Roman Catholic, but hardly distinguishable in effect from those of the Church of England) seem to have meshed with those of pre-contact Cree religion; there is evidently no perception of conflict or contradiction – all the signs point to partial syncretism between two systems which, historically and theologically alike, appear radically different one from the other.

Glecia Bear, in fact, offers the most telling comment in surveying the decline in liturgical practice and the increasing competition offered by charismatic denominations when she affirms her belief in the Creeness of high ritualism by contrasting the two in a simple disjunction: *pahkw-âyamihâwin ahpô môniyâwi-ayamihâwin[a] êkwa ôm ânohc kâ-ispayik* '[I don't know what one should believe,] the Catholic Church or the White-Man's religions and what is going on today.'

THE OUTLOOK IS BLEAK: with all the innovations and gadgets of recent times, there is a sense of impending doom, and the old women who have always viewed the land with its plants and animals as the primary source of their livelihood despair of their grandchildren's ability to escape starvation.

The aimless, hopeless, wayward drift of the young is the overriding preoccupation of their grandmothers.

The texts extol and, inevitably, romanticise to some extent the practical skills of a by-gone age. In reviewing the past, the old women harp upon the daily chores, the traditional competencies, the simple virtues of daily life – but their texts are also permeated by a darker, more tragic theme: the break-up of the traditional value system and the crumbling of the social fabric. The recurrent expressions of their grief focus on the ravages of alcoholism and culminate in anguished plaints about the plight of battered women and their abandoned children.

Setting

In a context where several types of bilingualism are common and ethnic designations are far from settled, it needs to be stressed that the women who gave their recollections to Freda Ahenakew to publish all speak Cree as their first language.

While Irene Calliou and Mary Wells explicitly introduce themselves as coming from Métis settlements, Cree is their first language, too. Readers should keep in mind that the term *âpihtawikosisân* 'Métis' as used in these texts is largely a political and legal term referring to those speakers of Cree (and, to a lesser extent, other Indigenous languages of the northern plains, including of course Métchif) who for one reason or another – many of them entirely accidental – do not appear on the treaty lists drawn up by the Government of Canada.

The continuing presence of French, which has long played a major role in many of the settlements which grew out of fur-trade posts and in the surrounding areas, is especially obvious in Glecia Bear's speech; besides French surnames such as *Morin* or *Séguin* she also pronounces Christian names such as *Joseph* (in the reserve name, *Joseph Bighead*) and *David* and surnames such as *Sinclair* as one would in French, with nasalised vowels and stress on the last syllable.

THE CREE LANGUAGE is spoken in a number of distinct dialects which are as readily identifiable to Cree speakers as the 'BBC' or American English dialects heard in most commercial films are to speakers of English. Two of the major dialects are represented in this book (with some minor dialect differences to be reviewed in the Notes): while Janet Feitz speaks Woods Cree, all the other narrators included in this book are speakers of Plains Cree.

One of the most striking differences between these two major dialects of the Cree language is a large set of words which systematically have the sound *ð* (the symbol *ð* represents the th-sound of English *they*) in Woods Cree and the sound *y* in Plains Cree, e.g., *kahkiðaw / kahkiyaw* 'all', *ðôtin / yôtin* 'wind' or *wâhðaw / wâhyaw* 'far away'.

But not every Plains Cree *y* corresponds to a Woods Cree *ð*; in the very first sentence of Chapter 1 we find Woods Cree *kayâsîs* 'quite some time ago' which exhibits *y* just like its Plains Cree counterpart, *kayâsês*. (This last example and the noun *kinosîwak* 'fish' in the next, the equivalent of Plains Cree *kinosêwak*, also illustrate a more problematic kind of discrepancy between the sound systems of Woods Cree and Plains Cree: Plains Cree *ê* often but not always corresponds to *î* in Woods Cree.)

Another diagnostic for the two major dialects which is particularly obvious is the use of verb forms with the plural marker *-wâw* in Woods Cree where Plains Cree has the plural marker *-ik*. The phrase *ê-osîhakwâw kinosîwak* 'I was filleting the fish', for example, which occurs in the second sentence of Chapter 1, would appear in Plains Cree as *ê-osîhakik kinosêwak;* as it happens, the second paragraph of Chapter 1 contains many more instances of such verb forms.

Even amongst the Plains Cree speakers represented in this book there is a further division of a minor type: Glecia Bear's speech belongs to a northern variety of Plains Cree and displays certain northern features (she occasionally, but not always, will tend to *î* instead of *ê* or use the plural marker *-wâw* instead of the *-ik* expected in Plains Cree) which are not shared by the other Plains Cree speakers, whose speech is typical of the more common, southern variety of Plains Cree.

WITH THE EXCEPTION OF Janet Feitz (who comes from the northern community of La Ronge, which is part of the Churchill River system), all of the narrators belong to the Plains Cree groups which traditionally hunted north of the North Saskatchewan River and eventually settled within the ambit of Carlton House and Fort Pitt. The former goes beyond *maskêko-sâkahikanihk* 'at Muskeg Lake' (which on modern maps appears as *Paddling Lake*) and *yêkawiskâwikamâhk* 'at Sandy Lake' (the *Hines Lake* of modern maps) to reach as far north as *kwâkopîwi-sâkahikanihk* 'at Green Lake'. The Fishing Lake and Elizabeth Métis colonies extend westward from the Alberta-Saskatchewan border, about halfway between the North Saskatchewan River and Cold Lake.

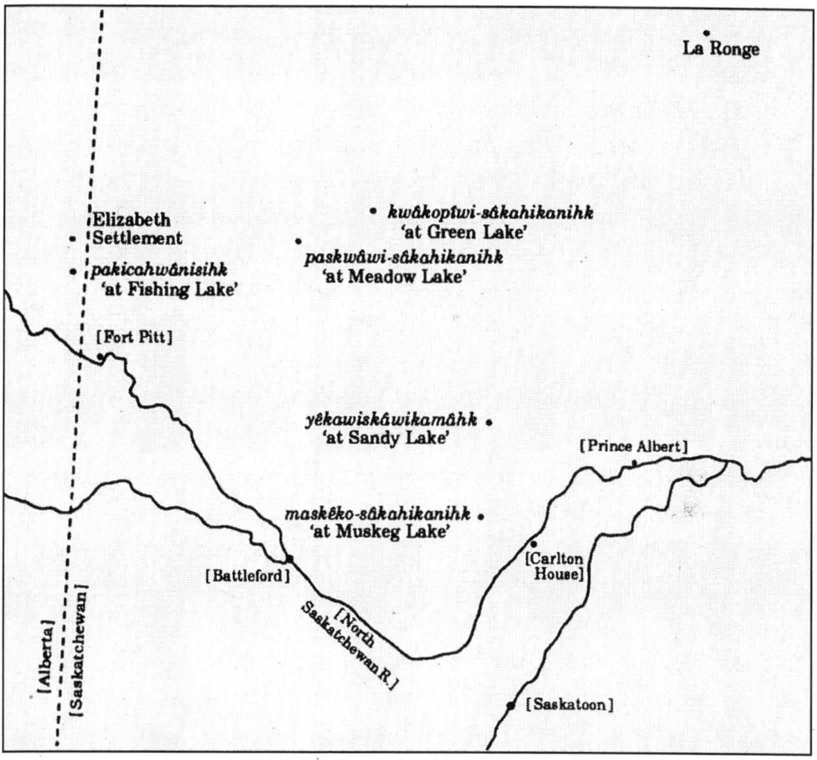

MINNIE FRASER BELONGED to the Anglican Church, which has played an important role amongst *atâhk-akohp*'s band at *yêkawiskâwikamâhk* 'at Sandy Lake' for over a century, while Glecia Bear is a Roman Catholic, which is also the dominant form of Christianity amongst *opitihkwâhakêw*'s band at *maskêko-sâkahikanihk* 'at Muskeg Lake'. With their high ceremonialism, these two manifestations of Catholicism seem to have been especially successful in integrating themselves into the pre-existing patterns of Cree religion.

MINNIE FRASER AND GLECIA BEAR are her relatives, well known to Freda Ahenakew since she was a child on *atâhk-akohp*'s reserve at *yêkawiskâwikamâhk* 'at Sandy Lake': Minnie Fraser was a member of her immediate family group (on her father's side) and a direct neighbour, and Glecia Bear, too, is her aunt (on her mother's side).

She has also known Alpha Lafond and Rosa Longneck since the time when, as a young woman, she married into *opitihkwâhakêw*'s reserve.

The other three she met more recently: Irene Calliou (from Fishing Lake) and Mary Wells (from Elizabeth) were her students in a Cree grammar and writing course, and Janet Feitz is the mother of another of the many Cree language teachers she has been teaching over the past decade.

MOST OF THE TEXTS in this book were recorded during 1988 (Glecia Bear, Irene Calliou, Mary Wells, and Alpha Lafond and Rosa Longneck); the record of Minnie Fraser's story was made in October 1986, only six months before her death, and Janet Feitz told of her experiences in January 1989 (Chapter 3) and again in January 1990 (Chapter 1).

Minnie Fraser was the oldest by far of the seven narrators: at the time she told her story she was almost ninety-one years old. Glecia Bear gives her age (in Chapter 8) as seventy-five, and Janet Feitz probably comes next, while Alpha Lafond and Rosa Longneck were sixty-two and sixty-eight, respectively, and Irene Calliou and Mary Wells in their late fifties at the time they recorded their texts for Freda Ahenakew.

Editorial Presentation

The form of presentation adopted for this book attempts to preserve, so far as possible, both the authenticity and the spontaneity of these documents.

There is, of course, much that simply cannot be saved in the transfer from spoken performance to printed page. Even an audio-recording already lacks the facial expressions, the gestures, the body language, and no written representation of more than a few sentences has yet been able to capture the rise and fall in pitch and volume, the deliberate changes in size of oral cavity, in timbre, in the tone of voice, etc. A speaker's mode of presentation is in part culturally determined but to a significant degree it is also a matter of individual personality and style.

The audio-recordings from which the texts in this book have been transcribed exhibit substantial differences in the manner in which the individual narrators speak their texts. While Janet Feitz's delivery, for example, is matter-of-fact to the point of appearing distant (an impression heightened and broken at once by the irony which marks the end of her first bear story), Glecia Bear's tone leaves little doubt that, in reporting her interviews with women of an earlier generation, she sides with the old against the presumed superiority of the new. When she upbraids the younger generation for neglecting their children, her voice carries extra force, and she rises to dramatic heights in denouncing the young women who hand their infants over into the care of cows rather than raising them with their own milk. Her personal engagement is unmistakable as she relates the thoughts of an old woman who sees her daughters battered without being able to intervene and, of course, in the emotionally charged account of her own arranged marriage.

IT IS NOT ONLY the gulf between oral performance (or its pale reflexion in an audio-recording) and printed page which separates most readers from the original Cree texts: there is also the thicket of translation into another language. Yet this is the only route available to English speakers – short of learning Cree themselves – by which Cree texts can be approached and appreciated. (The common alternative of asking for reminiscences to be told in English is worse: not only do many older people not speak English at all, but even when they do, their command may not be equal to what they might wish to say.)

Translation is always problematic: in trying to match an original, translators easily slip into unidiomatic, even clumsy prose; in striving for fluency, they inevitably risk distortion. In this book, we have chosen fidelity to the original over elegance in English: just as the original Cree texts have been left unsmoothed, so the translations reflect the absence of smoothing.

Clearly, it would have been possible – even easier in many cases – to depart from the relatively literal rendition which we consider appropriate for these texts and to choose a much freer translation. But that would have meant glossing over many characteristic aspects of Cree style, emphasis, syntax, distribution of information over clauses, choice of words, etc. All too easily, moreover, the path from literal to free translation leads down a slippery slope which can only end in a quagmire of approximation and paraphrase.

The dividing line between translation and interpretation is fine and fuzzy at once, and where we have erred in one direction or the other, we can only plead that translation is an art, not a science. When in doubt, we have deliberately chosen to stay on the side of caution, sacrificing fluency and idiomaticity in English to the goal of faithfully following the Cree original.

IN PRINCIPLE, the original being translated is the spoken text; in reality, however, it is the printed edition of the text. The term *edition* is here used in a technical, philological sense which is quite different from that of the term *editing* which is current in commercial publishing (and, of course, in computer jargon).

Where a new work is to be published, one kind of editor accepts or rejects the manuscript, another checks it for internal coherence (in the case of a novel) or defensibility (in a political or scholarly work), and a third reads it for style and consistency of presentation. The latter two steps are called *editing* and *copy-editing*, respectively, and *editing* is further used for a fourth task: that of actually revising or re-writing the manuscript.

In the case of an existing text, on the other hand, the editor's task is the very opposite of revision or re-writing. The document in question is typically of surpassing interest for its antiquity, inherent value, or authority: a sacred text in Hebrew or Sanskrit, a scientific treatise in Arabic or Greek, commercial contracts and tax records in Sumerian or Latin, poems, plays, letters, speeches in a modem European language – or a spoken document in Cree. In documentary editing, the editor's purpose is to present the text intact, in as authentic a state as can be recovered, in the form of a CRITICAL EDITION.

The principles followed in the preparation of a critical edition have developed primarily in the context of the biblical texts and those of the Greek and Latin classics – that is, all in languages well known in their internal structure, richly documented in grammars and dictionaries, and embedded in familiar, thoroughly studied cultures. The scholarly world is infinitely less knowledgeable with respect to the Cree language and, similarly, Cree culture. Despite this serious handicap, these are the models we have attempted to follow in this book – with appropriate modifications and within the limitations of space, time, and circumstance.

THE FIRST AND FOREMOST task of the editor in the philological sense of the term is to establish the text. In the traditional field of manuscript editing, the process of textual criticism begins with the identification and reading of the surviving manuscripts so that they can be grouped and ranked in order of reliability. In the new field of editing acoustic records, the first and most challenging step is to transcribe fully what is on the tape.

Although laymen tend to regard this as a simple matter – confusing it with the typist's task of taking a letter off a dictating machine – the transcription of spontaneous speech is in fact a serious problem. It would be straightforward only if shortcuts were permitted and if one could substitute an approximation for what is really there. In terms of fidelity, in fact, the demands of audio-philology far exceed the level normally expected of court or parliamentary recorders; often enough, the most appropriate parallel seems to be the work of the acousticians who try to analyse the record left on an airplane's flight recorder after a crash. The language may be known, the contents may be perfectly familiar in general terms, but when each scrap of information needs to be identified and interpreted, it is common for indeterminacies to remain.

The same is found in editing texts recorded on audio-tape. There is almost always background noise; there are slamming doors and screaming children. There are external interruptions, when the tape-recorder is shut off in mid-sentence. There are slurred words, or words that trail off in mid-production, and stretches where two or more people speak all at once. In short, any spontaneously produced spoken text will contain passages which remain impenetrable even to the most fluent speaker and careful student of the language.

FOR THE INTEGRITY of the text to be preserved, the distinction between the text itself and the editorial apparatus needs to be maintained at all times. Any queries or comments – especially in the case of passages which are difficult to follow or impossible to comprehend – as well as inserts intended to elaborate on the text are kept separate by typographical means.

In this book, all editorial matter is enclosed in square brackets, and we have been quite pedantic in their use, including them even for the chapter titles and section headings given in the translation, all of which are editorial additions. (The only exceptions to this rule are the section numbers, which are printed bold-face, and the chapter titles which appear in the running heads.)

While brief comments, e.g., [*pronounced as French*], are included in the text and marked by square brackets, longer comments take the form of notes; these usually deal with linguistic aspects of the text but commentary may also be required with respect to the pragmatic context: additional facts concerning biographical, geographical, historical, biological matters, the transport system, the kinship system – in short, the 'real world' being discussed in the text but which may not be fully intelligible without further explication.

THE TEXTS IN THIS BOOK are much closer to normal conversation in every aspect of their style than the prose to which most readers are accustomed. (Even so-called 'interviews' usually undergo much shaping and polishing before they appear in magazines or collections, as highly contrived specimens of written prose.)

We have also refrained from re-arranging sections within each text – they have been preserved integrally. (The only liberty taken by the editors has been to impose the order in which the texts appear, and the decision to treat as separate texts the three distinct segments of Glecia Bear's long recording session of 25 November 1988, interrupted as they were by long periods when the recorder was turned off and she was engaged in discussion of the texts being recorded with Freda Ahenakew.) In consequence, one and the same topic may come up in a number of different contexts, and prose of considerable substance or power may be interspersed with rather more mundane conversational passages.

Some of the asides directed to Freda Ahenakew and her responses, most of which deal with microphones and tapes that need to be turned over, are omitted from this edition so as not to distract the reader from the text itself. Especially in Chapter 6, there are also a number of instances where the recording was interrupted to allow for discussion of the next topic and where the opening of the subsequent section may have been missed because the speaker began before the tape-recorder could be switched on again. All external breaks or omissions are fully marked, either by editorial comment or by a sequence of three dots (also always in square brackets) indicating ellipsis.

WHERE THE SPEECH of a narrator differs from the shared norm, these individual features have usually been preserved without comment. Instances which might give rise to questions are confirmed as correctly printed by the editorial flag [*sic*].

Even within the southern variety of Plains Cree spoken by the five speakers from the area near the North Saskatchewan River (and also by Freda Ahenakew), there are minor regional discrepancies. While Freda Ahenakew, for example, uses the vowel *a* in the third syllable of ***kiskinahamawêw*** 'she teaches her', both of the speakers from ***maskêko-sâkahikanihk*** 'at Muskeg Lake' use *o* in the same position, ***kiskinohamawêw***. Such minor regional variations have not been standardised in this book.

As might be expected, each speaker uses a few words which are not common in the central Saskatchewan dialect of ***atâhk-akohp***'s band as spoken by Freda Ahenakew, or the closely related dialects of Peter Vandall and Joe Douquette, whose texts were published in 1987. Some of the specific differences in the sound system, in the inflexional system of noun and verb stems, in the formation of stems and, finally, in the constructions which hold all these elements together in sentences and the larger discourse are discussed in the Notes which follow the texts.

THE EDITORIAL and typographical conventions and abbreviations used in this book are summarised in the introduction to the Notes.

I

Life in the Bush

1.
Encounters with Bears

Janet Feitz

[FA:] êkwa aw êkwa kotak iskwêw, *La Ronge* ohci, ê-wî-âc-- ê-wî-âcimostâkoyahk, '*Janet Feitz*' isiyîhkâsow, owanihikêw, ê-papâ-pêyakwâcihot mân ôwanihikêskanâhk.

êkosi, kiya!

I

[1] aya ôma kâ-wî-âcimostâtakwâw, mitoni kayâsîs ôma kâ-wî-âtotamân ê-kî-ay-ispaðihikowân ôma, ê-pa-pîyakowân niwanihikîskanâhk; acimosis wið âta wiða, mâna mâka mâna niwîcîwâw.

[2] êkwa ôma pîyakwâw ê-kîsikâk ê-kî-- ê-kî-nâtaðapêyân, êkwân êkwa nikapân, ê-osîhakwâw kinosîwak, êkwa kâ-nitaw-âkotakwâw êkwa akwâwânisihk, ê-wî-aya-wîskwaswakwâw, namêstikwak ê-wî-osîhakwâw. êkwân êkwa nipimahkamikisin kinosêwak ê-osîhakwaw, êkwa nâsipîtimihk mâka wið ôma kâ-itahkamikisiyân. kîtahtawê kâ-pê-nâsipêpahtât êkwa awa nicêmisis, ê-âpasâpit mân îtê k-ôhcipahtât, êkotê ê-itâpit, ê-sêkisit, êkota kisiwâk pê-apiw ita ôma k-ôsîhikinosêwêyân; mîcisowinâhtik ê-ayâk nâsipêtimihk, êkota ôma k-ôsîhakwâw kinosêwak. êkwa ôma nikospin êkwa niwîcîwâw, mitoni kostâciw, namwâc kîkwây niwâpahtên kis-- anima kâ-kostahk; êkwân êkwa, nicakwâwânisihk nititohtân, nitakotâwak êkwa ôko nikinosêmak kâ-wîskwaswakwâw – ê-kî-pônamân wiða mîna pitamâ. êkwân êkwa nipîhtokwân êkwa, wâskahikanisihk ê--, êkotê êkwa mîna nipimahkamikisin. âskaw niwaðawân ê-nitawi-pônamân. êkwa ôm ê-ay-itahkamikisiyân, nitat-îkwa-âpihtâ-kîsikani-mîcison [*sic*], êkwân êkwa nititohtân ita kâ-wîskwaswakwâw kinosîwak, nipônasin, namôða mistahi nipônên, wið ôma ê-itêðihtamân êkwa ê-wî-kawisimowân êkwa ê-wî-aðiwîpiyân. êkwân ê-kî-pônasiyân, êkwâni nipîhtokwân êkwa, êkwân êkwa nikawisimon ê-pa-pimisiniyân ê-ayamihcikêyân,

[FA:] And now another woman, this one from La Ronge, is going to tell us a story, her name is Janet Feitz, she is a trapper and she goes around by herself on her trapline.

Now it is your turn!

I [The Value of a Bear]

[1] This story which I am going to tell you, what I am going to tell about, happened to me quite some time ago while I was alone on my trapline; although I did have a little dog with me.

[2] Now one day, after I had checked my nets, I beached my boat and was filleting the fish, and then I went to hang them on the drying rack, for I was going to smoke them and make smoked fish. So now I was working away and filleting the fish, and I was working close to the water. Suddenly now my little dog came running towards the water, glancing back to where he was coming from, he looked back there, he was scared, and he came to sit close to where I was cleaning the fish; there was a table close to the water, this is where I was filleting the fish. Now I went away from the water with him, he was really afraid, but I did not see what it was of which he was afraid; then I went over to my drying rack and hung up the fillets which I was smoking – and I had first made a fire. So then I went inside, into my little cabin, and there, too, I was working along. Sometimes I went outside to go and add wood to the fire. And now, while working about in this way, I began to have my lunch, and then I went to where I was smoking the fish and added a little wood to the fire, I did not make a big fire, for I thought I would go to bed and have a rest. When I had added a little wood to the fire, I went inside and then I went to bed and was lying down reading when all

kîtahtawê êkwa mâk âwa --, mâka mîn âwa nicêmisis, sôskwâc êkwa kwayask mikisimow, kwayask ê-kostâcit. êkwâni nitêpwâtâw êkwa, "pônwêwita!" ê-itak; âhci piko, *porch*ihk [*sic*] anita, êkota pîhtokwamik [*sic*], êkota kâ-mikisimot, kwayask ê-sîkisit, êkwâni nitawâc êkwa niwaniskân ê-nitawâpênikêyân. êkwâni kâ-paspâpiyân îtê isi nicakwâwânis k-âyâk, awêsk âw êkota, ohpimês nicakwâwânisihk kâ-cîpatapit maskwa. kwayask ê-pî-itâpit anitê ita ôma kâ-paspâpimak ita, êkwân â, nipîhtokwahâw êkwa nicêmisis, êkwân êkwa niwaðawân, sipwêhtêw wið âwa maskwa, namwâ-- namôða mâka wiða sôhki-pimi-kotiskâwêw; mâka nipimwasinâtâw êkwa mihti, "awas, îkatêhtê, maskwa! namôða kîða kâ-wî-asamitân kinosêw," nititâw. â, êkwân êkwa, nipîhtokwân êkwa mîna. êkwâni pîðisk at-ôtâkosin, kêyâpic kâh-kostâciw awa nicêmisis. êkwân êkwa, k-êtêðihtamân, "â, piko ta-pîhtokwahakwâw nikinosêmisak, nika-pê-nîpâ-kimotamâk wîð âwa, êwakwaðiw êtokw âw ôhci kâ-pê-itahkamikisit, kinosêwa ê-pasot awa maskwa," nititêðihtên. êkwân êkwa ispî miton ê-at-ôtâkosik, êkwân êkwa kâ-pîhtokwahakwâw êkwa ôko nikinosêmisak, *porch*ihk anita miscikosa mân ê-pimâskwamoki, êkota k-âh-akotakwâw. êkwa nicîmisis wîða mîna nikî-waðawîtisahwâw, wîða môð âðisk pîhtokwamihk [*sic; cf.* pîhtokwamik] nikanawîðimâw ('waðawîstim' nitisiðîhkâtâw mâna, wîða waðawîtimihk ê-wîkit; namôða wiða pîhtokwamihk [*sic; cf.* pîhtokwamik] wîkiw). êkwa ispî êkwa ê-wî-tipiskâk, sâsay mîna kâ-matwê-mwêstâtwêwitahk, ê-kostâcit. êkwâni niwaniskân êkwa mîna, ê-paspâpiyân, namwâc awiyak niwâpamâw, sôskwât namwâc.

[3] êkwân êkwa, kâwi nikawisimon. êkwa ê-kî-nipâyân, sâsay mîn êkwa mîna mwîstâtwêwitam, sôskwâc î-- î-mawimohkêt, ê-kostâcit sôskwâc. êkwân êkwa mîna niwaniskân ê--, nitîpwâtâw niwî-nôtinâw, "kawisimo!" ê-itak, namwâc pônwêwitam. êkwâni nicakwâwânisihk ici nititâpin, namwâc awiyak niwâpamâw êkotê. êkwân êkwa nâsipêtimihk êkwa, sâkahikanihk isi k-îtâpiyân [*sic*], êkwa ita mân ê-kwâpikêyân anima nâsipîskanaw, awîsk âw êkota, kâ-pimitapit wîð âwa maskwa, ê-ay-apit êkotê nâsipîtimihk. tânis îtokwê ê-itêðihtahk, sâkahikanihk wiða k-îtâpit [*sic*], ê-ay-asawâpit êkotê isi. êkwân êkwa, namôða pônwêwitam awa nicêmisis. êkwân

of a sudden my little dog was again barking mightily, he was mightily afraid. Now I called out to him, "Keep quiet!" I said to him; he still continued to bark, there in the porch, indoors, he was mightily scared, and at last I got up to check. Now I looked out the window in the direction of my drying rack, and what was that! just a little to the side from my drying rack, sitting straight up, there was a bear. He was looking straight in the direction from which I was looking out at him, so then, well, I put my little dog inside the cabin and then I went out, but the bear left, he was not exactly racing away; but I picked up a stick and threw it at him, saying to him: "Go away, get away from here, Bear! You are not the one to whom I am going to feed fish!" I said to him. Well, and then I went back inside again. Then, finally, it was becoming dusk, and my little dog was still afraid. So now I thought, "I must take my fillets inside, the bear will come and steal them from me in the dark of the night, obviously that is the reason why he is coming around, he smells the fish," I thought. And then, as it was really getting to be evening, I brought my fillets inside, onto the porch, and I hung them all up on rods that were nailed up along there. And I had also put my little dog outside for I did not keep him indoors (*waðawîstim* [*sc.* 'Outside-Dog'] I used to call him for he lived outside; he did not live indoors). And then, when it was getting dark, again already he could be heard barking with fear. Now I got up again and looked out the window, but I could not see anyone, no one at all.

[3] And so I went back to bed. No sooner had I fallen asleep when he again made a nuisance of himself by barking, he was howling miserably, he was definitely afraid. Now I got up again, I called out to him and I was going to hit him, "Lie down!" I said to him, but he would not cease barking. Now I looked towards my drying rack, but I could not see anyone there. Then I looked towards the water, towards the lake, and there, on the path down to the water, where I usually fetch my water, what was that! There, sitting across the path, was the bear, sitting there at the shore. I wonder what he thought, for he was looking towards the lake, he was keeping watch in that direction. And then my little dog would not cease barking. So then

êkwa *porch*ihk anita kâ-pîhtokwahak, êkota ê-osîhtamawak nipîwin ta-nipât, êkwa nititâw kita-pônwêwitahk.

[4] namôða wiða mîna niwî-pâskiswâw awa maskwa, wið îkâ kita-kî-kitamwak, ê-pêyakowân ôma, êkwa ê-kiðipi-misiwanâtahk masko-wiyâs, kâ-nipahat maskwa êkos îsi kâ-kîsopwêk. êkwan êkwa, wâpanwêwitam wîð âwa nicêmisis, ê-kostât anihi, mâk îspî ê-ati-wâpahk ê-waniskâyân, ê-koskomit êkwa mîna, êkota kos ôma kâ-pimohtêt êkwa awa maskwa, nitiskwâhtêmihk êkota. êkota ê-pa-pimohtêt, nicakwâwânisihk nêtê êkotê ê-nitawi-mâh-miðâhcikêt, ê-matwê-wâh-waskawipitahk nicakwâwânâhcikosa, mâka wiða îkâ kîkwây ê-astêk. êkwâni pê-waðawîw êkota ohci, wâskahikanis aðisk mân ânima nicakwâwânis, êkwâni pê-waðawîw, êkwân âspin k-âti-ka-kospit, ê-ati-wâpaniðik ôma, êkwan âspin.

[5] â, kwayask êkwa nipakwâtâw awa maskwa ê-takosihk. êkwa nitaðapiy kêyâpic mîn ê-akohcihk. êkwân îwako ê-kîsikâk, k-êtêðihtamân ê-wiðasowâtisowân, "â, cîskwa, nika-manipitâw nitaðapiy, osâm awa maskwa nika-mwîstâcihkâk, wêpinaki -- wêpinaki kinosîw nâsipêtimihk," nititâw -- nititêðihtên. êkwân êkwa êwako ê-kîsikâk, nimanipitâw êkwa nitaðapiy. êkwa aðisk mîna nicêmisis mâna, namôða ninakatahwâw; mayaw ôma kita-pôsiyân, êkwâni wîst âsokanihk pê-cîpatapiw; namôða wiða pôsi-kwâskohtiw, pâtimâ mâna, "pôsi!" k-êtak, êkwêðâc kâ-pôsit. mitoni mâna nêscâmocakosihk, êkotê mân ê-astâyân anâskânis, êkota mân ê-apit. â, êkwân êkwa kâ-nitawi-manipitak nitaðapiy.

[6] êkwâni nôsîhikinosîwân, niwîskwaswâwak aniki, namêstikwak ê-osîhakwâw. êkwâni kapê-kîsik êkwa mîna nipimahkamikisin ôma. êkwa anih âya, k-êskosâwâtakwâw kinosêwak, nitasiwaðâwak aya, mahkahkohk, ê-nitawi-wêpinakwâw akâmihk, êkâ ê-wî-asamak ana maskwa, osâm kita-kisâcît.

[7] êkwa êwako ê-tipiskâk, ninahahðâwak nikinosêmak, wiða ê-- ê-takosihk awa, êkwa ê-kostak kita-pê-kimotamawit. tâpwê, mayaw mâka mîn ê-at-âkwâ-tipiskâk, sâsay nicêmisis mâka

I brought him into the porch and made a bed there for him to sleep and told him to stop barking.

[4] I was not going to shoot the bear for I would not be able to eat all of him, being alone, and bear-meat spoils quickly when you kill a bear in warm weather like that. And my little dog barked all through the night, he was afraid of him, but then, as dawn broke and I was getting up, he startled me again, there was the bear walking by my door. He was walking by there, sniffing around my drying rack over there, he could be seen shaking the rails of my drying rack, but of course there was nothing on it. Now he came away from there, out of there, for my drying rack had a little shelter over it, now he came out of there, and as dawn broke, he went off into the bush and was gone.

[5] Well, I very much disliked having this bear here. And my net was still in the water. Then, it was that day that I thought I would make a plan, "Well, wait, I will pull in my net, for the bear will not leave me alone if I throw fish on the shore [*sc.* in cleaning it]," I said to him -- I thought. That day, then, I pulled in my net. And I usually do not leave my little dog behind when I go by boat; as soon as I get into my boat, he, too, comes and sits up on the dock; he does not jump into the boat, he waits, and only when I say to him, "Get in!", only then does he get in. Right at the bow I put a little blanket, and there he usually sits. Well, then I went to pull in my net.

[6] Then I cleaned the fish, I smoked the fillets, making smoked fish. And so I kept working along all day. And then I put what I had cut off in filleting the fish into a tub and went across the lake to throw it away, I was not going to provide food for that bear lest he stay.

[7] Then that night I put my fillets away, for the bear was in the vicinity and I was afraid he would come and steal them from me. True enough, as soon as it was getting later in the evening, again

mîna kâ-kostâcit. êkwâni nipaspâpin, awêsk âwa kâ-pê-na-nâsipêt awa maskwa, onikahp aðisk êkota ayâw, mîskanâhk, êkota ê-pê-na-nôkosit na-nisihkâc ê-pê-pa-pimohtêt, êkwa mîn ôm ê-pê-kiyokêt. êkwani kos ôm êkota kâ-pê-itohtêt nicakwâwânisihk anita, mâka sâsay nikî-nahahðâwak nikinosêmisak, êkota kos ôm êkwa k-âpit, ê-cîpatapit. ê-n-- ê-pî-itâpit mâna niwâskahikanisihk, âskaw ê-kitâpamât nicêmisisa, êkot[a] âw ê-kakwâtaki-mwîstâtwêwitahk wîð âwa, ê-mikitât, ê-ohtiskawapîstawât anihi maskwa awa nicêmisis, ê-mikitât, êkwa wîð âwa mosci mâna ê-kitâpamât. êkwa êkota ê-cîpatapit ana maskwa, kinwîsk êkota k-âpit, miton êtokwê nîso-tipahikan nânitaw. namôða nipisiskêðimâw; kîsâc wiða mîna nikî-âwatôpân, wiða waðawî-- êkâ ê-nôhtê-waðawîyân êkota anima kisiwâk ê-ayât.

[8] êkwâni, kîtahtawê êkwa, kâ-pimi-nâsipêt êkwa mîna. êkwa itê anima mâna k-ôsîhikinosîwêyân âsokanihk kisiwâk, êkota ôm êkwa k-îtohtêt [*sic*], ê-matwê-wâh-wâskâskahk anima mîcisowinâhtik, mâka wiða kahkiðaw kîkwây ê-wêpinamân, matwê-mâh-mônâtihkêw êkota, nitôt [*sic*] mîna matwê-wâh-wâskâskam. êkwân êkwa mîna kâ-pêci-kospit, êkota waðawîtimihk nîkihk, êkota ôma kâ-pa-pimohtêt, aspin êkwa mîn ê-kospit.

[9] â, êkwân êkwa, mâka tahto-kîsikâw mitâtô-- nitâcimostawâwak ôko, taht ôrêtiyowa mâna kâ-nitohtahkwâw kîwêtinohk (ayâwak aðisk orêtiyowa, ê-ayamihitowâhk mâna), êkota nitâh-âcimâw awa maskwa, êkwa mihcêt awiyak nititik, "â, nipah! pâskis êwakw âna, ê-mwîstâtahkamikisit! maskwayân ana ka-kî-atâwâkân," nititikwak. "namwâc, namwâc nika-kî-nipahâw; pikwanita [*sic*] kita-wiyakihtâyân wiyâs, êkâ kita-kî-kitâyân êkwa mi-- ta-misiwanâtahk wiyâs, namwâc." â, êkwân êkwa, pîðisk -- pîyak awa, kisiwâk kâ-wîkit awiyak, pîðisk niwî-nôtinik, "nipah êwakw âna kâ-mwîstâtwêwêmat maskwa, kita-pônwêwitaman!" nititik -- nititâw -- [*sic*]. êkwâni, "namwâc," nititâw, "namwâ [*sic*] mosciwâk ka-nipahak."

[10] êkwâni, kîhtwâm êkwa (pêyak-ispaðiw aw êkota maskwa ayâw, niyânan-kîsikâw mwêhc êkota ê-itahkamikisit awa maskwa), êkwa

already my little dog was afraid. Now I looked out, and what was that! the bear was coming down to the water, for it was a portage, and there on the trail he was coming into view, walking slowly, coming to visit again. Then he came to where I had my drying rack but I had already put my fillets away, and this is where he now stayed, sitting upright. He would look towards my cabin, sometimes he looked at my little dog, this one was making such a terrible racket and was barking at him, my little dog sitting with his face towards the bear and barking at him, and the bear in turn simply looking at him. And there the bear sat upright, staying there for a long time, it must have been about two full hours. I did not bother him; I had hauled my water beforehand for I did not want to go outside when he was close by there.

[8] Then, all of a sudden, he made his way to the water again. Then he went to where I usually clean the fish, close to the dock, he could be seen walking around and around the table, but I had thrown everything away, he could be seen digging around there and also going around and around my boat. Then he was making his way back away from the water, he came walking by the outside of my cabin, and away he went into the bush.

[9] Well, then, each day I told about this to all those who usually listen on the radio up north (for they have [*sc.* two-way] radios and we talk to one another), I kept telling about the bear on the radio, and many said to me, "Well, kill him! Shoot that one, he is being troublesome! You will be able to sell the bearhide," they said to me. "No way, I will not be able to kill him; I would waste the meat for no good purpose, as I would not be able to eat all of it and then the meat would spoil, no way." Well, and then, finally, one who lived close by spoke harshly to me, "Kill that bear you are complaining about, so that you will quit talking about it!" he said to me -- I said to him --. And then, "No way," I said to him, "under no circumstances will I be able to kill him."

[10] And then the next time (the bear was there for a week, for exactly five days the bear was hanging around there), and then one day,

pêyakwâw ê-kîsikâk, mêkwâc nâsipêtimihk ê-itahkamikisiyân (ê-nânapâcihtâyân nitôt [*sic*], ê-kîsipêkînamân, kwayask ê-nânapâcihtâyân, ê-wî-nahastâyân; wîpac ê-wî-ohpahowân), êkwâni, ninitomâw êkwa aw ôpimiðâw, "niyânano-kîsikâki pê-nâtahôhkan!" nititâw awa, "mitâtaht-tipahikan ê-kîkisîpâyâk; kîyâm nika-kîwân, osâm nipakwâtâw awa maskwa k-êtahkamikisit," nitit-- nititâw awa k-ītwêstamawit [*sic*] – wið êkâ nîða *La Ronge* ê-kî-takopaðik nitayamiwin, kotak pikw âwiyak ê-itôtamawit.

[11] êkwâni tâpwê, ê-nîwo-kîsikâk êkospî, wâpahki t-ês-ôhpahowân, êkota êkwa miton êkâ kâ-wawêyatêðihtahk awa maskwa. kapê-kîsik kos ôm êkwa nicakwâwânisihk osâm piko ê-apit anita, kâh-kwêkwask ê-itohtêt, anit[a] êtêhkê isi namahtinihk ê-apit nicakwâwânisihk, âskaw kihciniskihk, âskaw awasîw [*sic*] ohci, tîpiðâhk ê-- tâpiskôc ê-kanawêðimit, êkâ waðawîtimihk tit-îtahkamikisiwak [*sic*]. êkwân êkwa, ôta kos âw ê-ay-apit awa maskwa kapê-kisik, "pâskac êkwa ê-pê-ohtiskawapit," nititâcimon ôm ôrêtiyow ê--, ê-ay-ayamihak ana pêyak iskwêw kisiwâk êkota. "mâcikôci, kik-âcimostâtin ê-itahkamikisit," nititwân, ê-ayamiyân anita orêtiyow, kisik ê-paspâpimak awa maskwa waðawîtimihk. "ê-isîhcikêt kos âwa maskwa! nicakwâwânisihk ohpimês anita ê-âpit; êkwa kos âwa, ê-nânapâcihisot kwayask, ê-sîkahahk, ê-- ê-nôskwâtahk ospitona, êkwa wâskikanihk mîna misiwê, êkwân ê-ohpinahk ocihciya, awasîw [*sic*] aya, wîhtawakaya [*sic*] ômis [*sic*] ê-âh-itôtahk, î-sîkahot," nititâw. "iyikohk [*sic*] kos âw êkwa mîn ê-ohpinahk ospiton, ê-cîhcîkinahk kos ôm ôtê ôkana [*sic*]" (ê-otihkomit êtokw âwa maskwa), "êkos ân[a] ê-isîhcikêt, ê-câh-cîhcîkît; êkwa misiwê mîna, wîhcikwana [*sic*] ê-nânapâcihtât – matwân cî aw[a] ê-itêðihtahk kita-kiskinawâpamak ê-isîhcikêt," nititwân ê-pâhpiyân. "êkos êtokw âna, êkây êtokw ân[a] ê-ohci-kâsihkwêyan, ê-itêðimisk, k-ôh-is-îtôtahk êwakw âna maskwa, ê-itisk êtokw âna ta-kâsihkwêyan," nititik êkwa awa kâ-ay-ayamihak. êkwân êkwa kâ-kîs-âcimak awa maskwa.

[12] miton êkwa nipakwâtâw; ê-nêwo-kîsikâk ê-otâkosik ôma, wâpahki wið âta wiða t-ôhpahowân ta-tapasîhak, ay[a] ôti êkâ ê-nôhtê-wîc-âyâmak; ôta pêyak-ispaðiw ê-wîc-âyâmak. êkwân

while I was working along by the water (fixing up my boat, washing it and properly fixing it up, for I was going to put it away and fly out soon), then I asked the pilot to come, "Come and get me on Friday!" I told him, "At ten o'clock in the morning; I will simply go home, because I hate the bear hanging around here," I said to the one who was relaying my message for me – as my own transmission cannot reach La Ronge, I have to have someone else do this for me.

[11] And indeed, it was Thursday then, I would be flying out the next day, it was then that the bear behaved in a very odd way. He stayed by my drying rack for most of that day, going back and forth there, sitting to the left of my drying rack and then sometimes to the right, sometimes on the other side, just as if keeping watch over me so that I would not work outside. And so this bear sat there all day, "Now he has even come to sit facing me," I told about this on the radio, talking to one woman who lives close by. "Just wait, I will tell you what he does," I said, as I talked there on the radio and at the same time watched the bear outside through the window. "The things this bear is doing! He is sitting a little away from my drying rack; and he is properly primping himself, combing his fur -- licking his arms, and also all over his chest, then lifting his paws and doing this [*gesture, despite the fact that the original telling took place over a two-way radio*] behind his ears, combing himself," I said to her. "And now he is lifting his arm so high, scratching his armpits there" (I guess the bear had lice), "and this is what he is doing, he keeps scratching himself; and then all over, he is taking care of his knees – I wonder if he thinks I should follow his example," I said with a laugh. "That must be it, it must be that he thinks you did not wash your face, that is why that bear is doing this, he must be telling you to wash your face," the one I was talking to said to me. And then I was finished telling about the bear [*sc.* on the radio].

[12] Now I disliked him a great deal; it was Thursday evening, and at least I was to fly out the next day and flee from him for I did not want to live with him; I had been living with him here for a week.

êkwa êkosi k-îtêyihtamân [*sic*], "cîskwa, nika-pâskiswâw, aya, nik-êsi-pâskisikân itê isi k-âpit, kita-tapasît." êkwân êkwa, kâ-sipwêhtêt êkwa, mitoni wâhðawês kâ-matwê-cîpatapit, mâka wiða misiwê ê-paskwâk, matwê wâhðaw apiw, ê-pê-ohtiskawapit, êkotê ê-osâpamit. êkwa ê-kostamân ta-waðawîyân, "nânitaw isi pê-nâcipahici," ê-itêðimak; nicêmisis wîð îtwêwitam ôma ê-kostât, mâka namwâ [*sic*] nipîhtokwahâw.

[13] êkwan êkwa k-ôtinamân êkwa nipâskisikan, anima '*thirty-thirty*' k-êtahkwâw mâna; êkwâni k-âsiwatâyân pêyak môsosiniy, êkwan êkwa k-îsi-wêpahamân [*sic*]. êkwani kâ-pâskihtênamân êkwa niwâsînamân, anima piko sakimîwayânêkin, êwako piko ê-itamok, namôða mîn êwako nikî-âhtinên, ât[a] ê-kakwê-âh-îkatê-wêpahamân, mâka namwâc, ê-manâ-pîkonamân anima, anim êwakw ânima pîwâpisk, wiða sakimîskâhk. êkwân êkwa êkota kâ-nîpawiyân, pâskac ê-tîhtapiyân, êkwa nipâskisikan anima ê-tahkohtastâyân anita wâsênamânihk. êkwân êkwa k-ôwiðâpamak, ohpimê ita k-âpit, êkota! – êkota k-êsi-- k-îtâpiyân [*sic*] ôma, êkwa kâ-tasinamân anima nipâskisikan. êkwa, namwâc kos ôma kîkwây ê-pîhtamân, tâhôc [*sic; cf.* tâpiskôc] ê-kipipaðiki nihtawakaya [*sic*], êkwa orêtiyow ôm âwiyak ê-ay-ayamihit, namwâc kos ôma kwayask ê-pîhtawak, î-kipihtêpaðiyân anima kâ-matwêwêk, wið pîhtokwamihk [*sic; cf.* pîhtokwamik]. êkwân êkwa, pitamâ êkwa mîna kâ-- nihtawakaya [*sic*] kâ-pâh-pôhtâskwahamân, "tânis ôma ê-ispaðiki," êkwâni nikisîwênên êkwa nôrêtiyôm, kisîwêw awa k-ây-ayamihit. êkwa, "kipîhtên nâ kâ-matwêwêk?" ê-i-- ê-itak; "êy, yôho! namwâc wiða nama cî êkây ê-mâkonat an[a] ôcipâson," k-êsit, kita-kî-mâkonak aðisk ocipâson ana, kita-pîhtahk ê-matwêwêðik, mâka wið êkây êkos ê-kî-tôtamân, wið ê-kî-nîsohkiniskêyân. êkwâni kos ôm âta wiða kâ-tapasît ana maskwa.

[14] êkwan ê-niyânano-kîsikâk (nikîsi-mamanân êwako ê-otâkosik, ê-asiwacikêyân ê--, wiða wâpahki ta-pê-nâtahokawiyân), êkwân êkwa âsokanihk, mitoni kisip-âyihk, êkotê ôma kâ-nitaw-âscikêyân, kisik ê-asawâpamak awa maskwa, kita-takosihk, mâka wið ê-kî-pâskiswak mâna mâka tapasîw. êkwa mitâtaht-tipahikan,

And so I thought, "Wait, I will shoot at him, I will shoot in the direction where he sits so that he will flee." And then he left, he could be seen sitting upright quite some distance away, but it was treeless everywhere and he could be seen sitting at quite a distance, sitting so as to face me and watching me from there. And I was afraid to go outside, "What if he comes running for me," I thought about him; my little dog was still barking in fear of him, but I did not take him indoors.

[13] And then I took my gun, what they call a 30-30; and then I put one bullet in, and then I cocked it. Then I opened my window, only the screen, only that was still in it but I could not move that although I was trying to push it aside, but I could not, I did not want to tear the metal screen for the mosquitoes were thick. And then I stood there, actually sitting up on something, and propped my gun up there on the window. And then I put my sights on him, a little off from where he sat, I aimed for that point and then I pulled the trigger of my gun. Then I did not hear anything, as though my ears were blocked, and someone was talking to me on the radio but I could not hear her at all properly, my ears were blocked by the gun blast for it was indoors. And then I first of all poked my ears, "What is the matter with them," then I turned my radio up, the one who was talking to me spoke louder. "Did you hear the gun blast?" I said to her; "Hey, yooho! No, maybe you did not push down the transmission button," she said to me, of course I should have pushed it down for her to hear the gun blast, but I could not do that for I needed both hands [*sc.* on the gun]. But then the bear did flee.

[14] Then on Friday (I had finished getting ready the evening before, putting things into boxes, for I would be picked up the next day), then I went and put everything at the end of the dock, all the while watching for the bear to arrive, but he had fled after I had shot at him. At ten o'clock the plane could already be heard coming, and

sâsay k-â--, âta wiða kâ-pê-pîhtâkwahk pimiðâkan, êkwân êkwa nitâcimostawâw êkwa aw ôpimiðâw, "pêyak-ispaðiw ôta ê-wîc-âyâmak awa maskwa; anohc kâ-kîkisêpâyâk namîskwa ôta takosin," nititâw. "yôh, kita-kî-pîsiwak wið ôma nipâpâ, kita-pê-nipahât," k-îsit [*sic*]. "êy, tâpwê pikw âni, pîðisk kipâpâ kita-nipahât anihi maskwa, nipakwâtâw aw ê-itahkamikisit ôta; ahpô êtokwê ta-pîhtokwêw niwâskahikanis," nititâw. êkwân êkwa nitôhpahonân.

[15] êkwa êkospî anima, ê-at-îhkihk *nineteen-eighty-two* pakahkam, k-âti-pasitêk kos ôma niwanihikêskanaw, misiwê êkota ê-pasitêk. êkwa êkotê kos ôm ê-nitawi-twêhocik otâstawêhikêwak, kâ-miskawâcik kos ôma êkoni, anihi maskwa, mitoni kisiwâk nîkihk,

[FA:] – ê-pimâtisit? –

êkota isi ê-nipit ana maskwa, êkwa kos ôma nama kîkwây ostikwân. awiyak îtokwê ê-kî-pâskiswât, êkwa ê-manâhot ostikwân anima,

[FA:] – mitoni nayêstaw ostikwân? –

kâ-sîpaskwâtahkwâw mâna, êkos îtokw ê-isîhcikêt. êkwa anik êkota kâ-kî-ayâcik aya, môsôkimâwak aniki, mistah ê-kâh-kakwêcimicik aya, "tânis ôm ê-isîhcikêyan kâ--, ê-kî-itakotâyan cî masko-tâpakwâna kâ-nipahat maskwa," ê-isicik – êkwa wið ôma ê-kî-manâcihimak, êkâ ê-kî-ohci-wî-nipahimak; êkwa nîð ê-atâmimicik ê-nipahimak.

[16] êkwan êkota ê-iskw-âcimikosit awa maskwa; êkwân âta wiða ê-kî-nakatahwak.

[SW:] tâpwê êsa.

[JF:] miton êsa kî--, kîyâpic – kîyâpic pêyak niwî-atôtên.

[FA:] âha; âha.

II

[17] aya, kotak mîna niwî-âtotên, maskwa ê-wî-âcimak. êkwa aya, ahpô êtokwê awiyak 'masko-nôcokwêsiw' nika-wî-isiðîhkâtik, mâka kiyâm êkos îsi.

then I told the pilot, "I have been living here with this bear for a week; but this morning he has not yet shown up here," I told him. "Oh, I should have brought my dad along to kill him," he said to me. "Hey, by all means have your dad kill that bear at last, I dislike him hanging around here; he might even get inside my cabin," I said to him. And then we lifted off.

[15] And then there was a forest fire that summer, in 1982, I believe, in the area of my trapline, the whole area burnt out. And when the firefighters went to land there, they found that bear, quite close to my place,

[FA:] – alive? –

they found the carcass of that bear there, and its head was gone. Someone must have shot it and taken the head as a trophy,

[FA:] – the head and nothing else? –

when they stuff them, that is what he must have done. And the game wardens who were there questioned me closely, "What were you doing, had you been setting bear-traps when you killed the bear," they said to me – when on the contrary I had been sparing him and would not kill him; and now they were blaming me for killing him.

[16] And that is all there is to tell about this bear; of course I had left him behind when I took the float-plane out.

[SW:] Indeed.

[JF:] It was really --, still – I am going to tell one more story.

[FA:] Yes; yes.

II [The Bear Who Got Away]

[17] Well, I will also tell another story, I am going to tell about a bear. Perhaps someone is now going to call me *masko-nôcokwêsiw* [*sc.* 'Bear-Old-Woman'), but that's all right, too.

[18] aya, pîyakwâw ôma mîn ê-sîkwâk, êkotê ê-is-ôhpahowân, êkwa pêyak aw îskwêw, *Charl--* aya, *'Rosie Charles'* isiðîhkâsow, "â, nisikosê, ka-wîcîwitin, kâ-wî-nitawi-sîkwanisiyan," k-îsit [*sic*]. "â, tîniki," nititâw, "kika-wîcîwin;" êkwân êkwa nikî-ohpahonân.

[19] mâka mîn îkotî anima ay-ihkin ôm ê-kî-twêhowâhk, sâsay mistahi kî-mêscipaðiw kôna. êkwa êkotê anim ê-ay-itahkamikisiyâhk, môða niwanihikânân, mistahi mâk âya, nikâh-kaskikwâsonân êkwa nipahkêkinohkânân, êkos îsi kîkwây ê-ay-itôtamâhk; kapê-ayi nicanawânân. êkwa pêyakwâw ê-kîsikâk, ê-nâcakwêsit ê-kî-wâposo-câpakwêsiyâhk, "â, nisikosê, awiyak kos âwa kikimotamâkonaw aya, wâposwa, tâhôc [*sic; cf.* tâpiskôc] kos âwa maskwa ê-tak-- ê-takosihk," k-îtwît [*sic*]. ê-takohtahât, pêyak wið âta wiða pêsiwêw, mâka kotak[a] ânihi iyawis ê-wanihât; ê-âh-- ê-âh-ocipitât awiyak, ê-sipwêhtahât.

[20] êkwa kos ôma, wîpac at[i] êkospî, kâ-misi-mispok, miton êtokwê pîyak-misit ê-mispok. êkwân êkwa, "â, mitoni wið êkwa aðâkonêwa kicâpakwânisinawa," itwêw. "â, êðiwêhk nîða nika-natâkwêsin [*sic*] ôta kisiwâk ôhi [*sic*] kâ-kî-akotâyân, mahti kê-nipahak," nititwân; êkwâni nisipwêhtân. êkwa wîsta, ohpimê isi wîsta sipwêhtêw, ê-nâcakwêsit, wiða pâh-piskihc ê-isi-câpakwêsiyâhk. nîða nîkân nitakosinin; nama kîkwây nipîtân, kahkiðaw kîkwây aðâkonêw, îkwaðiw [*sic*] ê-misi-mispok.

[21] nîða mâka wîpac kâ-kî-nâtakwêyân, mâka wîða namôða wîpac. kêtahtawê kâ-takosihk, "â, nikiskîðimâw êkwa awiyak kâ-kimotamâkowahk wâposwa," itwêw, "maskwa aw îsa, nimâtahâw êkwa, ita ês ê--, aya, ê-ohtinât niwâposoma," itwêw; "êkwa ôtê isi-sipwêhtêw." â, êkwân êkwa, "â, cîskwa, kika-tâpakwamahwânaw ana maskwa." êkwân êkwa, ninitonên nitâpakwâna, nîwo pakahkam masko-tâpakwâna kâ-kî-ayâyân. êkwân êkon êkwa nitakotânân, mâk îsa namôða maskawâw anima tâpakwânêyâpiy; tâpakwâtêw wîða, paskipitamiðiwa. êkw ânih êkwa kotaka nîsta nitâpakwâna, namôð êkwa nikî-âpacihtân – iyawis nimaninên, wið ê-paskipitahk misawâc ana.

[18] Well, one spring I was also flying out there, and one woman, her name was Rosie Charles, "Well, my aunt, I will go with you when you go to your trapline in the spring," she said to me. "Well, thank you," I said to her, "you will come with me;" and then we had flown out.

[19] And it so happened that, over there, much of the snow was already gone when we landed. And we were busy over there, we did not trap but we were doing a lot of sewing and tanning hides, we were doing things like that; we were busy all along. And one day she went to check the rabbit snares we had set, "Well, my aunt, someone has stolen our rabbits from us, it seems that a bear has arrived," she said. She brought one rabbit, she did bring one anyway, but all the rest she lost; someone pulled them out and took them away.

[20] And soon afterwards there was a big snowfall, it must have snowed at least a foot. And then, "Well, our snares are buried deep in the snow now," she said. "Well, as for me, I will nevertheless check those which I set close-by to see if I will have killed one," I said; and so I went off. And she, too, went off in a different direction to check her snares, for we were setting our snares in separate areas. I arrived home first; I did not bring back anything, everything was covered by snow, it had snowed so much.

[21] I had gone early to check my snares but she had not. After a while, when she came back, "Well, now I know the one who has been stealing our rabbits from us," she said, "it is a bear, and I tracked him from where he took my rabbits," she said; "he went off in this [*gesture*] direction." Well, and then, "Well, wait, we will snare that bear." And then I looked for my snares, I believe I had four snares for bears. Then we set those, but evidently that snare wire was not strong; she snared him but he broke the snare wire. And the same with the other snares I had, I could not use them now, I took all of them down again – with that bear breaking the snare wire in any case.

[22] êkwân êkwa, "â, pîminahkwân kik-âpacihtânânaw; itwêwak aniki mâna, 'k-ôsâwâpêkahk anima, aya, pîminahkwân, êwakw ê-miðwâsik maskwa ohci,' itwêwak ôma mâna," nititâw. â, êkwân êkwa mâna kâ-ca-cîpatapiyâhk ôma, kisik ê-ayamiyâhk ê-tâpakwânihkêyâhk, maskwa wîð âw ê-tâpakwamahwâyâhk. êkwani, ê-otâkosik êkwa, êkwân êkwa kâ-kospiyâhk êkwa mîna, mâka timikoniw kwayask, ninitawi-tâpakwamahwânân. tâpwê mîna, êsa kî-pimohtêw, mâka namôða nitâpakwâtânân; sâ-sâpohtêw -- aya oti ê-mâh-miyâskahk,

[FA:] – ê-pâh-patiskahk; –

[JF:] – êha; –

êkwâni, ê-wâpahk, namôða nipisiskêðihtênân nitâpakwâninâna, êkos îsi namôða nôh-tâpakwamahwânân; pâtimâ kîsopwêki, kôna ana mêscipaðici, êkwêðâc mîna. pêðisk [*sic*] êkwa mêscipaðiw awa kôna, â, êkwân êkwa mîna kâ-nitawi-tâpakwêyâhk. kîhkîhk mîna, wîða mîna sâsay mîn ê-tâpakwâtât; paskinam ani--, anima pîminahkwân awa maskwa, â, mâka wiða *thirty-thirty* ê-tahkonamâhk. â, êkwân êkwa, kâ-pimitisahwâyâhk êkwa; ninîkânohtân, otâskanâhk wîð âwa, wiða nîð ê-nîmâskwêyân, ohtitaw piko nîkân nîða. kîtahtawê k-âti-m--, ita awa ê-ati-pimohtêt, êkota k-âstêk anima pîminahkwân, ê-ati-kêcikopitahk êtokw ânima.

[23] êkwân â, sâsay mîna kotaka nôsîhtânân tâpakwâna, wið êkospî anim ê-kî-itikawiyâhk mîna, "awiyak nipahâci maskwa, wîsopiy anima mistakihtêw, êwako kit-ôtinahk awiyak kit-âtâwâkêt, mistahi k-ôhtisin sôniyâw[a] [*sic*]," ê-itikawiyâhk mîna; êwak ôm ôhc îðikohk kâ-nôcihâyâhk awa maskwa. êkwâni nikospinân, êkwa mîn ê-oðakoyâhk; nipâh-patakwâtânân.

[24] êkwân îkwa, "â, niwi--, êkwâni nîða niwî-nâtakwân," k-êsit. "îhi," nititâw, "pâskisikan ôma tahkona, kâwið[a] âsiwatâhkan môsosiniy! pâtimâ wâpamaci, namôð ânima wîhkât nitasiwatân môsosiniy, ta-pimohtatâyân pâskisikan," nititâw, "pâtimâ awiyak kâ-wâpamak, êkwêðâc êkota [*?sic*]." â, êkwâni, kâ-mamanêt êkwa. êkwa êkosi k-êtak, "kîspin tâpakwâsoc[i] âna maskwa, kâ-- aya, okwayâhk, okwayâhk kakwê-pâskiswâhkan! kîspin wiða wiyawihk wî-pâskiswaci, kika-pistahên anima wîsopiy," ê-itak; namwâc

[22] And then, "Well, we will use rope; they always say, 'That yellow rope is good for bears,' they always say," I said to her. Well, and so we sat talking and making snares, we were setting snares for that bear. And then, in the evening, we went into the bush again, but the snow was very deep, we went to set our snares for him. And he had indeed gone by again, but we did not snare him; he went right through --, actually he went around it,

[FA:] – he missed it; –

[JF:] – yes; –

then, in the morning, we did not bother with our snares, we did not set snares for him in this way; only later, when it was warm and the snow melted, only then would we try again. Finally the snow melted, well, and now we again went to set snares. And, with perseverance, she again was the one to snare him; but the bear also broke that rope, well, but we were carrying a 30-30. Well, now we followed him; I walked in the lead and she in the rear, for I carried the gun, it was appropriate for me to be ahead. Suddenly there lay that rope, where the bear had been going along, he must have pulled it off as he went.

[23] Then, well, already again we made more snares, for at that time we had also been told, "If someone kills a bear, the gall-bladder is very valuable, for someone to take it and sell it, you will get paid lots of money for it," we had been told; this was the reason we were so keen to go after this bear. And so we went into the bush, and again we were out of luck [?]; we kept missing him.

[24] And then, "Well, now I am going to check the snares," she said to me. "Yes," I said to her, "take this gun, but do not put a shell in! Wait until you see him, I never put the shell in when I am carrying a gun," I said to her, "only when I see someone, only then." Well, now she got ready [?]. And I said to her, "If you snare that bear, shoot him in the neck, in the neck! For if you are going to shoot him in the body, you will accidentally hit the gall-bladder," I said to her; she could not stop laughing, so funny did she find that. And so she went

ê-kî-pôni-pâhpit, iðikohk ê-wawêyatêðihtahk. êkwân âspin kospiw; takosin. sâsay mîna, nistwâw ê-paskakwâkot; iðikohk ês êkâ ê-miðwâsik anima pîminạhkwân. êkwa mîn ânima tâpakwânêyâpiy, êkwa êkâ kotak kîkwây ê-ayâyâhk; "â, êkwâni mâna mâka ê-kîhikoyahk," nititâw.

[25] êkwâni namwâ [*sic*] nôhci-nipahânân ana maskwa. pîyak wiða pahkêkin nikî-kîsinênân, ê-kî-pâsamâhk ê-- ê-otinamâhk opîwaya, êkwa ê-kî-pâsamâhk êkwa ê-wîskwasamâhk; êwako wiða nikî-kîsihtânân. êkwa kâ--, êkwân êkwa mîna k-- âya, kâ-kâh-kwâskwêpicikêyâhk ê-pimâhocikîsiyâhk, ê-nipahâyâhkwâw namêkosisak. îẏako ê-kîsikâk kâ-wî-pê-ohpahowâhk, ê-- wîpac ê-kîkisêpâyâk, kâ-papâmiskâyâhk – wiða nîso mîn ôsa [*sic*] ê-ayâyâhk, ôcisisa [*sic*], pậh-pêyak ê-âpacihtâyâhk. nisto kos ôma wîða ê-nipahât namêkosisa, êkwa pîyak wiða nîða ninipahâw; îyakonik oski-kinosêwak ê-pî-kîwê-nîmâyâhk.

[26] êkwâni wîða pakahkam êkota ê-iskw-âcimikosit mîn êwako maskwa,

[FA:] – êkwa ê-kî-kîhikoyêk –

nikî-kîhikonân êkwâni, aspin.

into the bush; she arrived back. Already again the bear had broken her snare, for the third time; so unsuitable was that rope. And that snare wire, too, but we did not have anything else; "Well, and so he got away on us again," I said to her.

[25] And so we failed to kill that bear. We did, however, finish one hide, we dried it and took the hair off, and then dried and smoked it; we did finish that one. And then we also went casting for fish, each in a little boat, and we caught a few small trout. It was the day that we were going to fly back, it was early in the morning, when we were paddling about – for we had two boats, two little boats, and we used one each. She caught three small trout, and I caught one, too; these were fresh fish we brought back home with us.

[26] And about him, too, this is all there is to tell about that bear, I believe,

[FA:] – and he got away on you –

he did get away on us, he was gone.

[FA:] ᐁᑲᐧ ᐊᐘ ᐁᑲᐧ ᑯᑕᐠ ᐃᐢᑫᐧᐤ, La Ronge ᐅᐦᒋ,
ᐁ ᐑ ᐋᒋᒧᐢᑖᑯᔭᕽ, 'Janet Feitz' ᐃᓯᔩᐦᑳᓱᐤ,
ᐅᐘᓂᐦᐃᑫᐤ, ᐁ ᐸᐹ ᐯᔭᑳᐧᒋᐦᐅᐟ ᒫᓇ ᐅᐘᓂᐦᐃᑫᐢᑲᓈᕽ.
ᐁᑯᓯ, ᑭᔭ.

I

[1] ᐊᔭ ᐆᒪ ᑳ ᐑ ᐋᒋᒧᐢᑖᑕᑳᐧᐤ, ᒥᑐᓂ ᑲᔮᓭᐢ ᐆᒪ ᑳ ᐑ ᐋᑐᑕᒫᐣ ᐁ ᑮ ᐊᔨᐢᐸᔫᐦᐃᑯᐚᐣ ᐆᒪ, ᐁ ᐸ ᐯᔭᑯᐚᐣ ᓂᐘᓂᐦᐃᑫᐢᑲᓈᕽ, ᐊᒋᒧᓯᐢ ᐏᔭ ᐋᑕ ᐏᔭ, ᒫᓇ ᒫᑲ ᒫᓇ ᓂᐑᒉᐚᐤ.

[2] ᐁᑲᐧ ᐆᒪ ᐯᔭᑳᐧᐤ ᐁ ᑮᓯᑳᐠ ᐁ ᑮ ᓈᑕᔭᐯᔮᐣ, ᐁᑳᐧᓂ ᐁᑲᐧ ᓂᑲᐹᐣ, ᐁ ᐅᔩᐦᐊᑳᐧᐤ ᑭᓄᓰᐘᐠ, ᐁᑲᐧ ᑳ ᓂᑕᐏ ᐊᑯᑕᑳᐧᐤ ᐁᑲᐧ ᐊᑳᐧᐚᓂᓯᕽ, ᐁ ᐑ ᐊᔭ ᐑᐢᑲᐧᓴᐧᑳᐧᐤ, ᓇᒣᐢᑎᑲᐧᐠ ᐁ ᐑ ᐅᔩᐦᐋᑳᐧᐤ. ᐁᑳᐧᓂ ᐁᑲᐧ ᓂᐱᒪᐦᑲᒥᑭᓯᐣ ᑭᓄᓭᐘᐠ ᐁ ᐅᔩᐦᐊᑲᐧᐤ, ᐁᑲᐧ ᓈᓯᐲᑎᒥᕽ ᒫᑲ ᐏᔭ ᐆᒪ ᑳ ᐃᑕᐦᑲᒥᑭᓯᔮᐣ. ᑮᑕᐦᑕᐍ ᑳ ᐯ ᓈᓯᐯᐸᐦᑖᐟ ᐁᑲᐧ ᐊᐘ ᓂᒉᒥᓯᐢ, ᐁ ᐋᐸᓵᐱᐟ ᒫᓇ ᐃᑌ ᑳ ᐅᐦᒋᐸᐦᑖᐟ, ᐁᑯᑌ ᐁ ᐃᑖᐱᐟ, ᐁ ᓭᑭᓯᐟ, ᐁᑯᑕ ᑭᓯᐚᐠ ᐯ ᐊᐱᐤ ᐃᑕ ᐆᒪ ᑲ ᐅᔩᐦᐃᑭᓄᓭᐍᔮᐣ, ᒦᒋᓯᐏᓈᐦᑎᐠ ᐁ ᐊᔮᐠ ᓈᓯᐯᑎᒥᕽ, ᐁᑯᑕ ᐆᒪ ᑳ ᐅᔩᐦᐋᑳᐧᐤ ᑭᓄᓭᐘᐠ. ᐁᑲᐧ ᐆᒪ ᓂᑯᐢᐱᐣ ᐁᑲᐧ ᓂᐑᒉᐚᐤ, ᒥᑐᓂ ᑯᐢᑖᒋᐤ, ᓇᒫᐧᐨ ᑮᑳᐧᐩ ᓂᐚᐸᐦᑌᐣ ᐊᓂᒪ ᑳ ᑯᐢᑕᕽ, ᐁᑳᐧᓂ ᐁᑲᐧ, ᓂᒐᑳᐧᐚᓂᓯᕽ ᓂᑎᑐᐦᑖᐣ, ᓂᑕᑯᑖᐘᐠ ᐁᑲᐧ ᐆᑯ ᓂᑭᓄᓭᒪᐠ ᑳ ᐑᐢᑲᐧᓴᐧᑳᐧᐤ – ᐁ ᑮ ᐴᓇᒫᐣ ᐏᔭ ᒦᓇ ᐱᑕᒫ. ᐁᑳᐧᓂ ᐁᑲᐧ ᓂᐲᐦᑐᑳᐧᐣ ᐁᑲᐧ, ᐚᐢᑲᐦᐃᑲᓂᓯᕽ ᐁᑯᑌ ᐁᑲᐧ ᒦᓇ ᓂᐱᒪᐦᑲᒥᑭᓯᐣ. ᐋᐢᑲᐤ ᓂᐘᔭᐚᐣ ᐁ ᓂᑕᐏ ᐴᓇᒫᐣ. ᐁᑲᐧ ᐆᒪ ᐁ ᐊᔨᑕᐦᑲᒥᑭᓯᔮᐣ, ᓂᑕᑎ ᐁᑲᐧ ᐋᐱᐦᑖ ᑮᓯᑲᓂᒦᒋᓯᐣ, ᐁᑳᐧᓂ ᐁᑲᐧ ᓂᑎᑐᐦᑖᐣ ᐃᑕ ᑳ ᐑᐢᑲᐧᓴᐧᑳᐧᐤ ᑭᓄᓭᐘᐠ, ᓂᐴᓇᓯᐣ, ᓇᒨᔭ ᒥᐢᑕᐦᐃ ᓂᐴᓀᐣ, ᐏᔭ ᐆᒪ ᐁ ᐃᑌᔨᐦᑕᒫᐣ ᐁᑲᐧ ᐁ ᐑ ᑲᐏᓯᒧᐚᐣ ᐁᑲᐧ ᐁ ᐑ ᐊᔨᐍᐲᔮᐣ. ᐁᑳᐧᓂ ᐁ ᑮ ᐴᓇᓯᔮᐣ, ᐁᑳᐧᓂ ᓂᐲᐦᑐᑳᐧᐣ ᐁᑲᐧ, ᐁᑳᐧᓂ ᐁᑲᐧ ᓂᑲᐏᓯᒧᐣ ᐁ ᐸ ᐱᒥᓯᓂᔮᐣ ᐁ ᐊᔭᒥᐦᒋᑫᔮᐣ, ᑮᑕᐦᑕᐍ ᐁᑲᐧ ᒫᑲ ᐊᐘ ᓂᒉᒥᓯᐢ, ᓲᐢᑲᐧᐨ ᐁᑲᐧ ᑲᐧᔭᐢᐠ ᒥᑭᓯᒧᐤ, ᑲᐧᔭᐢᐠ ᐁ ᑯᐢᑖᒋᐟ. ᐁᑳᐧᓂ ᓂᑌᐹᐧᑖᐤ ᐁᑲᐧ, «ᐴᓀᐧᐏᑕ.» ᐁ ᐃᑕᐠ, ᐋᐦᒋ ᐱᑯ, porchᐃᕽ ᐊᓂᑕ, ᐁᑯᑕ ᐲᐦᑐᑲᐧᒥᐠ, ᐁᑯᑕ ᑳ ᒥᑭᓯᒧᐟ, ᑲᐧᔭᐢᐠ ᐁ ᓭᑭᓯᐟ, ᐁᑳᐧᓂ ᓂᑕᐚᐨ ᐁᑲᐧ ᓂᐘᓂᐢᑳᐣ ᐁ ᓂᑕᐚᐯᓂᑫᔮᐣ. ᐁᑳᐧᓂ ᑳ ᐸᐢᐹᐱᔮᐣ ᐃᑌ ᐃᓯ ᓂᒐᑳᐧᐚᓂᐢ ᑳ ᐊᔮᐠ, ᐊᐍᐢᑲ ᐊᐘ ᐁᑯᑕ, ᐅᐦᐱᒣᐢ ᓂᒐᑳᐧᐚᓂᓯᕽ ᑳ ᒌᐸᑕᐱᐟ ᒪᐢᑲᐧ. ᑲᐧᔭᐢᐠ ᐁ ᐯ ᐃᑖᐱᐟ ᐊᓂᑌ ᐃᑕ ᐆᒪ ᑳ ᐸᐢᐹᐱᒪᐠ ᐃᑕ, ᐁᑳᐧᓂ, ᐋ, ᓂᐲᐦᑐᑲᐧᐦᐋᐤ ᐁᑲᐧ ᓂᒉᒥᓯᐢ, ᐁᑳᐧᓂ ᐁᑲᐧ ᓂᐘᔭᐚᐣ, ᓯᐯᐧᐦᑌᐤ ᐑᔭ ᐊᐘ ᒪᐢᑲᐧ, ᓇᒨᔭ ᒫᑲ ᐏᔭ ᓲᐦᑭ ᐱᒥ ᑯᑎᐢᑳᐍᐤ, ᒫᑲ ᓂᐱᒪᐧᓯᓈᑖᐤ ᐁᑲᐧ ᒥᐦᑎ, «ᐊᐘᐢ, ᐄᑲᑌᐦᑌ, ᒪᐢᑲᐧ. ᓇᒨᔭ ᑮᔭ ᑳ ᐑ ᐊᓴᒥᑖᐣ ᑭᓄᓭᐤ,» ᓂᑎᑖᐤ. ᐋ, ᐁᑳᐧᓂ ᐁᑲᐧ, ᓂᐲᐦᑐᑳᐧᐣ ᐁᑲᐧ ᒦᓇ. ᐁᑳᐧᓂ ᐲᔨᐢᐠ ᐊᑎ ᐅᑖᑯᓯᐣ, ᑫᔮᐱᐨ ᑳᐦ ᑯᐢᑖᒋᐤ ᐊᐘ ᓂᒉᒥᓯᐢ. ᐁᑳᐧᓂ ᐁᑲᐧ, ᑳ ᐃᑌᔨᐦᑕᒫᐣ,

«ᐋ, ᐱᑯ ᑕ ᐲᐦᑐᑲᐧᐦᐋᑳᐧᐤ ᓂᑭᓄᓴᒥᓴᐠ, ᓂᑲ ᐯ ᓃᐹ ᑭᒧᑕᒫᐠ ᐄᐧᖬ ᐊᐊᐧ, ᐁᐊᐧᑲᐧᖨᐤ ᐁᑐᑫᐧ ᐊᐊᐧ ᐅᐦᒋ ᑳ ᐯ ᐃᑕᐦᑲᒥᑭᓯᐟ, ᑭᓄᓴᐊᐧ ᐁ ᐸᓯᐟ ᐊᐊᐧ ᒪᐢᑲᐧ,» ᓂᑎᑌᖨᐦᑌᐣ. ᐁᑳᐧᓂ ᐁᑲᐧ ᐃᐢᐲ ᒥᑐᓂ ᐁ ᐊᑎ ᐅᑖᑯᓯᐠ, ᐁᑳᐧᓂ ᐁᑲᐧ ᑳ ᐲᐦᑐᑲᐧᐦᐋᑳᐧᐤ ᐁᑲᐧ ᐆᑯ ᓂᑭᓄᓴᒥᓴᐠ, porchᐃᕽ ᐊᓂᑕ ᒥᐢᒋᑯᓴ ᒫᓇ ᐁ ᐱᒫᐢᑲᐧᒧᑭ, ᐁᑯᑕ ᑳ ᐋᐦ ᐊᑯᑕᑳᐧᐤ. ᐁᑲᐧ ᓂᒉᒥᓯᐢ ᐄᐧᖬ ᒦᓇ ᓂᑮ ᐊᐧᖬᐄᐧᑎᓴᐦᐋᐧᐤ, ᐃᐧᖬ ᒨᖬ ᐊᖨᐢᐠ ᐲᐦᑐᑲᐧᒥᐠ ᓂᑲᓇᐁᐧᖨᒫᐤ (ᐊᐧᖬᐄᐧᐢᑎᑦ ᓂᑎᓯᖩᐦᑳᑖᐤ ᒫᓇ, ᐃᐧᖬ ᐊᐧᖬᐄᐧᑎᒥᕽ ᐁ ᐄᐧᑭᐟ, ᓇᒨᖬ ᐃᐧᖬ ᐲᐦᑐᑲᐧᒥᐠ ᐄᐧᑭᐤ). ᐁᑲᐧ ᐃᐢᐲ ᐁᑲᐧ ᐁ ᐄᐧᑎᐱᐢᑳᐧᐠ, ᓵᓴᐩ ᒦᓇ ᑳ ᒪᑌᐧ ᒣᐧᐢᑖᑌᐧᐃᐧᑕᕽ, ᐁ ᑯᐢᑖᒋᐟ. ᐁᑳᐧᓂ ᓂᐊᐧᓂᐢᑳᐣ ᐁᑲᐧ ᒦᓇ, ᐁ ᐸᐢᐹᐱᔮᐣ, ᓇᒫᐧᐨ ᐊᐃᐧᔭᐠ ᓂᐋᐧᐸᒫᐤ, ᓰᐢᑲᐧᐟ ᓇᒫᐧᐨ.

[3] ᐁᑳᐧᓂ ᐁᑲᐧ, ᑳᐃᐧ ᓂᑲᐃᐧᓯᒧᐣ. ᐁᑲᐧ ᐁ ᑮ ᓂᐹᔮᐣ, ᓵᓴᐩ ᒦᓇ ᐁᑲᐧ ᒦᓇ ᒦᐧᐢᑖᑌᐧᐃᐧᑕᑦ, ᓰᐢᑳᐧᐨ ᐁ ᒪᐃᐧᒧᐦᑫᐟ, ᐁ ᑯᐢᑖᒋᐟ ᓰᐢᑳᐧᐨ. ᐁᑳᐧᓂ ᐁᑲᐧ ᒦᓇ ᓂᐊᐧᓂᐢᑳᐣ, ᓂᑌᐹᐧᑖᐤ ᓂᐄᐧ ᓅᑎᓈᐤ, «ᑲᐃᐧᓯᒧ,» ᐁ ᐃᑕᐠ, ᓇᒫᐧᐨ ᐳᓄᐧᐃᐧᑕᑦ. ᐁᑳᐧᓂ ᓂᒐᑲᐧᐋᐧᓂᓯᕽ ᐃᒋ ᓂᑎᑖᐱᐣ, ᓇᒫᐧᐨ ᐊᐃᐧᔭᐠ ᓂᐋᐧᐸᒫᐤ ᐁᑯᑌ. ᐁᑳᐧᓂ ᐁᑲᐧ ᓈᓯᐯᑎᒥᕽ ᐁᑲᐧ, ᓵᑲᐦᐃᑲᓂᕽ ᐃᓯ ᑳ ᐃᑖᐱᔮᐣ, ᐁᑲᐧ ᐃᑕ ᒫᓇ ᐁ ᑳᐧᐱᑫᔮᐣ ᐊᓂᒪ ᓈᓯᐯᐢᑲᓇᐤ, ᐊᐁᐧᐢᑲ ᐊᐊᐧ ᐁᑯᑕ, ᑳ ᐱᒥᑕᐱᐟ ᐄᐧᖬ ᐋᐊᐧ ᒪᐢᑲᐧ, ᐁ ᐊᔭᐱᐟ ᐁᑯᑌ ᓈᓯᐲᑎᒥᕽ. ᑖᓂᓯ ᐁᑐᑫᐧ ᐁ ᐃᑌᖨᐦᑕᕽ, ᓵᑲᐦᐃᑲᓂᕽ ᐃᐧᖬ ᑳ ᐃᑖᐱᐟ, ᐁ ᐊᔭᓴᐋᐧᐱᐟ ᐁᑯᑌ ᐃᓯ. ᐁᑳᐧᓂ ᐁᑲᐧ, ᓇᒨᖬ ᐴᓄᐧᐃᐧᑕᑦ ᐊᐊᐧ ᓂᒉᒥᓯᐢ. ᐁᑳᐧᓂ ᐁᑲᐧ porchᐃᕽ ᐊᓂᑕ ᑳ ᐲᐦᑐᑲᐧᐦᐊᐠ, ᐁᑯᑕ ᐁ ᐅᓰᐦᑕᒪᐊᐧᐠ ᓂᐯᐃᐧᐣ ᑕ ᓂᐹᐟ, ᐁᑲᐧ ᓂᑎᑖᐤ ᑭᑕ ᐴᓄᐧᐃᐧᑕᕽ.

[4] ᓇᒨᖬ ᐃᐧᖬ ᒦᓇ ᓂᐄᐧᐹᐢᑭᓵᐧᐤ ᐊᐊᐧ ᒪᐢᑲᐧ, ᐃᐧᖬ ᐁᑳ ᑭᑕ ᑮ ᑭᑕᒪᐧᐠ, ᐁ ᐯᔭᑯᐋᐧᐣ ᐆᒪ, ᐁᑲᐧ ᐁ ᑭᖨᐱᒥᓯᐊᐧᓈᑕᕽ ᒪᐢᑯᐃᐧᔮᐢ, ᑳ ᓂᐸᐦᐊᐟ ᒪᐢᑲᐧ ᐁᑯᓯ ᐃᓯ ᑳ ᑮᓯᐯᐧᐠ. ᐁᑳᐧᓂ ᐁᑲᐧ, ᐋᐧᐸᓄᐧᐃᐧᑕᑦ ᐄᐧᖬ ᐊᐊᐧ ᓂᒉᒥᓯᐢ, ᐁ ᑯᐢᑖᐟ ᐊᓂᐦᐃ, ᒫᑲ ᐃᐢᐲ ᐁ ᐊᑎ ᐋᐧᐸᕽ ᐁ ᐊᐧᓂᐢᑳᔭᐣ, ᐁ ᑯᐢᑯᒥᐟ ᐁᑲᐧ ᒦᓇ, ᐁᑯᑕ ᑯᓴ ᐆᒪ ᑳ ᐱᒧᐦᑌᐟ ᐁᑲᐧ ᐊᐊᐧ ᒪᐢᑲᐧ, ᓂᑎᐢᑳᐧᐦᑌᒥᕽ ᐁᑯᑕ. ᐁᑯᑕ ᐁ ᐸ ᐱᒧᐦᑌᐟ, ᓂᒐᑳᐧᐋᐧᓂᓯᕽ ᓄᑌ ᐁᑯᑌ ᐁ ᓂᑕᐃᐧᒫᐦᒥᖭᐦᒋᑫᐟ, ᐁ ᒪᑌᐧ ᐋᐧᐦ ᐊᐧᐢᑲᐃᐧᐱᑕᕽ ᓂᒐᑳᐧᐋᐧᓈᐦᒋᑯᓴ, ᒫᑲ ᐃᐧᖬ ᐁᑳ ᑮᑲᐧᐩ ᐁ ᐊᐢᑌᐠ. ᐁᑳᐧᓂ ᐯ ᐊᐧᖬᐄᐧᐤ ᐁᑯᑕ ᐅᐦᒋ, ᐋᐧᐢᑲᐦᐃᑲᓂᐢ ᐊᖨᐢᐠ ᒫᓇ ᐊᓂᒪ ᓂᒐᑳᐧᐋᐧᓂᐢ, ᐁᑳᐧᓂ ᐯ ᐊᐧᖬᐄᐧᐤ, ᐁᑳᐧᓂ ᐊᐢᐱᐣ ᑳ ᐊᑎ ᑲ ᑯᐢᐱᐟ, ᐁ ᐊᑎ ᐋᐧᐸᓂᖨᐠ ᐆᒪ, ᐁᑳᐧᓂ ᐊᐢᐱᐣ.

[5] ᐋ, ᑲᐧᔭᐢᐠ ᐁᑲᐧ ᓂᐸᑳᐧᑖᐤ ᐊᐊᐧ ᒪᐢᑲᐧ ᐁ ᑕᑯᓯᕽ. ᐁᑲᐧ ᓂᑕᖬᐱᐩ ᑫᔮᐱᐨ ᒦᓇ ᐁ ᐊᑯᐦᒋᕽ. ᐁᑳᐧᓂ ᐁᐊᐧᑯ ᐁ ᑮᓯᑳᐠ, ᑳ ᐃᑌᖨᐦᑕᒫᐣ ᐁ ᐃᐧᖬᓯᐋᐧᑎᓯᐋᐧᐣ, «ᐋ, ᒉᐢᑲᐧ, ᓂᑲ ᒪᓂᐱᑖᐤ ᓂᑕᖬᐱᐩ, ᐅᓰᑦ ᐊᐊᐧ ᒪᐢᑲᐧ ᓂᑲ ᒣᐧᐢᑖᒋᐦᑳᐠ, ᐁᐧᐱᓇᑭ ᑭᓄᓴᐤ ᓈᓯᐯᑎᒥᕽ,» ᓂᑎᑌᖨᐦᑌᐣ. ᐁᑳᐧᓂ ᐁᑲᐧ ᐁᐊᐧᑯ ᐁ ᑮᓯᑳᐠ, ᓂᒪᓂᐱᑖᐤ ᐁᑲᐧ ᓂᑕᖬᐱᐩ. ᐁᑲᐧ ᐊᖨᐢᐠ ᒦᓇ ᓂᒉᒥᓯᐢ ᒫᓇ, ᓇᒨᖬ ᓂᓇᑲᑕᐦᐋᐧᐤ, ᒪᔭᐤ ᐆᒪ ᑭᑕ ᐴᓯᔮᐣ, ᐁᑳᐧᓂ ᐄᐧᐢᑕ ᐋᓯᑲᓂᕽ ᐯ ᒌᐸᑕᐱᐤ, ᓇᒨᖬ ᐃᐧᖬ ᐴᓯ ᑳᐧᐢᑯᐦᑎᐤ, ᐹᑎᒫ ᒫᓇ, «ᐴᓯ.» ᑳ ᐃᑕᐠ, ᐁᑫᐧᖭᐨ ᑳ ᐴᓯᐟ. ᒥᑐᓂ ᒫᓇ ᓄᐢᒑᒍᒐᑯᓯᕽ, ᐁᑯᑌ ᒫᓇ ᐁ ᐊᐢᑖᔮᐣ ᐊᓈᐢᑲᓂᐢ, ᐁᑯᑕ ᒫᓇ ᐁ ᐊᐱᐟ. ᐋ, ᐁᑳᐧᓂ ᐁᑲᐧ ᑳ ᓂᑕᐃᐧᒪᓂᐱᑕᐠ ᓂᑕᖬᐱᐩ.

[6] ᐁᑳᐧᓂ ᓅᓰᐦᐃᑭᓄᓰᐋᐧᐣ, ᓂᐄᐧᐢᑲᐧᓵᐧᐊᐧᐠ ᐊᓂᑭ, ᓇᒣᐢᑎᑲᐧᐠ ᐁ ᐅᓰᐦᐊᑳᐧᐤ. ᐁᑳᐧᓂ ᑲᐯ ᑮᓯᐠ ᐁᑲᐧ ᒦᓇ ᓂᐱᒪᐦᑲᒥᑭᓯᐣ ᐆᒪ. ᐁᑲᐧ ᐊᓂᐦᐃ ᐊᔭ, ᑳ ᐃᐢᑯᓵᐊᐧᑖᐧᐤ ᑭᓄᓴᐊᐧᐠ, ᓂᑕᓯᐊᐧᖭᐊᐧᐠ ᐊᔭ, ᒪᐦᑲᐦᑯᕽ, ᐁ ᓂᑕᐃᐧ ᐁᐧᐱᓇᑳᐧᐤ ᐊᑳᒥᕽ, ᐁᑳ ᐁ ᐄᐧ ᐊᓴᒪᐠ ᐊᓇ ᒪᐢᑲᐧ, ᐅᓵᒼ ᑭᑕᑮᓵᒌᐟ.

[7] ᐁᑲᐧ ᐁᐊᐧᑯ ᐁ ᑎᐱᐢᑳᐠ, ᓂᓇᐦᐊᐦᖭᐊᐧᐠ ᓂᑭᓄᓴᒪᐠ, ᐃᐧᖬ ᐁ ᑕᑯᓯᕽ ᐊᐊᐧ, ᐁᑲᐧ ᐁ ᑯᐢᑕᐠ ᑭᑕ ᐯ ᑭᒧᑕᒪᐃᐧᐟ. ᑖᐯᐧ, ᒪᔭᐤ ᒫᑲ ᒦᓇ ᐁ ᐊᑎ ᐋᑳᐧᑎᐱᐢᑳᐠ, ᓵᓴᐩ ᓂᒣᒥᓯᐢ ᒫᑲ ᒦᓇ ᑳ ᑯᐢᑖᒋᐟ. ᐁᑳᐧᓂ ᓂᐸᐢᐹᐱᐣ, ᐊᐁᐧᐢᑲ ᐊᐊᐧ ᑳ ᐯ ᓇᓈᓯᐯᐟ ᐊᐊᐧ ᒪᐢᑲᐧ, ᐅᓂᑲᐦᑊ ᐊᖨᐢᐠ ᐁᑯᑕ ᐊᔮᐤ, ᒣᐢᑲᓈᕽ, ᐁᑯᑕ ᐁ ᐯ ᓇ ᓅᑯᓯᐟ ᓇᓂᓯᐦᑳᐨ ᐁ ᐯ ᐸ ᐱᒧᐦᑌᐟ, ᐁᑲᐧ ᒦᓇ ᐆᒪ ᐁ ᐯ ᑭᔪᑫᐟ. ᐁᑲᐧᓂ ᑯᓴ ᐆᒪ ᐁᑯᑕ ᑳ ᐯ ᐃᑐᐦᑌᐟ ᓂᒐᑳᐧᐋᐧᓂᓯᕽ ᐊᓂᑕ, ᒫᑲ ᓵᓴᐩ ᓂᑮ ᓇᐦᐊᐦᖭᐊᐧᐠ ᓂᑭᓄᓴᒥᓴᐠ, ᐁᑯᑕ ᑯᓴ ᐆᒪ ᐁᑲᐧ ᑳ ᐊᐱᐟ, ᐁ ᒌᐸᑕᐱᐟ. ᐁ ᐯ ᐃᑖᐱᐟ ᒫᓇ ᓂᐋᐧᐢᑲᐦᐃᑲᓂᓯᕽ, ᐋᐧᐢᑲᐤ ᐁ ᑭᑖᐸᒫᐟ ᓂᒣᒥᓯᓴ, ᐁᑯᑕ ᐊᐊᐧ ᐁ ᑲᑳᐧᑕᑭ ᒣᐧᐢᑖᑌᐧᐃᐧᑕᕽ ᐄᐧᖬ ᐊᐊᐧ, ᐁ ᒥᑭᑖᐟ, ᐁ ᐅᐦᑎᐢᑲᐊᐧᐲᐢᑕᐋᐧᐟ ᐊᓂᐦᐃ ᒪᐢᑲᐧ ᐊᐊᐧ ᓂᒣᒥᓯᐢ, ᐁ ᒥᑭᑖᐟ, ᐁᑲᐧ ᐄᐧᖬ ᐊᐊᐧ ᒧᐢᒋ ᒫᓇ ᐁ ᑭᑖᐸᒫᐟ. ᐁᑲᐧ ᐁᑯᑕ ᐁ ᒌᐸᑕᐱᐟ ᐊᓇ ᒪᐢᑲᐧ, ᑭᓀᐧᐢᐠ ᐁᑯᑕ ᑳ ᐊᐱᐟ, ᒥᑐᓂ ᐁᑐᑫᐧ ᓃᓯᑎᐸᐦᐃᑲᐣ ᓈᓂᑕᐤ. ᓇᒨᖬ ᓂᐱᓯᐢᑫᖨᒫᐤ, ᑮᓵᐨ ᐃᐧᖬ ᒦᓇ ᓂᑮ ᐋᐊᐧᑑᐹᐣ, ᐃᐧᖬ ᐁᑳ ᐁ ᓅᐦᑌ ᐊᐧᖬᐄᐧᔮᐣ ᐁᑯᑕ ᐊᓂᒪ ᑭᓯᐋᐧᐠ ᐁ ᐊᔮᐟ.

[8] ᐁᑳᐧᓂ, ᑮᑕᐦᑕᐁᐧ ᐁᑲᐧ, ᑳ ᐱᒥ ᓈᓯᐯᐟ ᐁᑲᐧ ᒦᓇ. ᐁᑲᐧ ᐃᑌ ᐊᓂᒪ ᒫᓇ ᑳ ᐅᓰᐦᐃᑭᓄᓴᐁᐧᔮᐣ ᐋᓯᑲᓂᕽ ᑭᓯᐋᐧᐠ, ᐁᑯᑕ ᐆᒪ ᐁᑲᐧ ᑳ ᐃᑐᐦᑌᐟ, ᐁ ᒪᑌᐧ ᐋᐧᐦ ᐋᐧᐢᑳᐢᑲᕽ ᐊᓂᒪ ᒦᒋᓯᐃᐧᓈᐦᑎᐠ, ᒫᑲ ᐃᐧᖬ ᑲᐦᑭᖬᐤ ᑮᑲᐧᐩ ᐁ ᐁᐧᐱᓇᒫᐣ, ᒪᑌᐧ ᒫᐦ ᒨᓈᑎᐦᑫᐤ ᐁᑯᑕ, ᓂᑑᐟ ᒦᓇ ᒪᑌᐧ ᐋᐧᐦ ᐋᐧᐢᑳᐢᑲᒼ. ᐁᑳᐧᓂ ᐁᑲᐧ ᒦᓇ ᑳ ᐯᒋ ᑯᐢᐱᐟ, ᐁᑯᑕ ᐊᐧᖬᐄᐧᑎᒥᕽ ᓃᑭᕽ, ᐁᑯᑕ ᐆᒪ ᑳ ᐸ ᐱᒧᐦᑌᐟ, ᐊᐢᐱᐣ ᐁᑲᐧ ᒦᓇ ᐁ ᑯᐢᐱᐟ.

[9] ᐋ, ᐁᑳᐧᓂ ᐁᑲᐧ, ᒫᑲ ᑕᐦᑐ ᑮᓯᑳᐤ ᓂᑖᒋᒧᐢᑕᐋᐧᐊᐧᐠ ᐆᑯ, ᑕᐦᑐ ᐅ≷ᐁᑎᔪᐊᐧ ᒫᓇ ᑳ ᓂᑐᐦᑕᐦᑳᐧᐤ ᑮᐁᐧᑎᓄᕽ (ᐊᔮᐊᐧᐠ ᐊᖨᐢᐠ ᐅ≷ᐁᑎᔪᐊᐧ, ᐁ ᐊᔭᒥᐦᐃᑐᐋᐧᕽ ᒫᓇ), ᐁᑯᑕ ᓂᑖᐦ ᐋᒋᒫᐤ ᐊᐊᐧ ᒪᐢᑲᐧ, ᐁᑲᐧ ᒥᐦᒉᐟ ᐊᐃᐧᔭᐠ ᓂᑎᑎᐠ, «ᐋ, ᓂᐸᐦ. ᐹᐢᑭᐢ ᐁᐊᐧᑯ ᐊᓇ, ᐁ ᒣᐧᐢᑖᑕᐦᑲᒥᑭᓯᐟ. ᒪᐢᑲᐧᔮᐣ ᐊᓇ ᑲ ᑮ ᐊᑖᐋᐧᑲᐣ,» ᓂᑎᑎᑲᐧᐠ. «ᓇᒫᐧᐨ, ᓇᒫᐧᐨ ᓂᑲ ᑮ ᓂᐸᐦᐋᐤ, ᐱᑲᐧᓂᑕ ᑭᑕ ᐃᐧᔭᑭᐦᑖᔮᐣ ᐃᐧᔮᐢ, ᐁᑳ ᑭᑕ ᑮ ᑭᑖᔮᐣ ᐁᑲᐧ ᑕᒥᓯᐊᐧᓈᑕᕽ ᐃᐧᔮᐢ, ᓇᒫᐧᐨ.» ᐋ, ᐁᑳᐧᓂ ᐁᑲᐧ, ᐯᔭᐠ ᐊᐊᐧ, ᑭᓯᐋᐧᐠ ᑳ ᐄᐧᑭᐟ ᐊᐃᐧᔭᐠ, ᐲᖨᐢᐠ ᓂᐄᐧ ᓅᑎᓂᐠ, «ᓂᐸᐦ ᐁᐊᐧᑯ ᐊᓇ ᑳ ᒣᐧᐢᑖᑌᐧᐁᐧᒪᐟ ᒪᐢᑲᐧ, ᑭᑕ ᐴᓀᐧᐃᐧᑕᒫᐣ.» ᓂᑎᑎᐠ. ᐁᑳᐧᓂ, «ᓇᒫᐧᐨ,» ᓂᑎᑖᐤ, «ᓇᒫᐧᐨ ᒧᐢᒋᐋᐧᐠ ᑲ ᓂᐸᐦᐊᐠ.»

[10] ᐁᑳᐧᓂ, ᑮᐦᑖᐧᒼ ᐁᑲᐧ (ᐯᔭᐠ ᐃᐢᐸᖨᐤ ᐊᐊᐧ ᐁᑯᑕ ᒪᐢᑲᐧ ᐊᔮᐤ, ᓂᔮᓇᐣ ᑮᓯᑳᐤ ᒣᐧᐦᒋ ᐁᑯᑕ ᐁ ᐃᑕᐦᑲᒥᑭᓯᐟ ᐊᐊᐧ ᒪᐢᑲᐧ), ᐁᑲᐧ ᐯᔭᑳᐧᐤ ᐁ ᑮᓯᑳᐠ, ᒣᑳᐧᐨ ᓈᓯᐯᑎᒥᕽ ᐁ ᐃᑕᐦᑲᒥᑭᓯᔮᐣ (ᐁ ᓈᓇᐹᒋᐦᑖᔮᐣ ᓂᑑᐟ, ᐁ ᑮᓰᐯᑭᓇᒫᐣ, ᑲᐧᔭᐢᐠ ᐁ ᓈᓇᐹᒋᐦᑖᔮᐣ, ᐁ ᐄᐧ ᓇᐦᐊᐢᑖᔮᐣ, ᐄᐧᐸᐨ ᐁ ᐄᐧ ᐅᐦᐸᐦᐅᐋᐧᐣ), ᐁᑳᐧᓂ, ᓂᓂᑐᒫᐤ ᐁᑲᐧ ᐊᐊᐧ ᐅᐱᒥᖬᐤ,

«ᓂᔮᓇᓄ ᑮᓯᑳᑭ ᐯ ᓈᑕᐦᐆᐦᑲᐣ.» ᓂᑎᑖᐤ ᐊᐊᐧ, «ᒥᑖᑕᐦᐟ ᑎᐸᐦᐃᑲᐣ ᐁ ᑮᑭᓭᐹᔮᐠ, ᑭᔮᒼ ᓂᑲ ᑮᐋᐧᐣ, ᐅᓵᒼ ᓂᐸᑳᐧᑖᐤ ᐊᐊᐧ ᒪᐢᑲᐧ ᑳ ᐃᑕᐦᑲᒥᑭᓯᐟ,» ᓂᑎᑖᐤ ᐊᐊᐧ ᑳ ᐃᑌᐧᐢᑕᒪᐃᐧᐟ – ᐃᐧᖬ ᐁᑳ ᓃᖬ La Ronge ᐁ ᑮ ᑕᑯᐸᖨᐠ ᓂᑕᔭᒥᐃᐧᐣ, ᑯᑕᐠ ᐱᑯ ᐊᐃᐧᔭᐠ ᐁ ᐃᑑᑕᒪᐃᐧᐟ.

[11] ᐁᑳᐧᓂ ᑖᐯᐧ, ᐁ ᓀᐅᐧ ᑮᓯᑳᐠ ᐁᑯᐢᐲ, ᐋᐧᐸᐦᑭ ᑕ ᐃᓯ ᐅᐦᐸᐦᐅᐋᐧᐣ, ᐁᑯᑕ ᐁᑲᐧ ᒥᑐᓂ ᐁᑳ ᑳ ᐊᐧᐃᐧᔭᑌᖨᐦᑕᕽ ᐊᐊᐧ ᒪᐢᑲᐧ. ᑲᐯ ᑮᓯᐠ ᑯᓴ ᐆᒪ ᐁᑲᐧ ᓂᒐᑳᐧᐋᐧᓂᓯᕽ ᐅᓵᒼ ᐱᑯ ᐁ ᐊᐱᐟ ᐊᓂᑕ, ᑳᐦ ᑫᐧᑲᐧᐢᐠ ᐁ ᐃᑐᐦᑌᐟ, ᐊᓂᑕ ᐃᑌᐦᑫ ᐃᓯ ᓇᒪᐦᑎᓂᕽ ᐁ ᐊᐱᐟ ᓂᒐᑳᐧᐋᐧᓂᓯᕽ, ᐋᐢᑲᐤ ᑭᐦᒋᓂᐢᑭᕽ, ᐋᐢᑲᐤ ᐊᐊᐧᓴ ᐅᐦᒋ, ᑌᐱᖭᕽ ᑖᐱᐢᑰᐨ ᐁ ᑲᓇᐁᐧᖨᒥᐟ, ᐁᑳ ᐊᐧᖬᐄᐧᑎᒥᕽ ᑎᑕ ᐃᑕᐦᑲᒥᑭᓯᐊᐧᐠ. ᐁᑳᐧᓂ ᐁᑲᐧ, ᐆᑕ ᑯᓴ ᐊᐊᐧ ᐁ ᐊᔭᐱᐟ ᐊᐊᐧ ᒪᐢᑲᐧ ᑲᐯ ᑮᓯᐠ, «ᐹᐢᑲᐨ ᐁᑲᐧ ᐁ ᐯ ᐅᐦᑎᐢᑲᐊᐧᐱᐟ,» ᓂᑖᒋᒧᐣ ᐆᒪ ᐅᕒᐁᑎᔪᐤ, ᐁ ᐊᔭᔭᒥᐦᐊᐠ ᐊᓇ ᐯᔭᐠ ᐃᐢᑫᐧᐤ ᑭᓯᐋᐧᐠ ᐁᑯᑕ. «ᒫᒋᑯᒋ, ᑭᑲ ᐋᒋᒧᐢᑖᑎᐣ ᐁ ᐃᑕᐦᑲᒥᑭᓯᐟ,» ᓂᑎᑖᐧᐣ, ᐁ ᐊᔭᒥᔮᐣ ᐊᓂᑕ ᐅᕒᐁᑎᔪᐤ, ᑭᓯᐠ ᐁ ᐸᐢᐹᐱᒪᐠ ᐊᐊᐧ ᒪᐢᑲᐧ ᐊᐧᖬᐄᐧᑎᒥᕽ. «ᐁ ᐃᓰᐦᒋᑫᐟ ᑯᓴ ᐊᐊᐧ ᒪᐢᑲᐧ. ᓂᒐᑳᐧᐋᐧᓂᓯᕽ ᐅᐦᐱᒉᐢ ᐊᓂᑕ ᐁ ᐋᐱᐟ, ᐁᑲᐧ ᑯᓴ ᐊᐊᐧ, ᐁ ᓈᓇᐹᒋᐦᐃᓯᐟ ᑲᐧᔭᐢᐠ, ᐁ ᓰᑲᐦᐊᕽ, ᐁ ᓅᐢᑳᐧᑕᕽ ᐅᐢᐱᑐᓇ, ᐁᑲᐧ ᐋᐧᐢᑭᑲᓂᕽ ᒦᓇ ᒥᓯᐁᐧ, ᐁᑳᐧᓂ ᐁ ᐅᐦᐱᓇᕽ ᐅᒋᐦᒋᔭ, ᐊᐊᐧᓴ ᐊᔭ, ᐄᐧᐦᑕᐊᐧᑲᔭ ᐆᒥᓯ ᐁ ᐋᐦ ᐃᑑᑕᕽ, ᐁ ᓰᑲᐦᐅᐟ,» ᓂᑎᑖᐤ. «ᐃᖨᑯᕽ ᑯᓴ ᐊᐊᐧ ᐁᑲᐧ ᒦᓇ ᐁ ᐅᐦᐱᓇᕽ ᐅᐢᐱᑐᐣ, ᐁ ᒌᐦᒌᑭᓇᕽ ᑯᓴ ᐆᒪ ᐆᑌ ᐆᑲᓇ» (ᐁ ᐅᑎᐦᑯᒥᐟ ᐁᑐᑫᐧ ᐊᐊᐧ ᒪᐢᑲᐧ –), «ᐁᑯᓯ ᐊᓇ ᐁ ᐃᓰᐦᒋᑫᐟ, ᐁ ᒨᐦ ᒌᐦᒌᑮᐟ, ᐁᑲᐧ ᒥᓯᐁᐧ ᒦᓇ, ᐄᐧᐦᒋᑲᐧᓇ ᐁ ᓈᓇᐹᒋᐦᑖᐟ – ᒪᑖᐧᐣ ᒌ ᐊᐊᐧ ᐁ ᐃᑌᖨᐦᑕᕽ ᑭᑕ ᑭᐢᑭᓇᐋᐧᐸᒪᐠ ᐁ ᐃᓰᐦᒋᑫᐟ,» ᓂᑎᑖᐧᐣ ᐁ ᐹᐦᐱᔮᐣ. «ᐁᑯᓯ ᐁᑐᑫᐧ ᐊᓇ, ᐁᑳ ᐁᑐᑫᐧ ᐊᓇ ᐁ ᐅᐦᒋ ᑳᓯᐦᑫᐧᔭᐣ, ᐁ ᐃᑌᖨᒥᐢᐠ, ᑳ ᐆᐦ ᐃᓯ ᐃᑑᑕᕽ ᐁᐊᐧᑯ ᐊᓇ ᒪᐢᑲᐧ, ᐁ ᐃᑎᐢᐠ ᐁᑐᑫᐧ ᐊᓇ ᑕ ᑳᓯᐦᑫᐧᔭᐣ,» ᓂᑎᑎᐠ ᐁᑲᐧ ᐊᐊᐧ ᑳ ᐊᔭᔭᒥᐦᐊᐠ. ᐁᑳᐧᓂ ᐁᑲᐧ ᑳ ᑮᓯ ᐋᒋᒪᐠ ᐊᐊᐧ ᒪᐢᑲᐧ.

[12] ᒥᑐᓂ ᐁᑲᐧ ᓂᐸᑳᐧᑖᐤ, ᐁ ᓀᐅᐧ ᑮᓯᑳᐠ ᐁ ᐅᑖᑯᓯᐠ ᐆᒪ, ᐋᐧᐸᐦᑭ ᐃᐧᖬ ᐋᑕ ᐃᐧᖬ ᑕ ᐅᐦᐸᐦᐅᐋᐧᐣ ᑕᑕᐸᓰᐦᐊᐠ, ᐊᔭ ᐅᑎ ᐁᑳ ᐁ ᓅᐦᑌ ᐄᐧᒋ ᐊᔮᒪᐠ, ᐆᑕ ᐯᔭᐠ ᐃᐢᐸᖨᐤ ᐁ ᐄᐧᒋ ᐊᔮᒪᐠ. ᐁᑳᐧᓂ ᐁᑲᐧ ᐁᑯᓯ ᑳ ᐃᑌᖨᐦᑕᒫᐣ, «ᒉᐢᑲᐧ, ᓂᑲ ᐹᐢᑭᓵᐧᐤ, ᐊᔭ, ᓂᑲ ᐃᓯ ᐹᐢᑭᓯᑲᐣ ᐃᑌ ᐃᓯ ᑳ ᐊᐱᐟ, ᑭᑕ ᑕᐸᓰᐟ.» ᐁᑳᐧᓂ ᐁᑲᐧ, ᑳ ᓯᐯᐧᐦᑌᐟ ᐁᑲᐧ, ᒥᑐᓂ ᐋᐧᐦᖬᐁᐧᐢ ᑳ ᒪᑌᐧ ᒌᐸᑕᐱᐟ, ᒫᑲ ᐃᐧᖬ ᒥᓯᐁᐧ ᐁ ᐸᐢᑳᐧᐠ, ᒪᑌᐧ ᐋᐧᐦᖬᐤ ᐊᐱᐤ, ᐁ ᐯ ᐅᐦᑎᐢᑲᐊᐧᐱᐟ, ᐁᑯᑌ ᐁ ᐅᓵᐸᒥᐟ. ᐁᑲᐧ ᐁ ᑯᐢᑕᒫᐣ ᑕ ᐊᐧᖬᐄᐧᔮᐣ, «ᓈᓂᑕᐤ ᐃᓯ ᐯ ᓈᒋᐸᐦᐃᒋ,» ᐁ ᐃᑌᖨᒪᐠ, ᓂᒉᒥᓯᐢ ᐄᐧᖬ ᐃᑌᐧᐃᐧᑕᒼ ᐆᒪ ᐁ ᑯᐢᑖᐟ, ᒫᑲ ᓇᒫᐧᐨ ᓂᐲᐦᑐᑲᐧᐦᐋᐤ.

[13] ᐁᑲᐧᓂ ᐁᑲᐧ ᑳ ᐅᑎᓇᒫᐣ ᐁᑲᐧ ᓂᐹᐢᑭᓯᑲᐣ, ᐊᓂᒪ ‘thirty-thirty’ ᑳ ᐃᑕᐦᑳᐧᐤ ᒫᓇ, ᐁᑳᐧᓂ ᑲ ᐊᓯᐊᐧᑖᔮᐣ ᐯᔭᐠ ᒨᓯᓯᓂᐩ, ᐁᑲᐧᓂ ᐁᑲᐧ ᑳ ᐃᓯ ᐁᐧᐸᐦᐊᒫᐣ. ᐁᑲᐧᓂ ᑳ ᐹᐢᑭᐦᑌᓇᒫᐣ ᐁᑲᐧ ᓂᐋᐧᓴᓇᒫᐣ, ᐊᓂᒪ ᐱᑯ ᓴᑭᒉᐊᐧᔮᓀᑭᐣ, ᐁᐊᐧᑯ ᐱᑯ ᐁ ᐃᑕᒧᐠ, ᓇᒨᖬ ᒦᓇ ᐁᐊᐧᑯ ᓂᑮ ᐋᐦᑎᓀᐣ, ᐋᑕ ᐁ ᑲᑫᐧ ᐋᐦ ᐄᑲᑌ ᐁᐧᐸᐦᐊᒫᐣ, ᒫᑲ ᓇᒫᐧᐨ,

ᐁ ᒪᓈ ᐲᑯᓇᒫᐤ ᐊᓂᒪ, ᐊᓂᒪ ᐁᐊᐧᑯ ᐊᓂᒪ ᐲᐋᐧᐱᐢᐠ, ᐃᐧᖧ ᓴᑭᒣᐢᑳᕽ. ᐁᑳᐧᓂ ᐁᑲᐧ ᐁᑯᑕ ᑳ ᓃᐸᐃᐧᔮᐤ, ᐹᐢᑲᐨ ᐁ ᑌᐦᑕᐱᔮᐤ, ᐁᑲᐧ ᓂᐹᐢᑭᓯᑲᐤ ᐊᓂᒪ ᐁ ᑕᐦᑯᐦᑕᐢᑖᔮᐤ ᐊᓂᑕ ᐋᐧᓴᓇᒫᓂᕽ. ᐁᑳᐧᓂ ᐁᑲᐧ ᑳ ᐅᐃᐧᖫᐸᒪᐠ, ᐅᐦᐱᒣ ᐃᑕ ᑳ ᐊᐱᐟ, ᐁᑯᑕ ᑳ ᐃᑖᐱᔮᐤ ᐆᒪ, ᐁᑲᐧ ᑳ ᑕᓯᓇᒫᐤ ᐊᓂᒪ ᓂᐹᐢᑭᓯᑲᐤ. ᐁᑲᐧ, ᓇᒫᐧᐨ ᑯᓴ ᐆᒪ ᑮᑳᐧᐩ ᐁ ᐯᐦᑕᒫᐤ, ᑖᐱᐢᑰᐨ ᐁ ᑭᐱᐸᖬᑭ ᓃᐦᑕᐊᐧᑲᔭ, ᐁᑲᐧ ᐅᕒᐁᑎᐨᐤ ᐆᒪ ᐊᐃᐧᔭᐠ ᐁ ᐊᔭᔭᒥᐦᐃᐟ, ᓇᒫᐧᐨ ᑯᓴ ᐆᒪ ᑲᐧᔭᐢᐠ ᐁ ᐯᐦᑕᐊᐧᐠ, ᐁ ᑭᐱᐦᑌᐸᖬᔮᐤ ᐊᓂᒪ ᑳ ᒪᑌᐧᐁᐧᐠ, ᐃᐧᖧ ᐲᐦᑐᑲᐧᒥᐠ. ᐁᑳᐧᓂ ᐁᑲᐧ, ᐱᑕᒫ ᐁᑲᐧ ᒦᓇ ᓃᐦᑕᐊᐧᑲᔭ ᑳ ᐹᐦᐴᐦᑖᐢᑲᐧᐦᐊᒫᐤ, «ᑖᓂᓯ ᐆᒪ ᐁ ᐃᐢᐸᖬᑭ,» ᐁᑲᐧᓂ ᓂᑮᔫᐁᐧᓄᐤ ᐁᑲᐧ ᓅᕒᐁᑎᐨᐤ, ᑭᔫᐁᐧᐤ ᐊᐊᐧ ᑳ ᐊᔭᔭᒥᐦᐃᐟ. ᐁᑲᐧ, «ᑭᐯᐦᑌᐤ ᓈ ᑳ ᒪᑌᐧᐁᐧᐠ.» ᐁ ᐃᑕᐠ, «ᐁᐩ, ᐨᐦᐅ. ᓇᒫᐧᐨ ᐃᐧᖧ ᓇᒪ ᒌ ᐁᑲ ᐁ ᒫᑯᓇᐟ ᐊᓇ ᐅᒋᐹᓯᐤ,» ᑳ ᐃᓯᐟ, ᑭᑕ ᑮ ᒫᑯᓇᐠ ᐊᖬᐢᐠ ᐅᒋᐹᓯᐤ ᐊᓇ, ᑭᑕ ᐯᐦᑕᕽ ᐁ ᒪᑌᐧᐁᐧᖬᐠ, ᒫᑲ ᐃᐧᖧ ᐁᑳ ᐁᑯᓯ ᐁ ᑮ ᑑᑕᒫᐤ, ᐃᐧᖧ ᐁ ᑮ ᓃᓯᐦᑭᓂᐢᑫᔮᐤ. ᐁᑳᐧᓂ ᑯᓴ ᐆᒪ ᐋᑕ ᐃᐧᖧ ᑳ ᑕᐸᔫᐟ ᐊᓇ ᒪᐢᑲᐧ.

[14] ᐁᑳᐧᓂ ᐁ ᓂᔮᓇᓄ ᑮᓯᑳᐠ (– ᓂᑮᓯ ᒪᒪᓈᐤ ᐁᐊᐧᑯ ᐁ ᐅᑖᑯᓯᐠ, ᐁ ᐊᓯᐊᐧᒋᑫᔮᐤ, ᐃᐧᖧ ᐋᐧᐸᐦᑭ ᑕ ᐯ ᓈᑕᐦᐅᑲᐃᐧᔮᐤ), ᐁᑳᐧᓂ ᐁᑲᐧ ᐋᐧᓯᑲᓂᕽ, ᒥᑐᓂ ᑭᓯᐱ ᐊᖬᕽ, ᐁᑯᑌ ᐆᒪ ᑳ ᓂᑕᐃᐧ ᐊᐢᒋᑫᔮᐤ, ᑭᓯᐠ ᐁ ᐊᓴᐋᐧᐸᒪᐠ ᐊᐊᐧ ᒪᐢᑲᐧ, ᑭᑕ ᑕᑯᓯᕽ, ᒫᑲ ᐃᐧᖧ ᐁ ᑮ ᐹᐢᑭᓴᐧᐠ ᒫᓇ ᒫᑲ ᑕᐸᔫᐤ. ᐁᑲᐧ ᒥᑖᑕᐦᐟ ᑎᐸᐦᐃᑲᐤ, ᓵᓴᐩ ᐋᑕ ᐃᐧᖧ ᑳ ᐯ ᐯᐦᑖᑲᐧᕽ ᐱᒥᖫᑲᐤ, ᐁᑳᐧᓂ ᐁᑲᐧ ᓂᑖᒋᒧᐢᑕᐋᐧᐤ ᐁᑲᐧ ᐊᐊᐧ ᐅᐱᒥᖫᐤ, «ᐯᔭᐠ ᐃᐢᐸᖬᐤ ᐆᑕ ᐁ ᐄᐧᒋ ᐊᔫᒪᐠ ᐊᐊᐧ ᒪᐢᑲᐧ, ᐊᓄᐦᐨ ᑳ ᑮᑭᓭᐹᔮᐠ ᓇᒣᐢᑲᐧ ᐆᑕ ᑕᑯᓯᐤ,» ᓂᑎᑖᐤ. «ᐨᐦ, ᑭᑕ ᑮ ᐯᓯᐋᐧᐠ ᐃᐧᖧ ᐆᒪ ᓂᐹᐹ, ᑭᑕ ᐯ ᓂᐸᐦᐋᐧᐟ,» ᑳ ᐃᓯᐟ. «ᐁᐩ, ᑖᐯᐧ ᐱᑯ ᐊᓂ, ᐲᖬᐢᐠ ᑭᐹᐹ ᑭᑕ ᓂᐸᐦᐋᐧᐟ ᐊᓂᐦᐃ ᒪᐢᑲᐧ, ᓂᐸᑳᐧᑖᐤ ᐊᐊᐧ ᐁ ᐃᑕᐦᑲᒥᑭᓯᐟ ᐆᑕ, ᐊᐦᐴ ᐁᑐᑫᐧ ᑕ ᐲᐦᑐᑫᐧᐤ ᓂᐋᐧᐢᑲᐦᐃᑲᓂᐢ,» ᓂᑎᑖᐤ. ᐁᑳᐧᓂ ᐁᑲᐧ ᓂᑑᐦᐸᐦᐅᓈᐤ.

[15] ᐁᑲᐧ ᐁᑯᐢᐲ ᐊᓂᒪ, ᐁ ᐊᑎ ᐃᐦᑭᕽ nineteen-eighty-two ᐸᑲᐦᑲᐣ, ᑳ ᐊᑎ ᐸᓯᑌᐠ ᑯᓴ ᐆᒪ ᓂᐊᐧᓂᐦᐃᑫᐢᑲᓇᐤ, ᒥᓯᐁᐧ ᐁᑯᑕ ᐁ ᐸᓯᑌᐠ. ᐁᑲᐧ ᐁᑯᑌ ᑯᓴ ᐆᒪ ᐁ ᓂᑕᐃᐧ ᑌᐧᐦᐅᒋᐠ ᐅᑖᐢᑕᐁᐧᐦᐃᑫᐊᐧᐠ, ᑳ ᒥᐢᑲᐋᐧᒋᐠ ᑯᓴ ᐆᒪ ᐁᑯᓂ, ᐊᓂᐦᐃ ᒪᐢᑲᐧ, ᒥᑐᓂ ᑭᓯᐋᐧᐠ ᓃᑭᕽ, ᐁᑯᑕ ᐃᓯ ᐁ ᓂᐱᐟ ᐊᓇ ᒪᐢᑲᐧ, ᐁᑲᐧ ᑯᓴ ᐆᒪ ᓇᒪ ᑮᑳᐧᐩ ᐅᐢᑎᑳᐧᐤ. ᐊᐃᐧᔭᐠ ᐁᑐᑫᐧ ᐁ ᑮ ᐹᐢᑭᓵᐧᐟ, ᐁᑲᐧ ᐁ ᒪᓈᐦᐅᐟ ᐅᐢᑎᑳᐧᐤ ᐊᓂᒪ, ᑳ ᔫᐸᐢᑳᐧᑕᐦᑳᐧᐤ ᒫᓇ, ᐁᑯᓯ ᐁᑐᑫᐧ ᐁ ᐃᔫᐦᒋᑫᐟ. ᐁᑲᐧ ᐊᓂᑭ ᐁᑯᑕ ᑳ ᑮ ᐊᔮᒋᐠ ᐊᔭ, ᒨᔫᑭᒫᐊᐧᐠ ᐊᓂᑭ, ᒥᐢᑕᐦᐃ ᐁ ᑳᐦᑲᑫᐧᒋᒥᒋᐠ ᐊᔭ, «ᑖᓂᓯ ᐆᒪ ᐁ ᐃᔫᐦᒋᑫᔭᐤ, ᐁ ᑮ ᐃᑕᑯᑖᔭᐤ ᒌ ᒪᐢᑯ ᑖᐸᑳᐧᓇ ᑳ ᓂᐸᐦᐋᐧᐟ ᒪᐢᑲᐧ,» ᐁ ᐃᓯᒋᐠ – ᐁᑲᐧ ᐃᐧᖧ ᐆᒪ ᐁ ᑮ ᒪᓈᒋᐦᐃᒪᐠ, ᐁᑳ ᐁ ᑮ ᐅᐦᒋ ᐄᐧ ᓂᐸᐦᐃᒪᐠ, ᐁᑲᐧ ᓃᖧ ᐁ ᐊᑖᒥᒥᒋᐠ ᐁ ᓂᐸᐦᐃᒪᐠ.

[16] ᐁᑳᐧᓂ ᐁᑯᑕ ᐁ ᐃᐢᑯ ᐋᐧᒋᒥᑯᓯᐟ ᐊᐊᐧ ᒪᐢᑲᐧ, ᐁᑳᐧᓂ ᐋᑕ ᐃᐧᖧ ᐁ ᑮ ᓇᑲᑕᐦᐊᐧᐠ.

II

[17] ᐊᔭ, ᑯᑕᐠ ᒦᓇ ᓂᐄᐧ ᐋᐧᑐᑌᐣ, ᒪᐢᑲᐧ ᐁ ᐄᐧ ᐋᐧᒋᒪᐠ. ᐁᑲᐧ ᐊᔭ, ᐊᐦᔮ ᐁᑐᑫᐧ ᐊᐃᐧᔭᐠ ᒪᐢᑯ ᓅᒍᑫᐧᓯᐤ ᓂᑲ ᐄᐧ ᐃᓯᔩᐦᑳᑎᐠ, ᒫᑲ ᑭᔮᒼ ᐁᑯᓯ ᐃᓯ.

[18] ᐊᔭ, ᐯᔮᑳᐧᐤ ᐆᒪ ᒦᓇ ᐁ ᓰᑳᐧᐠ, ᐁᑯᑌ ᐁ ᐃᓯ ᐅᐦᐸᐦᐅᐋᐧᐣ, ᐁᑲᐧ ᐯᔭᐠ ᐊᐊᐧ ᐃᐢᑫᐧᐤ, ‘Rosie Charles’ ᐃᓯᔩᐦᑳᓱᐤ, «ᐋ, ᓂᓯᑯᓴ, ᑲ ᐄᐧᒉᐃᐧᑎᐣ, ᑳ ᐄᐧ ᓂᑕᐃᐧ ᓰᑲᐧᓂᓯᔭᐣ,» ᑳ ᐃᓯᐟ. «ᐋ, ᑌᓂᑭ,» ᓂᑎᑖᐤ, «ᑭᑲ ᐄᐧᒉᐃᐧᐣ,» ᐁᑳᐧᓂ ᐁᑲᐧ ᓂᑮ ᐅᐦᐸᐦᐅᓈᐣ.

[19] ᒫᑲ ᒦᓇ ᐁᑯᑌ ᐊᓂᒪ ᐊᔨᐦᑭᐣ ᐆᒪ ᐁ ᑮ ᑌᐧᐦᐅᐋᐧᕽ, ᓵᓴᐩ ᒥᐢᑕᐦᐃ ᑮ ᒉᐢᒋᐸᔨᐤ ᑰᓇ. ᐁᑲᐧ ᐁᑯᑌ ᐊᓂᒪ ᐁ ᐊᔨᑕᐦᑲᒥᑭᓯᔮᕽ, ᒨᔨ ᓂᐊᐧᓂᐦᐃᑳᓈᐣ, ᒥᐢᑕᐦᐃ ᒫᑲ ᐊᔭ, ᓂᑳᐦ ᑲᐢᑭᑳᐧᓱᓈᐣ ᐁᑲᐧ ᓂᐸᐦᑫᑭᓄᐦᑳᓈᐣ, ᐁᑯᓯ ᐃᓯ ᑮᑳᐧᐩ ᐁ ᐊᔨᑑᑕᒫᕽ, ᑲᐯ ᐊᔨ ᓂᒐᓇᐋᐧᓈᐣ. ᐁᑲᐧ ᐯᔮᑳᐧᐤ ᐁ ᑮᓯᑳᐠ, ᐁ ᓈᒐᑫᐧᓯᐟ ᐁ ᑮ ᐋᐧᐳᓯ ᒑᐸᑫᐧᓯᔮᕽ, «ᐋ, ᓂᓯᑯᓴ, ᐊᐃᐧᔭᐠ ᑯᓴ ᐊᐊᐧ ᑭᑭᒧᑕᒫᑯᓇᐤ ᐊᔭ, ᐋᐧᐳᓴᐧ, ᑖᐱᐢᑯᐨ ᑯᓴ ᐊᐊᐧ ᒪᐢᑲᐧ ᐁ ᑕᑯᓯᕽ,» ᑳ ᐃᑌᐧᐟ. ᐁ ᑕᑯᐦᑕᐦᐋᐟ, ᐯᔭᐠ ᐃᐧᔨ ᐋᑕ ᐃᐧᔨ ᐯᓯᐁᐧᐤ, ᒫᑲ ᑯᑕᑲ ᐊᓂᐦᐃ ᐃᔭᐃᐧᐢ ᐁ ᐊᐧᓂᐦᐋᐟ, ᐁ ᐋᐦ ᐅᒋᐱᑖᐟ ᐊᐃᐧᔭᐠ, ᐁ ᓯᐯᐧᐦᑕᐦᐋᐟ.

[20] ᐁᑲᐧ ᑯᓴ ᐆᒪ, ᐄᐧᐸᐨ ᐊᑎ ᐁᑯᐢᐲ, ᑳᒥᓯᒥᐢᐳᐠ, ᒥᑐᓂ ᐁᑐᑫᐧ ᐯᔭᐠᒥᓯᐟ ᐁ ᒥᐢᐳᐠ. ᐁᑳᐧᓂ ᐁᑲᐧ, «ᐋ, ᒥᑐᓂ ᐃᐧᔨ ᐁᑲᐧ ᐊᔩᑯᓄᐊᐧ ᑭᒑᐸᑳᐧᓂᓯᓇᐊᐧ,» ᐃᑌᐧᐤ. «ᐋ, ᐁᔨᐁᐧᕽ ᓃᔨ ᓂᑲ ᓈᑕᑫᐧᓯᐣ ᐆᑕ ᑭᓯᐋᐧᐠ ᐆᐦᐃ ᑳ ᑮ ᐊᑯᑖᔮᐣ, ᒪᐦᑎ ᑫᓂᐸᐦᐊᐧᐠ,» ᓂᑎᑖᐧᐣ, ᐁᑳᐧᓂ ᓂᓯᐯᐧᐦᑖᐣ. ᐁᑲᐧ ᐄᐧᐢᑕ, ᐅᐦᐱᒉ ᐃᓯ ᐄᐧᐢᑕ ᓯᐯᐧᐦᑌᐤ, ᐁ ᓈᒐᑫᐧᓯᐟ, ᐃᐧᔨ ᐹᐦ ᐱᐢᑭᐦᐨ ᐁ ᐃᓯ ᒑᐸᑫᐧᓯᔩᕽ. ᓃᔨ ᓃᑲᐣ ᓂᑕᑯᓯᓂᐣ, ᓇᒪ ᑮᑳᐧᐩ ᓂᐯᑖᐣ, ᑲᐦᑭᔨᐤ ᑮᑳᐧᐩ ᐊᔩᑯᓄᐤ, ᐁᑲᐧᔨᐤ ᐁ ᒥᓯᒥᐢᐳᐠ.

[21] ᓃᔨ ᒫᑲ ᐄᐧᐸᐨ ᑳ ᑮ ᓈᑕᑫᐧᔮᐣ, ᒫᑲ ᐄᐧᔨ ᓇᒨᔨ ᐄᐧᐸᐨ. ᑫᑕᐦᑕᐁᐧ ᑳ ᑕᑯᓯᕽ, «ᐋ, ᓂᑭᐢᑫᔨᒫᐤ ᐁᑲᐧ ᐊᐃᐧᔭᐠ ᑳ ᑭᒧᑕᒫᑯᐊᐧᕽ ᐋᐧᐳᓴᐧ,» ᐃᑌᐧᐤ, «ᒪᐢᑲᐧ ᐊᐊᐧ ᐁᓴ, ᓂᒫᑕᐦᐋᐤ ᐁᑲᐧ, ᐃᑕ ᐁᓴ ᐁ ᐅᐦᑎᓈᐟ ᓂᐋᐧᐳᓯᒪ,» ᐃᑌᐧᐤ, «ᐁᑲᐧ ᐆᑌ ᐃᓯ ᓯᐯᐧᐦᑌᐤ.» ᐋ, ᐁᑳᐧᓂ ᐁᑲᐧ, «ᐋ, ᒉᐢᑲᐧ, ᑭᑲ ᑖᐸᑲᐧᒪᐦᐋᐧᓇᐤ ᐊᓇ ᒪᐢᑲᐧ.» ᐁᑳᐧᓂ ᐁᑲᐧ, ᓂᓂᑐᓄᐣ ᓂᑖᐸᑳᐧᓇ, ᓄᐅᐧ ᐸᑲᐦᑲᒼ ᒪᐢᑯ ᑖᐸᑳᐧᓇ ᑳ ᑮ ᐋᔮᔭᐣ. ᐁᑳᐧᓂ ᐁᑯᓂ ᐁᑲᐧ ᓂᑕᑯᑖᓈᐣ, ᒫᑲ ᐁᓴ ᓇᒨᔨ ᒪᐢᑲᐋᐧᐤ ᐊᓂᒪ ᑖᐸᑳᐧᓄᔮᐱᐩ, ᑖᐸᑳᐧᑌᐤ ᐄᐧᔨ, ᐸᐢᑭᐱᑕᒥᔨᐊᐧ. ᐁᑯᐧ ᐊᓂᐦᐃ ᐁᑲᐧ ᑯᑕᑲ ᓃᐢᑕ ᓂᑖᐸᑳᐧᓇ, ᓇᒨᔨ ᐁᑲᐧ ᓂᑮ ᐋᐸᒋᐦᑖᐣ – ᐃᔭᐃᐧᐢ ᓂᒪᓂᓄᐣ, ᐃᐧᔨ ᐁ ᐸᐢᑭᐱᑕᕽ ᒥᓴᐋᐧᐨ ᐊᓇ.

[22] ᐁᑳᐧᓂ ᐁᑲᐧ, «ᐋ, ᐲᒥᓇᐦᑳᐧᐣ ᑭᑲ ᐋᐸᒋᐦᑖᓈᓇᐤ, ᐃᑌᐧᐊᐧᐠ ᐊᓂᑭ ᒫᓇ, ᑳ ᐅᓵᐋᐧᐯᑲᕽ ᐊᓂᒪ, ᐊᔭ, ᐲᒥᓇᐦᑳᐧᐣ, ᐁᐊᐧᑯ ᐁ ᒥᔩᐧᓯᐠ ᒪᐢᑲᐧ ᐅᐦᒋ, ᐃᑌᐧᐊᐧᐠ

ᐆᒪ ᒫᓇ,» ᓂᑎᑖᐤ. ᐋ, ᐁᑳᐧᓂ ᐁᑲᐧ ᒫᓇ ᑳ ᒉᒦᐸᑕᐱᔮᕽ ᐆᒪ, ᑭᓯᐠ ᐁ ᐊᔭᒥᔮᕽ ᐁ ᑖᐸᑳᐧᓂᐦᑫᔮᕽ, ᒪᐢᑲᐧ ᐐᔭ ᐊᐊᐧ ᐁ ᑖᐸᑲᐧᒪᐦᐋᐧᔮᕽ. ᐁᑳᐧᓂ, ᐁ ᐅᑖᑯᓯᐠ ᐁᑲᐧ, ᐁᑳᐧᓂ ᐁᑲᐧ ᑳ ᑯᐢᐱᔮᕽ ᐁᑲᐧ ᒦᓇ, ᒫᑲ ᑎᒥᑯᓂᐤ ᑲᐧᔭᐢᐠ, ᓂᓂᑕᐃᐧ ᑖᐸᑲᐧᒪᐦᐋᐧᓈᐣ. ᑖᐯᐧ ᒦᓇ, ᐁᓴ ᑮ ᐱᒧᐦᑌᐤ, ᒫᑲ ᓇᒨᔭ ᓂᑖᐸᑳᐧᑖᓈᐣ, ᓵᓵᐳᐦᑌᐤ – ᐊᔭ ᐅᑎ ᐁ ᒫᐦᒥᔮᐢᑲᕽ, ᐁᑳᐧᓂ, ᐁ ᐋᐧᐸᕽ, ᓇᒨᔭ ᓂᐱᓯᐢᑫᔨᐦᑌᓈᐣ ᓂᑖᐸᑳᐧᓂᓈᓇ, ᐁᑯᓯ ᐃᓯ ᓇᒨᔭ ᓅᐦ ᑖᐸᑲᐧᒪᐦᐋᐧᓈᐣ, ᐹᑎᒫ ᑮᓯᐯᐧᑭ, ᑰᓇ ᐊᓇ ᒣᐢᒋᐸᔨᒋ, ᐁᑫᐧᔭ- ᒦᓇ. ᐱᔨᐢᐠ ᐁᑲᐧ ᒣᐢᒋᐸᔨᐤ ᐊᐊᐧ ᑰᓇ, ᐋ, ᐁᑳᐧᓂ ᐁᑲᐧ ᒦᓇ ᑳ ᓂᑕᐃᐧ ᑖᐸᑫᐧᔮᕽ. ᑭᐦᑭᕽ ᒦᓇ, ᐄᐧᔭ ᒦᓇ ᓵᓴᐩ ᒦᓇ ᐁ ᑖᐸᑳᐧᑖᐟ, ᐸᐢᑭᓇᑦ ᐊᓂᒪ ᐲᒥᓇᐦᑳᐧᐣ ᐊᐊᐧ ᒪᐢᑲᐧ, ᐋ, ᒫᑲ ᐃᐧᔭ thirty-thirty ᐁ ᑕᐦᑯᓇᒫᕽ. ᐋ, ᐁᑳᐧᓂ ᐁᑲᐧ, ᑳ ᐱᒥᑎᓴᐦᐋᐧᔮᕽ ᐁᑲᐧ, ᓂᓃᑳᓅᐦᑖᐣ, ᐅᑖᐢᑲᓈᕽ ᐄᐧᔭ ᐊᐊᐧ, ᐃᐧᔭ ᓃᔭ ᐁ ᓃᒫᐢᑫᐧᔮᐣ, ᐅᐦᑎᑖᐤ ᐱᑯ ᓃᑲᐣ ᓃᔭ. ᑮᑕᐦᑕᐁᐧ, ᐃᑕ ᐊᐊᐧ ᐁ ᐊᑎ ᐱᒧᐦᑌᐟ, ᐁᑯᑕ ᑳ ᐊᐢᑌᐠ ᐊᓂᒪ ᐲᒥᓇᐦᑳᐧᐣ, ᐁ ᐊᑎ ᑫᒋᑯᐱᑕᕽ ᐁᑐᑫᐧ ᐊᓂᒪ.

[23] ᐁᑳᐧᓂ ᐋ, ᓵᓴᐩ ᒦᓇ ᑯᑕᑲ ᓅᓰᐦᑖᓈᐣ ᑖᐸᑳᐧᓇ, ᐃᐧᔭ ᐁᑯᐢᐲ ᐊᓂᒪ ᐁ ᑮ ᐃᑎᑲᐃᐧᔮᕽ ᒦᓇ, «ᐊᐃᐧᔭᐠ ᓂᐸᐦᐋᒋ ᒪᐢᑲᐧ, ᐄᐧᓯᐱᐩ ᐊᓂᒪ ᒥᐢᑕᑭᐦᑌᐤ, ᐁᐊᐧᑯ ᑭᑕ ᐅᑎᓇᕽ ᐊᐃᐧᔭᐠ ᑭᑕ ᐊᑖᐋᐧᑫᐟ, ᒥᐢᑕᐦᐃ ᑳ ᐅᐦᑎᓯᐣ ᓰᓂᔮᐊᐧ,» ᐁ ᐃᑎᑲᐃᐧᔮᕽ ᒦᓇ, ᐁᐊᐧᑯ ᐆᒪ ᐅᐦᒋ ᐃᔨᑯᕽ ᑳ ᓅᒋᐦᐋᐧᔮᕽ ᐊᐊᐧ ᒪᐢᑲᐧ. ᐁᑳᐧᓂ ᓂᑯᐢᐱᓈᐣ, ᐁᑲᐧ ᒦᓇ ᐁ ᐅᔨᑯᔮᕽ, ᓂᐹᐦ ᐸᑕᑳᐧᑖᓈᐣ.

[24] ᐁᑳᐧᓂ ᐁᑲᐧ, «ᐋ, ᐁᑳᐧᓂ ᓃᔭ ᓂᐄᐧ ᓈᑕᑳᐧᐣ,» ᑳ ᐃᓯᐟ. «ᐄᐦᐃ,» ᓂᑎᑖᐤ, «ᐹᐢᑭᓯᑲᐣ ᐆᒪ ᑕᐦᑯᓇ, ᑳᐃᐧᔭ ᐊᓯᐊᐧᑖᐦᑲᐣ ᒨᓯᓯᓂᐩ. ᐹᑎᒫ ᐋᐧᐸᒪᒋ, ᓇᒨᔭ ᐊᓂᒪ ᐄᐧᐦᑳ- ᓂᑕᓯᐊᐧᑖᐣ ᒨᓯᓯᓂᐩ, ᑕ ᐱᒧᐦᑕᑖᔮᐣ ᐹᐢᑭᓯᑲᐣ,» ᓂᑎᑖᐤ, «ᐹᑎᒫ ᐊᐃᐧᔭᐠ ᑳ ᐋᐧᐸᒪᐠ, ᐁᑫᐧᔭ- ᐁᑯᑕ.» ᐋ, ᐁᑳᐧᓂ, ᑳ ᒪᒪᒍᐟ ᐁᑲᐧ. ᐁᑲᐧ ᐁᑯᓯ ᑳ ᐃᑕᐠ, «ᑮᐢᐱᐣ ᑖᐸᑳᐧᓯᒋ ᐊᓇ ᒪᐢᑲᐧ, ᐊᔭ, ᐅᑲᐧᔮᕽ, ᐅᑲᐧᔮᕽ ᑲᑫᐧ ᐹᐢᑭᓵᐧᐦᑲᐣ. ᑮᐢᐱᐣ ᐃᐧᔭ ᐃᐧᔭᐃᐧᕽ ᐄᐧ ᐹᐢᑭᓴᐧᒋ, ᑭᑲ ᐱᐢᑕᐦᐁᐣ ᐊᓂᒪ ᐋᐧᓯᐱᐩ,» ᐁ ᐃᑕᐠ, ᓇᒫᐧ- ᐁ ᑮ ᐴᓂ ᐹᐦᐱᐟ, ᐃᔨᑯᕽ ᐁ ᐊᐧᐁᐧᔭᑌᔨᐦᑕᕽ. ᐁᑳᐧᓂ ᐊᐢᐱᐣ ᑯᐢᐱᐤ, ᑕᑯᓯᐣ. ᓵᓴᐩ ᒦᓇ, ᓂᐢᑖᐧᐤ ᐁ ᐸᐢᑲᑳᐧᑯᐟ, ᐃᔨᑯᕽ ᐁᓴ ᐁᑳ ᐁ ᒥᔮᐧᓯᐠ ᐊᓂᒪ ᐲᒥᓇᐦᑳᐧᐣ. ᐁᑲᐧ ᒦᓇ ᐊᓂᒪ ᑖᐸᑳᐧᓄᔮᐱᐩ, ᐁᑲᐧ ᐁᑳ ᑯᑕᐠ ᑮᑳᐧᐩ ᐁ ᐋᔮᔭᕽ, «ᐋ, ᐁᑳᐧᓂ ᒫᓇ ᒫᑲ ᐁ ᑮᐦᐃᑯᔭᕽ,» ᓂᑎᑖᐤ.

[25] ᐁᑳᐧᓂ ᓇᒫᐧ ᓅᐦᒋ ᓂᐸᐦᐋᐧᓈᐣ ᐊᓇ ᒪᐢᑲᐧ. ᐯᔭᐠ ᐃᐧᔭ ᐸᐦᑫᑭᐣ ᓂᑮ ᑮᓯᑐᓈᐣ, ᐁ ᑮ ᐹᓴᒫᕽ ᐁ ᐅᑎᓇᒫᕽ ᐅᐲᐊᐧᔭ, ᐁᑲᐧ ᐁ ᑮ ᐹᓴᒫᕽ ᐁᑲᐧ ᐁ ᐄᐧᐢᑲᐧᓴᒫᕽ, ᐁᐊᐧᑯ ᐃᐧᔭ ᓂᑮ ᑮ ᓰᐦᑖᓈᐣ. ᐁᑳᐧᓂ ᐁᑲᐧ ᒦᓇ ᑳ ᑳᐦᑳᐧᐢᑫᐧᐱᒋᑫᔮᕽ ᐁ ᐱᒫᐦᐅᒋᑫᓯᔮᕽ, ᐁ ᓂᐸᐦᐋᐧᔮᐦᑳᐧᐤ ᓇᒣᑯᓯᓴᐠ. ᐁᐊᐧᑯ ᐁ ᑮᓯᑲᐠ ᑳ ᐄᐧ ᐯ ᐅᐦᐸᐦᐅᐋᐧᕽ, ᐄᐧᐸ- ᐁ ᑮᑭᓴᐹᔭᐠ, ᑳ ᐸᐹᒥᐢᑳᔭᕽ – ᐃᐧᔭ ᓃᓯ ᒦᓇ ᐆᓴ ᐁ ᐊᔮᔭᕽ, ᐆᒋᓯᓴ, ᐹᐦ ᐯᔭᐠ ᐁ ᐋᐸᒋᐦᑖᔭᕽ. ᓂᐢᑐ ᑯᓴ ᐆᒪ ᐄᐧᔭ ᐁ ᓂᐸᐦᐋᐧᐟ ᓇᒣᑯᓯᓴ, ᐁᑲᐧ ᐯᔭᐠ ᐃᐧᔭ ᓃᔭ ᓂᓂᐸᐦᐋᐧᐤ, ᐁᐊᐧᑯᓂᐠ ᐅᐢᑭ ᑭᓄᓴᐊᐧᐠ ᐁ ᐯ ᑮᐁᐧ ᓃᒫᔭᕽ.

[26] ᐁᑳᐧᓂ ᐄᐧᔭ ᐸᑲᐦᑲᑦ ᐁᑯᑕ ᐁ ᐃᐢᑯ ᐋᒋᒥᑯᓯᐟ ᒦᓇ ᐁᐊᐧᑯ ᒪᐢᑲᐧ, ᓂᑮ ᑮᐦᐃᑯᓈᐣ ᐁᑳᐧᓂ, ᐊᐢᐱᐣ.

2.
Daily Life

Glecia Bear

[FA:] hâw, êkwa ani âsay mîna.
[GB:] kâwi êkwa ka-mâcihtâyahk.
[FA:] êha.

I

[1] â, êkw âni nik-âtotên êkwa aya; misiw îtê ayis nikî-pê-atoskân ôma, nikî-pê-- atoskêwin ê-kî-pê-otinamân, ê-papâm-âtoskêyân, êkwa mâna kêhtê-ayak misiw îtê, *ten reserves* ê-kî-kiyo-- ê-kî-pimohtâtamân ê-atoskâtamân mîna; kîwêtinohk ôtê misiwê, *Waterhen*, *Joseph* [*pronounced as French*] *Bighead*, *Mudie Lake*, *ten* ôho *reserves* ôtê, wâhyaw mîn ôtê *north*, ê-atoskâtamân.

[2] êkwa mâna kêhtê-ayak mâna, kahkiyaw kîkway ê-kî-kâh-kakwêcimakik mân ê-kî-kiyokawakik. *ten years* ê-kî-atoskêyân *fish-plant*, êkwa *F.S.I.* ê-kî-atoskawakik, mitoni kinwêsêskamik mîn âkota nikî-atoskân *F.S.I.*; êkwa *old-folk's home* ôta ôma paskwâwi-sâkahikanihk, nistam ê-osîhtâhk, êkota ê-kî-mâtatoskêyân mîna; êkwa mîna *Indian Hospital* nikî-atoskân, kahkiyaw nitawâsimisak ê-kî-atoskêcik êkota; ohpimê êkwa ayi ê-kî-atoskêcik ê-wâh-onâpêmicik, niy êkwa êkotê nikî-nitaw-âtoskân mîna. nikî-pê-kakwâtakatoskân misiwê. mîcisowikamikohk ê-kî-pê-atoskêyân, *thirty-five dollars a month* ê-kî---kî-sôniyâhkêyân, *six o'clock in the morning* êkotê ê-kî-takohtêyân ê-mostohtêyâcihoyân; êkwa ê-- ê-kî-pê-kîwêyân, ê-âpihtâ-tipiskâk mân ê-pê-kîwê-mostohtêyân. iyikohk ê-kî-kakwâtakatoskêyân, askihkwak ê-wêpinakik, *slop-pails* ê-misi-mâh-misikiticik, kahkiyaw kîkway ê-kî-pê-tôtamân. piyis mâka kâ-kî-ati-miyo-sôniyâhkêyân, "*F.S.I.* ê-atoskêyân," wahwâ nititêyihtên êkwa, "miton ê-mâh-- ê-miyo-sôniyâhkêyân."

[FA:] Right, now we can start again.
[GB:] Now we will begin again.
[FA:] Yes.

I [*Interviews with Old Women*]

[1] Well, now I will also tell about it; for I used to work all over, I took a job, I used to go about in my work and visit old people all over, I used to travel to ten reserves all over in this work; all over the north, Waterhen, Joseph Bighead, Mudie Lake, and also farther north, I worked at these ten reserves over there.

[2] And I would visit old people and ask them questions about everything. I had worked at a fish plant for ten years, and I had worked for the F.S.I. people, I also worked there for a very long time, at the F.S.I. [*sc.* Federation of Saskatchewan Indians]; and at the old folks' home here in ***pâskwawi-sâkahikanihk***, I had begun to work there when they first opened it; and I had also worked at the Indian Hospital [*sc.* at Battleford], and all my children [*sc.* daughters] had worked there too; when they got married and worked elsewhere, then I for my part had also gone and worked there. I have always worked terribly hard and all over. I used to work in a restaurant for thirty-five dollars a month, I used to get there at six o'clock in the morning, travelling there on foot; and I would come home at midnight, also on foot. I worked so terribly hard, emptying pails, very big slop-pails, I have done everything. But finally I began to make good money, oh my, then I thought, "I am really making good money working for F.S.I."

II

[3] êkota ohc êkwa, *Health-and-Welfare* êkwa kâ-kî-atoskêyân êkwa mîna. êkotê anim êkwa, misiw îtê kâ-papâmâcihoyân. êkwa ôkik kêhtê-ayak mâna kâ-ka-kiyokawakik mâna, ê-kî-wa-wîtapimakik ê-pa-pîkiskwâtakwâw, âskaw mân îyikohk kinwêsêskamik mân âkotê ê-kî-kisâtamân ôta ôma *Waterhen*, kêhtê-ayak ê-kî-pîkiskwâtakik mâna. kahkiyaw kîkway ê-kî-wî-kakwê-kiskêyihtamân mâna, tânisi n--, kayâs kîkway tânisi ê-kî-pê-ispayik.

[4] *well*, nôhkom aw êkwa kâ-wîhtamawak êkwa, "nôhkom!" nititâw, "tânis ôma ê-kî-- kiyawâw kayâs ê-kî-pê-isi-pimâcihoyêk?" nititâw; miton ê-kêhtê-ayiwit awa nôcikwêsiw. êkwa kêyâpic ê-pimâtisit; '*Larocque*' awa ka-- isiyîhkâsow nôcikwêsiw *Waterhen* ohci, êwakw âna kâ-pa-pîkiskwâtak. "tânisi ê-kî-isi-wîkiyêk ôma nistam," nititâw, ana nôcikwêsiw; "ayihk aya, ma kîkway kayâs ôma kîkway ohc-îhtakok, môniyâwi-kîkway ôma ôta, kîkway ahpô ôho wâskahikana, êkâ kîkway ê-ohci-ihtakoki," ê-ay-itak.

[5] "nôsisim!" nititik, "ê-k-- aya, ê-kî-osîhtâyâhk mâna pahkêkinwa, êkwa kâ-minahocik ôkik nâpêwak; ê-kî-mâwacihtâyâhk mâna pahkêkinwa, êkwa ê-kâh-kîsinamâhk, mîkiwâhp pahkêkino-mîkiwâhp ê-kî-osîhtâyâhk," itwêw. êkwa, "nayêstaw êkotow[a] ê-kî-pê-wiyâhtamâhk," ê-itwêt, "nâpêwak pahkwêkinîtâs[a] [*sic; cf.* pahkêkinwêtâsa] ê-kî-osîhtamawâyâhkwâw, pahkêkin ohci papakiwayâna, mitâsa, maskisin[a] êkotowa ohci, astisak [*sic*]. nîstanân êkotow[a] ê-wiyâhtamâhk," itwêw, "ma kîkway wiya papakiwânêkin ohci-ihtakon," itwêw, "kîkway êkos îsi, mîna ma kîkway wîhkâc asapâp aw ânohc êkwa, kîkway kâ-âh-âpacihâcik, môy kîkway ohci-ihtakon êkos îs," îtwêw.

[6] êkwa, "kîkway mâk ê-kaskikwâcikâkêyan, nôhkom?" nititâw. "môswa ohc," îtwêw, "ê-otinamâhk, otâhk ospiskwaniwâhk," itwêw, "êwakw ânim ê-pâsamâhk, 'astinwân' isiyîhkâtêw," itwêw. "êwakw ân[i] ânima mân ê-kî-kaskikwâcikâkêyâhk," itwêw awa nôcikwêsiw.

II [*Running a Household*]

[3] And from then on I also worked for Health-and-Welfare. It was then that I travelled about all over. And when I would be visiting these old people, I would sit with them and talk to them, sometimes I would stay for a such a long time over there at Waterhen and talk to the old people. I wanted to try to know everything, how things had been in the old days.

[4] Well, I told this one old woman about it, "Grandmother!" I said to her, "How did your family live in the old days?" I said to her; this old woman was very old. And she is still alive, Larocque is the name of this little old woman from Waterhen, she was the one to whom I was talking. "How did you live at first," I said to this old woman; "you know, when there was none of this White-Man's stuff here in the old days, not even these houses, when there were none of them," I said to her.

[5] "Grandchild!" she said to me, "We used to prepare the hides when the men had killed an animal; we used to collect the hides when we had finished them, and we made a lodge, a lodge made from hides," she said. And, "That kind [*sc.* hide] is all we wore," she said, "we made hide pants for the men, shirts made from leather, pants, moccasins made from that kind, mitts. We [*sc.* the women] too wore that kind," she said, "there was no cloth available then," she said, "or anything like that, and there was never anything like the thread of today, what they all use now, there was never anything like that," she said.

[6] Then, "But what did you sew with, Grandmother?" I said to her. "We took it from the moose," she said, "back there from their back," she said, "and we dried that, 'loin-sinew' it is called," she said, "it was that with which we used to sew," this old woman said.

[7] "sâponikan mâka, kîkwây mâk ê-ay-âpacihtâyêk, êkâ kîkway ê-ihtakoki?" nititâw. "â, nâ--, apisimôsoso-oskanis [*sic*]," itwêw, "kîkway, êkota ohci mân ê-kî-osîhtât ninâpêm sâponikan," itwêw. "asiniya ohci mân ê-kî-tâsahahk mâna," itwêw, ana nôcikwêsiw. "môy âyis mîna kîkway môhkomâna," itwêw, "ohci-ihtakonwa," itwêw; "oskan ê-kî-- mâna," itwêw, "ê-kî-âpacihtâcik," itwêw, "môhkomân ê-kî-osîhtamâsocik," itwêw, "êwakw ân[a] âna, asiniy[a] ânih," îtwêw, "mân ê-kî-tâsahikâkêcik, ê-kî-os-- ê-kî-papakipotâcik mâna, môhkomân[a] ê-osîhtâcik," itwêw.

[8] êkwa k--, "ayihk mâka," nititâw, "kîkwây mâk ê-mit-- ê-mîciswâtamêk?" nitit--, "ohci, ê-ohci-mîcisoyêk, wiyâkana êkâ ê-ohci-ihtakok[i]?" ê-itak. "waskway, kahkiyaw kîkway waskway ohc," îtwêw, "wiyâkan[a] ê-kî-osîhtâhk," itwêw; "êkwa nipiy mîna," itwêw, "êkotowihk ê-kî-âwatâhk," itwêw, "ê-osîhâ-- ê-osîhihcik askihkwak," itwêw, "êkota ohci anima nipiy ê-kî-âwatâhk," itwêw.

[9] êkwa, "tânisi mâk êkâ kîkway pakâhcikanaskihkwak ê-ohci-ihtakocik?" ni-- ê-itak ôma. "nôsisim!" itwêw, "kayâs ma kîkway ohci-pakâhtâniwan, wiy êkâ askihkwak ê-ihtako-- [*sc.* ê-ihtakocik], kahkiyaw kîkway ê-kî-mosci-nawacîhk, kotawânihk, wayawîtimihk," ê-itwêt ana nôcikwêsiw; kahkiyaw kîkway ê-kî-maskatêpot, itwêw, wayawîtimihk, itwêw. "êkwa ôk--, wiya pîhc-âyihk kâ-- kâ-pipohk kâ-kî-ayâyâhk," itwêw, "êkota mân ê-kî-ihtakok, akwâwân ê-kî-osîhtâhk," itwêw, "pîhc-âyihk," itwêw.

[10] "tânisi mâk êkwa mîn êkâ ê-ocipohkâhtêk pahkêkin ê-- ôma êkot[a] ê-pônikâtêk?" nititâw. "môy," îtwêw, "mis-- misâw ayis," itwêw, "êkwa nêtê anima ispimihk ayis tawâw," itwêw, "kahkiyaw êkotê kîkway ispayiw," itwêw, awa nôcikwêsiw.

[11] "kîkway mâk ê-kî-otakohpiyêk?" êkwa mîna kâ-itak. "ay[i]," îtwêw, "môswêkin," itwêw, "ê-kî-mâtahamâhk mâna," itwêw, ôma itwêw, "êkwa, ê-kî-aya---nakatamâhk anih ôpîwaya," itwêw, ana, "kâ-pê-pâsamâhk êkwa," itwêw; "êwakw ân[i] ânima," itwêw, "ôma mâna ôkik minahikwak ê-kî---mâna---naha---otinâyâhkwâw, êkonik

[7] "But what about needles, what did you use since there were no needles?" I said to her. "Well, some small deerbone," she said, "my husband used to make needles from that," she said. "He used to grind it to a point with a stone," that old woman said. "For there were no knives, either," she said, "there were none," she said; "a bone," she said, "they used," she said, "and they made a knife for themselves," she said; "it was that one," she said, "with that stone they used to grind the bone to an edge, they used to thin it to an edge when they made knives," she said.

[8] And then, "But then," I said to her, "what did you eat from?" I said to her, "from what did you eat since there were no dishes?" I said to her. "Birch-bark, everything was made of birch-bark," she said, "they made dishes," she said; "and for water as well," she said, "in that kind [*sc.* birch-bark vessels] one hauled water," she said, "pails were made of it," she said, "and the water was hauled in those," she said.

[9] And then, "What did you do, since there were no boiling pots?" I said to her. "Grandchild," she said, "in the old days one did not do any boiling, since there were no pots, one simply roasted everything, on the campfire, outside," that old woman said; she used to roast everything on a spit, she said, outside, she said. "And then, since we used to be inside in the winter," she said, "there would be a rack there, one would make a rack," she said, "inside," she said.

[10] "But how was it that the hide [*sc.* of the tent-cover] would not shrivel when a fire was made in there?" I said to her. "It did not," she said, "for the lodge was big," she said, "and up there at the top it was open," she said, "everything went up there," she said, this old woman.

[11] "But what did you have for blankets?" I also said to her. "Oh," she said, "moosehide," she said, "we would scrape it," she said, this she said, "and then we would leave the hair on it," she said, that one, "when we came to dry it," she said; "that was the way," she said,

mân ê-kî-anâskêyâhk mîkiwâhpihk," itwêw, "êkwa ispî, êwakw ânim âkota mâna môswêkin ê-kî-astâyâhk," itwêw. "êkwa apisimôsoso-pahkêkinosa ê-yôskâki," itwêw, "ê-kî-mâmawokwâtamâhk mâna êkon," îtwêw. "êwakw ânima mân ê-kî-otanâskasowiniyâhk, waskic mân ê-kî-astâyâhk êkotow[a] âyi, anihi, môswêkinohk anima, opîway[a] ânihi; êkw êkotow[a] ânima mîna môswêkin mâna," itwêw, "ê-kî-- mân ê-kîsinamâhk, mâka mâna ê-kî-wâpiskâk," itwêw, "môy ê-kaskâpasamâhk," itw--, "kîkway ôm âkos îsi k-âpacihtâyâhk," itwêw, "ita kâ-nipâyâhk," itwêw. "êkw ân[i] ânihi ê-kî-otakwanahoyâhk mîna," itwêw; "aspiskwêsimon apisimôsoswayân mîna," itwêw, "ê-kipokwâtâyâhk," itwêw, "êkwa mwâskosiwân[a] [*sic; cf.* mâskosiwâna] ânihi mâna, êkotow[a] ânihi mân êkotowihk ê-kî-sâkaskinahtâyâhk ê-kipokwâtamâhk, êkon ânihi mân ê-kî-otaspiskwêsimoniyâhk," itwêw ana nôcikwêsiw, "kahkiyaw kîkway môswêkin êkwa apisimôsoswayân," itwêw, "ê-kî-âpacihtâyâhk," itwêw, "êkotowa pikw ê-kî-wiyâhtamâhk," itwêw.

[12] êkwa mîna ni-- êkwa nikakwêcimâw, "kîkway mâk êmihkwânis ê-is-âpacihâyêk?" nititâw, "kîkwây kitâpacihtânâwâw?" nititâw. "'êsisak' isiyîhkâtêw, mâna sâkahikanihk mân âyâwak anikik," itwêw, "akwanâ-- akwanâpiwêhikâsosiwak mâna," itwêw, "êkotow[a] ânikik," itwêw, "êkon [*sic*] ânikik mân mîciswâkêyâhk," itwêw; "êkwa môy kîkway mask--, kayâs *tea* ê-ohci-ihtakok," itwêw, "nayêstaw maskêko-*litea* [*sic*], êk ôho - *rose-bushes* anikik, êkwa âya,

[FA:] – okiniyak; –

[GB:] – âha; –

êkonik mîna mân ê-kî-pakâsimây-- --tâyâhk [*sic; sc.*-pakâhtâyâhk] anihi miscikosa," itwêw, "êy, wîhkasin mistahi, kisik kinanâtahowâkân," itwêw.

[13] êkwa ôma nititâw, "tânisi mân ê-kî-kisîpêkistikwânêyêk, kîkwây kâpacihtânâwâw [*sic; cf.* kitâpacihtânâwâw]?" nikî-itâw. "nôsisim!" itwêw, "anohc kiyawâw iyikohk ôma," itwêw, "kâ-wa-- kâ-wâh-wâpistikwânêyêk, kâ-pâh-paskwasêsipayiki [*sic*] kistikwâniwâwa," itwêw ana nôcikwêsiw, "iyikohk kahkiyaw kîkway ê-âpacihtâyêk môniyâwi-kîkway kistikwâniwâhk," itwêw, "niyanân,

"and we would take these spruce boughs and we would put them on the floor in the lodge," she said, "and then we would place that moosehide there," she said. "And soft deerhides," she said, "we would sew together," she said. "And we would use that as sheets, we would put these on top of the hair-side of the moosehide; and that kind also, the moosehide," she said, "we would finish, but it would be left white," she said, "we did not smoke it," she said, "when we used things like this," she said, "for where we slept," she said. "And we also used that kind [*sc.* moosehide] as covers," she said; "and for pillows also deerhide," she said, "we sewed them closed," she said, "and then we would use bulrushes, we would fill that kind [*sc.* bulrushes] into that kind [*sc.* deerhide pillowcases] and sew them closed, and these we would use as pillows," that old woman said, "we would use moosehide and deerhide," she said, "for everything," she said, "that is all we wore," she said.

[12] And then I also asked her, "But what did you use as spoons?" I said to her, "what did you use?" I said to her. "The name is 'shells', they are in the lake," she said, "and they usually have little covers," she said, "they were that kind," she said, "with these we used to eat," she said; "and there was no tea in the old days," she said, "there was only Labrador tea and also the rose-bushes and,

[FA:] – rosehips; –

[GB:] – yes; –

those too we would boil, boiling the branches [*sc.* of the Labrador tea]," she said, "hey, it tastes very good, and at the same time you use it medicinally," she said.

[13] And then I said to her, "How did you use to wash your hair, what did you use?" I had said to her. "Grandchild!" she said, "Today all of you," she said, "have so much white hair and your heads go bald," that old woman said, "since you use so much of all that White-Man's stuff on your heads," she said, "as for us, we used none of that; when we would want to have a bath, when we would want to wash

ma kîkway; kâ-kî-wî-pakâsimoyâhk, kâ-wî-kisîpêkistikwânêyâhk," itwêw, "matotisânihk ê-kî-pîhtikwêyâhk," itwêw, "êkot[a] ânim êkwa ê-pakâsimoyâhk," itwêw, "ê-kanâ-- ê-kanâcihisoyâhk," itwêw, "nistikwâninâhk mîn," îtwêw, "namôy wîhkâc kîkway ohci-pê-âpatan ôho kîkway ka-pê-kiskêyihtâkwahk ôho," itwêw; "mihcêt anohc kêhtê-ayak, âsônê ôkik kayâs môy ôhci-wâpistikwânêwak," itwêw; "ayis môy kîkway ohci--, pîtos kîkway ohc-âpacihcikâtêw," itwêw; "kikî-kanâtisin pêyakwan, kâ-pîhtikwêyan matotisânihk," itwêw, "kikanâcihon kwayas," itwêw.

III

[14] êkw âw êkwa kotak mîna nôcikwêsiw êkwa ê-kiyokawak, "nôhkom!" nititâw; "kayâs ôm," ê-it-- nititâw, "awîna kikî-pê-pamihikowâw kâ-wî-ocawâsimisiyêk," ê-itak aw êkwa nôcikwêsiw, kotak awa, â, mâk êwako kî-pôni-pimâtisiw êwako, *'Mrs Blackbird'* kî-isiyîhkâsow.

[15] "nôsisim! anohc ôma mân êk ôma," itwêw, "âhkosîwikamikohk, kahkiyaw awiyak kâ-itohtêt kâ-nihtâwikihâwasot," itwêw, "niyan-- niyanân ê-kî-pamihisoyâhk," itwêw, "kâ--, môy âwiyak nôhci-pamihikonân," itwêw, "nikî-pamihisonân," itwêw; "â, sôskwât mân âhpô sakâhk nikî-itohtânân, êkotê ê-nihtâwikahâyâhkik awâsisak, êkotê ohc êkwa ê-pêsiwâyâhkwâw," itwêw, "ê-pamihisoyâhk. môy wîhkâ [*sic*] nôhci-pimisininân, ka-pê-pimisiniyâhk, êkos ânima tâpwê piko ê-maskihkîwâpôhkatisoyâhk, êkosi tâpwê piko ayi, ê-atoskêyâhk, môy wîhkât nôhci-pimisininân," itwêw, "têpiyâhk ê-nihtâwikicik awâsisak, êkosi nitatoskânân; têpiyâhk mân ê-kî-sîhtwâhpisosoyâhk ôt[a] ôma natânâhk," itwêw, "maskihkiy, nêhiyawi-maskihkiy kisik ê-minihkwêyâhk," itwêw; "â, anohc kâ-kîsikâk, êwak ôhc êtikwê ayisiyiniw kâ-maskawâtisit," itwêw, ê-itwêt ana nôcikwêsiw – mitoni sôskwâc.

our hair," she said, "we would go into the sweat-lodge," she said, "there we had a bath," she said, "and cleaned ourselves," she said, "and also on our heads," she said, "none of these things were ever used so far as anyone would know," she said; "still today, many old people, especially those of the old times, do not have white hair," she said; "for none of these strange things were used," she said; "you were just as clean when you went into the sweat-lodge," she said, "you cleaned yourself properly," she said.

III [*Midwifery*]

[14] And then I also visited another little old woman, "Grandmother," I said to her; "in the old days," I said to her, "who used to be midwife to you all when you were about to give birth?" I then said to this old woman, another one, well, but that one has since died, Mrs Blackbird had been her name.

[15] "Grandchild! Today it is the rule," she said, "that every woman goes into the hospital when she gives birth to a child," she said, "as for us, we used to be midwife to ourselves," she said, "we did not have a midwife," she said, "we used to be midwife to ourselves," she said; "well, we would even simply go off into the bush, giving birth to the children there and then bringing them back from there," she said, "and be midwife to ourselves. We never used to lie down, we never would be lying down, we straight away made a medicine drink for ourselves, and we straight away were back at work, we never used to lie down," she said, "the children had no sooner been born when we were back at work; so long as we would have a support tied around here [*gesture*], around our abdomen," she said, "and at the same time we also drank medicine, Cree medicine," she said; "well, today, that must be the reason why people are strong," she said, that old woman said

– it was really something!

[16] êkwa, "kîkwây mâk êkwa mâna kitâpacihtânâwâw," nititâw ôma, "ayis mistahi mihko wêpinikâtêw, nôhkom?" ê-itak ana nôcikwêsiw. "â, nôsisim," itwêw, "askiya! askiya mân," îtwêw, "mistah êkon ânihi ê-kî-âpatahk[i]," îtwêw, "ê-kî-wêwêkinamâhk mâna," itwêw, "êkon ânih," îtwêw, "ê-kî-âpacihtâyâhk ôm," îtwêw, "niyanân," itwêw; "anohc kâ-kîsikâk kêyâpic ôma kâ-pimâtisiyâhk," itwêw, "ê-kî-pê-wâpahtamâhk ê-- ê-âyimahk, êkwa mîna nika-kî-itwân ê-- ê-kî-miyo-pimâcihohk kayâs; kahkiyaw kîkway ayis kî-ihtakon sakâwi-pimâcihowin," itwêw. "anohc êkw âsay mîn êwakw ân[i] ânima, êkwa wâpiskiwiyâs kâ-misiwanâcihtât, kahkiyaw kîkway ê-nipahtamâkoyahk, kahkiyaw kîkway ôho nanâtohk kîkway piscipowina ê-âpacihtâcik, ê-sîkahâhtahkik askiya piscipowin ohci; kâ-pâh-pâhkisikêcik ôma, kahkiyaw kîkway ê-nipahtâcik," itwêw. "êkwa ê-kî-miy---pakitinahk manitow ka-ohci-pimâcihohk," itwêw, "kahkiyaw kîkway kikî-pê-miyikonaw, mînisa, kahkiyaw kîkway, (wâposwa, sîsîpa, piyêwak [*sic*], kinosêwak [*sic*]), kahkiyaw (môswak) kîkway ê-kî-pê-mêkit. môy wîhkâ [*sic*] ayisiyiniw ohci-nôhtêhkatêw," itwêw, "tâpitawi kîkway kwayas kî-ayâniwan," itwêw. "êkwa, nâpêwak wiyawâw ê-kî-ôs[a]-ôsîhtamâsocik [*sic*], waskwayi-ôsa," itwêw, "kahkiyaw kîkway mâna ê-kî--, ê-kî-papâmicimêcik mâna," itwêw, "ê-kî-nipahcikêcik," itwêw.

[17] "êy, kî-miywâsin," itwêw, nôcikwêsiw ana, "nititêyihtên niy ê-kî-miyw-âyâyâhk," itwêw; "anohc ôm êkwa, kahkiyaw kîkway môniyâwi-kîkway ispî êkwa kâ-ispayik awa (pahkwêsikan môy wîhkât ohci-pê-kiskêyihtâkwan ka-kî-ihtakot), anohc êkwa, kahkiyaw kîkway êkwa êkon ânih," îtwêw, "ôho nanâtohk kîkway êkwa ka-mîcihk," itwêw; "êwak ôhci ayisiyiniw kinwês kî-pimâtisiw, môy ôhci-nihtâ-âhkosiw," itwêw, "ayis ê-miywâsiniyik, ê-kanâtahk [*sic; sc.* ê-kanâtaniyik] kîkway, ê-kî-- ê-kî-pê-mîcit," itwêw, "êkwa mîna, anohc êkwa môy nika-kî-itwan kîkway ê-kanâtahk, kîkway ka-nipahtâhk isi," itwêw, "ôma sakâwi-mîciwin, osâm mistahi kahkiyaw kîkway piscipowin, misiwê kîkway wîstawâw êkwa ê-ati-mîcicik môswak," itwêw, "êkwa kahkiyaw kîkway, ê-ati-wî-nipahikocik êkwa," itwêw, "kîstanaw êkwa êwakw ânima ê-ati-mîciyâhk," itwêw.

[16] And, "But then what would you use," I said to her, "for much blood is lost, Grandmother?" I said to that old woman. "Well, Grandchild," she said, "moss! We would use moss," she said, "a lot of that was used," she said, "we would wrap it up," she said, "and that," she said, "we would use," she said, "we for our part," she said; "we who are still alive today," she said, "we have seen difficult times, and I can also say that we had a good life in the old days; for everything was there for making one's life in the bush," she said. "And today the White-Skin has destroyed that, too, he has killed everything that was ours, they use all kinds of these poisons and spray the earth with poison; and when they drop bombs [*sc.* as part of military exercises at the Cold Lake base], they kill everything," she said. "And God has put these things down for people to live on," she said, "He has given us everything, berries, He has been giving out everything, (rabbits, ducks, prairie-chickens, fish), all things (moose). Man never used to go hungry," she said, "and one always had enough," she said. "And the men, they used to make birch-bark canoes for themselves," she said, "and they would go about in their canoes," she said, "and kill every kind of game," she said.

[17] "Hey, life used to be good," she said, that old woman, "I for my part think we used to have a good life," she said; "and today, now that all this stuff, this White-Man's stuff has come about (it had never been known for flour to exist), and today, there are all these things," she said, "all these various things to eat," she said; "that is the reason why people used to live long and did not fall ill often," she said, "for they ate good, clean food," she said, "and today, also, I cannot say that anything is clean, when one kills something," she said, "the bush food, for there is too much poison in everything, and the moose, too, eat everything all over," she said, "and they are being killed by everything," she then said, "and then we, too, are eating that," she said.

[18] "êkwa ê-kî-ma-miyo---ma-miyo-wa-wîkihk [*sic*] mâna," itwêw ôma, "pikw îtê kî-papâmipicinâniwan, môy wîhkât pêyakwanohk ayisiyiniw ohc-âyâw," itwêw, "ê-kî-papâmipicihk, ôsihk mân ê-kî-papâmipicihk, ê-papâmi-nîmâwinihkêhk kici kâ-pipohk," itwêw, "êkos ê-minahocik nâpêwak, kâhkêwakwa (kahkiyaw kîkway ê-kî-nipahtâcik)," itwêw, "ê-osîhtâyâhk," itwêw. "môy âyis mîna kîkway ohc-âtâwâkâniwan pahkêkin," itwêw, "kahkiyaw kikî-kanawêyihtamâson. awâsis kâ-nihtâwikit, êkotowa wâspison, pahkêkin, êkotowa wiya ê-- ê-pohtiskahk – kahkiyaw kîkway pahkêkin," itwêw; "êkosi êkwa ka-kî-- ka-kîsowâspisowak mîna awâsisak," itwêw. "ê-nôhay-- ê-nôhay-- ê-nôhihcik awâsisak," itwêw, "ma kîkway ayiwâk ka-kî-nitawêyihcikâtêk mâna," itwêw, "nitay-itêyihtên mân ânohc kâ-mâmitonêyihtamân," itwêw. "anohc kahkiyaw kîkway ê-tipahahkik, ahpô âsiyânihkêpison[a] ê-tipahahkwâw, kahkiyaw kîkway môniyâwi-kîkway ê-- ê-pimitisahahkik," itwêw, "êkwa ê-mêstinikêcik," itwêw, ana nôcikwêsiw. nikî-mâmaskâsihtawâw mân ê-ay-- kâ-kî-ac-- âh-âcimôhaki.

IV

[19] êkwa mîna, pêyak awa nê--, kotak êkwa nôcikwêsiw, *Mudie Lake* êkwa êwakw âna, pêyak mîna ê-kâh-kakwêcimak ôma, kahkiyaw kîkway. "môy wîhkâc ê-ayihk--, ê-ohci-ihtakok kîkway, ôho ayamihâwina, ôm ânohc êkwa iyikohk kâ-ihtakok[i]," îtwêw ana nôcikwêsiw, "kây-- kayâs ê-kî-ay-- kâ-kî-mawimoscikêyan," itwêw, "awa kâ-tipêyimikoyahk, ispimihk kâ-kitâpamikoyahk," itwêw, "kipîkiskwâtânaw ê-mawimostawâyahk," itwêw. "êkosi nawac êkw êtikwê kî-nitohtâkowisinâniwan," itwêw, "ayis kwayask kikî-isi-pimâtisin, ma kîkway kôhci-pê-maci-kikiskâkon; êkwa kayâs ayisiyiniw kîkway kâ-nipahtât, ê-kî-papâmohtêhk ê-- ê-asamihcik kotakak ayisiyiniwak," itwêw; "ê-asamacik, kîkway k-âyâyan, piko wîstawâw ê-asamacik," itwêw. "anohc kâ-kîsikâk, namôy kîkway, pêyak kîkway ayisiyiniw ka-mosc-âsamik, kîkway ka-nipahtât kîkway, piko k-âtâwêyan," itwêw. "ahpô êkw ânohc kâ-pîhtikwêyan wâskahikanihk, môy âhpô kiminahikawin maskihkîwâpoy

[18] "And one used to have good dwellings then," she said, "one camped about just any place, the people never stayed in one place," she said, "one moved about with one's camp, one moved about by boat, going about and getting food ready for the winter," she said, "and so the men would kill game, and (they killed everything)," she said, "and we prepared dried meat," she said. "And of course one did not sell the hides," she said, "you kept them all for yourself. When a child was born, the mossbag was of that kind, of hide, the baby wore that kind [*sc.* a mossbag] – everything was of hide," she said; "and so the children also were warmly swaddled," she said. "And the children were breastfed," she said, "what more could one wish for," she said, "I usually think when I think back today," she said. "Today they pay for everything, they even pay for diapers, they follow every one of the White-Man's things," she said, "and they spend all their money on them," she said, that old woman. I was amazed to hear her story, when I had her telling me stories.

IV [*Drinking and Prophesies*]

[19] And then I also asked another little old woman, this one from Mudie Lake, about everything. "In the old days this thing did not exist, the fact that today there are so many religions," that old woman said, "in the old days when you worshipped," she said, "the one who is master over us all, who watches us from above," she said, "we speak to him in our worship," she said. "At that time, it seems, one's worship received more of a hearing," she said, "for you lived properly, there was no evil in you; and when a person killed something in the old days, one went about and food was provided for other people," she said; "you fed them when you had something, you had an obligation to feed them, too," she said. "Today there is none of that, not one person will give you food for nothing when they kill game; you have to buy it from them," she said. "Even when you go into a house today, you are not even given tea to drink,"

êkwa," itwêw, "ayis môniyâwi-kîkway ê-pimitisahahkwâw," itwêw, "kahkiyaw kîkway nipîmakan. kayâs ê-kî-wîhkohtohk, ahpô ayisiyiniw pêyak kâ-minahot, kahkiyaw ê-kî-wîhkomihcik ayisiyiniwak, ê-kî-misi-piminawasohk mâna mistaskihkohk, wayawîtimihk," itwêw. "êkwa ê-kî-wîhkomihcik êkwa êkotê ê-mîcisohk wayawîtimihk," itwêw, "ê-wîhkomacik," itwêw; "môy wîhkâc anohc êwako kîkway wâpahcikâtêw," ê-itwêt ana nôcikwêsiw.

[20] "êk ôma k--, kâ-wîkihtocik ôkik ayamihêwikamikohk," itwêw, "kayâs ma kîkway êwakw ânima wîkihtowin; kâ-miskamâsoyan awiyak, nâpêw, kâ-wîkimat, êkosi tâpwê piko kiwîkimâw, môy wîhkât kipaskêwihâw," itwêw. "kâ-kî-isi-wîkimat, êkos âni tâpwê piko ê-wîc-âyâmat," itwêw, "ma kîkway kihci-wîkihtowin, êkosi kinwês ê-wîc-âyâhtohk isko pêyak ka-nakasiwêt," itwêw. "anohc êkwa," itwêw, "âtiht têpiyâhk ê-wîkihtocik, matwân cî anih âhcanisa ohci, têpiyâhk âtiht ê-wî-kakwê-ayâwâcik ê-miyosiyit ka-wâsihkopayiyit," itwêw; "mâka môy kiskisiwak manitowa," itwêw, "ê-wî-- kâ-wîkihtahikocik, wanikiskisiwak êkon ânih," îtwêw, "anih ê-mamacikastâkêcik anihi âhcanisa. pêyak-pîsim, ahpô âskaw môy pêyak-pîsim âtiht, ê-wîc-âyâmâcik onâpêmiwâwa ê-wêpinâcik," itwêw, "môy âkosi ohc-îspayiw," itwêw; "kayâs kî-mânacihtâniwan kahkiyaw kîkway," itwêw, "ê-kî-pê-miyo-pimâtisihk."

[21] "mihcêtwâw mâna," itwêw, "kâ-pa-pimisiniyân ê-wî--, mâna niwî-ma-môskwêyihtên mân ê-mâmitonêyihtamân," itwêw, "anohc nitawâsimisak, tânisi nîst ê-pê-is-ôhpikicik, minihkwêwin anim îyikohk ê-otinahkwâw, ocawâsimisiwâwa ê-wêpinâcik, ê-misi-nâh-nôcihihcik ôkik nitânisak mân," îtwêw, "onâpêmiwâwa ê-mâh-misi-nâh-nôcihikocik [*sic*]," itwêw. "mâka môy nikî-nâtamâwason," itwêw, "ê-kaskihtamâsocik anima kâ-nôcihihcik," itwêw, "ê-papâmâcihocik êkwa ê-wî--, ocawâsimisiwâwa ê-nakatâcik," itwêw; "namôy nikî-nâtamâwason," itwêw. "mâka mâna nik-- nikîmôci-môskwêyihtên mâna," itwêw, "iyikohk ê-kî-pakwâtamân ê-isi-pimâtisicik," itwêw.

she said, "for they follow the White-Man's customs," she said, "everything is dead. In the old days they used to hold a feast, if a person killed even a single animal, all the people used to be invited, and they would do a great deal of cooking in a big pot, outside," she said. "And people were invited and everyone ate outside," she said, "you invited them," she said; "none of that is ever seen today," that old woman said.

[20] "And this business of people getting married in church," she said, "in the old days there was none of that marrying business; when you found someone, a man for yourself to marry, you straight away married him, you never separated from him," she said. "As you had married him, so you remained with him by virtue of that fact," she said, "there was no church marriage, and thus they lived together until one of them would depart this world," she said. "And today," she said, "some only marry for the sake of getting married, I wonder if some merely want to try and have that nice ring that will glitter," she said; "but they do not remember that it is God," she said, "who joins them in marriage, they forget Him," she said, "they show off with that ring. For one month, or sometimes not even for a month, they live with their husbands and then they leave them," she said, "that did not use to happen," she said; "in the old days one used to have respect for everything," she said, "and one used to lead a proper life."

[21] "Many times," she said, "when I am lying down thinking, I almost cry when I think about it," she said, "how my very own children, too, have come to grow up, they take alcohol to such an extent, they abandon their children, and my daughters are always being beaten," she said, "their husbands always beat them so severely," she said. "But I cannot take up for my children," she said, "they deserve it when they are beaten," she said, "they run around and leave their children behind," she said; "I cannot take up for my children," she said. "But in secret I always cry because of it," she said, "so much do I hate the way they live," she said.

[22] "kiyâm ayisiyiniw mêtoni ka-miyo-pimâtisiw, tâpiskô [*sic*] ôma niya nika-kî-itwân," itwêw, "nama kîkway maci-kîkway nôhci-pê-nôcihtan," itwêw ana nôhkom. "ê-kî-pê-miyo-pimâtisiyân, namôy wîhkât nôhci-pêyakon nânitaw kâ-itohtêyân, ninâpêm ê-kî-wîcêwak, awâsisak ê-ayâwâyâhkwâw, iyawis ê-sipwêhtahâyâhkik," itwêw; "anohc êkwa, môy êwakw ânima kîkway êkwa wîhkâc wâpahcikâtêw," itwêw, "iyikohk ê-kitimâkahk; kitimâkisinâniwan," itwêw. "nôsisimisak mâna, mihcêtwâw mân ê-mâmitonêyimakwâw, ê-kitimâkisicik ê-wâpahtahkwâw ê-pakamahomiht okâwîwâwâ," itwêw, "ê-- ê-wâpahtahkik êwako," itwêw. "êkwa mwêstas, ê-itêyihtamân," itwêw, "namôy ânima wîhkâc anikik awâsisak ka-wanikiskisiwak, tânisi kîkway kâ-pê-isi-wâpahtihikocik ôhtâwiwâwa anihi, kâ-nôtiniskwêwêyit, ahpô êtikwê wîstawâw ka-kakwê-âsô-kiskinawâpiwak, ê-itêyimakik mâna," itwêw, "kîs-ôhpikitwâwi," ê-itwêt awa nôcikwêsiw.

[23] "mistah âyiman. êkwa iyikohk ê-wî-kitimâkahk ôma nîkân, ati sâsay ahpô nôkwan," itwêw, "iyikohk ê-kitimâkahk," itwêw. "nama kîkway atoskêwin, nama kîkway," itwêw, "kayâs kimosôminaw ê-kî-itwêt," itwêw, "ê-tâpwêt," itwêw, "'mwêstas at[i] ôtê,' ê-kî-itwêt kayâs, kimosôminaw êsa," itwêw, "'môy kîkway, wîpac ka-ihtakon êkwa ôtê ati nîkân, namôy âsiskîhk kîkway ka-pimipayiw, nayêwac ka-pimipayiw kîkway,' ê-kî-itwêt awa, ê-kî-kiskinawêhikêt aw êsa pêyak kisêyinîsis," itwêw. "tâpwê anim âkosi sâsay ê-ispayik anima kâ-kî-itwêt," itwêw, "'nayêwac kîkway ka-pimipayiw,' kâ-kî-itwêt," itwêw, "êwak ôm êtik ôm âkwa [*sic*] pimiyâkan [*sic*] êkwa," itwêw, "nayêwac kâ-pimipayik," itwêw. "'kîkway ani ka-ihtakon, kêtahtawê ka-misiwanâcihcikêmakahk, wâpiskiwiyâs ka-misiwanâcihât ayisiyiniwa, mwêstas at[i] ôt[ê],' ê-kî-itwêt," itwêw, "sâsay ôma kahkiyaw êwak ôma kîkway ê-ati-wâpahtamahk," itwêw. "tâpiskôc ôma minihkwêwin kâ-misiwanâcihikocik ân--."

[*external break*]

[FA:] ---moyani [*sc.* wî-acimoyani] mîna.

[GB:] êy, wîpac êtikw êkwa nika-mêscitonêsinin, wâcistakâc!

[22] "It does not matter if a person really leads a proper life, as I will be able to say for myself," she said, "I have never done anything bad," this grandmother of mine said. "I have been living a proper life, I have never gone alone when I went some place, I went with my husband, and when we had children we took them with us, the whole lot," she said; "now today, you never see that anymore," she said, "there is so much misery; people are miserable," she said. "Many times I think of my grandchildren, they are so miserable when they see their mother being beaten," she said, "when they see that," she said. "And later, I think," she said, "those children will never forget what their father has shown them, when he beat up his wife, and they may even themselves try to follow the example set for them, I tend to think about them," she said, "when they are grown up," the old woman said.

[23] "Life is very difficult. And there is going to be so much misery in the future, that is even becoming visible already," she said, "there is so much misery," she said. "There is no work, nothing," she said, "our grandfather had said this long ago," she said, "and he spoke the truth," she said, "'Later in the future,' he had said long ago, our grandfather," she said, "'there will be nothing then, in the future, soon nothing will travel on the ground, everything will travel through the air,' he had said, one little old man had prophesied," she said. "It is true, and some of what he had said is happening already," she said, "'Everything will travel through the air,' as he had said," she said, "that must be the airplane now," she said, "which travels through the air," she said. "'There will be something that will at some time destroy things, the White-Skin will destroy people, later on there in the future,' he had said," she said, "and we have already begun to see all these things," she said. "'For instance the alcohol which is destroying them" --

[*external break*]

[FA:] -- if you want to tell more.

[GB:] Hey, soon now I will probably wear my mouth out, by golly!

[24] êkw êwakw âw êkwa, awa nô-- kôhkominaw êkwa mîna ê- kâ-itwêt êkwa, "êy," itwêw, "pikw ân[i] êkâ kâ-pakicîyahk, nôsisim!" itwêw; "kêyiwêhk ani, âhkamêyimo kîsta, kakêskimik kitawâsimisak, kakêskimik kôsisimak! pikw ânima êkâ ka-pakicîyan, k-âhkamêyimohk ka-kakwê-kwêskinihcik; ahpô êtikwê piyis kâh-mâmitonêyihtamwak, tânisi ê-pê-ispayik kayâs," itwêw. "mâk âyis, âta wiya mîn ê-pîwêyihtahkwâw ôma, kîkway kâ-wîhtamâhcik," itwêw.

[25] "mistah âni wî-kitimâkan ôtê mwêstas ka-nipahâhkatosocik ayisiyiniwak," itwêw, "âsay ati-nôkwan," itwêw. "sôskwâ [*sic*] mâna nimâmaskâtên, tânisi ka-kî-isi-pimâtisicik osk-âyak – kiyânaw wiya kika-pimâtisinaw, wiya kiyânaw kikaskihtânaw kîkway ka-kî-nipahtamâsoyahk, kayâsi-pimâcihowin ka-otinamahk," itwêw. "mâk ôkik osk-âyak, ma kîkway ayis kiskêyihtamwak," itwêw; "kîkway piko ê-kiskêyihtahkwâw, ka-pôsapicik sêhkêpayîsa, ka-papâmi-minihkwêcik, ka-papâmi-miyawâtahkwâw, môy wiya mâmitonêyimêwak onîkihikowâwa, kêhtê-aya ahpô ka-mâmitonêyimâcik tânisi ka-kî-isi-manâcihâcik," itwêw, "ka-pîkwêyihtamihâcik," itwêw, "mihcêtwâw mistahi mâtowin ihtakon minihkwêwin ohc," îtwêw, "ê-nipahisihkik ayisiyiniwak, awâsisak," itwêw, "minihkwêwin anima kahkiyaw ê-tôcikêmakahk," itwêw.

[24] And then that one, that grandmother of ours, also said, "Hey," she said, "we must not give up, Grandchild!" she said; "you, too, persevere nevertheless, counsel your children, counsel your grandchildren! You must not give up in this, one must persevere to try to turn them around; one day perhaps they might think about how things had been in the old days," she said. "But, of course, they have a low opinion of the things about which they are told," she said.

[25] "There is going to be a great deal of misery there, later, when people will starve," she said, "it is becoming visible already," she said. "I simply find it mind-boggling, how these young people will be able to survive – we for our part will survive for we are able to kill things for ourselves and to take up the traditional way of life," she said. "But these young people, of course, they do not know anything," she said; "the only thing they do know is to get into a car and to go about drinking and to go about having a good time, for they do not think about their parents, that they would even think about how they might show respect to the old people," she said, "or that they would cause them terrible worry," she said, "many times there is much crying because of alcohol," she said, "when people get killed in an accident, also children," she said, "and all that is the fault of alcohol," she said.

I

[1] ᐋ, ᐁᑲᐧ ᐊᓂ ᓂᑲ ᐋᑐᑌᐣ ᐁᑲᐧ ᐊᔭ, ᒥᓯᐁᐧ ᐃᑌ ᐊᔨᐢ ᓂᑮ ᐯ ᐊᑐᐢᑳᐣ ᐆᒪ, ᐊᑐᐢᑫᐃᐧᐣ ᐁ ᑮ ᐯ ᐅᑎᓇᒫᐣ, ᐁ ᐸᐹᒥ ᐊᑐᐢᑫᔮᐣ, ᐁᑲᐧ ᒫᓇ ᑫᐦᑌ ᐊᔭᐠ ᒥᓯᐁᐧ ᐃᑌ, ten reserves ᐁ ᑮ ᐱᒧᐦᑖᑕᒫᐣ ᐁ ᐊᑐᐢᑳᑕᒫᐣ ᒦᓇ, ᑮᐁᐧᑎᓄᕽ ᐆᑌ ᒥᓯᐁᐧ, Waterhen, Joseph Bighead, Mudie Lake, ten ᐆᐦᐅ reserves ᐆᑌ, ᐋᐧᐦᔭᐤ ᒦᓇ ᐆᑌ north, ᐁ ᐊᑐᐢᑳᑕᒫᐣ.

[2] ᐁᑲᐧ ᒫᓇ ᑫᐦᑌ ᐊᔭᐠ ᒫᓇ, ᑲᐦᑭᔭᐤ ᑮᑲᐧᕀ ᐁ ᑮ ᑳᐦ ᑲᑫᐧᒋᒪᑭᐠ ᒫᓇ ᐁ ᑮ ᑭᔪᑲᐊᐧᑭᐠ. ten years ᐁ ᑮ ᐊᑐᐢᑫᔮᐣ fish-plant, ᐁᑲᐧ F.S.I. ᐁ ᑮ ᐊᑐᐢᑲᐊᐧᑭᐠ, ᒥᑐᓂ ᑭᓀᐧᓴᐢᑲᒥᐠ ᒦᓇ ᐁᑯᑕ ᓂᑮ ᐊᑐᐢᑳᐣ F.S.I., ᐁᑲᐧ old-folk's home ᐆᑕ ᐆᒪ ᐸᐢᑳᐧᐃᐧ ᓵᑲᐦᐃᑲᓂᕽ, ᓂᐢᑕᒼ ᐁ ᐅᓰᐦᑖᕽ, ᐁᑯᑕ ᐁ ᑮ ᒫᑕᑐᐢᑫᔮᐣ ᒦᓇ, ᐁᑲᐧ ᒦᓇ Indian Hospital ᓂᑮ ᐊᑐᐢᑳᐣ, ᑲᐦᑭᔭᐤ ᓂᑕᐋᐧᓯᒥᓴᐠ ᐁ ᑮ ᐊᑐᐢᑫᒋᐠ ᐁᑯᑕ, ᐅᐦᐱᒣ ᐁᑲᐧ ᐊᔨ ᐁ ᑮ ᐊᑐᐢᑫᒋᐠ ᐁ ᐋᐧᐦᐅᓈᐯᒥᒋᐠ, ᓂᔭ ᐁᑲᐧ ᐁᑯᑌ ᓂᑮ ᓂᑕᐃᐧ ᐊᑐᐢᑳᐣ ᒦᓇ. ᓂᑮ ᐯ ᑲᑳᐧᑕᑲᑐᐢᑳᐣ ᒥᓯᐁᐧ. ᒦᒋᓱᐃᐧᑲᒥᑯᕽ ᐁ ᑮ ᐯ ᐊᑐᐢᑫᔮᐣ, thirty-five dollars a month ᐁ ᑮ ᓲᓂᔮᐦᑫᔮᐣ, six o'clock in the morning ᐁᑯᑌ ᐁ ᑮ ᑕᑯᐦᑌᔮᐣ ᐁ ᒧᐢᑐᐦᑌᔮᒋᐦᐅᔮᐣ, ᐁᑲᐧ ᐁ ᑮ ᐯ ᑮᐁᐧᔮᐣ, ᐁ ᐋᐱᐦᑖ ᑎᐱᐢᑳᐠ ᒫᓇ ᐁ ᐯ ᑮᐁᐧ ᒧᐢᑐᐦᑌᔮᐣ. ᐃᔨᑯᕽ ᐁ ᑮ ᑲᑳᐧᑕᑲᑐᐢᑫᔮᐣ, ᐊᐢᑭᐦᑲᐧᐠ ᐁ ᐁᐧᐱᓇᑭᐠ, slop-pails ᐁ ᒥᓯ ᒫᐦ ᒥᓯᑭᑎᒋᐠ, ᑲᐦᑭᔭᐤ ᑮᑲᐧᕀ ᐁ ᑮ ᐯ ᑑᑕᒫᐣ. ᐱᔨᐢ ᒫᑲ ᑳ ᑮ ᐊᑎ ᒥᔪ ᓲᓂᔮᐦᑫᔮᐣ, «F.S.I. ᐁ ᐊᑐᐢᑫᔮᐣ,» ᐋᐧᐦᐋᐧ ᓂᑎᑌᔨᐦᑌᐣ ᐁᑲᐧ, «ᒥᑐᓂ ᐁ ᒥᔪ ᓲᓂᔮᐦᑫᔮᐣ.»

II

[3] ᐁᑯᑕ ᐅᐦᒋ ᐁᑲᐧ, Health-and-Welfare ᐁᑲᐧ ᑳ ᑮ ᐊᑐᐢᑫᔮᐣ ᐁᑲᐧ ᒦᓇ. ᐁᑯᑌ ᐊᓂᒪ ᐁᑲᐧ, ᒥᓯᐁᐧ ᐃᑌ ᑳ ᐸᐹᒫᒋᐦᐅᔮᐣ. ᐁᑲᐧ ᐆᑭᐠ ᑫᐦᑌ ᐊᔭᐠ ᒫᓇ ᑳ ᑲ ᑭᔪᑲᐊᐧᑭᐠ ᒫᓇ, ᐁ ᑮ ᐊᐧ ᐄᐧᑕᐱᒪᑭᐠ ᐁ ᐸ ᐲᑭᐢᑳᐧᑕᑳᐧᐤ, ᐋᐢᑲᐤ ᒫᓇ ᐃᔨᑯᕽ ᑭᓀᐧᓴᐢᑲᒥᐠ ᒫᓇ ᐁᑯᑌ ᐁ ᑮ ᑭᓵᑕᒫᐣ ᐆᑕ ᐆᒪ Waterhen, ᑫᐦᑌ ᐊᔭᐠ ᐁ ᑮ ᐲᑭᐢᑳᐧᑕᑭᐠ ᒫᓇ. ᑲᐦᑭᔭᐤ ᑮᑲᐧᕀ ᐁ ᑮ ᐄᐧᑲᑫᐧᑭᐢᑫᔨᐦᑕᒫᐣ ᒫᓇ, ᑲᔮᐢ ᑮᑲᐧᕀ ᑖᓂᓯ ᐁ ᑮ ᐯ ᐃᐢᐸᔨᐠ.

[4] well, ᓅᐦᑯᒼ ᐊᐊᐧ ᐁᑲᐧ ᑳ ᐄᐧᐦᑕᒪᐊᐧᐠ ᐁᑲᐧ, «ᓅᐦᑯᒼ.» ᓂᑎᑖᐤ, «ᑖᓂᓯ ᐆᒪ ᑭᔭᐋᐧᐤ ᑲᔮᐢ ᐁ ᑮ ᐯ ᐃᓯ ᐱᒫᒋᐦᐅᔦᐠ.» ᓂᑎᑖᐤ, ᒥᑐᓂ ᐁ ᑫᐦᑌ ᐊᔨᐃᐧᐟ ᐊᐊᐧ ᓅᒋᑫᐧᓯᐤ. ᐁᑲᐧ ᑫᔮᐱᐨ ᐁ ᐱᒫᑎᓯᐟ, 'Larocque' ᐊᐊᐧ ᐃᓯᔩᐦᑳᓱᐤ ᓅᒋᑫᐧᓯᐤ Waterhen ᐅᐦᒋ, ᐁᐊᐧᑯ ᐊᓇ ᑳ ᐸ ᐲᑭᐢᑳᐧᑕᐠ. «ᑖᓂᓯ ᐁ ᑮ ᐃᓯ ᐄᐧᑭᔦᐠ ᐆᒪ ᓂᐢᑕᒼ,» ᓂᑎᑖᐤ, ᐊᓇ ᓅᒋᑫᐧᓯᐤ, «ᐊᔨᕽ ᐊᔭ, ᒪ ᑮᑲᐧᕀ ᑲᔮᐢ ᐆᒪ ᑮᑲᐧᕀ ᐅᐦᒋ ᐃᐦᑕᑯᐠ, ᒨᓂᔮᐃᐧ ᑮᑲᐧᕀ ᐆᒪ ᐆᑕ, ᑮᑲᐧᕀ ᐊᐦᐴ ᐆᐦᐅ ᐋᐧᐢᑲᐦᐃᑲᓇ, ᐁᑳ ᑮᑲᐧᕀ ᐁ ᐅᐦᒋ ᐃᐦᑕᑯᑭ,» ᐁ ᐊᔨᑕᐠ.

[5] «ᓅᓯᓯᒼ.» ᓂᑎᑎᐠ, «ᐊᔭ, ᐁ ᑮ ᐅᓰᐦᑖᔮᕽ ᒫᓇ ᐸᐦᑫᑭᓇᐧ, ᐁᑲᐧ ᑳᒥᓇᐦᐅᒋᐠ ᐆᑭᐠ ᓈᐯᐊᐧᐠ, ᐁ ᑮ ᒫᐊᐧᒋᐦᑖᔮᕽ ᒫᓇ ᐸᐦᑫᑭᓇᐧ, ᐁᑲᐧ ᐁ ᑳᐦᑮᓯᓇᒫᕽ, ᒦᑭᐋᐧᐦᑊ, ᐸᐦᑫᑭᓄ ᒦᑭᐋᐧᐦᑊ ᐁ ᑮ ᐅᓰᐦᑖᔮᕽ,» ᐃᑌᐧᐤ. ᐁᑲᐧ, «ᓇᔦᐢᑕᐤ ᐁᑯᑐᐊᐧ ᐁ ᑮ ᐯ ᐃᐧᔮᐦᑕᒫᕽ,» ᐁ ᐃᑌᐧᐟ, «ᓈᐯᐊᐧᐠ ᐸᐦᑫᑭᓀᐧᑖᓴ ᐁ ᑮ ᐅᓰᐦᑕᒪᐋᐧᔮᐦᑳᐧᐤ, ᐸᐦᑫᑭᐣ ᐅᐦᒋ ᐸᐸᑭᐋᐧᔮᓇ, ᒥᑖᓴ, ᒪᐢᑭᓯᓇ ᐁᑯᑐᐊᐧ ᐅᐦᒋ, ᐊᐢᑎᓴᐠ. ᓃᐢᑕᓈᐣ ᐁᑯᑐᐊᐧ ᐁ ᐃᐧᔮᐦᑕᒫᕽ,» ᐃᑌᐧᐤ, «ᒪ ᑮᑲᐧᐩ ᐃᐧᔭ ᐸᐸᑭᐋᐧᓀᑭᐣ ᐅᐦᒋ ᐃᐦᑕᑯᐣ,» ᐃᑌᐧᐤ, «ᑮᑲᐧᐩ ᐁᑯᓯ ᐃᓯ, ᒦᓇ ᒪ ᑮᑲᐧᐩ ᐄᐧᐦᑳᐨ ᐊᓴᐹᑊ ᐊᐊᐧ ᐊᓄᐦᐨ ᐁᑲᐧ, ᑮᑲᐧᐩ ᑳ ᐋᐦ ᐋᐸᒋᐦᐋᒋᐠ, ᒨᔭ ᑮᑲᐧᐩ ᐅᐦᒋ ᐃᐦᑕᑯᐣ ᐁᑯᓯ ᐃᓯ,» ᐃᑌᐧᐤ.

[6] ᐁᑲᐧ, «ᑮᑲᐧᐩ ᒫᑲ ᐁ ᑲᐢᑭᑳᐧᒋᑳᑫᔭᐣ, ᓅᐦᑯᒼ.» ᓂᑎᑖᐤ. «ᒨᓴᐧ ᐅᐦᒋ,» ᐃᑌᐧᐤ, «ᐁ ᐅᑎᓇᒫᕽ, ᐅᑖᕽ ᐅᐢᐱᐢᑲᐧᓂᐋᐧᕽ,» ᐃᑌᐧᐤ, «ᐁᐊᐧᑯ ᐊᓂᒪ ᐁ ᐹᓵᒫᕽ, ᐊᐢᑎᓈᐧᐣ ᐃᓯᔩᐦᑳᑌᐤ,» ᐃᑌᐧᐤ. «ᐁᐊᐧᑯ ᐊᓂ ᐊᓂᒪ ᒫᓇ ᐁ ᑮ ᑲᐢᑭᑳᐧᒋᑳᑫᔮᕽ,» ᐃᑌᐧᐤ ᐊᐊᐧ ᓅᒋᑫᐧᓯᐤ.

[7] «ᓵᐳᓂᑲᐣ ᒫᑲ, ᑮᑳᐧᐩ ᒫᑲ ᐁ ᐊᐩ ᐋᐸᒋᐦᑖᔦᐠ, ᐁᑳ ᑮᑲᐧᐩ ᐁ ᐃᐦᑕᑯᑭ.» ᓂᑎᑖᐤ. «ᐋ, ᐊᐱᓯᒨᓱᓱᐅᐢᑲᓂᐢ,» ᐃᑌᐧᐤ, «ᑮᑲᐧᐩ, ᐁᑯᑕ ᐅᐦᒋ ᒫᓇ ᐁ ᑮ ᐅᓰᐦᑖᐟ ᓂᓈᐯᒼ ᓵᐳᓂᑲᐣ,» ᐃᑌᐧᐤ. «ᐊᓯᓂᔭ ᐅᐦᒋ ᒫᓇ ᐁ ᑮ ᑖᓴᐦᐊᕽ ᒫᓇ,» ᐃᑌᐧᐤ, ᐊᓇ ᓅᒋᑫᐧᓯᐤ. «ᒨᔭ ᐊᔨᐢ ᒦᓇ ᑮᑲᐧᐩ ᒨᐦᑯᒫᓇ,» ᐃᑌᐧᐤ, «ᐅᐦᒋ ᐃᐦᑕᑯᓇᐧ,» ᐃᑌᐧᐤ, «ᐅᐢᑲᐣ ᒫᓇ,» ᐃᑌᐧᐤ, «ᐁ ᑮ ᐋᐸᒋᐦᑖᒋᐠ,» ᐃᑌᐧᐤ, «ᒨᐦᑯᒫᐣ ᐁ ᑮ ᐅᓰᐦᑕᒫᓱᒋᐠ,» ᐃᑌᐧᐤ, «ᐁᐊᐧᑯ ᐊᓇ ᐊᓇ, ᐊᓯᓂᔭ ᐊᓂᐦᐃ,» ᐃᑌᐧᐤ, «ᒫᓇ ᐁ ᑮ ᑖᓴᐦᐃᑳᑫᒋᐠ, ᐁ ᑮ ᐸᐸᑭᐳᑖᒋᐠ ᒫᓇ, ᒨᐦᑯᒫᓇ ᐁ ᐅᓰᐦᑖᒋᐠ,» ᐃᑌᐧᐤ.

[8] ᐁᑲᐧ, «ᐊᔨᕽ ᒫᑲ,» ᓂᑎᑖᐤ, «ᑮᑳᐧᐩ ᒫᑲ ᐁ ᒦᒋᓵᐧᑕᒣᐠ.» ᓂᑎᑖᐤ, «ᐅᐦᒋ, ᐁ ᐅᐦᒋ ᒦᒋᓱᔦᐠ, ᐃᐧᔮᑲᓇ ᐁᑳ ᐁ ᐅᐦᒋ ᐃᐦᑕᑯᑭ.» ᐁ ᐃᑕᐠ. «ᐊᐧᐢᑲᐧᐩ, ᑲᐦᑭᔭᐤ ᑮᑲᐧᐩ ᐊᐧᐢᑲᐧᐩ ᐅᐦᒋ,» ᐃᑌᐧᐤ, «ᐃᐧᔮᑲᓇ ᐁ ᑮ ᐅᓰᐦᑖᕽ,» ᐃᑌᐧᐤ, «ᐁᑲᐧ ᓂᐱᐩ ᒦᓇ,» ᐃᑌᐧᐤ, «ᐁᑯᑐᐃᐧᕽ ᐁ ᑮ ᐋᐊᐧᑖᕽ,» ᐃᑌᐧᐤ, «ᐁ ᐅᓰᐦᐃᐦᒋᐠ ᐊᐢᑭᐦᑲᐧᐠ,» ᐃᑌᐧᐤ, «ᐁᑯᑕ ᐅᐦᒋ ᐊᓂᒪ ᓂᐱᐩ ᐁ ᑮ ᐋᐊᐧᑖᕽ,» ᐃᑌᐧᐤ.

[9] ᐁᑲᐧ, «ᑖᓂᓯ ᒫᑲ ᐁᑳ ᑮᑲᐧᐩ ᐸᑳᐦᒋᑲᓇᐢᑭᐦᑲᐧᐠ ᐁ ᐅᐦᒋ ᐃᐦᑕᑯᒋᐠ.» ᐁ ᐃᑕᐠ ᐆᒪ. «ᓅᓯᓯᒼ.» ᐃᑌᐧᐤ, «ᑲᔮᐢ ᒪ ᑮᑲᐧᐩ ᐅᐦᒋ ᐸᑳᐦᑖᓂᐊᐧᐣ, ᐃᐧᔭ ᐁᑳ ᐊᐢᑭᐦᑲᐧᐠ ᐁ ᐃᐦᑕᑯᒋᐠ, ᑲᐦᑭᔭᐤ ᑮᑲᐧᐩ ᐁ ᑮ ᒧᐢᒋ ᓇᐊᐧᒌᕽ, ᑯᑕᐋᐧᓂᕽ, ᐊᐧᔭᐄᐧᑎᒥᕽ,» ᐁ ᐃᑌᐧᐟ ᐊᓇ ᓅᒋᑫᐧᓯᐤ, ᑲᐦᑭᔭᐤ ᑮᑲᐧᐩ ᐁ ᑮ ᒪᐢᑲᑌᐳᐟ, ᐃᑌᐧᐤ, ᐊᐧᔭᐄᐧᑎᒥᕽ, ᐃᑌᐧᐤ. «ᐁᑲᐧ ᐃᐧᔭ ᐲᐦᒋ ᐊᔨᕽ ᑳ ᐱᐳᕽ ᑳ ᑮ ᐊᔮᔮᕽ,» ᐃᑌᐧᐤ, «ᐁᑯᑕ ᒫᓇ ᐁ ᑮ ᐃᐦᑕᑯᐠ, ᐊᑳᐧᐋᐧᐣ ᐁ ᑮ ᐅᓰᐦᑖᕽ,» ᐃᑌᐧᐤ, «ᐲᐦᒋ ᐊᔨᕽ,» ᐃᑌᐧᐤ.

[10] «ᑖᓂᓯ ᒫᑲ ᐁᑲᐧ ᒦᓇ ᐁᑳ ᐁ ᐅᒋᐳᐦᑳᐦᑌᐠ ᐸᐦᑫᑭᐣ ᐆᒪ ᐁᑯᑕ ᐁ ᐴᓂᑳᑌᐠ.» ᓂᑎᑖᐤ. «ᒨᔭ,» ᐃᑗᐤ, «ᒥᓵᐤ ᐊᔨᐢ,» ᐃᑗᐤ, «ᐁᑲᐧ ᓀᑌ ᐊᓂᒪ ᐃᐢᐱᒥᕽ ᐊᔨᐢ ᑕᐚᐤ,» ᐃᑗᐤ, «ᑲᐦᑭᔭᐤ ᐁᑯᑌ ᑮᑲᐧᐩ ᐃᐢᐸᔨᐤ,» ᐃᑗᐤ, ᐊᐘ ᓅᒋᑫᐧᓯᐤ.

[11] «ᑮᑲᐧᐩ ᒫᑲ ᐁ ᑮ ᐅᑕᑯᐦᐱᓴᐠ.» ᐁᑲᐧ ᒦᓇ ᑳ ᐃᑕᐠ. «ᐊᔨ,» ᐃᑗᐤ, «ᒨᓴᐧᑭᐣ,» ᐃᑗᐤ, «ᐁ ᑮ ᒫᑕᐦᐋᒫᕽ ᒫᓇ,» ᐃᑗᐤ, ᐆᒪ ᐃᑗᐤ, «ᐁᑲᐧ, ᐁ ᑮ ᓇᑲᑕᒫᕽ ᐊᓂᐦᐃ ᐅᐲᐘᔭ,» ᐃᑗᐤ, ᐊᓇ, «ᑳ ᐯ ᐹᓴᒫᕽ ᐁᑲᐧ,» ᐃᑗᐤ, «ᐁᐘᑯ ᐊᓂ ᐊᓂᒪ,» ᐃᑗᐤ, «ᐆᒪ ᒫᓇ ᐆᑭᐠ ᒥᓇᐦᐃᑲᐧᐠ ᐁ ᑮ ᒫᓇ ᐅᑎᓈᔮᐦᑳᐧᐤ, ᐁᑯᓂᐠ ᒫᓇ ᐁ ᑮ ᐊᓈᐢᑫᔮᕽ ᒦᑭᐚᐦᐱᕽ,» ᐃᑗᐤ, «ᐁᑲᐧ ᐃᐢᐲ, ᐁᐘᑯ ᐊᓂᒪ ᐁᑯᑕ ᒫᓇ ᒨᓴᐧᑭᐣ ᐁ ᑮ ᐊᐢᑖᔮᕽ,» ᐃᑗᐤ. «ᐁᑲᐧ ᐊᐱᓯᒨᓯᓯ ᐸᐦᑫᑭᓅᓴ ᐁ ᐚᐢᑲᑭ,» ᐃᑗᐤ, «ᐁ ᑮ ᒪᒪᐃᐧᑳᐧᑕᒫᕽ ᒫᓇ ᐁᑯᓂ,» ᐃᑗᐤ. «ᐁᐘᑯ ᐊᓂᒪ ᒫᓇ ᐁ ᑮ ᐅᑕᓈᐢᑲᓯᐃᐧᓂᔮᕽ, ᐘᐢᑭᐨ ᒫᓇ ᐁ ᑮ ᐊᐢᑖᔮᕽ ᐁᑯᐘ ᐊᔨ, ᐊᓂᐦᐃ, ᒨᓴᐧᑭᓅᕽ ᐊᓂᒪ, ᐅᐲᐘᔭ ᐊᓂᐦᐃ, ᐁᑲᐧ ᐁᑯᐘ ᐊᓂᒪ ᒦᓇ ᒨᓴᐧᑭᐣ ᒫᓇ,» ᐃᑗᐤ, «ᒫᓇ ᐁ ᑮᓯᓇᒫᕽ, ᒫᑲ ᒫᓇ ᐁ ᑮ ᐚᐱᐢᑳᐠ,» ᐃᑗᐤ, «ᒨᔭ ᐁ ᑲᐢᑳᐸᓴᒫᕽ,» ᐃᑗᐤ, «ᑮᑲᐧᐩ ᐆᒪ ᐁᑯᓯ ᐃᓯ ᑲ ᐚᐸᒥᐦᑖᔮᕽ,» ᐃᑗᐤ, «ᐃᑕ ᑳ ᓂᐹᔮᕽ,» ᐃᑗᐤ. «ᐁᑲᐧ ᐊᓂ ᐊᓂᐦᐃ ᐁ ᑮ ᐅᑕᑲᐧᓇᐦᐆᔮᕽ ᒦᓇ,» ᐃᑗᐤ, «ᐊᐢᐱᐢᑫᐧᓯᒧᐣ ᐊᐱᓯᒨᓯᓴᐧᔮᐣ ᒦᓇ,» ᐃᑗᐤ, «ᐁ ᑭᐳᑳᐧᑖᔮᕽ,» ᐃᑗᐤ, «ᐁᑲᐧ ᒫᐧᐢᑯᓯᐚᓇ ᐊᓂᐦᐃ ᒫᓇ, ᐁᑯᐘ ᐊᓂᐦᐃ ᒫᓇ ᐁᑯᐃᐧᕽ ᐁ ᑮ ᓵᑲᐢᑭᓇᐦᑖᔮᕽ ᐁ ᑭᐳᑳᐧᑕᒫᕽ, ᐁᑯᓂ ᐊᓂᐦᐃ ᒫᓇ ᐁ ᑮ ᐅᑕᐢᐱᐢᑫᐧᓯᒧᓂᔮᕽ,» ᐃᑗᐤ ᐊᓇ ᓅᒋᑫᐧᓯᐤ, «ᑲᐦᑭᔭᐤ ᑮᑲᐧᐩ ᒨᓴᐧᑭᐣ ᐁᑲᐧ ᐊᐱᓯᒨᓯᓴᐧᔮᐣ,» ᐃᑗᐤ, «ᐁ ᑮ ᐚᐸᒥᐦᑖᔮᕽ,» ᐃᑗᐤ, «ᐁᑯᐘ ᐱᑯ ᐁ ᑮ ᐃᐧᔮᐦᑕᒫᕽ,» ᐃᑗᐤ.

[12] ᐁᑲᐧ ᒦᓇ ᐁᑲᐧ ᓂᑲᑫᐧᒋᒫᐤ, «ᑮᑲᐧᐩ ᒫᑲ ᐁᒥᐦᑳᐧᓂᐢ ᐁ ᐃᓯ ᐚᐸᒥᐦᐚᓴᐠ.» ᓂᑎᑖᐤ, «ᑮᑳᐧᐩ ᑭᑖᐸᒥᐦᑖᓈᐚᐤ.» ᓂᑎᑖᐤ. «ᐁᓯᓴᐠ ᐃᓯᔩᐦᑳᑌᐤ, ᒫᓇ ᓵᑲᐦᐃᑲᓂᕽ ᒫᓇ ᐊᔮᐘᐠ ᐊᓂᑭᐠ,» ᐃᑗᐤ, «ᐊᑲᐧᓈᐱᐍᐦᐃᑳᓯᓯᐘᐠ ᒫᓇ,» ᐃᑗᐤ, «ᐁᑯᐘ ᐊᓂᑭᐠ,» ᐃᑗᐤ, «ᐁᑯᓂᐠ ᐊᓂᑭᐠ ᒫᓇ ᐁ ᒦᒋᓵᐧᑫᔮᕽ,» ᐃᑗᐤ, «ᐁᑲᐧ ᒨᔭ ᑮᑲᐧᐩ ᑲᔮᐢ tea ᐁ ᐅᐦᒋ ᐃᐦᑕᑯᐠ,» ᐃᑗᐤ, «ᓇᓴᐢᑕᐤ ᒪᐢᑫᑯ litea, ᐁᑲᐧ ᐆᐦᐅ – rose bushes ᐊᓂᑭᐠ, ᐅᑭᓂᔭᐠ, ᐁᑯᓂᐠ ᒦᓇ ᒫᓇ – ᐁ ᑮ ᐸᑳᐦᑖᔮᕽ ᐊᓂᐦᐃ ᒥᐢᒋᑯᓴ,» ᐃᑗᐤ, «ᐁᐩ, ᐄᐧᐦᑲᓯᐣ ᒥᐢᑕᐦᐃ, ᑭᓯᐠ ᑭᓈᑕᐦᐅᐚᑳᐣ,» ᐃᑗᐤ.

[13] ᐁᑲᐧ ᐆᒪ ᓂᑎᑖᐤ, «ᑖᓂᓯ ᒫᓇ ᐁ ᑮ ᑭᓰᐯᑭᐢᑎᑳᐧᓀᓴᐠ, ᑮᑲᐧᐩ ᑭᑲ ᐚᐸᒥᐦᑖᓈᐚᐤ.» ᓂᑮ ᐃᑖᐤ. «ᓅᓯᓯᒼ.» ᐃᑗᐤ, «ᐊᓄᐦᐨ ᑭᔭᐚᐤ ᐃᔨᑯᕽ ᐆᒪ,» ᐃᑗᐤ, «ᑳ ᐚᐦ ᐚᐱᐢᑎᑳᐧᓀᓴᐠ, ᑳ ᐹᐦ ᐸᐢᑲᐧᓴᓯᐸᔨᑭ ᑭᐢᑎᑳᐧᓂᐚᐘ,» ᐃᑗᐤ ᐊᓇ ᓅᒋᑫᐧᓯᐤ, «ᐃᔨᑯᕽ ᑲᐦᑭᔭᐤ ᑮᑲᐧᐩ ᐁ ᐚᐸᒥᐦᑖᓴᐠ ᒧᓂᔮᐃᐧ ᑮᑲᐧᐩ ᑭᐢᑎᑳᐧᓂᐚᕽ,» ᐃᑗᐤ, «ᓂᔭᓈᐣ, ᒪ ᑮᑲᐧᐩ, ᑳ ᑮ ᐄᐧ ᐸᑳᓯᒧᔮᕽ, ᑳ ᐄᐧ ᑭᓰᐯᑭᐢᑎᑳᐧᓀᔮᕽ,» ᐃᑗᐤ, «ᒪᑐᑎᓵᓂᕽ ᐁ ᑮ ᐲᐦᑎᑫᐧᔮᕽ,» ᐃᑗᐤ, «ᐁᑯᑕ ᐊᓂᒪ ᐁᑲᐧ ᐁ ᐸᑳᓯᒧᔮᕽ,» ᐃᑗᐤ, «ᐁ ᑲᓈᒋᐦᐃᓱᔮᕽ,» ᐃᑗᐤ, «ᓂᐢᑎᑳᐧᓂᓈᕽ ᒦᓇ,» ᐃᑗᐤ, «ᓇᒨᔭ ᐄᐧᐦᑳᐨ ᑮᑲᐧᐩ ᐅᐦᒋ ᐯ ᐚᐸᑕᐣ ᐆᐦᐅ ᑮᑲᐧᐩ ᑲ ᐯ ᑭᐢᑫᔨᐦᑖᑲᐧᕽ ᐆᐦᐅ,» ᐃᑗᐤ, «ᒥᐦᒉᐟ ᐊᓄᐦᐨ

ᑫᐦᑌ ᐊᔭᐠ, ᐋᓰᓀ ᐆᑭᐠ ᑲᔮᐢ ᒨᔭ ᐅᐦᒋ ᐋᐧᐱᐢᑎᑳᐧᓀᐊᐧᐠ,» ᐃᑌᐧᐤ, «ᐊᔨᐢ ᒨᔭ ᐲᑐᐢ ᑮᑳᐧᐩ ᐅᐦᒋ ᐋᐸᒋᐦᒋᑳᑌᐤ,» ᐃᑌᐧᐤ, «ᑭᑮ ᑲᓈᑎᓯᐣ ᐯᔭᑲᐧᐣ, ᑳ ᐲᐦᑎᑫᐧᔭᐣ ᒪᑐᑎᓵᓂᕽ,» ᐃᑌᐧᐤ, «ᑭᑲᓈᒋᐦᐅᐣ ᑲᐧᔭᐢ,» ᐃᑌᐧᐤ.

III

[14] ᐁᑲᐧ ᐋᐊᐧ ᐁᑲᐧ ᑯᑕᐠ ᒦᓇ ᓅᒋᑫᐧᓯᐤ ᐁᑲᐧ ᐁ ᑭᔦᑲᐊᐧᐠ, «ᓅᐦᑯᒼ.» ᓂᑎᑖᐤ, «ᑳᔮᐢ ᐆᒪ,» ᓂᑎᑖᐤ, «ᐊᐄᐧᓇ ᑭᑮ ᐯ ᐸᒥᐦᐃᑯᐋᐧᐤ ᑳ ᐄᐧ ᐅᒐᐋᐧᓯᒥᓯᔦᐠ,» ᐁ ᐃᑕᐠ ᐋᐊᐧ ᐁᑲᐧ ᓅᒋᑫᐧᓯᐤ, ᑯᑕᐠ ᐊᐊᐧ, ᐋ, ᒫᑲ ᐁᐊᐧᑯ ᑮ ᐴᓂ ᐱᒫᑎᓯᐤ ᐁᐊᐧᑯ, 'Mrs Blackbird' ᑮ ᐃᓯᔩᐦᑳᓱᐤ.

[15] «ᓅᓯᓯᒼ. ᐊᓄᐦᐨ ᐆᒪ ᒫᓇ ᐁᑲᐧ ᐆᒪ,» ᐃᑌᐧᐤ, «ᐋᐦᑯᓰᐃᐧᑲᒥᑯᕽ, ᑲᐦᑭᔭᐤ ᐊᐃᐧᔭᐠ ᑳ ᐃᑐᐦᑌᐟ ᑳ ᓂᐦᑖᐃᐧᑭᐦᐋᐊᐧᓯᐟ,» ᐃᑌᐧᐤ, «ᓂᔭᓈᐣ ᐁ ᑮ ᐸᒥᐦᐃᓯᔮᕽ,» ᐃᑌᐧᐤ, «ᒨᔭ ᐊᐃᐧᔭᐠ ᓅᐦᒋ ᐸᒥᐦᐃᑯᓈᐣ,» ᐃᑌᐧᐤ, «ᓂᑮ ᐸᒥᐦᐃᓯᓈᐣ,» ᐃᑌᐧᐤ, «ᐋ, ᓰᐢᑲᐧᐟ ᒫᓇ ᐊᐦᐴ ᓴᑳᕽ ᓂᑮ ᐃᑐᐦᑖᓈᐣ, ᐁᑯᑌ ᐁ ᓂᐦᑖᐃᐧᑲᐦᐋᔮᐦᑭᐠ ᐊᐋᐧᓯᓴᐠ, ᐁᑯᑌ ᐅᐦᒋ ᐁᑲᐧ ᐁ ᐯᓯᐋᐧᔮᐦᑳᐧᐤ,» ᐃᑌᐧᐤ, «ᐁ ᐸᒥᐦᐃᓯᔮᕽ. ᒨᔭ ᐄᐧᐦᑳ ᓅᐦᒋ ᐱᒥᓯᓂᓈᐣ, ᑳ ᐯ ᐱᒥᓯᓂᔮᕽ, ᐁᑯᓯ ᐊᓂᒪ ᑖᐯᐧ ᐱᑯ ᐁ ᒪᐢᑭᐦᑮᐋᐧᐳᐦᑲᑎᓯᔮᕽ, ᐁᑯᓯ ᑖᐯᐧ ᐱᑯ ᐊᔨ, ᐁ ᐊᑐᐢᑫᔮᕽ, ᒨᔭ ᐄᐧᐦᑳᐟ ᓅᐦᒋ ᐱᒥᓯᓂᓈᐣ,» ᐃᑌᐧᐤ, «ᑌᐱᔮᕽ ᐁ ᓂᐦᑖᐃᐧᑭᒋᐠ ᐊᐋᐧᓯᓴᐠ, ᐁᑯᓯ ᓂᑕᑐᐢᑲᓈᐣ, ᑌᐱᔮᕽ ᒫᓇ ᐁ ᑮ ᔩᐦᑖᐧᐦᐱᓯᓯᔮᕽ ᐆᑕ ᐆᒪ ᓇᑖᓈᕽ,» ᐃᑌᐧᐤ, «ᒪᐢᑭᐦᑭᐩ, ᓀᐦᐃᔭᐃᐧ ᒪᐢᑭᐦᑭᐩ ᑭᓯᐠ ᐁ ᒥᓂᐦᑫᐧᔮᕽ,» ᐃᑌᐧᐤ, «ᐋ, ᐊᓄᐦᐨ ᑳ ᑮᓯᑳᐠ, ᐁᐊᐧᑯ ᐅᐦᒋ ᐁᑎᑫᐧ ᐊᔨᓯᔨᓂᐤ ᑳ ᒪᐢᑲᐋᐧᑎᓯᐟ,» ᐃᑌᐧᐤ, ᐁ ᐃᑌᐧᐟ ᐊᓇ ᓅᒋᑫᐧᓯᐤ

— ᒥᑐᓂ ᓰᐢᑲᐧᐨ.

[16] ᐁᑲᐧ, «ᑮᑳᐧᐩ ᒫᑲ ᐁᑲᐧ ᒫᓇ ᑭᑖᐸᒋᐦᑖᓈᐋᐧᐤ,» ᓂᑎᑖᐤ ᐆᒪ, «ᐊᔨᐢ ᒥᐢᑕᐦᐃ ᒥᐦᑯ ᐁᐧᐱᓂᑳᑌᐤ, ᓅᐦᑯᒼ.» ᐁ ᐃᑕᐠ ᐊᓇ ᓅᒋᑫᐧᓯᐤ. «ᐋ, ᓅᓯᓯᒼ,» ᐃᑌᐧᐤ, «ᐊᐢᑭᔭ. ᐊᐢᑭᔭ ᒫᓇ,» ᐃᑌᐧᐤ, «ᒥᐢᑕᐦᐃ ᐁᑯᓂ ᐊᓂᐦᐃ ᐁ ᑮ ᐋᐸᑕᐦᑭ,» ᐃᑌᐧᐤ, «ᐁ ᑮ ᐁᐧᐁᐧᑭᓇᒫᕽ ᒫᓇ,» ᐃᑌᐧᐤ, «ᐁᑯᓂ ᐊᓂᐦᐃ,» ᐃᑌᐧᐤ, «ᐁ ᑮ ᐋᐸᒋᐦᑖᔮᕽ ᐆᒪ,» ᐃᑌᐧᐤ, «ᓂᔭᓈᐣ,» ᐃᑌᐧᐤ, «ᐊᓄᐦᐨ ᑳ ᑮᓯᑳᐠ ᑫᔮᐱᐨ ᐆᒪ ᑳ ᐱᒫᑎᓯᔮᕽ,» ᐃᑌᐧᐤ, «ᐁ ᑮ ᐯ ᐋᐧᐸᐦᑕᒫᕽ ᐁ ᐋᔨᒪᕽ, ᐁᑲᐧ ᒦᓇ ᓂᑲ ᑮ ᐃᑖᐧᐣ ᐁ ᑮ ᒥᔦ ᐱᒫᒋᐦᐅᕽ ᑲᔮᐢ, ᑲᐦᑭᔭᐤ ᑮᑳᐧᐩ ᐊᔨᐢ ᑮ ᐃᐦᑕᑯᐣ ᓴᑳᐃᐧ ᐱᒫᒋᐦᐅᐃᐧᐣ,» ᐃᑌᐧᐤ. «ᐊᓄᐦᐨ ᐁᑲᐧ ᐋᓴᐩ ᒦᓇ ᐁᐊᐧᑯ ᐊᓂ ᐊᓂᒪ, ᐁᑲᐧ ᐋᐧᐱᐢᑭᐃᐧᔩᐢ ᑳ ᒥᓯᐊᐧᓈᒋᐦᑖᐟ, ᑲᐦᑭᔭᐤ ᑮᑳᐧᐩ ᐁ ᓂᐸᐦᑕᒫᑯᔭᕽ, ᑲᐦᑭᔭᐤ ᑮᑳᐧᐩ ᐆᐦᐅ ᓇᓈᑐᕽ ᑮᑳᐧᐩ ᐱᐢᒋᐳᐃᐧᓇ ᐁ ᐋᐸᒋᐦᑖᒋᐠ, ᐁ ᔩᑲᐦᐋᐦᑕᐦᑭᐠ ᐊᐢᑭᔭ ᐱᐢᒋᐳᐃᐧᐣ ᐅᐦᒋ, ᑳ ᐹᐦ ᐹᐦᑭᓯᑫᒋᐠ ᐆᒪ, ᑲᐦᑭᔭᐤ ᑮᑳᐧᐩ ᐁ ᓂᐸᐦᑖᒋᐠ,» ᐃᑌᐧᐤ. «ᐁᑲᐧ ᐁ ᑮ ᐸᑭᑎᓇᕽ ᒪᓂᑐᐤ ᑳ ᐅᐦᒋ ᐱᒫᒋᐦᐅᕽ,» ᐃᑌᐧᐤ, «ᑲᐦᑭᔭᐤ ᑮᑳᐧᐩ ᑭᑮ ᐯ ᒥᔨᑯᓇᐤ, ᒦᓂᓴ, ᑲᐦᑭᔭᐤ ᑮᑳᐧᐩ, (— ᐋᐧᐳᓴᐧ, ᔩᔩᐸ, ᐱᔦᐊᐧᐠ, ᑭᓄᓭᐊᐧᐠ —), ᑲᐦᑭᔭᐤ (— ᒨᓴᐧᐠ —) ᑮᑳᐧᐩ

ᐁ ᑮ ᐯ ᒣᑭᐟ. ᒨᔭ ᐄᐧᐦᑳ ᐊᔨᓯᔨᓂᐤ ᐅᐦᒋ ᓅᐦᑌᐦᑲᑌᐤ,» ᐃᑌᐧᐤ, «ᑖᐱᑕᐃᐧ ᑮᑲᐧᐩ ᑲᐧᔭᐢ ᑮ ᐊᔮᓂᐊᐧᐣ,» ᐃᑌᐧᐤ. «ᐁᑲᐧ, ᓈᐯᐊᐧᐠ ᐃᐧᔭᐋᐧᐤ ᐁ ᑮ ᐆᓴ ᐅᓰᐦᑕᒫᓯᒋᐠ, ᐊᐧᐢᑲᐧᔨ ᐆᓴ,» ᐃᑌᐧᐤ, «ᑲᐦᑭᔭᐤ ᑮᑲᐧᐩ ᒫᓇ ᐁ ᑮ ᐸᐹᒥᒋᒣᒋᐠ ᒫᓇ,» ᐃᑌᐧᐤ, «ᐁ ᑮ ᓂᐸᐦᒋᑫᒋᐠ,» ᐃᑌᐧᐤ.

[17] «ᐁᐩ, ᑮ ᒥᔫᐧᓯᐣ,» ᐃᑌᐧᐤ, ᓅᒋᑫᐧᓯᐤ ᐊᓇ, «ᓂᑎᑌᔨᐦᑌᐣ ᓂᔭ ᐁ ᑮ ᒥᔪ ᐊᔮᔭᕽ,» ᐃᑌᐧᐤ, «ᐊᓄᐦᐨ ᐆᒪ ᐁᑲᐧ, ᑲᐦᑭᔭᐤ ᑮᑲᐧᐩ ᒧᓂᔮᐃᐧ ᑮᑲᐧᐩ ᐃᐢᐲ ᐁᑲᐧ ᑳ ᐃᐢᐸᔨᐠ ᐊᐊᐧ (– ᐸᐦᑫᐧᓯᑲᐣ ᒨᔭ ᐄᐧᐦᑳᐟ ᐅᐦᒋ ᐯ ᑭᐢᑫᔨᐦᑖᑲᐧᐣ ᑲ ᑮ ᐃᐦᑕᑯᐟ –), ᐊᓄᐦᐨ ᐁᑲᐧ, ᑲᐦᑭᔭᐤ ᑮᑲᐧᐩ ᐁᑲᐧ ᐁᑯᓂ ᐊᓂᐦᐃ,» ᐃᑌᐧᐤ, «ᐆᐦᐅ ᓇᓈᑐᕽ ᑮᑲᐧᐩ ᐁᑲᐧ ᑲ ᒦᒋᕽ,» ᐃᑌᐧᐤ, «ᐁᐊᐧᑯ ᐅᐦᒋ ᐊᔨᓯᔨᓂᐤ ᑭᓀᐧᐢ ᑮ ᐱᒫᑎᓯᐤ, ᒨᔭ ᐅᐦᒋ ᓂᐦᑖ ᐋᐦᑯᓯᐤ,» ᐃᑌᐧᐤ, «ᐊᔨᐢ ᐁ ᒥᔫᐧᓯᓂᔨᐠ, ᐁ ᑲᓈᑕᓂᔨᐠ ᑮᑲᐧᐩ, ᐁ ᑮ ᐯ ᒦᒋᐟ,» ᐃᑌᐧᐤ, «ᐁᑲᐧ ᒦᓇ, ᐊᓄᐦᐨ ᐁᑲᐧ ᒨᔭ ᓂᑲ ᑮ ᐃᑖᐧᐣ ᑮᑲᐧᐩ ᐁ ᑲᓈᑕᕽ, ᑮᑲᐧᐩ ᑲ ᓂᐸᐦᑖᕽ ᐃᓯ,» ᐃᑌᐧᐤ, «ᐆᒪ ᓴᑳᐃᐧ ᒦᒋᐃᐧᐣ, ᐅᓵᒼ ᒥᐢᑕᐦᐃ ᑲᐦᑭᔭᐤ ᑮᑲᐧᐩ ᐱᐢᒋᐳᐃᐧᐣ, ᒥᓯᐁᐧ ᑮᑲᐧᐩ ᐄᐧᐢᑕᐋᐧᐤ ᐁᑲᐧ ᐁ ᐊᑎ ᒦᒋᒋᐠ ᒨᓴᐧᐠ,» ᐃᑌᐧᐤ, «ᐁᑲᐧ ᑲᐦᑭᔭᐤ ᑮᑲᐧᐩ, ᐁ ᐊᑎ ᐄᐧ ᓂᐸᐦᐃᑯᒋᐠ ᐁᑲᐧ,» ᐃᑌᐧᐤ, «ᑮᐢᑕᓇᐤ ᐁᑲᐧ ᐁᐊᐧᑯ ᐊᓂᒪ ᐁ ᐊᑎ ᒦᒋᔮᕽ,» ᐃᑌᐧᐤ.

[18] «ᐁᑲᐧ ᐁ ᑮ ᒪᒥᔪ ᐊᐧ ᐄᐧᑭᕽ ᒫᓇ,» ᐃᑌᐧᐤ ᐆᒪ, «ᐱᑯ ᐃᑌ ᑮ ᐸᐹᒥᐱᒋᓈᓂᐊᐧᐣ, ᒨᔭ ᐄᐧᐦᑳᐟ ᐯᔭᑲᐧᓄᕽ ᐊᔨᓯᔨᓂᐤ ᐅᐦᒋ ᐊᔮᐤ,» ᐃᑌᐧᐤ, «ᐁ ᑮ ᐸᐹᒥᐱᒋᕽ, ᐆᓯᕽ ᒫᓇ ᐁ ᑮ ᐸᐹᒥᐱᒋᕽ, ᐁ ᐸᐹᒥ ᓃᒫᐃᐧᓂᐦᑫᕽ ᑭᒋ ᑳ ᐱᔭᕽ,» ᐃᑌᐧᐤ, «ᐁᑯᓯ ᐁ ᒥᓇᐦᐅᒋᐠ ᓈᐯᐊᐧᐠ, ᑳᐦᑫᐊᐧᑲᐧ (– ᑲᐦᑭᔭᐤ ᑮᑲᐧᐩ ᐁ ᑮ ᓂᐸᐦᑖᒋᐠ –),» ᐃᑌᐧᐤ, «ᐁ ᐅᓰᐦᑖᔭᕽ,» ᐃᑌᐧᐤ. «ᒨᔭ ᐊᔨᐢ ᒦᓇ ᑮᑲᐧᐩ ᐅᐦᒋ ᐊᑖᐋᐧᑳᓂᐊᐧᐣ ᐸᐦᑫᑭᐣ,» ᐃᑌᐧᐤ, «ᑲᐦᑭᔭᐤ ᑭᑮ ᑲᓇᐁᐧᔨᐦᑕᒫᓯᐣ. ᐊᐋᐧᓯᐢ ᑳ ᓂᐦᑖᐃᐧᑭᐟ, ᐁᑯᑐᐊᐧ ᐋᐧᐢᐱᓯᐣ, ᐸᐦᑫᑭᐣ, ᐁᑯᑐᐊᐧ ᐃᐧᔭ ᐁ ᐳᐦᑎᐢᑲᕽ – ᑲᐦᑭᔭᐤ ᑮᑲᐧᐩ ᐸᐦᑫᑭᐣ,» ᐃᑌᐧᐤ, «ᐁᑯᓯ ᐁᑲᐧ ᑲ ᑮᓯᐋᐧᐢᐱᓯᐊᐧᐠ ᒦᓇ ᐊᐋᐧᓯᓴᐠ,» ᐃᑌᐧᐤ. «ᐁ ᓅᐦᐃᐦᒋᐠ ᐊᐋᐧᓯᓴᐠ,» ᐃᑌᐧᐤ, «ᒪ ᑮᑲᐧᐩ ᐊᔨᐋᐧᐠ ᑲ ᑮ ᓂᑕᐁᐧᔨᐦᒋᑲᑌᐠ ᒫᓇ,» ᐃᑌᐧᐤ, «ᓂᑕᔨ ᐃᑌᔨᐦᑌᐣ ᒫᓇ ᐊᓄᐦᐨ ᑳ ᒫᒥᑐᓀᔨᐦᑕᒫᐣ,» ᐃᑌᐧᐤ. «ᐊᓄᐦᐨ ᑲᐦᑭᔭᐤ ᑮᑲᐧᐩ ᐁ ᑎᐸᐦᐊᐦᑭᐠ, ᐊᐦᐴ ᐋᓯᔮᓂᐦᑫᐱᓯᓇ ᐁ ᑎᐸᐦᐊᐦᑳᐧᐤ, ᑲᐦᑭᔭᐤ ᑮᑲᐧᐩ ᒧᓂᔮᐃᐧ ᑮᑲᐧᐩ ᐁ ᐱᒥᑎᓴᐦᐊᐦᑭᐠ,» ᐃᑌᐧᐤ, «ᐁᑲᐧ ᐁ ᒣᐢᑎᓂᑫᒋᐠ,» ᐃᑌᐧᐤ, ᐊᓇ ᓅᒋᑫᐧᓯᐤ. ᓂᑮ ᒫᒪᐢᑳᓯᐦᑕᐋᐧᐤ ᒫᓇ ᐋᐦ ᐋᒋᒨᐦᐊᑭ.

IV

[19] ᐁᑲᐧ ᒦᓇ, ᐯᔭᐠ ᐊᐊᐧ ᑯᑕᐠ ᐁᑲᐧ ᓅᒋᑫᐧᓯᐤ, Mudie Lake ᐁᑲᐧ ᐁᐊᐧᑯ ᐊᓇ, ᐯᔭᐠ ᒦᓇ ᐁ ᑳᐦᑲᑫᐧᒋᒪᐠ ᐆᒪ, ᑲᐦᑭᔭᐤ ᑮᑲᐧᐩ. «ᒨᔭ ᐄᐧᐦᑳᐨ ᐁ ᐅᐦᒋ ᐃᐦᑕᑯᐠ ᑮᑲᐧᐩ, ᐆᐦᐅ ᐊᔭᒥᐦᐋᐃᐧᓇ, ᐆᒪ ᐊᓄᐦᐨ ᐁᑲᐧ ᐃᔨᑯᕽ ᑳ ᐃᐦᑕᑯᑭ,» ᐃᑌᐧᐤ ᐊᓇ ᓅᒋᑫᐧᓯᐤ, «ᑳᔮᐢ ᑳ ᑮ ᒪᐃᐧᒍᐢᒋᑫᔭᐣ,» ᐃᑌᐧᐤ, «ᐊᐊᐧ ᑳ ᑎᐯᔨᒥᑯᔭᕽ, ᐃᐢᐱᒥᕽ ᑳ ᑭᑖᐸᒥᑯᔭᕽ,»

ᐃᑘᐤ, «ᑭᐲᑭᐢᒁᑖᓇᐤ ᐁ ᒪᐏᒧᐢᑕᐚᔭᕽ,» ᐃᑘᐤ. «ᐁᑯᓯ ᓇᐘᐨ ᐁᑿ ᐁᑎᑵ ᑮ ᓂᑐᐦᑖᑯᐏᓯᓈᓂᐚᐣ,» ᐃᑘᐤ, «ᐊᔨᐢ ᑿᔭᐢᐠ ᑭᑮ ᐃᓯ ᐱᒫᑎᓯᐣ, ᒪ ᑮᑿᐩ ᑰᐦᒋ ᐯ ᒪᒋ ᑭᑭᐢᑳᑯᐣ, ᐁᑿ ᑲᔮᐢ ᐊᔨᓯᔨᓂᐤ ᑮᑿᐩ ᑳ ᓂᐸᐦᑖᐟ, ᐁ ᑮ ᐸᐹᒧᐦᑌᕽ ᐁ ᐊᓴᒥᐦᒋᐠ ᑯᑕᑲᐠ ᐊᔨᓯᔨᓂᐘᐠ,» ᐃᑘᐤ, «ᐁ ᐊᓴᒪᒋᐠ, ᑮᑿᐩ ᑳ ᐊᔮᔭᐣ, ᐱᑯ ᐑᐢᑕᐚᐤ ᐁ ᐊᓴᒪᒋᐠ,» ᐃᑘᐤ. «ᐊᓄᐦᐨ ᑳ ᑮᓯᑳᐠ, ᓇᒨᔭ ᑮᑿᐩ, ᐯᔭᐠ ᑮᑿᐩ ᐊᔨᓯᔨᓂᐤ ᑲ ᒧᐢᒋ ᐊᓴᒥᐠ, ᑮᑿᐩ ᑲ ᓂᐸᐦᑖᐟ ᑮᑿᐩ, ᐱᑯ ᑲ ᐊᑖᐍᔭᐣ,» ᐃᑘᐤ. «ᐊᐦᐴ ᐁᑿ ᐊᓄᐦᐨ ᑳ ᐲᐦᑎᑵᔭᐣ ᐚᐢᑲᐦᐃᑲᓂᕽ, ᒨᔭ ᐊᐦᐴ ᑭᒥᓇᐦᐃᑲᐏᐣ ᒪᐢᑭᐦᑮᐚᐳᐩ ᐁᑿ,» ᐃᑘᐤ, «ᐊᔨᐢ ᒨᓂᔮᐏ ᑮᑿᐩ ᐁ ᐱᒥᑎᓴᐦᐊᐦᒁᐤ,» ᐃᑘᐤ, «ᑲᐦᑭᔮᐤ ᑮᑿᐩ ᓂᐲᒪᑲᐣ. ᑲᔮᐢ ᐁ ᑮ ᐑᐦᑯᐦᑐᕽ, ᐊᐦᐴ ᐊᔨᓯᔨᓂᐤ ᐯᔭᐠ ᑳ ᒥᓇᐦᐅᐟ, ᑲᐦᑭᔮᐤ ᐁ ᑮ ᐑᐦᑯᒥᐦᒋᐠ ᐊᔨᓯᔨᓂᐘᐠ, ᐁ ᑮ ᒥᓯ ᐱᒥᓇᐘᓱᕽ ᒫᓇ ᒥᐢᑕᐢᑭᐦᑯᕽ, ᐘᔭᐑᑎᒥᕽ,» ᐃᑘᐤ. «ᐁᑿ ᐁ ᑮ ᐑᐦᑯᒥᐦᒋᐠ ᐁᑿ ᐁᑯᑌ ᐁ ᒦᒋᓱᕽ ᐘᔭᐑᑎᒥᕽ,» ᐃᑘᐤ, «ᐁ ᐏᐦᑰᒪᒋᐠ,» ᐃᑘᐤ, «ᒨᔭ ᐑᐦᑳᐨ ᐊᓄᐦᐨ ᐁᐘᑯ ᑮᑿᐩ ᐚᐸᐦᒋᑳᑌᐤ,» ᐁ ᐃᑘᐟ ᐊᓇ ᓅᒋᑵᓯᐤ.

[20] «ᐁᑿ ᐆᒪ ᑳ ᐑᑭᐦᑐᒋᐠ ᐆᑭᐠ ᐊᔭᒥᐦᐁᐏᑲᒥᑯᕽ,» ᐃᑘᐤ, «ᑲᔮᐢ ᒪ ᑮᑿᐩ ᐁᐘᑯ ᐊᓂᒪ ᐑᑭᐦᑐᐏᐣ, ᑳ ᒥᐢᑲᒫᓱᔭᐣ ᐊᐏᔭᐠ, ᓈᐯᐤ, ᑲ ᐑᑭᒪᐟ, ᐁᑯᓯ ᑖᐻ ᐱᑯ ᑭᐑᑭᒫᐤ, ᒨᔭ ᐑᐦᑳᐟ ᑭᐸᐢᑫᐏᐦᐋᐤ,» ᐃᑘᐤ. «ᑳ ᑮ ᐃᓯ ᐑᑭᒪᐟ, ᐁᑯᓯ ᐊᓂ ᑖᐻ ᐱᑯ ᐁ ᐑᒋ ᐊᔮᒪᐟ,» ᐃᑘᐤ, «ᒪ ᑮᑿᐩ ᑭᐦᒋ ᐑᑭᐦᑐᐏᐣ, ᐁᑯᓯ ᑭᓊᐢ ᐁ ᐑᒋ ᐊᔭᐦᑐᕽ ᐃᐢᑯ ᐯᔭᐠ ᑲ ᓇᑲᓯᐍᐟ,» ᐃᑘᐤ. «ᐊᓄᐦᐨ ᐁᑿ,» ᐃᑘᐤ, «ᐋᑎᐦᐟ ᑌᐱᔮᕽ ᐁ ᐑᑭᐦᑐᒋᐠ, ᒪᑤᐣ ᒌ ᐊᓂᐦᐃ ᐋᐦᒐᓂᓴ ᐅᐦᒋ, ᑌᐱᔮᕽ ᐋᑎᐦᐟ ᐁ ᐑ ᑲᑵ ᐊᔮᐚᒋᐠ ᐁ ᒥᔪᓯᔨᐟ ᑲ ᐚᓯᐦᑯᐸᔨᔨᐟ,» ᐃᑘᐤ, «ᒫᑲ ᒨᔭ ᑭᐢᑭᓯᐘᐠ ᒪᓂᑐᐘ,» ᐃᑘᐤ, «ᑳ ᐑᑭᐦᑕᐦᐃᑯᒋᐠ, ᐘᓂᑭᐢᑭᓯᐘᐠ ᐁᑯᓂ ᐊᓂᐦᐃ,» ᐃᑘᐤ, «ᐊᓂᐦᐃ ᐁ ᒪᒪᒋᑲᐢᑖᑫᒋᐠ ᐊᓂᐦᐃ ᐋᐦᒐᓂᓴ. ᐯᔭᐠ ᐲᓯᒼ, ᐊᐦᐴ ᐋᐢᑲᐤ ᒨᔭ ᐯᔭᐠ ᐲᓯᒼ ᐋᑎᐦᐟ, ᐁ ᐑᒋ ᐊᔮᒪᒋᐠ ᐅᓈᐯᒥᐚᐘ ᐁ ᐍᐱᓈᒋᐠ,» ᐃᑘᐤ, «ᒨᔭ ᐁᑯᓯ ᐅᐦᒋ ᐃᐢᐸᔨᐤ,» ᐃᑘᐤ, «ᑲᔮᐢ ᑮ ᒪᓈᒋᐦᑖᓂᐘᐣ ᑲᐦᑭᔮᐤ ᑮᑿᐩ,» ᐃᑘᐤ, «ᐁ ᑮ ᐯ ᒥᔦ ᐱᒫᑎᓯᕽ.»

[21] «ᒥᐦᒉᑤᐤ ᒫᓇ,» ᐃᑘᐤ, «ᑳ ᐸᐱᒥᓯᓂᔮᐣ, ᒫᓇ ᓂᐑ ᒪ ᒨᐢᑵᔨᐦᑌᐣ ᒫᓇ ᐁ ᒫᒥᑐᓀᔨᐦᑕᒫᐣ,» ᐃᑘᐤ, «ᐊᓄᐦᐨ ᓂᑕᐚᓯᒥᓴᐠ, ᑖᓂᓯ ᓃᐢᑕ ᐁ ᐯ ᐃᓯ ᐅᐦᐱᑭᒋᐠ, ᒥᓂᐦᑵᐏᐣ ᐊᓂᒪ ᐃᔨᑯᕽ ᐁ ᐅᑎᓇᐦᒁᐤ, ᐅᒐᐚᓯᒥᓯᐚᐘ ᐁ ᐍᐱᓈᒋᐠ, ᐁ ᒥᓯ ᓈᐦ ᓅᒋᐦᐃᐦᒋᐠ ᐆᑭᐠ ᓂᑖᓂᓴᐠ ᒫᓇ,» ᐃᑘᐤ, «ᐅᓈᐯᒥᐚᐘ ᐁ ᒫᐦ ᒥᓯ ᓈᐦ ᓅᒋᐦᐃᑯᒋᐠ,» ᐃᑘᐤ. «ᒫᑲ ᒨᔭ ᓂᑮ ᓇᑕᒫᐘᓯᐣ,» ᐃᑘᐤ, «ᐁ ᑲᐢᑭᐦᑕᒫᓱᒋᐠ ᐊᓂᒪ ᑳ ᓅᒋᐦᐃᐦᒋᐠ,» ᐃᑘᐤ, «ᐁ ᐸᐹᒫᒋᐦᐅᒋᐠ ᐁᑿ, ᐅᒐᐚᓯᒥᓯᐚᐘ ᐁ ᓇᑲᑖᒋᐠ,» ᐃᑘᐤ, «ᓇᒨᔭ ᓂᑮ ᓇᑕᒫᐘᓯᐣ,» ᐃᑘᐤ. «ᒫᑲ ᒫᓇ ᓂᑮ ᒧᒋ ᒨᐢᑵᔨᐦᑌᐣ ᒫᓇ,» ᐃᑘᐤ, «ᐃᔨᑯᕽ ᐁ ᑮ ᐸᒁᑕᒫᐣ ᐁ ᐃᓯ ᐱᒫᑎᓯᒋᐠ,» ᐃᑘᐤ.

[22] «ᑭᔮᒼ ᐊᔨᓯᔨᓂᐤ ᒣᑐᓂ ᑲ ᒥᔦ ᐱᒫᑎᓯᐤ, ᑖᐱᐢᑰ ᐆᒪ ᓂᔭ ᓂᑲ ᑮ ᐃᑤᐣ,» ᐃᑘᐤ, «ᓇᒪ ᑮᑿᐩ ᒪᒋ ᑮᑿᐩ ᓅᐦᒋ ᐯ ᓅᒋᐦᑖᐣ,» ᐃᑘᐤ ᐊᓇ

ᓅᐦᑯᒼ. «ᐁ ᑮ ᐯ ᒥᔪ ᐱᒫᑎᓯᔮᐣ, ᓇᒨᔭ ᐄᐧᐦᑳᐟ ᓅᐦᒋ ᐯᔭᑯᐣ ᓈᓂᑖᐤ ᑳ ᐃᑐᐦᑌᔮᐣ, ᓂᓈᐯᒼ ᐁ ᑮ ᐄᐧᑫᐊᐧᐠ, ᐊᐋᐧᓯᓴᐠ ᐁ ᐊᔫᐋᐧᔫᐦᑳᐧᐤ, ᐃᔨᐃᐧᐢ ᐁ ᓯᐯᐧᐦᑕᐦᐋᔫᐦᑭᐠ,» ᐃᑌᐧᐤ, «ᐊᓅᐦᐨ ᐁᑲᐧ, ᒨᔭ ᐁᐊᐧᑯ ᐊᓂᒪ ᑮᑲᐧᐩ ᐁᑲᐧ ᐄᐧᐦᑳᐨ ᐋᐧᐸᐦᒋᑳᑌᐤ,» ᐃᑌᐧᐤ, «ᐃᔨᑯᕽ ᐁ ᑭᑎᒫᑲᕽ, ᑭᑎᒫᑭᓯᓈᓂᐊᐧᐣ,» ᐃᑌᐧᐤ. «ᓅᓯᓯᒥᓴᐠ ᒫᓇ, ᒥᐦᑫᑖᐧᐤ ᒫᓇ ᐁ ᒫᒥᑐᓀᔨᒪᑳᐧᐤ, ᐁ ᑭᑎᒫᑭᓯᒋᐠ ᐁ ᐋᐧᐸᐦᑕᐦᑳᐧᐤ ᐁ ᐸᑲᒪᐦᐅᒥᐦᐟ ᐅᑳᐃᐧᐋᐧᐋᐧ,» ᐃᑌᐧᐤ, «ᐁ ᐋᐧᐸᐦᑕᐦᑭᐠ ᐁᐊᐧᑯ,» ᐃᑌᐧᐤ. «ᐁᑲᐧ ᒣᐧᐢᑕᐢ, ᐁ ᐃᑌᔨᐦᑕᒫᐣ,» ᐃᑌᐧᐤ, «ᓇᒨᔭ ᐊᓂᒪ ᐄᐧᐦᑳᐨ ᐊᓂᑭᐠ ᐊᐋᐧᓯᓴᐠ ᑲ ᐊᐧᓂᑭᐢᑭᓯᐊᐧᐠ, ᑖᓂᓯ ᑮᑲᐧᐩ ᑳ ᐯ ᐃᓯ ᐋᐧᐸᐦᑎᐦᐃᑯᒋᐠ ᐆᐦᑖᐃᐧᐋᐧᐊᐧ ᐊᓂᐦᐃ, ᑳ ᓅᑎᓂᐢᑫᐧᐁᐧᔨᐟ, ᐊᐦᐆ ᐁᑎᑫᐧ ᐄᐧᐢᑕᐋᐧᐤ ᑲ ᑲᑫᐧ ᐋᐧᓲ ᑭᐢᑭᓇᐋᐧᐱᐊᐧᐠ, ᐁ ᐃᑌᔨᒪᑭᐠ ᒫᓇ,» ᐃᑌᐧᐤ, «ᑮᓯ ᐅᐦᐱᑭᑖᐧᐃᐧ,» ᐁ ᐃᑌᐧᐟ ᐊᐊᐧ ᓅᒋᑫᐧᓯᐤ.

[23] «ᒥᐢᑕᐦᐃ ᐋᔨᒪᐣ. ᐁᑲᐧ ᐃᔨᑯᕽ ᐁ ᐄᐧ ᑭᑎᒫᑲᕽ ᐆᒪ ᓃᑳᐣ, ᐊᑎ ᓵᓴᐩ ᐊᐦᐴ ᓅᑲᐧᐣ,» ᐃᑌᐧᐤ, «ᐃᔨᑯᕽ ᐁ ᑭᑎᒫᑲᕽ,» ᐃᑌᐧᐤ. «ᓇᒪ ᑮᑲᐧᐩ ᐊᑐᐢᑫᐃᐧᐣ, ᓇᒪ ᑮᑲᐧᐩ,» ᐃᑌᐧᐤ, «ᑳᔮᐢ ᑭᒧᓲᒥᓇᐤ ᐁ ᑮ ᐃᑌᐧᐟ,» ᐃᑌᐧᐤ, «ᐁ ᑖᐯᐧᐟ,» ᐃᑌᐧᐤ, «ᒣᐧᐢᑕᐢ ᐊᑎ ᐆᑌ, ᐁ ᑮ ᐃᑌᐧᐟ ᑳᔮᐢ, ᑭᒧᓲᒥᓇᐤ ᐁᓴ,» ᐃᑌᐧᐤ, «ᒨᔭ ᑮᑲᐧᐩ, ᐄᐧᐸᐨ ᑲ ᐃᐦᑕᑯᐟ ᐁᑲᐧ ᐆᑌ ᐊᑎ ᓃᑳᐣ, ᓇᒨᔭ ᐊᓯᐢᑮᕽ ᑮᑲᐧᐩ ᑲ ᐱᒥᐸᔨᐤ, ᓇᔦᐊᐧᐨ ᑲ ᐱᒥᐸᔨᐤ ᑮᑲᐧᐩ, ᐁ ᑮ ᐃᑌᐧᐟ ᐊᐊᐧ, ᐁ ᑮ ᑭᐢᑭᓇᐁᐧᐦᐃᑫᐟ ᐊᐊᐧ ᐁᓴ ᐯᔭᐠ ᑭᓴᔨᓃᓯᐢ,» ᐃᑌᐧᐤ. «ᑖᐯᐧ ᐊᓂᒪ ᐁᑯᓯ ᓵᓴᐩ ᐁ ᐃᐢᐸᔨᐠ ᐊᓂᒪ ᑳ ᑮ ᐃᑌᐧᐟ,» ᐃᑌᐧᐤ, «ᓇᔦᐊᐧᐨ ᑮᑲᐧᐩ ᑲ ᐱᒥᐸᔨᐤ, ᑳ ᑮ ᐃᑌᐧᐟ,» ᐃᑌᐧᐤ, «ᐁᐊᐧᑯ ᐆᒪ ᐁᑎᑫᐧ ᐆᒪ ᐁᑲᐧ ᐱᒥᔮᑲᐣ ᐁᑲᐧ,» ᐃᑌᐧᐤ, «ᓇᔦᐊᐧᐨ ᑳ ᐱᒥᐸᔨᐠ,» ᐃᑌᐧᐤ. «ᑮᑲᐧᐩ ᐊᓂ ᑲ ᐃᐦᑕᑯᐣ, ᑫᑕᐦᑕᐁᐧ ᑲ ᒥᓯᐊᐧᓈᒋᐦᒋᑫᒪᑲᕽ, ᐋᐧᐱᐢᑭᐃᐧᔮᐢ ᑲ ᒥᓯᐊᐧᓈᒋᐦᐋᐧᐟ ᐊᔨᓯᔨᓂᐊᐧ, ᒣᐧᐢᑕᐢ ᐊᑎ ᐆᑌ, ᐁ ᑮ ᐃᑌᐧᐟ,» ᐃᑌᐧᐤ, «ᓵᓴᐩ ᐆᒪ ᑲᐦᑭᔭᐤ ᐁᐊᐧᑯ ᐆᒪ ᑮᑲᐧᐩ ᐁ ᐊᑎ ᐋᐧᐸᐦᑕᒪᕽ,» ᐃᑌᐧᐤ. «ᑖᐱᐢᑰᐨ ᐆᒪ ᒥᓂᐦᑫᐧᐃᐧᐣ ᑳ ᒥᓯᐊᐧᓈᒋᐦᐃᑯᒋᐠ.»

– ᐁᐩ, ᐄᐧᐸᐨ ᐁᑎᑫᐧ ᐁᑲᐧ ᓂᑲ ᒣᐢᒋᑐᓀᓯᓂᐣ, ᐋᐧᒋᐢᑕᑳᐨ. –

[24] ᐁᑲᐧ ᐁᐊᐧᑯ ᐊᐊᐧ ᐁᑲᐧ, ᐊᐊᐧ ᑰᐦᑯᒥᓇᐤ ᐁᑲᐧ ᒦᓇ ᑳ ᐃᑌᐧᐟ ᐁᑲᐧ, «ᐁᐩ,» ᐃᑌᐧᐤ, «ᐱᑯ ᐊᓂ ᐁᑳ ᑲ ᐸᑭᒦᔭᕽ, ᓅᓯᓯᒼ.» ᐃᑌᐧᐤ, «ᑫᔨᐁᐧᕽ ᐊᓂ, ᐋᐦᑲᒣᔨᒧ ᑮᐢᑕ, ᑲᑫᐢᑭᒥᐠ ᑭᑕᐋᐧᓯᒥᓴᐠ, ᑲᑫᐢᑭᒥᐠ ᑰᓯᓯᒪᐠ. ᐱᑯ ᐊᓂᒪ ᐁᑳ ᑲ ᐸᑭᒦᔭᐣ, ᑲ ᐋᐦᑲᒣᔨᒧᕽ ᑲ ᑲᑫᐧ ᑫᐧᐢᑭᓂᐦᒋᐠ, ᐊᐦᐴ ᐁᑎᑫᐧ ᐱᔨᐢ ᑳᐦ ᒫᒥᑐᓀᔨᐦᑕᒪᐧᐠ, ᑖᓂᓯ ᐁ ᐯ ᐃᐢᐸᔨᐠ ᑳᔮᐢ,» ᐃᑌᐧᐤ. «ᒫᑲ ᐊᔨᐢ, ᐋᑕ ᐃᐧᔭ ᒦᓇ ᐁ ᐲᐁᐧᔨᐦᑕᐦᑳᐧᐤ ᐆᒪ, ᑮᑲᐧᐩ ᑳ ᐄᐧᐦᑕᒫᐦᒋᐠ,» ᐃᑌᐧᐤ.

[25] «ᒥᐢᑕᐦᐃ ᐊᓂ ᐄᐧ ᑭᑎᒫᑲᐣ ᐆᑌ ᒣᐧᐢᑕᐢ ᑲ ᓂᐸᐦᐋᐧᐦᑲᑐᓯᒋᐠ ᐊᔨᓯᔨᓂᐊᐧᐠ,» ᐃᑌᐧᐤ, «ᐋᐧᓴᐩ ᐊᑎ ᓅᑲᐧᐣ,» ᐃᑌᐧᐤ. «ᓲᐢᑳᐧᐟ ᒫᓇ ᓂᒫᒪᐢᑳᑌᐣ, ᑖᓂᓯ ᑲ ᑮ ᐃᓯ ᐱᒫᑎᓯᒋᐠ ᐅᐢᑭ ᐊᔭᐠ – ᑭᔮᓇᐤ ᐃᐧᔭ ᑭᑲ ᐱᒫᑎᓯᓇᐤ, ᐃᐧᔭ ᑭᔮᓇᐤ ᑭᑲᐢᑭᐦᑖᓇᐤ ᑮᑲᐧᐩ ᑲ ᑮ ᓂᐸᐦᑕᒫᓯᔭᕽ, ᑲᔮᓯ ᐱᒫᒋᐦᐅᐃᐧᐣ ᑲ ᐅᑎᓇᒪᕽ,» ᐃᑌᐧᐤ. «ᒫᑲ ᐆᑭᐠ ᐅᐢᑭ ᐊᔭᐠ, ᒪ ᑮᑲᐧᐩ ᐊᔨᐢ ᑭᐢᑫᔨᐦᑕᒪᐧᐠ,» ᐃᑌᐧᐤ, «ᑮᑲᐧᐩ ᐱᑯ ᐁ ᑭᐢᑫᔨᐦᑕᐦᑳᐧᐤ, ᑲ ᐆᓴᐱᒋᐠ

ᓴᐦᑫᐸᔩᓴ, ᑲ ᐸᐹᒥ ᒥᓂᐦᑵᒋᐢ, ᑲ ᐸᐹᒥ ᒥᔭᐚᑕᐦᒁᐤ, ᒨᔭ ᐏᔭ ᒫᒥᑐᓀᔨᒣᐘᐠ ᐅᓃᑭᐦᐃᑯᐚᐘ, ᑫᐦᑌ ᐊᔭ ᐊᐦᔩ ᑲ ᒫᒥᑐᓀᔨᒫᒋᐠ ᑖᓂᓯ ᑲ ᑮ ᐃᓯ ᒪᓈᒋᐦᐋᒋᐠ,» ᐃᑘᐤ, «ᑲ ᐲᑵᔨᐦᑕᒥᐦᐋᒋᐠ,» ᐃᑘᐤ, «ᒥᐦᒉᑤᐤ ᒥᐢᑕᐦᐃ ᒫᑐᐏᐣ ᐃᐦᑕᑯᐣ ᒥᓂᐦᑵᐏᐣ ᐅᐦᒋ,» ᐃᑘᐤ, «ᐁ ᓂᐸᐦᐃᓯᐦᑭᐠ ᐊᔨᓯᔨᓂᐘᐠ, ᐊᐚᓯᓴᐠ,» ᐃᑘᐤ, «ᒥᓂᐦᑵᐏᐣ ᐊᓂᒪ ᑲᐦᑭᔭᐤ ᐁ ᒨᒋᑫᒪᑲᕽ,» ᐃᑘᐤ.

3.
Then and Now

Janet Feitz

[FA:] *my glasses* ôma ê-wanastâyân.
[JF:] ôh.
[FA:] anohc ôma *January 12th, La Ronge* ôma ê-ayâyâhk,
'*Janet Feitz*' isiyîhkâsow aw ê-wî-âcimostâkoyâhk.
êkosi, sôskwâc kiya ka-mâtâcimon.
kikâh-ki-âcimostawinân tânimayikohk
ê-itahtopiponêyan, êkosi.

[1] namôða wiða niwî-wîhtên ê-itahtw-âskîwinêyân, êwako wiða namôða kîkwây kiwî-âcimostâtinâwâw. mâka niwî-âtotên, nîst ê-pî-isi-kiskisiyân, pî-otâskanâhk ê-kî-pê-is-ôhpikihikawiyâhk ê-awâsisîwiyâhk.

[2] anohc kâ-kîsikâk ôma, ôtênaw ôm îta k-âyâyâhk, ihtâwin oti, mistahi pîtosinâkwan mîna ê-kiskisiyân ê-kî-pê-isinâkwahk kayâhtê. namôð ôhci-mihcêtiw môniyâw êkospî êkoni kîsikâwa; êkwa mîna namôða nanâtohk nôhc-îsi-mîcisonân atâwêwikamikohk ohti [*sic*], tâhôc [*sic; cf.* tâpiskôc] anohc kâ-kîsikâk kistikâna, kaskâpiskahikana, nanâtohk êkos îsi. ê-kî-pî-is-ôhpikihikawiyâhk nîðanân, ê-kî-pî-mâcîcik nôhtâwinânak [*sic; cf.* nôhtâwînânak], nôhkominânak, wiyâs ê-mîciyâhk, ðîwahikanak, ê-pakitahwâcik, kinosêw ê-mowâyâhk; namôða nanâtohk kîkwây nôhci-mîcinân, mâka nititîðihtên ê-kî-miðoskâkot aðisiðiniw êkospî nawac omîciwin, ispî anohc kâ-kîsikâk.

[3] êkwa mîna mâna nikî--, ê-kî-pî-isi-pamihikawiyâhk, ê-kî-aya--- wanihikîskanâhk mâna ---itohtahikawiyâhk [*sic*], êkotî ê-pamihikawiyâhk, ê-asamikawiyâhk êkotê, êkwa mîna ê-wanihikêcik mîna ninîkihikonânak, êkota ohc âya, mâna mâk âhtaya kâ-nipahâcik, kî-pî-itohtahêwak mân âtâwêwikamikohk, ê-pî-nâtâcik pahkwêsikana, *tea,* sôkâw, pimiy êkos îsi kîkwây; wâsaskocînikanisa, êkos îsi kîkwâya mân ê-kî-pî-nâtahkwâw.

[FA:] I have misplaced my glasses.
[JF:] Oh.
[FA:] Today is January 12 and we are at La Ronge and Janet Feitz is going to tell us a story.

So now it is your turn to start telling a story right away. You could tell us how old you are, go ahead.

[1] I am not going to say how old I am, I am telling you none of that. But I am going to tell what I myself still remember, how we had been raised back then when we were children.

[2] Today, this town where we are, this community, looks very different from the way I remember it looking before. In those days, there were not many White people; and we also did not eat all the various kinds of food from the store, not like today, vegetables, canned goods, various things like that. The way we were raised, our fathers used to hunt, and our grandmothers [*sc.* used to prepare the animals], we ate meat and pounded meat, they fished with nets and we ate fish; we did not eat all the various kinds of food, but I think the food then was better for people than today's.

[3] And we also used to --, the way we were looked after, we used to be taken out on the trapline, there we were looked after and there we were provided with food, and our parents also trapped [*sc.* as well as hunting], and when they killed fur-bearing animals, they used to take them to the store, and with that they got flour, tea, sugar, lard, things like that; they also used to get candles and things like these.

[4] êkwa mîna, namôð ôsâm ohci osâmêyatinwa êkospi, êkoni anihi kîsikâwa kayâs, ôho 'wanihikana' k-êcikâtêki, osâm piko mâna, 'mistiko-wanihikana' itamwak, êkoni ê-kî-âpacihtâcik. êkwa nawac pî-otâskanâhk mâna, nikî-âcimostâkonân nimosôm, êkâ sôskwâc ê-ohc-îhtakwahki [*sic*] êkoni ôho wanihikana, nayêstaw êsa mâna, êkotowahk kâ-kî-âpatahki, mistiko-wanihikana; êkwa mîn âta wiða mîna mân âya kî-osîhtâwak, pîminahkwânis êsa mâna kâ-kî-ohci-osîhtâcik, tâpakwâna, pisiwa ê-nipahâcik êkwa wâposwa mîna. nikî-wâpamâw nôhkomipan ê-osîhtât êkotow[a] ânihi câpakwânisa, ê-apiscâpêkasik pîminahkwânis ohci, êkwa mîna mâna kî-wîpakwêpaðiwak mân ânik â, wâposwak, ê-ohpipaðicik, ê-koðâwêkocihkwâw; êkosi mîna kâ-kî-isi-tâpakwamahwâcik êkospî anima, wâposwa. mistahi pîtos anohc kâ-kîsikâk nîsta nitisi-câpakwêsin, mîn êkospî anima kâ-kî-isi-wâpahkêyân mâna. pîyakwâw nikî-kocihtân, nîso iskwêsisak ê-kiskinohamawakwâw, tânisi kit-êsi-ohpipaðit kiwâposom, tâpakwâsoci, êkwa --

[*external break*]

[FA:] osâm ês ânima ê-kî-îwâsênamân.

[JF:] ôh.

êkosi.

[5] êkwa mîna mâna kâ-nîpihk, nikî-- k-âyamihcikêyâhk, êkospi nikî-sipwêhoðikawinân mîna mân êkospî, êko-- êkos ânima isi [*sic*] ê-otaminahikawiyâhk [*sic*], ohpimê ê-ayâyâhk; êkwa k-âyamihcikêyâhk mîna, êkota wiða mîna mihcêt kîkwây nikî-kiskinohamâkawinân mâna mâka; mâka namôð ôsâm nitâpacihikonân, nititîðihtên mâna, âtiht kîkwây ê-kî-kiskinohamâkawiyâhk, awîn âna kâ-kî-kihci-okimâwit êkospî, awîn âna kâ-kî-ômis-îsîhcikêt nikî-itikawinân mâna; êkwa misiwîskamik mîna mâna nikî-wîhtamâkawinân, tânihi êkoni – kaskitêwiyâsak itê kâ-wîkicik, *German*ak [*sic*] itê kâ-wîkicik, nanâtohk êkos îsi kîkwây. mâka pêyak wiða kihci-kîkwây ê-itêðihtamân nîða ê-kî-kiskinohamâkawiyâhk êkospî, kihci-masinahikan mân ê-kî-ayamihtâyâhk tahto-- tahto-kîsikâw, âpihtaw-tipahikan mâna kâ-kî-kiskinohamâkawiyâhk êwak ôma kihci-masinahikanihk ohci. êkwa mân ê-kî-miskôtamâhk [*sic*], ê-âkaðâsîmowâhk mâka wiða – wið êkâ ê-ohci-pakitinikawiyâhk ta-nêhiðawêyâhk iskôlihk.

[4] And in those days long ago, there also were not so many [metal] 'traps', as they are called, they mostly used what they called 'wooden traps'. And even further back, our grandfather used to tell us, there were none of these [metal] traps at all, the only ones that were in use were that kind, the wooden traps; although they also made snares, using a string to make them, and they killed lynx and also rabbits. I used to see my late grandmother making these little snares, with a thin string, and the rabbits had their necks snapped when they were catapulted up and dangled in mid-air; and that is how they used to snare rabbits then. Today I, too, do my snaring quite differently from the way I used to see them do it then. Once I tried to teach two little girls how your rabbit would spring up when caught in a snare, and --

[*external break*]

[FA:] I had turned it [*sc.* the tape-recorder] too low.

[JF:] Oh.

Ready.

[5] And in the summers, while we were school-children, they used to take us by boat at that time, and that is how they kept us busy, we stayed away [*sc.* from town]; and when we were in school we were also taught many things; but some of the things we were taught were not particularly useful to us, I tend to think, we were told who the king was at the time and who did what; and we were also instructed about the whole world, which ones – where the Africans live and where the Germans live and all kinds of things like that. But we were taught one important thing, I think, at that time, we used to read the Bible every day, for half an hour daily we were taught about the Bible. And we also discussed it, in English of course – for we were not allowed to speak Cree in school.

[6] êkwa anohc kâ-kîsikâk, mistahi pîtos mâna mâka ispaðiw; k-âyamihcikêcik êkwa ôko, namôða kiskinohamawâwak kîkwây kihci-masinahikanihk ohci, tâhôt [*sic; cf.* tâpiskôt] kayâhtê kâ-kî-pê-isi-kiskinohamâhcik. êkwa mîna mân ê-kiskisiyân, kâ-pê-ohpikihikawiyâhk nîstanân ôma, tahto-kîkisîpâyâw mân ê-kî-ayamihâyâhk, tahtwâw ê-mwayê-kawisimowâhk ê-kî-ayamihâyâhk; êkwa anohc kâ-kîsikâk êkwa, êwako mîna kahkiðaw kiwanihtânânaw. tâpw êcik ân[i] ê-kî-pî-miðo-pamihikawiyâhk pî-kayâs, êkwa anohc êkwa, mitoni kahkiðaw kîkwây ê-ati-wanihtâyâhk, kayâhtê kîhtê-ayak kâ-kî-pê-isi-kiskinohamâkoyâhkwâw.

[*external break*]

[7] êkwa mîna mâna kayâs, ôma kâ-pimohtêhonâniwik, namôð âðisk ohc-îhtakonwa mayaw ôtê itêhkêskamik ôho 'pimiðâkana' k-êcikâtêki. nistam nîst ê-kiskisiyân ê-wâpahtamân pimiðâkan, nipîhk ê-kî-twêhômakahk, tâhôc [*sic; cf.* tâpiskôc] ôsi [*sic*] ê-kî-isinâkwahk. êkwa mâna, aniki kâ-nitaw-âstawêhikêcik, êkwa *Prince Albert* mîna mân ôhci âtiht awiyak ê-kî-nitaw-âyamihcikêt, *'John Hastings', 'Abby Halkett'* kî-itâwak aniki nîso nâpêwak, êkonik nikî-wâpamâwak ê-kapâcik anim ôhci pimiðâkan; êkonik nistam ê-wâpamakwâw ê-pimiðâcik. êkwa (*nineteen-twenty* pakahkam nânitaw ôma, nistam kâ-kî-wâpahtamâhk pimiðâkan, nânitaw *twenty-nine,* namôða mwêhci nikiskisin), êkwa aya, kâ-sipwêhotêhocik mîn ôk ôwanihikêwak, kâ-sipwêhotêhowâhk mâna (ôsa [*sic*] nayêstaw kî-âpatanwa êkospî, ê-pimiskâyan mîna, namôða mîna mwâsi ohc-îhtakow *'engine'* k-êtiht êkospî anima, osâm piko mâna kahkið[aw] âwiyak [*sic*] kî-pimiskâw), êkwa ôma kâ-misi-ðôtihk, êkota wiða mâna kî-osîhtâwak aya, ðâhkâstimona, aya, ê-pimâsicik, êkâ ê-pimiskâcik, mêskoc ðôtinwa ê-pimohtahikocik.

[8] êkwa, namwâc wiða nôhci-otisâpahtên kit-ôsîhtâcik ôho 'waskway-ôsa' k-êcikâtêki mâna, mâka nikî-wâpahtên wiða nîst êkoni anih ôsa [*sic*], kayâs mitoni; êkospî âtiht awiyak kêyâpic kî-âpacihtâw êkoni ôho 'waskway-ôsa' k-êcikâtêki. êkwa mîna mân ê-kî-pisiskâpamakwâw êkonik ôki [*sic*] k-âpacihtâcik anihi

[6] But today things are very different; the school-children are taught nothing about the Bible, nothing like the way they used to be taught about it before. And I also remember, as we ourselves were being brought up, each morning we used to pray, and every night before we went to bed we used to pray; and now today we also have lost all that. It is true, in the old days we used to be looked after properly, and today we are losing absolutely everything that the old people used to teach us before.

[*external break*]

[7] And travel, furthermore, used to be by boat long ago, for there were no 'planes' yet, as they are called, in this part of the world. The first time I myself remember seeing a plane, it landed on the water, it looked like a boat. And the ones who went fire-fighting [*sc.* used planes], and occasionally someone coming back from school at Prince Albert, these two men were called John Hastings and Abby Halkett, I saw them get off the float-plane; they were the first ones I saw fly. And then (it was about 1920, I believe, that we first saw a plane, about '29, I don't remember exactly), and when the trappers canoed out, when we canoed out (only boats were in use then, you paddled along, there were hardly any 'engines' then, as they are called, almost everyone used to paddle along), and when there was a strong wind, then they used to make sails and sail before the wind, not paddling but, instead, being taken along by Wind himself.

[8] I am not old enough to have seen them make 'birch-bark canoes' as they are called, but I did see these canoes very long ago; at that time some people still made use of these 'birchbark canoes' as they are called. And I used to notice the people who used these

waskway-ôsa, êkâ mwâs[i] ê-ohci-kikaskisinêcik, kâ-wî-kapâcik; ê-kî-pakastawê-tahkoskêcik, êk ôtôtiwâw [*sic*] nisihkâc ê-nâtakâsinahkwâw, êkâ êtokwê mâna mâka ta-pîkohtatâcik.

[9] êkwa ôma kâ-wî-âtotamân, kâ-wanihikâniwik mâna, kayâs ohci mihcêt ôko wanihikîskanawa ê-ayâcik, ohtâwîwâwa, omosômipaniwâwa; nimosômipan, êkâ ê-ohci-pimâtisit, êkwa nipâpâ êkwaðiw wanihikîskanaw ê-kî-at-âyât, êkwa êkâ ê-pimâtisit nipâpâ, nîtisânak êkwa, êkwa ôsisima nipâpâ, êkonik êkwa anohc kâ-kîsikâk êkotê wanihikîwak. îyakoni ôho wanihikîskanawa, ê-itêðihtamân mâna, kâ-nakataskêt awiyak, namôða kita-kî-wêpinikâtêki êkoni ôho ihtâwina, kita-kî-kakwê-miciminikâtêki kahkiðaw, wið êkoni ê-nakatamâkawiyahk, êkota ohci kita-pimâcihisowahk. wîðawâw wiða môniyâwâk mâna mâka *life-insurance* ayâwak êkos îsi kîkwâya, êkota ohci ê-ati-pami-- ê-ati-pamihimiht o-- aya, ocawâsimisiwâwa mîna wîwiwâwa; êkwa îwakw îtokw ânima kîðânaw, êwako mâna mâka kita-kî-icikâtêk '*life-insurance*', animiðiw kâ-nakatamâkowahkwâw kôhtâwînawak kita-- kit-ôhci-asamâwasowahk mîna kit-ôhci-pamihoyahk [*sic*] – wiða kayâhtê, wiða nîhiðaw wîð êkâ êkos îsi ê-kî-mâwacisôniyâwêt kita-nakatamawât otawâsimisa mîna kotaka awiya, ita ohti [*sic*] ta-pimâcihisoðit. êkwa anohc ôma kâ-kîsikâk, mihcêtîs awiyak itohtêw wanihikîskanâhk, mâka mîna mihcît namwâc itohtêwak. kayâs aðisk namôð ôhc-îhtakon '*family-allowance*' k-êcikâtêk, êkwa mîna kêhtêwasinahikana namwâc ohc-îhtakonwa. kahkiðaw awiyak piko ê-kî-atoskêt, ê-asamisot; mâka wið ânohc êkwa kâ-kîsikâk, îwakw îtok ôhc êk[â] âwiyak êkwa kâ-wî-kakwê-waskawît kit-âsamisot – misawâc ê-mosci-mîðiht sôniyâwa, ê-mosci-pamihiht. nîða mâka wið ê-iteðihtamân, namôða kwayask î-ihkihk, îwakw ânima k-îhkihk [*sic*]; wið ôti wið ê-isi-wâpahtamân nîsta, ê-kitâpahtamân êwak ôma kayâhtê isi-pimâcihowin mîn ânohc kâ-kîsikâk. êkonik ôko mâna kâ-kî-pimohtêhocik iðiniwak kayâs, kî-maskawisîwak, ahpô awâsisak kî-maskawisîwak, mistah ônikahpihk kî-nayahcikîwak, mistahi kî-- kî-waskawîwak. sôskwâc kî-isi-sôhkâtisiw aðisiðiniw;

birch-bark canoes, they hardly ever wore shoes when they would come ashore; they used to step into the water and gently guide their canoes to shore so as not to damage them, I guess.

[9] And what I am going to tell about, the trapping, many people have traplines from way back, from their fathers and their late grandfathers; when my late grandfather died, my dad got that trapline, and when my dad died, then my siblings and my father's grandchildren, they trap there today. These traplines, I tend to think, when someone dies, these trapline areas should not be given up, an attempt should be made to hold onto all of them, for they have been left for us to make our living from them. The Whites usually have life-insurance and things like that, and their children and wives are looked after by that; and, in our case, that could be called our life-insurance, I suppose, what our fathers have left for us, with which to feed our children and to live from – for the Crees cannot pile up money in that fashion, beforehand, in order to leave it for their children or anyone else to live on. And today quite a few go to the trapline, but many also do not go. Long ago of course there was no family-allowance as it is called, and there also were no old-age pension cheques. Everybody had to work at feeding himself; but today that is why people will not even try to do something in order to feed themselves – for they are simply given money anyways, they are simply looked after. But, as for me, I think that what is happening is not right; at least that is how I myself see it, when I look at the life as it used to be and that of today. These people who used to travel by boat long ago, they used to be strong, even the children used to be strong, they used to carry big loads at portages, they used to work a great deal. People used to be very fit physically;

namôða mîn ôhc-âhkosiskiw awiyak, êkâ êtokwê mâna mâka nanâtohk kîkwây ê-ohci-mîcit, nayêstaw kinosêwa, wiyâs êkos îsi ê-mîcicik; êkwa mîn ôs--, êkâ osâm ê-ohci-pîhtwâniwik mîn êkospî. êkwa anohc kâ-kîsikâk, namwâc îkwa nikiskîðimâw awiyak kwayask kita-maskawisît. niwâpahkân wiða mân ê-kâh-kocîcik ôko, ê-kâh-kakwê-mawinêhotocik, ê-nayahcikîcik; mâka nikêhcinâhon, namôð êkwaðikohk wîhkâc ohci-nayahcikêwak, mîna kayâhtê kâ-kî-pê-isi-maskawisîcik ôko iðiniwak, mâk îtokwê ohci, êkâ kâ-kî-âhkosiskicik, êkâ nanâtohk kîkwây ê-ohci-mîticik [*sic*] êkwa mîna, iðikohk mîn ê-kî-waskawîhtâcik, ita ohci maskawisîwin ê-kî-kâhcitinahkwâw. êkosi mân ê-itêðihtamân, mâka wið anohc êkwa kâ-kîsikâk, iðikohk nanâtohk kîkwây kitôninâhk ê-asiwatâyahk; mihcît êtokw âni kîkwây êkwa anohc, nawac kimâðiskâkonânaw, ispî wiða kwayask kik-êtiskâkowahk, ta-maskawîskâkowahk. mihcêtin mâna mâka kîkwây, ahpô pîhtwâwin mîn ôma kâ-kîskwêskâkot, êkwa minihkwêwin mîna, iðikohk mistahi ê-âpatahk; namôð ôma mâmaskâc, iðikohk mihcît êkwa, iðikohk mâna k-âhkosiyahk.

[JF:] *I can't think of anything else.*
[FA:] kisâkaskinahtân.
[JF:] mâk ânima, mâk ânim--

and they were not sickly, for they did not eat all the various kinds of food, I suppose, they only ate fish, meat, and things like that; and there also was not much smoking at that time. And now today I do not know anyone who would really be strong. I watch today when they keep trying, in competition with one another, to carry loads on their backs; but, I am certain, they never carry as much as they used to carry before, when the people had been strong, but I guess it is because they were not sickly, they did not eat all the various kinds of food and also kept at their work so much, gaining their strength from that. This is what I tend to think, but today we always put all kinds of things in our mouths; many of these things of today are probably bad for us, instead of being good for us and making us strong. There are many things, for example the smoking that makes one crazy, and also the drinking of which there is so much; it is no wonder that so many of us should be sick.

[JF:] I can't think of anything else.
[FA:] You have filled it [*sc.* the tape] up.
[JF:] But that one --

[FA:] ᐁᑯᓯ, ᓰᐢᑳᐧᐨ ᑭᔭ ᑲ ᒫᑖᒋᒧᐣ. ᑭᑳᐦ ᑮ ᐋᒋᒧᐢᑕᐃᐧᓈᐣ
ᑖᓂᒪᔨᑯᕽ ᐁ ᐃᑕᐦᑐᐱᐳᓀᔭᐣ, ᐁᑯᓯ.

[1] ᓇᒨᔭ ᐃᐧᔭ ᓂᐄᐧ ᐄᐧᐦᑌᐣ ᐁ ᐃᑕᐦᑐ ᐊᐢᑮᐃᐧᓀᔮᐣ, ᐁᐊᐧᑯ ᐃᐧᔭ ᓇᒨᔭ ᑮᑳᐧᐩ ᑭᐄᐧ ᐋᒋᒧᐢᑖᑎᓈᐋᐧᐤ. ᒫᑲ ᓂᐄᐧ ᐋᑐᑌᐣ, ᓃᐢᑕ ᐁ ᐯ ᐃᓯ ᑭᐢᑭᓯᔮᐣ, ᐯ ᐅᑖᐢᑲᓈᕽ ᐁ ᑮ ᐯ ᐃᓯ ᐅᐦᐱᑭᐦᐃᑲᐃᐧᔮᕽ ᐁ ᐊᐋᐧᓯᓰᐃᐧᔮᕽ.

[2] ᐊᓄᐦᐨ ᑳ ᑮᓯᑳᐠ ᐆᒪ, ᐆᑌᓇᐤ ᐆᒪ ᐃᑕ ᑳ ᐊᔮᔭᕽ, ᐃᐦᑖᐃᐧᐣ ᐅᑎ, ᒥᐢᑕᐦᐃ ᐲᑐᓯᓈᑲᐧᐣ ᒦᓇ ᐁ ᑭᐢᑭᓯᔮᐣ ᐁ ᑮ ᐯ ᐃᓯᓈᑲᐧᕽ ᑲᔮᐦᑌ. ᓇᒨᔭ ᐅᐦᒋ ᒥᐦᒉᑎᐤ ᒨᓂᔮᐤ ᐁᑯᐢᐲ ᐁᑯᓂ ᑮᓯᑳᐊᐧ, ᐁᑲᐧ ᒦᓇ ᓇᒨᔭ ᓇᓈᑐᕽ ᓅᐦᒋ ᐃᓯ ᒦᒋᓯᓈᐣ ᐊᑖᐁᐧᐃᐧᑲᒥᑯᕽ ᐅᐦᒋ, ᑖᐱᐢᑰᐨ ᐊᓄᐦᐨ ᑳ ᑮᓯᑳᐠ ᑭᐢᑎᑳᓇ, ᑲᐢᑳᐱᐢᑲᐦᐃᑲᓇ, ᓇᓈᑐᕽ ᐁᑯᓯ ᐃᓯ. ᐁ ᑮ ᐯ ᐃᓯ ᐅᐦᐱᑭᐦᐃᑲᐃᐧᔮᕽ ᓃᔭᓈᐣ, ᐁ ᑮ ᐯ ᒫᒌᒋᐠ ᓅᐦᑖᐄᐧᓈᓇᐠ, ᓅᐦᑯᒥᓈᓇᐠ, ᐃᐧᔮᐢ ᐁ ᒦᒋᔮᕽ, ᔩᐊᐧᐦᐃᑲᓇᐠ, ᐁ ᐸᑭᑕᐦᐋᐧᒋᐠ, ᑭᓄᓭᐤ ᐁ ᒧᐋᐧᔮᕽ, ᓇᒨᔭ ᓇᓈᑐᕽ ᑮᑳᐧᐩ ᓅᐦᒋ ᒦᒋᓈᐣ, ᒫᑲ ᓂᑎᑌᔨᐦᑌᐣ ᐁ ᑮ ᒥᔨᐢᑳᑯᐟ ᐊᔨᓯᔨᓂᐤ ᐁᑯᐢᐲ ᓇᐊᐧᐨ ᐅᒦᒋᐃᐧᐣ, ᐃᐢᐲ ᐊᓄᐦᐨ ᑳ ᑮᓯᑳᐠ.

[3] ᐁᑲᐧ ᒦᓇ ᒫᓇ ᐁ ᑮ ᐯ ᐃᓯ ᐸᒥᐦᐃᑲᐃᐧᔮᕽ, ᐊᐧᓂᐦᐃᑫᐢᑲᓈᕽ ᒫᓇ ᐁ ᑮ ᐃᑐᐦᑕᐦᐃᑲᐃᐧᔮᕽ, ᐁᑯᑌ ᐁ ᐸᒥᐦᐃᑲᐃᐧᔮᕽ, ᐁ ᐊᓴᒥᑲᐃᐧᔮᕽ ᐁᑯᑌ, ᐁᑲᐧ ᒦᓇ ᐁ ᐊᐧᓂᐦᐃᑫᒋᐠ ᒦᓇ ᓂᓃᑭᐦᐃᑯᓈᓇᐠ, ᐁᑯᑕ ᐅᐦᒋ ᐊᔭ, ᒫᓇ ᒫᑲ ᐊᐦᑕᔭ ᑳ ᓂᐸᐦᐋᐧᒋᐠ, ᑮ ᐯ ᐃᑐᐦᑕᐦᐁᐊᐧᐠ ᒫᓇ ᐊᑖᐁᐧᐃᐧᑲᒥᑯᕽ, ᐁ ᐯ ᓈᑖᒋᐠ ᐸᐦᑫᐧᓯᑲᓇ, tea, ᓲᑳᐤ, ᐱᒥᐩ ᐁᑯᓯ ᐃᓯ ᑮᑳᐧᐩ, ᐋᐧᓴᐢᑯᒉᓂᑲᓂᓴ, ᐁᑯᓯ ᐃᓯ ᑮᑳᐧᔭ ᒫᓇ ᐁ ᑮ ᐯ ᓈᑕᐦᑳᐧᐤ.

[4] ᐁᑲᐧ ᒦᓇ, ᓇᒨᔭ ᐅᓵᑦ ᐅᐦᒋ ᐅᓵᒉᔭᑎᓇᐧ ᐁᑯᐢᐲ, ᐁᑯᓂ ᐊᓂᐦᐃ ᑮᓯᑳᐊᐧ ᑲᔮᐢ, ᐆᐦᐅ ᐊᐧᓂᐦᐃᑲᓇ ᑳ ᐃᒥᑳᑌᑭ, ᐅᓵᑦ ᐱᑯ ᒫᓇ, ᒥᐢᑎᑯ ᐊᐧᓂᐦᐃᑲᓇ ᐃᑕᒪᐧᐠ, ᐁᑯᓂ ᐁ ᑮ ᐋᐸᒋᐦᑖᒋᐠ. ᐁᑲᐧ ᓇᐊᐧᐨ ᐯ ᐅᑖᐢᑲᓈᕽ ᒫᓇ, ᓂᑮ ᐋᒋᒧᐢᑖᑯᓈᐣ ᓂᒧᓲᑦ, ᐁᑳ ᓰᐢᑳᐧᐨ ᐁ ᐅᐦᒋ ᐃᐦᑕᑲᐧᐦᑭ ᐁᑯᓂ ᐆᐦᐅ ᐊᐧᓂᐦᐃᑲᓇ, ᓇᓭᐢᑕᐤ ᐁᓴ ᒫᓇ, ᐁᑯᑐᐊᐧᕽ ᑳ ᑮ ᐋᐸᑕᐦᑭ, ᒥᐢᑎᑯ ᐊᐧᓂᐦᐃᑲᓇ, ᐁᑲᐧ ᒦᓇ ᐋᑕ ᐃᐧᔭ ᒦᓇ ᒫᓇ ᐊᔭ ᑮ ᐅᔩᐦᑖᐊᐧᐠ, ᐲᒥᓇᐦᑳᐧᓂᐢ ᐁᓴ ᒫᓇ ᑳ ᑮ ᐅᐦᒋ ᐅᔩᐦᑖᒋᐠ, ᑖᐸᑳᐧᓇ, ᐱᓯᐊᐧ ᐁ ᓂᐸᐦᐋᐧᒋᐠ ᐁᑲᐧ ᐋᐧᐳᓴᐧ ᒦᓇ. ᓂᑮ ᐋᐧᐸᒫᐤ ᓅᐦᑯᒥᐸᐣ ᐁ ᐅᔩᐦᑖᐟ ᐁᑯᑐᐊᐧᕽ ᐊᓂᐦᐃ ᒫᐸᑳᐧᓂᓴ, ᐁ ᐊᐱᐢᒫᐯᑲᓯᐠ ᐲᒥᓇᐦᑳᐧᓂᐢ ᐅᐦᒋ, ᐁᑲᐧ ᒦᓇ ᒫᓇ ᑮ ᐁᐧᐸᑫᐧᐸᔨᐊᐧᐠ ᒫᓇ ᐊᓂᑭ, ᐋ, ᐋᐧᐳᓴᐧᐠ, ᐁ ᐅᐦᐱᐸᔨᒋᐠ, ᐁ ᑯᔮᐁᐧᑯᒋᐦᑳᐧᐤ, ᐁᑯᓯ ᒦᓇ ᑳ ᑮ ᐃᓯ ᑖᐸᑳᐧᒪᐦᐋᐧᒋᐠ ᐁᑯᐢᐲ ᐊᓂᒪ, ᐋᐧᐳᓴᐧ. ᒥᐢᑕᐦᐃ ᐲᑐᐢ ᐊᓄᐦᐨ ᑳ ᑮᓯᑳᐠ ᓃᐢᑕ ᓂᑎᓯ ᒫᐸᑫᐧᓯᐣ, ᒦᓇ ᐁᑯᐢᐲ ᐊᓂᒪ ᑳ ᑮ ᐃᓯ ᐋᐧᐸᐦᑫᔮᐣ ᒫᓇ. ᐯᔮᑳᐧᐤ ᓂᑮ ᑯᒋᐦᑖᐣ, ᓃᓯ ᐃᐢᑫᐧᓯᓴᐠ ᐁ ᑭᐢᑭᓄᐦᐊᒪᐊᐧᑳᐧᐤ, ᑖᓂᓯ ᑭᑕ ᐃᓯ ᐅᐦᐱᐸᔨᐟ ᑭᐋᐧᐳᓯᑦ, ᑖᐸᑳᐧᓯᒋ.

[5] ᐁᑲᐧ ᒦᓇ ᒫᓇ ᑳᓃᐱᕽ, ᑳ ᐊᔭᒥᐦᒋᑫᔮᕽ, ᐁᑯᐢᐲ ᓂᑮ ᓯᐯᐧᐃᐧᔪᑲᐃᐧᓈᐣ ᒦᓇ ᒫᓇ ᐁᑯᐢᐲ, ᐁᑯᓯ ᐊᓂᒪ ᐃᓯ ᐁ ᐅᑕᒥᓇᐦᐃᑲᐃᐧᔮᕽ, ᐅᐦᐱᒣ ᐁ ᐊᔮᔮᕽ, ᐁᑲᐧ ᑳ ᐊᔭᒥᐦᒋᑫᔮᕽ ᒦᓇ, ᐁᑯᑕ ᐃᐧᔭ ᒦᓇ ᒥᐦᒉᐟ ᑮᑳᐧᐩ ᓂᑮ ᑭᐢᑭᓄᐦᐊᒫᑲᐃᐧᓈᐣ ᒫᓇ ᒫᑲ, ᒫᑲ ᓇᒨᔭ ᐅᓵᒼ ᓂᑖᐸᒋᐦᐃᑯᓈᐣ, ᓂᑎᑌᔨᐦᑌᐣ ᒫᓇ, ᐋᑎᐦᐟ ᑮᑳᐧᐩ ᐁ ᑮ ᑭᐢᑭᓄᐦᐊᒫᑲᐃᐧᔮᕽ, ᐊᐄᐧᓇ ᐊᓇ ᑳ ᑮ ᑭᐦᒋ ᐅᑭᒫᐃᐧᐟ ᐁᑯᐢᐲ, ᐊᐄᐧᓇ ᐊᓇ ᑳ ᑮ ᐆᒥᓯ ᐃᓰᐦᒋᑫᐟ ᓂᑮ ᐃᑎᑲᐃᐧᓈᐣ ᒫᓇ, ᐁᑲᐧ ᒥᓯᐁᐧᐢᑲᒥᐠ ᒦᓇ ᒫᓇ ᓂᑮ ᐄᐧᐦᑕᒫᑲᐃᐧᓈᐣ, ᑲᐢᑭᑌᐃᐧᔮᓴᐠ ᐃᑌ ᑳ ᐄᐧᑭᒋᐠ, Germanᐊᐠ ᐃᑌ ᑳ ᐄᐧᑭᒋᐠ, ᓇᓈᑐᕽ ᐁᑯᓯ ᐃᓯ ᑮᑳᐧᐩ. ᒫᑲ ᐯᔭᐠ ᐃᐧᔭ ᑭᐦᒋ ᑮᑳᐧᐩ ᐁ ᐃᑌᔨᐦᑕᒫᐣ ᓃᔭ ᐁ ᑮ ᑭᐢᑭᓄᐦᐊᒫᑲᐃᐧᔮᕽ ᐁᑯᐢᐲ, ᑭᐦᒋ ᒪᓯᓇᐦᐃᑲᐣ ᒫᓇ ᐁ ᑮ ᐊᔭᒥᐦᑖᔮᕽ ᑕᐦᑐ ᑮᓯᑳᐤ, ᐋᐱᐦᑕᐤ ᑎᐸᐦᐃᑲᐣ ᒫᓇ ᑳ ᑮ ᑭᐢᑭᓄᐦᐊᒫᑲᐃᐧᔮᕽ ᐁᐊᐧᑯ ᐆᒪ ᑭᐦᒋ ᒪᓯᓇᐦᐃᑲᓂᕽ ᐅᐦᒋ. ᐁᑲᐧ ᒫᓇ ᐁ ᑮ ᒥᐢᑰᑕᒫᕽ, ᐁ ᐋᑲᔭᓰᒧᔭᕽ ᒫᑲ ᐃᐧᔭ – ᐃᐧᔭ ᐁᑳ ᐁ ᐅᐦᒋ ᐸᑭᑎᓂᑲᐃᐧᔮᕽ ᑕ ᓀᐦᐃᔭᐁᐧᔮᕽ ᐃᐢᑰᓫᐃᕽ.

[6] ᐁᑲᐧ ᐊᓄᐦᐨ ᑳ ᑮᓯᑳᐠ, ᒥᐢᑕᐦᐃ ᐲᑐᐢ ᒫᓇ ᒫᑲ ᐃᐢᐸᔨᐤ, ᑳ ᐊᔭᒥᐦᒋᑫᒋᐠ ᐁᑲᐧ ᐆᑯ, ᓇᒨᔭ ᑭᐢᑭᓄᐦᐊᒪᐋᐧᐊᐧᐠ ᑮᑳᐧᐩ ᑭᐦᒋ ᒪᓯᓇᐦᐃᑲᓂᕽ ᐅᐦᒋ, ᑖᐱᐢᑰᐨ ᑲᔮᐦᑌ ᑳ ᑮ ᐯ ᐃᓯ ᑭᐢᑭᓄᐦᐊᒫᐦᒋᐠ. ᐁᑲᐧ ᒦᓇ ᒫᓇ ᐁ ᑭᐢᑭᓯᔮᐣ, ᑳ ᐯ ᐅᐦᐱᑭᐦᐃᑲᐃᐧᔮᕽ ᓃᐢᑕᓈᐣ ᐆᒪ, ᑕᐦᑐ ᑮᑭᓭᐹᔮᐤ ᒫᓇ ᐁ ᑮ ᐊᔭᒥᐦᐋᔮᕽ, ᑕᐦᑖᐧᐤ ᐁ ᒪᐧᓭᑲᐃᐧᓯᒧᐋᐧᕽ ᐁ ᑮ ᐊᔭᒥᐦᐋᔮᕽ, ᐁᑲᐧ ᐊᓄᐦᐨ ᑳ ᑮᓯᑳᐠ ᐁᑲᐧ, ᐁᐊᐧᑯ ᒦᓇ ᑲᐦᑭᔭᐤ ᑭᐊᐧᓂᐦᑖᓈᓇᐤ. ᑖᐯᐧ ᐁᒋᑲ ᐊᓂ ᐁ ᑮ ᐯ ᒥᔫ ᐸᒥᐦᐃᑲᐃᐧᔮᕽ ᐯ ᑲᔮᐢ, ᐁᑲᐧ ᐊᓄᐦᐨ ᐁᑲᐧ, ᒥᑐᓂ ᑲᐦᑭᔭᐤ ᑮᑳᐧᐩ ᐁ ᐊᑎ ᐊᐧᓂᐦᑖᔭᕽ, ᑲᔮᐦᑌ ᑫᐦᑌ ᐊᔭᐠ ᑳ ᑮ ᐯ ᐃᓯ ᑭᐢᑭᓄᐦᐊᒫᑯᔮᐦᑳᐧᐤ.

[7] ᐁᑲᐧ ᒦᓇ ᒫᓇ ᑲᔮᐢ, ᐆᒪ ᑳ ᐱᒧᐦᑌᐦᐅᓈᓂᐃᐧᐠ, ᓇᒨᔭ ᐊᔨᐢᐠ ᐅᐦᒋ ᐃᐦᑕᑯᓇᐧ ᒪᔭᐤ ᐆᑌ ᐃᑌᐦᑫᐢᑲᒥᐠ ᐆᐦᐅ ᐱᒥᔮᑲᓇ ᑳ ᐃᒋᑳᑌᑭ. ᓂᐢᑕᒼ ᓃᐢᑕ ᐁ ᑭᐢᑭᓯᔮᐣ ᐁ ᐋᐧᐸᐦᑕᒫᐣ ᐱᒥᔮᑲᐣ, ᓂᐲᕽ ᐁ ᑮ ᑌᐧᐦᐅᒪᑲᕽ, ᑖᐱᐢᑰᐨ ᐆᓯ ᐁ ᑮ ᐃᓯᓈᑲᐧᕽ. ᐁᑲᐧ ᒫᓇ, ᐊᓂᑭ ᑳ ᓂᑕᐃᐧ ᐋᐧᐢᑕᐁᐧᐦᐃᑫᒋᐠ, ᐁᑲᐧ Prince Albert ᒦᓇ ᒫᓇ ᐅᐦᒋ ᐋᑎᐦᐟ ᐊᐃᐧᔭᐠ ᐁ ᑮ ᓂᑕᐃᐧ ᐊᔭᒥᐦᒋᑫᐟ, 'John Hastings', 'Abby Halkett' ᑮ ᐃᑖᐊᐧᐠ ᐊᓂᑭ ᓃᓯ ᓈᐯᐊᐧᐠ, ᐁᑯᓂᐠ ᓂᑮ ᐋᐧᐸᒫᐊᐧᐠ ᐁ ᑲᐹᒋᐠ ᐊᓂᒪ ᐅᐦᒋ ᐱᒥᔮᑲᐣ, ᐁᑯᓂᐠ ᓂᐢᑕᒼ ᐁ ᐋᐧᐸᒪᑳᐧᐤ ᐁ ᐱᒥᔮᒋᐠ. ᐁᑲᐧ (nineteen-twenty ᐸᑲᐦᑲᒼ ᓈᓂᑕᐤ ᐆᒪ, ᓂᐢᑕᒼ ᑳ ᑮ ᐋᐧᐸᐦᑕᒫᕽ ᐱᒥᔮᑲᐣ, ᓈᓂᑕᐤ twenty-nine, ᓇᒨᔭ ᒣᐧᐦᒋ ᓂᑭᐢᑭᓯᐣ), ᐁᑲᐧ ᐊᔭ, ᑳ ᓯᐯᐧᐦᐅᑌᐦᐅᒋᐠ ᒦᓇ ᐆᑯ ᐅᐊᐧᓂᐦᐃᑫᐊᐧᐠ, ᑳ ᓯᐯᐧᐦᐅᑌᐦᐅᐋᐧᕽ ᒫᓇ (ᐆᓴ ᓇᓭᐢᑕᐤ ᑮ ᐋᐸᑕᓇᐧ ᐁᑯᐢᐲ, ᐁ ᐱᒥᐢᑳᔮᐣ ᒦᓇ, ᓇᒨᔭ ᒦᓇ ᒫᐧᓯ ᐅᐦᒋ ᐃᐦᑕᑯᐤ 'engine' ᑳ ᐃᑎᐦᐟ ᐁᑯᐢᐲ ᐊᓂᒪ, ᐅᓵᒼ ᐱᑯ ᒫᓇ ᑲᐦᑭᔭᐤ ᐊᐃᐧᔭᐠ ᑮ ᐱᒥᐢᑳᐤ), ᐁᑲᐧ ᐆᒪ ᑳ ᒥᓯ ᔫᑎᕽ, ᐁᑯᑕ ᐃᐧᔭ ᒫᓇ ᑮ ᐅᓰᐦᑖᐊᐧᐠ ᐊᔭ, ᔭᐦᑳᐢᑎᒧᓇ, ᐊᔭ, ᐁ ᐱᒫᓯᒋᐠ, ᐁᑳ ᐁ ᐱᒥᐢᑳᒋᐠ, ᒣᐢᑯᐨ ᔫᑎᓇᐧ ᐁ ᐱᒧᐦᑕᐦᐃᑯᒋᐠ.

[8] ᐁᑲᐧ, ᓇᒫᐧᐨ ᐃᐧᔭ ᓅᐦᒋ ᐅᑎᓵᐸᐦᑌᐣ ᑭᑕ ᐅᓰᐦᑖᒋᐠ ᐆᐦᐅ ᐊᐧᐢᑲᐧᐩᐆᓴ ᑳ ᐃᒋᑳᑌᑭ ᒫᓇ, ᒫᑲ ᓂᑮ ᐋᐧᐸᐦᑌᐣ ᐃᐧᔭ ᓃᐢᑕ ᐁᑯᓂ ᐊᓂᐦᐃ ᐆᓴ, ᑲᔮᐢ ᒥᑐᓂ, ᐁᑯᐢᐲ ᐋᑎᐦᐟ ᐊᐃᐧᔭᐠ ᑫᔮᐱᐨ ᑮ ᐋᐧᐸᒋᐦᑖᐤ ᐁᑯᓂ ᐆᐦᐅ ᐊᐧᐢᑲᐧᐩᐆᓴ ᑳ ᐃᒋᑳᑌᑭ. ᐁᑲᐧ ᒦᓇ

ᒫᓇ ᐁ ᑮ ᐱᓯᐢᑳᐸᒪᑳᐧᐤ ᐁᑯᓂᐠ ᐆᑭ ᑳ ᐋᐸᒋᐦᑖᒋᐠ ᐊᓂᐦᐃ ᐊᐧᐢᑲᐧᐩ ᐆᓴ, ᐁᑳ ᒫᐧᓯ ᐁ ᐅᐦᒋ ᑭᑲᐢᑭᓯᓀᒋᐠ, ᑳ ᐄᐧ ᑲᐹᒋᐠ, ᐁ ᑮ ᐸᑲᐢᑕᐁᐧ ᑕᐦᑯᐢᑫᒋᐠ, ᐁᑲᐧ ᐅᑑᑎᐋᐧᐤ ᓂᓯᐦᑳᐧ- ᐁ ᓈᑕᑳᓯᓇᐦᑳᐧᐤ, ᐁᑳ ᐁᑐᑫᐧ ᒫᓇ ᒫᑲ ᑕ ᐲᑯᐦᑕᑖᒋᐠ.

[9] ᐁᑲᐧ ᐆᒪ ᑳ ᐄᐧ ᐋᐧᑐᑕᒫᐣ, ᑳ ᐊᐧᓂᐦᐃᑳᓂᐃᐧᐠ ᒫᓇ, ᑲᔮᐢ ᐅᐦᒋ ᒥᐦᒉᐟ ᐆᑯ ᐊᐧᓂᐦᐃᑫᐢᑲᓇᐊᐧ ᐁ ᐋᔮᒋᐠ, ᐅᐦᑖᐄᐧᐋᐧᐊᐧ, ᐅᒧᓲᒥᐸᓂᐋᐧᐊᐧ, ᓂᒧᓲᒥᐸᐣ, ᐁᑳ ᐁ ᐅᐦᒋ ᐱᒫᑎᓯᐟ, ᐁᑲᐧ ᓂᐹᐹ ᐁᑲᐧᖪᐤ ᐊᐧᓂᐦᐃᑮᐢᑲᓇᐤ ᐁ ᑮ ᐊᑎ ᐋᔮᐟ, ᐁᑲᐧ ᐁᑳ ᐁ ᐱᒫᑎᓯᐟ ᓂᐹᐹ, ᓃᑎᓵᓇᐠ ᐁᑲᐧ, ᐁᑲᐧ ᐆᓯᓯᒪ ᓂᐹᐹ, ᐁᑯᓂᐠ ᐁᑲᐧ ᐊᓄᐦᐨ ᑳ ᑮᓯᑳᐠ ᐁᑯᑌ ᐊᐧᓂᐦᐃᑫᐊᐧᐠ. ᐁᑯᓂ ᐆᐦᐅ ᐊᐧᓂᐦᐃᑫᐢᑲᓇᐊᐧ, ᐁ ᐃᑌᖪᐦᑕᒫᐣ ᒫᓇ, ᑳ ᓇᑲᑕᐢᑫᐟ ᐊᐃᐧᔭᐠ, ᓇᒨᖬ ᑭᑕ ᑮ ᐁᐧᐱᓂᑳᑌᑭ ᐁᑯᓂ ᐆᐦᐅ ᐃᐦᑖᐃᐧᓇ, ᑭᑕ ᑮ ᑲᑫᐧᒥᒋᒥᓂᑳᑌᑭ ᑲᐦᑭᖬᐤ, ᐃᐧᖬ ᐁᑯᓂ ᐁ ᓇᑲᑕᒫᑲᐃᐧᔭᕽ, ᐁᑯᑕ ᐅᐦᒋ ᑭᑕ ᐱᒫᒋᐦᐃᓱᐊᐧᕽ. ᐄᐧᖬᐋᐧᐤ ᐃᐧᖬ ᒨᓂᖭᐊᐧᐠ ᒫᓇ ᒫᑲ life-insurance ᐋᔮᐊᐧᐠ ᐁᑯᓯ ᐃᓯ ᑮᑳᐧᔭ, ᐁᑯᑕ ᐅᐦᒋ ᐁ ᐊᑎ ᐸᒥᐦᐃᒥᐦᐟ ᐅᒐᐋᐧᓯᒥᓯᐋᐧᐊᐧ ᒦᓇ ᐄᐧᐃᐧᐋᐧᐊᐧ, ᐁᑲᐧ ᐁᐊᐧᑯ ᐁᑐᑫᐧ ᐊᓂᒪ ᑮᖬᓇᐤ, ᐁᐊᐧᑯ ᒫᓇ ᒫᑲ ᑭᑕ ᑮ ᐃᒥᑳᑌᐠ 'life-insurance', ᐊᓂᒥᖪᐤ ᑳ ᓇᑲᑕᒫᑯᐊᐧᐦᑳᐧᐤ ᑰᐦᑖᐄᐧᓇᐊᐧᐠ ᑭᑕ ᐅᐦᒋ ᐊᓴᒫᐊᐧᓱᐊᐧᕽ ᒦᓇ ᑭᑕ ᐅᐦᒋ ᐸᒥᐦᐅᔭᕽ – ᐃᐧᖬ ᑲᔮᐦᑌ, ᐃᐧᖬ ᓀᐦᐃᖬᐤ ᐄᐧᖬ ᐁᑳ ᐁᑯᓯ ᐃᓯ ᐁ ᑮ ᒫᐊᐧᒋᓲᓂᔮᐁᐧᐟ ᑭᑕ ᓇᑲᑕᒪᐋᐧᐟ ᐅᑕᐋᐧᓯᒥᓴ ᒦᓇ ᑯᑕᑲ ᐊᐃᐧᔭ, ᐃᑕ ᐅᐦᒋ ᑕ ᐱᒫᒋᐦᐃᓱᖪᐟ. ᐁᑲᐧ ᐊᓄᐦᐨ ᐆᒪ ᑳ ᑮᓯᑳᐠ, ᒥᐦᒉᑏᐢ ᐊᐃᐧᔭᐠ ᐃᑐᐦᑌᐤ ᐊᐧᓂᐦᐃᑫᐢᑲᓈᕽ, ᒫᑲ ᒦᓇ ᒥᐦᒌᐟ ᓇᒫᐧᐨ ᐃᑐᐦᑌᐊᐧᐠ. ᑲᔮᐢ ᐊᖪᐢᐠ ᓇᒨᖬ ᐅᐦᒋ ᐃᐦᑕᑯᐣ 'family-allowance' ᑳ ᐃᒥᑳᑌᐠ, ᐁᑲᐧ ᒦᓇ ᑫᐦᑌᐊᐧᓯᓇᐦᐃᑲᓇ ᓇᒫᐧᐨ ᐅᐦᒋ ᐃᐦᑕᑯᓇᐧ. ᑲᐦᑭᖬᐤ ᐊᐃᐧᔭᐠ ᐱᑯ ᐁ ᑮ ᐊᑐᐢᑫᐟ, ᐁ ᐊᓴᒥᓱᐟ, ᒫᑲ ᐃᐧᖬ ᐊᓄᐦᐨ ᐁᑲᐧ ᑳ ᑮᓯᑳᐠ, ᐁᐊᐧᑯ ᐁᑐᑫᐧ ᐅᐦᒋ ᐁᑳ ᐊᐃᐧᔭᐠ ᐁᑲᐧ ᑳ ᐄᐧ ᑲᑫᐧ ᐊᐧᐢᑳᐄᐧᐟ ᑭᑕ ᐊᓴᒥᓱᐟ – ᒥᓴᐋᐧᐨ ᐁ ᒧᐢᒋ ᒦᖪᐦᐟ ᓲᓂᔮᐊᐧ, ᐁ ᒧᐢᒋ ᐸᒥᐦᐃᐦᐟ. ᓃᖬ ᒫᑲ ᐃᐧᖬ ᐁ ᐃᑌᖪᐦᑕᒫᐣ, ᓇᒨᖬ ᑲᐧᔭᐢᐠ ᐁ ᐃᐦᑭᕽ, ᐁᐊᐧᑯ ᐊᓂᒪ ᑳ ᐃᐦᑭᕽ, ᐃᐧᖬ ᐅᑎ ᐃᐧᖬ ᐁ ᐃᓯ ᐚᐸᐦᑕᒫᐣ ᓃᐢᑕ, ᐁ ᑭᑖᐸᐦᑕᒫᐣ ᐁᐊᐧᑯ ᐆᒪ ᑲᖬᐦᑌ ᐃᓯ ᐱᒫᒋᐦᐅᐃᐧᐣ ᒦᓇ ᐊᓄᐦᐨ ᑳ ᑮᓯᑳᐠ. ᐁᑯᓂᐠ ᐆᑯ ᒫᓇ ᑳ ᑮ ᐱᒧᐦᑌᐦᐅᒋᐠ ᐃᖪᓂᐊᐧᐠ ᑲᖭᐢ, ᑮ ᒪᐢᑲᐃᐧᓰᐊᐧᐠ, ᐊᐦᖭ ᐊᐋᐧᓯᓴᐠ ᑮ ᒪᐢᑲᐃᐧᓰᐊᐧᐠ, ᒥᐢᑕᐦᐃ ᐅᓂᑲᐦᐱᕽ ᑮ ᓇᔭᐦᒋᑫᐊᐧᐠ, ᒥᐢᑕᐦᐃ ᑮ ᐊᐧᐢᑳᐃᐧᐊᐧᐠ. ᓲᐢᑳᐧᐨ ᑮ ᐃᓯ ᓲᐦᑳᑎᓯᐤ ᐊᖪᓯᖪᓂᐤ, ᓇᒨᖬ ᒦᓇ ᐅᐦᒋ ᐋᐦᑯᓯᐢᑭᐤ ᐊᐃᐧᔭᐠ, ᐁᑳ ᐁᑐᑫᐧ ᒫᓇ ᒫᑲ ᓇᓈᑐᕽ ᑮᑳᐧᐩ ᐁ ᐅᐦᒋ ᒦᒋᐟ, ᓇᓭᐢᑕᐤ ᑭᓄᓴᐊᐧ, ᐃᐧᔮᐢ ᐁᑯᓯ ᐃᓯ ᐁ ᒦᒋᒋᐠ, ᐁᑲᐧ ᒦᓇ ᐁᑳ ᐅᓵᐨ ᐁ ᐅᐦᒋ ᐲᐦᑖᐧᓂᐃᐧᐠ ᒦᓇ ᐁᑯᐢᐲ. ᐁᑲᐧ ᐊᓄᐦᐨ ᑳ ᑮᓯᑳᐠ, ᓇᒫᐧᐨ ᐁᑲᐧ ᓂᑭᐢᑫᖪᒫᐤ ᐊᐃᐧᔭᐠ ᑲᐧᔭᐢᐠ ᑭᑕ ᒪᐢᑲᐃᐧᓰᐟ. ᓂᐋᐧᐸᐦᑳᐣ ᐃᐧᖬ ᒫᓇ ᐁ ᑳᐦᑯᒦᒋᐠ ᐆᑯ, ᐁ ᑳᐦ ᑲᑫᐧ ᒪᐃᐧᓀᐦᐅᑐᒋᐠ, ᐁ ᓇᔭᐦᒋᑮᒋᐠ, ᒫᑲ ᓂᑫᐦᒋᓈᐦᐅᐣ, ᓇᒨᖬ ᐁᑲᐧᖪᑯᕽ ᐄᐧᐦᑳᐨ ᐅᐦᒋ ᓇᔭᐦᒋᑫᐊᐧᐠ, ᒦᓇ ᑲᔮᐦᑌ ᑳ ᑮ ᐯ ᐃᓯ ᒪᐢᑲᐃᐧᓰᒋᐠ ᐆᑯ ᐃᖪᓂᐊᐧᐠ, ᒫᑲ ᐁᑐᑫᐧ ᐅᐦᒋ, ᐁᑳ ᑳ ᑮ ᐋᐦᑯᓯᐢᑭᒋᐠ, ᐁᑳ ᓇᓈᑐᕽ ᑮᑳᐧᐩ ᐁ ᐅᐦᒋ ᒦᒋᒋᐠ ᐁᑲᐧ ᒦᓇ, ᐃᖪᑯᕽ ᒦᓇ ᐁ ᑮ ᐊᐧᐢᑳᐃᐧᐦᑖᒋᐠ, ᐃᑕ ᐅᐦᒋ ᒪᐢᑲᐃᐧᓰᐃᐧᐣ ᐁ ᑮ ᑳᐦᒋᑎᓇᐦᑳᐧᐤ. ᐁᑯᓯ ᒫᓇ ᐁ ᐃᑌᖪᐦᑕᒫᐣ, ᒫᑲ ᐃᐧᖬ ᐊᓄᐦᐨ ᐁᑲᐧ ᑳ ᑮᓯᑳᐠ, ᐃᖪᑯᕽ ᓇᓈᑐᕽ ᑮᑳᐧᐩ ᑭᑑᓂᓈᕽ ᐁ ᐊᓯᐋᐧᑖᔭᕽ, ᒥᐦᒉᐟ ᐁᑐᑫᐧ ᐊᓂ ᑮᑳᐧᐩ ᐁᑲᐧ ᐊᓄᐦᐨ, ᓇᐊᐧᐨ ᑭᒫᖪᐢᑲᑯᓈᓇᐤ, ᐃᐢᐲ

ᐏᔭ ᑿᔭᐢᐠ ᑭᑲ ᐃᑎᐢᑳᑯᐘᕽ, ᑕᒪᐢᑲᐑᐢᑳᑯᐘᕽ. ᒥᐦᒉᑎᐤ ᒫᓇ ᒫᑲ ᑮᒁᐩ, ᐊᐦᔮ ᐲᐦᑤᐏᐤ ᒦᓇ ᐆᒪ ᑳ ᑮᐢᑵᐢᑳᑯᐟ, ᐁᑿ ᒥᓂᐦᑵᐏᐤ ᒦᓇ, ᐃᔨᑯᕽ ᒥᐢᑕᐦᐃ ᐁ ᐋᐸᑕᕽ, ᓇᒨᔭ ᐆᒪ ᒫᒪᐢᑳᐨ, ᐃᔨᑯᕽ ᒥᐦᒉᐟ ᐁᑿ, ᐃᔨᑯᕽ ᒫᓇ ᑳ ᐋᐦᑯᓯᔭᕽ.

4.
His First Moose

Minnie Fraser

[1] *well,* mân âyihk, *his dad* ê-ay-âhkosiyit mâna mêkwâc, *they used to go out, Shellbrook way, eh, to go and trap,* êtikwê mâna êkos ê-kî-itatoskêt *the old man, eh.* êkwa mâna *this woman, she was very religious, Easter* k-êspayiyik, tita--, *from there –*

> "ta-wawêyîw," kî-itêwak omâmâwâwa, *Eliza* awa nicâhkosipan, *and,* "ê-ka-kwayâcihtât kahkiyaw kîkway," itwêw, "naspâpan, miton êtikwê wîpac mân ê-waniskât, *Shellbrook* ê-isi-mostohtêt, *Snake Plain* ê-nitaw-âyamihât, êh, *and that way, wherever she was,* ê-mostohtêt,"

they didn't have nothing,

> "êkwa piko ta-mostohtêt;"

but when they lived at, aya,

> "*Ordale* k-âyâyâhk,"

– there was another one, 'Stump Lake' pakahkam kî-icikâtêw, êkotê anima mâna *the old lady* kayâs ê-kî-ayât, êkotê ê-kî-wîkicik *when my old man was a boy,* êkw ês ê-nitaw-âyamihâcik *Snake Plain, that's quite a ways from there.*

[2] êkwa *after church* êkwa ayihk, êtikwê ayis *you know,* êkwa mâna *her brother's* itohtêw, aniki macôhow's aniki, *you know, Birds* êkonik ôki, *she had how many brothers there,* ana kotak --, *his mother.*

[FA:] â, êwak ôhc êcik âna mâna kâ-kî-omâmâyân, "nisikos" kî-itwêw mâna, êkoni cî anihi?

[MF:] *yea;*

[1] Well, during the time that his dad [*sc.* the father of Norman, the speaker's late husband] was sick, they used to go out trapping in the direction of Shellbrook, that is the kind of work, I guess, which the old man [*sc.* Norman's father] had used to do. And this woman [*sc.* Norman's mother] was very religious, every Easter she would go from there –

> "She would get ready," they said about their mother, "and make all the preparations," my late sister-in-law Eliza said, "at the break of dawn, I guess, very early she would get up and walk to Shellbrook, she was going to church at Snake Plain, and she would walk there from wherever she might be,"

they had nothing,

> "and she had to go on foot;"

but when they lived at, well,

> "when we lived at Ordale,"

– they also lived at another place, I think it was called Stump Lake, that is where his mother had been staying long ago, and that is where they were living when my husband was a boy, and now they were going to church in Snake Plain, which is quite a distance from there.

[2] And after church now, I guess, she used to go, you know, to her brother's house, to *macôhow's* house, you know, his mother was a Bird and she had many brothers there.

[FA:] Oh, that is the reason, then, why my late mom spoke of her as "my aunt," was that her?

[MF:] Yes;

well, êkonik aniki, *how many Birds* ayihk, kî-ay--, *her brothers* êkot[a] ânima kî--, kî-ayâwak; êkwa aya, êkotê mâna *dinner* nitaw-âyâwak. *this time* êkwa ayihk, *after dinner* ôhi pêyak ôh ôsisa, kisiwâk êkota *church* nawac ê-wîkit, êkota itohtêwak êsa. êkwa ês âwa *this woman*, êtikwê kî-kwayâti-cî---pakâsimêw (*'ducks'* nik-êtwân),

[FA:] – êha, *gophers*; –

[MF:] – awas! –

[FA:] – *gophers*, môy nânitaw, nikî-wîhkistâwak aniki, kêyâpic êtik--, *that's nothing wrong*. –

[GP:] – môy nânitaw, *that's nothing wrong with that, that's the way they survived*. –

aya, *they went* ôhi ê-kiyokawâcik, *you know, and I guess they ate --, they ate gophers* ôhi ê-pakâsoyit, êh, *and* êtikwê ma-misi-mîcisowak, êtikwê wâhyaw ê-ohtohtêcik. êkw ês âya, êtikwê *the old man* ê-nâpêsisiwit, osîmis[a] ê-mâmitonêyimât, ôtê [*gesture*] êsa k-âsiwahât ôh ôtê, *inside*.

[FA:] anikwacâsa?

[MF:] êha.

[3] êkwa, êkos êkwa sipwêhtêwak êkwa ê-kîwêcik, wahwâ, ê-kisâstêk; miton ês âwa nôcikwêsiw, "ayiwêpitân," itêw êsa okosisa, êh; ayiwêpiwak êkota. ê-- ê-pasikôcik êkwa, kâ-nitonikêt ês ôtê. "tânis," itêw, "kîkway cî ê-nitonaman?" – "êha, nisîmisak ôta ê-kî-pêtamawakik *gopher*, ôt[a] ê-kî-asiwahimak," ôtê ês ê-nitonikêt aw ôtê, ôtê kâ-pimîwit êsa ê-kî-pahkisimât, "ê-pahkisimat êsa." miton ês ê-misi-mâtot, ê-mawîhkâtât anihi.

[FA:] êha, ê-kî-wî-kîwêhtatamâkêt.

[MF:] êha;

êkwa, "cêskw," îtwêw êsa, itik omâmâwa, "êkây nânitaw itêyihta, nikosis!" itêw êsa.

well, they were the ones, well, there were many Birds living there and they were her brothers; and they used to go there for dinner. And now, after dinner – this time they had gone to the place of this one uncle's of hers, he lived closer to the church; and this woman had cooked boiled (ducks, I will say),

[FA:] – rather, gophers; –

[MF:] – go on! –

[FA:] – gophers, it's alright, I loved the taste of them, I probably still would, there is nothing wrong with that. –

[GP:] – It's alright, there is nothing wrong with that, that is the way they survived. –

well, they went to visit them, you know, and I guess they ate these boiled gophers, and they must have eaten many for they had come from afar. And then my husband, who was a little boy, must have been thinking of his younger brothers and sisters, and he put one in here [*gesture*; *sc.* down the front of his shirt], inside.

[FA:] A gopher?

[MF:] Yes.

[3] And so they left on their way home, oh my, it was a hot day; and the old lady [*sc.* Norman's mother] said to her son, "Let's rest;" and they stopped to rest there. When they got up, now he was searching for something in there [*gesture*]. "What is the matter?" she said to him, "Are you looking for something?" – "Yes, I had brought a gopher in here for my younger brothers and sisters, I had put it in here for them," he searched in there, and all he found in there was a grease spot on himself, he had dropped the gopher, "You have dropped it." He cried very hard, sobbing over the gopher.

[FA:] Yes, he had been taking it home for them.

[MF:] Yes;

"Wait," she now said, his mother said to him, "don't fret about it, my son!" she said to him.

[4] "êkwa ê-ocihcihkwanapit êkota kâ-kî-omâmâyân, ê-ayamihât," itwêw; "'ocihcihkwanapi kîsta!' nititik," itwêw. "ê-nitotamâkêstamawit," itwêw, "ôtê ninîkânimihk, ta-nihtâ-nôcihcikêyân, ta-nihtâ-mâcîyân," ê-itwêt, "ê-kî-isi-nitotamawit, anim êwako – têpiyâhk êkâ ê-môskomak ôm ê-misi-mâtoyân," itwêw. "êkos êkw ê-kî-ayamihâyâhk, êkw âni nipasikônân ê-sipwêhtêyâhk."

– *thirteen* ôma kâ-kî-itwêt pakahkam ê-itahtopiponêt, môswa nistam ê-kî-nipahât.

[GP:] *the same year, eh?*

[MF:] êha.

[5] "ayihk," itwêw,

– opâpâwa kâ-pôni-pimâtisiyit, êkwa êkôtê âhci pikw ê-nitawi-nôcihcikêt an[a] îskwêw, êkwa wîst êtikwê ê-oskinîkiwiyinîsiwit –

"êkwa ôm," îtwêw, "*ducks* âsay ninâh-nipahâwak," itwêw, "kinwês ê-ayâyâhk," itwêw, "ê-mônahaskwêyâhk," itwêw. "'wahwâ, nisaskatamâwak êk ôki, nikosis! ôki sîsîpak; ôtê isi nawac wâhyaw misi-sâkahikan ayâw, *Shellbrook* ôm ôtê isi, êkotê ayâw, mistah âniki mâna miyosiwak êkotê sîsîpak,' nititik," itwêw. "'êkotê maht êkwa kakwê-nitaw--;' êkw ân[i] êkotê k-êtohtêyân, tâpwê," itwêw, "miton îhtakowak êkotê," itwêw, "*eight different kinds of ducks* ê-nipahakik, nipê-kîwêhtahâwak, wâ, nimamistêyimon [*sic; cf.* nimamihtêyimon] êkw ê-pêsiwakik anik," îtwêw.

[4] "And then my late mom knelt down there and prayed," he said; "'You kneel down, too!' she said to me," he said. "She asked this for me," he said, "that, in the life ahead of me, I should be a good trapper and a good hunter," he said, "that is what she asked for me – I had almost made her break into tears with all my crying. And so, when we had prayed, now we got up and left."

– he was thirteen, I think he had said, when he killed a moose for the first time.

[GP:] The same year?

[MF:] Yes.

[5] "Well," he said,

– after his dad had died, this woman [*sc.* Norman's mother] still went out to go trapping over there, and he must have been just a youngster –

"It was then," he said, "I was already killing ducks," he said, "we stayed there a long time," he said, "we were digging seneca-root," he said. "'Oh my, I am tired of eating these ducks, my son, in that direction [*gesture*], quite a distance away, there lies a big lake over there, in the direction of Shellbrook, there the ducks are really good,' she said to me," he said. "'Please try to go over there --;' and when I went over there, it was true," he said, "there were many over there," he said, "I killed eight different kinds of ducks and I was bringing them home, well, I was proud of myself that I was bringing them home," he said.

[6] " -- [*?record*] nipîhk, sisonê sâkahikanihk ê-pê-pimohtêyân êkwa, kîkway? – kêtisk ês ê-- ê-pimohtêt," itwêw, "nipiy kêyâpic ê-âh-asiwacipayik ôm ît[a] ê-kî-tahko--- tahkoskêt," itwêw. "wahwâ, nimosômipan mân êkosi kâ-kî-itwêt, ê-kînikâyik ômis îsi môswa ita kâ-pimohtêt, nikêhcinâhon môswa awa," ê-itwêt êsa. "niwêpinâwak nisîsîpimisak," itwêw, "êkwa ôm îtê, kotakihk nimiskên it[ê] ês ê-kî-ati-kapât ômis îs," îtwêw, "ati-sakâw êkota; êkw ât[i]-îspatinâw," itwêw. "ôtê is îsi," itwêw, "ômisi ê-wî-itohtêyân," itwêw, "kêt--, ôm îspatinâw, âpistaw-âyihk [*sic; cf.* âpihtaw-] êtikwê ômis ê-wî-itohtêyân," itwêw; "ê-sâkêwêyân, kî-matwê-apiw nêtê, ê-mîcisot," itwêw.

– êkot[ê] êkwa kâ-ohci-pâskiswât êsa, ê-kî-nipahât anihi, *his first moose.*

[FA:] êkosi wêpinêw cî osîsîpima?
[MF:] matwân cî.

[7] "êkos êkwa," itwêw, "â, nipê-kîwân êkwa," itwêw. "'tânisi, kîkway cî kinip-- kinipahâwak sîsîpak?' nititik," itwêw. "'êha, mâka niwêpinâwak.'" – "'îh! tânêhki mâka k-ôh-wêpinacik,' nititik," itwêw. "'aya, ê-nipahak môswa.'" – "'â, awas!' nititik," itwêw. "'tâpwê' – 'kakwêyâhok!'"

– "â, kakwêyâhok!" ê-itât ês ôsîmisa, awa *'John-George'* kâ-kî-itiht, *Tommy*, "misatimwak nâtitisahohkok!" ê-nâtitisahwâcik, êkwa mêton ê-kakwêyâhot, cîkahikan,

[GP:] – *well,* ma cî *the old lady wouldn't believe her* [*sic; sc. him*], *at first;* –
[MF:] – êha; –

[6] "-- in the water, as I came walking along the lake, what was this? – it had just gone by," he said, "the water was still trickling into the hoofprints," he said. "Oh my, my late grandfather had said that the tracks where a moose has gone are pointed like this [*gesture*], and I was certain that this was a moose," he said. "I threw away my ducks," he said, "and then I found another set of hoofprints where it had come out of the water, like this [*gesture*]," he said, "the bush began there; and then a hill," he said. "It was in this direction," he said, "and I was going to go this way [*gesture*]," he said, "I was going to go this way about halfway up the hill," he said; "when I came out into view, there it was in plain view, sitting over there and chewing the cud," he said.

– Then he shot it from there, he did kill it, his first moose.

[FA:] And so he threw his ducks away?
[MF:] I wonder.

[7] "And so," he said, "well, now I went back [*sc.* to the camp]," he said. "'What happened? Did you kill any ducks?' she said to me," he said. "'Yes, but I threw them away.'" – "'What? But why did you throw them away?' she said to me," he said. "'Well, I killed a moose.'" – "'Oh, go on!' she said to me," he said. "'It is true' – 'Hurry up!'"

– "Well, hurry up!" he said to his younger siblings, to John-George, as he was called, and to Tommy, "Go get the horses!" They went for the horses, and he was really rushing around, an axe,

[GP:] – well, wasn't it that his mother wouldn't believe him at first; –
[MF:] – yes; –

môhkomân, êkwa cîkahikan, kik-ês-âpacihtâcik sôskwâc, ê-pâh-pîhciwêpinahk êkota *in* --

"'îh! piyisk awa wâh-tâpwêhtawak [*sic*],' nititik," itwêw.

[FA:] – omâmâwa? –

[MF:] – êha; –

– môy ê-wî-tâpwêhtawât, "konit," ê-itêyihtahk. êkwa mâk ânih êkwa kâ-pâh-pôsiwêpinamiyit (êk ôhi *horses* ê-pêtitisahwâ--, nititik [*sic*]) –

"miton ê-kakwêyâhocik êkwa," itwêw, "ê-wiyahpicikêcik," itwêw. "êkwa an[i]," îtwêw, "kâ--, ê-kîsi-pôsiyâhk êkwa," itwêw. "ayê, nama kîkway nimanâtâstimâwak," itwêw, "sakâsa ôhi, ômayikohk," itwêw, "mitoni konit êkoni ê-ati-tahkohcipicikêyân, wahwâ, nimâh-mâkohâwâk," itwêw, "'êkw ânim îta, êk ôta piko ta-nakîyahk,' nititwân, 'anim îspatinâw,'" itwêw. "'îh! êkota ôma kâ-kî-itohtêyân,' ê-itak," itwêw, "'anima *hill* ômisi ê-itohtêyân,'" itwêw, "'îh! nâha kâ-pimisihk,' nititâw," itwêw. "wahwâ, mwayês ahpô êkota itohtêyâhk, iyikohk ê-nanâskomât manitowa," itwêw. "êkwa an[i]," îtwêw, "kâ-pahkonâyâhk êkwa," itwêw, "êkos îsi sôskwâc, nipâh-pôsiwêpinênân êkwa êkos îsi nikîwehtatânân," itwêw. "êkwa nîpiya nikâh-kaskatwânên," itwêw, "êkota ê-nîhciwêpinamâhk," itwêw. "êkwa an[i] êkwa," itwêw, "nâpêsisak," itwêw, "êy, kâ-sîhkimakik," itwêw, "ta-nâtahkik mihta. êkwa mîn ânih âkwâwâna (mistikwa *a certain way* ê-kî-isinâkwahki, ayis mân ômisi kî-itamohtâwak), êkoni anihi ê-nâtahkik êkwa. wahwâ, miton êkwa, akwâwân ôm ê-osîhtâyâhk, âsay wiya kâ-kî-omâmâyân," itwêw, "ê-mâci-pânisâwêt," itwêw. "êkos," îtwêw,

a knife and axe, the things they would use, he threw them into the wagon-box --

> "'Look, I am going to believe him yet!' she said about me," he said.
>
> [FA:] – his mother? –
>
> [MF:] – yes; –

– she wouldn't believe him, she thought, "He is just kidding." But now, when he was throwing these things onto the wagon (and with them [*sc.* his brothers] driving the horses to the camp, he said to me) –

> "Now they really hurried," he said, "with the harnessing," he said. "And then," he said, "when we had got on," he said, "wow, I did not spare them [*sc.* the passengers] in any way," he said, "I really just drove over the little bushes," he said, "just like this," he said, "oh my, I really scared them," he said, "'And this is the place, this is where we have to stop,' I said to them, 'this hill,'" he said. "'Look, this is the way I went,' I said to her," he said, "'I went up this hill this way [*gesture*],'" he said, "'look, there it lies,' I said to her," he said. "Oh my, before we even went there, she was already thanking God," he said. "And then," he said, "we skinned it," he said, "and just threw the meat on the wagon and took it back [*sc.* to the camp] like that," he said. "Then I broke off leafy branches," he said, "and threw the meat down on them," he said. "And then," he said, "I told the boys," he said, "to go for firewood. And also for drying-racks" (the poles had to be a certain way [*sc.* forked], because they used to put the rails on like this [*gesture*]), "now they went for these. Oh my, and then we built the drying-rack," he said, "my late mom had already begun to cut the meat into sheets," he said. "And so," he said, "of course,"

"ayis," itwêw, "ê-takohtêyâhk êkwa," itwêw, "êkwa nôsîhtânân anima akwâwân," itwêw, "êkwa ê-pônamâhk, 'nahiyikohk pâh-pônamok!' itêw ôhi nâpêsisa," itwêw. "êkwa niya --,"

– ê-pâh-pîkinisâwâtamawât êtikwê omâmâwa; êkotê ês ê-ati-pânisamiyit.

[8] "êkos," îtwêw,

– êkwa *Mary-Jane* ayis (mîn âwa kâ-kî-nicawi-nipic [*sic*] awa *States*, êh), êkwa aniki *two boys, John-George* êkwa *Tommy*, êkwa *the old man* ê-kî-nêwicik; êkwa *Eliza*? îh! mwâc, *Eliza* pakahkam -- môy ôm ôhci ê-ma-mâmiskômât êkoni, *she must have been married already,* wîpac ayis pakahkam ê-kî-onâpêmit.

[GP:] *she was the oldest, Eliza.*

"êkos," îtwêw, "ayihk; ê-pânisâwêt êkwa kapê-ayihk," itwêw, "wahwâ, miton êkwa akwâwân iyikohk," itwêw. "sôskwât nahiyikohk ê-wiyinot awa môswa," itwêw. "â, kêtahtawê êkwa," itwêw, "wiyinwa êkwa," itwêw, "miton ê-wiyinot, êkoni êkw ê-cîsâwâtahk ôhi wiyinwa êkwa," itwêw. "awa *Mary-Jane* ê-apisîsisit," itwêw, "*supper* ê-ayâyâhk," itwêw, "mâk ê-at-ôtâkosik," itwêw; "akwâwânihk ôma cîkâhtaw êkota," itwêw, "êkw âwa *Mary-Jane* êkot[a] ê-apit," itwêw, "mâka môy ê-misikitit. êkwa aya, awa nimâmâ êkw ê-cîsâwâtahk êkwa wiyinwa," itwêw. "êkota pêyak awa nayêstaw mistik ê-cimasot, kisiwâk," itwêw, "kâ-pê-twêhot êkota ôhow," itwêw, "ê-pê-kâh-kitot," itwêw, "êkwa awa *Mary-Jane* ê-wîsaki-kostât, ê-misi-mâh-mâtot," itwêw. "'kây, êkâya mâto! ê-nôhtêhkatêt ana wîst ôm ê-- ê-wâpamiko-- ê-wâpahtahk ôma wiyâs ê-nôhtê-mîcit,' itêw kâ-kî-omâmâyân," itwêw. "êkos âna ôhow, konita mân ômis [*gesture*] ê-itôtahk,

he said, "as we arrived," he said, "now we built the drying-rack," he said, "and as we made a fire, she said to the boys," he said, "'Make a good drying fire!' and I --,"

– he was cutting the meat into chunks for his mom, I guess; and she was cutting it into sheets over there.

[8] "And so," he said,

– there were four of them, Mary-Jane of course (the one who later died in the States), and the two boys, John-George and Tommy, and my husband; and Eliza? Look, not Eliza, I think, he did not mention her, she must have been married already, for I think she married early.

[GP:] Eliza was the oldest.

"And so," he said, "well; now she kept cutting the meat into sheets," he said, "oh my, we had a big drying rack," he said. "This moose had just the right amount of fat," he said. "Well, and after a while," he said, "now it was time to cut up the fat," he said, "it was really fat, and now she cut the fat into pieces," he said. "Mary-Jane was small," he said, "and we were having supper," he said, "but it was getting to be dusk," he said; "and Mary-Jane," he said, "was sitting close to the drying rack there," he said, "but she was little. And now my mom was cutting up the fat," he said. "Close by a lone tree that stood there," he said, "when an owl came and landed on that tree," he said, "it came and kept hooting," he said, "and Mary-Jane was terribly afraid of it and kept crying hard," he said. "'Don't, don't cry! That one is hungry, too, and it sees this meat and wants to eat it,' my late mom told her," he said. "And so that owl just did this [*gesture*], tâpiskôc kîkway ê-pâh-pîmiskwêyit, mitoni ê-wî-wâpahtahk ôma kîkway," itwêw; "kêtahtawê kâ-sipwêhât," itwêw.

[9] "wahwâ," itwêw, êkwa ani, ispî êkwa ê-pâstêki ôhi," itwêw. "'â, môy êkwa nika-kîwânân,' nititêyihtên, itwêw "'mitoni kinwês nika-mîcinân,'" itwêw, " – ayiwâk ihkin ê-âti-pâstêyiki, 'maht êkwa kîwêtan, aya, kinêpiko-maskotêhk itohtêtân,' k-êsit nimâmâ," itwêw. "'wahwâ, nimâmâ!'" –

[GP:] – *but in the meantime, back at Snake Plain* –

– êkwa aw îtwêw, 'macôhow' kâ-kî-itiht wîwa (êtikwê *outside* ê-ay-ayât, ê-pa-pônahk *outside,* matwân cî ê-pahkwêsikanihkêt), ayihk, ê-pê-pîhtikwêt, "wahwâ," itêw êsa, onâpêma, "kiya mâna, êkây wîhkâc kîkway ê-pîkwêyihtamihikoyan! kayâs ôma kitânisinaw, nayêstaw awâsis[a] ê-pici-- ê-picicik, êkâ ahpô nânitaw ê-wî-kakwê-kiskêyihtaman itê t-âyâcik, tânisi t-ês-âyâcik," itêw ês ônâpêma, êkos âti-wayawîw kâwi. êkwa âsay mîna kîkway êtikwê ê-wî-nâtahk *in the tent* – kâ-matwê-misi-pâh-pâhpiyit, "iyaw, tânis êkwa ê-ma-môhcw-âyâyan cî êkwa?" itêw ês ônâpêma. "namôy," îtik êsa, aya, "ê-wawiyatêyimak aw," îtwêw, "awa, ay-- ay-- aya, môniyâs ês ê-kî-nipahât apisi-- môswa, êkw ê-akwâwêt kitânisinaw, êkwa awa iskwêsis ê-- ê-wîsaki-kosit anima ê-nitaw--" (*you know*, ê-nitawâpênawât), êkwa sôskwac kâ-- ê-mêkwâ-mîcisocik, kâhkêwak ê-mîcicik, sôskwât miyw-âyâwak," ê-itwêt. êkos ânima tâpwê ê-kî-ihkiniyik, matwân cî anima *one or two days after* kâ-takopiciyit. –

turning its head this way and that, as if trying to see something," he said; "then suddenly it flew away," he said.

[9] "Oh my," he said, "and then, when the sheets of meat were dry," he said, "'Well, we won't go home now,' I thought," he said, "'we will have lots to eat for a long time,'" he said, "– and would you believe it, as the sheets of meat were getting dry, my mom said to me, 'Let's go home now, let's go to ***kinêpiko-maskotêhk*** [*sc.* Snake Plain],'" he said. "'Oh my, Mom!'" –

[GP:] – but in the meantime, back at Snake Plain –

– And the wife of *macôhow*, as he was called, said (she must have been outside, she had a fire going outside, I wonder if she was making bannock), well, as she came inside, "Oh my," she said to her husband, "you, you never worry about anything! It's been ages since our daughter has gone off, with only children in her camp, and you are not even trying to find out where they are or how they are doing," she said to her husband, and with that she went back outside. And then she must have gone into the tent again to fetch something – she could hear him laughing and laughing, "Ho! What now? Have you gone crazy now?" she said to her husband. "No," he said to her, "I am laughing with joy about him," he said, "about *môniyâs* [*sc.* Norman], he has killed a moose, and our daughter is hanging up the meat to dry, and the little girl was terribly afraid of me, you know, when I went --" (you know, he had gone to check on them [*sc.* in the form of an owl]), "and, indeed, they were in the midst of eating at the time, they were eating dried meat, they are having a good life," he said. And this is truly what had happened, it was one or two days after this, I am not quite sure, that she [*sc.* their daughter] arrived with her camp. –

> "'wahwâ, nimâmâ! êkây êkotê itohtêtân, mâka mîna kika-mêscasahkân [*sic*],' nititâw," itwêw, "êkotê ê-takohtêyâhk," itwêw, "kâ-kî-mônahaskwêyâhk," itwêw, "konit êkw êkoni ê-itohtatâcik;"

– aya, ohkoma êkwa omosôma ayihk, 'macôhow' kâ-kî-itiht, êkwa *and her --, his mother* –

> "mîciwin nayêstaw ê-kî-pêtâcik. ayiwâk ihkin pêminawasocik aniyê, ê-wîhkohkêmocik, ta-pê-mâh-mîcihk kâhkêwak; konit êk ômis ê-iskotêhkêhk *outside*," itwêw.

– êkot[a] ânima macôhôsis kâ-kî-ayâcik, êkota, *Snake Plain; Willy Dreaver* mîna mân êkota kî-ayâw piyisk, êkota ôma; –

> "ayihk, êkwa mâninakis [*?record*] ayisiyiniwak ôma ê-pê-mîcisocik, mitoni ê-mihcêtihk," itwêw.

– *well,* wâh-kîwêyici, ê-kîsi-mîcisôhât, kâhkêwakwa ê-miyât awa nôcikwêsiw, anihi omâmâwa, *the old man.* kahkiyaw êkosi,

> "ayiwâk ihkin, awînipan êkwa kâhkêwakwa ê-kîsi--, – ê-mêstasahkêt," ê-itwêt.

êwako kâ-kî-isi-kostahk.

> "êkos," îtwêw, "sôskwâc ê-- êwakw ânima kâ-kî-kostamân sêmâk sôskwâc, kahkiyaw mêstasahkêw," itwêw.

[10] mâk êsa, *that's the first,* kayâs kâ-nipahtât awiyak kîkway, osk-âya nistam, êkos ê-kî-itôtamihk, ê-wîhkohkêhiht tâpiskôc, êkwa mîn ê-asahkêhk *like, you know.* êkos êtikw ânim ânima k-ôh-- k-ôh-itôtamâht.

> "'Oh my, Mom! Let's not go over there, for you will again give all our meat out to feed people,' I said to her," he said, "and when we arrived there," he said, "the seneca-root we had dug," he said, "they too immediately took it there [sc. to town, in order to sell it];"

– well, his grandmother and his grandfather, well, *macôhow*, as he was called, and his mother –

> "they brought back nothing but food. And would you believe it, they cooked and cooked, inviting people to come and eat dried meat; they made a fire outside like this [*gesture*]," he said.

– It was there where *macôhow*'s son and his family lived, there at Snake Plain; Willy Dreaver also lived there later, it was there; –

> "Well, and then people just kept coming to eat, there were very many of them," he said.

– Well, and when they would be about to go home, when she had given them to eat, the old lady gave them more dried meat to take along, my husband's mom. And so everything was gone,

> "and would you believe it, there was none of the dried meat left – she gave it all out to feed people," he said.

That is what he had been afraid of.

> "And so it was," he said, "exactly what I had been afraid of at the outset, she had given it all out to feed people," he said.

[10] But in the old days, when someone made a kill, when a young person killed his first animal, this is what you used to do, to hold a feast for him and also to give out the meat, you know. That must have been the reason why she did that to him.

[1] well, ᒫᓇ ᐊᔨᕽ, his dad ᐁ ᐊᔮᐦᑯᓯᔨᐟ ᒫᓇ ᒣᒁᐨ, they used to go out, Shellbrook way, eh, to go and trap, ᐁᑎᑵ ᒫᓇ ᐁᑯᓯ ᐁ ᑮ ᐃᑕᑐᐢᑵᐟ the old man, eh. ᐁᑿ ᒫᓇ this woman, she was very religious, Easter ᑳ ᐃᐢᐸᔨᔨᐠ, from there –

> «ᑕ ᐘᐌᔩᐤ,» ᑮ ᐃᑌᐘᐠ ᐅᒫᒫᐚᐘ, Eliza ᐊᐘ ᓂᒑᐦᑯᓯᐸᐣ,
> and, «ᐁ ᑲ ᑿᔮᒋᐦᑖᐟ ᑲᐦᑭᔭᐤ ᑮᑿᐩ,» ᐃᑗᐤ, «ᓇᐢᐹᐸᐣ, ᒥᑐᓂ
> ᐁᑎᑵ ᐚᐸᐨ ᒫᓇ ᐁ ᐘᓂᐢᑳᐟ, Shellbrook ᐁ ᐃᓯ ᒧᐢᑐᐦᑌᐟ,
> Snake Plain ᐁ ᓂᑕᐏ ᐊᔭᒥᐦᐋᐟ, ᐁᐦ, and that way,
> wherever she was, ᐁ ᒧᐢᑐᐦᑌᐟ,»

they didn't have nothing,

> «ᐁᑿ ᐱᑯ ᑕ ᒧᐢᑐᐦᑌᐟ,»

but when they lived at, ᐊᔭ,

> «Ordale ᑳ ᐊᔮᔮᕽ,»

– there was another one, 'Stump Lake' ᐸᑲᐦᑲᑦ ᑮ ᐃᒋᑳᑌᐤ, ᐁᑯᑌ ᐊᓂᒪ ᒫᓇ the old lady ᑲᔮᐢ ᐁ ᑮ ᐊᔮᐟ, ᐁᑯᑌ ᐁ ᑮ ᐑᑭᒋᐠ when my old man was a boy, ᐁᑿ ᐁᓴ ᐁ ᓂᑕᐏ ᐊᔭᒥᐦᐋᒋᐠ Snake Plain, that's quite a ways from there.

[2] ᐁᑿ after church ᐁᑿ ᐊᔨᕽ, ᐁᑎᑵ ᐊᔨᐢ you know, ᐁᑿ ᒫᓇ her brother's ᐃᑐᐦᑌᐤ, ᐊᓂᑭ ᒪᒨᐦᐅᐤ's ᐊᓂᑭ, you know, Birds ᐁᑯᓂᐠ ᐆᑭ, she had how many brothers there, ᐊᓇ ᑯᑕᐠ –, his mother. well, ᐁᑯᓂᐠ ᐊᓂᑭ, how many Birds ᐊᔨᕽ, her brothers ᐁᑯᑕ ᐊᓂᒪ ᑮ ᐊᔮᐘᐠ, ᐁᑿ ᐊᔭ, ᐁᑯᑌ ᒫᓇ dinner ᓂᑕᐏ ᐊᔮᐘᐠ. this time ᐁᑿ ᐊᔨᕽ, after dinner ᐆᐦᐃ ᐯᔭᐠ ᐆᐦᐃ ᐅᓯᓴ, ᑭᓯᐚᐠ ᐁᑯᑕ church ᓇᐘᐨ ᐁ ᐑᑭᐟ, ᐁᑯᑕ ᐃᑐᐦᑌᐘᐠ ᐁᓴ. ᐁᑿ ᐁᓴ ᐊᐘ this woman, ᐁᑎᑵ ᑮ ᑿᔮᒋ ᐸᑳᓯᒣᐤ – 'ducks' ᓂᑲ ᐃᑛᐣ –

> [FA:] – ᐁᐦᐊ, gophers –
> [MF:] – ᐊᐘᐢ –
> [FA:] – gophers, ᒨᔭ ᓈᓂᑕᐤ, ᓂᑮ ᐑᐦᑭᐢᑖᐘᐠ ᐊᓂᑭ, ᑫᔮᐱᐨ ᐁᑎᑵ, that's nothing wrong.
> [GP:] – ᒨᔭ ᓈᓂᑕᐤ, that's nothing wrong with that, that's the way they survived.

– ᐊᔭ, they went ᐆᐦᐃ ᐁ ᑭᔪᑲᐚᒋᐠ, you know, and I guess they ate gophers ᐆᐦᐃ ᐁ ᐸᑳᓯᔨᐟ, ᐁᐦ, and ᐁᑎᑵ ᒪᒥᓯ ᒦᒋᓱᐘᐠ, ᐁᑎᑵ ᐚᐦᔭᐤ ᐁ ᐅᐦᑐᐦᑌᒋᐠ. ᐁᑿ ᐁᓴ ᐊᔭ, ᐁᑎᑵ the old man ᐁ ᓈᐯᓯᓯᐏᐟ, ᐅᓰᒥᓴ ᐁ ᒫᒥᑐᓀᔨᒫᐟ, ᐆᑌ ᐁᓴ ᑳ ᐊᓯᐘᐦᐚᐟ ᐆᐦᐃ ᐆᑌ, inside.

[FA:] ᐊᓂᑿᒑᓴ.
[MF:] ᐁᐦᐊ.

[3] ᐁᑿ, ᐁᑯᓯ ᐁᑿ ᓯᐍᐦᑌᐘᐠ ᐁᑿ ᐁ ᑮᐍᒋᐠ, ᐘᐦᐚ, ᐁ ᑭᓵᐢᑌᐠ, ᒥᑐᓂ ᐁᓴ ᐊᐘ ᓅᒋᑵᓯᐤ, «ᐊᔨᐍᐱᑖᐣ,» ᐃᑌᐤ ᐁᓴ ᐅᑯᓯᓴ, ᐁᐦ, ᐊᔨᐍᐱᐘᐠ ᐁᑯᑕ. ᐁ ᐸᓯᑰᒋᐠ ᐁᑿ, ᑳ ᓂᑐᓂᑫᐟ ᐁᓴ ᐆᑌ. «ᑖᓂᓯ,» ᐃᑌᐤ, «ᑮᑿᐩ ᒌ ᐁ ᓂᑐᓇᒪᐣ.» – «ᐁᐦᐊ, ᓂᓰᒥᓴᐠ ᐆᑕ ᐁ ᑮ ᐯᑕᒪᐘᑭᐠ gopher, ᐆᑕ ᐁ ᑮ ᐊᓯᐘᐦᐃᒪᐠ,» ᐆᑌ ᐁᓴ ᐁ ᓂᑐᓂᑫᐟ ᐊᐘ ᐆᑌ, ᐆᑌ ᑳ ᐱᒦᐏᐟ ᐁᓴ ᐁ ᑮ ᐸᐦᑭᓯᒫᐟ, «ᐁ ᐸᐦᑭᓯᒪᐟ ᐁᓴ.» ᒥᑐᓂ ᐁᓴ ᐁ ᒥᓯ ᒫᑐᐟ, ᐁ ᒪᐑᐦᑳᑖᐟ ᐊᓂᐦᐃ.

[FA:] ᐁᐦᐊ, ᐁ ᑮ ᐑ ᑮᐍᐦᑕᑕᒫᑫᐟ.
[MF:] ᐁᐦᐊ,

ᐁᑿ, «ᒉᐢᑿ,» ᐃᑗᐤ ᐁᓴ, ᐃᑎᐠ ᐅᒫᒪᐘ, «ᐁᑳᔭ ᓈᓂᑕᐤ ᐃᑌᔨᐦᑕ, ᓂᑯᓯᐢ.» ᐃᑌᐤ ᐁᓴ.

[4] «ᐁᑿ ᐁ ᐅᒋᐦᒋᐦᑿᓇᐱᐟ ᐁᑯᑕ ᑳ ᑮ ᐅᒫᒫᔮᐣ,
ᐁ ᐊᔭᒥᐦᐋᐟ,» ᐃᑗᐤ, «ᐅᒋᐦᒋᐦᑿᓇᐱ ᑮᐢᑕ. ᓂᑎᑎᐠ,»
ᐃᑗᐤ. «ᐁ ᓂᑐᑕᒫᑫᐢᑕᒪᐏᐟ,» ᐃᑗᐤ, «ᐆᑌ ᓂᓃᑳᓂᒥᕽ,
ᑕ ᓂᐦᑖ ᓅᒋᐦᒋᑫᔮᐣ, ᑕ ᓂᐦᑖ ᒫᒌᔮᐣ,» ᐁ ᐃᑗᐟ,
«ᐁ ᑮ ᐃᓯ ᓂᑐᑕᒪᐏᐟ, ᐊᓂᒪ ᐁᐘᑯ – ᑌᐱᔮᕽ ᐁᑳ ᐁ ᒨᐢᑯᒪᐠ
ᐆᒪ ᐁ ᒥᓯ ᒫᑐᔮᐣ,» ᐃᑗᐤ. «ᐁᑯᓯ ᐁᑿ ᐁ ᑮ ᐊᔭᒥᐦᐋᔮᕽ, ᐁᑿ
ᐊᓂ ᓂᐸᓯᑰᓈᐣ ᐁ ᓯᐍᐦᑌᔮᕽ.»

– thirteen ᐆᒪ ᑳ ᑮ ᐃᑗᐟ ᐸᑲᐦᑲᐨ ᐁ ᐃᑕᐦᑐᐱᐳᓀᐟ, ᒨᓷ ᓂᐢᑕᐨ ᐁ ᑮ ᓂᐸᐦᐚᐟ.

[GP:] the same year, eh?
[MF:] ᐁᐦᐊ.

[5] «ᐊᔨᕽ,» ᐃᑌᐤ,
– ᐅᐹᐹᐊᐧ ᑳ ᐴᓂ ᐱᒫᑎᓯᔨᐟ, ᐁᑲᐧ ᐁᑯᑌ ᐋᐦᒋ ᐱᑯ ᐁ ᓂᑕᐃᐧ ᓅᒋᐦᒋᑫᐟ ᐊᓇ ᐃᐢᑫᐧᐤ, ᐁᑲᐧ ᐄᐧᐢᑕ ᐁᑎᑫᐧ ᐁ ᐅᐢᑭᓃᑭᐃᐧᔨᓃᓯᐃᐧᐟ –

«ᐁᑲᐧ ᐆᒪ,» ᐃᑌᐤ, «ducks ᐋᓴᕀ ᓂᓈᐦ ᓂᐸᐦᐋᐊᐧᐠ,» ᐃᑌᐤ, «ᑭᓄᐧᐢ ᐁ ᐊᔮᔮᕽ,» ᐃᑌᐤ, «ᐁ ᒨᓇᐦᐊᐢᑫᐧᔮᕽ,» ᐃᑌᐤ. «ᐊᐧᐦᐋᐧ, ᓂᓴᐢᑲᑕᒫᐊᐧᐠ ᐁᑲᐧ ᐆᑭ, ᓂᑯᓯᐢ. ᐆᑭ ᓰᓰᐸᐠ, ᐆᑌ ᐃᓯ ᓇᐊᐧᐨ ᐋᐧᐦᔭᐤ ᒥᓯ ᓵᑲᐦᐃᑲᐣ ᐊᔮᐤ, Shellbrook ᐆᒪ ᐆᑌ ᐃᓯ, ᐁᑯᑌ ᐊᔮᐤ, ᒥᐢᑕᐦᐃ ᐊᓂᑭ ᒫᓇ ᒥᔪᓯᐊᐧᐠ ᐁᑯᑌ ᓰᓰᐸᐠ, ᓂᑎᑎᐠ,» ᐃᑌᐤ. «ᐁᑯᑌ ᒪᐦᑎ ᐁᑲᐧ ᑲᑫᐧᓂᑕᐃᐧ~, ᐁᑲᐧ ᐊᓂ ᐁᑯᑌ ᑳ ᐃᑐᐦᑌᔮᐣ, ᑖᐯᐧ,» ᐃᑌᐤ, «ᒥᑐᓂ ᐃᐦᑕᑯᐊᐧᐠ ᐁᑯᑌ,» ᐃᑌᐤ, «eight different kinds of ducks ᐁ ᓂᐸᐦᐊᑭᐠ, ᓂᐯ ᑮᐍᐦᑕᐦᐋᐊᐧᐠ, ᐋᐧ, ᓂᒪᒥᐦᑌᔨᒧᐣ ᐁᑲᐧ ᐁ ᐯᓯᐊᐧᑭᐠ ᐊᓂᑭ,» ᐃᑌᐤ.

[6] « – ᓂᐲᕽ, ᓯᓰᓄ ᓵᑲᐦᐃᑲᓂᕽ ᐁ ᐯ ᐱᒧᐦᑌᔮᐣ ᐁᑲᐧ, ᑮᑲᐧᕀ. – ᑫᑎᐢᐠ ᐁᓴ ᐁ ᐱᒧᐦᑌᐟ,» ᐃᑌᐤ, «ᓂᐱᕀ ᑫᔮᐱᐨ ᐁ ᐋᐦ ᐊᓯᐊᐧᒋᐸᔨᐠ ᐆᒪ ᐃᑕ ᐁ ᑮ ᑕᐦᑯᐢᑫᐟ,» ᐃᑌᐤ. «ᐊᐧᐦᐋᐧ, ᓂᒧᓲᒥᐸᐣ ᒫᓇ ᐁᑯᓯ ᑳ ᑮ ᐃᑌᐧᐟ, ᐁ ᑮᓂᑳᔨᐠ ᐆᒥᓯ ᐃᓯ ᒧᓴᐧ ᐃᑕ ᑳ ᐱᒧᐦᑌᐟ, ᓂᑫᐦᒋᓈᐦᐅᐣ ᒧᓴᐧ ᐊᐊᐧ,» ᐁ ᐃᑌᐧᐟ ᐁᓴ. «ᓂᐍᐱᓈᐊᐧᐠ ᓂᓰᓰᐱᒥᓴᐠ,» ᐃᑌᐤ, «ᐁᑲᐧ ᐆᒪ ᐃᑌ, ᑯᑕᑭᕽ ᓂᒥᐢᑫᐣ ᐃᑌ ᐁᓴ ᐁ ᑮ ᐊᑎ ᑲᐹᐟ ᐆᒥᓯ ᐃᓯ,» ᐃᑌᐤ, «ᐊᑎ ᓴᑳᐤ ᐁᑯᑕ, ᐁᑲᐧ ᐊᑎ ᐃᐢᐸᑎᓈᐤ,» ᐃᑌᐤ. «ᐆᑌ ᐃᓯ ᐃᓯ,» ᐃᑌᐤ, «ᐆᒥᓯ ᐁ ᐄᐧ ᐃᑐᐦᑌᔮᐣ,» ᐃᑌᐤ, «ᐆᒪ ᐃᐢᐸᑎᓈᐤ, ᐋᐱᐦᑕᐃᐧ ᐊᔨᕽ ᐁᑎᑫᐧ ᐆᒥᓯ ᐁ ᐄᐧ ᐃᑐᐦᑌᔮᐣ,» ᐃᑌᐤ, «ᐁ ᓵᑫᐍᔮᐣ, ᑮ ᒪᑌᐧ ᐊᐱᐤ ᓄᑌ, ᐁ ᒦᒋᓱᐟ,» ᐃᑌᐤ.

– ᐁᑯᑌ ᐁᑲᐧ ᑳ ᐅᐦᒋ ᐹᐢᑭᓵᐧᐟ ᐁᓴ, ᐁ ᑮ ᓂᐸᐦᐋᐟ ᐊᓂᐦᐃ, his first moose.

[FA:] ᐁᑯᓯ ᐍᐱᓄᐤ ᒌ ᐅᓰᓰᐱᒪ.

[MF:] ᒪᑖᐧᐣ ᒌ.

[7] «ᐁᑯᓯ ᐁᑲᐧ,» ᐃᑌᐤ, «ᐋ, ᓂᐯ ᑮᐋᐧᐣ ᐁᑲᐧ,» ᐃᑌᐤ. «ᑖᓂᓯ, ᑮᑲᐧᕀ ᒌ ᑭᓂᐸᐦᐋᐊᐧᐠ ᓰᓰᐸᐠ. ᓂᑎᑎᐠ,» ᐃᑌᐤ. «ᐁᐦᐊ, ᒫᑲ ᓂᐍᐱᓈᐊᐧᐠ.» – «ᐄᐦ. ᑖᓄᐦᑭ ᒫᑲ ᑳ ᐆᐦ ᐍᐱᓇᒋᐠ, ᓂᑎᑎᐠ,» ᐃᑌᐤ. «ᐊᔭ, ᐁ ᓂᐸᐦᐊᐠ ᒧᓴᐧ.» – «ᐋ, ᐊᐊᐧᐢ. ᓂᑎᑎᐠ,» ᐃᑌᐤ. «ᑖᐯᐧ – ᑲᑫᐧᔮᐦᐅᐠ.»

– « ᐋ, ᑲᑫᐧᔩᐦᐅᐠ. » ᐁ ᐃᑖᐟ ᐁᓴ ᐅᓰᒥᓴ, ᐊᐊᐧ 'John-George' ᑳ ᑮ ᐃᑎᐦᐟ, Tommy, « ᒥᓴᑎᒪᐧᐠ ᓈᑎᑎᓴᐦᐅᐦᑯᐠ. » ᐁ ᓈᑎᑎᓴᐦᐋᐧᒋᐠ, ᐁᑲᐧ ᒣᑐᓂ ᐁ ᑲᑫᐧᔩᐦᐅᐟ, ᒌᑲᐦᐃᑲᐣ, – ᒨᐦᑯᒫᐣ, ᐁᑲᐧ ᒌᑲᐦᐃᑲᐣ, ᑭᑲ ᐃᓯ ᐋᐸᒋᐦᑖᒋᐠ ᓰᐢᑳᐧᐨ, ᐁ ᐹᐦ ᐲᐦᒋᐁᐧᐱᓇᕽ ᐁᑯᑕ in –

« ᐄᐦ. ᐱᔨᐢᐠ ᐊᐊᐧ ᐋᐧᐦ ᑖᐯᐧᐦᑕᐊᐧᐠ, ᓂᑎᑎᐠ, » ᐃᑌᐧᐤ.

– ᒨᔨ ᐁ ᐄᐧ ᑖᐯᐧᐦᑕᐋᐧᐟ, « ᑯᓂᑕ, » ᐁ ᐃᑌᔨᐦᑕᕽ. ᐁᑲᐧ ᒫᑲ ᐊᓂᐦ ᐁᑲᐧ ᑳ ᐹᐦ ᐴᓯᐁᐧᐱᓇᒥᔨᐟ –

« ᒥᑐᓂ ᐁ ᑲᑫᐧᔩᐦᐅᒋᐠ ᐁᑲᐧ, » ᐃᑌᐧᐤ, « ᐁ ᐃᐧᔨᐦᐱᒋᑫᒋᐠ, » ᐃᑌᐧᐤ. « ᐁᑲᐧ ᐊᓂ, » ᐃᑌᐧᐤ, « ᐁ ᑮᓯ ᐴᓯᔩᕽ ᐁᑲᐧ, » ᐃᑌᐧᐤ. « ᐊᔭ, ᓇᒪ ᑮᑲᐧᐩ ᓂᒪᓈᑖᐢᑎᒫᐊᐧᐠ, » ᐃᑌᐧᐤ, « ᓴᑳᓴ ᐆᐦᐃ, ᐆᒪᔨᑯᕽ, » ᐃᑌᐧᐤ, « ᒥᑐᓂ ᑯᓂᑕ ᐁᑯᓂ ᐁ ᐊᑎ ᑕᐦᑯᐦᒋᐱᒋᑫᔩᐣ, ᐊᐧᐦᐋᐧ, ᓂᒫᐦ ᒫᑯᐦᐋᐊᐧᐠ, » ᐃᑌᐧᐤ, « ᐁᑲᐧ ᐊᓂᒪ ᐃᑕ, ᐁᑲᐧ ᐆᑕ ᐱᑯ ᑕᓇᑮᔩᕽ, ᓂᑎᑖᐧᐣ, ᐊᓂᒪ ᐃᐢᐸᑎᓈᐤ, » ᐃᑌᐧᐤ. « ᐄᐦ. ᐁᑯᑕ ᐆᒪ ᑳ ᑮ ᐃᑐᐦᑌᔩᐣ, ᐁ ᐃᑕᐠ, » ᐃᑌᐧᐤ, « ᐊᓂᒪ hill ᐆᒥᓯ ᐁ ᐃᑐᐦᑌᔩᐣ, » ᐃᑌᐧᐤ, « ᐄᐦ. ᓈᐦᐊ ᑳ ᐱᒥᓯᕽ, ᓂᑎᑖᐤ, » ᐃᑌᐧᐤ. « ᐊᐧᐦᐋᐧ, ᒪᐧᔭᐢ ᐊᐦᐴ ᐁᑯᑕ ᐃᑐᐦᑌᔩᕽ, ᐃᔨᑯᕽ ᐁ ᓇᓈᐢᑯᒫᐟ ᒪᓂᑐᐊᐧ, » ᐃᑌᐧᐤ. « ᐁᑲᐧ ᐊᓂ, » ᐃᑌᐧᐤ, « ᑳ ᐸᐦᑯᓈᔩᕽ ᐁᑲᐧ, » ᐃᑌᐧᐤ, « ᐁᑯᓯ ᐃᓯ ᓰᐢᑳᐧᐨ, ᓂᐹᐦ ᐴᓯᐁᐧᐱᓀᓈᐣ ᐁᑲᐧ ᐁᑯᓯ ᐃᓯ ᓂᑮᐁᐧᐦᑕᑖᓈᐣ, » ᐃᑌᐧᐤ. « ᐁᑲᐧ ᓃᐱᔨ ᓂᑳᐦ ᑲᐢᑲᑖᐧᓀᐣ, » ᐃᑌᐧᐤ, « ᐁᑯᑕ ᐁ ᓃᐦᒋᐁᐧᐱᓇᒫᕽ, » ᐃᑌᐧᐤ. « ᐁᑲᐧ ᐊᓂ ᐁᑲᐧ, » ᐃᑌᐧᐤ, « ᓈᐯᓯᓴᐠ, » ᐃᑌᐧᐤ, « ᐁᐩ, ᑳ ᓲᐦᑭᒪᑭᐠ, » ᐃᑌᐧᐤ, « ᑕ ᓈᑕᐦᑭᐠ ᒥᐦᑕ. ᐁᑲᐧ ᒦᓇ ᐊᓂᐦᐃ ᐊᑳᐧᐋᐧᓇ (ᒥᐢᑎᑲᐧ a certain way ᐁ ᑮ ᐃᓯᓈᑲᐧᐦᑭ, ᐊᔨᐢ ᒫᓇ ᐆᒥᓯ ᑮ ᐃᑕᒧᐦᑖᐊᐧᐠ) ᐁᑯᓂ ᐊᓂᐦᐃ ᐁ ᓈᑕᐦᑭᐠ ᐁᑲᐧ. ᐊᐧᐦᐋᐧ, ᒥᑐᓂ ᐁᑲᐧ, ᐊᑳᐧᐋᐧᐣ ᐆᒪ ᐁ ᐅᓰᐦᑖᔩᕽ, ᐋᓴᐩ ᐃᐧᔨ ᑳ ᑮ ᐅᒫᒫᔩᐣ, » ᐃᑌᐧᐤ, « ᐁ ᒫᒋ ᐹᓂᓵᐁᐧᐟ, » ᐃᑌᐧᐤ. « ᐁᑯᓯ, » ᐃᑌᐧᐤ, « ᐊᔨᐢ, » ᐃᑌᐧᐤ, « ᐁ ᑕᑯᐦᑌᔩᕽ ᐁᑲᐧ, » ᐃᑌᐧᐤ, « ᐁᑲᐧ ᓅᓰᐦᑖᓈᐣ ᐊᓂᒪ ᐊᑳᐧᐋᐧᐣ, » ᐃᑌᐧᐤ, « ᐁᑲᐧ ᐁ ᐴᓇᒫᕽ, ᓇᐦᐃᔨᑯᕽ ᐹᐦ ᐴᓇᒧᐠ. ᐃᑌᐤ ᐆᐦᐃ ᓈᐯᓯᓴ, » ᐃᑌᐧᐤ.

– ᐁ ᐹᐦ ᐲᑭᓂᓵᐋᐧᑕᒪᐋᐧᐟ ᐁᑎᑫᐧ ᐅᒫᒫᐊᐧ, ᐁᑯᑌ ᐁᓴ ᐁ ᐊᑎ ᐹᓂᓴᒥᔨᐟ.

[8] « ᐁᑯᓯ, » ᐃᑌᐧᐤ, –

– ᐁᑲᐧ Mary-Jane ᐊᔨᐢ (ᒦᓇ ᐊᐊᐧ ᑳ ᑮ ᓂᒐᐃᐧᓂᐱᐨ ᐊᐊᐧ States, ᐁᐦ), ᐁᑲᐧ ᐊᓂᑭ two boys, John-George ᐁᑲᐧ Tommy, ᐁᑲᐧ the old man ᐁ ᑮ ᓀᐃᐧᒋᐠ, ᐁᑲᐧ Eliza. ᐄᐦ. ᒫᐧᐨ, Eliza ᐸᑲᐦᑲᒼ – ᒨᔭ ᐆᒪ ᐅᐦᒋ ᐁ ᒪ ᒫᒥᐢᑰᒫᐟ ᐁᑯᓂ, she must have been married already, ᐄᐧᐸᐨ ᐊᔨᐢ ᐸᑲᐦᑲᒼ ᐁ ᑮ ᐅᓈᐯᒥᐟ.

> «ᐁᑯᓯ,» ᐃᑘᐤ, «ᐊᔨᕽ, ᐁ ᐹᓂᓵᐍᐟ ᐁᑲᐧ ᑲᐯ ᐊᔨᕽ,» ᐃᑘᐤ, «ᐊᐧᐦᐋᐧ, ᒥᑐᓂ ᐁᑲᐧ ᐊᑳᐧᐋᐧᐣ ᐃᔨᑯᕽ,» ᐃᑘᐤ. «ᓲᐢᑳᐧᐟ ᓇᐦᐃᔨᑯᕽ ᐁ ᐃᐧᔨᓄᐟ ᐊᐊᐧ ᒨᓴᐧ,» ᐃᑘᐤ. «ᐋ, ᑫᑕᐦᑕᐍ ᐁᑲᐧ,» ᐃᑘᐤ, «ᐃᐧᔨᓇᐧ ᐁᑲᐧ,» ᐃᑘᐤ, «ᒥᑐᓂ ᐁ ᐃᐧᔨᓄᐟ, ᐁᑯᓂ ᐁᑲᐧ ᐁ ᒌᓵᐋᐧᑕᕽ ᐆᐦᐃ ᐃᐧᔨᓇᐧ ᐁᑲᐧ,» ᐃᑘᐤ. «ᐊᐊᐧ Mary-Jane ᐁ ᐊᐱᓰᓯᓯᐟ,» ᐃᑘᐤ, «supper ᐁ ᐊᔮᔮᕽ,» ᐃᑘᐤ, «ᒫᑲ ᐁ ᐊᑎ ᐅᑖᑯᓯᐠ,» ᐃᑘᐤ, «ᐊᑳᐧᐋᐧᓂᕽ ᐆᒪ ᒌᑲᐦᑕᐤ ᐁᑯᑕ,» ᐃᑘᐤ, «ᐁᑲᐧ ᐊᐊᐧ Mary-Jane ᐁᑯᑕ ᐁ ᐊᐱᐟ,» ᐃᑘᐤ, «ᒫᑲ ᒨᔭ ᐁ ᒥᓯᑭᑎᐟ. ᐁᑲᐧ ᐊᔭ, ᐊᐊᐧ ᓂᒫᒫ ᐁᑲᐧ ᐁ ᒌᓵᐋᐧᑕᕽ ᐁᑲᐧ ᐃᐧᔨᓇᐧ,» ᐃᑘᐤ, «ᐁᑯᑕ ᐯᔭᐠ ᐊᐊᐧ ᓇᓭᐢᑕᐤ ᒥᐢᑎᐠ ᐁ ᒋᒪᓯᐟ, ᑭᓯᐋᐧᐠ,» ᐃᑘᐤ, «ᑳ ᐯ ᑌᐧᐦᐅᐟ ᐁᑯᑕ ᐆᐦᐅᐤ,» ᐃᑘᐤ, «ᐁ ᐯ ᑳᐦ ᑭᑐᐟ,» ᐃᑘᐤ, «ᐁᑲᐧ ᐊᐊᐧ Mary-Jane ᐁ ᐄᐧᓴᑭ ᑯᐢᑖᐟ, ᐁ ᒥᓯ ᒫᐦ ᒫᑐᐟ,» ᐃᑘᐤ. «ᑳᐩ, ᐁᑳᔭ ᒫᑐ. ᐁ ᓅᐦᑌᐦᑲᑌᐟ ᐊᓇ ᐄᐧᐢᑕ ᐆᒪ ᐁ ᐋᐧᐸᐦᑕᕽ ᐆᒪ ᐃᐧᔮᐢ ᐁ ᓅᐦᑌᒦᒋᐟ, ᐃᑌᐤ ᑳ ᑮ ᐅᒫᒫᔮᐣ,» ᐃᑘᐤ. «ᐁᑯᓯ ᐊᓇ ᐆᐦᐅᐤ, ᑯᓂᑕ ᒫᓇ ᐆᒥᓯ ᐁ ᐃᑑᑕᕽ, ᑖᐱᐢᑰᐨ ᑮᑲᐧᐩ ᐁ ᐹᐦ ᐲᒥᐢᑫᐧᔨᐟ, ᒥᑐᓂ ᐁ ᐄᐧ ᐋᐧᐸᐦᑕᕽ ᐆᒪ ᑮᑲᐧᐩ,» ᐃᑘᐤ, «ᑫᑕᐦᑕᐍ ᑳ ᓯᐯᐧᐦᐋᐧᐟ,» ᐃᑘᐤ.

[9] «ᐋᐧᐦᐋᐧ,» ᐃᑘᐤ, «ᐁᑲᐧ ᐊᓂ, ᐃᐢᐲ ᐁᑲᐧ ᐁ ᐹᐢᑌᑭ ᐆᐦᐃ,» ᐃᑘᐤ. «ᐋ, ᒨᔭ ᐁᑲᐧ ᓂᑲ ᑮᐋᐧᓈᐣ, ᓂᑎᑌᔨᐦᑌᐣ,» ᐃᑘᐤ «ᒥᑐᓂ ᑭᓀᐧᐢ ᓂᑲ ᒦᒋᓈᐣ,» ᐃᑘᐤ, «– ᐊᔨᐋᐧᐠ ᐃᐦᑭᐣ ᐁ ᐊᑎ ᐹᐢᑌᔨᑭ, ᒪᐦᑎ ᐁᑲᐧ ᑮᐍᑕᐣ, ᐊᔭ, ᑭᓀᐱᑯ ᒪᐢᑯᑌᕽ ᐃᑐᐦᑌᑖᐣ, ᑳ ᐃᓯᐟ ᓂᒫᒫ,» ᐃᑘᐤ. «ᐋᐧᐦᐋᐧ, ᓂᒫᒫ.» –

[GP:] – but in the meantime, back at Snake Plain –

– ᐁᑲᐧ ᐊᐊᐧ ᐃᑘᐤ, ᒪᒨᐦᐅᐤ ᑳ ᑮ ᐃᑎᐦᐟ ᐄᐧᐊᐧ (ᐁᑎᑫᐧ outside ᐁ ᐊᔭᔮᐟ, ᐁ ᐸᐴᓇᕽ outside, ᒪᑖᐧᐣ ᒌ ᐁ ᐸᐦᑫᐧᓯᑲᓂᐦᑫᐟ), ᐊᔨᕽ, ᐁ ᐯ ᐲᐦᑎᑫᐧᐟ, «ᐋᐧᐦᐋᐧ,»

ᐃᑌᐤ ᐁᓴ, ᐅᓈᐯᒪ, «ᑭᔭ ᒫᓇ, ᐁᑳᔭ ᐄᐧᐦᑳᐨ ᑮᑲᐧᐩ
ᐁ ᐲᑫᐧᔨᐦᑕᒥᐦᐃᑯᔭᐣ. ᑲᔮᐢ ᐆᒪ ᑭᑖᓂᓯᓇᐤ, ᓇᔦᐢᑕᐤ
ᐊᐋᐧᓯᓴ ᐁ ᐱᒋᒋᐠ, ᐁᑳ ᐊᐦᐴ ᓈᓂᑕᐤ ᐁ ᐄᐧ ᑲᑫᐧ ᑭᐢᑫᔨᐦᑕᒪᐣ
ᐃᑌ ᑕ ᐊᔮᒋᐠ, ᑖᓂᓯ ᑕ ᐃᓯ ᐊᔮᒋᐠ,» ᐃᑌᐤ ᐁᓴ ᐅᓈᐯᒪ,
ᐁᑯᓯ ᐊᑎ ᐊᐧᔭᐄᐧᐤ ᑳᐃᐧ. ᐁᑲᐧ ᐋᓴᐩ ᒦᓇ ᑮᑳᐧᐩ ᐁᑎᑫᐧ
ᐁ ᐄᐧ ᓈᑕᕽ in the tent – ᑳ ᒪᑌᐧᒥᓯ ᐹᐦ ᐹᐦᐱᔨᐟ, «ᐃᔭᐤ,
ᑖᓂᓯ ᐁᑲᐧ ᐁ ᒪ ᒨᐦᒍ ᐊᔮᔭᐣ ᒌ ᐁᑲᐧ.» ᐃᑌᐤ ᐁᓴ ᐅᓈᐯᒪ.
«ᓇᒨᔭ,» ᐃᑎᐠ ᐁᓴ, ᐊᔭ, «ᐁ ᐊᐧᐃᐧᔭᑌᔨᒪᐠ ᐊᐊᐧ,»
ᐃᑌᐧᐤ, «ᐊᐊᐧ, ᐊᔭ, ᒨᓂᔮᐢ ᐁᓴ ᐁ ᑮ ᓂᐸᐦᐋᐟ ᒨᓴᐧ, ᐁᑲᐧ
ᐁ ᐊᑳᐧᐁᐧᐟ ᑭᑖᓂᓯᓇᐤ, ᐁᑲᐧ ᐊᐊᐧ ᐃᐢᑫᐧᓯᐢ ᐁ ᐄᐧᓴᑭ ᑯᓯᐟ
ᐊᓂᒪ» (you know, ᐁ ᓂᑕᐋᐧᐯᓇᐋᐧᐟ), «ᐁᑲᐧ ᓰᐢᑲᐧᐨ
ᐁ ᒉᑳᐧ ᒦᒋᓱᒋᐠ, ᑳᐦᑫᐊᐧᐠ ᐁ ᒦᒋᒋᐠ, ᓰᐢᑳᐧᐟ ᒥᔦ ᐊᔮᐊᐧᐠ,»
ᐁ ᐃᑌᐧᐟ. ᐁᑯᓯ ᐊᓂᒪ ᑖᐯᐧ ᐁ ᑮ ᐃᐦᑭᓂᔨᐠ, ᒪᑖᐧᐣ ᒌ
ᐊᓂᒪ one or two days after ᑳ ᑕᑯᐱᒋᔨᐟ. –

«ᐊᐧᐦᐋᐧ, ᓂᒫᒫ. ᐁᑳᔭ ᐁᑯᑌ ᐃᑐᐦᑌᑖᐣ, ᒫᑲ ᒦᓇ
ᑭᑲ ᒉᐢᒐᓴᐦᑳᐣ, ᓂᑎᑖᐤ,» ᐃᑌᐧᐤ, «ᐁᑯᑌ ᐁ ᑕᑯᐦᑌᔮᕽ,»
ᐃᑌᐧᐤ, «ᑳ ᑮ ᒨᓇᐦᐊᐢᑫᐧᔮᕽ,» ᐃᑌᐧᐤ, «ᑯᓂᑕ ᐁᑲᐧ ᐁᑯᓂ
ᐁ ᐃᑐᐦᑕᑖᒋᐠ,»

– ᐅᐦᑯᒪ ᐁᑲᐧ ᐅᒧᓰᒪ ᐊᔨᕽ, ᒪᒨᐦᐅᐤ ᑳ ᑮ ᐃᑎᐦᐟ, ᐁᑲᐧ and his mother –

«ᒦᒋᐃᐧᐣ ᓇᔦᐢᑕᐤ ᐁ ᑮ ᐯᑖᒋᐠ. ᐊᔨᐋᐧᐠ ᐃᐦᑭᐣ ᐯᒥᓇᐊᐧᓯᒋᐠ
ᐊᓂᔦ, ᐁ ᐄᐧᐦᑯᐦᑫᒧᒋᐠ, ᑕ ᐯ ᒫᐦ ᒦᒋᕽ ᑳᐦᑫᐊᐧᐠ, ᑯᓂᑕ ᐁᑲᐧ ᐆᒥᓯ
ᐁ ᐃᐢᑯᑌᐦᑫᕽ outside,» ᐃᑌᐧᐤ.

– ᐁᑯᑕ ᐊᓂᒪ ᒪᒨᐦᐆᓯᐢ ᑳ ᑮ ᐊᔮᒋᐠ, ᐁᑯᑕ, Snake Plain, Willy Dreaver ᒦᓇ
ᒫᓇ ᐁᑯᑕ ᑮ ᐊᔮᐤ ᐱᔨᐢᐠ, ᐁᑯᑕ ᐆᒪ,

«ᐊᔨᕽ, ᐁᑲᐧ ᒫᓂᓇᑭᐢ ᐊᔨᓯᔨᓂᐊᐧᐠ ᐆᒪ ᐁ ᐯ ᒦᒋᓱᒋᐠ, ᒥᑐᓂ
ᐁ ᒥᐦᒉᑎᕽ,» ᐃᑌᐧᐤ.

– well, ᐋᐧᐦ ᑮᐁᐧᔨᒋ, ᐁ ᑮᓯ ᒦᒋᓲᐦᐋᐟ, ᑳᐦᑫᐊᐧᑲᐧ ᐁ ᒥᔮᐟ ᐊᐊᐧ ᓅᒋᑫᐧᓯᐤ, ᐊᓂᐦᐃ
ᐅᒫᒫᐊᐧ, the old man. ᑲᐦᑭᔭᐤ ᐁᑯᓯ,

«ᐊᔨᐋᐧᐠ ᐃᐦᑭᐣ, ᐊᐄᐧᓂᐸᐣ ᐁᑲᐧ ᑳᐦᑫᐊᐧᑲᐧ ᐁ ᒉᐢᑕᓴᐦᑫᐟ,»
ᐁ ᐃᑌᐧᐟ.

ᐁᐊᐧᑯ ᑳ ᑮ ᐃᓯ ᑯᐢᑕᕽ.

> «ᐁᑯᓯ,» ᐃᑎᐧᐤ, «ᓲᐢᑳᐧᐨ ᐁᐊᐧᑫᐧ ᐊᓂᒪ ᑳ ᑮ ᑯᐢᑕᒫᐣ ᓴᒫᐠ
> ᓲᐢᑳᐧᐨ, ᑲᐦᑭᔭᐤ ᒉᐢᑕᓴᐦᑫᐤ,» ᐃᑎᐧᐤ.

[10] ᒫᑲ ᐁᓴ, that's the first, ᑲᔮᐢ ᑳ ᓂᐸᐦᑖᐟ ᐊᐃᐧᔭᐠ ᑮᑲᐧᐩ, ᐅᐢᑭ ᐊᔭ ᓂᐢᑕᑦ, ᐁᑯᓯ ᐁ ᑮ ᐃᑑᑕᒥᕽ, ᐁ ᐄᐧᐦᑯᐦᑫᐦᐃᐦᐟ ᑖᐱᐢᑰᐨ, ᐁᑲᐧ ᒥᓇ ᐁ ᐊᓴᐦᑫᕽ like, you know. ᐁᑯᓯ ᐁᑎᑫᐧ ᐊᓂᒪ ᐊᓂᒪ ᑳ ᐆᐦ ᐃᑑᑕᒫᐦᐟ.

II

Reserve Life

5.
Lost and Found

Glecia Bear

[GB:] â, êkos êtikw êkwa --
[FA:] cêskwa.
êkw ê-wî-âcimostâkoyahk êkwa,
ê-kî-wanisihkik osîmisa êsa kayâs.

[1] nisîmis awa, ayi, *'Gigi'* isiyîhkâsow, kwâkopîwi-sâkahikanihk, ayinânêw ê-itahtopiponêt, pêyakosâp niy ê-itahtopiponêyân. êkwa nikî-- nikî-nitaw-âyamihân êwakw ânima kîkisêpâ ê-ni-- ê-nitawi-saskamoyân, nimâmâ aw ê-wîcêwak ê-nitawi-saskamoyân anima. ê-pê-kîwêyâhk êkwa, nipâpâ êkwa – nikî-wîhtamâkonân sâsay, otâkosihk is ê-wîhtamâkoyâhk, mostos aw ê-wî-otawâsimisit nânitaw ôtê sakâhk; êkwa, "aswahohk!" itwêw, "tasamânihk [*sic*];" (kayâs mâna kî-tasamânihkêwak [*sic*] êkota mostoswak ê-asikâpawicik), "asawâpamihk êwakw ân[a] ânîcâniw [*sic; cf.* ônîcâniw]!" itwêw, "sêskisici, pimitisahwâhkêk!" nitit-- nititik awa nipâpâ; "ki-- ka-pimitisahwâwâw, mâk êkây cîk ôhci ka-pimitisahwâyêk, ka-- nâh-nakîci, ka-kiskêyihtam ê-pimitisahwâyêk, piko wâhyaw -- wâhyawês ohci piko ka-p-- ka-pimitisahwâyêk, êkâ ka-wâpamikoyêk," itwêw.

[2] êk ôma, mwêhc êkwa ê-pê-takosiniyâhk awa nimâmâ, ayamihêwikamikohk ohci ê-pê-takohtêyâhk, mostos awa, tâpwê ôho nipâpâ kâ-kî-itwêt k-âsawâpamâyâhk, mwêhci kâ-pimi-sipwêhtêt ana mostos, ây, êy, kwayask tôhtôsâpoy ay-ayâw; ê-wî-ati-sêskisit. tâpwê pikw êkwa kâ-pîhtikwêpahtâyân êkwa nêtê aya, ê-wîsâmak ana nisîmis. "wîcêwin," nititâw awa, "ka-nitawi-- ka-pimitisahwâyahk ana mostos!" nitit-- – nipapâsimâw, sâsâkihtiw, êkos îsi, môya wâhyaw êtikwê ê-itêyihtamâhk ayis. sâsâkihtiw, niya wiya kêyâpit nipohtiskên nicayiwinisisa ôma kâ-kî-nitawi-saskamoyân. mâka môya nimît-- nimîcison, êkwa ayi – kayâs ayis mâna, piko môya ka-mîcisoyan, k-âcimisoyan ka-saskamoyan, môy tâpiskôc anohc. kikî-oc-- kikî-ocihcihkwanapin ê-saskamonahikawiyan ayamihêwikamikohk, anohc êkwa kinîpawin ê-sa--, kicihcîhk êkwa kimiyikawin êkwa

[GB:] Well, and now, I guess --
[FA:] Wait.
Now she is going to tell us how she and her little sister were lost long ago.

[1] My little sister is called *Gigi*, we lived at *kwâkopîwi-sâkahikanihk*, she was eight years old, and I, I was eleven years old. And I had been to church early that morning to take communion, I had gone with my mom to take communion. On our way home, my dad – he had told us, telling us the previous evening already, that one cow would be calving somewhere in the bush over here; so he had said, "Watch out for her at the smudge!" (they used to make smudges long ago, with the cows standing about there), "Look out for that female!" he had said, "When she goes into the bush, then you all follow her!" my dad had said to me; "you follow her, but you should not follow her too closely, for when she stops now and then [*sc.* during contractions], she will know that you are following her, you have to follow her from afar -- from a little distance, so that she will not see you," he had said.

[2] And then, just as we were getting home, my mom and I, as we were arriving home from church, at that moment the cow, the very one for which my dad had told us to look out, was going off, wow, hey, she had lots of milk; she was heading into the bush. So I straight away ran inside over there and asked my little sister along. "Come with me," I said to her, "to follow that cow!" I said to her – I rushed her, she was barefoot but came like that, for we did not think it would be far. She was barefoot but I, I still wore the clothes in which I had gone to communion. But I had not eaten – for in the old days you had to fast before you went to confession and communion, not like today. You used to kneel in church when you were given communion, whereas today you stand and the host is put in your

saskamowin, ê-saskamonahisoyan; mîna môy âyamihêwiyiniw, konit êkwa ayisiyiniw kitati-saskamonahik; mistahi pîtos ahpô êwakw ânima êkw ânohc ayamihâwin k-ây-ispayik. kîkwây êtikwê ka-kî-tâpwêwakêyihtamihk, pahkw-âyamihâwin ahpô môniyâwi-ayamihâwin[a] êkwa ôm ânohc kâ-ispayik; kayâs kî-kihcêyihcikâtêw pahkw-âyamihâwin. tâspwâw wiya niya kêyâpic êwako ê-pimitisahamân misakâmê; kîkwây ninîkihikwak kâ-kî-kiskinahamawicik, môy wîhkât ka-kî-pakitinamân, êkosi ka-isi-nakataskêyân, kîkwây kâ-kî-nakatamawicik.

[3] êkos êkwa, kâ-sipwêhtêyâhk awa nisîmis awa, nipimitisahok, tâpwê nipâpâ kâ-kî-itwêt, "wâhyaw ohci pimitisahohk!" kâ-itwêt. mayaw kâ-- ana kâ-wî-nakît mostos, êkosi mân ê-kî-nawakipayihoyâhk ê-apiyâhk; têpiyâhk ê-ati-wâpamâyâhk ê-ati-nôkosit, tânitê kâ-itohtêt.

[4] wahwâ, kêtahtawê êkot[ê] ê-takohtêyâhk, pôt âw ôtê kî-pimicikâpawiw awa (kinwês mâk ê-pimohtêyâhk, mitoni wâhyaw anim êtikw ê-ocawâsimisit), êkotê kâ-pimicikâpawit ê-nôhâwasot. wahwâ, êkw âni kâ-itohtêyâhk, wah, nimôcikêyihcênân êkotê, wahwâ, moscosos awa ê-- ê-nônic awa. nipakwahcêhonis awa, nisîpêkiskâwasâkâs ohci, *belt* ana kâ-tahkopitak okwayâhk, awa nisîmis êkwa êkoni ê-miciminât; êkwa niya ê-îkinak ana mostos, iyikohk mistahi tôhtôsâpoy ê-ayât; konit ê-pâh-pâhpiyâhk êkota, ê-mêtawâkêyâhk anima tôhtôsâpoy, ê-âh-îkinamawak awa nisîmis wîhkwâkanihk. ê-kî-sîkopitimâyâhk êkw ânih ôtôhtôsima awa mostos êkwa, nitah-- nitahkitisahwâw êkwa. tâpwê êkwa kâ-sipwêhtêt, nitat-âskowânân awa moscosos ê-pimitisahwât, nêsowisiw awa moscosos awa.

[5] wahwâ, kêtahtawê êkwa, sîpîsis ê-pimihtik, êkot[a] êkwa ana mostos êkwa môya wî-âsowaham ana. kâ-pasastêhwak êkw âna mostos, êkwa ê-pâhkopêtisahwâyâhk êkwa, kâ-wi-- (tâpwê piko, êcik âni itê ê-tastôstôkahk anima), k-âti-kotâwipayit ana mostos, ê-waskawît tahk âyiwâk ê-ati-kotâwipayit, ana mostos. êkos îs êkwa, moscosos an[a] êkwa, an[a] ît[a] âna kâ-tahkopitât anima nipakwahtêhon ohci – moscosos ana kâ-tahkopitak êkwa êkota,

hand and you put it in your mouth yourself; also, it is not the priest but an ordinary person who is giving you communion; things are done very differently in church today. I do not know what one should believe, the Catholic Church or the White-Man's religions and what is going on today; in the old days, the Catholic Church was highly thought of. In fact, I myself still follow it all the way; what my parents had taught me, I would never let that go, and I will die with what my parents have left to me.

[3] And so we took off, with my little sister following me, exactly as my dad had said, "Follow her from a distance!" he had said. As soon as the cow was about to come to a halt, we would duck down and stay there; so long as we continued to keep her in view to see where she was going.

[4] Oh my, as we arrived over there, all at once there she stood sideways [*sc.* at a right angle to the path] (but we had walked a long way, it must have been far off where she had her calf), there she stood sideways, suckling her calf. Oh my, and now we went over there, oh, we were excited; oh my, the little calf was sucking. When I had tied it fast with my belt, from my sweater, around its neck, then my little sister held it [*sc.* the calf]; and then I, I milked the cow, she had so much milk; we just kept laughing, then, as we played with the milk, with me squirting it on my little sister's face. When we had drained the milk from her teats, I drove the cow forward. And, indeed, she started walking, with us following behind the calf as it followed her, the calf was quite weak.

[5] Oh my, after a while there ran a creek, and there now the cow refused to cross. Then I whipped her and we chased her into the water (as it turned out, in fact, into a bog), and then the cow began sinking into it, and as she moved she began to sink in deeper and deeper. So now, as she [*sc.* my little sister] had tied the calf around the neck with my belt – with that [*sc.* belt] I tied the calf up, I tied

n-- sakâhk êkotâ, nitahkopitâw. êkos êkwa wî-nitawi-wîhtamâhk, awa mostos awa êkwa ê-ati-kotâwipayit awa; aspin âta wiy âpihtaw kêyâpic ê-nôkosit, êkwa kâ-sipwêhtêyâhk.

[6] êcik ân[i] êkwa, êkos êkwa ê-wanisiniyâhk. êkwa sâsay ôm ê-- ê-ati-takwâkik kâ-tâh-tahkâyâk ati. wahwahwâ, êkw âni kâ-pimohtêyâhk kâ-pimohtêyâhk, ê-mâtot awa nisîmis, êkwa niy ê-têpwêyân ê-têpwêyân nîsta, ka-kakwê-pêhtâkawiyâhk. êy, ê-sâ-sêkwâhtawîyâhk ita ê-kâh-kawisik-- ê-kâh-kawisihkik ôkik minahikwak, ita kâ-cawâsik ê-sîpâhtawîyâhk mân ê-pimohtêyâhk.

[7] piyis êkwa ê-tipiskâk êkwa, ôh, êkw ân[i] êkwa kâ-kimiwahk. sîpâ êkwa minahikohk, âsay mitoni nisikwâskocininân; sîpâ êkwa minahikohk êkwa k-âpiyân êkwa ayi, misi-minahik awa, êkot[a] êkwa ê-- ê-âpiyân, êkwa aw ânima nisîpêkiskâwasâkâs, ôta ê-tahkonak awa nisîmis ê-nawakapiyân, ê-akwanahak êkw âkota ê-wî-kakwê-kîsônak ôma, kanakê wiya ka-kîsôsit. kapê-tipisk êkos êkota êkwa, tâpwê ê-- nipâw, nîsta ninipân. ê-wî-wa-waniskâyâhk, ôh, kwayas pâh-pâkisitêpayiw ê-kîskicihk awa nisîmis awa. êkwa kayâs maskimotêkin ayis piko kikî-wiyâhtên – êkotowa pîhtawêsâkân, sîscâskwahonis [*sic; cf.* sîhcâskwahonis], kitôhtôsimak êkocow[a] ôhci maskimotêkin ê-kî-- ê-kî-osîhtâhk, êkotowa piko kikî-wiyâhtên. êkwa, kâ-itak êkw âna nisîmis, "nipîhtawêsâkân ôma nika-kêcikonên, nika-titipahpitên kisita," nititâw. tâpwê êkwa kâ-kêcikonamân anima nipîhtawêsâkân, nitâskipitên âpihtaw, niwâh-wêwêkahpitâw êkwa oh--, osita, êwak ôhc ânima.

[8] âsay mîn êkwa kâ-sipwêhtêyâhk êkwa, nipimohtânân kapê-kisik, iyikohk âsay mîna kâ-pimohtêyâhk. ma kîkwây ê-mîciyâhk, nistam kâ-tipiskâk anima k-ât-ôtâkosik ninôhtêhkatânân; ê-nôhtê-minihkwêt awa nisîmis, maskêkohk wiya mân ê-- ê-- ê-- kâ-otihtamâhk, ê-wâtihkêyân isko nipiy ka-miskamân, êkwa mâna nicihciy ohc ê-minahak anima nipiy. êkosi mâna nisipwêyâcihonân kâwi.

it up there in the bush. So now we were about to go and tell about the cow sinking in; from the distance, half of her could still be seen when we left.

[6] And with that, as it turned out, we were lost. It was already early fall, when it begins to get cold. Oh my oh my, and now we walked and walked, and my little sister was crying, and I myself was yelling and yelling so that we might be heard. Hey, we were crawling under fallen spruce-trees, we would crawl through underneath, where there was a little opening, as we went along.

[7] At last it was night, oh, and now it rained. So then I sat under a spruce-tree, our clothes were already quite torn by the branches; sitting under a spruce-tree, it was a big spruce-tree where I sat, there I held my little sister, huddled over her and covering her with my sweater so as to keep her warm, so that she, at least, would be warm. All night we were there like that, and she did indeed sleep, and I slept too. As we were waking up, oh, my little sister had badly swollen feet since she had cut herself. And in the old days, of course, all you had to wear was flour-sacking – slips made from that kind, and the brassiere for your breasts was also made from that kind, from flour-sacks, that kind was all you had to wear. Then I said to my little sister, "I will take off my slip and bind your feet with it," I said to her. And so I took off my slip and tore it in half and then wrapped her feet up with it.

[8] So now we left again, walking all day, and again we walked so much. We had nothing to eat, and the first night we felt hungry, towards evening; as my sister wanted to drink, I dug a hole when we reached a muskeg until I found water, and then gave her water to drink with my cupped hands. And so we would travel on some more.

[9] wâ, piyis êkwa sôs-- sôskwâc êkwa ayi, sâ-sikohtatâw anihi, mîna mân âhtahpitamân [*sic*] anima, nipîhcawêsâkânis anima ohci kâ-wi--, osita kâ-titipahpitamwak, mêscihtatâw. êkwa êwak ôma êkwa nisîhcâskwahonis [*sic*] êkwa (nitôhtôsimihk anim ôhci êkw âni, *my brassiere* âhk îtâp êtikw ânima), êwakw ân[i] ânim êk ôhci êkwa mîna kâ-titipahpitak, âpihtaw êkwa êwakw ânima mîn ê-tâskipitamân ê-wêwêkahpitamwak, katiskaw wanaskoc ôtê ôh ôsicisa. â, môy kinwês mêstâskocihcâw, wanihtâw anima pêyak ê-manâskocihtât. "môy êkwa, ma kîkw--, niwî-pimohtân ayiwâk," nititik. êkosi mât--, ê-mâtot iyikohk, piyis môy âhpô ê-pêhtâkosit, iyikohk ê-mâh-mâtot ahpô.

[10] kâ-nayômak êkwa; nîsta wiya ninêstosin; êkwa misikitiw anima êkwayikohk, ayinânêw ê-itahtopiponêt êkwa ê-kî-wiyinot. kâ-nayômak êkwa, ê-pimohtêyân ê-pimohtêyân, ê-nayômak. â, âsay mîn êkwa ê-tipiskâk, âsay mîn êkwa minahik, âsay mîna ninitonawâw, sêkw-âyihk êkota k-âyâyâhk. êkot[a] êkwa sêkw-âyihk êkwa ê-ayâyâhk, wâcistakâc, kâ-wâh-wâsaskotêpayik êkwa, iyikohk ê-maci-kîsikâk êkos ânima êwakw ânima tipiskâw. mâka môy nisâpopânân, minahikohk ayis sîpâ nitayânân, mâka sâpopêwa wiya nitayiwinisinân[a] ânima kâ-pimohtêyâhk, âh? êkot[a] êkwa sîpâ êkwa kâ--, âsay mîna k-âpiyân, âsay mîna pêyakwan, ê-cahkonak [*sic*] awa nisîmis, â, sîpêkiskâwasâkâs anima, wâcistakâc, sikwâskocin. êwakw ân[i] ânim[a] êkwa, âsay mîn ôhc êkwa, wiy êkwa n--, niy êkwa nama kîkway nitâpacihtân, wiy êkwa niwêwêkinâw êkota, âsay mîna nipâw, wiy ê-nêstosit. nîsta ninipân; ê-ati-wâpahk, kêtahtawê kâ-pêhtawak ôhow ê-kâh-kitot êkota, tahkohc êkota minahikohk. ê-koskopayit, koskomik awa wîsta nisîmis, sêmâk mâtow, "ê-wî-nôtinikoyahk," ê-itwêt ôho, otahtahkwana ôho mân ânis îsi ê-taswêkiwêpinât awa ôhow. nîst âkosi nititêyihtên, ê-pê-itapit mân ânima ita k-âpiyâhk.

[11] *well*, "kika-sipwêhtânaw," nititâw awa nisîmis; âsay mîna, nisipwêhtânân. âsay mâka mîn ê-nayômak ôm êkwa, sâsay mîn ê-sipwêhtêyâhk. wiy îyikohk ê-pâkisitêpayit ê--, nîsta wiya nisikwâskocinin niskâtihk misiwê, mâka niya wiya miscikwaskisinisa nikî-kikiskên êkospî. êkw ân[i] êkwa, aw ôhow êkwa, mayaw

[9] Well, at last she simply wore out the rags on her feet, as I kept moving them around, the little slip with which I had bound her feet, she wore it out completely. And now I used my brassiere (the cloth from my breasts, it was much like a bra), now I also used that to bandage her again, tearing it in half and wrapping it around her little feet, barely covering the tips. Well, it was not long before, being in the bush, she had none of that left, also having lost one by getting it caught. "Now I am not going to walk any farther," she said to me. And with that she cried so much that, finally, she could not even be heard any more, so much had she been crying.

[10] I carried her on my back now; but I, too, was tired; and she was quite big, she was eight and she used to be fat. I carried her on my back now, walking and walking and carrying her on my back. Well, and again it was night, and again I looked for a spruce-tree for us to stay underneath there. There we stayed, underneath, oh my God, there was lightning now, it was such a bad storm that night. But we did not get wet for we were beneath a spruce-tree, but our clothes got wet when we were walking, eh? And again I sat underneath there, the same thing again, holding my little sister, well, with that little sweater, oh my God, she was torn ragged. And again I used that one, I had nothing to use for myself, but I wrapped her up with that, and again she fell asleep for she was tired. I slept too; towards dawn, suddenly I heard an owl hooting there, on that spruce-tree above. My little sister woke up, the owl woke her up, too, and she started crying right away, "It is going to attack us," she said about it, as the owl would flap its wings like that [*gesture*]. I thought so, too, as it looked at us where we sat.

[11] Well, "We will leave," I said to my little sister; and again we left. But I was again carrying her on my back, as we left again. Her feet were so swollen and I, too, had cuts all over my legs but I wore oxfords that day. And now, indeed, as soon as we left, straight

ê-sipwêhtêyâhk, tâpwê piko kâ-sipwêpiyât [*sic*]; wâhyawês mitoni nêt[ê] êkwa kâ--, mîtosihk êkwa nêtê kâ-- k-âkosît. kâ-pê-kwêsk-âyât, êkos îs ânima, otahtahkwana mân ânis îs ê-isi-wêpinât, pâskac ê-pêhtâkosit kisik, ê-taswêkiwêpinât, tâpiskô [*sic*] ê-wî-nôtinikoyâhk. cîki ê-at-âyâyâhk, sâsay mîna kâ-sipwêpiyât [*sic*], sâsay mîna êkotê êkwa minahikohk akosîw. pêyakwan êkosi, itêhkê is ôma k-âyâyâhk pê-itâpiw, êkos ânima mân ê-itôtahk, ê-pêhtâkosit. "wahwâ," kâ-itak awa nisîmis, "ka-pimitisahwânaw awa," nititâw, "ahpô êtikwê awa ê-wî-kiskinohtahikoyâhk awa, kâ-itôtahk," nititâw. "namôy!" êtwêw [*sic*], "ê-wî-nôtinikoyahk ana, kâ-itôtahk," itwêw awa nisimis, "môy kika-- kika-pimitisahwânaw," itwêw. "môya," nititâw, "pim-- ka-pimitisahwânaw mahti," nititâw.

[12] tâpwê êkwa, kâ-pimitisahwâyâhk, âsay mîn âkos âna ôhow. nânitaw êtikwê anima nêwâw ê-âhci-twêhot ana ôhow mâna, êkwa ê-pimitisahwâ-- nipimitisahwânân êkwa. *boy*, kêtahtawê kâ-pêhtamân tâpiskôc awiyak ê-têpwêt. nitêpwân, mâk âyis nimiyiskwân, môy êkwayikohk nikisîwân. pêhtamwak mâk ês ânikik, *'Alec Bishop'* ana kî-isiyîhkâsow, *Louis Morin, Salamon* [*sic; pronounced as French*] *Morin*, êkwa *Johnny Sinclair* [*pronounced as French*]. êcik âni ê-itasiwêcik, nâh-nêwo, ê-wî-nâh-nêwicik ôkik ê-- nâpêwak; *Hudson's Bay store* ohci ê-miyihcik pâskisikana, môsosiniya, *rubbers*, ê-miyihcik ka-nitonâkoyâhkwâw; kapê-ay ôma ês ê-nitonâkoyâhkwâw anima nistam kâ-wanisiniyâhk, nistam anima k-âti-- kâ-kîsikâk. nîkân êsa misiwê kî-papâmipayiwak, ê-p-- ê-papâmi-nitonâkawiyâhk wâskahikanihk ê-- ôma, âh? êkos êkwa kiskêyihtamwak êkwa ayi, ê-wanisiniyâhk.

[13] êkos ânim êsa, êkâ kî-nakatâyâhk ana mostos anim îta kâ-micimoskowêt anima, k-âti-kotâwipayit anima,

> (*David* [*pronounced as French*] *Merasty,* ominahowiyiniw, êwakw ân[a] êsa, kî-masinahikêhâw êwakw ân[a] ê-mitihtikoyâhk, âh? mâk êkwa niwanahâhtikonân ê-kî-ayi--, îh! anim îyikohk kâ-kimiwahk, â, môya piyis êtikwê nôkwan ôm îta kâ-pimohtêyâhk, nikî-- nikî-mitihtikonân wiya –

away the owl also flew off; landing on a tree over there, quite a distance ahead of us. It turned to face us, in the same way [*sc.* as before], moving its wings like that [*gesture*] and, on top of it all, making [*sc.* strange] noises at the same time and flapping its wings as if it were going to attack us. When we got close, again it flew off, again landing on a spruce-tree over there. In the same manner, it looked towards where we were, doing the same thing, making [*sc.* strange] noises. "Oh my," I said to my little sister, "we will follow it," I said to her, "maybe it is going to show us the way when it does that," I said to her. "No!" she said, "it is going to attack us when it does that," said my little sister, "we will not follow it," she said. "No," I said to her, "we will follow it and see," I said to her.

[12] And indeed we again followed the owl, in the same way. It must have changed its perch about four times, and we followed it. *Boy*, all at once it seemed as if I heard someone yelling. I yelled but, of course, my voice was weak, I was not loud enough. But they heard it, Alec Bishop was his name, and Louis Morin, Salamon Morin, and Johnny Sinclair. It appears they had planned teams of four, these men would go in fours; they had been given guns, shells, and rubber overshoes by the Hudson's Bay store to search for us; they had been searching for us all the time since first we had got lost, since that first day. First of all they had gone around everywhere on horseback, looking for us in all the houses, eh? and then they knew that we were lost.

[13] If we had not left that cow where she got stuck in the bog, where she was sinking in,

> (David Merasty, a hunter, had been hired to track us, eh? but lost our tracks, look! because it had rained so much, well, finally our tracks were no longer visible, I guess, but he had tracked us –

tâspwâw kî-nitawi-miskawêw anihi mostoswa. ôtê isk ôkwayâhk, ana mostos êkwa sâsay ê-îsi--, mâka kêyâpit ê-pimâtisit, pê-wîhtam êsa êkwa, nêtê kwâkopîwi-sakâhikanihk ê-miskawât anihi mostoswa; nipâpâw[a] êkwa ê-pê-wîhtamawât. êkosi nipâpâ mêkiw, anihi mostoswa ka-pê-pâskisomiht; êkosi kî-pê-nipahêwak anihi mostoswa, anihi mîna moscososa.)

nikâh-kî-miskâkawinân êwako tipiskâw, *lantrens* [*sic*] ê-miyihcik êsa, kahkiyaw ôkik nâpêwak *Hudson's Bay* ohci ê-ohcîstamâhcik ê--, ê-âpacihtâcik *lantrens* [*sic*] ôho, âh? – kayâs êkamâ kîkwây *flashlights*. êk ôkik êkwa kâ-pêhtawâyâhkik, aw êkwa kâ-matwê-têpwêt, sêmâk nik-- nikiskêyihtên, nâpêw êkwa, âha.

[14] êkwa êsa itwêw awa êkwa, wâpikwayâs, *Louis* wâpikwayâs, "ta-tapasîwak ahpô êtikwê," itwêw êsa, "anis îsi wâskâhtê--, ka-wâskâhtêwak ôkik nâpêwak, ôm îtê tâpiskô [*sic*] kâ-pêhtawâyâhkwâw, ka-tapasîwak nânitaw isi, kostah-- kostahkwâwi, kotak ayisiyiniw kîkway itêyihtahkwâw[i]," îtwêw awa. êkos ês[a] êkwa awa pêyak êkwa pê-taskamohtêw êkwa, ê-pê-nâtikoyâhk, itê isi kâ-pêhtâkoyâhk. ê-matwê-têpwêt, â, nik-- êkwa mitoni nikêhcinâhon êkwa ayisiyiniw, "kimiskâkawinaw," nititâw awa nisîmis. nitêpwân, mâk âyis nikohtaskway, kâ-pê-sâkêwêt êkota *Alec Bishop*. tâpwê piko ê-pê-wâh-otihtinikoyâhk ê-matôt, ê-wâh-ocêmikoyâhk awa kisêyinîsis – môy, êkospî osk-âyiwiw, môy kisêyinîwiw.

[15] êkosi tâpwê pikw êkwa pâskisikan anima kâ-tahkonahk, nistwâw matwêwêhtâw. êkos ânikik môy kinwês ôkik kâ-wâskâhtêcik, êkota pê-takos-- pê-takopahtâwak. pâh-pêyak mistatimwa mîna miyâwak, mîciwin ê-pimohtatâcik êkota, môsosiniya, kahkiyaw kîkway, âh? wîstawâw ka-mîcisocik êkwa miskâkawiyâhki ka-piminawatikawiyâhk. êkos êkw âkota, sêmâk aw êkwa kotawêw *Louis* wâpikwayâs, ka-kakwê-mîcisoyâhk. ôh, môya kinwês, âsay kâ-- misiwê kâ-matwêwêhtâhk, aw êkwa kâ-matwêwêhtât, misiw îtê konita kâ-pêhtâkwahk[i] êkwa, nipah--, ôkik kîkway wîstawâw ê-miskâkawiyâhk ka-kiskêyihtâkwahk, misiwê matwêwêhtâwak. êkos êkwa, êkot[a] êkwa, niminahi--,

as a matter of fact, he had gone and found the cow.
She had already sunk in up to her neck but she
was still alive, he went back over there to
kwâkopîwi-sâkahikanihk to tell that he had found the
cow; he came back to tell my dad about it. So my dad
gave the cow up to be shot; and they came and killed
that cow, and also the calf.)

we would have been found the same night, they were given lanterns, all the men were provided with lanterns from the Hudson's Bay store to use, eh? – there were no flashlights in the old days. And those whom we now heard, the one who was yelling now, I knew right away that now it was a man [*sc*. not an animal], yes.

[14] And *wâpikwayâs*, Louis *wâpikwayâs* had said, "They may even run away," he had said, "let the men go around that way [*gesture*], over here where we think we have heard them, just in case they run away if they get scared and think it might be some strange person," he had said. And so one man had come straight across towards us to come and fetch us, towards where they had heard us. He could be heard yelling, well, and now I knew for certain that it was a human being, "We have been found," I said to my little sister. I yelled but, of course, my throat [*sc*. was weak], then Alec Bishop came into view there. Straight away he came and grabbed both of us and cried, he kissed both of us, this old man – no, he was young then, he was not an old man.

[15] And so, with the gun which he carried, he straight away shot three times. So it was not long before the others, who had gone around, came running there. Each of them had also been given a horse to ride, they carried food, shells, and everything, eh? for themselves to eat and to cook for us when we would be found. So then Louis *wâpikwayâs* right away made a fire so that we could try to eat. Oh, and it was not long before shots were fired all over, when he had fired his shots, shooting was now heard just everywhere, so that it would be known to these people, too, that we had been found, they were firing shots all over. So then they were going to give

tea êkwa niwî-minahikawinân ka-mîcisoyâhk, êy, kahkiyaw kîkway, *Hudson's Bay* wiy ôhci sôskwâ [*sic*] mîciwin ê-mêkihk. môy nikaskihtânân ahpô, ka-kohcipayihtâyâhk anima, *tea* anima, namôy nikî-mîcisonân, mwâc sôskwâc!

[16] êkos êkwa k--, êkwa *Louis* wâpikwayâs êkwa itwêw, ka-têht-- ka-têhtapiyâhk êkwa niyanân, êkw âna mistatim ê-sakâpêkinâcik nitêhtapinân êkwa ê-kîwêhtahikawiyâhk êkwa. nêt[ê] êkwa ê-takosiniyâhk, êkwa nîkinâhk êkwa, ayi (– kani tâpwê awa ôhow, ispî êkwa kâ-miskâkoyâhkik ôkik, an[a] êkwa ôhow, aspin ê-sipwêpiyât [*sic*], ana ôhow, êwakw ân[a] ê-kiskinohtahikoyâhk). nêt[ê] êkwa nîkinâhk êkwa ê-takosiniyâhk êkwa ê-sâkêwêyâhk êkwa, wâcistakâc wa-- mistatimwak, sôskwât êkw ê-ihtasit kwâkopîwi-sâkahikanihk ayisiyiniw, êkota ê-ayât, sôskwâ [*sic*] mistatimwak konita k-ay-- k-ây-itapicik, êkotê anima, *wagons* kiyikaw. êkw êcik âni mân e--, kisik ê-ayamihâcik, ayamihêwiyiniw êkota ê-ayât, ôma ka-kakwê-miskâkawiyâhk, êkota sôskwâ [*sic*] ê-ayamihât ayamihêwiyiniw, êkot[a] ânima kahkiyaw, ka-kakwê-miskâkawiyâhk.

[17] ê-sâkêwêyâhk êkwa, anima nêta [*sic*] n--, wiya niya sâsay ê-oskinîkiskwêsisiwiyân, "môy niwî--, môy niwî-itohtân niy âkotê," nititâw awa *Alec Bishop*, "iyikohk kâ-sikwâskociniyân," nititâw. "êy, êkây nânitaw itêyihta, *my girl*," nititik *Alec Bishop*, "iyikohk ka-miywêyihtâkwahk ê-miskâkawiyêk," itwêw, "mistah ôma ê-kitimâkêyimohk ôma," itwêw, "êkây kîkway nêpêwisiwin kikiskâkok!" itwêw, "kitakohtahitinân." êy, *boy*, êkotê ê-takohtêyâhk, konit âyisiyiniwak ka-ocêmikoyâhkwâw. *'Frank Séguin'* kî-isiyîhkâsow *Hudson's Bay store*, mistikôsiw [*sic*], êwakw âna konit ê-pê-âkwaskitinikoyâhk ê-- ê-mâtot; êkos êkwa, itwêw awa *Frank Séguin*, ayihk aya, "ayiwinisa," itwêw, "awiyak ka-pê-nâtam nêtê atâwêwikamikohk kîkway ka-pohtiskahkik," itwêw. tâpwê êkwa, êkotê êkwa itohtê-- itohtêw êkwa, awa kâ-- kâ-kî-wiyôhkomiyân [*sic*], ê-nâtahk êkwa kîkway êkota, *Hudson's-Bay*-ayiwinisa [*sic*], sôskwâc ê-miyikoyâhk an[a] ê-pohtayiwinisahikoyâhk.

us tea to drink there, so that we might eat, hey, everything, for the food had simply been given out by the Hudson's Bay. We were not even able to swallow the tea, we certainly could not eat at all!

[16] So then Louis *wâpikwayâs* said that we would ride on horseback, and we rode as they led the horse and we were taken home. Then, as we arrived over there at our house (– I forgot, this owl truly just flew away, that owl, once we had been found by these men, it was that owl that showed us the way home). As we arrived over there at our house and came into view, oh my God the horses, simply everybody in *kwâkopîwi-sâkahikanihk* was there, there simply were horses everywhere, and also wagons. They had apparently been praying all the while, with the priest there, that we might be found, the priest and everyone else had simply been praying there that we might be found.

[17] As we came into view now, over there, I of course was a young girl already, "I am not going to go over there," I told Alec Bishop, "with my clothes so torn up," I said to him. "Hey, do not think about it, my girl," Alec Bishop said to me, "there will be such joy that you have been found," he said, "since there was a lot of misery," he said, "do not let modesty get in the way!" he said, "We have brought you back." Hey, *boy*, and as we arrived over there, all kinds of people were just kissing us. Frank Séguin was the name of the Hudson's Bay store manager, a Frenchman, he came and just hugged us amid tears; and then he said, "As for clothes," he said, "let someone come and fetch something at the store over there for them to wear," he said. And, indeed, my late grandmother went over there and fetched things, Hudson's Bay clothes, he simply gave them to us and fitted us out with clothes.

[18] êkos êkwa êkot[a] êkwa, sâsay mîn êkw âkota niwi--, ês ê-kî-piminawasohk êkw ê-wî-asamikawiyâhk, ma kîkway, môy niwî-mîcisonân, môy nikî-mîcisonân, nikohtaskwânân[a] ê-wîsakêyihtamâhk. tâpwê piko wiy âwa nisîmis awa, nipêwinihk ê-kî-pimisimiht, êkosi tâpwê piko ê-itihkwâmit, ê-kîsôsimâcik; osita, iyikohk ê-kîskicihk, akâminakasiy[a] ê-kâh-kêcikwahomâcik; iyikohk ê-- ê-kîskicihk osicisa.

[19] aya cî êkwa ekosi -- êkw âwa nimâmâ ayi, môy kayâs ê-kî-isi-tahkopitâwasot, *Alice Derocher* asic êsa mân ê-- wîscawâw ê-nîsicik ê-nîso-sipwêhtêcik, âhci piko ê-nit-- wîstawâw ê-nitonâkoyâhkwâw; ê-papâmi-mâtot êsa nimâmâ.

[20] mâcika, êkos âta wiya ê-kî-miskâkawiyâhk, êkos êkwa kâh-kîwêwak êkwa kî--, ê-kî-kîs-âyamihâcik ê-- âsay mîna, êkota âsay mîn âkota niya nisaskamonahikawin, mâka nisîmis wiya mêskw [*sic*] âkospî ê-ohci-saskamot; nisaskamonahikawin nîsta. êkos êtikwê êkwa nîst êkwa ê-pimisiniyân, êkosi tâpwê piko nîsta kâ-isi-nipâyân; pâtos [*sic*] kîkisêpâ kâ-ka-koskopayiyân.

[21] nikî-kakwâtakâcihonân ani; nikî-wapâhtên ê-âyimahk, ayisiyiniw kâ-wanisihk. êkwa môy wîhkâc ê-ohci-kostâciyâhk ahpô wâkayôs kîkway ka-kostâyâhk, ê-mâmaskâtamân ê-kaski-tipiskâk kâ-kitocik, kîkway ka-sêkihikoyân, nama kîkway! nama kîkway ê-ohci-mâmitonêyihtamân. anohc êkwa, nânitaw ka-wanisiniyân, nikâh-nipahi-sêkisin! na-- nîso-kîsikâw ê-wanisiniyâhk, ôm êkw âya *next day*, mwêhc ânima ê-âpihtâ-kîsikâk kâ-miskâkawiyâhk.

[22] êkwa nêtê ê-wâpahtamân pêyakwayak, anis îsi (nimosôm n-- ayis mâna nâcowêw kî-nihtâ-tâpakwêw), anis îsi ê-kîskatahikâtêki anihi nîpisiya ôho, ê-kîskatahikâtêki anis îsi s--, sâkahikanisis pêyak êkotê anima ê-takohtêyâhk. kâ-wâpahtamân anih êkos îsi, êkwa maskosîsa mask-- ê-astêki anis îsi, ita tâpiskô [*sic*] [a]wiyak ê-kî-apit, êkw âwa nisîmis kâ-itak, "îh!" nititâw, "kiwî-takosininaw," nititâw, nistam anim ê-tipiskâk, ê-at-ôtâkosik, "kiwî-takosininaw," nititâw, "kimosôminaw êtikwê ôho mâka mîna ôta nânitaw ê-kî-tâpakwêt," nititâw ôma; "ôt[a] êtikwê mân âhpô ê-kî-pa-pîhtwât ôma, kâ-isinâkwahk," nititâw.

[18] So then again now they were going to -- they had cooked already and we were going to be fed, but we still would not eat anything, we could not eat as our throats still hurt. And as soon as my little sister had been put to bed, she fell asleep straight away even as they tucked her in for warmth; her feet were so cut up, and they pulled the thorns out with a needle; so cut up were her feet.

[19] And so --, and my mom, although she had just recently had a baby, had nevertheless gone out, together with Alice Derocher, the two of them together, and had searched for us; my mom crying as they went about.

[20] And now, of course, that we had been found, now the people went home after they had finished praying again, and then I was again given communion, but my little sister had not yet had her first communion at that time; I, on the other hand, was given communion. And I, too, when I lay down, must have fallen asleep immediately; it was morning before I woke up.

[21] We really had had a terrible time; I saw how hard it is when a person is lost. And we never were afraid, we were not even afraid of bears or anything else, and with the thunder, in the dark of the night, I marvel that I did not think of anything, anything at all, of which to be scared. If I were to be lost some place today, I would be scared to death! We were lost for two days, and were found exactly at noon on the following [*sc.* the third] day.

[22] And over there [*sc.* in the bush] I had seen one place, like that [*gesture*] (for my grandfather *nâcowêw* used to do much snaring), with the willows cut like that [*gesture*], they were cut like that [*gesture*], we had arrived at a little lake over there. When I saw the willows like this, and the grass piled up like that [*gesture*], as if someone had sat there, I had said to my little sister, "Look!" I had said to her, "we are nearly at home," that was the first night, towards evening, "we are nearly at home," I had said to her, "our grandfather must have done some snaring around here," I had said to her; "he must even have sat here and smoked, by the way it looks," I had said to her.

[23] mâk êsa môya, êcik âni mân êtik ôma kâ-mâcîcik, k-âsawâpicik ôma, êwak ôhc ânim êtikwê ês ânima, kî-itwêw nimosôm, anima kâ-kîskatahikâsocik anikik, êkwa nêma maskosîsa k-âstêki mân ôma, k-âs-- k-âswahikâcik [*sic; cf.* k-âswahikêcik] kâ-mâcîcik ôma; êkotowihk anim êsa ê-kî-otihtamâhk. konit ê-papâmohtêyân êkota, ê-papâmi-nitonamân, "ahpô êtikwê kîkway kî-ay-- kî-ay-- kî-ay-iskwahtamwak, kîkway ê-wêpinahkik," ê-itêyihtamân, konit âkot[a] ê-papâmi-nitonamân kîkway ka-mîciyâhk.

[24] êkos êtikwê.

[23] But it had not been that, it appears it must have been hunters on the lookout [*sc.* for game], it must have been for that, according to what my grandfather said, that the willow-bushes had been cut and the grass piled up over there, for the hunters watching for game; it was that kind of a place which we had reached. I had walked around there, looking around for something, thinking, "Perhaps they had something left over and have thrown it away," as I had looked around for something for us to eat.

[24] That is all, I guess.

[1] ᓂᓰᒥᐢ ᐊᐊᐧ, 'Gigi' ᐃᓯᔩᐦᑳᓯᐤ, ᑳᐧᑯᐲᐃᐧᓵᑲᐦᐃᑲᓂᕽ, ᐊᔨᓈᓀᐤ ᐁ ᐃᑕᐦᑐᐱᐳᓀᐟ, ᐯᔭᑯᓵᑊ ᓂᔭ ᐁ ᐃᑕᐦᑐᐱᐳᓀᔮᐣ. ᐁᑲᐧ ᓂᑮ ᓂᑕᐃᐧ ᐊᔭᒥᐦᐋᐣ ᐁᐊᐧᑯ ᐊᓂᒪ ᑮᑭᓭᐹ ᐁ ᓂᑕᐃᐧ ᓴᐢᑲᒧᔮᐣ, ᓂᒫᒫ ᐊᐊᐧ ᐁ ᐄᐧᒉᐊᐧᐠ ᐁ ᓂᑕᐃᐧ ᓴᐢᑲᒧᔮᐣ ᐊᓂᒪ. ᐁ ᐯ ᑮᐁᐧᔮᕽ ᐁᑲᐧ, ᓂᐹᐹ ᐁᑲᐧ – ᓂᑮ ᐄᐧᐦᑕᒫᑯᓈᐣ ᓵᓴᐩ, ᐅᑖᑯᓯᕽ ᐃᓯ ᐁ ᐄᐧᐦᑕᒫᑯᔮᕽ, ᒧᐢᑐᐢ ᐊᐊᐧ ᐁ ᐄᐧ ᐅᑕᐋᐧᓯᒥᓯᐟ ᓈᓂᑖᐤ ᐆᑌ ᓴᑳᕽ, ᐁᑲᐧ, «ᐊᓴᐧᐦᐅᕽ.» ᐃᑌᐧᐤ, «ᐊᑎᓴᒫᓂᕽ,» (ᑲᔮᐢ ᒫᓇ ᑮ ᐊᑎᓴᒫᓂᐦᑫᐊᐧᐠ ᐁᑯᑕ ᒧᐢᑐᓴᐧᐠ ᐁ ᐊᓯᑳᐸᐃᐧᒋᐠ), «ᐊᓴᐋᐧᐸᒥᕽ ᐁᐊᐧᑯ ᐊᓇ ᐅᓃᒑᓂᐤ.» ᐃᑌᐧᐤ, «ᓭᐢᑭᓯᒋ, ᐱᒥᑎᓴᐦᐋᐧᐦᑫᐠ.» ᓂᑎᑎᐠ ᐊᐊᐧ ᓂᐹᐹ, «ᑲ ᐱᒥᑎᓴᐦᐋᐧᐋᐧᐤ, ᒫᑲ ᐁᑳᔭ ᒌᑭ ᐅᐦᒋ ᑲ ᐱᒥᑎᓴᐦᐋᐧᔦᐠ, ᓈᐦ ᓇᑮᒋ, ᑲ ᑭᐢᑫᔨᐦᑕᑦ ᐁ ᐱᒥᑎᓴᐦᐋᐧᔦᐠ, ᐱᑯ ᐋᐧᐦᔭᐁᐧᐢ ᐅᐦᒋ ᐱᑯ ᑲ ᐱᒥᑎᓴᐦᐋᐧᔦᐠ, ᐁᑳ ᑲ ᐋᐧᐸᒥᑯᔦᐠ,» ᐃᑌᐧᐤ.

[2] ᐁᑲᐧ ᐆᒪ, ᒣᐧᐦᒋ ᐁᑲᐧ ᐁ ᐯ ᑕᑯᓯᓂᔮᕽ ᐊᐊᐧ ᓂᒫᒫ, ᐊᔭᒥᐦᐁᐃᐧᑲᒥᑯᕽ ᐅᐦᒋ ᐁ ᐯ ᑕᑯᐦᑌᔮᕽ, ᒧᐢᑐᐢ ᐊᐊᐧ, ᑖᐯᐧ ᐆᐦᐅ ᓂᐹᐹ ᑳ ᑮ ᐃᑌᐧᐟ ᑳ ᐊᓴᐋᐧᐸᒫᔮᕽ, ᒣᐧᐦᒋ ᑳ ᐱᒥ ᓯᐯᐧᐦᑌᐟ ᐊᓇ ᒧᐢᑐᐢ, ᐋᐩ, ᐁᐩ, ᑲᐧᔭᐢᐠ ᑑᐦᑑᓵᐳᐩ ᐊᔮᐤ, ᐁ ᐄᐧ ᐊᑎ ᓭᐢᑭᓯᐟ. ᑖᐯᐧ ᐱᑯ ᐁᑲᐧ ᑳ ᐲᐦᑎᑫᐧᐸᐦᑖᔮᐣ ᐁᑲᐧ ᓄᑌ ᐊᔭ, ᐁ ᐄᐧᓵᒪᐠ ᐊᓇ ᓂᓰᒥᐢ. «ᐄᐧᒉᐃᐧᐣ,» ᓂᑎᑖᐤ ᐊᐊᐧ, «ᑲ ᓂᑕᐃᐧ ᐱᒥᑎᓴᐦᐋᐧᔭᕽ ᐊᓇ ᒧᐢᑐᐢ.» ᓂᑎᑖᐤ – ᓂᐸᐹᓯᒫᐤ, ᓵᓴᑭᐦᑎᐤ, ᐁᑯᓯ ᐃᓯ, ᒨᔭ ᐋᐧᐦᔭᐤ ᐁᑎᑫᐧ ᐁ ᐃᑌᔨᐦᑕᒫᕽ ᐊᔨᐢ. ᓵᓴᑭᐦᑎᐤ, ᓂᔭ ᐃᐧᔭ ᑫᔮᐱᐨ ᓂᐳᐢᑎᐢᑫᐣ ᓂᒐᔨᐃᐧᓂᓯᓴ ᐆᒪ ᑳ ᑮ ᓂᑕᐃᐧ ᓵᐢᑲᒧᔮᐣ. ᒫᑲ ᒨᔭ ᓂᒦᒋᓱᐣ, ᐁᑲᐧ ᐊᔨ – ᑲᔮᐢ ᐊᔨᐢ ᒫᓇ, ᐱᑯ ᒨᔭ ᑲᒦᒋᓱᔭᐣ, ᑳ ᐋᒋᒥᓱᔭᐣ ᑲ ᓴᐢᑲᒧᔭᐣ, ᒨᔭ ᑖᐱᐢᑰᐨ ᐊᓄᐦᐨ. ᑭᑮ ᐅᒋᐦᒋᐦᑲᐧᓇᐱᐣ ᐁ ᓴᐢᑲᒧᓇᐦᐃᑲᐃᐧᔭᐣ ᐊᔭᒥᐦᐁᐃᐧᑲᒥᑯᕽ, ᐊᓄᐦᐨ ᐁᑲᐧ ᑭᓃᐸᐃᐧᐣ, ᑭᒋᐦᒌᕽ ᐁᑲᐧ ᑭᒥᔨᑲᐃᐧᐣ ᐁᑲᐧ ᓴᐢᑲᒧᐃᐧᐣ, ᐁ ᓴᐢᑲᒧᓇᐦᐃᓱᔭᐣ, ᒦᓇ ᒨᔭ ᐊᔭᒥᐦᐁᐃᐧᔨᓂᐤ, ᑯᓂᑕ ᐁᑲᐧ ᐊᔨᓯᔨᓂᐤ ᑭᑕᑎ ᓴᐢᑲᒧᓇᐦᐃᐠ, ᒥᐢᑕᐦᐃ ᐲᑐᐢ ᐊᐦᐴ ᐁᐊᐧᑯ ᐊᓂᒪ ᐁᑲᐧ ᐊᓄᐦᐨ ᐊᔭᒥᐦᐋᐃᐧᐣ ᑳ ᐊᔨᐢᐸᔨᐠ. ᑮᑳᐧᐩ ᐁᑎᑫᐧ ᑲ ᑮ ᑖᐯᐧᐊᐧᑫᔨᐦᑕᒥᕽ, ᐸᐦᑯ ᐊᔭᒥᐦᐋᐃᐧᐣ ᐊᐦᐴ ᒨᓂᔮᐃᐧ ᐊᔭᒥᐦᐋᐃᐧᓇ ᐁᑲᐧ ᐆᒪ ᐊᓄᐦᐨ ᑳ ᐃᐢᐸᔨᐠ, ᑲᔮᐢ ᑮ ᑭᐦᒉᔨᐦᒋᑳᑌᐤ ᐸᐦᑯ ᐊᔭᒥᐦᐋᐃᐧᐣ. ᑖᓯᐹᐧᐤ ᐃᐧᔭ ᓂᔭ ᑫᔮᐱᐨ ᐁᐊᐧᑯ ᐁ ᐱᒥᑎᓴᐦᐊᒫᐣ ᒥᓴᑳᒣ, ᑮᑳᐧᐩ ᓂᓃᑭᐦᐃᑲᐧᐠ ᑳ ᑮ ᑭᐢᑭᓇᐦᐊᒪᐃᐧᒋᐠ, ᒨᔭ ᐄᐧᐦᑳᐨ ᑲ ᑮ ᐸᑭᑎᓇᒫᐣ, ᐁᑯᓯ ᑲ ᐃᓯ ᓇᑲᑕᐢᑫᔮᐣ, ᑮᑳᐧᐩ ᑳ ᑮ ᓇᑲᑕᒪᐃᐧᒋᐠ.

[3] ᐁᑯᓯ ᐁᑲᐧ, ᑳ ᓯᐯᐧᐦᑌᔮᕽ ᐊᐊᐧ ᓂᓰᒥᐢ ᐊᐊᐧ, ᓂᐱᒥᑎᓴᐦᐅᐠ, ᑖᐯᐧ ᓂᐹᐹ ᑳ ᑮ ᐃᑌᐧᐟ, «ᐋᐧᐦᔭᐤ ᐅᐦᒋ ᐱᒥᑎᓴᐦᐅᕽ.» ᑳ ᐃᑌᐧᐟ. ᒪᔭᐤ ᐊᓇ ᑳ ᐄᐧ ᓇᑮᐟ ᒧᐢᑐᐢ, ᐁᑯᓯ ᒫᓇ ᐁ ᑮ ᓇᐊᐧᑭᐸᔨᐦᐅᔮᕽ ᐁ ᐊᐱᔮᕽ, ᑌᐱᔮᕽ ᐁ ᐊᑎ ᐋᐧᐸᒫᔮᕽ ᐁ ᐊᑎ ᓅᑯᓯᐟ, ᑖᓂᑌ ᑳ ᐃᑐᐦᑌᐟ.

[4] ᐊᐧᐦᐋᐧ, ᑫᑕᐦᑕᐁᐧ ᐁᑯᑌ ᐁ ᑕᑯᐦᑌᔮᕽ, ᔫᑎ ᐊᐊᐧ ᐆᑌ ᑮ ᐱᒥᒋᑳᐸᐃᐧᐤ ᐊᐊᐧ (ᑭᓀᐧᐢ ᒫᑲ ᐁ ᐱᒧᐦᑌᔮᕽ, ᒥᑐᓂ ᐋᐧᐦᔭᐤ ᐊᓂᒪ ᐁᑎᑫᐧ ᐁ ᐅᒐᐋᐧᓯᒥᓯᐟ), ᐁᑯᑌ ᑳ ᐱᒥᒋᑳᐸᐃᐧᐟ ᐁ ᓅᐦᐋᐧᐊᐧᓯᐟ. ᐊᐧᐦᐋᐧ, ᐁᑲᐧ ᐊᓂ ᑳ ᐃᑐᐦᑌᔮᕽ, ᐊᐧᐦ, ᓂᒨᒋᑫᔨᐦᑌᓈᐣ ᐁᑯᑌ, ᐊᐧᐦᐋᐧ, ᒧᐢᒍᓯᐢ ᐊᐊᐧ ᐁ ᓅᓂᐨ ᐊᐊᐧ. ᓂᐸᑲᐧᐦᒉᐦᐅᓂᐢ ᐊᐊᐧ, ᓂᓰᐯᑭᐢᑳᐊᐧᓵᑳᐢ ᐅᐦᒋ, belt ᐊᓇ ᑳ ᑕᐦᑯᐱᑕᐠ ᐅᑲᐧᔮᕽ, ᐊᐊᐧ ᓂᓰᒥᐢ ᐁᑲᐧ ᐁᑯᓂ ᐁ ᒥᒋᒥᓈᐟ, ᐁᑲᐧ

ᓂᔭ ᐁ ᐄᑭᓇᐠ ᐊᓇ ᒧᐢᑐᐢ, ᐃᔨᑯᕽ ᒥᐢᑕᐦᐃ ᑑᐦᑑᓵᐸᐩ ᐁ ᐊᔮᐟ, ᑯᓂᑕ ᐁ ᐹᐦᐹᐦᐱᔮᕽ ᐁᑯᑕ, ᐁ ᒣᑕᐚᑫᔮᕽ ᐊᓂᒪ ᑑᐦᑑᓵᐸᐩ, ᐁ ᐚᐦ ᐄᑭᓇᒪᐘᐠ ᐊᐘ ᓂᓰᒥᐢ ᐑᐦᑿᑲᓂᕽ. ᐁ ᑮ ᓰᑯᐱᑎᒫᔮᕽ ᐁᑾ ᐊᓂᐦᐃ ᐅᑑᐦᑑᓯᒪ ᐊᐘ ᒧᐢᑐᐢ ᐁᑾ, ᓂᑕᐦᑭᑎᓴᐦᐚᐤ ᐁᑾ. ᑖᐻ ᐁᑾ ᑳ ᓯᐻᐦᑌᐟ, ᓂᑕᑎ ᐊᐢᑯᐚᓈᐣ ᐊᐘ ᒧᐢᒍᓯᐢ ᐁ ᐱᒥᑎᓴᐦᐚᐟ, ᓀᓯᐏᓯᐤ ᐊᐘ ᒧᐢᒍᓯᐢ ᐊᐘ.

[5] ᐘᐦᐚ, ᑫᑕᐦᑕᐍ ᐁᑾ, ᓰᐲᓯᐢ ᐁ ᐱᒥᐦᑎᐠ, ᐁᑯᑕ ᐁᑾ ᐊᓇ ᒧᐢᑐᐢ ᐁᑾ ᒨᔭ ᐑ ᐚᓯᐘᐦᐊᐨ ᐊᓇ. ᑳ ᐸᓴᐢᑌᐦᐘᐠ ᐁᑾ ᐊᓇ ᒧᐢᑐᐢ, ᐁᑾ ᐁ ᐹᐦᑯᐯᑎᓴᐦᐚᔮᕽ ᐁᑾ, (ᑖᐻ ᐱᑯ, ᐁᒋᑲ ᐊᓂ ᐃᑌ ᐁ ᑕᐢᑑᐢᑑᑲᕽ ᐊᓂᒪ), ᑳ ᐊᑎ ᑯᑖᐏᐸᔨᐟ ᐊᓇ ᒧᐢᑐᐢ, ᐁ ᐘᐢᑲᐑᐟ ᑕᐦᑭ ᐊᔨᐚᐠ ᐁ ᐊᑎ ᑯᑖᐏᐸᔨᐟ, ᐊᓇ ᒧᐢᑐᐢ. ᐁᑯᓯ ᐃᓯ ᐁᑾ, ᒧᐢᒍᓯᐢ ᐊᓇ ᐁᑾ, ᐊᓇ ᐃᑕ ᐊᓇ ᑳ ᑕᐦᑯᐱᑖᐟ ᐊᓂᒪ ᓂᐸᑾᐦᑌᐦᐅᐣ ᐅᐦᒋ – ᒧᐢᒍᓯᐢ ᐊᓇ ᑳ ᑕᐦᑯᐱᑕᐠ ᐁᑾ ᐁᑯᑕ, ᓴᑳᕽ ᐁᑯᑕ, ᓂᑕᐦᑯᐱᑖᐤ. ᐁᑯᓯ ᐁᑾ ᐁ ᐑ ᓂᑕᐏ ᐑᐦᑕᒫᕽ, ᐊᐘ ᒧᐢᑐᐢ ᐊᐘ ᐁᑾ ᐁ ᐊᑎ ᑯᑖᐏᐸᔨᐟ ᐊᐘ, ᐊᐢᐱᐣ ᐋᑕ ᐏᔭ ᐋᐱᐦᑕᐤ ᑫᔮᐱ- ᐁ ᓅᑯᓯᐟ, ᐁᑾ ᑳ ᓯᐻᐦᑌᔮᕽ.

[6] ᐁᒋᑲ ᐊᓂ ᐁᑾ, ᐁᑯᓯ ᐁᑾ ᐁ ᐘᓂᓯᓂᔮᕽ. ᐁᑾ ᓵᓴᐩ ᐆᒪ ᐁ ᐊᑎ ᑕᑿᑭᐠ ᑳ ᑖᐦ ᑕᐦᑳᔮᐠ ᐊᑎ. ᐘᐦᐘᐦᐚ, ᐁᑾ ᐊᓂ ᑳ ᐱᒧᐦᑌᔮᕽ ᑳ ᐱᒧᐦᑌᔮᕽ, ᐁ ᒫᑐᐟ ᐊᐘ ᓂᓰᒥᐢ, ᐁᑾ ᓂᔭ ᐁ ᑌᐻᔮᐣ ᐁ ᑌᐻᔮᐣ ᓃᐢᑕ, ᑲ ᑲᑵ ᐯᐦᑖᑲᐏᔮᕽ. ᐁᐩ, ᐁ ᓵ ᓴᑾᐦᑖᐑᔮᕽ ᐃᑕ ᐁ ᑳᐦᑲᐏᓯᐦᑭᐠ ᐆᑭᐠ ᒥᓇᐦᐃᑾᐠ, ᐃᑕ ᑳ ᒐᐚᓯᐠ ᐁ ᓰᐸᐦᑖᐑᔮᕽ ᒫᓇ ᐁ ᐱᒧᐦᑌᔮᕽ.

[7] ᐱᔨᐢ ᐁᑾ ᐁ ᑎᐱᐢᑳᐠ ᐁᑾ, ᐆᐦ, ᐁᑾ ᐊᓂ ᐁᑾ ᑳ ᑭᒥᐘᕽ. ᓰᐹ ᐁᑾ ᒥᓇᐦᐃᑯᕽ, ᐋᓴᐩ ᒥᑐᓂ ᓂᓯᑿᐢᑯᒋᓂᓈᐣ, ᓰᐹ ᐁᑾ ᒥᓇᐦᐃᑯᕽ ᐁᑾ ᑳ ᐊᐱᔮᐣ ᐁᑾ ᐊᔨ, ᒥᓯ ᒥᓇᐦᐃᐠ ᐊᐘ, ᐁᑯᑕ ᐁᑾ ᐁ ᐊᐱᔮᐣ, ᐁᑾ ᐊᐘ ᐊᓂᒪ ᓂᓰᐯᑭᐢᑳᐘᓵᑳᐢ, ᐆᑕ ᐁ ᑕᐦᑯᓇᐠ ᐊᐘ ᓂᓰᒥᐢ ᐁ ᓇᐚᑲᐱᔮᐣ, ᐁ ᐊᑾᓇᐦᐘᐠ ᐁᑾ ᐁᑯᑕ ᐁ ᐑ ᑲᑵ ᑮᓲᓇᐠ ᐆᒪ, ᑲᓇᑫ ᐏᔭ ᑲ ᑮᓲᓯᐟ. ᑲᐯ ᑎᐱᐢᐠ ᐁᑯᓯ ᐁᑯᑕ ᐁᑾ, ᑖᐻ ᓂᐹᐤ, ᓃᐢᑕ ᓂᓂᐹᐣ. ᐁ ᐑ ᐘ ᐚᓂᐢᑳᔮᕽ, ᐆᐦ, ᑾᔭᐢ ᐹᐦ ᐹᑭᓯᑌᐸᔨᐤ ᐁ ᑮᐢᑭᒋᕽ ᐊᐘ ᓂᓰᒥᐢ ᐊᐘ. ᐁᑾ ᑲᔮᐢ ᒪᐢᑭᒧᑌᑭᐣ ᐊᔨᐢ ᐱᑯ ᑭᑮ ᐏᔮᐦᑌᐣ – ᐁᑯᑐᐘ ᐲᐦᑕᐍᓵᑳᐣ, ᓰᐦᒑᐢᑾᐦᐅᓂᐢ, ᑭᑑᐦᑑᓯᒪᐠ ᐁᑯᒍᐘ ᐅᐦᒋ ᒪᐢᑭᒧᑌᑭᐣ ᐁ ᑮ ᐅᓰᐦᑖᕽ, ᐁᑯᑐᐘ ᐱᑯ ᑭᑮ ᐏᔮᐦᑌᐣ. ᐁᑾ, ᑳ ᐃᑕᐠ ᐁᑾ ᐊᓇ ᓂᓰᒥᐢ, «ᓂᐲᐦᑕᐍᓵᑳᐣ ᐆᒪ ᓂᑲ ᑫᒋᑯᓀᐣ, ᓂᑲ ᑎᑎᐸᐦᐱᑌᐣ ᑭᓯᑕ,» ᓂᑎᑖᐤ. ᑖᐻ ᐁᑾ ᑳ ᑫᒋᑯᓇᒫᐣ ᐊᓂᒪ ᓂᐲᐦᑕᐍᓵᑳᐣ, ᓂᑖᐢᑭᐱᑌᐣ ᐋᐱᐦᑕᐤ, ᓂᐚᐦ ᐍᐍᑲᐦᐱᑖᐤ ᐁᑾ, ᐅᓯᑕ, ᐁᐘᑯ ᐅᐦᒋ ᐊᓂᒪ.

[8] ᐋᓴᐩ ᒦᓇ ᐁᑾ ᑳ ᓯᐻᐦᑌᔮᕽ ᐁᑾ, ᓂᐱᒧᐦᑖᓈᐣ ᑲᐯ ᑮᓯᐠ, ᐃᔨᑯᕽ ᐋᓴᐩ ᒦᓇ ᑳ ᐱᒧᐦᑌᔮᕽ. ᒪ ᑮᑿᐩ ᐁ ᒦᒋᔮᕽ, ᓂᐢᑕᐨ ᑳ ᑎᐱᐢᑳᐠ ᐊᓂᒪ ᑳ ᐊᑎ ᐅᑖᑯᓯᐠ ᓂᓅᐦᑌᐦᑲᑖᓈᐣ, ᐁ ᓅᐦᑌᒥᓂᐦᑵᐟ ᐊᐘ ᓂᓰᒥᐢ, ᒪᐢᑫᑯᕽ ᐏᔭ ᒫᓇ ᑳ ᐅᑎᐦᑕᒫᕽ,

ᐁ ᐋᐧᑎᐦᑫᔮᐣ ᐃᐢᑯ ᓂᐱᐩ ᑲᒥᐢᑲᒫᐣ, ᐁᑲᐧ ᒫᓇ ᓂᒋᐦᒋᐩ ᐅᐦᒋ ᐁ ᒥᓇᐦᐊᐠ ᐊᓂᒪ ᓂᐱᐩ. ᐁᑯᓯ ᒫᓇ ᓂᓯᐯᐧᔮᒋᐦᐅᓈᐣ ᑳᐃᐧ.

[9] ᐋᐧ, ᐱᔨᐢ ᐁᑲᐧ ᓲᐢᑳᐧᐨ ᐁᑲᐧ ᐊᔨ, ᓵᓯᑯᐦᑕᑖᐤ ᐊᓂᐦᐃ, ᒦᓇ ᒫᓇ ᐋᐦᑕᐦᐱᑕᒫᐣ ᐊᓂᒪ, ᓂᐲᐦᒐᐁᐧᓵᑲᓂᐢ ᐊᓂᒪ ᐅᐦᒋ, ᐅᓯᑕ ᑳᑎᑎᐸᐦᐱᑕᒪᐧᐠ, ᒣᐢᒋᐦᑕᑖᐤ. ᐁᑲᐧ ᐁᐊᐧᑯ ᐆᒪ ᐁᑲᐧ ᓂᓰᐦᒑᐢᑲᐧᐦᐅᓂᐢ ᐁᑲᐧ (ᓂᓅᐦᓅᓯᒥᕽ ᐊᓂᒪ ᐅᐦᒋ ᐁᑲᐧ ᐊᓂ, my brassiere ᐋᐦᑭ ᐃᑖᑊ ᐁᑎᑫᐧ ᐊᓂᒪ), ᐁᐊᐧᑯ ᐊᓂ ᐊᓂᒪ ᐁᑲᐧ ᐅᐦᒋ ᐁᑲᐧ ᒦᓇ ᑳᑎᑎᐸᐦᐱᑕᐠ, ᐋᐱᐦᑕᐤ ᐁᑲᐧ ᐁᐊᐧᑯ ᐊᓂᒪ ᒦᓇ ᐁ ᑖᐢᑭᐱᑕᒫᐣ ᐁ ᐁᐧᐁᐧᑲᐦᐱᑕᒪᐧᐠ, ᑲᑎᐢᑲᐤ ᐊᐧᓇᐢᑯᐨ ᐆᑌ ᐆᐦᐅ ᐅᓯᒋᓴ. ᐋ, ᒨᔭ ᑭᓀᐧᐢ ᒣᐢᑖᐢᑯᒋᐦᒑᐤ, ᐊᐧᓂᐦᑖᐤ ᐊᓂᒪ ᐯᔭᐠ ᐁ ᒪᓈᐢᑯᒋᐦᑖᐟ. «ᒨᔭ ᐁᑲᐧ ᓂᐄᐧ ᐱᒧᐦᑖᐣ ᐊᔨᐋᐧᐠ,» ᓂᑎᑎᐠ. ᐁᑯᓯ ᐁ ᒫᑐᐟ ᐃᔨᑯᕽ, ᐱᔨᐢ ᒨᔭ ᐊᐦᔮ ᐁ ᐯᐦᑖᑯᓯᐟ, ᐃᔨᑯᕽ ᐁ ᒫᐦᒫᑐᐟ ᐊᐦᔮ.

[10] ᑳ ᓇᔫᒪᐠ ᐁᑲᐧ, ᓃᐢᑕ ᐃᐧᔭ ᓂᓀᐢᑐᓯᐣ, ᐁᑲᐧ ᒥᓯᑭᑎᐤ ᐊᓂᒪ ᐁᑲᐧᔨᑯᕽ, ᐊᔨᓈᓀᐤ ᐁ ᐃᑕᐦᑐᐱᐳᓀᐟ ᐁᑲᐧ ᐁ ᑮ ᐃᐧᔨᓄᐟ. ᑳ ᓇᔫᒪᐠ ᐁᑲᐧ, ᐁ ᐱᒧᐦᑌᔮᐣ ᐁ ᐱᒧᐦᑌᔮᐣ, ᐁ ᓇᔫᒪᐠ. ᐋ, ᐋᓴᐩ ᒦᓇ ᐁᑲᐧ ᐁ ᑎᐱᐢᑳᐠ, ᐋᓴᐩ ᒦᓇ ᐁᑲᐧ ᒥᓇᐦᐃᐠ, ᐋᓴᐩ ᒦᓇ ᓂᓂᑐᓇᐋᐧᐤ, ᓴᑳᐧ ᐊᔨᕽ ᐁᑯᑕ ᑳ ᐊᔮᔭᕽ. ᐁᑯᑕ ᐁᑲᐧ ᓴᑳᐧ ᐊᔨᕽ ᐁᑲᐧ ᐁ ᐊᔮᔭᕽ, ᐋᐧᒋᐢᑕᑲᐧᐨ, ᑳ ᐋᐧᐦ ᐋᐧᓴᐢᑯᑌᐸᔨᐠ ᐁᑲᐧ, ᐃᔨᑯᕽ ᐁ ᒪᒋ ᑮᓯᑳᐠ ᐁᑯᓯ ᐊᓂᒪ ᐁᐊᐧᑯ ᐊᓂᒪ ᑎᐱᐢᑳᐤ. ᒫᑲ ᒨᔭ ᓂᓵᐳᐹᓈᐣ, ᒥᓇᐦᐃᑯᕽ ᐊᔨᐢ ᓰᐹ ᓂᑕᔮᓈᐣ, ᒫᑲ ᓵᐳᐯᐊᐧ ᐃᐧᔭ ᓂᑕᔨᐃᐧᓂᓯᓈᓇ ᐊᓂᒪ ᑳ ᐱᒧᐦᑌᔮᕽ, ᐋᐦ. ᐁᑯᑕ ᐁᑲᐧ ᓰᐹ ᐁᑲᐧ, ᐋᓴᐩ ᒦᓇ ᑳ ᐊᐱᔮᐣ, ᐋᓴᐩ ᒦᓇ ᐯᔭᑲᐧᐣ, ᐁ ᒐᐦᑯᓇᐠ ᐊᐊᐧ ᓂᓰᒥᐢ, ᐋ, ᓰᐯᑭᐢᑳᐊᐧᓵᑲᐢ ᐊᓂᒪ, ᐋᐧᒋᐢᑕᑳᐧᐨ, ᓯᑳᐧᐢᑯᒋᐣ. ᐁᐊᐧᑯ ᐊᓂ ᐊᓂᒪ ᐁᑲᐧ, ᐋᓴᐩ ᒦᓇ ᐅᐦᒋ ᐁᑲᐧ, ᐃᐧᔭ ᐁᑲᐧ ᓂᔭ ᐁᑲᐧ ᓇᒪ ᑮᑲᐧᐩ ᓂᑖᐸᒋᐦᑖᐣ, ᐃᐧᔭ ᐁᑲᐧ ᓂᐁᐧᐁᐧᑭᓈᐤ ᐁᑯᑕ, ᐋᓴᐩ ᒦᓇ ᓂᐹᐤ, ᐃᐧᔭ ᐁ ᓀᐢᑐᓯᐟ. ᓃᐢᑕ ᓂᓂᐹᐣ, ᐁ ᐊᑎ ᐋᐧᐸᕽ, ᑫᑕᐦᑕᐁᐧ ᑳ ᐯᐦᑕᐊᐧᐠ ᐆᐦᐅᐤ ᐁ ᑳᐦᑭᑐᐟ ᐁᑯᑕ, ᑕᐦᑯᐦᐨ ᐁᑯᑕ ᒥᓇᐦᐃᑯᕽ. ᐁ ᑯᐢᑯᐸᔨᐟ, ᑯᐢᑯᒥᐠ ᐊᐊᐧ ᐄᐧᐢᑕ ᓂᓰᒥᐢ, ᓴᒫᐠ ᒫᑐᐤ, «ᐁ ᐄᐧ ᓅᑎᓂᑯᔭᕽ,» ᐁ ᐃᑌᐧᐟ ᐆᐦᐅ, ᐅᑕᐦᑕᐦᑲᐧᓇ ᐆᐦᐅ ᒫᓇ ᐊᓂᓯ ᐃᓯ ᐁ ᑕᓴᐧᑭᐁᐧᐱᓈᐟ ᐊᐊᐧ ᐆᐦᐅᐤ. ᓃᐢᑕ ᐁᑯᓯ ᓂᑎᑌᔨᐦᑌᐣ, ᐁ ᐯ ᐃᑖᐱᐟ ᒫᓇ ᐊᓂᒪ ᐃᑕ ᑳ ᐊᐱᔮᕽ.

[11] well, «ᑭᑲ ᓯᐯᐧᐦᑖᓇᐤ,» ᓂᑎᑖᐤ ᐊᐊᐧ ᓂᓰᒥᐢ, ᐋᓴᐩ ᒦᓇ, ᓂᓯᐯᐧᐦᑖᓈᐣ. ᐋᓴᐩ ᒫᑲ ᒦᓇ ᐁ ᓇᔫᒪᐠ ᐆᒪ ᐁᑲᐧ, ᓵᓴᐩ ᒦᓇ ᐁ ᓯᐯᐧᐦᑌᔮᕽ. ᐃᐧᔭ ᐃᔨᑯᕽ ᐁ ᐹᑭᓯᑌᐸᔨᐟ, ᓃᐢᑕ ᐃᐧᔭ ᓂᓯᑳᐧᐢᑯᒋᓂᐣ ᓂᐢᑳᑎᕽ ᒥᓯᐁᐧ, ᒫᑲ ᓂᔭ ᐃᐧᔭ ᒥᐢᒋᑲᐧᐢᑭᓯᓂᓴ ᓂᑮ ᑭᑭᐢᑫᐣ ᐁᑯᐢᐲ. ᐁᑲᐧ ᐊᓂ ᐁᑲᐧ, ᐊᐊᐧ ᐆᐦᐅᐤ ᐁᑲᐧ, ᒪᔭᐤ ᐁ ᓯᐯᐧᐦᑌᔭᕽ, ᑖᐯᐧ ᐱᑯ ᑳ ᓯᐯᐧᐱᐦᐋᐟ, ᐋᐧᐦᔭᐁᐧᐢ ᒥᑐᓂ ᓀᑌ ᐁᑲᐧ, ᒦᑐᓯᕽ ᐁᑲᐧ ᓀᑌ ᑳ ᐊᑯᓰᐟ. ᑳ ᐯ ᑫᐧᐢᑭ ᐊᔮᐟ, ᐁᑯᓯ ᐃᓯ ᐊᓂᒪ, ᐅᑕᐦᑕᐦᑲᐧᓇ ᒫᓇ ᐊᓂᓯ ᐃᓯ ᐁ ᐃᓯ ᐁᐧᐱᓈᐟ, ᐹᐢᑲᐨ ᐁ ᐯᐦᑖᑯᓯᐟ ᑭᓯᐠ, ᐁ ᑕᓴᐧᑭᐁᐧᐱᓈᐟ, ᑖᐱᐢᑰᐨ ᐁ ᐄᐧ ᓅᑎᓂᑰᔭᕽ. ᒦᑭ ᐁ ᐊᑎ ᐊᔮᔭᕽ, ᓵᓴᐩ ᒦᓇ ᑳ ᓯᐯᐧᐱᐦᐋᐟ, ᓵᓴᐩ ᒦᓇ ᐁᑯᑌ ᐁᑲᐧ ᒥᓇᐦᐃᑯᕽ ᐊᑯᓰᐤ. ᐯᔭᑲᐧᐣ ᐁᑯᓯ, ᐃᑌᐦᑫ ᐃᓯ ᐆᒪ ᑳ ᐊᔮᔭᕽ ᐯ ᐃᑖᐱᐤ, ᐁᑯᓯ ᐊᓂᒪ ᒫᓇ ᐁ ᐃᑑᑕᕽ, ᐁ ᐯᐦᑖᑯᓯᐟ. «ᐊᐧᐦᐋᐧ,» ᑳ ᐃᑕᐠ ᐊᐊᐧ ᓂᓰᒥᐢ, «ᑲ ᐱᒥᑎᓴᐦᐋᐧᓇᐤ ᐊᐊᐧ,» ᓂᑎᑖᐤ, «ᐊᐦᔮ ᐁᑎᑫᐧ ᐊᐊᐧ ᐁ ᐄᐧ ᑭᐢᑭᓄᐦᑕᐦᐃᑯᔮᕽ ᐊᐊᐧ,

ᑳ ᐃᑑᑕᕽ,» ᓂᑎᑖᐤ. «ᓇᒨᔭ.» ᐃᑘᐤ, «ᐁ ᐐ ᓅᑎᓂᑯᔭᕽ ᐊᓇ, ᑳ ᐃᑑᑕᕽ,» ᐃᑘᐤ ᐊᐘ ᓂᓯᒥᐢ, «ᒨᔭ ᑭᑲ ᐱᒥᑎᓴᐦᐚᓇᐤ,» ᐃᑘᐤ. «ᒨᔭ,» ᓂᑎᑖᐤ, «ᑲ ᐱᒥᑎᓴᐦᐚᓇᐤ ᒪᐦᑎ,» ᓂᑎᑖᐤ.

[12] ᑖᐻ ᐁᑿ, ᑳ ᐱᒥᑎᓴᐦᐚᔮᕽ, ᐋᓴᐩ ᒦᓇ ᐁᑯᓯ ᐊᓇ ᐆᐦᐅᐤ. ᓈᓂᑕᐤ ᐁᑎᑵ ᐊᓂᒪ ᓀᐚᐤ ᐁ ᐋᐦᒋ ᑘᐦᐅᐟ ᐊᓇ ᐆᐦᐅᐤ ᒫᓇ, ᐁᑿ ᓂᐱᒥᑎᓴᐦᐚᓈᐣ ᐁᑿ. boy, ᑫᑕᐦᑕᐍ ᑳ ᐯᐦᑕᒫᐣ ᑖᐱᐢᑰᐨ ᐊᐎᔭᐠ ᐁ ᑌᐻᐟ. ᓂᑌᐺᐣ, ᒫᑲ ᐊᔭᐢ ᓂᒥᔭᐢᒁᐣ, ᒨᔭ ᐁᑿᔭᑯᕽ ᓂᑭᓰᐚᐣ. ᐯᐦᑕᒷᐠ ᒫᑲ ᐁᓴ ᐊᓂᑭᐠ, 'Alec Bishop' ᐊᓇ ᑮ ᐃᓯᔮᐦᑳᓱᐤ, Louis Morin, Salamon Morin, ᐁᑿ Johnny Sinclair. ᐁᒋᑲ ᐊᓂ ᐁ ᐃᑕᓯᐍᒋᐠ, ᓈᐦ ᓀᐓ, ᐁ ᐐ ᓈᐦ ᓀᐎᒋᐠ ᐆᑭᐠ ᓈᐯᐘᐠ, Hudson's Bay Store ᐅᐦᒋ ᐁ ᒥᔭᐦᒋᐠ ᐹᐢᑭᓯᑲᓇ, ᒨᓯᓯᓂᔭ, rubbers, ᐁ ᒥᔭᐦᒋᐠ ᑲ ᓂᑐᓈᑯᔮᐦᒁᐤ, ᑲᐯ ᐊᔭ ᐆᒪ ᐁᓴ ᐁ ᓂᑐᓈᑯᔮᐦᒁᐤ ᐊᓂᒪ ᓂᐢᑕᑦ ᑳ ᐘᓂᓯᓂᔮᕽ, ᓂᐢᑕᑦ ᐊᓂᒪ ᑳ ᑮᓯᑲᐠ. ᓃᑲᐣ ᐁᓴ ᒥᓯᐍ ᑮ ᐸᐹᒥᐸᔭᐘᐠ, ᐁ ᐸᐹᒥ ᓂᑐᓈᑲᐑᔮᕽ ᐚᐢᑲᐦᐃᑲᓂᕽ ᐆᒪ, ᐋᐦ. ᐁᑯᓯ ᐁᑿ ᑭᐢᑫᔭᐦᑕᒷᐠ ᐁᑿ ᐊᔭ, ᐁ ᐘᓂᓯᓂᔮᕽ.

[13] ᐁᑯᓯ ᐊᓂᒪ ᐁᓴ, ᐁᑳ ᑮ ᓇᑲᑖᔮᕽ ᐊᓇ ᒧᐢᑐᐢ ᐊᓂᒪ ᐃᑕ ᑳ ᒥᒋᒧᐢᑯᐍᐟ ᐊᓂᒪ, ᑳ ᐊᑎ ᑯᑖᐏᐸᔭᐟ ᐊᓂᒪ,

> (David Merasty, ᐅᒥᓇᐦᐅᐏᔭᓂᐤ, ᐁᐘᑯ ᐊ ᓇ ᐁᓴ, ᑮ ᒪᓯᓇᐦᐃᑫᐦᐚᐤ ᐁᐘᑯ ᐊᓇ ᐁ ᒥᑎᐦᑎᑯᔮᕽ, ᐋᐦ. ᒫᑲ ᐁᑿ ᓂᐘᓇᐦᐚᐦᑎᑯᓈᐣ, ᐄᐦ. ᐊᓂᒪ ᐃᔭᑯᕽ ᑳ ᑭᒥᐘᕽ, ᐋ, ᒨᔭ ᐱᔭᐢ ᐁᑎᑵ ᓅᒁᐣ ᐆᒪ ᐃᑕ ᑳ ᐱᒧᐦᑌᔮᕽ, ᓂᑮ ᒥᑎᐦᑎᑯᓈᐣ ᐎᔭ – ᑖᓯᐺᐤ ᑮ ᓂᑕᐏᒥᐢᑫᐍᐤ ᐊᓂᐦᐃ ᒧᐢᑐᔕ. ᐆᑌ ᐃᐢᑯ ᐅᑿᔮᕽ, ᐊᓇ ᒧᐢᑐᐢ ᐁᑿ ᓵᓴᐩ ᒫᑲ ᑫᔮᐱᐨ ᐁ ᐱᒫᑎᓯᐟ, ᐯ ᐐᐦᑕᑦ ᐁᓴ ᐁᑿ, ᓀᑌ ᒁᑯᐲᐏᓵᐦᐃᑲᓂᕽ ᐁ ᒥᐢᑲᐚᐟ ᐊᓂᐦᐃ ᒧᐢᑐᔕ, ᓂᐹᐹᐘ ᐁᑿ ᐁ ᐯ ᐐᐦᑕᒪᐚᐟ. ᐁᑯᓯ ᓂᐹᐹ ᒣᑭᐤ, ᐊᓂᐦᐃ ᒧᐢᑐᔕ ᑲᐯ ᐹᐢᑭᓯᒥᐦᐟ, ᐁᑯᓯ ᑮ ᐯ ᓂᐸᐦᐁᐘᐠ ᐊᓂᐦᐃ ᒧᐢᑐᔕ, ᐊᓂᐦᐃ ᒦᓇ ᒧᐢᒍᓯᓴ.)

ᓂᑳᐦ ᑮ ᒥᐢᑳᑲᐏᓈᐣ ᐁᐘᑯ ᑎᐱᐢᑳᐤ, lanterns ᐁ ᒥᔭᐦᒋᐠ ᐁᓴ, ᑲᐦᑭᔭᐤ ᐆᑭᐠ ᓈᐯᐘᐠ Hudson's Bay ᐅᐦᒋ ᐁ ᐅᐦᒌᐢᑕᒫᐦᒋᐠ, ᐁ ᐋᐸᒋᐦᑖᒋᐠ lanterns ᐆᐦᐅ, ᐋᐦ. – ᑲᔮᐢ ᐁᑲᒫ ᑮᑿᐩ flashlights. ᐁᑿ ᐆᑭᐠ ᐁᑿ ᑳ ᐯᐦᑕᐚᔮᐦᑭᐠ, ᐊᐘ ᐁᑿ ᑳ ᒪᑘ ᑌᐻᐟ, ᓵᒫᐠ ᓂᑭᐢᑫᔭᐦᑌᐣ, ᓈᐯᐤ ᐁᑿ, ᐋᐦᐊ.

[14] ᐁᑿ ᐁᓴ ᐃᑘᐤ ᐊᐘ ᐁᑿ, ᐚᐱᑿᔮᐢ, Louis ᐚᐱᑿᔮᐢ, «ᑕ ᑕᐸᓰᐘᐠ ᐊᐦᔮ ᐁᑎᑵ,» ᐃᑘᐤ ᐁᓴ, «ᐊᓂᓯ ᐃᓯ ᑲ ᐚᐢᑳᐦᑌᐘᐠ ᐆᑭᐠ ᓈᐯᐘᐠ, ᐆᒪ ᐃᑌ ᑖᐱᐢᑰᐨ ᑳ ᐯᐦᑕᐚᔮᐦᒁᐤ, ᑲ ᑕᐸᓰᐘᐠ ᓈᓂᑕᐤ ᐃᓯ, ᑯᐢᑕᐦᒁᐏ, ᑯᑕᐠ ᐊᔭᓯᔭᓂᐤ ᑮᑿᐩ ᐃᑌᔭᐦᑕᐦᒁᐏ,» ᐃᑘᐤ ᐊᐘ. ᐁᑯᓯ ᐁᓴ ᐁᑿ ᐊᐘ ᐯᔭᐠ ᐁᑿ ᐯ ᑕᐢᑲᒧᐦᑌᐤ ᐁᑿ, ᐁ ᐯ ᓈᑎᑯᔮᕽ, ᐃᑌ ᐃᓯ ᑳ ᐯᐦᑖᑯᔮᕽ. ᐁ ᒪᑘ ᑌᐻᐟ, ᐋ, ᐁᑿ ᒥᑐᓂ ᓂᑫᐦᒋᓈᐦᐅᐣ ᐁᑿ ᐊᔭᓯᔭᓂᐤ, «ᑭᒥᐢᑳᑲᐏᓇᐤ,» ᓂᑎᑖᐤ ᐊᐘ ᓂᓰᒥᐢ. ᓂᑌᐺᐣ, ᒫᑲ ᐊᔭᐢ ᓂᑯᐦᑕᐢᑿᐩ,

ᑳ ᐯ ᓵᑫᐁᐧᐟ ᐁᑯᑕ Alec Bishop. ᑖᐯᐧ ᐱᑯ ᐁ ᐯ ᐋᐧᐦᐅᑎᐦᑎᓂᑯᔮᕽ ᐁ ᒫᑐᐟ, ᐁ ᐋᐧᐦᐅᒣᒥᑯᔮᕽ ᐊᐊᐧ ᑭᓭᔨᓃᓯᐢ – ᒨᔭ, ᐁᑯᐢᐲ ᐅᐢᑭ ᐊᔨᐃᐧᐤ, ᒨᔭ ᑭᓭᔨᓃᐃᐧᐤ.

[15] ᐁᑯᓯ ᑖᐯᐧ ᐱᑯ ᐁᑲᐧ ᐹᐢᑭᓯᑲᐣ ᐊᓂᒪ ᑳ ᑕᐦᑯᓇᕽ, ᓂᐢᑖᐧᐤ ᒪᑌᐧᐁᐧᐦᑖᐤ. ᐁᑯᓯ ᐊᓂᑭᐠ ᒨᔭ ᑭᓀᐧᐢ ᐆᑭᐠ ᑳ ᐋᐧᐢᑳᐦᑌᒋᐠ, ᐁᑯᑕ ᐯ ᑕᑯᐸᐦᑖᐊᐧᐠ. ᐹᐦ ᐯᔭᐠ ᒥᐢᑕᑎᒪᐧ ᒦᓇ ᒥᔮᐊᐧᐠ, ᒦᒋᐃᐧᐣ ᐁ ᐱᒧᐦᑕᑖᒋᐠ ᐁᑯᑕ, ᒨᓱᓯᓂᔭ, ᑲᐦᑭᔭᐤ ᑮᑲᐧᐩ, ᐋᐦ. ᐄᐧᐢᑕᐋᐧᐤ ᑲ ᒦᒋᓱᒋᐠ ᐁᑲᐧ ᒥᐢᑳᑲᐃᐧᔮᐦᑭ ᑲ ᐱᒥᓇᐊᐧᑎᑲᐃᐧᔮᕽ. ᐁᑯᓯ ᐁᑲᐧ ᐁᑯᑕ, ᓴᒫᐠ ᐊᐊᐧ ᐁᑲᐧ ᑯᑕᐁᐧᐤ Louis ᐋᐧᐱᑲᐧᔮᐢ, ᑲ ᑲᑫᐧ ᒦᒋᓱᔮᕽ. ᐆᐦ, ᒨᔭ ᑭᓀᐧᐣ, ᐋᓴᐩ ᒥᓯᐁᐧ ᑳ ᒪᑌᐧᐁᐧᐦᑖᕽ, ᐊᐊᐧ ᐁᑲᐧ ᑳ ᒪᑌᐧᐁᐧᐦᑖᐟ, ᒥᓯᐁᐧ ᐃᑌ ᑯᓂᑕ ᑳ ᐯᐦᑖᑲᐧᐦᑭ ᐁᑲᐧ, ᐆᑭᐠ ᑮᑲᐧᐩ ᐄᐧᐢᑕᐋᐧᐤ ᐁ ᒥᐢᑳᑲᐃᐧᔮᕽ ᑲ ᑭᐢᑫᔨᐦᑖᑲᐧᕽ, ᒥᓯᐁᐧ ᒪᑌᐧᐁᐧᐦᑖᐊᐧᐠ. ᐁᑯᓯ ᐁᑲᐧ, ᐁᑯᑕ ᐁᑲᐧ, tea ᐁᑲᐧ ᓂᐄᐧᒥᓇᐦᐃᑲᐃᐧᓈᐣ ᑲ ᒦᒋᓱᔮᕽ, ᐁᐩ, ᑲᐦᑭᔭᐤ ᑮᑲᐧᐩ, Hudson's Bay ᐃᐧᔭ ᐅᐦᒋ ᓲᐢᑳᐧᐨ ᒦᒋᐃᐧᐣ ᐁ ᒣᑭᕽ. ᒨᔭ ᓂᑲᐢᑭᐦᑖᓈᐣ ᐊᐦᔭ, ᑲ ᑯᐦᒋᐸᔨᐦᑖᔮᕽ ᐊᓂᒪ, tea ᐊᓂᒪ, ᓇᒨᔭ ᓂᑮ ᒦᒋᓱᓈᐣ, ᒫᐧᐨ ᓲᐢᑳᐧᐨ.

[16] ᐁᑯᓯ ᐁᑲᐧ, ᐁᑲᐧ Louis ᐋᐧᐱᑲᐧᔮᐢ ᐁᑲᐧ ᐃᑌᐤ, ᑲ ᑌᐦᑕᐲᔮᕽ ᐁᑲᐧ ᓂᔭᓈᐣ, ᐁᑲᐧ ᐊᓇ ᒥᐢᑕᑎᒼ ᐁ ᓵᑲᐯᑭᓈᒋᐠ ᓂᑌᐦᑕᐱᓈᐣ ᐁᑲᐧ ᐁ ᑮᐁᐧᐦᑕᐦᐃᑲᐃᐧᔮᕽ ᐁᑲᐧ. ᓀᑌ ᐁᑲᐧ ᐁ ᑕᑯᓯᓂᔮᕽ, ᐁᑲᐧ ᓃᑭᓈᕽ ᐁᑲᐧ, ᐊᔨ (ᑲᓂ ᑖᐯᐧ ᐊᐊᐧ ᐆᐦᐅᐤ, ᐃᐢᐲ ᐁᑲᐧ ᑳ ᒥᐢᑳᑯᔮᐦᑭᐠ ᐆᑭᐠ, ᐊᓇ ᐁᑲᐧ ᐆᐦᐅᐤ, ᐊᐢᐱᐣ ᐁ ᓯᐯᐧᐱᐦᐋᐧᐟ, ᐊᓇ ᐆᐦᐅᐤ, ᐁᐊᐧᑯ ᐊᓇ ᐁ ᑭᐢᑭᓄᐦᑕᐦᐃᑯᔮᕽ). ᓀᑌ ᐁᑲᐧ ᓃᑭᓈᕽ ᐁᑲᐧ ᐁ ᑕᑯᓯᓂᔮᕽ ᐁᑲᐧ ᐁ ᓵᑫᐁᐧᔮᕽ ᐁᑲᐧ, ᐋᐧᒋᐢᑕᑳᐨ ᒥᐢᑕᑎᒪᐧᐠ, ᓲᐢᑳᐧᐨ ᐁᑲᐧ ᐁ ᐃᐦᑕᓯᐟ ᑳᐧᑯᐲᐃᐧᓵᑲᐦᐃᑲᓂᕽ ᐊᔨᓯᔨᓂᐤ, ᐁᑯᑕ ᐁ ᐊᔮᐟ, ᓲᐢᑳᐧᐨ ᒥᐢᑕᑎᒪᐧᐠ ᑯᓂᑕ ᑳ ᐊᔨᑕᐱᒋᐠ, ᐁᑯᑌ ᐊᓂᒪ, wagons ᑭᔨᑲᐤ. ᐁᑲᐧ ᐁᒋᑲ ᐊᓂ ᒫᓇ ᑭᓯᐠ ᐁ ᐊᔭᒥᐦᐋᐧᒋᐠ, ᐊᔭᒥᐦᐁᐃᐧᔨᓂᐤ ᐁᑯᑕ ᐁ ᐊᔮᐟ, ᐆᒪ ᑲ ᑲᑫᐧ ᒥᐢᑳᑲᐃᐧᔮᕽ, ᐁᑯᑕ ᓲᐢᑳᐧᐨ ᐁ ᐊᔭᒥᐦᐋᐧᐟ ᐊᔭᒥᐦᐁᐃᐧᔨᓂᐤ, ᐁᑯᑕ ᐊᓂᒪ ᑲᐦᑭᔭᐤ, ᑲ ᑲᑫᐧ ᒥᐢᑳᑲᐃᐧᔮᕽ.

[17] ᐁ ᓵᑫᐁᐧᔮᕽ ᐁᑲᐧ, ᐊᓂᒪ ᓀᑕ, ᐃᐧᔭ ᓂᔭ ᓵᓴᐩ ᐁ ᐅᐢᑭᓃᑭᐢᑫᐧᓯᓯᐃᐧᔮᐣ, « ᒨᔭ ᓂᐄᐧ ᐃᑐᐦᑖᐣ ᓂᔭ ᐁᑯᑌ, » ᓂᑎᑖᐤ ᐊᐊᐧ Alec Bishop, « ᐃᔨᑯᕽ ᑳ ᓯᑲᐧᐢᑯᒋᓂᔮᐣ, » ᓂᑎᑖᐤ. « ᐁᐩ, ᐁᑳᔭ ᓈᓂᑕᐤ ᐃᑌᔨᐦᑕ, my girl, » ᓂᑎᑎᐠ Alec Bishop, « ᐃᔨᑯᕽ ᑲ ᒥᔦᐧᔨᐦᑖᑲᐧᕽ ᐁ ᒥᐢᑳᑲᐃᐧᔦᐠ, » ᐃᑌᐤ, « ᒥᐢᑕᐦᐃ ᐆᒪ ᐁ ᑭᑎᒫᑫᔨᒧᕽ ᐆᒪ, » ᐃᑌᐤ, « ᐁᑳᔭ ᑮᑲᐧᐩ ᓀᐯᐃᐧᓯᐃᐧᐣ ᑭᑭᐢᑳᑯᐠ. » ᐃᑌᐤ, « ᑭᑕᑯᐦᑕᐦᐃᑎᓈᐣ. » ᐁᐩ, boy, ᐁᑯᑌ ᐁ ᑕᑯᐦᑌᔮᕽ, ᑯᓂᑕ ᐊᔨᓯᔨᓂᐊᐧᐠ ᑳ ᐅᒣᒥᑯᔭᐦᑳᐧᐤ. 'Frank Séguin' ᑮ ᐃᓯᔩᐦᑳᓱᐤ Hudson's Bay store, ᐁᐧᒥᐢᑎᑰᓯᐤ, ᐁᐊᐧᑯ ᐊᓇ ᑯᓂᑕ ᐁ ᐯ ᐋᑲᐧᐢᑭᑎᓂᑯᔮᕽ ᐁ ᒫᑐᐟ, ᐁᑯᓯ ᐁᑲᐧ, ᐃᑌᐤ ᐊᐊᐧ Frank Séguin, ᐊᔨᕽ ᐊᔭ, « ᐊᔨᐃᐧᓂᓴ, » ᐃᑌᐤ, « ᐊᐃᐧᔭᐠ ᑲ ᐯ ᓈᑕᒼ ᓀᑌ ᐊᑖᐁᐧᐃᐧᑲᒥᑯᕽ ᑮᑲᐧᐩ ᑲ ᐳᐦᑎᐢᑲᐦᑭᐠ, » ᐃᑌᐤ. ᑖᐯᐧ ᐁᑲᐧ, ᐁᑯᑌ ᐁᑲᐧ ᐃᑐᐦᑌᐤ ᐁᑲᐧ, ᐊᐊᐧ ᑳ ᑮ ᐅᐋᐧᐦᑯᒥᔮᐣ, ᐁ ᓈᑕᕽ ᐁᑲᐧ ᑮᑲᐧᐩ ᐁᑯᑕ, Hudson's Bay ᐊᔨᐃᐧᓂᓴ, ᓲᐢᑳᐧᐨ ᐁ ᒥᔨᑯᔮᕽ ᐊᓇ ᐁ ᐳᐦᑕᔨᐃᐧᓂᓴᐦᐃᑯᔮᕽ.

[18] ᐁᑯᓯ ᐁᑲᐧ ᐁᑯᑕ ᐁᑲᐧ, ᓵᓴᐩ ᒦᓇ ᐁᑲᐧ ᐁᑯᑕ, ᐁᓴ ᐁ ᑮ ᐱᒥᓇᐊᐧᓱᕽ ᐁᑲᐧ ᐁ ᐄᐧ ᐊᓴᒥᑲᐃᐧᔮᕽ, ᒪ ᑮᑲᐧᐩ, ᒨᔭ ᓂᐄᐧᒥᒋᓯᓈᐣ, ᒨᔭ ᓂᑮᒦᒋᓯᓈᐣ, ᓂᑯᐦᑕᐢᑳᐧᓈᓇ ᐁ ᐄᐧᓴᑫᔨᐦᑕᒫᕽ. ᑖᐯᐧ ᐱᑯ ᐃᐧᔭ ᐊᐊᐧ ᓂᓰᒥᐢ ᐊᐊᐧ, ᓂᐯᐃᐧᓂᕽ ᐁ ᑮ ᐱᒥᓯᒥᐦᐟ, ᐁᑯᓯ ᑖᐯᐧ ᐱᑯ ᐁ ᐃᑎᐦᑳᐧᒥᐟ, ᐁ ᑮᓰᓯᒫᒋᐠ, ᐅᓯᑕ, ᐃᔨᑯᕽ ᐁ ᑮᐢᑭᒋᕽ, ᐊᑳᒥᓇᑲᓯᔭ ᐁ ᑳᐦ ᑫᒋᑲᐧᐦᐅᒫᒋᐠ, ᐃᔨᑯᕽ ᐁ ᑮᐢᑭᒋᕽ ᐅᓯᒋᓴ.

[19] ᐊᔭ ᒌ ᐁᑲᐧ ᐁᑯᓯ – ᐁᑲᐧ ᐊᐊᐧ ᓂᒫᒫ ᐊᔨ, ᒨᔭ ᑲᔮᐢ ᐁ ᑮ ᐃᓯ ᑕᐦᑯᐱᑖᐊᐧᓱᐟ, Alice Derocher ᐊᓯᒋ ᐁᓴ ᒫᓇ ᐄᐧᐢᒐᐋᐧᐤ ᐁ ᓃᓯᒋᐠ ᐁ ᓃᓱ ᓯᐯᐧᐦᑌᒋᐠ, ᐋᐦᒋ ᐱᑯ ᐄᐧᐢᑕᐋᐧᐤ ᐁ ᓂᑐᓈᑯᔮᐦᑳᐧᐤ, ᐁ ᐸᐹᒥ ᒫᑐᐟ ᐁᓴ ᓂᒫᒫ.

[20] ᒫᒋᑲ, ᐁᑯᓯ ᐋᑕ ᐃᐧᔭ ᐁ ᑮ ᒥᐢᑳᑲᐃᐧᔮᕽ, ᐁᑯᓯ ᐁᑲᐧ ᑳᐦ ᑮᐁᐧᐊᐧᐠ ᐁᑲᐧ, ᐁ ᑮ ᑮᓯ ᐊᔭᒥᐦᐋᒋᐠ ᐋᓴᐩ ᒦᓇ, ᐁᑯᑕ ᐋᓴᐩ ᒦᓇ ᐁᑯᑕ ᓂᔭ ᓂᓴᐢᑲᒧᓇᐦᐃᑲᐃᐧᐣ, ᒫᑲ ᓂᓰᒥᐢ ᐃᐧᔭ ᒉᐢᑲᐧ ᐁᑯᐢᐲ ᐁ ᐅᐦᒋ ᓴᐢᑲᒧᐟ, ᓂᓴᐢᑲᒧᓇᐦᐃᑲᐃᐧᐣ ᓃᐢᑕ. ᐁᑯᓯ ᐁᑎᑫᐧ ᐁᑲᐧ ᓃᐢᑕ ᐁᑲᐧ ᐁ ᐱᒥᓯᓂᔮᐣ, ᐁᑯᓯ ᑖᐯᐧ ᐱᑯ ᓃᐢᑕ ᑳ ᐃᓯ ᓂᐹᔮᐣ, ᐹᑐᐢ ᑮᑭᓭᐹ ᑳ ᑲ ᑯᐢᑯᐸᔨᔮᐣ.

[21] ᓂᑮ ᑲᑳᐧᑕᑳᒋᐦᐅᓈᐣ ᐊᓂ, ᓂᑮ ᐋᐧᐸᐦᑌᐣ ᐁ ᐋᔨᒪᕽ, ᐊᔨᓯᔨᓂᐤ ᑳ ᐊᐧᓂᓯᕽ. ᐁᑲᐧ ᒨᔭ ᐄᐧᐦᑳᐨ ᐁ ᐅᐦᒋ ᑯᐢᑖᒋᔮᕽ ᐊᐦᔭ ᐋᐧᑲᐋᐢ ᑮᑲᐧᐩ ᑲ ᑯᐢᑖᔮᕽ, ᐁ ᒫᒪᐢᑳᑕᒫᐣ ᐁ ᑲᐢᑭ ᑎᐱᐢᑳᐠ ᑳ ᑭᑐᒋᐠ, ᑮᑲᐧᐩ ᑲ ᓴᑭᐦᐃᑯᔮᐣ, ᓇᒪ ᑮᑲᐧᐩ. ᓇᒪ ᑮᑲᐧᐩ ᐁ ᐅᐦᒋ ᒫᒥᑐᓀᔨᐦᑕᒫᐣ. ᐊᓄᐦᐨ ᐁᑲᐧ, ᓈᓂᑕᐤ ᑲ ᐊᐧᓂᓯᓂᔮᐣ, ᓂᑳᐦ ᓂᐸᐦᐃ ᓴᑭᓯᐣ. ᓃᓱ ᑮᓯᑳᐤ ᐁ ᐊᐧᓂᓯᓂᔮᕽ, ᐆᒪ ᐁᑲᐧ ᐊᔭ next day, ᒉᐧᐦᒋ ᐊᓂᒪ ᐁ ᐋᐱᐦᑖ ᑮᓯᑳᐠ ᑳ ᒥᐢᑳᑲᐃᐧᔮᕽ.

[22] ᐁᑲᐧ ᓀᑌ ᐁ ᐋᐧᐸᐦᑕᒫᐣ ᐯᔭᑲᐧᔭᐠ, ᐊᓂᓯ ᐃᓯ (ᓂᒧᓲᒼ ᐊᔨᐢ ᒫᓇ ᓈᒍᐁᐧᐤ ᑮ ᓂᐦᑖ ᑖᐸᑫᐧᐤ), ᐊᓂᓯ ᐃᓯ ᐁ ᑮᐢᑲᑕᐦᐃᑳᑌᑭ ᐊᓂᐦᐃ ᓃᐱᓯᔭ ᐆᐦᐅ, ᐁ ᑮᐢᑲᑕᐦᐃᑳᑌᑭ ᐊᓂᓯ ᐃᓯ, ᓵᑲᐦᐃᑲᓂᓯᐢ ᐯᔭᐠ ᐁᑯᑌ ᐊᓂᒪ ᐁ ᑕᑯᐦᑌᔮᕽ. ᑳ ᐋᐧᐸᐦᑕᒫᐣ ᐊᓂᐦᐃ ᐁᑯᓯ ᐃᓯ, ᐁᑲᐧ ᒪᐢᑯᓰᓴ ᐁ ᐊᐢᑌᑭ ᐊᓂᓯ ᐃᓯ, ᐃᑕ ᑖᐱᐢᑰᐨ ᐊᐃᐧᔭᐠ ᐁ ᑮ ᐊᐱᐟ, ᐁᑲᐧ ᐊᐊᐧ ᓂᓰᒥᐢ ᑳ ᐃᑕᐠ, «ᐄᐦ.» ᓂᑎᑖᐤ, «ᑭᐄᐧ ᑕᑯᓯᓂᓇᐤ,» ᓂᑎᑖᐤ, ᓂᐢᑕᒼ ᐊᓂᒪ ᐁ ᑎᐱᐢᑳᐠ, ᐁ ᐊᑎ ᐅᑖᑯᓯᐠ, «ᑭᐄᐧ ᑕᑯᓯᓂᓇᐤ,» ᓂᑎᑖᐤ, «ᑭᒧᓲᒥᓇᐤ ᐁᑎᑫᐧ ᐆᐦᐅ ᒫᑲ ᒦᓇ ᐆᑕ ᓈᓂᑕᐤ ᐁ ᑮ ᑖᐸᑫᐧᐟ,» ᓂᑎᑖᐤ ᐆᒪ, «ᐆᑕ ᐁᑎᑫᐧ ᒫᓇ ᐊᐦᔭ ᐁ ᑮ ᐸ ᐲᐦᑖᐧᐟ ᐆᒪ, ᑳ ᐃᓯᓈᑲᐧᕽ,» ᓂᑎᑖᐤ.

[23] ᒫᑲ ᐁᓴ ᒨᔭ, ᐁᒋᑲ ᐊᓂ ᒫᓇ ᐁᑎᑫᐧ ᐆᒪ ᑳ ᒫᒌᒋᐠ, ᑳ ᐊᓴᐋᐧᐱᒋᐠ ᐆᒪ, ᐁᐊᐧᑯ ᐅᐦᒋ ᐊᓂᒪ ᐁᑎᑫᐧ ᐁᓴ ᐊᓂᒪ, ᑮ ᐃᑌᐧᐤ ᓂᒧᓲᒼ, ᐊᓂᒪ ᑳ ᑮᐢᑲᑕᐦᐃᑳᓱᒋᐠ ᐊᓂᑭᐠ, ᐁᑲᐧ ᓀᒪ ᒪᐢᑯᓲᓴ ᑳ ᐊᐢᑌᑭ ᒫᓇ ᐆᒪ, ᑳ ᐊᓴᐧᐦᐃᑫᒋᐠ ᑳ ᒫᒌᒋᐠ ᐆᒪ, ᐁᑯᑐᐃᐧᕽ ᐊᓂᒪ ᐁᓴ ᐁ ᑮ ᐅᑎᐦᑕᒫᕽ. ᑯᓂᑕ ᐁ ᐸᐹᒧᐦᑌᔮᐣ ᐁᑯᑕ, ᐁ ᐸᐹᒥ ᓂᑐᓇᒫᐣ, «ᐊᐦᔭ ᐁᑎᑫᐧ ᑮᑲᐧᐩ

ᑮ ᐊᔭᐢᑲᐧᐦᑕᒪᐧᐠ, ᑮᑲᐧ+ ᐁ ᐍᐱᓇᐦᑭᐠ,» ᐁ ᐃᑌᔭᐦᑕᒫᐟ, ᑯᓂᑕ ᐁᑯᑕ ᐁ ᐸᐹᒥ ᓂᑐᓇᒫᐟ ᑮᑲᐧ+ ᑲ ᒦᒋᔮᕽ.

[24] ᐁᑯᓯ ᐁᑎᑫᐧ.

6.
Household Chores

Irene Calliou

[FA:] aw âwa pêyak iskwêw, ê-wî-âcimostâkoyahk anohc; ka-wîhtâmakonaw ê-isiyîhkâsot êkwa tânitê ohci wiya – êkosi sôskwâc ka-mâc-âcimon, *Irene*.

[IC:] êha.

[1] aya, *Irene Calliou* niya, 'pakicahwânisihk' isiyîhkâtêw anima, aya, âpihtawikosisânaskîhk, êkotê ohci niya. êkwa nimosôm ê-wî-âcimak, amisko-sâkahikanihk ê-kî-ayâcik, êkota mâna nîstanân ê-kî-ayâyâhk ê-awâsisîwiyâhk; 'apisihkwês' kî-isiyîhkâsow nimosôm, '*Alphonse* apisihkwês' ('*Alphonse Smallface*') ê-kî-isiyîhkâsot nimosôm. mâka nôhkom wiya môy nikiskisin, tânis ê-kî-isiyîhkâsot. êwakw âwa nimosôm kâ-wî-âcimak; miton ê-kî-nihtâ-minahot awa nimosôm, ê-kiskisiyân. kâ-takwâkik mâna, môswa ê-kî-nihtâ-nipahât, apisimôsoswa, êkwa nôhkom awa mân ê-osîhtât wiyâs ôma, ê-pâsahk, kâhkêwakwa ê-osîhtât. êkwa mâna mîna nimosôm ê-kî-pakitahwât, atihkamêkwa ê-kî-mâh-misi-nip-- -nipahât; êkoni mîna mâna nôhkom ê-kî-pânisâwêt ê-kaskâpaswât. â, kî-wîhkitisiwak mâna. nimâmâ mân êkota wîst ê-kî-wîcihtâsot.

[2] êkwa, êkwa k-ât-âhkwatiniyik ôma, êkota mân ê-kî-mâh-misi-pakitahwât nimosôm, kêyâpic. êkw ê-kî-- ê-kî-osîhtât mâna mîtosihk, sakâhk, 'akocikan' mâna kî-isiyîhkâtamwak, êkota mân ê-kî-- ê-kî-ahât kinosêwa ka-- k-âhkwaciyit, ka-mowihcik ka-- kâ-pipohk, mihcêt mân êkota, ê-kî-têpipayihk mâna.

[3] êkwa mâna mîna kâ-miyoskamik, ê-kî-nihtâ-nôcihcikêt, ê-kî-wanihikêt, wacaskwa ê-nâh-ni---misi-nipahât [*sic*], amiskwa; êkwa nôhkom ê-kî-wîcihtâsot mîn êkota ê-pahkonikêt. êkwa ê-kiskisiyân mân ê-awâsisîwiyâhk nimis, êkospî, ê-kî-maskahtoyâhk mân âmiskwâyowa, ê-kî-nawacîyâhk mân îskotêhk, ahpô kotawânâpiskohk tahkohc; êkw ê-mîciyâhk mân ôhi. êkwa nipâpâ mâna wîsta, nôhtâwiy ê-kî-wî-- ê-kî-wîcêwât nimosôma,

[FA:] This is the one, this woman here is going to tell us stories today; she will tell us her name and where she is from – alright, you can just start telling us your story, Irene.

[IC:] Okay.

[1] Well, I am Irene Calliou, from the place called *pakicahwânisihk,* well, the Métis Settlement over there, that is where I am from. And now I am going to tell about my grandfather, they used to live at *amisko-sâkahikanihk,* and there we, too, used to live when we were children; my grandfather's name was *apisihkwês,* Alphonse *apisihkwês* (Alphonse Smallface) was my grandfather's name. But as for my grandmother, I do not remember her name. It is this one, my grandfather, that I am going to tell about; my grandfather used to be a very good hunter, I remember. In the fall he used to be good at killing moose and also deer, and then my grandmother would prepare the meat, drying it and making dried meat. And then also my grandfather used to set out nets, and he used to kill lots of whitefish; and these my grandmother used to fillet and smoke. Oh, they did taste good. My mom, too, used to help with that.

[2] Then, then at freeze-up, my grandfather still used to catch lots of fish in his net. And in the poplars, in the bush, he used to make what they called a 'storage-box', and there he used to put the fish to freeze, to be eaten in the winter; plenty of them, and they used to have enough.

[3] And then also in spring he used to be a good trapper, he used to set traps and he killed lots of muskrat and beaver; and my grandmother used to help with that, too, with the skinning. And I remember, at that time when we were children, how my older sister and I used to fight over the beaver-tails; we used to roast them at the fire or on top of the stove and then eat them. And my dad, too,

ê-nitawi-nôcihcikêcik ê-miyoskamik; mihcêt mân ê-kî-pêsiwâcik wacaskwa.

[4] êkwa kâ-miyoskaminiyik, ê-kî-mâh-misi-nipahât sîsîpa; ê-kiskisiyân mâna p--, nitawi-nôcihâci mâna sîsîpa ê-kî-- ê-nitawi-nakiskawâyâhk mân ê-âh-asawâpamâyâhk ka-pêcâstamohtêt, ê-pê-misi-tahkonât mâna sîsîpa, êkwa nimis êkwa niya mân ê-kî-nakiskawâyâhk awa nimosôm; ê-kî-miyikoyâhk mâna sîsîpa ka-tahk---tâh-tahkonâyâhkik. iyikohk mân ê-kî-môcikêyihtamâhk ê-miywêyihtamâhk, êkwa mâna nimâmâ ni-- êkwa nôhkom ê-kî-osîhâcik. êkwa sîsîpâwa mân ê-kî-- ê-kî-nitonahk, sâkahikanihk êkota; ôsi mân ê-kî-ayât, êkota mîna mân ê-kî-wîcêwâyâhk. ê-kî-kakâyawisît nimosôm; ê-kî--

[*external break*]

[5] êkwa, nôhkom mâna êkwa nim-- nimâmâ ê-kî-pahkêkinohkêcik ôhi pahkêkinwa kî-minahoci awa nimosôm, ê-kî-ka-kanawâpahkêyâhk mâna, ê-kî-- ê-kî-osîhâcik ôhi pahkêkinwa; êkwa mwêstas mâna ê-kî-- ê-kî-kaskikwâsocik, maskisina, kahkiyaw kîkway ê-osîhtâcik.

[6] êkwa nôhkom, ê-kiskisiyân mâna kâh-wî-pahkwêsikanihkêci, kinosêwi-wa--, wâhkwana mân ê-kî-ahât êkota pahkwêsikanihk, pahkwêsikana ê-kîsiswât. ê-kî-wîhkitisit mâna, *ban-- bannock* ê-kî-osîhât; ê-kiskisiyân mân ê-kî-wîhkitisit êwakw âna, wayawîtimihk mâna pâskac ê-kî-kîsiswât. êkwa wâposwa mîna mâna ê-kî-tâpakwêcik iskwêwak, ê-mâh-misi-nipahâcik wâposwa; êkoni mîna mâna ê-kaskâ-- ê-kaskâpaswâcik. nanâtohk mâna iskwêwak (ê-kî-kakâyawisîcik) ê-kî-tôtahkik, ê-kiskisiyân; ê-kisîpêkinikêcik, *washboard*

– ôta –

ê-âpacihtâcik, ma kîkway êko-- êkospî ôhi môniyâw-âya ê-kî-âpacihtâcik.

[*external break*]

[7] êkwa sîsîpak mîna, kâh-nipahâci mâna nimosôm, otakisiya mîna mân ânih ê-kî-kanâcihtâcik, iyikohk -- niyanân mîn

my father used to go along with my grandfather and they would go trapping in the spring; they used to bring home plenty of muskrats.

[4] And in the spring they used to kill lots of ducks; I remember how we would go and meet him when he went hunting for ducks and how we would watch for him to come back, carrying back many ducks, and then my older sister and I used to wait for my grandfather; he used to give us ducks to carry. We used to be so excited and happy, and then my mom and my grandmother would prepare them. And he [*sc.* my grandfather] used to search for duck-eggs, there at the lake; he used to have a boat and we would go along with him. My grandfather worked hard; he used to --

[*external break*]

[5] And then my grandmother and my mom used to make hides of the skins when my grandfather had made a kill, we used to watch, they used to prepare the hides; and later they used to sew, making moccasins and everything else.

[6] And my grandmother, I remember when she was going to make bannock, she used to put fish-eggs into the bannock, when she cooked bannock. The bannock used to taste good, and she used to make it [*sc.* this special bannock]; I remember how that tasted good – to top it off, she cooked it outside [*sc.* on an open fire]. And the women also used to snare rabbits, killing lots of rabbits; and these, too, they would smoke. The women used to do all kinds of things (they used to work hard), I remember; doing the laundry with a washboard,

– here –

they did not have these White gadgets [*sc.* washing-machines] to use.

[*external break*]

[7] And then the ducks, every time my grandfather had killed them, they used to clean out the guts, and we as children used to

ê-kî-wîcihtâsoyâhk ê-awâsisîwiyâhk, ê-kanâcihtâyâhk anihi otakisiya ê-nawacîyâhk iskôtêhk. êkwa otitâmiyawa mîna, môswa ohci, ê-kî-kanâcihtâcik. ma kîkway ohci-wêpinamwak, kahkiyaw ê-kî-âpacihtâcik ê-mît-- ê-mîciyâhk.

– awas; êkosi pitamâ.

[*external break*]

[8] êkwa nimosôm mâna ê-kî-âpacihât ôhi îkihtawitâpâna, êkotowahk mân ê-kiskisiyân ê-kî-- ê-kî-âpacihât; kî-minahoci, êkotowahk mân ê-kî-âp-- ê-is-âpacihât sakâhk, ê-nâtahk anima wiyâs. êkwa otâpânâskwa mîna, wâh-nitawi-pakitahwâci (wâhyaw ayis êkot[a] ôhci sâkahikan itê mâna kâ-kî-pakitahwât), misatimwa êkwa otâpânâskwa ê-kî-âpacihât.

– êkosi piko, awas.

[*external break*]

[9] êkwa iskwêwak mîna mâna ê-kî-misi-mâh-mawisocik; takwahiminâna ê-kî-mawis---misi-mawisocik ê-takwahahkik, ê-pâsahkik; misâskwatômina mîna ê-kî-pâsahkik. êkwa aya, îwahikana ê-kî-mâh-mis-ôsîhâcik, os-- môsowiyâs ohci, êkwa mân ê-kî-asiwatâcik ôhi, ôh âya –

– tânisi ê-isiyîhkâtêki anihi? –

[FA:] – *I can't think of it, birch-basket,* waskwayiwat; –

[IC:] – êha, –

waskwayiwatihk mâna ê-kî-asiwatâ---asiwatâcik ôhi mînisa, aya mîna mân âya, ê-kî-misi-mâh-mawisocik aya,

– *cranberries?* –

[FA:] – wîsakîmina; –

wîsakîmina, êkotowa-- êkotowihk mîna mân ê-kî-asiwatâcik, êkwa kâ-piponiyik mâna, wayawîtimihk ê-astâcik ê-âh-- ê-âhkwatihtâcik.

– êkosi pitamâ.

[*external break*]

[10] êkw âwâ-- awâsisak mâna ê-kî-mêtawâkêcik aya, ê-miyihcik anihi wîhkwaya, kinosêwak [*sic*] ohci, pîhc-âyihk ohci kinosêwa [*sic*]. êkw ânihi pihêwak ohci, paspaskiwak êkwa kotakak aniki pihêwak, wahkway[a] [*sic; cf.* wîhkwaya] ânih ê-kî-pôtâtahkik mâna,

help with that, cleaning the guts and roasting them on the fire. And also the stuff inside a moose, they also used to clean that. They did not throw away anything, they used to make use of everything and we ate it.

– Go on, that's it for now.
[*external break*]

[8] And my grandfather used to use the travois, that kind I remember him using; when he had made a kill, he used to use that kind in the bush to bring back the meat. And also a wagon, every time he went to fish (for the lake was far from here where he used to fish), he used to use horses and a wagon.

– That's it, go on.
[*external break*]

[9] And the women also used to do a lot of berrying; they picked lots of chokecherries, crushing and drying them; they also used to dry saskatoons. And they used to make lots of pounded meat, from moose-meat, and they used to put it in –

– what are they called? –
[FA:] – I can't think of it, birch-basket, birch-bark basket; –
[IC:] – yes, –

they used to put the berries into birch-bark baskets, and they also used to pick lots of, well,

– cranberries? –
[FA:] – cranberries; –

cranberries, that kind -- in that kind they used to put them, and then in winter they would place them outside and freeze them.

– That's it for now.
[*external break*]

[10] And the children used to play with these, the airbladders of the fish, from inside the fish, were given to them. And from the prairie-chickens, too, and from partridges and other kinds of chickens, they

ê-pâsamâhk; ẹ-kî-mêtawâkêyâhk, nîkân mân ê-kanâcihtâyâhk; ê-kî-pôtâtamâhk ê-mêtawâkêyâhk mâna, ê-tahkopitamâhk kî-pôtâtamihki.

– êkosi pitamâ.

[*external break*]

[11] êkwa kinosêwa ôh--, wâwikaniwâhk ohc âni--, ê-kî-mêtawâkêyâhk mâna ê-wa-osîkahoniyâhk, ê-kî-sîkahoyâhk mân ôhc êkoni, êkwa iskwêwak mân ê-kî-osîhâcik awâsisîhkâna, ê-wa-wâspitâcik.

– êkosi pitamâ.

[*external break*]

[FA:] êkwa.

[12] êkwa nimis êkwa niya mân ê-kî-mêtawêyâhk sakâhk, tâpiskôc wâskahikanis mân ê-kî-osîhtâyâhk, êkota ê-mêtawêyâhk; ahpô papakwânikamikos [*sic*] mân ê-kî-osîhtâyâhk.

[13] êkwa nôhkom mân âya, îwahikana k-ôsîhât, ê-kî-âpacihtât mân âya – â, pimîhkân ê-ôsîhât, êkw âya, takwahiminâna êkota mân ê-kî-astât êkwa misâskwatômina; kî-wîhkasin mâna pimîhkân.

[14] êkwa kotak mîna kîkway ê-kî-- ê-kiskisiyân, nôhkom mân ê-kî-ocipitahk anihi,

– tânisi – môy nikiskêyihtên tânis ê-isiyîhkâtêk[i] ânihi *wild rhubarb*; –

[FA:] – môy nîsta; –

wild rhubarb anihi ê-kî-ocipitahk ê-pîhtonahk êkwa ê-pîkinisahk, mîcimâpôhk ê-kî-astât; ê-kî-wîhkasik mân ânima mîcimâpoy. êkwa mîna mâna misâskwatômina mîn êkota ê-kî-astât mîcimâpôhk, ê-mîcimâpôhkâkêt; êkwa pahkwêsikana ê-itêhwât, êkota ê-astât. kî-wîhkasin mâna mîcimâpoy.

[15] êkwa iskwêwak mîna kotak kîkway aya, ê-kî-tôtahkik, nanâtohk mâna ê-kî-is-âtoskêcik, askiya ê-kî-akotâcik sisonê s-- maskêkohk, ê-pâsahkik; êkwa mân îsk-- iskwêwak mâna ê-kî-mêkicik, êkwa nimâmâ wîsta ê-kî-âpacihtât nisîmis ê-pêpîwit,

used to blow up the air-sacks and dry them; we used to play with them, first cleaning them out; we used to blow them up and play with them, tying them shut when they were blown up.

– That's it for now.
[*external break*]

[11] And the fish, we used to play with their backbones, using them as combs, we used to comb our hair with these, and the women used to make dolls and wrap them in mossbags.

– That's it for now.
[*external break*]

[FA:] And then.

[12] And my sister and I used to play in the bush, we used to make it like a little house and play there; or we used to make a little tent.

[13] And when my grandmother used to make pounded meat, she used to use – she prepared pemmican, she used to put in chokecherries and saskatoons; the pemmican did taste good.

[14] And I also remember another thing, my grandmother used to pull up these,

– what – I don't know what they are called,
these wild rhubarbs; –

[FA:] – I don't, either; –

she used to pull up these wild rhubarbs and peel them and cut them up, she used to put them into soup; that soup used to taste good. And then she also put saskatoons in there, in the soup, making soup with them; stirring in flour for thickening and putting them [*sc*. the berries] in there. The soup did taste good.

[15] And the women also used to do other things, they used to work at all kinds of things, they used to hang up moss along the swamp and dry it; and the women used to give it out [*sc*. as a gift], and my mom herself used to use it when my little sister was an infant,

– *what do you call a mossbag?* –

[FA:] – ê-kî-wâspitihcik, –

ê-kî-wâspitihcik aya pêpîsisak, askiy[a] ânih ê-kî-âpatahki; ma kîkway êkospi wiy âsiyâna kîkway ohc-âtâwêwak ahpô ê-ohc-âpacihâcik.

[16] êkwa, nôhkom mâna ê-kî-osîhtât anihi --, ê-kî-osîhtât aya, waskwayiwata, nanâtohk mân ê-kî-is-âpacihtâcik, mînisa ê-asiwatâcik, okaskikwâsowina mân ê-kî-asiwatât êkota, nanâtohk is ê-kî-isi---itâpatahki [*sic*].

[17] êkwa nim-- nimosôm mân ê-kî-- matotisân ê-kî-osîhtât, ê-kî-matotisit. êkwa êkota mân ê-kî-pîkiskwêt, ê-nanâskômât êtokwê kâ-tipêyihcikêyit, ê-nanâskomât, iyikohk mâna ê-kî-- ê-kî-mâh-misi-nipahtât kîkway, êtokwê.

[18] êkwa mâna mîna, nikî-wa-- nikî-wâpahtên, môy -- môy tâpwê mâka nikiskisin, ê-kî-nipâkwêsimohk. êkwa mâna ê-kî--, îskwêwak mâna, mihcêt mân îskwêwak ê-kî-itohtêcik sakâhk ê-nitaw-- – 'mêstan' kî-isiyîhkâtêwak, anihi mâna ê-kî-nâtâcik mîtosihk, ê-kî-pîhtoswâcik aya, mîtosa, êkwa mês-- mêstan an[a], ê-kî-otinâcik; êkwa mân ê-kî-asamihcik ôki kâ-nipâkwêsimocik, â, môy nikiskêyihtên tânêhki k-ôh-- k-âsamihcik, môy -- kîkway êtokwê ohci.

– êkosi pitamâ.

[*external break*]

[19] êkwa, iskwêwak mîna mân âya, ôm ê-kî-tôtahkik, wa--

[FA:] – waskway cî? –

waskwaya mâna ê-kî-papâm-âya--, môhkomân ahpô cîkahikanis ê-kî-tahkonahkik, ê-kî-cîkahwâcik apisis êkwa miscikos mân êkota ê-sêkonahkik; êkw ânim âya, *syrup* anim âya ê-kî-ohcikawahk êkota; êkwa askihkosa mâna sîpâ êkot[a] ê-âstât ê-wâpanastâcik aya, ê-ohcikawahk êkota, êkwa kîkisêpâ mân ê-kî-papâm-- ê-papâmi-nâtâcik anih âskihkosa. môy mâka nikis-- nikiskisin tânisi mân ê-kî-tôtahkik, matwân cî ê-kî-pakâhtâcik ahpô --. mâka

– what do you call a mossbag? –
[FA:] – they used to be wrapped up in them, –
the infants used to be wrapped up in a mossbag, that moss was used; they did not buy or use any diapers then.

[16] And my grandmother used to prepare those -- she used to prepare birch-bark baskets, they used to use them for all kinds of purposes, putting berries in, and she used to keep her sewing in there, they were used for all kinds of things.

[17] And my grandfather used to prepare a sweat-lodge, he used to use the sweat-lodge. And he used to speak his prayers in there, giving thanks to the Lord, I guess, giving thanks to him for having killed so many things, I guess.

[18] And then I did see a Sun-Dance, but I don't remember very much. And the women, many women used to go into the bush – they called it 'sap', they went to get that from the poplars, they used to take the bark off the poplars, and they used to get the sap; and those who danced the Sun-Dance were given that to eat, well, I don't remember why they were given it to eat, for what purpose.
– That's it for now.
[*external break*]

[19] And then the women used to do that,
[FA:] – birch? –
the birches, they used to take a knife or a hatchet, they used to chop into them a little, and insert a little stick in there; and that stuff, that syrup, used to drip out there; then one placed a little pail underneath there, they placed it overnight, and it dripped out there, and in the morning they would go around and fetch the pails. But I don't remember how they used to treat this [*sc.* the syrup], I wonder if they boiled it or --. But

niyanân wiya k-âwâsisîwiyâhk mâna ê-kiskisiyân ê-kî-minihkwêyâhk mâna, êwakw ânima ê-kî-- ê-kî-wîhkasik.
– êkosi.

[20]
[FA:] aya mâka pikiw? kîstawâw cî mâna kikî-mâwasakonâwâw ôh âya --
[IC:] *spruce-gum* cî ana?
[FA:] *spruce-gum*.
[IC:] êha; niyanân wiy ê-awâsisîwiyâhk ê-kî-- ê-kî-nitaw-ôtinâyâhk mân ê-mâmâkwamâyâhk. kî-miyosiw mâna êwakw âna, ê-mâmâkwa-- ê-mâmâkwamiht.
[FA:] sisonê sâkahikanihk mâka, kikî-mowâwâw -- kikî-manâhonâwâw cî mâna ka-mîciyêk anihi mâskosiwâna?
[IC:] êha, ê-kî-ocipitamâhk mâna, wanaskoc mân ânihi, êkon ânihi, âha.
[FA:] êha, wâpiskâwa.
[IC:] êha, êkotowahk mân ê-kî-mîciyâhk mâna.
[*external break*]
[FA:] êkosi.

[21] â, aya, iskwêwak aya, mîna mân âya, ê-kî-osîhâcik mâna ayapiya, miton ê-mâh-mis-ôsîhâcik êkotowahk, ê-kâh-kinwâpêkisiyit; êkoni mân ê-kî-âp-- ê-âpacihât -- ê-âpacihâcik aya kâ-pakitahwâcik, êkwa nimosôm mîna mân âya, asâma ê-kî-osîhât; ê-kî-kanawâpamâyâhk mân ê-osîhât êkotowahk, ê-mâh-misi-osîhât, ê-atotiht k-osîhât.
– êkos êtokwê.
[FA:] tânisi mâka ê-kî-- ê-kî-mâcîwâkêt cî mâna wîsta?
êha, kâ-piponiyik mâna ê-kî-- ê-kî-postiskahk kâ-mâcît.
[*external break*]
-- *birch* êtokwê, ê-kî-âpacihât, --
[FA:] êskwa! *birch* --
[*external break*]
[FA:] êkosi.

we used to drink it when we were children, I remember, and it tasted good.

– That's it.

[20]

[FA:] What about rosin? Did you, too, use to collect the --

[IC:] Do you mean spruce-gum?

[FA:] Spruce-gum.

[IC:] Yes; we used to go and get it when we were children, and chew on it. That used to be good to chew on.

[FA:] What about along the lake, did you eat them -- did you gather the reeds to eat?

[IC:] Yes, we used to pull them out, these things at the end, it was them, yes.

[FA:] Yes, they are white [*sc.* the ends, which are under water].

[IC:] Yes, we used to eat that kind.

[*external break*]

[FA:] Now.

[21] Well, the women also used to make nets, they used to make many of that kind, long strung-out ones; these she used -- they used when they fished, and my grandfather also used to make snowshoes; we used to watch him make that kind, making lots of them, he was asked to make them.

– That's it, I guess.

[FA:] For what did he use to -- did he, too, use them to hunt with?

Yes, in winter he used to put them on when he went hunting.

[*external break*]

-- birch he used, I guess.

[FA:] Wait! birch --

[*external break*]

[FA:] Go ahead.

[22] aya, ayisiyiniwak mân ôki kâ-kî-pê-kiyokawâcik mâna, nimosôm[a] êkwa nôhkoma ê-kî-mâ--, nôhkom mân ê-kî-mâh-mis-âsamât wiyâs ahpô kinosêwa, êkos îsi ê-kî-nihtâ-asahkêcik; ê-kî-- ê-kî-piminawasot mân ê-misi-piminawasot ê-asamât êkwa, kotaka -- kotak mîn ê-kî-asamât mâna, ka-kîwêhtatâcik [*sic*].

[23] êkwa, kotak kîkway mîn ê-kiskisiyân mâna k-âwâsisîwiyâhk, môy ê-ôhci-pakitinikawiyâhk, pîhc-âyihk k-âyâyâhk kîspin kêhtê-ayak kâ-pê-kiyokêcik; wayawîtimihk piko ê-ayâyâhk.

[FA:] kikî-âh-âcimostâkawinâwâw cî mâna, kîstawâw?

[24] êha, wîsahkêcâhk, âta wiya mâna kî-âcimêw, nôhkom ahpô nimosôm [*laughs*]. môy tâpwê nikiskisin êkoni, âcimowinisa mâna nimosôm ê-kî-âtotahk. wîsahkêcâhk piko mâna nikiskisin âtiht, ê-kî-âcimât, omikiy wiyê [*sic*] kâ-mîcit wîsahkêcâhk, êwakw ânima wiya nikiskisin mitoni [*laughs*].

– êkosi pitamâ.

[*external break*]

[FA:] êkosi.

[25] âskaw mâna mîna mâna nikî-wîcêwânân nôhkom, êkwa nimâmâ, âskaw ê-kî-wîcihiwêt wîst êkota. ê-kî-mônahahk mâna maskihkiya, nôhkom; êkwa kî-mônahahki mâna, êkota ê-ahât cistêmâwa. môy mâna nô-- nôhci-kiskêyihtên tânêhki, êkospî, cistêmâwa k-âhât.

[26] êkwa mâna mih--, mistahi maskihkiy mâna kî-kiskêyihtamwak nimosôm êkwa nôhkom. ê-kî-wâh-osîhtamawâcik mân âyisiyiniwa miskîsik-maskihkiy, môy nikiskêyihtên mâka, môy nôh-kiskinohamâkawin kîkway êkota. ahpô kêyâpic nimâmâ êwakw ânima maskihkiy kiskêyihtam, ê-miywâsiniyiki nisk-- miskîsikwa ohci.

– êkosi pitamâ.

[*external break*]

[22] Well, the people who used to come to visit them, my grandfather and my grandmother, my grandmother used to give them lots of meat or fish to eat, in this way they were always giving out food; she used to cook, cooking lots of food and then feeding them, and she also used to give them more food, for them to take home.

[23] And another thing I remember from when we were children, we were not allowed to stay inside if Elders came to visit; we had to stay outside.

[FA:] Did you, too, use to have stories told to you?

[24] Yes, especially about Wisahketchahk, my grandmother or my grandfather used to tell stories about him. I don't remember much of the little stories which my grandfather used to tell. I only remember a few about Wisahketchahk, he used to tell stories about him, I well remember the one where Wisahketchahk ate his own scab.

– That's it for now.
[*external break*]

[FA:] Now.

[25] Sometimes we also used to go along with my grandmother, and my mom, too, sometimes used to go along. My grandmother used to dig up medicinal roots; and once she had dug them up, she placed tobacco there [*sc.* in the hole]. I did not know then why she put tobacco in.

[26] And my grandfather and my grandmother used to know a lot about medicine. They used to prepare various medicines for people, eye-medicine, but I don't know it, I was not taught what was in it. Even now, my mom still knows that medicine, it is good medicine for the eyes.

– That's it for now.
[*external break*]

[27] â, nimosôm êkwa, nâpêwa kotak[a] ê-kî-- ê-kî-wîcêwât, nâpêwak ôki ê-kî-nitawi-nawatahikêcik, 'nêyâhk' mâna kî-isiyîhkâtamwak, itê ê-nitawi-nawatahikêhk mâna; kaskitêsipa ê-nawatahwâcik. mihcêt mân ê-kî-- ê-kî-mâh-misi-nipahâcik, êkwa mwêstas mâna ê-kî-papâmi-asahkêcik, kotaka ayisiyiniwa ê-papâm-âsamâcik ôhi sîsîpa.

[28] êkwa mîna mâna nimosôm mân ê-kî-â-- ê-kî-kakêskimikoyâhk. "kêhtê-ayisiyiniw kâkikê manâcih! êkây wîhkâc nêpêwisi kêhtê-ayisiyiniw ka-pîkiskwâtat!" ê-kî-itikoyâhk mâna. êkos-- êkosi mâna nititôtên mâna niya anohc kâ-kîsikâk. kiyâm ât[a] âwiyak êkây ê-nisitawêyimak ninitawi-pîkiskwâtâw mâna. n-- takahkêyihtamwak ôki kêhtê-ayisiyiniwak ka-pîkis-- kwayask ka-pîkiskwâtihcik, kwayask ê-kitâpamihcik.

– êkosi pitamâ.
[*external break*]

[29] êkwa mâna -- mâna mîna nimosôm ê-kî-pîhtwâtahk ôhi cikâsipakwa, ê-kî-misi-nâtahk mân ê-kî-- ê-pâsahk, mihkwâpêmakwa asici. êkoni mîn ê-pâsahk, ê-kâskahahk ôhi, mihkwâpêmakwa, êkwa êkoni mân ê-kî-pîhtwâtahk, ôspwâkanihk [*sic*] ê-kî-pîhtwât. môy wîhkâc wiya nikiskisin cistêmâwa awiyak k-âpacihât.

– êkosi pitamâ.
[*external break*]

[30] êkwa mâna mîn âna nôhkom êkwa nimâmâ mân ê-kî-kaskikwâsocik mistahi. kahkiyaw mân âyiwinisa ê-kî-osîhtamâkoyâhkik, môy kîkway ê-ohc-âtâwêcik, ahpô asikana ê-kî-osîhâcik, astisa, astotina, maskisina, miskotâkaya, kahkiyaw sôskwâc mân ê-kî-osîhtâcik, mistah ê-kî-kaskikwâsocik iskwêwak; êkospî wiya môy wîhkâc ohc-âtâwêwak kîkway.

[FA:] aya mâka akohpa?

akohpa mîna kî-mâh-misi-- ê-kî-osîhtamâsocik, ê-nanâtohkokwâsocik; môy ôhc-âtâwêwak.

[FA:] aspiskwêsimona?

[27] Well, and my grandfather went along with other men, the men used to go shooting ducks on the fly, they used to call it ***nêyâhk*** where one went shooting ducks on the fly; shooting black-ducks on the fly. They used to kill them in large numbers, and later they used to go around feeding people, feeding other people with these ducks.

[28] And my grandfather also used to counsel us. "Always treat older people with respect! Don't ever be too shy to speak to older people!" he used to say to us. I still do that today. Even if I don't know someone, I go and speak to them. Older people like being addressed properly and being treated with proper respect.

– That's it for now.
[*external break*]

[29] And my grandfather used to smoke these leaves, he used to go and collect lots and dry them; along with red willows. They scraped and dried the red willows [*sc*. after removing the bark], and he used to smoke them; he used to smoke them in his pipe. I don't remember anyone ever using tobacco.

– That's it for now.
[*external break*]

[30] And my grandmother and my mom also used to sew a great deal. They made all our clothes for us, they did not buy anything, they even used to make socks, mitts, hats, shoes, coats, they just made everything, the women used to sew a great deal; at that time, of course, they never used to buy anything.

[FA:] What about blankets, then?

They also made lots of blankets for themselves, sewing patchwork-quilt blankets; they did not buy them.

[FA:] Pillows?

êkotowahk mîna ê-kî-osîhtâcik, sîsîp-opîwaya ohci. êkwa, wâposwayâna mân ê-kî-osîhâcik, *there was -- uh,* sîsîp-akohpa, sîsîp-opîway[a] ôhci êkotowahk mîn ê-kî-osîhtâcik kî--; kîsowâwa mâna, êkoni akohpa, k-osîhtâcik.

[FA:] maskisina mâka?

[IC:] *moccasins?*

[FA:] âha.

âsay wiy êwakw ânima niwîhtên. êkosi.

They also made that kind, from duck-feathers. And they prepared rabbit-skins, there were duck-blankets, that kind they used to make also, from duck-feathers; they were warm, the blankets which they made.

[FA:] What about shoes, then?

[IC:] Moccasins?

[FA:] Yes.

I told about that already. This is it.

[FA:] ᐊᐊᐧ ᐊᐊᐧ ᐯᔭᐠ ᐃᐢᑫᐧᐤ, ᐁ ᐄᐧ ᐋᒋᒧᐢᑖᑯᔭᕽ ᐊᓄᐦᐨ, ᑲ ᐄᐧᐦᑕᒫᑯᓇᐤ ᐁ ᐃᓯᔩᐦᑳᓱᐟ ᐁᑲᐧ ᑖᓂᑌ ᐅᐦᒋ ᐃᐧᔭ – ᐁᑯᓯ ᓲᐢᑳᐧᐨ ᑲ ᒫᒋ ᐋᒋᒧᐣ, Irene.

[1] ᐊᔭ, Irene Calliou ᓂᔭ, ᐸᑭᒐᐦᐋᐧᓂᓯᕽ ᐃᓯᔩᐦᑳᑌᐤ ᐊᓂᒪ, ᐊᔭ, ᐋᐱᐦᑕᐃᐧᑯᓯᓵᓇᐢᑮᕽ, ᐁᑯᑌ ᐅᐦᒋ ᓂᔭ. ᐁᑲᐧ ᓂᒧᓲᒼ ᐁ ᐄᐧ ᐋᒋᒪᐠ, ᐊᒥᐢᑯ ᓵᑲᐦᐃᑲᓂᕽ ᐁ ᑮ ᐊᔮᒋᐠ, ᐁᑯᑕ ᒫᓇ ᓃᐢᑖᓈᐣ ᐁ ᑮ ᐊᔮᔭᕽ ᐁ ᐊᐋᐧᓯᓰᐃᐧᔮᕽ, ᐊᐱᓯᐦᑫᐧᐢ ᑮ ᐃᓯᔩᐦᑳᓱᐤ ᓂᒧᓲᒼ, ‘Alphonse’ ᐊᐱᓯᐦᑫᐧᐢ, ‘Alphonse Small-Face’ ᐁ ᑮ ᐃᓯᔩᐦᑳᓱᐟ ᓂᒧᓲᒼ. ᒫᑲ ᓅᐦᑯᒼ ᐃᐧᔭ ᒨᔭ ᓂᑭᐢᑭᓯᐣ, ᑖᓂᓯ ᐁ ᑮ ᐃᓯᔩᐦᑳᓱᐟ. ᐁᐊᐧᑯ ᐊᐊᐧ ᓂᒧᓲᒼ ᑳ ᐄᐧ ᐋᒋᒪᐠ, ᒥᑐᓂ ᐁ ᑮ ᓂᐦᑖᒥᓇᐦᐅᐟ ᐊᐊᐧ ᓂᒧᓲᒼ, ᐁ ᑭᐢᑭᓯᔮᐣ. ᑳᑕᑳᐧᑭᐠ ᒫᓇ, ᒨᓴᐧ ᐁ ᑮ ᓂᐦᑖ ᓂᐸᐦᐋᐟ, ᐊᐱᓯᒨᓯᓴᐧ, ᐁᑲᐧ ᓅᐦᑯᒼ ᐊᐊᐧ ᒫᓇ ᐁ ᐅᔫᐦᑖᐟ ᐃᐧᔮᐢ ᐆᒪ, ᐁ ᐹᓴᕽ, ᑳᐦᑫᐊᐧᑲᐧ ᐁ ᐅᔫᐦᑖᐟ. ᐁᑲᐧ ᒫᓇ ᒦᓇ ᓂᒧᓲᒼ ᐁ ᑮ ᐸᑭᑕᐦᐋᐧᐟ, ᐊᑎᐦᑲᒣᑲᐧ ᐁ ᑮ ᒫᐦᒥᓯ ᓂᐸᐦᐋᐟ, ᐁᑯᓂ ᒦᓇ ᒫᓇ ᓅᐦᑯᒼ ᐁ ᑮ ᐹᓂᓵᐁᐧᐟ ᐁ ᑲᐢᑳᐸᓵᐧᐟ. ᐋ, ᑮ ᐃᐧᐦᑭᑎᓯᐊᐧᐠ ᒫᓇ. ᓂᒫᒫ ᒫᓇ ᐁᑯᑕ ᐄᐧᐢᑕ ᐁ ᑮ ᐄᐧᒋᐦᑖᓯᐟ.

[2] ᐁᑲᐧ, ᐁᑲᐧ ᑳ ᐊᑎ ᐋᐦᑲᐧᑎᓂᔮᐠ ᐆᒪ, ᐁᑯᑕ ᒫᓇ ᐁ ᑮ ᒫᐦᒥᓯ ᐸᑭᑕᐦᐋᐧᐟ ᓂᒧᓲᒼ, ᑫᔮᐱᐨ. ᐁᑲᐧ ᐁ ᑮ ᐅᔫᐦᑖᐟ ᒫᓇ ᒦᑐᓯᕽ, ᓴᑳᕽ, ᐊᑯᒋᑲᐣ ᒫᓇ ᑮ ᐃᓯᔩᐦᑳᑕᒪᐧᐠ, ᐁᑯᑕ ᒫᓇ ᐁ ᑮ ᐊᐦᐋᐧᐟ ᑭᓄᓴᐊᐧ ᑲ ᐋᐦᑲᐧᒋᔮᐟ, ᑲ ᒧᐃᐧᐦᒋᐠ ᑳ ᐱᐳᕽ, ᒥᐦᒉᐟ ᒫᓇ ᐁᑯᑕ, ᐁ ᑮ ᑌᐱᐸᔮᕽ ᒫᓇ.

[3] ᐁᑲᐧ ᒫᓇ ᒦᓇ ᑳᒥᔪᐢᑲᒥᐠ, ᐁ ᑮ ᓂᐦᑖ ᓅᒋᐦᒋᑫᐟ, ᐁ ᑮ ᐊᐧᓂᐦᐃᑫᐟ, ᐊᐧᒐᐢᑲᐧ ᐁ ᒫᐦᒥᓯ ᓂᐸᐦᐋᐟ, ᐊᒥᐢᑲᐧ, ᐁᑲᐧ ᓅᐦᑯᒼ ᐁ ᑮ ᐄᐧᒋᐦᑖᓯᐟ ᒦᓇ ᐁᑯᑕ ᐁ ᐸᐦᑯᓂᑫᐟ. ᐁᑲᐧ ᐁ ᑭᐢᑭᓯᔮᐣ ᒫᓇ ᐁ ᐊᐋᐧᓯᓰᐃᐧᔮᕽ ᓂᒥᐢ ᐁᑯᐢᐲ, ᐁ ᑮ ᒪᐢᑲᐦᑐᔮᕽ ᒫᓇ ᐊᒥᐢᑳᐧᔪᐊᐧ, ᐁ ᑮ ᓇᐊᐧᒌᔮᕽ ᒫᓇ ᐃᐢᑯᑌᕽ, ᐊᐦᐳ ᑯᑕᐋᐧᓈᐱᐢᑯᕽ ᑕᐦᑯᐦᐨ, ᐁᑲᐧ ᐁ ᒦᒋᔮᕽ ᒫᓇ ᐆᐦᐃ. ᐁᑲᐧ ᓂᐸᐹ ᒫᓇ ᐄᐧᐢᑕ, ᓅᐦᑖᐃᐧᐩ ᐁ ᑮ ᐄᐧᒉᐋᐧᐟ ᓂᒧᓲᒪ, ᐁ ᓂᑕᐃᐧ ᓅᒋᐦᒋᑫᒋᐠ ᐁ ᒥᔪᐢᑲᒥᐠ, ᒥᐦᒉᐟ ᒫᓇ ᐁ ᑮ ᐯᓯᐋᐧᒋᐠ ᐊᐧᒐᐢᑲᐧ.

[4] ᐁᑲᐧ ᑳᒥᔪᐢᑲᒥᓂᔮᐠ, ᐁ ᑮ ᒫᐦᒥᓯ ᓂᐸᐦᐋᐟ ᓰᓰᐸ, ᐁ ᑭᐢᑭᓯᔮᐣ ᒫᓇ, ᓂᑕᐃᐧ ᓅᒋᐦᐋᒋ ᒫᓇ ᓰᓰᐸ ᐁ ᑮ ᓂᑕᐃᐧ ᓇᑭᐢᑲᐋᐧᔮᕽ ᒫᓇ ᐁ ᐋᐦ ᐊᓴᐋᐧᐸᒫᔮᕽ ᑲ ᐯᒑᐢᑕᒧᐦᑌᐟ, ᐁ ᐯᒥᓯ ᑕᐦᑯᓈᐟ ᒫᓇ ᓰᓰᐸ, ᐁᑲᐧ ᓂᒥᐢ ᐁᑲᐧ ᓂᔭ ᒫᓇ ᐁ ᑮ ᓇᑭᐢᑲᐋᐧᔮᕽ ᐊᐊᐧ ᓂᒧᓲᒼ, ᐁ ᑮ ᒥᔮᑯᔮᕽ ᒫᓇ ᓰᓰᐸ ᑲ ᑖᐦ ᑕᐦᑯᓈᔭᐦᑭᐠ. ᐃᔮᑯᕽ ᒫᓇ ᐁ ᑮ ᒨᒋᑫᔭᐦᑕᒫᕽ ᐁ ᒥᔪᐧᔭᐦᑕᒫᕽ, ᐁᑲᐧ ᒫᓇ ᓂᒫᒫ ᐁᑲᐧ ᓅᐦᑯᒼ ᐁ ᑮ ᐅᔩᐦᐊᒋᐠ. ᐁᑲᐧ ᓰᓰᐸᐊᐧ ᒫᓇ ᐁ ᑮ ᓂᑐᓇᕽ, ᓵᑲᐦᐃᑲᓂᕽ ᐁᑯᑕ, ᐆᓯ ᒫᓇ ᐁ ᑮ ᐊᔮᐟ, ᐁᑯᑕ ᒦᓇ ᒫᓇ ᐁ ᑮ ᐄᐧᒉᐋᐧᔮᕽ. ᐁ ᑮ ᑲᑳᔭᐃᐧᓰᐟ ᓂᒧᓲᒼ.

[5] ᐁᑲᐧ, ᓅᐦᑯᒼ ᒫᓇ ᐁᑲᐧ ᓂᒫᒫ ᐁ ᑮ ᐸᐦᑫᑭᓄᐦᑫᒋᐠ ᐆᐦᐃ ᐸᐦᑫᑭᓇᐧ ᑮ ᒥᓇᐦᐅᒋ ᐊᐊᐧ ᓂᒧᓲᒼ, ᐁ ᑮ ᑲ ᑲᓇᐋᐧᐸᐦᑫᔮᕽ ᒫᓇ, ᐁ ᑮ ᐅᔫᐦᐊᒋᐠ ᐆᐦᐃ ᐸᐦᑫᑭᓇᐧ, ᐁᑲᐧ ᒉᐧᐢᑕᐢ ᒫᓇ ᐁ ᑮ ᑲᐢᑭᑳᐧᓯᒋᐠ, ᒪᐢᑭᓯᓇ, ᑲᐦᑭᔭᐤ ᑮᑲᐧᐩ ᐁ ᐅᔫᐦᑖᒋᐠ.

[6] ᐁᑲᐧ ᓅᐦᑯᒼ, ᐁ ᑭᐢᑭᓯᔮᐣ ᒫᓇ ᑳᐦ ᐄᐧ ᐸᐦᑫᐧᓯᑲᓂᐦᑫᒋ, ᑭᓄᓴᐃᐧ ᐋᐧᐦᑲᐧᓇ ᒫᓇ ᐁ ᑮ ᐊᐦᐋᐧᐟ ᐁᑯᑕ ᐸᐦᑫᐧᓯᑲᓂᕽ, ᐸᐦᑫᐧᓯᑲᓇ ᐁ ᑮᓯᓵᐧᐟ. ᐁ ᑮ ᐄᐧᐦᑭᑎᓯᐟ ᒫᓇ, bannock ᐁ ᑮ ᐅᓰᐦᐋᐧᐟ, ᐁ ᑭᐢᑭᓯᔮᐣ ᒫᓇ ᐁ ᑮ ᐄᐧᐦᑭᑎᓯᐟ ᐁᐊᐧᑯ ᐊᓇ, ᐊᐧᔭᐄᐧᑎᒥᕽ ᒫᓇ ᐹᐢᑲᐨ ᐁ ᑮ ᑮᓯᓵᐧᐟ. ᐁᑲᐧ ᐋᐧᐳᓴᐧ ᒦᓇ ᒫᓇ ᐁ ᑮ ᑖᐸᑫᐧᒋᐠ ᐃᐢᑫᐧᐊᐧᐠ, ᐁ ᒫᐦ ᒥᓯ ᓂᐸᐦᐋᐧᒋᐠ ᐋᐧᐳᓴᐧ, ᐁᑯᓂ ᒦᓇ ᒫᓇ ᐁ ᑲᐢᑲᐸᓵᐧᒋᐠ. ᓇᓈᑐᕽ ᒫᓇ ᐃᐢᑫᐧᐊᐧᐠ (ᐁ ᑮ ᑲᑳᔭᐃᐧᓰᒋᐠ) ᐁ ᑮ ᑑᑕᐦᑭᐠ, ᐁ ᑭᐢᑭᓯᔮᐣ, ᐁ ᑭᓰᐯᑭᓂᑫᒋᐠ, washboard ᐁ ᐋᐸᒋᐦᑖᒋᐠ, ᒪ ᑮᑲᐧᐩ ᐁᑯᐢᐲ ᐆᐦᐃ ᒨᓂᔮᐃᐧ ᐊᔭ ᐁ ᑮ ᐋᐸᒋᐦᑖᒋᐠ.

[7] ᐁᑲᐧ ᓰᓰᐸᐠ ᒦᓇ, ᑳ ᓂᐸᐦᐋᒋ ᒫᓇ ᓂᒧᓲᒼ, ᐅᑕᑭᓯᔭ ᒦᓇ ᒫᓇ ᐊᓂᐦᐃ ᐁ ᑮ ᑲᓈᒋᐦᑖᒋᐠ, ᓂᔭᓈᐣ ᒦᓇ ᐁ ᑮ ᐄᐧᒋᐦᑖᓱᔮᕽ ᐁ ᐊᐋᐧᓯᓰᐃᐧᔮᕽ, ᐁ ᑲᓈᒋᐦᑖᔮᕽ ᐊᓂᐦᐃ ᐅᑕᑭᓯᔭ ᐁ ᓇᐋᐧᒦᔮᕽ ᐃᐢᑯᑌᕽ. ᐁᑲᐧ ᐅᑎᑖᒥᔭᐊᐧ ᒦᓇ, ᒨᓴᐧ ᐅᐦᒋ, ᐁ ᑮ ᑲᓈᒋᐦᑖᒋᐠ. ᒪ ᑮᑲᐧᐩ ᐅᐦᒋ ᐁᐧᐱᓇᒪᐧᐠ, ᑲᐦᑭᔭᐤ ᐁ ᑮ ᐋᐸᒋᐦᑖᒋᐠ ᐁ ᒦᒋᔮᕽ.

[8] ᐁᑲᐧ ᓂᒧᓲᒼ ᒫᓇ ᐁ ᑮ ᐋᐸᒋᐦᐋᐧᐟ ᐆᐦᐃ ᐄᑭᐦᑕᐃᐧᑖᐹᓇ, ᐁᑯᑐᐊᐧᕽ ᒫᓇ ᐁ ᑭᐢᑭᓯᔮᐣ ᐁ ᑮ ᐋᐸᒋᐦᐋᐧᐟ, ᑮ ᒥᓇᐦᐅᒋ, ᐁᑯᑐᐊᐧᕽ ᒫᓇ ᐁ ᑮ ᐃᓯ ᐋᐸᒋᐦᐋᐧᐟ ᓴᑳᕽ, ᐁ ᓈᑕᕽ ᐊᓂᒪ ᐃᐧᔮᐢ. ᐁᑲᐧ ᐅᑖᐹᓈᐢᑲᐧ ᒦᓇ, ᐋᐧᓂᑕᐃᐧᐸᑭᑕᐦᐋᐧᒋ (ᐋᐧᐦᔭᐤ ᐊᔨᐢ ᐁᑯᑕ ᐅᐦᒋ ᓵᑲᐦᐃᑲᐣ ᐃᑌ ᒫᓇ ᑳ ᑮ ᐸᑭᑕᐦᐋᐧᐟ), ᒥᓴᑎᒪᐧ ᐁᑲᐧ ᐅᑖᐹᓈᐢᑲᐧ ᐁ ᑮ ᐋᐸᒋᐦᐋᐧᐟ.

[9] ᐁᑲᐧ ᐃᐢᑫᐧᐊᐧᐠ ᒦᓇ ᒫᓇ, ᐁ ᑮ ᒥᓯ ᒫᐦᒪᐃᐧᓯᒋᐠ, ᑕᑲᐧᐦᐃᒥᓈᓇ ᐁ ᑮ ᒥᓯ ᒪᐃᐧᓯᒋᐠ ᐁ ᑕᑲᐧᐦᐊᐦᑭᐠ, ᐁ ᐹᓴᐦᑭᐠ, ᒥᓵᐢᑲᐧᑑᒥᓇ ᒦᓇ ᐁ ᑮ ᐹᓴᐦᑭᐠ. ᐁᑲᐧ ᐊᔭ, ᐄᐊᐧᐦᐃᑲᓇ ᐁ ᑮ ᒫᐦᒥᓯ ᐅᓰᐦᐋᒋᐠ, ᒨᓯᐃᐧᔮᐢ ᐅᐦᒋ, ᐁᑲᐧ ᒫᓇ ᐁ ᑮ ᐊᓯᐋᐧᑖᒋᐠ ᐆᐦᐃ, ᐆᐦᐃ ᐊᔭ, ᐊᐧᐢᑲᐧᔨᐊᐧᑎᕽ ᒫᓇ ᐁ ᑮ ᐊᓯᐋᐧᑖᒋᐠ ᐆᐦᐃ ᒦᓂᓴ, ᐊᔭ ᒦᓇ ᒫᓇ ᐊᔭ, ᐁ ᑮ ᒥᓯ ᒫᐦᒪᐃᐧᓯᒋᐠ ᐊᔭ, ᐄᐧᓴᑮᒥᓇ, ᐁᑯᑐᐃᐧᕽ ᒦᓇ ᒫᓇ ᐁ ᑮ ᐊᓯᐋᐧᑖᒋᐠ, ᐁᑲᐧ ᑳ ᐱᐳᓂᔨᐠ ᒫᓇ, ᐊᐧᔭᐄᐧᑎᒥᕽ ᐁ ᐊᐢᑖᒋᐠ ᐁ ᐋᐧᐦᑲᐧᑎᐦᑖᒋᐠ.

[10] ᐁᑲᐧ ᐊᐋᐧᓯᓴᐠ ᒫᓇ ᐁ ᑮ ᒣᑕᐋᐧᑫᒋᐠ ᐊᔭ, ᐁ ᒥᔨᐦᒋᐠ ᐊᓂᐦᐃ ᐄᐧᐦᑲᐧᔭ, ᑭᓄᓴᐊᐧ ᐅᐦᒋ, ᐲᐦᒋ ᐊᔨᕽ ᐅᐦᒋ ᑭᓄᓴᐊᐧ. ᐁᑲᐧ ᐊᓂᐦᐃ ᐱᐦᐁᐊᐧᐠ ᐅᐦᒋ, ᐸᐢᐸᐢᑭᐊᐧᐠ ᐁᑲᐧ ᑯᑕᑲᐠ ᐊᓂᑭ ᐱᐦᐁᐊᐧᐠ, ᐄᐧᐦᑲᐧᔭ ᐊᓂᐦᐃ ᐁ ᑮ ᐴᑖᑕᐦᑭᐠ ᒫᓇ, ᐁ ᐹᓴᒫᕽ, ᐁ ᑮ ᒣᑕᐋᐧᑫᔮᕽ, ᓃᑳᐣ ᒫᓇ ᐁ ᑲᓈᒋᐦᑖᔮᕽ, ᐁ ᑮ ᐴᑖᑕᒫᕽ ᐁ ᒣᑕᐋᐧᑫᔮᕽ ᒫᓇ, ᐁ ᑕᐦᑯᐱᑕᒫᕽ ᑮ ᐴᑖᑕᒥᐦᑭ.

[11] ᐁᑲᐧ ᑭᓄᓴᐊᐧ ᐋᐧᐃᐧᑲᓂᐋᐧᕽ ᐅᐦᒋ ᐁ ᑮ ᒣᑕᐋᐧᑫᔮᕽ ᒫᓇ ᐁ ᐊᐧ ᐅᓰᑲᐦᐅᓂᔮᕽ, ᐁ ᑮ ᓰᑲᐦᐅᔮᕽ ᒫᓇ ᐅᐦᒋ ᐁᑯᓂ, ᐁᑲᐧ ᐃᐢᑫᐧᐊᐧᐠ ᒫᓇ ᐁ ᑮ ᐅᓰᐦᐋᒋᐠ ᐊᐋᐧᓯᓰᐦᑲᓇ, ᐁ ᐊᐧ ᐋᐧᐢᐱᑖᒋᐠ.

[12] ᐁᑲᐧ ᓂᒥᐢ ᐁᑲᐧ ᓂᔭ ᒫᓇ ᐁ ᑮ ᒣᑕᐁᐧᔮᕽ ᓴᑳᕽ, ᑖᐱᐢᑰᐨ ᐋᐧᐢᑲᐦᐃᑲᓂᐢ ᒫᓇ ᐁ ᑮ ᐅᓰᐦᑖᔮᕽ, ᐁᑯᑕ ᐁ ᒣᑕᐁᐧᔮᕽ, ᐊᐦᐴ ᐸᐸᑳᐧᓂᑲᒥᑯᐢ ᒫᓇ ᐁ ᑮ ᐅᓰᐦᑖᔮᕽ.

[13] ᐁᑲᐧ ᓅᐦᑯᒼ ᒫᓇ ᐊᔭ, ᐄᐚᐦᐃᑲᓇ ᑳ ᐅᓰᐦᐚᐟ, ᐁ ᑮ ᐋᐸᒋᐦᑖᐟ ᒫᓇ ᐊᔭ – ᐚ, ᐱᒦᐦᑳᐣ ᐁ ᐅᓰᐦᑖᐟ, ᐁᑲᐧ ᐊᔭ, ᑕᑲᐧᐦᐃᒥᓈᓇ ᐁᑯᑕ ᒫᓇ ᐁ ᑮ ᐊᐢᑖᐟ ᐁᑲᐧ ᒥᓵᐢᑲᐧᑑᒥᓇ, ᑮ ᐑᐦᑲᓯᐣ ᒫᓇ ᐱᒦᐦᑳᐣ.

[14] ᐁᑲᐧ ᑯᑕᐠ ᒦᓇ ᑮᑲᐧᐩ ᐁ ᑭᐢᑭᓯᔮᐣ, ᓅᐦᑯᒼ ᒫᓇ ᐁ ᑮ ᐅᒋᐱᑕᕽ ᐊᓂᐦᐃ, (ᑖᓂᓯ – ᒨᔭ ᓂᑭᐢᑫᔦᐦᑌᐣ, ᑖᓂᐢ ᐁ ᐃᓯᔩᐦᑳᑌᑭ ᐊᓂᐦᐃ wild rhubarb,) wild rhubarb ᐊᓂᐦᐃ ᐁ ᑮ ᐅᒋᐱᑕᕽ ᐁ ᐲᐦᑐᓇᕽ ᐁᑲᐧ ᐁ ᐲᑭᓂᓴᕽ, ᒦᒋᒫᐳᕽ ᐁ ᑮ ᐊᐢᑖᐟ, ᐁ ᑮ ᐑᐦᑲᓯᐠ ᒫᓇ ᐊᓂᒪ ᒦᒋᒫᐳᐩ. ᐁᑲᐧ ᒦᓇ ᒫᓇ ᒥᓵᐢᑲᐧᑑᒥᓇ ᒦᓇ ᐁᑯᑕ ᐁ ᑮ ᐊᐢᑖᐟ ᒦᒋᒫᐳᕽ, ᐁ ᒦᒋᒫᐳᐦᑳᑫᐟ, ᐁᑲᐧ ᐸᐦᑫᐧᓯᑲᓇ ᐁ ᐃᑌᐦᐚᐟ, ᐁᑯᑕ ᐁ ᐊᐢᑖᐟ. ᑮ ᐑᐦᑲᓯᐣ ᒫᓇ ᒦᒋᒫᐳᐩ.

[15] ᐁᑲᐧ ᐃᐢᑫᐧᐘᐠ ᒦᓇ ᑯᑕᐠ ᑮᑲᐧᐩ ᐊᔭ, ᐁ ᑮ ᑑᑕᐦᑭᐠ, ᓇᓈᑐᕽ ᒫᓇ ᐁ ᑮ ᐃᓯ ᐊᑐᐢᑫᒋᐠ, ᐊᐢᑭᔭ ᐁ ᑮ ᐊᑯᑖᒋᐠ ᓯᓯᓀ ᒪᐢᑫᑯᕽ, ᐁ ᐹᓴᐦᑭᐠ, ᐁᑲᐧ ᒫᓇ ᐃᐢᑫᐧᐘᐠ ᒫᓇ ᐁ ᑮ ᒉᑭᒋᐠ, ᐁᑲᐧ ᓂᒫᒫ ᐐᐢᑕ ᐁ ᑮ ᐋᐸᒋᐦᑖᐟ ᓂᓰᒥᐢ ᐁ ᐯᐲᐏᐟ, ᐁ ᑮ ᐚᐢᐱᑎᐦᒋᐠ ᐊᔭ ᐯᐲᓯᓴᐠ, ᐊᐢᑭᔭ ᐊᓂᐦᐃ ᐁ ᑮ ᐋᐸᑕᐦᑭ, ᒪ ᑮᑲᐧᐩ ᐁᑯᐢᐲ ᐏᔭ ᐋᓯᔮᓇ ᑮᑲᐧᐩ ᐅᐦᒋ ᐊᑖᐍᐘᐠ ᐊᐦᐴ ᐁ ᐅᐦᒋ ᐋᐸᒋᐦᐋᒋᐠ.

[16] ᐁᑲᐧ, ᓅᐦᑯᒼ ᒫᓇ ᐁ ᑮ ᐅᓰᐦᑖᐟ ᐊᓂᐦᐃ –, ᐁ ᑮ ᐅᓰᐦᑖᐟ ᐊᔭ, ᐘᐢᑲᐧᔦᐘᑕ, ᓇᓈᑐᕽ ᒫᓇ ᐁ ᑮ ᐃᓯ ᐋᐸᒋᐦᑖᒋᐠ, ᒦᓂᓴ ᐁ ᐊᓯᐚᑖᒋᐠ, ᐅᑲᐢᑮᑲᐧᓯᐏᓇ ᒫᓇ ᐁ ᑮ ᐊᓯᐚᑖᐟ ᐁᑯᑕ, ᓇᓈᑐᕽ ᐃᓯ ᐁ ᑮ ᐃᑖᐸᑕᐦᑭ.

[17] ᐁᑲᐧ ᓂᒧᓲᒼ ᒫᓇ ᒪᑐᑎᓵᐣ ᐁ ᑮ ᐅᓰᐦᑖᐟ, ᐁ ᑮ ᒪᑐᑎᓯᐟ. ᐁᑲᐧ ᐁᑯᑕ ᒫᓇ ᐁ ᑮ ᐲᑭᐢᑫᐧᐟ, ᐁ ᓇᓈᐢᑯᒫᐟ ᐁᑐᑫᐧ ᑳ ᑎᐯᔦᐦᒋᑫᔦᐟ, ᐁ ᓇᓈᐢᑯᒫᐟ, ᐃᔦᑯᕽ ᒫᓇ ᐁ ᑮ ᒫᐦᒥᓯ ᓂᐸᐦᑖᐟ ᑮᑲᐧᐩ, ᐁᑐᑫᐧ.

[18] ᐁᑲᐧ ᒫᓇ ᒦᓇ, ᓂᑮ ᐚᐸᐦᑌᐣ, ᒨᔭ ᑖᐯᐧ ᒫᑲ ᓂᑭᐢᑭᓯᐣ, ᐁ ᑮ ᓂᐹᑫᐧᓯᒧᕽ. ᐁᑲᐧ ᒫᓇ ᐃᐢᑫᐧᐘᐠ ᒫᓇ, ᒥᐦᒉᐟ ᒫᓇ ᐃᐢᑫᐧᐘᐠ ᐁ ᑮ ᐃᑐᐦᑌᒋᐠ ᓴᑳᕽ ᐁ ᓂᑕᐏ –, ᒉᐢᑕᐣ ᑮ ᐃᓯᔩᐦᑳᑌᐘᐠ, ᐊᓂᐦᐃ ᒫᓇ ᐁ ᑮ ᓈᑖᒋᐠ ᒦᑐᓯᕽ, ᐁ ᑮ ᐲᐦᑑᓵᐧᒋᐠ ᐊᔭ, ᒦᑐᓴ, ᐁᑲᐧ ᒉᐢᑕᐣ ᐊᓇ, ᐁ ᑮ ᐅᑎᓈᒋᐠ, ᐁᑲᐧ ᒫᓇ ᐁ ᑮ ᐊᓴᒥᐦᒋᐠ ᐆᑭ ᑳ ᓂᐹᑫᐧᓯᒧᒋᐠ, ᐚ, ᒨᔭ ᓂᑭᐢᑫᔦᐦᑌᐣ ᑖᓀᐦᑭ ᑳ ᐆᐦ ᐊᓴᒥᐦᒋᐠ, ᑮᑲᐧᐩ ᐁᑐᑫᐧ ᐅᐦᒋ.

[19] ᐁᑲᐧ, ᐃᐢᑫᐧᐘᐠ ᒦᓇ ᒫᓇ ᐊᔭ, ᐆᒪ ᐁ ᑮ ᑑᑕᐦᑭᐠ, ᐘᐢᑲᐧᔭ ᒫᓇ ᐁ ᑮ ᐸᐹᒥ ᐊᔭ –, ᒨᐦᑯᒫᐣ ᐊᐦᐴ ᒌᑲᐦᐃᑲᓂᐢ ᐁ ᑮ ᑕᐦᑯᓇᐦᑭᐠ, ᐁ ᑮ ᒌᑲᐦᐚᒋᐠ ᐊᐱᓯᐢ ᐁᑲᐧ ᒥᐢᒋᑯᐢ ᒫᓇ ᐁᑯᑕ ᐁ ᓴᑯᓇᐦᑭᐠ, ᐁᑲᐧ ᐊᓂᒪ ᐊᔭ, syrup ᐊᓂᒪ ᐊᔭ ᐁ ᑮ ᐅᐦᒋᑲᐘᕽ ᐁᑯᑕ, ᐁᑲᐧ ᐊᐢᑭᐦᑯᐢ ᒫᓇ ᓰᐹ ᐁᑯᑕ ᐁ ᐊᐢᑖᐟ ᐁ ᐚᐸᓇᐢᑖᒋᐠ ᐊᔭ, ᐁ ᐅᐦᒋᑲᐘᕽ ᐁᑯᑕ, ᐁᑲᐧ ᑮᑭᓭᐹ ᒫᓇ ᐁ ᐸᐹᒥ ᓈᑖᒋᐠ ᐊᓂᐦᐃ ᐊᐢᑭᐦᑯᐢ. ᒨᔭ ᒫᑲ ᓂᑭᐢᑭᓯᐣ ᑖᓂᓯ ᒫᓇ ᐁ ᑮ ᑑᑕᐦᑭᐠ, ᒪᑖᐧᐣ ᒌ ᐁ ᑮ ᐸᑳᐦᑖᒋᐠ ᐊᐦᐴ –. ᒫᑲ ᓂᔦᓈᐣ ᐏᔭ ᑳ ᐊᐚᓯᓰᐏᔮᕽ ᒫᓇ ᐁ ᑭᐢᑭᓯᔮᐣ ᐁ ᑮ ᒥᓂᐦᑫᐧᔮᕽ ᒫᓇ, ᐁᐘᑯ ᐊᓂᒪ ᐁ ᑮ ᐑᐦᑲᓯᐠ.

[20] [FA:] ᐊᔭ ᒫᑲ ᐱᑭᐤ. ᑮᐢᑕᐚᐤ ᒦ ᒫᓇ ᑭᑮᒫᐘᓴᑯᓈᐚᐤ ᐆᐦᐃ ᐊᔭ –
[IC:] spruce-gum ᒦ ᐊᓇ.
[FA:] spruce-gum.
[IC:] ᐁᐦᐊ, ᓂᔭᓈᐣ ᐏᔭ ᐁ ᐊᐚᓯᔩᐏᔮᕽ ᐁ ᑮ ᓂᑕᐏᐅᑎᓈᔮᕽ ᒫᓇ ᐁ ᒫ ᒫᑿᒫᔮᕽ. ᑮᒥᐘᓯᐤ ᒫᓇ ᐁᐘᑯ ᐊᓇ, ᐁ ᒫ ᒫᑿᒥᐦᐟ.
[FA:] ᓯᓯᓀ ᓵᑲᐦᐃᑲᓂᕽ ᒫᑲ, ᑭᑮᒫᓈᐦᐆᓈᐚᐤ ᒦ ᒫᓇ ᑲᒦᒋᔦᐠ ᐊᓂᐦᐃ ᒫᐢᑯᓯᐚᓇ.
[IC:] ᐁᐦᐊ, ᐁ ᑮ ᐅᒋᐱᑕᒫᕽ ᒫᓇ, ᐘᓇᐢᑯ- ᒫᓇ ᐊᓂᐦᐃ, ᐁᑯᓂ ᐊᓂᐦᐃ, ᐚᐦᐊ.
[FA:] ᐁᐦᐊ, ᐚᐱᐢᑳᐘ.
[IC:] ᐁᐦᐊ, ᐁᑯᑐᐘᕽ ᒫᓇ ᐁ ᑮ ᒦᒋᔮᕽ ᒫᓇ.

[21] ᐚ, ᐊᔭ, ᐃᐢᑫᐘᐠ ᐊᔭ, ᒦᓇ ᒫᓇ ᐊᔭ, ᐁ ᑮ ᐅᓲᐦᐚᒋᐠ ᒫᓇ ᐊᔭᐱᔭ, ᒥᑐᓂ ᐁ ᒫᐦᒥᓯ ᐅᓲᐦᐚᒋᐠ ᐁᑯᑐᐘᕽ, ᐁ ᑳᐦᑭᓈᐌᑭᓯᐸᐟ, ᐁᑯᓂ ᒫᓇ ᐁ ᑮ ᐚᐸᒋᐦᐚᐟ – ᐁ ᐚᐸᒋᐦᐚᒋᐠ ᐊᔭ ᑳᐸᑭᑕᐦᐚᒋᐠ, ᐁᑿ ᓂᒧᓲᒼ ᒦᓇ ᒫᓇ ᐊᔭ, ᐊᓵᒪ ᐁ ᑮ ᐅᓲᐦᐚᐟ, ᐁ ᑮ ᑲᓇᐚᐸᒫᔮᕽ ᒫᓇ ᐁ ᐅᓲᐦᐚᐟ ᐁᑯᑐᐘᕽ, ᐁ ᒫᐦᒥᓯ ᐅᓲᐦᐚᐟ, ᐁ ᐊᑐᑎᐦᐟ ᑲ ᐅᓲᐦᐚᐟ.
[FA:] ᑖᓂᓯ ᒫᑲ ᐁ ᑮ ᒫᒦᐚᑵᐟ ᒦ ᒫᓇ ᐐᐢᑕ.
ᐁᐦᐊ, ᑳ ᐱᐳᓂᐹᐠ ᒫᓇ ᐁ ᑮ ᐳᐢᑎᐢᑳᕽ ᑳᒫᒦᐟ. – birch ᐁᑐᑵ, ᐁ ᑮ ᐚᐸᒋᐦᐚᐟ.

[22] ᐊᔭ, ᐊᐹᓯᐹᓂᐘᐠ ᒫᓇ ᐆᑭ ᑳ ᑮ ᐯ ᑭᔦᑲᐚᒋᐠ ᒫᓇ, ᓂᒧᓲᒪ ᐁᑿ ᓅᐦᑯᒪ, ᓅᐦᑯᒼ ᒫᓇ ᐁ ᑮ ᒫᐦᒥᓯ ᐊᓵᒫᐟ ᐏᔮᐢ ᐊᐦᐹ ᑭᓄᓭᐘ, ᐁᑯᓯ ᐃᓯ ᐁ ᑮ ᓂᐦᑖ ᐊᓴᐦᑫᒋᐠ, ᐁ ᑮ ᐱᒥᓇᐘᓱᐟ ᒫᓇ ᐁ ᒥᓯ ᐱᒥᓇᐘᓱᐟ ᐁ ᐊᓵᒫᐟ ᐁᑿ, ᑯᑕᐠ ᒦᓇ ᐁ ᑮ ᐊᓵᒫᐟ ᒫᓇ, ᑲ ᑮᐌᐦᑕᑖᒋᐠ.

[23] ᐁᑿ, ᑯᑕᐠ ᑮᑿᐩ ᒦᓇ ᐁ ᑭᐢᑭᓯᔫᐣ ᒫᓇ ᑳ ᐊᐚᓯᔩᐏᔮᕽ, ᒨᔭ ᐁ ᐅᐦᒋ ᐸᑭᑎᓂᑲᐏᔮᕽ, ᐲᐦᒋ ᐊᐹᕽ ᑳ ᐊᔮᔮᕽ ᑮᐢᐱᐣ ᑫᐦᑌ ᐊᔭᐠ ᑳ ᐯ ᑭᔦᑫᒋᐠ, ᐘᔭᐑᑎᒥᕽ ᐱᑯ ᐁ ᐊᔮᔮᕽ.

[FA:] ᑭᑮ ᐚᐦ ᐋᒋᒧᐢᑖᑲᐏᓈᐚᐤ ᒦ ᒫᓇ, ᑮᐢᑕᐚᐤ.

[24] ᐁᐦᐊ, ᐑᓴᐦᑫᒫᕽ, ᐋᑕ ᐃᔭ ᒫᓇ ᑮ ᐋᒋᒣᐤ, ᓅᐦᑯᒼ ᐊᐦᐹ ᓂᒧᓲᒼ. ᒨᔭ ᑖᐻ ᓂᑭᐢᑭᓯᐣ ᐁᑯᓂ, ᐋᒋᒧᐏᓂᓴ ᒫᓇ ᓂᒧᓲᒼ ᐁ ᑮ ᐋᑐᑕᕽ. ᐑᓴᐦᑫᒫᕽ ᐱᑯ ᒫᓇ ᓂᑭᐢᑭᓯᐣ ᐋᑎᐦᐟ, ᐁ ᑮ ᐋᒋᒫᐟ, ᐅᒥᑭᐩ ᐏᔦ ᑳᒦᒋᐟ ᐑᓴᐦᑫᒫᕽ, ᐁᐘᑯ ᐊᓂᒪ ᐃᔭ ᓂᑭᐢᑭᓯᐣ ᒥᑐᓂ.

[25] ᐋᐢᑳᐤ ᒫᓇ ᒦᓇ ᒫᓇ ᓂᑮ ᐑᒣᐚᓈᐣ ᓅᐦᑯᒼ, ᐁᑿ ᓂᒫᒫ, ᐋᐢᑳᐤ ᐁ ᑮ ᐑᒋᐦᐃᐌᐟ ᐑᐢᑕ ᐁᑯᑕ. ᐁ ᑮ ᒨᓇᐦᐊᕽ ᒫᓇ ᒪᐢᑭᐦᑭᔭ, ᓅᐦᑯᒼ, ᐁᑿ ᑮ ᒨᓇᐦᐊᐦᑭ ᒫᓇ, ᐁᑯᑕ ᐁ ᐊᐦᐚᐟ ᒋᐢᑌᒫᐘ. ᒨᔭ ᒫᓇ ᓅᐦᒋ ᑭᐢᑫᔮᐦᑌᐣ ᑖᓀᐦᑭ, ᐁᑯᐢᐲ, ᒋᐢᑌᒫᐘ ᑲ ᐊᐦᐚᐟ.

[26] ᐁᑲᐧ ᒫᓇ ᒥᐢᑕᐦᐃ ᒪᐢᑭᐦᑭᐩ ᒫᓇ ᑮ ᑭᐢᑫᔨᐦᑕᒪᐧᐠ ᓂᒧᓲᒼ ᐁᑲᐧ ᓅᐦᑯᒼ. ᐁ ᑮ ᐋᐧᐦ ᐅᓰᐦᑕᒪᐋᐧᒋᐠ ᒫᓇ ᐊᔨᓯᔨᓂᐊᐧ ᒥᐢᑮᓯᐠ ᒪᐢᑭᐦᑭᐩ, ᒨᔭ ᓂᑭᐢᑫᔨᐦᑌᐣ ᒫᑲ, ᒨᔭ ᓅᐦ ᑭᐢᑭᓄᐦᐊᒫᑲᐃᐧᐣ ᑮᑳᐧᐩ ᐁᑯᑕ. ᐊᐦᔮ ᑫᔮᐱᐨ ᓂᒫᒫ ᐁᐊᐧᑯ ᐊᓂᒪ ᒪᐢᑭᐦᑭᐩ ᑭᐢᑫᔨᐦᑕᒼ, ᐁ ᒥᔮᐧᓯᓂᔨᑭ ᒥᐢᑮᓯᑲᐧ ᐅᐦᒋ.

[27] ᐋ, ᓂᒧᓲᒼ ᐁᑲᐧ, ᓈᐯᐊᐧ ᑯᑕᑲ ᐁ ᑮ ᐄᐧᒉᐋᐧᐟ, ᓈᐯᐊᐧᐠ ᐆᑭ ᐁ ᑮ ᓂᑕᐃᐧᓇᐊᐧᑕᐦᐃᑫᒋᐠ, ᓀᔮᕽ ᒫᓇ ᑮ ᐃᔨᔫᐦᑳᑕᒪᐧᐠ, ᐃᑌ ᐁ ᓂᑕᐃᐧᓇᐊᐧᑕᐦᐃᑫᕽ ᒫᓇ, ᑲᐢᑭᑌᓯᐸ ᐁ ᓇᐊᐧᑕᐦᐋᐧᒋᐠ. ᒥᐦᒉᐟ ᒫᓇ ᐁ ᑮ ᒫᐦᒥᓯ ᓂᐸᐦᐋᐧᒋᐠ, ᐁᑲᐧ ᒉᐧᐢᑕᐢ ᒫᓇ ᐁ ᑮ ᐸᐹᒥ ᐊᓴᐦᑫᒋᐠ, ᑯᑕᑲ ᐊᔨᓯᔨᓂᐊᐧ ᐁ ᐸᐹᒥ ᐊᓴᒫᒋᐠ ᐆᐦᐃ ᓲᓯᐸ.

[28] ᐁᑲᐧ ᒦᓇ ᒫᓇ ᓂᒧᓲᒼ ᒫᓇ ᐁ ᑮ ᑲᑫᐢᑭᒥᑯᔮᕽ. «ᑫᐦᑌ ᐊᔨᓯᔨᓂᐤ ᑳᑭᑫ ᒪᓈᒋᐦ. ᐁᑳᔭ ᐄᐧᐦᑳᐨ ᓀᐯᐃᐧᓯ ᑫᐦᑌ ᐊᔨᓯᔨᓂᐤ ᑲ ᐲᑭᐢᑳᐧᑕᐟ.» ᐁ ᑮ ᐃᑎᑯᔮᕽ ᒫᓇ. ᐁᑯᓯ ᒫᓇ ᓂᑎᑑᑌᐣ ᒫᓇ ᓂᔭ ᐊᓄᐦᐨ ᑳ ᑮᓯᑳᐠ. ᑭᔮᒼ ᐋᑕ ᐊᐃᐧᔭᐠ ᐁᑳᔭ ᐁ ᓂᓯᑕᐁᐧᔨᒪᐠ ᓂᓂᑕᐃᐧ ᐲᑭᐢᑳᐧᑖᐤ ᒫᓇ. ᑕᑲᐦᑫᔨᐦᑕᒪᐧᐠ ᐆᑭ ᑫᐦᑌ ᐊᔨᓯᔨᓂᐊᐧᐠ ᑲᐧᔭᐢᐠ ᑲ ᐲᑭᐢᑳᐧᑎᐦᒋᐠ, ᑲᐧᔭᐢᐠ ᐁ ᑭᑖᐸᒥᐦᒋᐠ.

[29] ᐁᑲᐧ ᒫᓇ ᒦᓇ ᓂᒧᓲᒼ ᐁ ᑮ ᐲᐦᑖᐧᑕᕽ ᐆᐦᐃ ᒋᑳᓯᐸᑲᐧ, ᐁ ᑮ ᒥᓯ ᓈᑕᕽ ᒫᓇ ᐁ ᐹᓴᕽ, ᒥᐦᑳᐧᐯᒪᑲᐧ ᐊᓯᒋ. ᐁᑯᓂ ᒦᓇ ᐁ ᐹᓴᕽ, ᐁ ᑳᐢᑲᐦᐊᕽ ᐆᐦᐃ, ᒥᐦᑳᐧᐯᒪᑲᐧ, ᐁᑲᐧ ᐁᑯᓂ ᒫᓇ ᐁ ᑮ ᐲᐦᑖᐧᑕᕽ, ᐅᐢᐹᐧᑲᓂᕽ ᐁ ᑮ ᐲᐦᑖᐧᐟ. ᒨᔭ ᐄᐧᐦᑳᐨ ᐃᐧᔭ ᓂᑭᐢᑭᓯᐣ ᒋᐢᑌᒫᐊᐧ ᐊᐃᐧᔭᐠ ᑳ ᐋᐸᒋᐦᐋᐟ.

[30] ᐁᑲᐧ ᒫᓇ ᒦᓇ ᐊᓇ ᓅᐦᑯᒼ ᐁᑲᐧ ᓂᒫᒫ ᒫᓇ ᐁ ᑮ ᑲᐢᑭᑳᐧᓱᒋᐠ ᒥᐢᑕᐦᐃ. ᑲᐦᑭᔭᐤ ᒫᓇ ᐊᔨᐃᐧᓂᓴ ᐁ ᑮ ᐅᓰᐦᑕᒫᑯᔮᐦᑭᐠ, ᒨᔭ ᑮᑳᐧᐩ ᐁ ᐅᐦᒋ ᐊᑖᐁᐧᒋᐠ, ᐊᐦᔮ ᐊᓯᑲᓇ ᐁ ᑮ ᐅᓰᐦᐋᐧᒋᐠ, ᐊᐢᑎᓴ, ᐊᐢᑐᑎᓇ, ᒪᐢᑭᓯᓇ, ᒥᐢᑯᑖᑲᔭ, ᑲᐦᑭᔭᐤ ᓲᐢᑳᐧᐨ ᒫᓇ ᐁ ᑮ ᐅᓰᐦᑖᒋᐠ, ᒥᐢᑕᐦᐃ ᐁ ᑮ ᑲᐢᑭᑳᐧᓱᒋᐠ ᐃᐢᑫᐧᐊᐧᐠ, ᐁᑯᐢᐲ ᐃᐧᔭ ᒨᔭ ᐄᐧᐦᑳᐨ ᐅᐦᒋ ᐊᑖᐁᐧᐊᐧᐠ ᑮᑳᐧᐩ.

[FA:] ᐊᔭ ᒫᑲ ᐊᑯᐦᐸ.

ᐊᑯᐦᐸ ᒦᓇ ᐁ ᑮ ᐅᓰᐦᑕᒫᓱᒋᐠ, ᐁ ᓇᓈᑐᐦᑯᑳᐧᓱᒋᐠ, ᒨᔭ ᐅᐦᒋ ᐊᑖᐁᐧᐊᐧᐠ.

[FA:] ᐊᐢᐱᐢᑫᐧᓯᒧᓇ.

ᐁᑯᑐᐊᐧᕽ ᒦᓇ ᐁ ᑮ ᐅᓰᐦᑖᒋᐠ, ᓰᓰᑊ ᐅᐲᐊᐧᔭ ᐅᐦᒋ. ᐁᑲᐧ, ᐋᐧᐳᓴᐧᔭᓇ ᒫᓇ ᐁ ᑮ ᐅᓰᐦᐋᐧᒋᐠ, ᓰᓰᑊ ᐊᑯᐦᐸ, ᓰᓰᑊ ᐅᐲᐊᐧᔭ ᐅᐦᒋ ᐁᑯᑐᐊᐧᕽ ᒦᓇ ᐁ ᑮ ᐅᓰᐦᑖᒋᐠ, ᑮᓯᐋᐧᐊᐧ ᒫᓇ, ᐁᑯᓂ ᐊᑯᐦᐸ, ᑳ ᐅᓰᐦᑖᒋᐠ.

[FA:] ᒪᐢᑭᓯᓇ ᒫᑲ.

ᐋᓴᐩ ᐃᐧᔭ ᐁᐊᐧᑯ ᐊᓂᒪ ᓂᐄᐧᐦᑌᐣ. ᐁᑯᓯ.

7.
Fun and Games

Mary Wells

[FA:] hâw, êkwa kiya, êkây katâc mitoni cîki.

I

[1] â, apisis ê-wî-- ê-wî-âcimoyân, *'Mary Wells'* nitisiyîhkâson, â, *Elizabeth Settlement* ohci niya. ê-mêkwâ-awâsisîwiyân, nikiskisin, ispî *Elizabeth Settlement* ê-ispiciyâhk, ê-- ê-takwâkik *nineteen-thirty-nine,* êkotê kâ-kî-ispiciyâhk. â, nipâpâ nîtisânak nôhkom êkwa nimâmâ, êkwa nimâmâ ohcâwisa, wîsta êwakw ân[a] ôhi kahkiyaw aya, ocawâsimisa wîwa, êkwa *'Swans'* kotakak ê-isiyîhkâsocik ayisiyiniwak; êkonik piko nisto-- nisto-aya ayisiyiniwak êkotê nistam ê-kî-ispiciyâhk. êkwa nikiskisin, ê-piciyâhk ispî, mistatimwak ê-âpacihâyâhkik otâpânâskohk, êkotê êk ôma wâhyaw, wâhyawês ê-ispiciyâhk; nikiskisin mîn âyi, papakwânikamikohk ê-wîkiyâhk nistam.

II

[2] êkwa awa nôhkom mân âyi, ê-nitawi-nitâmisot, iyinimina ê-miskahk. wahwâ, môy wîhkâc ê-ohci-pê-kotistamân iyinimina, mistahi niwîhkistên, wâwîs sîwinikan asic êkot[ê] ê-apit. êkwa, kîhtwâm ê-nitâmisot nôhkom, ê-asamit mînisa, ê-nitotamâyân sîwinikan, "ma kîkway êkwa ka-kî-ahâw sîwinikan êkota kimînisimihk," nititik nimâmâ. "tânêhki mâka," ê-itak nimâmâ, "êkos îsi pikw ânih ê-wîhkasiki." – "â," nimâmâ kâ-isit, "apisis piko ê-ayâwâyâhk awa sîwinikan, êkwa kisîmis nawac t-âpacihât êkoni ispîhci kiya, kiya kimisikitin, ta-kî-- ka-nisitohtên, êkây katâc sîwinikan t-âpacihat," nititikawin. mâka, nikî-wâpamâw nimâmâ tânit[ê] ê-ahât ôhi sîwinikana, ayi, *in a syrup pail* kî-asiwahêw êkwa mîtosihk ê-akotât. wâ, mayaw êkâ awiyak ê-pê-itâpit ê-itêyihtamân, nikîhcêkosîn awa mîtos aw ê-nâtâhtawâtak sîwinikan. wâ, ê-kî-- ê-takwâhtawîyân êkotê ni-- ni-- sôskwâc nimoscicihcênamâyân [*sic*] ôm êkot[a] âskihkohk nic-- nitôtinâw awa sîwinikan. mâk ês âw êtokwê wîsta âmow aw êkotê ê-kî-pîhtokwêt ê-kakwê-tasi-kimotit

[FA:] So, now it is your turn, you don't have to be too close [*sc.* to the microphone].

I [*A New Settlement*]

[1] Well, I am going to tell a little bit, my name is Mary Wells, well, I am from the Elizabeth Settlement. I was a child at the time, I remember, when we moved to the Elizabeth Settlement, we moved there in the fall of 1939. Well, my dad and my brothers and sisters, my grandmother and my mom, and my mom's uncle, too, with all his children and his wife, and other people called Swan; at first only these three families had moved there. And I remember the time when we moved, we used horses with the wagons, it was far over there, we moved quite a ways; and I remember that at first we lived in tents.

II [*Just Deserts*]

[2] And my grandmother went berry-picking and found blueberries. Oh my, I had never tasted blueberries until then, I really liked the taste, especially with sugar on them. And my grandmother went berry-picking again and fed me some and I asked for sugar, but my mom told me: "There is not enough sugar for you to put on your berries." – "Why not?" I asked my mom, "they are only good like that." – "Well," my mom said to me, "we only have a bit of sugar, and your little brother should get that instead, you, you are big and will understand that you don't have to use sugar," I was told. But I had seen where my mom had stored the sugar, she had put it in a syrup pail and hung it in a tree. Well, as soon as I thought no one was looking that way, I went up the tree, climbing up for the sugar. Well, climbing up far enough to reach it, I just used my bare hands to dip into the pail for the sugar. But a bee must have gotten inside the pail, too, trying to steal the sugar, too, and wouldn't you know

wîsta ôhi sîwinikana, mâcika nicîsok! wâcistakâc, niwîsaki-cîsok, sôskwât ninîhcipayin êkota ohci mîtosihk; âh, iyikohk ta-kî-mâtoyân nimâton. nôhkom awa kâ-pâpahtât, "tânis, îskwêw?" ('iskwêw' mân ê-kî-isiyîhkâsit), êyikohk [*sic*] ê-mâtoyân ôma, "ê-cîsot awa âmow, nêtê sîwinikan ê-kakwê-otinamâsoyân," nititwân, pêskis ê-mâtoyân, "wâh-wahwâ, kiwawiyatisin!" k-êsit awa nôhkom, "ahpô êtokw êwako kika-kiskinohamâkon êkây kîhtwâm tita-kakwê-kimotiyan kîkway." namôy nikitimâkinâkawin ômayikohk ê-wîsaki-cîsot âmow.

III

[3] êwakw ânim êkwa ê-takwâkik, nipâpâ êkwa kâ-mâc-ôsîhtât ayi, wâskahikanis, aya, mistikwa ohci, êkwa ayi, pâmwayês tita-pipohk ôma, pipohk[i] êkota ta-wîkiyâhk. ê-kiskisiyân nimâmâ ê-wîcihak êkwa êwakw ânim âyi, wâskahikanis ayi, ê-sisowaskinikêyâhk. ê-kî-kîsîhtât êkwa êwakw ânima wâskahikan nipâpâ, kâ-- ma kîkway êkwa âpacihcikana mîna pîhc-âyihk ta-kî-âpatahki nitôh-ayânân; nipâpâ êkwa kâ-wiyatahahk ê-osîhtât ayi, mîcisowinâhtik, êkwa cêhcapiwinisa âyîtaw ohc êkota ê-sakahahk – kisâstaw mwêhci mân ôh âyi, mêkwâc êkw ânohc kâ-aya-- kâ-- wayawîtimihk kâ-mîcisohk mân ânima mîcisowinâhtikwa, êkos îsi kî-isinâkwaniyiw anima nipâpâ k-ôsîhtât ayi, mîcisowinâhtik. êkwa ê-osîhtât mîn âyi, akocikana, ita nimâmâ t-âhât askihkwa, wiyâkana t-âstât. misi-mistikowat mîna ê-osîhtât, êkota mihta t-âsiwatêki. êkwa, nipêwin-- nipêwina êkwa mîna ê-osîhtât, mistiko-nipêwina. êkwa wiya nimâmâ êkw âya, *canvas*, êwakw ânim êkwa wiy ê-wiyikwâtahk êkw êkota maskosiya ê-asiwatât, êkon ânih êkwa ê-aspisiniyâhk, mâna nikiskisin ê-awâsisîwiyâhk. êkwa mohcihk, mohcihtak ôma, ma kîkway kayâs anas-- anâskânih-- kîkway ê-ohc-âstêk, anâskânihtakohk. nikiskisin mâna nimâmâ ê-wîcihak ayi, ê-kisîpêkinihtakwêyâhk êkwa, pihko mân ê-kî-âpaciht-- ê-âpacihtât êkwa ayi, kîkwây êtokwê mân âsic âya, êkota ê-kî-âpacihtât ê-kâs-- ê-kisîpêkinamâhk ôm âya, anâskânihtak, nipiy asic âta wiya mân ê-kî-âpacihtâyâhk. êkwa mâna, mêtoni ê-kî-kanâtâpâwêk ôm ânâskânihtak, ê-kî-mamihcisiyâhk mâna nimâmâ asici.

it, it stung me! By gosh, the sting really hurt, and I just fell down off the tree; oh, I cried as hard as I could. When my grandmother came running, "What's wrong, *iskwêw?*" (she used to call me *iskwêw),* I was crying so hard, "A bee stung me while I was trying to take some sugar for myself over there," I told her through my tears; "Oh my oh my, serves you right!" my grandmother said to me, "maybe this will teach you not to try and steal things again." No one felt sorry for me when the bee had stung me so hard.

III [*A New House*]

[3] It was that fall that my dad started to build a little house, with logs, before winter, for us to live in during the winter. I remember helping my mom to mud that house. My dad finished that house but we did not have any furniture that might be used inside; now my dad put the pieces together and made a dinner-table with an attached bench on either side – the dinner-table which my dad made looked very much like the picnic tables of today. And he built cupboards for my mom to put the pots and the dishes. He also made a big wooden box for the firewood. And then he also made beds, wooden beds. And then my mom sewed canvas covers and stuffed them with hay, and these we used as mattresses, I remember, when we were children. And it was the [*sc.* bare] floor, the wooden floor, in those days there was nothing [*sc.* such as linoleum, for example] on top of the floor-boards. I remember helping my mom to scrub the floors, we -- she used ashes, I don't know what else she used to scrub the floors with, although we also used water. And the floors used to be spotlessly clean, we used to be so proud, my mom and I.

IV

[4] êkwa nipâpâ mân âta wiya ê-kî-mâcît wîsta; êkwa aya, kahkiyaw kîkway nikî-pê-nanâtohk-ayi-- nikî-pê-mî---mîc-- -mî---mowâyâhkik [*sic*] nanâtohk pisiskisîsak, tâpiskôc aya, apisimôsos, wâpos, kâkwa, wînisakâcihp, êkwa aya pihêwak êkwa sîsîpak, anikwacâsak,

[FA:] – ê-kâh-kitowêyêkinikêyan. –

êkwa aya, ôhow mîna nikî-mowânân, êkwa câhcâhkayowak. câhcâhkayowak wiy âniki nikiskisin, nimâmâ ê-kî-aya---tasôhât, ê-kî-osîhtamâsot aya, napakihtakwa ê-kî-mâmawi-sakahahk êkota; miscikos[a] ê-cimatât êkota sîpâ êkwa ê-patakopitât ôh âyi, it[a] ê-mi-- ê-pê-mîcisoyit ayi, câhcâhkayowa, êkwa mîcimâpoy ê-osîhtamâkoyâhk.

[5] âskaw -- pêyakwâw mîna nikiskisin ayi, nipâpâ ê-mâcît. sôskwâc nama kîkway êsa kî-miskam ta-nipahtât, ê-pê-kîwêt êtokwê êsa kâ-pê-- kâ-pê-miskawât êkota aya, sikâkwa; *so* êkon êkwa nipahêw, pê-kîwêhtahêw. êkwa nôhkom êkwa ê-osîhât ôh âya, sikâkwa, êkw ê-kaskihkaswât kotawânâpiskohk. wahwâ, iyikohk ê-wîhkistâyâhk awa sikâk.

[6] môy wîhkâc nitôh-ayânân mîna kiscikânis, ayis ma kîkway ohc-îhtakow sôniyâw t-âtâwêhk kiscikânisa; *so,* kîkwây piko ê-kî-ohci-pimâcihoyâhk ê-ohci-pimâtisiyâhk wiyâs, pahkwêsikan êkwa mînisa.

[7] êkwa mân âwa nôhkom wiya kî-pîhtwâw. â, mihkwâpêmakwa mâna ê-kî-pîhtwâtahk; êkwa mâna ê-kî-wîcihak ayi, ê-osîhtât ôhi, ê-nitawi-kîskatahamâhk mân ôhi mihkwâpêmakosa êkwa ê-pîhtonamâhk ê-kâskahamâhk, êkwa mâna ê-k-- ê-kâspihkasahk mâna, kotawânâpiskohk ê-sêko-- ê-sêkwâpiskinahk.

V

[8] kêtahtawê êkwa aya, ispî êkwa aya ê-misikitiyân nawac ayi, nikî-kiskinohamâkosinân (piyisk kî-ihtakon

IV [*Our Livelihood I*]

[4] And my dad, on the other hand, used to go hunting; and we used to eat all kinds of animals, such as deer, rabbit, porcupine, badger, and prairie-chickens, ducks, squirrels,

[FA:] – You are rustling the paper. –

and we also ate owl, and blackbirds. I remember the blackbirds; my mom used to entrap them, she had made the trap for herself by nailing boards together; she propped it up with little sticks and when the blackbirds came to eat underneath the board, she jerked out the little sticks and brought the board down on the blackbirds, and then she made soup for us.

[5] Sometimes -- I remember one time when my dad went hunting. He just could not find anything to kill until, on his way home, he found a skunk; so he killed that and brought it back home. And then my grandmother prepared the skunk and cooked it on the stove until it was tender. Oh my, we very much liked the taste of that skunk.

[6] We never had a garden either, for there never was any money to buy seeds; so, the only things we used to do for a living and we used to live on were meat, bannock and berries.

[7] And my grandmother, she used to smoke. Well, she used to smoke red willows; and I used to help her prepare them, we cut the red willow branches and peeled the bark off and scraped the stick, and then she dried them crisp by putting them in the oven.

V [*A Little Girl's Inventiveness: Cigarettes*]

[8] At one time, when I was a little bigger, we were in school (finally there was a school-house at Elizabeth, where we went to

kiskinohamâtowikamik, *Elizabeth,* ita ê-kiskinohamâkosiyâhk), wâ, pêyakwâw (mâna okiskinohamâkêw ê-kî-nakatikoyâhk pêyak-tipahikan mân ê-nitawi-mîcisot), kêtahtawê nititâwak ôk îskwêsisak, "an-- aya, wâpahki ka-pîhtwânaw," nititâwak; "nah! kîkwây mâka kê-pîhtwâtamahk, tânitê k-ôhtinâyahk cistêmâw?" nititikwak. "nah! nikiskêyihtên niya, ê-is-ôsîhak cistêmâw," nititâwak iskwêsisak; "âhâ!" nititikwak. êkwa nititâw aw âya, nim-- nimis awa, "pêtâhkan itâp aya, nôhcâwîs ayi, omâcîwihkômân wâpahki." – "êha!" itwêw. â, êkosi; kêkisêpâ [*sic*] êkwa, kîhtwâm êkwa ê-kîsikâk, wâ, pêtâw nipâpâsis ôm ômâcîwihkomân. wâ, mayaw ê-kî-sipwêhtêt okiskinohamâkêw ê-kî-kîsi-mîcisoyâhk, nisipwêhtânân êkwa sakâhk êkw ê-nâtamâhk mihkwâpêmakwa, êkwa ê-osîhtâyâhk êkon ânihi. wah, kotawânâpiskohk tahkohc êkw êkota ê-kâspihkasamâhk. êk ôhi mân âya, aya, masinahikanêkinowatisihk mân ê-kî-nîmâyâhk ayi, mîciwinis, êkon êkwa --

[*external break*]

[MW:] êha, kinitohtâtin. *'cause* môy mâna sêmâk ayis anima --
[FA:] êha; êkosi.
[MW:] *okay.*

êkonî [*sic*] mân ôhi, maskimocisa kâ-kî-âpacihtâyâhk, it[a] ê-- ê-- nî-- nîmâwin[a] ê-sipwêhtatâyâhk, êkoni [*sic*] êkwa ôhi kâ-- kâ-tâh-tâtopitamâhk ôhi maskimocisa, êkot[a] êk ôhi mihkwâpêmakw[a] êkw âyi ê-- ê-wêwêkinamâhk, ê-osîhâyâhk-- ê-osîhâyâhkik ôk âyi pîhcwâwinisak êkwa ê-pîhtwâyâhk. mêtoni êsa n-- êtok ôma nikakwâhyakâpâs-- nikakwâhyakâpasikânân pîhc-âyihk, ê-wîhcêkimahkasikêyâhk ot[i] êtokwê. wâ, ê-pê-pîhtokwêt aw ôkiskinohamâkêwiskwêw, wahwâ, hm-hm-hm [*imitates sniffing noises*], konit ê--, hm-hm, ê-nâh-nitawâpasot. kiskêyihtam nânitaw ê-kî-itahkamikisiyâhk, mâka tâpiskôc êka niyanân, ma kîkway. wâ, piyis ês êtokwê, kâ-- kâ-k-- kâ-k--, awiya kâ-wîhtamâkot tânis ânima ê-kî-isîhcikêyâhk. êkosi; môy âta wiya nânitaw nititikonân. wahwâ, nânitaw nîso-kîsikâw ê-kî-ispayik ayi, kêtahtawê aw ôkiskinohamâkêw onâpêma kâ-tâh-têpwâtikoyâhk, misatimokamikohk nêtê ê-nitaw-âsamastimwêt; "âstam! ôtê, iskwêsisak," nititikonân. wâ, nitispahtânân êkotê;

school), well, this one time (the teacher used to leave us alone for an hour while she went to eat lunch), at one time I told the girls, "Now, tomorrow we will smoke," I told them; "Nonsense, what will we smoke? Where will we get tobacco?" they said to me. "Nonsense, I, I know how to make tobacco," I told those girls; "Right on!" they said to me. And I told my older cousin, "Tomorrow, bring your father's hunting-knife along!" – "Okay!" she said. Well, and so it was; in the morning, the next day, well, she brought along her dad's hunting-knife. Well, as soon as we had finished eating and the teacher had left, we went off into the bush to get red willows and then we prepared them. Oh, we dried them on top of the stove until crisp. And we used to take our lunches in paper bags, and these--

[*external break*]

[MW:] Yes, I heard you. Because it is not yet quite on--
[FA:] Yes, now.
[MW:] Okay.

and these little bags which we used to carry our lunches to school, we tore them up and rolled the red willows up in them, making cigarettes and smoking them. We must have made a great deal of smoke in that place, causing a foul smell with our smoking. Well, when the teacher came back in, oh my, *sniff-sniff-sniff*, she just went *sniff-sniff*, sniffing around. She knew we had been up to something, but we acted as if nothing had happened, nothing at all. Well, finally someone must have told her what we had done. And so it was; she did not say anything to us. Oh my, it was about two days later when all of a sudden the teacher's husband was calling us from the barn over there where he had gone to feed the horses; "Come here! Over here, you girls!" he said to us. Well, we ran over there; and he gave each of us a

kâ-mâh-miyikoyâhk ôh âya, pîhcwâwinisa. êy, takahkêyihtamwak ôki iskwêsisak wiyawâw, wâ, "êkâya," nititâwak, "êkây ka-p--, êkâya sêmâk -- ka-saskahwânawak," nititâwak ôk îskwêsisak. "mô-- môy kwayas nititêyihtên ôma niy âwa kâ-pîhtwâhikoyahk awa nâpêw," nititâwak, "môy wîhkâc nitâpwêhtên ayisiyiniw, nâpêw, ta-pîhtwâhât awâsisa," nititâwak, "ki-- nânitaw kîkway anim êkotê êtokw ê-kî-astât," nititâwak ôk îskwêsisak. êkosi, kâw êkwa kiskinohamâtowikamikohk nêtê nititohtânân. wâ, tâpwê êkw êkotê ê-kî-takohtêyâhk nipâh-pâskêkinânânak ôki kâ-s-- kâ-pîhtwâhikawiyâhk. nâh, êsa ôm ôta ayi, mistatimo-mêy[a] ê-pâstêyik[i] ês êkot[a] ê-kî-wâh-wêwêkinahk, êkoni ôhi kâ-pîhtwâhikoyâhk ôhi, m-- nitak ôt[i] êkâ ê-saskahwâyâhkik, mâskôt tâh-kî-mâyâpasowak, nititêyihtên.

VI

[9] êkwa ôm âya, êkwa kîhtwâm mîna nik-âtotên ôm âya, ispî êkwa aya nawac aya, kinwês ê-ayâyâhk ekôta *Elizabeth*. kêtahtawê ayi, kâ-mâc-âya-nâh-nîmihitowinihkêcik ôk âyisiyiniwak (êkwa môy wîhkâc niwâpahtê-- ê-wâpahtamâhk ôm ê-nîmihitôhk ôma niyanân k-âwâsisîwiyâhk), êkwa mân âya, kâ-nîmihitowinihkêt aw âyisiyiniw, aya, wîhkihkasikanihk mân êkôta sôniyâs[a] ê-kî-ahâcik; êkw âwiyak miskwamâci êkon ânihi sôniyâsa, piko ta-nîmihitowinihkêt, wîkiwâhk mâka mân ê-kî-nâh-nîmihitowinihkêcik. wahwâ, kêtahtawê nôhtâwiy, kâ-miskwamât sôniyâsa; êkôsi, nîmihitowinihkêw êkwa. wahwâ, "aciyaw kika-kitâpahkân," nititikawin. wâ, ê-piyasêyimoyân, môy nikî-pêhon, "ta-tipiskâk ôma ta-wî-nîmihitohk," t-- ê-isit awa nimâmâ. wahwâ, piyis âta wiya kâ-tipiskâk, âh, kâ-mâci-takwâwahitocik ôk âyisiyiniwak, kêtahtawê pêyak kâ-nâkatâpamak aw ôskinîkiskwêw, wâcistakâc, iyikohk ê-katawatêyimak, iyikohk ê-takahkisîhot! pâskac ê-mihkwâyik ôma sênipânasâkay ê-postiskahk, astotin asici ê-kikiskahk êkwa m-- mistikwaskisin[a] ê-postiskahk, mêtoni ê-âh-ispâhkwanêyâyiki; wâh-wahwâ, nitakahkinawâw, wâcistakâc! môy wîhkâc ahpô ayis niya maskisina nitôh-wâpahtên, nayêstaw pahkêkinwêskisina mân ê-kî-kikiskamâhk êkwa aya, waskitaskisin[a] âsici, êkây kâ-- ka-sâpopêyâhk, ka-sâpopêki nimaskisininâna. êkosi, nitapin êkw

cigarette. Hey, these girls, they were happy, well, but I told them, "Don't! Don't, don't light them right away," I told these girls. "It does not seem right to me that this man is giving us smokes," I told them; "I cannot believe that a grown-up, an adult, would give smokes to children," I told them, "he must have put something in there," I told these girls. With that we went back over there to the school. Well, and in fact when we got over there we each of us broke open the cigarette that he had given us to smoke. Ugh, in each one he had wrapped up dry horse-dung, this was what he had given us to smoke, and it was a good thing we did not light them, no doubt they would have given off a foul stench, I think.

VI [*A Little Girl's Inventiveness: Fancy Dress*]

[9] And then, I will tell about another time again, when we had been at Elizabeth for some time. Once, when the people started holding dances (we had never seen a dance, us, when we were children), now when someone held a dance, they used to put a coin in the cake; and the one who found that coin in his mouth had to hold the [next] dance at his place, for they used to hold the dances in their houses. Oh my, once my father found the coin in his mouth; and so he now held the dance. Oh my, I was told, "You can watch for a little while." Well, I was anxious and I could not wait, "Tonight will be the dance," my mom said to me. Oh my, finally it was night, oh, as groups of people began to arrive, suddenly I noticed one young woman, wow, I thought her so pretty, she was dressed so beautifully! She even wore a red satin dress, and she also had a hat on and she wore pumps with really high heels; oh my oh my, I really thought she looked beautiful, wow! For I, I had never even seen any shoes, we only used to wear hide-moccasins and rubber overshoes with them so that we wouldn't get wet, so that our moccasins wouldn't get wet. So, I

êkota, wahwâ, konit êkwa ê-itohtêyân aw ôskinîkiskwêw, oskotâkay ôm ê-nitawi-âh-âyinamwak; âh, wâcistakâc iyikohk ê-katawatêyimak! êkos âwa nimâmâ êkwa, "nitawi-kawisimo êkwa!" nititikawin, "êkoyikohk kinwês kikitâpahkân." êkosi ninitawi-kawisimon. ê, kîkisêpâ êkwa, môy nikî-wanikiskisin êwakw âw âya, iyikohk ê-kî-katawatêyimak aw îsk--, aw ôskinîkiskwêw. wâ, tânis êkwa, mâc-- êkwa ê-mâci-mêtawêyân êkwa, wâ, niwiyêyihtên, yâhk ês ê-wî-nitawi-nîmihitoyân, piko mâk êkwa ta-wawêsîyân ôma nîsta, tâpiskôc awa kâ-kî-takahkinawak awa oskinîkiskwêw. nimâmâ aw ôskotâkay kâ-nitawi-nitâhtâmak, ê-kî-ayât wîst ê-mihkwâyik miskotâkay. "mâmâ! maht ês âya, awihin kiskotâkay, ê-wî-mêtawâkêyân." êkw âwa nimâmâ nikitâpamik, "naah [*sic*]! ma cî mâka, môy kika-têpiskên, osâm ta-kinwâpêkan." – "namôya," nititâw nimâmâ, "nikiskêyihtên tânisi ta-tôtamân, ta-têpiskamân kiskotâkay." wâ, nitawihik oskotâkay, â, nipostiskên êk ôma miskotâkay, pîminahkwânis êk ôtê ê-kî-iskonamân ôma kîskasâkay, êkot[a] êkwa pîminahkwânis nitahkopitên, êk ôma kotak êkw êkôta niwaskitakotân; êkosi, nahiyikohk ispîhc-- iskwâw.

[10] âh, astotin mâk êkwa mîna piko, tânit[ê] êkwa t-ôhtinamân astotin? wâ, nima-mâmitonêyihtên. nikiskisopayin nimâmâ ê-kî-ayât astotin, mâka kayâs nama kîkway ayis, nayêstaw *tams* mân ê-kî-ayâhk. êkôsi, "mâmâ! maht ês âwihin *your tam*, ê-wî-pos-- nika-wî--, êwako nika-wî-postiskamân [*sic*]." â, nitawihik êkwa otastotin nimâmâ. êkwa, wiyâkanikamikohk êkwa k-êtohtêyân, êkw êkotê wiyâkan êkwa ê-nitawi-nâtamân, êwak ôm êkwa nêtê pîhc-âyihk *in the tam* êkwa nitasiwatân, êwakw êkw ê-postiskamân; wahwâ, tâpiskôt tâpwê ôm âstotin isinâkwan, itow[a] ân[a] ôskinîkiskwêw kâ-kî-postiskahk.

[11] wâ, maskisina êkwa, tânitê êkwa maskisina? wâ, êkwa ôhi piko waskicaskisinis[a] ê-postiskamân. nimâmitonêyihtên, wâ, niwiyêyihtên. nipîhtokwân kâwi nêtê nîkinâhk, "mâmâ! maht ês âya, nîso asapâpâhtikwak ê-nitawêyimakik," nititâw nimâmâ. "nac! tânisi mâk ê-wî-itâpacihacik asapâpâhtikwak?" – "ê-wî-mêtawâkêyân." â, êkôsi, "pakahkam pêyak nitayâwâw," itwêw awa nimâmâ. ê-nitonikêt êk ôkaskikwâsowatihk, kâ-otin--, pêyak ês ôh ê-kî-mêstinât ay âsapâpa, âta wiy âyâwêw. mâk ô-- kotak aw âsapâpâhtik, kêyâpic

sat there, oh my, I just went over to this young woman and kept running my hand over her dress; oh, by gosh, I thought her so pretty! And now my mom told me, "Go to bed now, you have watched long enough." So I went to bed. Hey, in the morning I could not forget how pretty I had thought that young woman. Well, what now? I was starting to play, well, I thought of what to do, I would pretend I was going to a dance, and now I, too, had to dress up like the young woman that had looked so beautiful to me. I went to borrow my mom's dress for she, too, had a red dress. "Mom, please lend me your dress to play with." My mom looked at me, "Don't be silly! It won't fit you, will it now, it will be too long." – "No," I said to my mom, "I know what to do for your dress to fit me." Well, she let me have her dress, well, and I put the dress on and with some twine now I pulled the skirt up to over here [*gesture*] and tied it up with the twine, and the other piece [*sc.* the blouse] I let hang over; with that, it was the right length.

[10] Oh, but I had to have a hat, too, and where would I get a hat? Well, I thought about it. It came to me that my mom had a hat, but in the old days, of course, there was no such thing, for they only used to have tams. With that, "Mom, please lend me your tam, I am going to wear it." Well, now my mom lent me her tam. And now I went to the pantry and took a plate and put that inside, in the tam, and put it on; well, this hat really looked like the kind that young woman had worn.

[11] Well, now for the shoes; where would I get shoes? Well, I only wore little rubber overshoes. I thought about it, well, I had an idea. I went back into the house again over there, "Mom! I want two thread-spools please," I said to my mom. "Hm, what are you going to do with thread-spools?" – "I am going to play with them." With that, my mom said to me, "I believe I may have one." Now she looked in her sewing box, and she had one on which she had used up all the thread. But there still was some thread on the other spool.

asapâp êkot[a] ê-akwamot. kâ-otinât nimâmâ êk ôhpimê êkwa masinahikanêkinohk ê-- titipisimêw ôh âsapâpa, iskohk ê-mêsci---mêstinât. wâ, nîso êk ôk âsapâpâhtikwak nimiyikawin, nitakahkêyihtên. kâ-otinamân pîminahkwânis, êkwa êkonik anik êkwa mîna nahkwanihk êkw êkot[a] ê-tâh-tahkopitakik ôk âsapâpâhtikwak, ê-- ê-ispâhkwanêyâki mistikwaskisina ê-postiskamân. wâ, miton ôt[a] ê-pâh-papâmohtêyân ôma, nitakahkwêwêsinin, nitakahkêyimison, mwêhc îyinitohk aw ôskinîkiskwêw awa kâ-kî-wâpamak, mwêhc êkosi nititêyimison ôma, ê-- yâhki ê-wî-nitawi-nîmihitoyân. pâskac aw âya, nipâpâ aya, ôta aya, wêy--

– *I forgot, what do you call that* --

[FA:] – kîkwây? –

âwataskosiwâkanihk, êkota ôma kâ-wî-nitawi-nîmihitoyân ôma, ê-- napakihtakwa ôhi -- ê-napakihtakohkâsot awa âwataskosiwâkan, êkotê êkwa ê-wî-nitawi-nîmihitoyân ôma. mâk ôm iyikohk (awa nôhkom awa nitawâc ê-wawiyatêyimak), kâ-pâh-papâmohtêyân ôma, "iyaw!" itwêw nôhkom, "tânisi mâka wiy âw îskwêw awa, ita kâ-papâm-ây-itwêwêsihk, tâpiskôc pâhkahâhkwân [*sic; cf.* pâhpahâhkwân] ê-kî-âhkwatiniyik[i] ôsita," nititik.

VII

[12] wâ, piyis êkwa âta wiy êkwa, ê-misikitiyâhk êkw âsay, nânitaw êtokwê nêwosâp ê-itahtopiponwêyâhk, kêyâpic mâka môy wîhkâc ê-ôhci-wâpahtamâhk ôtênaw, ôtênâhk ôh âtâwêwikamikohk ahpô, môy wîhkâc ê-ôhci-wîcihiwêyâhk. â, kêtahtawê pêyakwâw ê-takahki-kîsikâk ôm âya, ê-nikotwâsiko-kîsikâk, môniyâw mân âwa, akâmi-sîpîsisihk kî-wîkiw pêyak, êkotê ôma nititohtânân ôma, ê-nitawi-kiyokawâyâhk awa môniyâw. wâ, kâ-mâh-miyikoyâhk ôh âya, nâtitisahikêwasinahikana, ês êtokwê mihcêt ê-kî-ati-mâh-mâwacihtât. â, nitapi-- nikîwêhtatânân! pâmwayês takohtêyâhk nîkinâhk nêtê, âpihtaw iyikohk êtokwê nitapinân êkota êkwa, êkôni ôhi masinahikana ôhi êkot[a] ê-kâh-kitâpahtamâhk. wâh-wahwâ, iyikohk ê-mâh-miyonawâyâhkik ôk îskwêwak êkota ê-masinahikâsocik ôki, ayiwinisa nanâtohk ê-kikiskahkik. kahkiyaw pâskac ê-mâh-mihkotonêhocik!

My mom took it and wound the thread onto a separate piece of cardboard until she had taken it all off. Well, now I was given the two spools and I was happy. Taking some string now and tying the spools under my heels, I was wearing highheeled pumps. Well, as I kept walking all around there, back and forth, I made nice sounds with my heels and I liked the way I was, exactly like the young woman I had seen, I fancied myself exactly like her, as if I was going to a dance. As a final touch, my dad --

– I forgot, what do you call that --

[FA:] – What? –

on a hay-rack, that's where I was going to dance, the boards -- the hay-rack was made of lumber, that's where I was going to dance. But I was walking around, back and forth, so much (and I had to laugh at her in spite of it), that my grandmother said, "What now! What is it with this *iskwêw* that she goes around making such sounds back and forth like a chicken with frozen feet," she said about me.

VII [*A Little Girl's Inventiveness: Lipstick*]

[12] Well, at last we were bigger now, we must have been about fourteen already, but we still had never seen town or the stores in town, we had never gone along. Well, on one occasion, once when it was a nice day, a Saturday, we went to visit a certain White-Man who used to live across the creek. Well, he gave us these mail-order catalogues, of which he must have been collecting a lot. Well, we took them home! Before we arrived at our house over there, it must have been about halfway, we sat down; and there we looked at these books. Oh my oh my, all the women in the pictures looked so pretty to us, with all their various clothes. To top it all off, every one of them had lipstick on!

[13] êkosi, nikîwêhtatânân ôhi masinahikana. â, ninitawi-kiskinohamâkosinân êkwa kîhtwâm ê-kîsikâk, môy nikî-pônêyihtên ôma mihkotonêhon, ôm ê-mihkotonêhocik ôk îskwêwak, êkwa mâka mîna nitakâwâtamawâwak. wâ, kî-- êwakw ânim êkwa ê-kî-kîsi-mîcisoyâhk ayi, ê-âpihtâ-kîsikâk ômisi nititâw aw âya, nimis, nôhcâwîs otânisa: "maht êsa," nititâw, "wâpahk[i] âyi, pakamâkanis itâp a-- aya, kika-pêtân," nititâw awa nimis awa. "êha," itwêw, "tânisi mâk ê-wî-itâpacihtâyan pakamâkanis?" nititik. "môy ê-wî-wîhtamâtân," nititâw, "ka-wâpahtên wâpahki, tânis ê-wî-itâpacihtâyân," nititâw.

[14] êkosi, nikî-- nipê-kîwânân. kîhtwâm ê-wâpahk, wâ, pêtâw pakamâkanis, êkwa niy êkwa nisipwêhtatân tahto-kîkway ôhi ê-wî-âpacihtâyâhk êkwa; ê--, kîkway ôma nânitaw ê-wî-isi-môhcwahkamikisiyâhk âkamîna [*sic*]; êkosi. â, mâka mîna okiskinohamâkêw ê-kî-nitawi-mîcisot, ôm ê-nakatikoyâhk êkw âyi, itê mân ôh âya, wiyâkanikamikos ê-ay-ayât, êkotê ê-kanawêyihtahk ôh âpacihci-- kîkway ôhi ayi, k-âpacihtâyâhk mân âyi, kiskinohamâtowikamikohk, êk ôm âya, ê-mihkwâk, '*chalk*' isiyîhkâtêw (môy nikiskêyihtên tânis ê-isiyîhkâtêk ê-nêh-- ê-nêhiyawêhk), êwak ôm ôm ôma [*sic*] kâ-nâtamân ôma, ê-mihkwâk, êkwa pakamâkanis ohc âna, mêtoni miton ê-pîkinatahamân êwakw ânima iskohk mêton âyi, mwêhci pahkwêsikan iyikohk ayi ê-pîkinâk. êkot[a] êk ôm âya, wâpiski-pimiy êkw âsic êkota kâ-- kâ-takwastâyân êkwa, mêtoni kwayas êkwa nitôsîhtâyân [*sic*] mihkotonêhon.

[15] kahkiyaw êkwa tahto iskwêsisak ôki kiskinohamâtowikamikohk ê-ayâyâhk, iskohk ê-apisîsisicik ôk îskwêsisak aya, nânitaw pêyak iyikohk ê-m-- ê-kiskêyihtahkik masinahikan, kahkiyaw mîn êkonik nimihkotonêhwânânak. wahwâ, kêtahtawê okiskinohamâkêw takohtêw, wâh-wahwahwâ, nawac piko koskwêyihtam ôma, kahkiyaw ôm ê-nîpitêpiyâhk ôm âyi, kahkiyaw ê-mâh-mihkotonêyâhk. kêhcinâhow mîna môy wîhkâc ayis ôtênâhk, ôm ê-kicimâkisiyâhk kahkiyaw, "tânitê ôk êtok ôk ê-ohtinahkik?" nikî-itêyimikonân êtokwê mâna mihkotonêhon ê-kî-osîhtamâsoyâhk. êkosi; kêyâpic ôm ânohc iskohk kâ-kîsikâk

[13] So we took these books home. Well, the next day we went to school but I could not forget this lipstick, the women wearing lipstick, and as usual I envied them. Well, when we had finished eating at lunch-time, I said to my older cousin, the daughter of my father's brother, "C'mon," I said to her, "tomorrow you bring along a hammer," I said to this cousin of mine. "Okay," she said, "but what are you going to do with a hammer?" she said to me. "I am not going to tell you," I said to her, "tomorrow you will see what I am going to use it for," I said to her.

[14] So we went home. The next day, well, she brought a hammer, and now I, too, took along everything that we were going to need; and as usual we were going to do something crazy; that was that. Well, as usual the teacher went to eat and left us alone, and there in the cupboard where she kept these things that we used in school, this red 'chalk' it is called (I do not know what it is called in Cree), it was this red stuff that I went to get, and with the hammer I ground it down very, very fine until it was powdered exactly like flour. And now, when I mixed it with lard, I had indeed made real lipstick.

[15] Every one of the girls in the school, all the way down to the smallest ones who were only in Grade I, we put lipstick on all of them. Oh my, all of a sudden the teacher came in, oh my oh my oh my, she was kind of surprised as we all sat side-by-side, each one of us with lipstick. She was certain that we had never been to town for we were all of us poor, "I wonder where they got it?" she must have thought of us when in fact we had made lipstick for ourselves.

(êwakw ân[a] ân[a] êkwa aya, nitôcâhkosin êwakw ân[a] ân[a] îskw--, okiskinohamâkêw ê-kî-kiskinohamawit), môy wîhkâc mâka nitôh-âcimostawâw, ê-kî-- tânitê ê-kî-ohtinamâhk mihkotonêhon.

[*external break*]

VIII

[16] "-- ê-pê-kîwêyâhk ê-tipiskâk," itwêw, "êkwa awa nimâmâ ê-kî--, kâhkêwak ê-kî-osîhtât," itwêw, "êkwa pîhc-âyihk ômis îsi ê-- kî-nîpitêkotâw, sisonê kotawânâpiskohk," itwêw, "ta-pâstêyik[i]," îtwêw.

[17] êkwa mân ân[a] ôsîmis[a] âna k-âcimak ana, okiskinohamâkêwa kâ-kî-wîwit, ê-kî-miywêyihtahk êsa mân ê-mâcît, ê-nitawi-mâcît ês âkamîn [*sic*] êtokwê êsa, sâpo-- ê-sâpopatât ês ây êtokwê aya, opahkêkinwêskisina, êkotê ês ôma kîswân [*sic*] ôma k-âkotât ês ôh ôhi wîst ôh ômaskisina, sisonê kâhkêwak[wa] ôh ê-akotêyiki. *boy!* nîpâ-tipisk êtokwê awa nicâhkos êsa yâhk ê-nitawi-kimotit ôm âyi, kâhkêwak êkwa ê-wî-mîcicik êkwa *before* ta-kawisimocik. osîmis[a] ês ôm ômaskisiniyiw, miton ês ât[a] ê-kakwê-- ê-kakwê--, *she tried to tear a piece off and this,* 'kâhkêwak,' ê-itêyihtahk, wiy ôm ê-- mistikwâhkatotêwa ê-pâstêki *moccasins*. êkos îs ês ôcipitam êkwa ê-nitawi-kawisimocik (kîkwây kayâs, nayêstaw *lamp*), *boy!* konit ês êkwa mitoni --

[FA:] – ê-sâ-sîpêkahtahk. –

– "môy nikî-kîskahtên!" itêw ês ômisa, ê-saskahahkik *lamp,* pôt ês ôma, osîmisiwâwa omaskisiniyiw ê-kakwê-mîcicik!

[*external break*]

[FA:] êkosi.

That's how it was; and to this day (this one, that same woman, the teacher who used to teach me is now my sister-in-law), I have never yet told her where we got the lipstick.

[*external break*]

VIII [*A Tough Mistake*]

[16] "-- we were coming home at night," he said [*sc.* MW's husband], "and my mom had made dried meat," he said, "and she had hung it up inside the house, in a row like this [*gesture*], beside the stove," he said, "to dry," he said.

[17] And the younger brother of the one whose story I am telling, the one who was married to the school-teacher, he used to like hunting, and he must have gone out hunting and must have gotten his moccasins wet, and, as it happens, he, too, had hung his moccasins up beside where the dried meat was hanging. *Boy*, in the middle of the night, it appears, my sister-in-law [*sc.* their sister] must have gotten it into her head to go and steal this dried meat, and for them [*sc.* her and her older sister] to eat it before going to bed. It was her younger brother's moccasin, and although she really tried to tear a piece off, thinking it was a piece of dried meat, dried moccasins are hard as wood! She had merely pulled it off [*sc.* the line] like this, as they went to go to bed (what else was there in the old days but [*sc.* kerosene] lamps), *boy*! she really --

[FA:] – she was stretching it with her teeth. –

– "I can't bite a piece off it!" she said to her older sister, and they lit the lamp and what was this! they were trying to eat their younger brother's moccasin!

[*external break*]

[FA:] Go ahead.

IX

[18] â, kiyâm, âsay mîna nôhkom nik-âcimâw, osâm mistahi ê-kî-sâkihak nôhkom, nîsta mân ê-kî-sâkihit. mâka wiya, ê-kî-miywêyihtahk ê-pininawasot [*sic; cf.* -piminawasot] nôhkom, kâkikê wiya mân ê-kî-pininawatikoyâhk [*sic*]. isko iskwêyâc ê-kî-pininawasot [*sic*], ê-kî-misi-pahkwêsikanihkêt pêyakwâw kêkisêpâ [*sic*], êkw ânima kâ-mâc-âhkosit ê-pôn-âpihtâ-kîsikâyik; êwakw ânima, ê-âh-â-- [*?sic*] ê-tipiskâyik kâ-nakataskêt! ispî êkwa ê-nîpêpîstâht, opahkwêsikanima êkota ê-kî-mowimiht; êkoyikohk ê-kî-kakâyawisît nôhkom.

X

[19] êkwa wiya nimâmâ, mâna kî-osîhêw aya, apisimôsoswayâna, ê-kî-kîsinamâsot. âta mân ê-nî---kî-wîcihak, mâka môy wîhkac ê-ohci-nâkatohkêyân tânisi mwêhci mân ânima ê-kî-isîhât. êkos êkwa niy êwako niwanihtân, mâka môy --, môy nikask--, môy nikiskêyihtên tânisi ka-isi-kîsinakik, â, pahkêkinwak [*sic*]. êkwa mîna mâna ê-kî-osîhtât pahkêkinwêskisina, ay âstisa ê-kî-osîhât, aya, miskotâkaya mîna mân ê-kî-osîhtât, pahkêkinwêsâkaya ê-mîkisihkahtahk, kîskanakwêwayâna asici.

[20] êkwa, môy mâka nikiskisin, kîspin wîhkâc ka-kî-atâwâkêt, môy nikiskisin, mâk âhpô êtokwê mâna kî-atâwâkêw.

[21] êkwa mîna mâna nikiskisin nimâmâ, ê-kî-nihtâ-wanihikêt, sihkosa mân ê-kî-wanihikamawât. mihcêtwâw mân ê-kî-wîcêwak nâciwanihikanêci, tâniyikohk mâna sî--, sihkosak ôki, êkosi wiy âta wiy êkota mâna nikî-kiskinohamâk, tânisi k-êsi-pahkonakik ôki, sihkosak êkwa ta-sîpahwakik. êkwa nipâpâ, wîsta mâna kî-wanihikêw, mâka wacaskwa mâna piko ê-kî-wanihikamawât. êkwa kâ-miyoskaminiyik mâna wiya mîna kî-- kî-nitawi-pâskiswêw mâna wacaskwa. êkw âtimwa mân ê-kî-ayâwât pêyak, ê-nihtâ-nât---nâtahisipêt aw âtim, ahpô mâna wacaskwa kâ-pâskiswât ê-kî-nâtâyit, êkosi mâna mistahi ê-kî-itêyimat otêma. kêtahtawê êkw âw âya, atim aw êsa kâ-nitaw-ôtihtinât ayi, kâkwa! êy, êy, iyikohk ê-kî-kakwâhyakicihk ôtonihk misiwê, môy ôhci-kaskihtâw nipâpâ ê--, kahkiyaw ka-manipitimât,

IX [*My Grandmother*]

[18] Well, I suppose I will once again tell about my grandmother because I used to love her a great deal, and she used to love me, too. But as for her, my grandmother liked to cook, and it was always she who cooked for us. Until the last she used to cook, and one morning she had made lots of bannock, and it was then, after noon, that she fell ill; and it was that same night that she died! And so it was her own bannock that was eaten at her wake; so active had she been, my grandmother.

X [*Our Livelihood*]

[19] And as for my mom, she used to prepare deer-skins, finishing them for herself. Although I used to help her, I never took notice exactly how she used to finish them. And so, as far as I'm concerned, I lost it, I do not know how to finish hides. Well, she also used to make moccasins, she used to make mitts, and she used to make coats, too, she made beaded leather coats, and vests as well.

[20] But I cannot remember if she ever sold any, I do not remember, but she may have sold some.

[21] And I also remember that my mom was good at trapping, she used to trap for weasels. Many times I used to go with her when she went to check her traps, the weasels were plentiful, and that way she used to teach me how to skin the weasels and how to stretch their pelts. And my dad, too, used to set traps, but he used to trap only for muskrat. And in the spring he also used to go and shoot muskrat. And he used to have a dog, and that dog used to be good at retrieving ducks from the water, even when he shot a muskrat, the dog went to get it, and so he used to think the world of his dog. At one time this dog went and seized a porcupine! Hey, hey, he had the quills all over his mouth, so much so that my dad was not able

êkosi kî-nipahik anihi. wah, wah, â, m-- êkosi kî-nipiw an[a] âtim. kî-nipahi-mihtâtêw nipâpâ otêma, êkosi môy wîhkâc kîhtwâm ohci-miskawêw kotak[a] âtimwa êkoyikohk ayi, ê-nihtâ-nâtahisipêyit.

[22] êkwa mîna kîhtwâm awa nik-âcimâw awa nôhkom, tânisi mâna wiya pihêw[a] ê-kî-is-- ê-kî-is-âyi---nâh-nakwâtât. ê-kî-pêhot mâna ispî ôh âyi, kâ-nîmihitoyit, êkota mâna k-- ê-kî-nitawi-kitâpamât, êkwa mêtoni ê-wiyêyihtahk mwêhci tânit[a] ânima kâ-nîmihitoyit. êkwa mâna misiwê êkota mâna miscikosa ê-kî-wâh-- wâ-- ê-- kâh-wâh-wâkinahki mân êkotê ê-âh-sêkonahk [*sic*] asiskîhk, êkw êkota mân âya, câpakwânisa mân êkot[a] ê-kî-akotât. ayis ôki pihêwak kâ-nîmihitocik, konita mân ê-pimi-nâh-nawakiskwêsimocik, kâh-pimi-nawakiskwêsimotwâwi mân êkota, pimi-tâpakwâsowak, êkosi mâna misahkamik ê-- mân ê-kî-mâh-misi-nipahât pihêwa êkos îsi nôhkom. êkwa mâna ni-- mihcêtwâw nikî-- nikî-wîcêwâw kâh-nitawi-nâtakwêci; konita mân ôki pihêwak kî-âh-akocinwak – ê-k---kot-- ê-kî-kicimahihcik âta ê-nîmihitocik.

[23] êkwa, ispî êkwa mîna mitoni ê-misikitiyân, nisîmisak êkwa wîstawâw nîso, nâpêsisak, mêtoni ê-mâh-misikiticik, nikiskisin mâna nipâpâ ê-kî-kiskinohamâkoyâhk ayi, ê-nitawi-wiyahpicikêyâhk, misatimwak ôki ê-wiyahpitâyâhkik, êkwa mân ê-kî-nâtaskosiwêyâhk. pêskis mân âsic îyikohk ê-kî-mâsihitoyâhk, nâtaskosiwêyâhki maskosîhk. êwako mîna mâna ê-kiskisiyân ê-kî-miywêyihtamân ê-nâtaskosiwêyâhk, nipâpâ otêma t-âsamât.

[24] pêyakwâw pamwayês aya, mâka mîn ê-kî-mêscinêcik aya, aya, wâposwak, kêtahtawê ê-kakwâhyakêyaticik, sôskwâc mâna nipâpâ owîscihkânisa iyinitohk kî-wî-kâh-kitâyiwa, iyikohk mân ê-kî-mihcêticik wâposwak. kêtahtawê mîn êkonik kahkiyaw kâ-namatêcik. kêyâpic ôm âs--, anim ânohc kâ-kîsikâk, môy âni mihcêt wâposwak kâ-- kâ-wâpamâyâhkik niyanân nitaskînâhk. pêyak piko nikî-wâpamâw mêskanâhk ê-ay-apit wâposos, miton âta k-âkâwâtak êwakw âna, mâka mitoni kayâ-- môy âhpô êkwa nikiskisin tânisi wâposo-mîcîmâpoy ê-is-- ê-isiyîhkâtêk [*sic; sc.* ê-ispakwahk].

to pull them all out, and so they [*sc.* the quills] killed him. Oh, oh, so that dog died. My dad sorely missed his dog and never again found another dog that was so good at retrieving ducks from the water.

[22] And I will also tell about my grandmother again, how she used to snare prairie-chickens. She used to wait for the time when they were dancing, then she would go and watch them and determine exactly where it was that they danced. And then she used to bend little sticks and place both ends into the ground, all over that place, and then she used to hang little snares on them. For when the prairie-chickens dance, they just dance along with their heads bent down, and each time they dance along there with their heads bent down, they get caught as they move along, and in that way my grandmother used to kill a large number of prairie-chickens. And I used to go with her many times when she would go to check her snares; and all the prairie-chickens just used to hang there – they were treated cruelly even as they danced.

[23] And when I was quite a big girl, and both my younger brothers, too, were getting quite big, I remember that my dad used to teach us how to harness, and we harnessed the horses, and then we used to go and get hay. On those occasions, when we would go for hay, we also used to wrestle on the hay. That, too, I remember that I used to like going for hay, for my dad to feed his horses.

[24] At one time, before the rabbits had once again become scarce, they were all of a sudden plentiful and there were so many rabbits that they were simply just eating all of my dad's hay-stacks. And then again all of a sudden there were none of them. To this day, there still are not many rabbits that I have seen on our colony. I saw only one little rabbit sitting on the road and I really wanted that one but I do not even remember the taste of rabbit soup.

XI

[25] wâ, kot-- nikiskisin âsay mîna, pêyak kotak kîkway nik-âtotên. aya, aya ôm êkwa ê-kêhtê-ayiwiyân nîsta, nikî-- nikî-ohpikihânân nôsisiminân pêyak, nâpêsis. êkw âya, tôhtôsâpoy môy ê-ohci-kaskihtât ayi t-âpacihtât, ê-kî-mâyiskâkot mistahi, êkwa mân âwa nikisêyinîm mân ê-kî-- mâna wâposwa ê-kî-misi-- kâh-misi-nipahâci, wâposo-mîcimâpoy mâna ê-kî-osî-- ê-kî-oht--, ê-kî-ohc-ôhpikihâyâhk awa nôsisim, ê-kî-wîhkistahk wâposo-mîcimâpoy. wahwâ, kêtahtawê ôtênâhk ê-itohtêyâhk ayi, "mîcisowikamikohk awa nik-êtohtahâw," itwêw nitânis ôhi, ana, ana nôsisimis awa – mâk âya, kotak nitânis okosisa, môy âwa kâ-wî-itohtahât ayi, mîcisowikamikohk. â, ê-ay-apicik ês ôm êtokwê, ê-nitotahkik kîkway ka-mîcicik (â, '*Cory*' isiyîhkâsow awa nôsisim awa), êkw êtokwê aw îtêw nitânis, "*Cory*, kîkwây mâk ôma kiy ê-nôhtê-mîciyan ôm ôtê w-- kâ-pê-mîcisoyahk?" itêw êsa. "âw, wâposo-mîcimâpoy niya ni-- ê-wî-mîciyân," k-êtwêt êsa nôsisimis, môniyâwi-mîcisowikamikohk ôma wâposo-mîcimâpoy ê-nitotahk!

[*external break*].

XII

[26] ---kânak [*sc.* awâsisîhkânak] ôk âyi, ma kîkway ayis wîhkâc awâsisîhkânak ê-ohc-âyâwâyâhkik ta-mêtawâkêyâhk. wâ, êkospî aw âwa kâ-- kâ-kî-âcimak aw âya, nâp-- nâpêw ana kâ-miyikoyâhk anihi nâtitisahikêwasinahikana, wâ, êkot[a] êkwa mîna kâ-wiyêyihtamâhk aw âya, nikâwîs asici, ta-mê-- n-- ê-wiyiswâyâhkik êk ôk âya, awâsisîhkânak. kahkiyaw ôki niwiyiswânânak, nâpêwak, iskwêwak, awâsisak. tahto ê-ihtakocik ôk âya, ayisiyiniwak anit[a] âya, *Elizabeth* nitaskînâhk, kahkiyaw êkonik nitôsîhânânak êkwa. wahwâ, êkwa mân âscikêwikamikohk ê-kî-mêtawêyâhk, asici ana nikâwîs. wâ, kâ-nîmihitohk ês êkwa, kahkiyaw êk ôk âwâsisîhkânak ôk ê-pê-nîmihitocik! êkwa mân âya, okiskinohamâkêw nikî-ayâwâyâhk [*sic*] ayi, kisêyiniw (mêton êtokwê têpakohpomitanaw ê-itahtopiponwêt awa kisêyiniw, mân ê-kî-kiskinohamâkoyâhk, osâm konit îtê ôm ê-kî-ayâyâhk, môy mâna nitôh-- nôhc-âya--, okiskinohamâkêwak nitôhc-- ohci-miywêyihtamwak êkotê t-âyâcik, osâm wâhyaw, nama

XI [*Food Preferences*]

[25] Well, another -- I also remember another thing, I will tell you about one other thing. Now that I, too, was getting older, we raised one of our grandchildren, a boy. Now he could not tolerate milk, he was severely allergic to it, and with my husband killing lots of rabbits, we used to raise this grandchild of ours on rabbit soup, he really liked the taste of rabbit soup. Oh my, one time we were going to town, and my daughter said, "I'll take him to the restaurant," referring to him, that grandchild of mine – but he is the son of another daughter of mine, not of the one who was going to take him to the restaurant. Well, they must have been sitting there, ordering something to eat (well, my grandchild's name is Cory), and my daughter must have said to him, "Cory, what is it you want to have here where we've come to eat?" she said to him. "Well, as for me, I am going to eat rabbit soup," my grandson said, in a White restaurant he ordered rabbit soup!

[*external break*]

XII [*Coping with Boys*]

[26] -- dolls, for we never had dolls to play with. Well, at that time the one I have told about, the man who had given us the catalogues, well, we decided what to do, my aunt and I, and now we were cutting out these dolls. We cut them all out, men, women, and children. As many as there were people at our place, at Elizabeth Colony, we made them, all of them. Oh my, and we used to play in a shed, I and my aunt. Well, when there was a dance, all of the dolls came to dance! And we used to have a teacher, an old man (that old man must have been seventy years old when he used to teach us, we used to be so far away from anywhere that the teachers did not like to live there, it was too far out and there was no town close by). So at this

kî-- kîkway cîk ôtênaw). êkos ôma kâ-- kâ-nîmihi--, k-- âhki [*sic*] ôma kâ-nîmihitohk, kêtahtawê aw âya, aya (*my* -- nôhcâwîs awa, êkwa aya, êkwa nimâmâ wiy âya, o-- aya, ôstês--, osîmisa êtokwê), kêtahtawê kâ-- kâ-pê-itohtêcik ôki nâpêsisak, "â, ka-wîci-mêtawêmitinân," nititikonânak. êkosi; mâk êkwa an[i] êkwa, wîstawâw êkw ê-nîmihâcik ôh âtiht awâsisîhkân[a], ê-nîsonitocik ôk âwâsisîhkânak êkwa ê-nîmihâyâhkik mâna. wahwâ, kêtahtawê awa nôhcâwîs awa itwêw, "tânim êsa kiya?" nititik ôh âwâsisîhkân[a] ôhi, êkwa yâhki niy âwa pêyak, ôma niy âw âwâsisîhkân. wâ, n-- ê-nîpitêhâyâhkik mohcihk ôki, m-- ê-mêtawêyâhk. wâ, êkwa, "tân ês âya" ('*Flip*' kî-isiyîhkâsow awa okiskinohamâkêw, kisêyinîwi-okiskinohamâkêw), "*Flip* êsa, tân-- tâna?" â, êkw âwa wîsta kisêyinîwi-okiskinohamâkêw nitôsîhânân, nêtê wîhkwêhtakâhk apiw; kâ-o-- kâ-nitawi-nâtât awa nôhcâwîs ôh êkwa, "â, yâhk ês ê-wîsâmisk êsa *Flip*," nititik. â, êkw ân[i] ê-nîmihitôhât ôhi, yâhk êkwa awa niya kisêyiniw aw ê-wîcisimômak awa okiskinohamâkêw, k-âti-wayawîsimot ôm ôtê is âscikêwikamikosihk, "yâhk îtâp ês ê-kwâsihisk *Flip*" – aspin ê-kwâsihât nitawâsisîhkâna.

[27] kêtahtawê êkwa ayi, mîn âya ê-nitawi-kiskinohamâkosiyâhk, êkwa môy sêmâk kâwi nikî-wî-nitawi-mêtawânân, pôt êsa kâ-nitawi-pîhtokwêcik ôki nâpêsisak êkonik aniki, pêyakwan êkonik nâpêsisak, ni-- nôhcâwîsinânak ôki, kâ-w-- kâ-otinahkik ês âya, lamilâs, ês êkotê ê-itohtatâcik, kahkiyaw ês êkon ânihi nitawâsisîhkâninâna ômatowihk, aya, *on the wall* ês êkota kahkiyaw ê-pasakwahwâcik. ôh, ê-misiwanâcihâcik, êkos êkwa ma kîkway awâsisîhkânak nitayâwânânak, mîn-- ê-kakwâhyakihikoyâhkik nâpêsisak.

XIII

[28] aya, aya mîna mâna, nikî-osîhtamâsoyâhk [*sic*] ayi, awâsisîhkânak, konita mâna k-- ayânisa kâh-pitikwêkinamâhki, ê-wâwiyê-pitikwêkinamâhk, êkwa êkota wâpiskayiwinis mâna, ê-wâ-wêkin-- ê-wêwêkinamâhk. êkwa wiya mâna nimâmâ ê-kî-mîkis-- ê-kî-masinistahikêt, êkwa nikî-kiskinohamawit [*sic*] ta-masinistahikêyân; êkwa mân ôskîsikowâwa mân

make-believe dance, all of a sudden (my uncle [*sc.* my mother's parallel cousin] and, I guess, my mom's younger brother), all of a sudden these boys came there and said to us, "Well, we will play with you." So it was; and so they, too, now made some of the dolls dance, and we would make them dance together in pairs. Oh my, suddenly my uncle said, "Which one are you?" he said to me, referring to these dolls, and one of the dolls, as it were, was me, it was make-believe me. Well, we put them in a row on the floor in our playing. Well, and then, "Which one – ?" (the teacher's name, the old teacher's name was Flip), "Flip, which one is he?" Well, we had made that one, too, that old teacher, and he sat over there in the corner; my uncle went and fetched him and said to me: "Well, pretend that Flip asked you to dance." Well, and then he made them dance, pretending that I was dancing with this old man, this teacher, and he began to dance towards the door, out of the shed, "Pretend that Flip is running away with you," – and with that he ran away with my dolls.

[27] At one time, also, when we went to school, we were not going back to play right away, what was this? these boys had gone inside, these same boys, our uncles, and had gotten hold of some syrup and taken it in there and glued all these dolls of ours up like there [*gesture*], there on the wall. Oh, they ruined them, so then we didn't have dolls anymore, the boys were very mean to us.

XIII [*Coping with Other Girls*]

[28] We also used to make dolls for ourselves, we would just roll clothes up, into a ball, and then cover it with white cloth. And my mom used to do embroidery, and she used to teach me embroidery; and I used to embroider eyes, noses, and mouths

ê-kî-masinistahamâhk, oskiwaniwâwa otôniwâwa ôk âwâsisîhkânak. êkwa astotina, ascotinisa [*sic*] mân ê-osîhtamawâyâhkik, êkwa miskocâkâsa mâka wiya mâna ma kîkway ospitoniwâwa kîkway, wâspisonisa mân ê-kî-osîhtamawâyâhkik, êkw êkotê ê-sâkiskwêhpitâyâhkik ôk âwâsisîhkânak, êkosi mâna ê-kî-mêtawâkêyâhk. kayâs ayis ma kîkway, sôskwâc kahkiyaw kîkway mân âya, ê-kî-- ê-kî-miskamâsoyâhk ê-mêtawâkêyâhk. êkwa mân âya, wâskahikam--, sakâhk mân êkotê ê-kî-osîhtâyâhk mêtawêwikamikwa, konita mistikohk mân êkotê ê-kî-sakahamâhk ayi, â, akocikanisa; konita kahkiyaw kîkway mân âya, kayâs-âya, asiwacikana mân ê-kî-mêtawâkêyâhk. kêtahtawê awa nôhkom kâ-miyit ayi, ô-- ôh âya, minihkwâcikan mâna kâkikê ê-kî-ayât ê-miywâsiniyik. kêtahtawê (ê-pîwâpiskwâyik mâka), kêtahtawê ohcikawaniyiw ôma, ôm ôminihkwâcikan, wâ, kâ-miyit ôm êwako ta-mêtâwakêyân ôma nimêtawêwikamikohk; wahwâ, iyikohk ê-mamihcihikoyân ôma niy âyi, niya piko ê-ayâyân ôm âyi, aya, minihkwâcikan ê-miywâsik, mêtawêwikamikohk.

[29] êkosi mân ôki, kotakak mân ôki wîstawâw iskwêsisak ohpimê ê-wâh-wîkicik, êkwa mân ê-kiyokâtoyâhk. kêtahtawê ôki iskwêsisak ôki, *Martineau*-iskwêsisak nipê-kiyo-- nipê-kiyokâkwak. êtok ôma nitakâwâtamâkwak ôma niminihkwâcikan; wahwâ, kêtahtawê niwanihtân niminihkwâcikan, tânitê? – misiwê ninatonên [*sic*]. “wahwâ,” nititêyihtên, “nikêhcinâhon ôki iskwêsisak, nikotwâw ê-kimotamawicik,” nititêyiht-- nititêyihtên ôma niminihkwâcikan. wâ, êkwa an[i] êkwa, kahkiyaw êkwa kâ-papâmi-kiyokawakik êkwa, mahti ka-kakwê-wâpahtamân ôm âwîn[a] ê-kî-kimotamawit niminihkwâcikan. wâ, iskwêyâc ôk êkwa *Martineau*-iskwêsisak êkw êkotê êkwa, ninitaw-- ninitawi-kiyokân. mâka cîk ê-at-âyâyân, niwâpamâw awa pêyak iskwêsis kîkway ê-kât-- -- ê-kâciwêpinahk, ê-akwanahasit om âya, *tea*-- [*sc. tea-cloth*] aya, pâhkwahikâkanis ohci kîkway. êkosi, nitakohtân êkotê êkwa aya, yâhk îtâp ôma konit ê-maskihkîwâpôhkêcik, êkwa ê-wî-minahicik yâhki. wâ, ê-kî-kîsi-minihkwêyân ôma, yâhk îtâp maskihkîwâpoy êkwa, kâ-itohtêyân ôma nêtê êkwa, itê kâ-kî-kâcikêcik ôma, awîn ôma tâpwê êkota niminihkwâcikan kî-astêw, wiyawâw ês ê-kî-pê-kimotamawicik. wahwâ, mêton ê-pim-- nikisiwâsin ôm ê-kî-kimotamâkawiyân,

for these dolls. Also hats, we would make little hats for them, and little dresses. But there were no arms, we used to make mossbags for them and wrap the dolls up so that only their necks would stick out, that is the way we used to play with them. For in the old days there was nothing, we just used to find everything for ourselves and play with it. And little houses, we used to build play-houses in the bush, anywhere on a tree we used to nail up shelves; we used to play with any old thing, with containers. Once my grandmother gave me a nice cup that she had had for a long time. At one point it sprang a leak (it was a tin cup), well, and she gave it to me to play with in my play-house; oh my, it made me so proud, I was the only one to have a nice cup in my play-house.

[29] So then these other girls, they had their play-houses off in various places, and we would visit one another. One time these girls, the Martineau girls, came to visit me. They must have envied me my cup; oh my, all at once I lost my cup, where was it? – I looked for it everywhere. "Oh my," I thought, "I am sure one of these girls has stolen it from me," I thought with respect to my cup. Well, and then I went around visiting all of them, to try and see, perhaps, who had stolen my cup from me. Well, the last place I went to visit was that of the Martineau girls. But when I got close I saw one girl hiding something, fast, and covering it with a dish-towel. So then I arrived there, and they made make-believe tea and were going to offer it to me. Well, when I had finished the make-believe tea, then I went over there where they had hidden it, and what was that? There indeed was my cup, it was they who had come and stolen it from me. Oh my, I was angry that it had been stolen

ê-kî-mamihcisiyân nôhkom ê-kî-miyit. "ta-kî-nêpêwisiyêk ôm êkotê kâ-- kâ-pê-kimotiyêk, êkwa ê-kî-kakwêcimitakok, 'ma kîk-- môy niyanân,' ê-kî-isiyâhk." wahwâ, kêkâc nipakamahwâwak iyikohk ê-kisiwâhicik. wâ, konit êkw âta wiya ê-kîwêhtatâyân niminihkwâcikan, kâwi nimêtawêwikamikohk.

XIV

[30] askiya mân âyi, îwahikanak nikî-osîhcikâkêyâhk [*sic*], êkwa aya, âm--, âtiht mîna mân âya wiyâs, êkwa, kêtahtawê mîn âya, nititohtânân aya, ê-miskamâhk, nîpiya (kîkway êtokwê mâna ê-kî-ohpikihki sisonê sâkahikanisisihk; â, mwêhc âsêsinwa, ahpô aya, maskisinêkinwa mâna tâpiskôc ê-kî-isinâkwahki), êkoni mîna mân ê-kî-misi-manipitamâhk êkwa yâhk îtâp ê-maskisinihkêhkâsoyâhk, mêtoni mâna nanâtohk kâh-itêkinamâhk[i], êkwa mâna ê-kî-mâh-mâmâkwahtamâhk êkon ânihi nîpiy[a] ânihi, êk ôma kâ-taswêkinamâhk tâpiskôc ê-mîkisihkahtêki ê-isinâkwahki, êkwa mân ê-kî-kaskikwâtamâhk êkon ânihi ê-maskisinihkêyâhk ôh âya, nîpiya.

[31] kahkiyaw kîkway mâna k-âwâsisîwihk ayis ôm âya

[IC:] – *mud-pies* –

[MW:] – êha–

asiskîwi-pahkwêsikanak mîna mâna nikî-osîhânânak. êkwa awa mîna nim--, aya, nisîm -- nimis awa, kêtahtawê kâ-pê-itohtêt nimêtawêwikamikohk,

[MW:] – ôh, mâka môy ê-kiskêyihtamân tânis ê-isiyîhkâtêk, *mustard* –

[FA:] – *oh, mustard!* –

[MW:] – êha, êkotowahk ôm âya –

"êkotowahk ê-kî-osîhtâyân," itwêw, aya, pasakoskiw-âya -- pasakoskiw, tâpiskôc mîtosihk mâk ê-wa-ohcikawit mâna, êkotowahk ês ôh ê-kî-papâmi-kâh-- ê-kî-papâmi-wâh-otinât êkwa pahkwêsikan[a] âsic êkotê ê-takonât, êkosi mwêhc âya, *mustard* ê-osîhtât, ê-mamihcisit iyikohk. â, êkosi pêyakwâw êkota ê-kî-otahot ayi, wiyê [*sic*] nawac ê-kî-kiskêyihtahk ê-isi-- kîkway ê-isi-osîhtât.

from me, I had been proud that my grandmother had given it to me. "You should be ashamed of yourselves to have stolen it from me over there, and I had asked you about it and you had said, 'It wasn't us.'" Well, I almost hit them because they had angered me so much. Well, and now I just took my cup home again, back to my play-house.

XIV *[A Little Girl's Inventiveness: Mustard]*

[30] We had used moss to make pounded meat with, and some also to make meat with, and at one time we went to a place where we found leaves (what is it, I wonder, that used to grow beside a little lake; they look exactly like the vamp of a moccasin or like shoe-leather), of these we used to pull up a lot and act as if we were making moccasins with them, folding them in various ways, and then we also used to bite down on these leaves, and when we unfolded them, they looked as if they were beaded, and we used to sew these leaves, making moccasins from them.

[31] For when you were a child, you used everything,

[IC:] – mud-pies –

[MW:] – oh yes –

we also used to make mud-pies. And my older cousin also once came to my play-house

[MW:] – ah, but I don't know the word for mustard –

[FA:] – oh, mustard! –

[MW:] – yes, that kind –

"I have made that kind," she said, she had gone around and collected sticky stuff -- like the gum that drips from the trees, that kind, and mixed it with flour, thereby making it exactly like mustard, and she was so proud. Well, and so in that, she knew better than I how to make something, this once she did beat me.

I

[1] ᐋ, ᐊᐱᓯᐢ ᐁ ᐑ ᐋᒋᒧᔮᐣ, 'Mary Wells' ᓂᑎᓯᔩᐦᑳᓱᐣ, ᐋ, Elizabeth Settlement ᐅᐦᒋ ᓂᔭ. ᐁ ᒣᑳᐧ ᐊᐚᓯᓰᐏᔮᐣ, ᓂᑭᐢᑭᓯᐣ, ᐃᐢᐲ Elizabeth Settlement ᐁ ᐃᐢᐱᒋᔮᕽ, ᐁ ᑕᑳᐧᑭᐠ nineteen-thirty-nine, ᐁᑯᑌ ᑳ ᑮ ᐃᐢᐱᒋᔮᕽ. ᐋ, ᓂᐹᐹ ᓃᑎᓵᓇᐠ ᓅᐦᑯᒼ ᐁᑲᐧ ᓂᒫᒫ, ᐁᑲᐧ ᓂᒫᒪ ᐅᐦᒑᐏᓴ, ᐑᐢᑕ ᐁᐘᑯ ᐊᓇ ᐆᐦᐃ ᑲᐦᑭᔭᐤ ᐊᔭ, ᐅᒐᐚᓯᒥᓴ ᐑᐘ, ᐁᑲᐧ 'Swans' ᑯᑕᑲᐠ ᐁ ᐃᓯᔩᐦᑳᓱᒋᐠ ᐊᔨᓯᔨᓂᐘᐠ, ᐁᑯᓂᐠ ᐱᑯ ᓂᐢᑐ ᐊᔭ ᐊᔨᓯᔨᓂᐘᐠ ᐁᑯᑌ ᓂᐢᑕᒼ ᐁ ᑮ ᐃᐢᐱᒋᔮᕽ. ᐁᑲᐧ ᓂᑭᐢᑭᓯᐣ, ᐁ ᐱᒋᔮᕽ ᐃᐢᐲ, ᒥᐢᑕᑎᒪᐧᐠ ᐁ ᐚᐸᒋᐦᐋᔮᐦᑭᐠ ᐅᑖᐹᓈᐢᑯᕽ, ᐁᑯᑌ ᐁᑲᐧ ᐆᒪ ᐚᐦᔭᐤ, ᐚᐦᔭᐍᐢ ᐁ ᐃᐢᐱᒋᔮᕽ, ᓂᑭᐢᑭᓯᐣ ᒦᓇ ᐊᔨ, ᐸᐸᑳᐧᓂᑲᒥᑯᕽ ᐁ ᐑᑭᔮᕽ ᓂᐢᑕᒼ.

II

[2] ᐁᑲᐧ ᐊᐘ ᓅᐦᑯᒼ ᒫᓇ ᐊᔨ, ᐁ ᓂᑕᐏ ᓂᑖᒥᓲᐟ, ᐃᔨᓂᒥᓇ ᐁ ᒥᐢᑲᕽ. ᐘᐦᐚ, ᒨᔭ ᐑᐦᑳᐨ ᐁ ᐅᐦᒋ ᐯ ᑯᑎᐢᑕᒫᐣ ᐃᔨᓂᒥᓇ, ᒥᐢᑕᐦᐃ ᓂᐑᐦᑭᐢᑌᐣ, ᐚᐑᐢ ᓰᐏᓂᑲᐣ ᐊᓯᒋ ᐁᑯᑌ ᐁ ᐊᐱᐟ. ᐁᑲᐧ, ᑮᐦᑖᐧᒼ ᐁ ᓂᑖᒥᓲᐟ ᓅᐦᑯᒼ, ᐁ ᐊᓴᒥᐟ ᒦᓂᓴ, ᐁ ᓂᑐᑕᒫᔮᐣ ᓰᐏᓂᑲᐣ, «ᒪ ᑮᑲᐧᐩ ᐁᑲᐧ ᑳ ᑮ ᐊᐦᐋᐤ ᓰᐏᓂᑲᐣ ᐁᑯᑕ ᑭᒦᓂᓯᒥᕽ,» ᓂᑎᑎᐠ ᓂᒫᒫ. «ᑖᓀᐦᑭ ᒫᑲ,» ᐁ ᐃᑕᐠ ᓂᒫᒫ, «ᐁᑯᓯ ᐃᓯ ᐱᑯ ᐊᓂᐦᐃ ᐁ ᐑᐦᑲᓯᑭ.» – «ᐋ,» ᓂᒫᒫ ᑳ ᐃᓯᐟ, «ᐊᐱᓯᐢ ᐱᑯ ᐁ ᐋᔮᐚᔮᕽ ᐊᐘ ᓰᐏᓂᑲᐣ, ᐁᑲᐧ ᑭᓰᒥᐢ ᓇᐘ-ᑕ ᐚᐸᒋᐦᐋᐟ ᐁᑯᓂ ᐃᐢᐲᐦᒋ ᑭᔭ, ᑭᔭ ᑭᒥᓯᑭᑎᐣ, ᑲ ᓂᓯᑐᐦᑌᐣ, ᐁᑳᔭ ᑲᑖᐨ ᓰᐏᓂᑲᐣ ᑕ ᐚᐸᒋᐦᐊᐟ,» ᓂᑎᑎᑲᐏᐣ. ᒫᑲ, ᓂᑮ ᐚᐸᒫᐤ ᓂᒫᒫ ᑖᓂᑌ ᐁ ᐊᐦᐋᐟ ᐆᐦᐃ ᓰᐏᓂᑲᓇ, ᐊᔨ, in a syrup pail ᑮ ᐊᓯᐘᐦᐁᐤ ᐁᑲᐧ ᒦᑐᓯᕽ ᐁ ᐊᑯᑖᐟ. ᐚ, ᒪᔭᐤ ᐁᑳ ᐊᐏᔭᐠ ᐁ ᐯ ᐃᑖᐱᐟ ᐁ ᐃᑌᔨᐦᑕᒫᐣ, ᓂᑮᐦᑫᑯᓰᐣ ᐊᐘ ᒦᑐᐢ ᐊᐘ ᐁ ᓈᑖᐦᑕᐚᑕᐠ ᓰᐏᓂᑲᐣ. ᐚ, ᐁ ᑕᑳᐧᐦᑕᐑᔮᐣ ᐁᑯᑌ ᓲᐢᑳᐧᐨ ᓂᒧᐢᒋᒋᐦᑫᓇᒫᔮᐣ ᐆᒪ ᐁᑯᑕ ᐊᐢᑭᐦᑯᕽ ᓂᑑᑎᓈᐤ ᐊᐘ ᓰᐏᓂᑲᐣ. ᒫᑲ ᐁᓴ ᐊᐘ ᐁᑐᑫᐧ ᐑᐢᑕ ᐋᒧᐤ ᐊᐘ ᐁᑯᑌ ᐁ ᑮ ᐲᐦᑐᑫᐧᐟ ᐁ ᑲᑫᐧᑕᓯ ᑭᒧᑎᐟ ᐑᐢᑕ ᐆᐦᐃ ᓰᐏᓂᑲᓇ, ᒫᒋᑲ ᓂᒌᓱᐠ. ᐚᒋᐢᑕᑳᐨ, ᓂᐑᓴᑭ ᒌᓱᐠ, ᓲᐢᑳᐧᐟ ᓂᓃᐦᒋᐸᔨᐣ ᐁᑯᑕ ᐅᐦᒋ ᒦᑐᓯᕽ, ᐋᐦ, ᐃᔨᑯᕽ ᑕ ᑮ ᒫᑐᔮᐣ ᓂᒫᑐᐣ. ᓅᐦᑯᒼ ᐊᐘ ᑳ ᐹᐸᐦᑖᐟ, «ᑖᓂᓯ, ᐃᐢᑫᐧᐤ.» (ᐃᐢᑫᐧᐤ ᒫᓇ ᐁ ᑮ ᐃᓯᔩᐦᑳᓱᐟ), ᐃᔨᑯᕽ ᐁ ᒫᑐᔮᐣ ᐆᒪ, «ᐁ ᒌᓱᐟ ᐊᐘ ᐋᒧᐤ, ᓀᑌ ᓰᐏᓂᑲᐣ ᐁ ᑲᑫᐧ ᐅᑎᓇᒫᓱᔮᐣ,» ᓂᑎᑖᐧᐣ, ᐯᐢᑭᐢ ᐁ ᒫᑐᔮᐣ, «ᐚᐦ ᐘᐦᐚ, ᑭᐘᐏᔭᑎᓯᐣ.» ᑳ ᐃᓯᐟ ᐊᐘ ᓅᐦᑯᒼ, «ᐊᐦᐴ ᐁᑐᑫᐧ ᐁᐘᑯ ᑭᑲ ᑭᐢᑭᓅᐦᐊᒫᑯᐣ ᐁᑳᔭ ᑮᐦᑖᐧᒼ ᑎᑕ ᑲᑫᐧ ᑭᒧᑎᔭᐣ ᑮᑲᐧᐩ.» ᓇᒨᔭ ᓂᑭᑎᒫᑭᓈᑲᐏᐣ ᐆᒪᔨᑯᕽ ᐁ ᐑᓴᑭ ᒌᓱᐟ ᐋᒧᐤ.

III

[3] ᐁᐊᐧᑯ ᐊᓂᒪ ᐁᑲᐧ ᐁ ᑕᑳᐧᑭᐠ, ᓂᐹᐹ ᐁᑲᐧ ᑳ ᒫᒋ ᐅᓰᐦᑖᐟ ᐊᔨ, ᐋᐧᐢᑲᐦᐃᑲᓂᐢ, ᐊᔭ, ᒥᐢᑎᑲᐧ ᐅᐦᒋ, ᐁᑲᐧ ᐊᔨ, ᐹᒪᐧᔦᐢ ᑎᑕ ᐱᐳᕽ ᐆᒪ, ᐱᐳᐦᑭ ᐁᑯᑕ ᑕ ᐄᐧᑭᔮᕽ. ᐁ ᑭᐢᑭᓯᔮᐣ ᓂᒫᒫ ᐁ ᐄᐧᒋᐦᐊᐠ ᐁᑲᐧ ᐁᐊᐧᑯ ᐊᓂᒪ ᐊᔨ, ᐋᐧᐢᑲᐦᐃᑲᓂᐢ ᐊᔨ, ᐁ ᓯᓯᐊᐧᐢᑭᓂᑫᔮᕽ. ᐁ ᑮ ᑮᓰᐦᑖᐟ ᐁᑲᐧ ᐁᐊᐧᑯ ᐊᓂᒪ ᐋᐧᐢᑲᐦᐃᑲᐣ ᓂᐹᐹ, ᒪ ᑮᑲᐧᐩ ᐁᑲᐧ ᐋᐸᒋᐦᒋᑲᓇ ᒦᓇ ᐲᐦᒋ ᐊᔨᕽ ᑕ ᑮ ᐋᐸᑕᐦᑭ ᓂᑑᐦ ᐊᔮᓈᐣ, ᓂᐹᐹ ᐁᑲᐧ ᑳ ᐃᐧᔭᑕᐦᐊᕽ ᐁ ᐅᓰᐦᑖᐟ ᐊᔨ, ᒦᒋᓱᐃᐧᓈᐦᑎᐠ, ᐁᑲᐧ ᑫᐦᒐᐱᐃᐧᓂᓴ ᐊᔩᑕᐤ ᐅᐦᒋ ᐁᑯᑕ ᐁ ᓴᑲᐦᐊᕽ – ᑭᓵᐢᑕᐤ ᒉᐧᐦᒋ ᒫᓇ ᐆᐦᐃ ᐊᔨ, ᒉᑳᐧᐨ ᐁᑲᐧ ᐊᓄᐦᐨ ᐊᐧᔭᐄᐧᑎᒥᕽ ᑳ ᒦᒋᓱᕽ ᒫᓇ ᐊᓂᒪ ᒦᒋᓱᐃᐧᓈᐦᑎᑲᐧ, ᐁᑯᓯ ᐃᓯ ᑮ ᐃᓯᓈᑲᐧᓂᔨᐤ ᐊᓂᒪ ᓂᐹᐹ ᑳ ᐅᓰᐦᑖᐟ ᐊᔨ, ᒦᒋᓱᐃᐧᓈᐦᑎᐠ. ᐁᑲᐧ ᐁ ᐅᓰᐦᑖᐟ ᒦᓇ ᐊᔨ, ᐊᑯᒋᑲᓇ, ᐃᑕ ᓂᒫᒫ ᑕ ᐊᐦᐋᐧᐟ ᐊᐢᑭᐦᑲᐧ, ᐃᐧᔮᑲᓇ ᑕ ᐊᐢᑖᐟ. ᒥᓯ ᒥᐢᑎᑯᐊᐧᐟ ᒦᓇ ᐁ ᐅᓰᐦᑖᐟ, ᐁᑯᑕ ᒥᐦᑕ ᑕ ᐊᓯᐊᐧᑌᑭ. ᐁᑲᐧ, ᓂᐯᐃᐧᓇ ᐁᑲᐧ ᒦᓇ ᐁ ᐅᓰᐦᑖᐟ, ᒥᐢᑎᑯᓂᐯᐃᐧᓇ. ᐁᑲᐧ ᐃᐧᔭ ᓂᒫᒫ ᐁᑲᐧ ᐊᔭ, canvas, ᐁᐊᐧᑯ ᐊᓂᒪ ᐁᑲᐧ ᐃᐧᔭ ᐁ ᐃᐧᔨᑳᐧᑕᕽ ᐁᑲᐧ ᐁᑯᑕ ᒪᐢᑯᓯᔭ ᐁ ᐊᓯᐊᐧᑖᐟ, ᐁᑯᓂ ᐊᓂᐦᐃ ᐁᑲᐧ ᐁ ᐊᐢᐱᓯᓂᔮᕽ, ᒫᓇ ᓂᑭᐢᑭᓯᐣ ᐁ ᐊᐋᐧᓯᓰᐃᐧᔮᕽ. ᐁᑲᐧ ᒧᐦᒋᕽ, ᒧᐦᒋᐦᑕᐠ ᐆᒪ, ᒪ ᑮᑲᐧᐩ ᑲᔮᐢ ᑮᑲᐧᐩ ᐁ ᐅᐦᒋ ᐊᐢᑌᐠ, ᐊᓈᐢᑳᓂᐦᑕᑯᕽ. ᓂᑭᐢᑭᓯᐣ ᒫᓇ ᓂᒫᒫ ᐁ ᐄᐧᒋᐦᐊᐠ ᐊᔨ, ᐁ ᑭᔩᐯᑭᓂᐦᑕᑫᐧᔮᕽ ᐁᑲᐧ, ᐱᐦᑯ ᒫᓇ ᐁ ᐋᐸᒋᐦᑖᐟ ᐁᑲᐧ ᐊᔨ, ᑮᑲᐧᐩ ᐁᑐᑫᐧ ᒫᓇ ᐊᓯᒋ ᐊᔭ, ᐁᑯᑕ ᐁ ᑮ ᐋᐸᒋᐦᑖᐟ ᐁ ᑭᔩᐯᑭᓇᒫᕽ ᐆᒪ ᐊᔭ, ᐊᓈᐢᑳᓂᐦᑕᐠ, ᓂᐱᐩ ᐊᓯᒋ ᐋᑕ ᐃᐧᔭ ᒫᓇ ᐁ ᑮ ᐋᐸᒋᐦᑖᔮᕽ. ᐁᑲᐧ ᒫᓇ, ᒉᑐᓂ ᐁ ᑮ ᑲᓈᑖᐹᐁᐧᐠ ᐆᒪ ᐊᓈᐢᑳᓂᐦᑕᐠ, ᐁ ᑮ ᒪᒥᐦᒋᓯᔮᕽ ᒫᓇ ᓂᒫᒫ ᐊᓯᒋ.

IV

[4] ᐁᑲᐧ ᓂᐹᐹ ᒫᓇ ᐋᑕ ᐃᐧᔭ ᐁ ᑮ ᒫᒋᐟ ᐄᐧᐢᑕ, ᐁᑲᐧ ᐊᔭ, ᑲᐦᑭᔭᐤ ᑮᑲᐧᐩ ᓂᑮ ᐯ ᒧᐋᐧᔮᐦᑭᐠ – ᓇᓈᑐᕽ ᐱᓯᐢᑮᓴᐠ, ᑖᐱᐢᑰᐨ ᐊᔭ, ᐊᐱᓯᒨᓯᐢ, ᐋᐧᐳᐢ, ᑳᑲᐧ, ᐄᐧᓂᓴᑳᒋ‴, ᐁᑲᐧ ᐊᔭ ᐱᐦᐁᐊᐧᐠ ᐁᑲᐧ ᓰᓰᐸᐠ, ᐊᓂᑲᐧᒑᓴᐠ, ᐁᑲᐧ ᐊᔭ, ᐆᐦᐅᐤ ᒦᓇ ᓂᑮ ᒧᐋᐧᓈᐣ, ᐁᑲᐧ ᒑᐦᒑᐦᑲᔪᐊᐧᐠ. ᒑᐦᒑᐦᑲᔪᐊᐧᐠ ᐃᐧᔭ ᐊᓂᑭ ᓂᑭᐢᑭᓯᐣ, ᓂᒫᒫ ᐁ ᑮ ᑕᓲᐦᐋᐟ, ᐁ ᑮ ᐅᓰᐦᑕᒫᓱᐟ ᐊᔭ, ᓇᐸᑭᐦᑕᑲᐧ ᐁ ᑮ ᒫᒪᐃᐧᓴᑲᐦᐊᕽ ᐁᑯᑕ, ᒥᐢᒋᑯᓴ ᐁ ᒋᒪᑖᐟ ᐁᑯᑕ ᓰᐹ ᐁᑲᐧ ᐁ ᐸᑕᑯᐱᑖᐟ ᐆᐦᐃ ᐊᔨ, ᐃᑕ ᐁ ᐯ ᒦᒋᓯᔨᐟ ᐊᔨ, ᒑᐦᒑᐦᑲᔪᐊᐧ, ᐁᑲᐧ ᒦᒋᒫᐳᐩ ᐁ ᐅᓰᐦᑕᒫᑯᔮᕽ.

[5] ᐯᔭᑳᐧᐤ ᒦᓇ ᓂᑭᐢᑭᓯᐣ ᐊᔨ, ᓂᐹᐹ ᐁ ᒫᒋᐟ. ᓲᐢᑳᐧᐨ ᓇᒪ ᑮᑲᐧᐩ ᐁᓴ ᑮ ᒥᐢᑲᒼ ᑕ ᓂᐸᐦᑖᐟ, ᐁ ᐯ ᑮᐁᐧᐟ ᐁᑐᑫᐧ ᐁᓴ ᑳ ᐯ ᒥᐢᑲᐋᐧᐟ ᐁᑯᑕ ᐊᔭ, ᓯᑳᑲᐧ, so ᐁᑯᓂ ᐁᑲᐧ ᓂᐸᐦᐁᐤ, ᐯ ᑮᐁᐧᐦᑕᐦᐁᐤ. ᐁᑲᐧ ᓅᐦᑯᒼ ᐁᑲᐧ ᐁ ᐅᓲᐦᐋᐟ ᐆᐦᐃ ᐊᔭ, ᓯᑳᑲᐧ, ᐁᑲᐧ ᐁ ᑲᐢᑭᐦᑲᓵᐧᐟ ᑯᑕᐋᐧᓈᐱᐢᑯᕽ. ᐊᐧᐦᐋᐧ, ᐃᔨᑯᕽ ᐁ ᐄᐧᐦᑭᐢᑖᔮᕽ ᐊᐊᐧ ᓯᑳᐠ.

[6] ᒨᔮ ᐄᐧᐦᑳᐨ ᓂᑑᐦᐊᔮᓈᐣ ᒦᓇ ᑭᐢᒋᑳᓂᐢ, ᐊᔨᐢ ᒪ ᑮᑲᐧᐩ ᐅᐦᒋ ᐃᐦᑕᑯᐤ ᓰᓂᔮᐤ ᑕ ᐊᑖᐁᐧᕽ ᑭᐢᒋᑳᓂᓴ, so, ᑮᑲᐧᐩ ᐱᑯ ᐁ ᑮ ᐅᐦᒋ ᐱᒫᒋᐦᐅᔮᕽ ᐁ ᐅᐦᒋ ᐱᒫᑎᓯᔮᕽ ᐃᐧᔮᐢ, ᐸᐦᑫᐧᓯᑲᐣ ᐁᑲᐧ ᒦᓂᓴ.

[7] ᐁᑲᐧ ᒫᓇ ᐊᐊᐧ ᓅᐦᑯᒼ ᐃᐧᔭ ᑮ ᐲᐦᑖᐧᐤ. ᐋ, ᒥᐦᑳᐧᐯᒪᑲᐧ ᒫᓇ ᐁ ᑮ ᐲᐦᑖᐧᑕᕽ, ᐁᑲᐧ ᒫᓇ ᐁ ᑮ ᐄᐧᒋᐦᐊᐠ ᐊᔨ, ᐁ ᐅᓰᐦᑖᐟ ᐆᐦᐃ, ᐁ ᓂᑕᐃᐧ ᑮᐢᑲᑕᐦᐊᒫᕽ ᒫᓇ ᐆᐦᐃ ᒥᐦᑳᐧᐯᒪᑯᓴ ᐁᑲᐧ ᐁ ᐲᐦᑐᓇᒫᕽ ᐁ ᑳᐢᑲᐦᐊᒫᕽ, ᐁᑲᐧ ᒫᓇ ᐁ ᑳᐢᐱᐦᑲᓴᕽ ᒫᓇ, ᑯᑕᐋᐧᓈᐱᐢᑯᕽ ᐁ ᓴᑳᐧᐱᐢᑭᓇᕽ.

V

[8] ᑫᑕᐦᑕᐁᐧ ᐁᑲᐧ ᐊᔭ, ᐃᐢᐲ ᐁᑲᐧ ᐊᔭ ᐁ ᒥᓯᑭᑎᔮᐣ ᓇᐊᐧᐨ ᐊᔨ, ᓂᑮ ᑭᐢᑭᓄᐦᐊᒫᑯᓯᓈᐣ (ᐱᔨᐢᐠ ᑮ ᐃᐦᑕᑯᐣ ᑭᐢᑭᓄᐦᐊᒫᑐᐃᐧᑲᒥᐠ, Elizabeth, ᐃᑕ ᐁ ᑭᐢᑭᓄᐦᐊᒫᑯᓯᔮᕽ), ᐋᐧ, ᐯᔭᑳᐧᐤ (ᒫᓇ ᐅᑭᐢᑭᓄᐦᐊᒫᑫᐤ ᐁ ᑮ ᓇᑲᑎᑯᔮᕽ ᐯᔭᐠ ᑎᐸᐦᐃᑲᐣ ᒫᓇ ᐁ ᓂᑕᐃᐧ ᒦᒋᓯᐟ), ᑫᑕᐦᑕᐁᐧ ᓂᑎᑖᐊᐧᐠ ᐆᑭ ᐃᐢᑫᐧᓯᓴᐠ, «ᐊᔭ, ᐋᐧᐸᐦᑭ ᑲ ᐲᐦᑖᐧᓇᐤ,» ᓂᑎᑖᐊᐧᐠ, «ᓇᐦ. ᑮᑲᐧᐩ ᒫᑲ ᑫ ᐲᐦᑖᐧᑕᒪᕽ, ᑖᓂᑌ ᑲ ᐅᐦᑎᓈᔭᕽ ᒋᐢᑌᒫᐤ.» ᓂᑎᑎᑲᐧᐠ. «ᓇᐦ. ᓂᑭᐢᑫᔨᐦᑌᐣ ᓂᔭ, ᐁ ᐃᓯ ᐅᓰᐦᐊᐠ ᒋᐢᑌᒫᐤ,» ᓂᑎᑖᐊᐧᐠ ᐃᐢᑫᐧᓯᓴᐠ, «ᐋᐦᐋ.» ᓂᑎᑎᑲᐧᐠ. ᐁᑲᐧ ᓂᑎᑖᐤ ᐊᐊᐧ ᐊᔭ, ᓂᒥᐢ ᐊᐊᐧ, «ᐯᑖᐦᑲᐣ ᐃᑖᑊ ᐊᔭ, ᓅᐦᒑᐄᐧᐢ ᐊᔨ, ᐅᒫᒌᐃᐧᐦᑯᒫᐣ ᐋᐧᐸᐦᑭ.» – «ᐁᐦᐊ.» ᐃᑌᐧᐤ. ᐋ, ᐁᑯᓯ, ᑫᑭᓴᐹ ᐁᑲᐧ, ᑮᐦᑖᐧᒼ ᐁᑲᐧ ᐁ ᑮᓯᑳᐠ, ᐋᐧ, ᐯᑖᐤ ᓂᐸᐹᓯᐢ ᐆᒪ ᐅᒫᒌᐃᐧᐦᑯᒫᐣ. ᐋᐧ, ᒪᔭᐤ ᐁ ᑮ ᓯᐯᐧᐦᑌᐟ ᐅᑭᐢᑭᓄᐦᐊᒫᑫᐤ ᐁ ᑮ ᑮᓯ ᒦᒋᓯᔮᕽ, ᓂᓯᐯᐧᐦᑖᓈᐣ ᐁᑲᐧ ᓴᑳᕽ ᐁᑲᐧ ᐁ ᓈᑕᒫᕽ ᒥᐦᑳᐧᐯᒪᑲᐧ, ᐁᑲᐧ ᐁ ᐅᓰᐦᑖᔮᕽ ᐁᑯᓂ ᐊᓂᐦᐃ. ᐊᐧᐦ, ᑯᑕᐋᐧᓈᐱᐢᑯᕽ ᑕᐦᑯᐦᐨ ᐁᑲᐧ ᐁᑯᑕ ᐁ ᑳᐢᐱᐦᑲᓴᒫᕽ. ᐁᑲᐧ ᐆᐦᐃ ᒫᓇ ᐊᔭ, ᐊᔭ, ᒪᓯᓇᐦᐃᑲᓀᑭᓄᐊᐧᑎᓯᕽ ᒫᓇ ᐁ ᑮ ᓃᒫᔮᕽ ᐊᔨ, ᒦᒋᐃᐧᓂᐢ, ᐁᑯᓂ ᐁᑲᐧ, ᐁᑯᓂ ᒫᓇ ᐆᐦᐃ, ᒪᐢᑭᒧᒋᓴ ᑳ ᑮ ᐋᐸᒋᐦᑖᔮᕽ, ᐃᑕ ᓃᒫᐃᐧᓇ ᐁ ᓯᐯᐧᐦᑕᑖᔮᕽ, ᐁᑯᓂ ᐁᑲᐧ ᐆᐦᐃ ᑳ ᑖᐦ ᑖᑐᐱᑕᒫᕽ ᐆᐦᐃ ᒪᐢᑭᒧᒋᓴ, ᐁᑯᑕ ᐁᑲᐧ ᐆᐦᐃ ᒥᐦᑳᐧᐯᒪᑲᐧ ᐁᑲᐧ ᐊᔨ ᐁ ᐁᐧᐁᐧᑭᓇᒫᕽ, ᐁ ᐅᓰᐦᐋᔮᐦᑭᐠ ᐆᑭ ᐊᔨ ᐲᐦᒐᐧᐃᐧᓂᓴᐠ ᐁᑲᐧ ᐁ ᐲᐦᑖᐧᔮᕽ. ᒣᑐᓂ ᐁᓴ ᐁᑐᑫᐧ ᐆᒪ ᓂᑲᑳᐧᐦᔭᑳᐸᓯᑳᓈᐣ ᐱᐦᒋ ᐊᔨᕽ, ᐁ ᐄᐧᐦᒣᑭᒪᐦᑲᓯᑫᔮᕽ ᐅᑎ ᐁᑐᑫᐧ. ᐋᐧ, ᐁ ᐯ ᐲᐦᑐᑫᐧᐟ ᐊᐊᐧ ᐅᑭᐢᑭᓄᐦᐊᒫᑫᐃᐧᐢᑫᐧᐤ, ᐊᐧᐦᐋᐧ, hm-hm-hm ᑯᓂᑕ, hm-hm, ᐁ ᓈᐦ ᓂᑕᐋᐧᐸᓯᐟ. ᑭᐢᑫᔨᐦᑕᒼ ᓈᓂᑕᐤ ᐁ ᑮ ᐃᑕᐦᑲᒥᑭᓯᔮᕽ, ᒫᑲ ᑖᐱᐢᑯᐨ ᐁᑳ ᓂᔭᓈᐣ, ᒪ ᑮᑲᐧᐩ. ᐋᐧ, ᐱᔨᐢ ᐁᓴ ᐁᑐᑫᐧ, ᐊᐃᐧᔭ ᑳ ᐄᐧᐦᑕᒫᑯᐟ ᑖᓂᓯ ᐊᓂᒪ ᐁ ᑮ ᐃᓰᐦᒋᑫᔮᕽ. ᐁᑯᓯ, ᒨᔭ ᐋᑕ ᐃᐧᔭ ᓈᓂᑕᐤ ᓂᑎᑎᑯᓈᐣ. ᐊᐧᐦᐋᐧ, ᓈᓂᑕᐤ ᓃᓯ ᑮᓯᑳᐤ ᐁ ᑮ ᐃᐢᐸᔨᐠ ᐊᔨ, ᑫᑕᐦᑕᐁᐧ ᐊᐊᐧ ᐅᑭᐢᑭᓄᐦᐊᒫᑫᐤ ᐅᓈᐯᒪ ᑳ ᑖᐦ ᑌᐹᐧᑎᑯᔮᕽ, ᒥᓴᑎᒧᑲᒥᑯᕽ ᓀᑌ ᐁ ᓂᑕᐃᐧ ᐊᓴᒪᐢᑎᒣᐧᐟ, «ᐋᐢᑕᒼ. ᐆᑌ, ᐃᐢᑫᐧᓯᓴᐠ,» ᓂᑎᑎᑯᓈᐣ. ᐋᐧ, ᓂᑎᐢᐸᐦᑖᓈᐣ ᐁᑯᑌ, ᑳ ᒫᐦ ᒥᔨᑯᔮᕽ ᐆᐦᐃ ᐊᔭ, ᐲᐦᒐᐧᐃᐧᓂᓴ. ᐁᐩ, ᑕᑲᐦᑫᔨᐦᑕᒪᐧᐠ ᐆᑭ ᐃᐢᑫᐧᓯᓴᐠ ᐃᐧᔭᐋᐧᐤ, ᐋᐧ, «ᐁᑳᔭ,» ᓂᑎᑖᐊᐧᐠ, «ᐁᑳᔭ ᓴᒫᐠ – ᑲ ᓴᐢᑲᐦᐋᐧᓇᐊᐧᐠ,» ᓂᑎᑖᐊᐧᐠ ᐆᑭ ᐃᐢᑫᐧᓯᓴᐠ. «ᒨᔭ ᑲᐧᔭᐢ ᓂᑎᑌᔨᐦᑌᐣ ᐆᒪ ᓂᔭ ᐊᐊᐧ ᑳ ᐲᐦᑖᐧᐦᐃᑯᔭᕽ ᐊᐊᐧ ᓈᐯᐤ,» ᓂᑎᑖᐊᐧᐠ, «ᒨᔭ ᐄᐧᐦᑳᐨ ᓂᑖᐯᐧᐦᑌᐣ ᐊᔨᓯᔨᓂᐤ, ᓈᐯᐤ,

ᑕ ᐲᐦᑖᐧᐦᐚᐟ ᐊᐚᓯᓴ,» ᓂᑎᑖᐘᐠ, «ᓈᓂᑕᐤ ᑮᑲᐧᐩ ᐊᓂᒪ ᐁᑯᑌ ᐁᑐᑫᐧ ᐁ ᑮ ᐊᐢᑖᐟ,» ᓂᑎᑖᐘᐠ ᐆᑭ ᐃᐢᑫᐧᓯᓴᐠ. ᐁᑯᓯ, ᑳᐏ ᐁᑲᐧ ᑭᐢᑭᓅᐦᐊᒫᑐᐏᑲᒥᑯᕽ ᓄᑌ ᓂᑎᑐᐦᑖᓈᐣ. ᐚ, ᑖᐯᐧ ᐁᑲᐧ ᐁᑯᑌ ᐁ ᑮ ᑕᑯᐦᑌᔮᕽ ᓂᐹᐦ ᐹᐢᑫᑭᓈᓈᓇᐠ ᐆᑭ ᑳ ᐲᐦᑖᐧᐦᐃᑲᐏᔮᕽ. ᓈᐦ, ᐁᓴ ᐆᒪ ᐆᑕ ᐊᔨ, ᒥᐢᑕᑎᒧ ᒣᔭ ᐁ ᐹᐢᑌᔨᑭ ᐁᓴ ᐁᑯᑕ ᐁ ᑮ ᐚᐦ ᐍᐍᑭᓇᕽ, ᐁᑯᓂ ᐆᐦᐃ ᑳ ᐲᐦᑖᐧᐦᐃᑯᔮᕽ ᐆᐦᐃ, ᓂᑕᑲ ᐅᑎ ᐁᑳ ᐁ ᓴᐢᑲᐦᐚᔮᐦᑭᐠ, ᒫᐢᑰᐟ ᑖᐦ ᑮ ᒫᔮᐸᓰᐘᐠ, ᓂᑎᑌᔨᐦᑌᐣ.

VI

[9] ᐁᑲᐧ ᐆᒪ ᐊᔭ, ᐁᑲᐧ ᑮᐦᑖᐧᒼ ᒦᓇ ᓂᑲ ᐋᑐᑌᐣ ᐆᒪ ᐊᔭ, ᐃᐢᐲ ᐁᑲᐧ ᐊᔭ ᓇᐘᐨ ᐊᔭ, ᑭᓀᐧᐢ ᐁ ᐋᔮᔮᕽ ᐁᑰᑕ Elizabeth. ᑫᑕᐦᑕᐍ ᐊᔨ, ᑳ ᒫᒋ ᓈᐦ ᓃᒥᐦᐃᑐᐏᓂᐦᑫᒋᐠ ᐆᑭ ᐊᔨᓯᔨᓂᐘᐠ (ᐁᑲᐧ ᒨᔭ ᐑᐦᑳᐨ ᐁ ᐚᐸᐦᑕᒫᕽ ᐆᒪ ᐁ ᓃᒥᐦᐃᑐᕽ ᐆᒪ ᓂᔭᓈᐣ ᑳ ᐊᐚᓯᓰᐏᔮᕽ), ᐁᑲᐧ ᒫᓇ ᐊᔭ, ᑳ ᓃᒥᐦᐃᑐᐏᓂᐦᑫᐟ ᐊᐘ ᐊᔨᓯᔨᓂᐤ, ᐊᔭ, ᐑᐦᑭᐦᑲᓯᑲᓂᕽ ᒫᓇ ᐁᑯᑕ ᓲᓂᔮᓴ ᐁ ᑮ ᐊᐦᐋᒋᐠ, ᐁᑲᐧ ᐊᐏᔭᐠ ᒥᐢᑲᐧᒫᒋ ᐁᑯᓂ ᐊᓂᐦᐃ ᓲᓂᔮᓴ, ᐱᑯ ᑕ ᓃᒥᐦᐃᑐᐏᓂᐦᑫᐟ, ᐑᑭᐚᕽ ᒫᑲ ᒫᓇ ᐁ ᑮ ᓈᐦ ᓃᒥᐦᐃᑐᐏᓂᐦᑫᒋᐠ. ᐘᐦᐚ, ᑫᑕᐦᑕᐍ ᓅᐦᑖᐏᐩ, ᑳ ᒥᐢᑲᐧᒫᐟ ᓲᓂᔮᓴ, ᐁᑯᓯ, ᓃᒥᐦᐃᑐᐏᓂᐦᑫᐤ ᐁᑲᐧ. ᐘᐦᐚ, «ᐊᒋᔭᐤ ᑭᑲ ᑭᑖᐸᐦᑳᐣ,» ᓂᑎᑎᑲᐏᐣ. ᐚ, ᐁ ᐱᔭᓴᔨᒨᔮᐣ, ᒨᔭ ᓂᑮ ᐯᐦᐅᐣ, «ᑕ ᑎᐱᐢᑳᐠ ᐆᒪ ᑕ ᐑ ᓃᒥᐦᐃᑐᕽ,» ᐁ ᐃᓯᐟ ᐊᐘ ᓂᒫᒫ. ᐘᐦᐚ, ᐱᔨᐢ ᐚᑕ ᐃᐧᔭ ᑳ ᑎᐱᐢᑳᐠ, ᐚᐦ, ᑳ ᒫᒋ ᑕᑳᐧᐘᐦᐃᑐᒋᐠ ᐆᑭ ᐊᔨᓯᔨᓂᐘᐠ, ᑫᑕᐦᑕᐍ ᐯᔭᐠ ᑳ ᓈᑲᑖᐸᒪᐠ ᐊᐘ ᐅᐢᑭᓃᑭᐢᑫᐧᐤ, ᐚᒋᐢᑕᑳᐨ, ᐃᔨᑯᕽ ᐁ ᑲᑕᐘᑌᔨᒪᐠ, ᐃᔨᑯᕽ ᐁ ᑕᑲᐦᑭᓰᐦᐅᐟ. ᐹᐢᑲᐨ ᐁ ᒥᐦᑳᐧᔨᐠ ᐆᒪ ᓴᓂᐹᓇᓵᑲᐩ ᐁ ᐳᐢᑎᐢᑲᕽ, ᐊᐢᑐᑎᐣ ᐊᓯᒋ ᐁ ᑭᑭᐢᑲᕽ ᐁᑲᐧ ᒥᐢᑎᑲᐧᐢᑭᓯᓇ ᐁ ᐳᐢᑎᐢᑲᕽ, ᒣᑐᓂ ᐁ ᐋᐦ ᐃᐢᐹᐦᑲᐧᓀᔮᔨᑭ, ᐚᐦ ᐘᐦᐚ, ᓂᑕᑲᐦᑭᓇᐚᐤ, ᐚᒋᐢᑕᑳᐨ. ᒨᔭ ᐑᐦᑳᐨ ᐊᐦᐳ ᐊᔨᐢ ᓂᔭ ᒪᐢᑭᓯᓇ ᓂᑑᐦ ᐚᐸᐦᑌᐣ, ᓇᓭᐢᑕᐤ ᐸᐦᑫᑭᓀᐧᐢᑭᓯᓇ ᒫᓇ ᐁ ᑮ ᑭᑭᐢᑲᒫᕽ ᐁᑲᐧ ᐊᔭ, ᐘᐢᑭᑕᐢᑭᓯᓇ ᐊᓯᒋ, ᐁᑳᔭ ᑳ ᓵᐳᐯᔮᕽ, ᑳ ᓵᐳᐯᑭ ᓂᒪᐢᑭᓯᓂᓈᓇ. ᐁᑯᓯ, ᓂᑕᐱᐣ ᐁᑲᐧ ᐁᑯᑕ, ᐘᐦᐚ, ᑯᓂᑕ ᐁᑲᐧ ᐁ ᐃᑐᐦᑌᔮᐣ ᐊᐘ ᐅᐢᑭᓃᑭᐢᑫᐧᐤ, ᐅᐢᑯᑖᑲᐩ ᐆᒪ ᐁ ᓂᑕᐏ ᐚᐦ ᐚᔨᓇᒪᐧᐠ, ᐚᐦ, ᐚᒋᐢᑕᑳᐨ ᐃᔨᑯᕽ ᐁ ᑲᑕᐘᑌᔨᒪᐠ. ᐁᑯᓯ ᐊᐘ ᓂᒫᒫ ᐁᑲᐧ, «ᓂᑕᐏ ᑲᐏᓯᒧ ᐁᑲᐧ.» ᓂᑎᑎᑲᐏᐣ, «ᐁᑯᔨᑯᕽ ᑭᓀᐧᐢ ᑭᑭᑖᐸᐦᑳᐣ.» ᐁᑯᓯ ᓂᓂᑕᐏ ᑲᐏᓯᒧᐣ. ᐁ, ᑮᑭᓭᐹ ᐁᑲᐧ, ᒨᔭ ᓂᑮ ᐘᓂᑭᐢᑭᓯᐣ ᐁᐘᑯ ᐊᐘ ᐊᔭ, ᐃᔨᑯᕽ ᐁ ᑮ ᑲᑕᐘᑌᔨᒪᐠ ᐊᐘ ᐅᐢᑭᓃᑭᐢᑫᐧᐤ. ᐚ, ᑖᓂᓯ ᐁᑲᐧ, ᐁᑲᐧ ᐁ ᒫᒋ ᒣᑕᐍᔮᐣ ᐁᑲᐧ, ᐚ, ᓂᐏᓭᔨᐦᑌᐣ, ᔮᐦᑭ ᐁᓴ ᐁ ᐑ ᓂᑕᐏ ᓃᒥᐦᐃᑐᔮᐣ, ᐱᑯ ᒫᑲ ᐁᑲᐧ ᑕ ᐘᐍᓰᔮᐣ ᐆᒪ ᓃᐢᑕ, ᑖᐱᐢᑰᐨ ᐊᐘ ᑳ ᑮ ᑕᑲᐦᑭᓇᐘᐠ ᐊᐘ ᐅᐢᑭᓃᑭᐢᑫᐧᐤ. ᓂᒫᒫ ᐊᐘ ᐅᐢᑯᑖᑲᐩ ᑳ ᓂᑕᐏ ᓂᑖᐦᑖᒪᐠ, ᐁ ᑮ ᐊᔮᐟ ᐑᐢᑕ ᐁ ᒥᐦᑳᐧᔨᐠ ᒥᐢᑯᑖᑲᐩ. «ᒫᒫ. ᒪᐦᑎ ᐁᓴ ᐊᔭ, ᐊᐏᐦᐃᐣ ᑭᐢᑯᑖᑲᐩ, ᐁ ᐑ ᒣᑕᐚᑫᔮᐣ.» ᐁᑲᐧ ᐊᐘ ᓂᒫᒫ ᓂᑭᑖᐸᒥᐠ, «ᓈᐦ. ᒪ ᒌ ᒫᑲ, ᒨᔭ ᑭᑲ ᑌᐱᐢᑫᐣ, ᐅᓵᒼ ᑕ ᑭᓈᐧᐯᑲᐣ.» – «ᓇᒨᔭ,» ᓂᑎᑖᐤ ᓂᒫᒫ, «ᓂᑭᐢᑫᔨᐦᑌᐣ ᑖᓂᓯ ᑕ ᑑᑕᒫᐣ, ᑕ ᑌᐱᐢᑲᒫᐣ ᑭᐢᑯᑖᑲᐩ.» ᐚ, ᓂᑕᐏᐦᐃᐠ ᐅᐢᑯᑖᑲᐩ, ᐋ, ᓂᐳᐢᑎᐢᑫᐣ ᐁᑲᐧ ᐆᒪ

ᒥᐢᑯᑖᑲᐩ, ᐲᒥᓇᐦᑳᐧᓂᐢ ᐁᑲᐧ ᐆᑌ ᐁ ᑮ ᐃᐢᑯᓇᒫᐣ ᐆᒪ ᑮᐢᑲᓵᑲᐩ, ᐁᑯᑕ ᐁᑲᐧ ᐲᒥᓇᐦᑳᐧᓂᐢ ᓂᑕᐦᑯᐱᑌᐣ, ᐁᑲᐧ ᐆᒪ ᑯᑕᐠ ᐁᑲᐧ ᐁᑯᑕ ᓂᐊᐧᐢᑭᑕᑯᑖᐣ, ᐁᑯᓯ, ᓇᐦᐃᔨᑯᕽ ᐃᐢᑳᐧᐤ.

[10] ᐋᐦ, ᐊᐢᑐᑎᐣ ᒫᑲ ᐁᑲᐧ ᒦᓇ ᐱᑯ, ᑖᓂᑌ ᐁᑲᐧ ᑕᐅᐦᑎᓇᒫᐣ ᐊᐢᑐᑎᐣ. ᐋᐧ, ᓂᒪ ᒫᒥᑐᓀᔨᐦᑌᐣ. ᓂᑭᐢᑭᓯᐸᔨᐣ ᓂᒫᒫ ᐁ ᑮ ᐊᔮᐟ ᐊᐢᑐᑎᐣ, ᒫᑲ ᑲᔮᐢ ᓇᒪ ᑮᑲᐧᐩ ᐊᔨᐢ, ᓇᔦᐢᑕᐤ tams ᒫᓇ ᐁ ᑮ ᐊᔮᕽ. ᐁᑯᓯ, «ᒫᒫ. ᒪᐦᑎ ᐁᓴ ᐊᐃᐧᐦᐃᐣ your tam, ᐁᐊᐧᑯ ᐁ ᐄᐧ ᐳᐢᑎᐢᑲᒫᐣ.» ᐋ, ᓂᑕᐃᐧᐦᐃᐠ ᐁᑲᐧ ᐅᑕᐢᑐᑎᐣ ᓂᒫᒫ. ᐁᑲᐧ, ᐃᐧᔮᑲᓂᑲᒥᑯᕽ ᐁᑲᐧ ᑳ ᐃᑐᐦᑌᔮᐣ, ᐁᑲᐧ ᐁᑯᑌ ᐃᐧᔮᑲᐣ ᐁᑲᐧ ᐁ ᓂᑕᐃᐧ ᓈᑕᒫᐣ, ᐁᐊᐧᑯ ᐆᒪ ᐁᑲᐧ ᓀᑌ ᐲᐦᒋ ᐊᔨᕽ in the tam ᐁᑲᐧ ᓂᑕᓯᐊᐧᑖᐣ, ᐁᐊᐧᑯ ᐁᑲᐧ ᐁ ᐳᐢᑎᐢᑲᒫᐣ, ᐊᐧᐦᐋᐧ, ᑖᐱᐢᑰᐟ ᑖᐯᐧ ᐆᒪ ᐊᐢᑐᑎᐣ ᐃᓯᓈᑲᐧᐣ, ᐃᑐᐊᐧ ᐊᓇ ᐅᐢᑭᓃᑭᐢᑫᐧᐤ ᑳ ᑮ ᐳᐢᑎᐢᑲᕽ.

[11] ᐋᐧ, ᒪᐢᑭᓯᓇ ᐁᑲᐧ, ᑖᓂᑌ ᐁᑲᐧ ᒪᐢᑭᓯᓇ. ᐋᐧ, ᐁᑲᐧ ᐆᐦᐃ ᐱᑯ ᐊᐧᐢᑭᒪᐢᑭᓯᓂᓴ ᐁ ᐳᐢᑎᐢᑲᒫᐣ. ᓂᒫᒥᑐᓀᔨᐦᑌᐣ, ᐋᐧ, ᓂᐃᐧᔦᔨᐦᑌᐣ. ᓂᐲᐦᑐᑳᐧᐣ ᑳ ᐃᐧ ᓀᑌ ᓃᑭᓈᕽ, «ᒫᒫ. ᒪᑎ ᐁᓴ ᐊᔭ, ᓃᓯ ᐊᓴᐹᐹᐦᑎᑲᐧᐠ ᐁ ᓂᑕᐯᐧᔨᒪᑭᐠ,» ᓂᑎᑖᐤ ᓂᒫᒫ. «ᓇᐨ. ᑖᓂᓯ ᒫᑲ ᐁ ᐄᐧ ᐃᑖᐸᒋᐦᐊᒋᐠ ᐊᓴᐹᐹᐦᑎᑲᐧᐠ.» – «ᐁ ᐄᐧ ᒣᑕᐋᐧᑫᔮᐣ.» ᐁᑯᓯ, «ᐸᑲᐦᑲᒼ ᐯᔭᐠ ᓂᑕᔮᐋᐧᐤ,» ᐃᑌᐧᐤ ᐊᐊᐧ ᓂᒫᒫ. ᐁ ᓂᑐᓂᑫᐟ ᐁᑲᐧ ᐅᑲᐢᑭᑳᐧᓯᐊᐧᑎᕽ, ᐯᔭᐠ ᐁᓴ ᐆᐦᐃ ᐁ ᑮ ᒣᐢᑎᓈᐟ ᐊᔭ ᐊᓴᐹᐸ, ᐋᑕ ᐃᐧᔭ ᐊᔮᐁᐧᐤ. ᒫᑲ ᑯᑕᐠ ᐊᐊᐧ ᐊᓴᐹᐹᐦᑎᐠ, ᑫᔮᐱᐨ ᐊᓴᐹᑊ ᐁᑯᑕ ᐁ ᐊᑲᐧᒧᐟ. ᑳᐅᑎᓈᐟ ᓂᒫᒫ ᐁᑲᐧ ᐅᐦᐱᒣ ᐁᑲᐧ ᒪᓯᓇᐦᐃᑲᓀᑭᓄᕽ ᑎᑎᐱᓯᒣᐤ ᐆᐦᐃ ᐊᓴᐹᐸ, ᐃᐢᑯᕽ ᐁ ᒣᐢᑎᓈᐟ. ᐋᐧ, ᓃᓯ ᐁᑲᐧ ᐆᑭ ᐊᓴᐹᐹᐦᑎᑲᐧᐠ ᓂᒥᔨᑲᐃᐧᐣ, ᓂᑕᑲᐦᑫᔨᐦᑌᐣ. ᑳᐅᑎᓇᒫᐣ ᐲᒥᓇᐦᑳᐧᓂᐢ, ᐁᑲᐧ ᐁᑯᓂᐠ ᐊᓂᑭ ᐁᑲᐧ ᒦᓇ ᓇᐦᑲᐧᓂᕽ ᐁᑲᐧ ᐁᑯᑕ ᐁ ᑖᐦ ᑕᐦᑯᐱᑕᑭᐠ ᐆᑭ ᐊᓴᐹᐹᐦᑎᑲᐧᐠ, ᐁ ᐃᐢᐹᐦᑲᐧᓀᔭᑭ ᒥᐢᑎᑲᐧᐢᑭᓯᓇ ᐁ ᐳᐢᑎᐢᑲᒫᐣ. ᐋᐧ, ᒥᑐᓂ ᐆᑕ ᐁ ᐹᐦᐸᐹᒧᐦᑌᔮᐣ ᐆᒪ, ᓂᑕᑲᐦᑫᐧᐁᐧᓯᓂᐣ, ᓂᑕᑲᐦᑫᔨᒥᓯᐣ, ᒣᐧᐦᒋ ᐃᔨᓂᑐᕽ ᐊᐊᐧ ᐅᐢᑭᓃᑭᐢᑫᐧᐤ ᐊᐊᐧ ᑳ ᑮ ᐋᐧᐸᒪᐠ, ᒣᐧᐦᒋ ᐁᑯᓯ ᓂᑎᑌᔨᒥᓯᐣ ᐆᒪ, ᔮᐦᑭ ᐁ ᐄᐧ ᓂᑕᐃᐧ ᓃᒥᐦᐃᑐᔮᐣ. ᐹᐢᑲᐨ ᐊᐊᐧ ᐊᔭ, ᓂᐹᐹ ᐊᔭ, ᐆᑕ ᐊᔭ, ᐋᐊᐧᑕᐢᑯᓯᐋᐧᑲᓂᕽ, ᐁᑯᑕ ᐆᒪ ᑳ ᐄᐧ ᓂᑕᐃᐧ ᓃᒥᐦᐃᑐᔮᐣ ᐆᒪ, ᓇᐸᑭᐦᑕᑲᐧ ᐆᐦᐃ – ᐁ ᓇᐸᑭᐦᑕᑯᐦᑳᓯᐟ ᐊᐊᐧ ᐋᐊᐧᑕᐢᑯᓯᐋᐧᑲᐣ, ᐁᑯᑌ ᐁᑲᐧ ᐁ ᐄᐧ ᓂᑕᐃᐧ ᓃᒥᐦᐃᑐᔮᐣ ᐆᒪ. ᒫᑲ ᐆᒪ ᐃᔨᑯᕽ (ᐊᐊᐧ ᓅᐦᑯᒼ ᐊᐊᐧ ᓂᑕᐋᐧᐨ ᐁ ᐊᐧᐃᐧᔭᑌᔨᒪᐠ), ᑳ ᐹᐦᐸᐹᒧᐦᑌᔮᐣ ᐆᒪ, «ᐃᔭᐤ.» ᐃᑌᐧᐤ ᓅᐦᑯᒼ, «ᑖᓂᓯ ᒫᑲ ᐃᐧᔭ ᐊᐊᐧ ᐃᐢᑫᐧᐤ ᐊᐊᐧ, ᐃᑕ ᑳᐸᐹᒥ ᐊᔨᑌᐧᐁᐧᓯᕽ, ᑖᐱᐢᑰᐨ ᐹᐦᐸᐦᐋᐦᑳᐧᐣ ᐁ ᑮ ᐋᐦᑲᐧᑎᓂᔨᑭ ᐅᓯᑕ,» ᓂᑎᑎᐠ.

VII

[12] ᐋᐧ, ᐱᔨᐢ ᐁᑲᐧ ᐋᑕ ᐃᐧᔭ ᐁᑲᐧ, ᐁ ᒥᓯᑭᑎᔮᕽ ᐁᑲᐧ ᐋᓴᐩ, ᓈᓂᑕᐤ ᐁᑐᑫᐧ ᓀᐅᐧᓵᑊ ᐁ ᐃᑕᐦᑐᐱᐳᓀᐧᔭᕽ, ᑫᔮᐱᐨ ᒫᑲ ᒨᔭ ᐄᐧᐦᑳᐨ ᐁ ᐅᐦᒋ ᐋᐧᐸᐦᑕᒫᕽ ᐆᑌᓇᐤ, ᐆᑌᓈᕽ ᐆᐦᐃ ᐊᑖᐁᐧᐃᐧᑲᒥᑯᕽ ᐊᐦᐳ, ᒨᔭ ᐄᐧᐦᑳᐨ ᐁ ᐅᐦᒋ ᐄᐧᒋᐦᐃᐁᐧᔮᕽ. ᐋ, ᑫᑕᐦᑕᐁᐧ ᐯᔭᑳᐧᐤ ᐁ ᑕᑲᐦᑭ ᑮᓯᑳᐠ ᐆᒪ ᐊᔭ, ᐁ ᓂᑯᑖᐧᓯᑯ ᑮᓯᑳᐠ, ᒨᓂᔮᐤ ᒫᓇ ᐊᐊᐧ, ᐊᑳᒥ ᔮᐲᓯᓯᕽ ᑮ ᐄᐧᑭᐤ ᐯᔭᐠ, ᐁᑯᑌ ᐆᒪ ᓂᑎᑐᐦᑖᓈᐣ ᐆᒪ, ᐁ ᓂᑕᐃᐧ ᑭᔪᑲᐋᐧᔮᕽ

ᐊᐘ ᒨᓂᔮᐤ. ᐚ, ᑳ ᒫᐦᒥᔨᑯᔮᕽ ᐆᐦᐃ ᐊᔭ, ᓈᑎᑎᓴᐦᐃᑫᐘᓯᓇᐦᐃᑲᓇ, ᐁᓴ ᐁᑐᑵ ᒥᐦᒉᐟ ᐁ ᑮ ᐊᑎᒫᐦ ᒫᐘᒋᐦᒑᐟ. ᐚ, ᓂᑮᐍᐦᑕᑖᓈᐣ. ᐹᒷᔦᐢ ᑕᑯᐦᑌᔮᕽ ᓃᑭᓈᕽ ᓀᑌ, ᐋᐱᐦᑕᐤ ᐃᔨᑯᕽ ᐁᑐᑵ ᓂᑕᐱᓈᐣ ᐁᑯᑕ ᐁᑿ, ᐁᑯᓂ ᐆᐦᐃ ᒪᓯᓇᐦᐃᑲᓇ ᐆᐦᐃ ᐁᑯᑕ ᐁ ᑳᐦ ᑭᑖᐸᐦᑕᒫᕽ. ᐚᐦ ᐘᐦᐚ, ᐃᔨᑯᕽ ᐁ ᒫᐦ ᒥᔦᓇᐚᔮᐦᑭᐠ ᐆᑭ ᐃᐢᑵᐘᐠ ᐁᑯᑕ ᐁ ᒪᓯᓇᐦᐃᑳᓯᒋᐠ ᐆᑭ, ᐊᔨᐏᓂᓴ ᓇᓈᑐᕽ ᐁ ᑭᑭᐢᑲᐦᑭᐠ. ᑲᐦᑭᔭᐤ ᐹᐢᑲᐨ ᐁ ᒫᐦ ᒥᐦᑯᑐᓀᐦᐅᒋᐠ.

[13] ᐁᑯᓯ, ᓂᑮᐍᐦᑕᑖᓈᐣ ᐆᐦᐃ ᒪᓯᓇᐦᐃᑲᓇ. ᐚ, ᓂᓂᑕᐏ ᑭᐢᑭᓄᐦᐊᒫᑯᓯᓈᐣ ᐁᑿ ᑮᐦᑤᒼ ᐁ ᑮᓯᑳᐠ, ᒨᔭ ᓂᑮ ᐴᓀᔨᐦᑌᐣ ᐆᒪ ᒥᐦᑯᑐᓀᐦᐅᐣ, ᐆᒪ ᐁ ᒥᐦᑯᑐᓀᐦᐅᒋᐠ ᐆᑭ ᐃᐢᑵᐘᐠ, ᐁᑿ ᒫᑲ ᒦᓇ ᓂᑕᑳᐘᑕᒫᐘᐘᐠ. ᐚ, ᐁᐘᑯ ᐊᓂᒪ ᐁᑿ ᐁ ᑮ ᑮᓯ ᒦᒋᓱᔮᕽ ᐊᔨ, ᐁ ᐚᐱᐦᑖ ᑮᓯᑳᐠ ᐅᒥᓯ ᓂᑎᑖᐤ ᐊᐘ ᐊᔭ, ᓂᒥᐢ, ᓅᐦᒑᐑᐢ ᐅᑖᓂᓴ: «ᒪᐦᑎ ᐁᓴ,» ᓂᑎᑖᐤ, «ᐚᐸᐦᑭ ᐊᔨ, ᐸᑲᒫᑲᓂᐢ ᐃᑖᑊ ᐊᔭ, ᑭᑲ ᐯᑖᐣ,» ᓂᑎᑖᐤ ᐊᐘ ᓂᒥᐢ ᐊᐘ. «ᐁᐦᐊ,» ᐃᑘᐤ, «ᑖᓂᓯ ᒫᑲ ᐁ ᐑ ᐃᑖᐸᒋᐦᑖᔭᐣ ᐸᑲᒫᑲᓂᐢ.» ᓂᑎᑎᐠ. «ᒨᔭ ᐁ ᐑ ᐑᐦᑕᒫᑖᐣ,» ᓂᑎᑖᐤ, «ᑲ ᐚᐸᐦᑌᐣ ᐚᐸᐦᑭ, ᑖᓂᓯ ᐁ ᐑ ᐃᑖᐸᒋᐦᑖᔮᐣ,» ᓂᑎᑖᐤ.

[14] ᐁᑯᓯ, ᓂᐯ ᑮᐚᓈᐣ. ᑮᐦᑤᒼ ᐁ ᐚᐸᕽ, ᐚ, ᐯᑖᐤ ᐸᑲᒫᑲᓂᐢ, ᐁᑿ ᓂᔭ ᐁᑿ ᓂᓯᐻᐦᑕᑖᐣ ᑕᐦᑐ ᑮᑿᐩ ᐆᐦᐃ ᐁ ᐑ ᐚᐸᒋᐦᑖᔮᕽ ᐁᑿ, ᑮᑿᐩ ᐆᒪ ᓈᓂᑕᐤ ᐁ ᐑ ᐃᓯ ᒨᐦᒒᐦᑲᒥᑭᓯᔭᕽ ᐋᑲᒦᓇ, ᐁᑯᓯ. ᐚ, ᒫᑲ ᒦᓇ ᐅᑭᐢᑭᓄᐦᐊᒫᑫᐤ ᐁ ᑮ ᓂᑕᐏ ᒦᒋᓱᐟ, ᐆᒪ ᐁ ᓇᑲᑎᑯᔮᕽ ᐁᑿ ᐊᔨ, ᐃᑌ ᒫᓇ ᐆᐦᐃ ᐊᔭ, ᐏᔮᑲᓂᑲᒥᑯᐢ ᐁ ᐊᔭᔮᐟ, ᐁᑯᑌ ᐁ ᑲᓇᐍᔨᐦᑕᕽ ᐆᐦᐃ ᑮᑿᐩ ᐆᐦᐃ ᐊᔨ, ᑲ ᐚᐸᒋᐦᑖᔮᕽ ᒫᓇ ᐊᔨ, ᑭᐢᑭᓄᐦᐊᒫᑐᐏᑲᒥᑯᕽ, ᐁᑿ ᐆᒪ ᐊᔭ, ᐁ ᒥᐦᑷᐠ, ‘chalk’ ᐃᓯᔩᐦᑳᑌᐤ (ᒨᔭ ᓂᑭᐢᑫᔨᐦᑌᐣ ᑖᓂᓯ ᐁ ᐃᓯᔩᐦᑳᑌᐠ ᐁ ᓀᐦᐃᔭᐍᕽ), ᐁᐘᑯ ᐆᒪ ᐆᒪ ᐆᒪ ᑳ ᓈᑕᒫᐣ ᐆᒪ, ᐁ ᒥᐦᑷᐠ, ᐁᑿ ᐸᑲᒫᑲᓂᐢ ᐅᐦᒋ ᐊᓇ, ᒣᑐᓂ ᒥᑐᓂ ᐁ ᐲᑭᓇᑕᐦᐊᒫᐣ ᐁᐘᑯ ᐊᓂᒪ ᐃᐢᑯᕽ ᒣᑐᓂ ᐊᔨ, ᒹᐦᒋ ᐸᐦᑵᓯᑲᐣ ᐃᔨᑯᕽ ᐊᔨ ᐁ ᐲᑭᓈᐠ. ᐁᑯᑕ ᐁᑿ ᐆᒪ ᐊᔭ, ᐚᐱᐢᑭ ᐱᒥᐩ ᐁᑿ ᐊᓯᒋ ᐁᑯᑕ ᑳ ᑕᑿᐢᑖᔮᐣ ᐁᑿ, ᒣᑐᓂ ᑿᔭᐢ ᐁᑿ ᓂᑑᓰᐦᑖᔮᐣ ᒥᐦᑯᑐᓀᐦᐅᐣ.

[15] ᑲᐦᑭᔭᐤ ᐁᑿ ᑕᐦᑐ ᐃᐢᑵᓯᓴᐠ ᐆᑭ ᑭᐢᑭᓄᐦᐊᒫᑐᐏᑲᒥᑯᕽ ᐁ ᐊᔮᔭᕽ, ᐃᐢᑯᕽ ᐁ ᐊᐱᓰᓯᓯᒋᐠ ᐆᑭ ᐃᐢᑵᓯᓴᐠ ᐊᔭ, ᓈᓂᑕᐤ ᐯᔭᐠ ᐃᔨᑯᕽ ᐁ ᑭᐢᑫᔨᐦᑕᐦᑭᐠ ᒪᓯᓇᐦᐃᑲᐣ, ᑲᐦᑭᔭᐤ ᒦᓇ ᐁᑯᓂᐠ ᓂᒥᐦᑯᑐᓀᐦᐚᓈᓇᐠ. ᐘᐦᐚ, ᑫᑕᐦᑕᐍ ᐅᑭᐢᑭᓄᐦᐊᒫᑫᐤ ᑕᑯᐦᑌᐤ, ᐚᐦ ᐘᐦᐘᐦᐚ, ᓇᐘᐨ ᐱᑯ ᑯᐢᑵᔨᐦᑕᒼ ᐆᒪ, ᑲᐦᑭᔭᐤ ᐆᒪ ᐁ ᓃᐱᑌᐱᔮᕽ ᐆᒪ ᐊᔨ, ᑲᐦᑭᔭᐤ ᐁ ᒫᐦ ᒥᐦᑯᑐᓀᔮᕽ. ᑫᐦᒋᓈᐦᐅᐤ ᒦᓇ ᒨᔭ ᐑᐦᑳᐨ ᐊᔨᐢ ᐆᑌᓈᕽ, ᐆᒪ ᐁ ᑭᒋᒫᑭᓯᔮᕽ ᑲᐦᑭᔭᐤ, «ᑖᓂᑌ ᐆᑭ ᐁᑐᑵ ᐆᑭ ᐁ ᐅᐦᑎᓇᐦᑭᐠ.» ᓂᑮ ᐃᑌᔨᒥᑯᓈᐣ ᐁᑐᑵ ᒫᓇ ᒥᐦᑯᑐᓀᐦᐅᐣ ᐁ ᑮ ᐅᔩᐦᑕᒫᓯᔮᕽ. ᐁᑯᓯ, ᑫᔮᐱᐨ ᐆᒪ ᐊᓄᐦᐨ ᐃᐢᑯᕽ ᑳ ᑮᓯᑳᐠ (ᐁᐘᑯ ᐊᓇ ᐊᓇ ᐁᑿ ᐊᔭ, ᓂᑑᒑᐦᑯᓯᐣ ᐁᐘᑯ ᐊᓇ ᐊᓇ, ᐅᑭᐢᑭᓄᐦᐊᒫᑫᐤ ᐁ ᑮ ᑭᐢᑭᓄᐦᐊᒪᐏᐟ), ᒨᔭ ᐑᐦᑳᐨ ᒫᑲ ᓂᑑᐦ ᐚᒋᒧᐢᑕᐚᐤ, ᑖᓂᑌ ᐁ ᑮ ᐅᐦᑎᓇᒫᕽ ᒥᐦᑯᑐᓀᐦᐅᐣ.

VIII

[16] «– ᐁ ᐯ ᑮᐌᔮᕽ ᐁ ᑎᐱᐢᑳᐠ,» ᐃᑘᐤ, «ᐁᑿ ᐊᐘ ᓂᒫᒫ ᑳᐦᑫᐘᐠ ᐁ ᑮ ᐅᔩᐦᑖᐟ,» ᐃᑘᐤ, «ᐁᑿ ᐲᐦᒋ ᐊᔨᕽ ᐆᒥᓯ ᐃᓯ ᑮ ᓃᐱᑌᑯᑖᐤ, ᓯᓯᓭ ᑯᑖᐚᓈᐱᐢᑯᕽ,» ᐃᑘᐤ, «ᑕ ᐹᐢᑌᔨᑭ,» ᐃᑘᐤ.

[17] ᐁᑿ ᒫᓇ ᐊᓇ ᐅᔩᒥᓴ ᐊᓇ ᑳ ᐋᒋᒪᐠ ᐊᓇ, ᐅᑭᐢᑭᓄᐦᐊᒫᑫᐘ ᑳ ᑮ ᐄᐏᐟ, ᐁ ᑮ ᒥᔦᐧᔨᐦᑕᕽ ᐁᓴ ᒫᓇ ᐁ ᒫᒌᐟ, ᐁ ᓂᑕᐏᒫᒌᐟ ᐁᓴ ᐋᑲᒦᓇ ᐁᑐᑵ ᐁᓴ, ᐁ ᓵᔨᐸᑖᐟ ᐁᓴ ᐊᔭ ᐁᑐᑵ ᐊᔭ, ᐅᐸᐦᑫᑭᓌᐢᑭᓯᓇ, ᐁᑯᑌ ᐁᓴ ᐆᒪ ᑫᓵᐧᐣ ᐆᒪ ᑳ ᐊᑯᑖᐟ ᐁᓴ ᐆᐦᐃ ᐆᐦᐃ ᐑᐢᑕ ᐆᐦᐃ ᐅᒪᐢᑭᓯᓇ, ᓯᓯᓭ ᑳᐦᑫᐘᑿ ᐆᐦᐃ ᐁ ᐊᑯᑌᔨᑭ. boy. ᓃᐹᑎᐱᐢᐠ ᐁᑐᑵ ᐊᐘ ᓂᒨᐦᑯᐢ ᐁᓴ ᐴᑭ ᐁ ᓂᑕᐏᑭᒧᑎᐟ ᐆᒪ ᐊᔨ, ᑳᐦᑫᐘᐠ ᐁᑿ ᐁ ᐑᒦᒋᒋᐠ ᐁᑿ before ᑕ ᑲᐏᓯᒧᒋᐠ. ᐅᔩᒥᓴ ᐁᓴ ᐆᒪ ᐅᒪᐢᑭᓯᓂᔨᐤ, ᒥᑐᓂ ᐁᓴ ᐋᑕ she tried to tear a piece off and this, ᑳᐦᑫᐘᐠ, ᐁ ᐃᑌᔨᐦᑕᕽ, ᐏᔭ ᐆᒪ ᒥᐢᑎᑷᐦᑲᑐᑌᐘ ᐁ ᐹᐢᑌᑭ moccasins. ᐁᑯᓯ ᐃᓯ ᐁᓴ ᐅᒋᐱᑕᒼ ᐁᑿ ᐁ ᓂᑕᐏᑲᐏᓯᒧᒋᐠ (ᑮᑷᐩ ᑲᔮᐢ, ᓇᔦᐧᐢᑕᐤ lamp), boy ᑯᓂᑕ ᐁᓴ ᐁᑿ ᒥᑐᓂ – «ᒨᔭ ᓂᑮ ᑮᐢᑳᐦᑌᐣ.» ᐃᑌᐤ ᐁᓴ ᐅᒥᓴ, ᐁ ᓴᐢᑲᐦᐊᐦᑭᐠ lamp, ᐴᑎ ᐁᓴ ᐆᒪ, ᐅᔩᒥᓯᐚᐘ ᐅᒪᐢᑭᓯᓂᔨᐤ ᐁ ᑲᑵᒦᒋᒋᐠ.

IX

[18] ᐋ, ᑭᔮᒼ, ᐋᓴᐩ ᒦᓇ ᓅᐦᑯᒼ ᓂᑲ ᐋᒋᒫᐤ, ᐅᓵᒼ ᒥᐢᑕᐦᐃ ᐁ ᑮ ᓵᑭᐦᐊᐠ ᓅᐦᑯᒼ, ᓃᐢᑕ ᒫᓇ ᐁ ᑮ ᓵᑭᐦᐃᐟ. ᒫᑲ ᐏᔭ, ᐁ ᑮ ᒥᔦᐧᔨᐦᑕᕽ ᐁ ᐱᒥᓇᐘᓱᐟ ᓅᐦᑯᒼ, ᑳᑭᑫ ᐏᔭ ᒫᓇ ᐁ ᑮ ᐱᒥᓇᐘᑎᑯᔮᕽ. ᐃᐢᑯ ᐃᐢᑵᔮᐨ ᐁ ᑮ ᐱᒥᓇᐘᓱᐟ, ᐁ ᑮ ᒥᓯ ᐸᐦᑵᓯᑲᓂᐦᑫᐟ ᐯᔭᑷᐤ ᑫᑭᓭᐹ, ᐁᑿ ᐊᓂᒪ ᑳ ᒫᒋ ᐋᐦᑯᓯᐟ ᐁ ᐴᓂ ᐋᐱᐦᑖ ᑮᓯᑳᔨᐠ, ᐁᐘᑯ ᐊᓂᒪ, ᐁ ᑎᐱᐢᑳᔨᐠ ᑳ ᓇᑲᑕᐢᑫᐟ. ᐃᐢᐲ ᐁᑿ ᐁ ᓃᐯᐲᐢᑖᐦᐟ, ᐅᐸᐦᑵᓯᑲᓂᒪ ᐁᑯᑕ ᐁ ᑮ ᒧᐏᒥᐦᐟ, ᐁᑯᔨᑯᕽ ᐁ ᑮ ᑲᑳᔭᐏᓰᐟ ᓅᐦᑯᒼ.

X

[19] ᐁᑿ ᐏᔭ ᓂᒫᒫ, ᒫᓇ ᑮ ᐅᔩᐦᐁᐤ ᐊᔭ, ᐊᐱᓯᒨᓯᓴᐧᔮᓇ, ᐁ ᑮ ᑮᓯᓇᒫᓯᐟ. ᐋᑕ ᒫᓇ ᐁ ᑮ ᐑᒋᐦᐋᐠ, ᒫᑲ ᒨᔭ ᐑᐦᑳᐨ ᐁ ᐅᐦᒋ ᓈᑲᑐᐦᑫᔮᐣ ᑖᓂᓯ ᒷᐦᒋ ᒫᓇ ᐊᓂᒪ ᐁ ᑮ ᐃᔩᐦᐋᐟ. ᐁᑯᓯ ᐁᑿ ᓂᔭ ᐁᐘᑯ ᓂᐘᓂᐦᑖᐣ, ᒫᑲ ᒨᔭ ᓂᑭᐢᑫᔨᐦᑌᐣ ᑖᓂᓯ ᑲ ᐃᓯ ᑮᓯᓇᑭᐠ, ᐋ, ᐸᐦᑫᑭᓊᐠ. ᐁᑿ ᒦᓇ ᒫᓇ ᐁ ᑮ ᐅᔩᐦᑖᐟ ᐸᐦᑫᑭᓌᐢᑭᓯᓇ, ᐊᔭ ᐊᐢᑎᓴ ᐁ ᑮ ᐅᔩᐦᐋᐟ, ᐊᔭ, ᒥᐢᑯᑖᑲᔭ ᒦᓇ ᒫᓇ ᐁ ᑮ ᐅᔩᐦᑖᐟ, ᐸᐦᑫᑭᓌᓵᑲᔭ ᐁ ᒦᑭᓯᐦᑲᐦᑕᕽ, ᑮᐢᑲᓇᑵᐘᔮᓇ ᐊᓯᒋ.

[20] ᐁᑿ, ᒨᔭ ᒫᑲ ᓂᑭᐢᑭᓯᐣ, ᑮᐢᐱᐣ ᐑᐦᑳᐨ ᑲ ᑮ ᐊᑖᐚᑫᐟ, ᒨᔭ ᓂᑭᐢᑭᓯᐣ, ᒫᑲ ᐊᐦᐴ ᐁᑐᑵ ᒫᓇ ᑮ ᐊᑖᐚᑫᐤ.

[21] ᐁᑲᐧ ᒦᓇ ᒫᓇ ᓂᑭᐢᑭᓯᐣ ᓂᒫᒫ, ᐁ ᑮ ᓂᐦᑖ ᐊᐧᓂᐦᐃᑫᐟ, ᓯᐦᑯᓴ ᒫᓇ ᐁ ᑮ ᐊᐧᓂᐦᐃᑲᒪᐋᐧᐟ. ᒥᐦᒉᑖᐧᐤ ᒫᓇ ᐁ ᑮ ᐄᐧᒉᐊᐧᐠ ᓈᒋᐊᐧᓂᐦᐃᑲᓀᒋ, ᑖᓂᔨᑯᕽ ᒫᓇ ᓯᐦᑯᓴᐠ ᐆᑭ, ᐁᑯᓯ ᐃᐧᔭ ᐋᑕ ᐃᐧᔭ ᐁᑯᑕ ᒫᓇ ᓂᑮ ᑭᐢᑭᓄᐦᐊᒫᐠ, ᑖᓂᓯ ᑲ ᐃᓯ ᐸᐦᑯᓇᑭᐠ ᐆᑭ, ᓯᐦᑯᓴᐠ ᐁᑲᐧ ᑕᓰᐸᐦᐊᐧᑭᐠ. ᐁᑲᐧ ᓂᐹᐹ, ᐄᐧᐢᑕ ᒫᓇ ᑮ ᐊᐧᓂᐦᐃᑫᐤ, ᒫᑲ ᐊᐧᒐᐢᑲᐧ ᒫᓇ ᐱᑯ ᐁ ᑮ ᐊᐧᓂᐦᐃᑲᒪᐋᐧᐟ. ᐁᑲᐧ ᑳᒥᔦᐢᑲᒥᓂᔨᐠ ᒫᓇ ᐃᐧᔭ ᒦᓇ ᑮᓂᑕᐃᐧᐹᐢᑭᓴᐧᐤ ᒫᓇ ᐊᐧᒐᐢᑲᐧ. ᐁᑲᐧ ᐊᑎᒪᐧ ᒫᓇ ᐁ ᑮ ᐊᔮᐋᐧᐟ ᐯᔭᐠ, ᐁ ᓂᐦᑖ ᓈᑕᐦᐃᓯᐯᐟ ᐊᐊᐧ ᐊᑎᑦ, ᐊᐦᐴ ᒫᓇ ᐊᐧᒐᐢᑲᐧ ᑳ ᐹᐢᑭᓵᐧᐟ ᐁ ᑮ ᓈᑖᔨᐟ, ᐁᑯᓯ ᒫᓇ ᒥᐢᑕᐦᐃ ᐁ ᑮ ᐃᑌᔨᒫᐟ ᐅᑌᒪ. ᑫᑕᐦᑕᐁᐧ ᐁᑲᐧ ᐊᐊᐧ ᐊᔭ, ᐊᑎᑦ ᐊᐊᐧ ᐁᓴ ᑳᓂᑕᐃᐧᐅᑎᐦᑎᓈᐟ ᐊᔨ, ᑳᑲᐧ. ᐁᐩ, ᐁᐩ, ᐃᔨᑯᕽ ᐁ ᑮ ᑲᑳᐧᐦᔭᑭᒥᕽ ᐅᑑᓂᕽ ᒥᓯᐁᐧ, ᒨᔭ ᐅᐦᒋ ᑲᐢᑭᐦᑖᐤ ᓂᐹᐹ ᑲᐦᑭᔭᐤ ᑲᒪᓂᐱᑎᒫᐟ, ᐁᑯᓯ ᑮ ᓂᐸᐦᐃᐠ ᐊᓂᐦᐃ. ᐊᐧᐦ, ᐊᐧᐦ, ᐋ, ᐁᑯᓯ ᑮ ᓂᐱᐤ ᐊᓇ ᐊᑎᑦ. ᑮ ᓂᐸᐦᐃ ᒥᐦᑖᑌᐤ ᓂᐹᐹ ᐅᑌᒪ, ᐁᑯᓯ ᒨᔭ ᐄᐧᐦᑳᐨ ᑮᐦᑖᐧᑦ ᐅᐦᒋ ᒥᐢᑲᐁᐧᐤ ᑯᑕᑲ ᐊᑎᒪᐧ ᐁᑯᔨᑯᕽ ᐊᔨ, ᐁ ᓂᐦᑖ ᓈᑕᐦᐃᓯᐯᔨᐟ.

[22] ᐁᑲᐧ ᒦᓇ ᑮᐦᑖᐧᑦ ᐊᐊᐧ ᓂᑲ ᐋᒋᒫᐤ ᐊᐊᐧ ᓅᐦᑯᑦ, ᑖᓂᓯ ᒫᓇ ᐃᐧᔭ ᐱᐦᐁᐊᐧ ᐁ ᑮ ᐃᓯ ᓈᐦᓇᑳᐧᑖᐟ. ᐁ ᑮ ᐯᐦᐅᐟ ᒫᓇ ᐃᐢᐲ ᐆᐦᐃ ᐊᔨ, ᑳ ᓃᒥᐦᐃᑐᔨᐟ, ᐁᑯᑕ ᒫᓇ ᐁ ᑮ ᓂᑕᐃᐧᑭᑖᐸᒫᐟ, ᐁᑲᐧ ᒣᑐᓂ ᐁ ᐃᐧᔦᔨᐦᑕᕽ ᒣᐧᐦᒋ ᑖᓂᑕ ᐊᓂᒪ ᑳ ᓃᒥᐦᐃᑐᔨᐟ. ᐁᑲᐧ ᒫᓇ ᒥᓯᐁᐧ ᐁᑯᑕ ᒫᓇ ᒥᐢᒋᑯᓴ ᑳ ᐋᐧᐦ ᐋᐧᑭᓇᐦᑭ ᒫᓇ ᐁᑯᑌ ᐁ ᐋᐦ ᓴᑯᓇᕽ ᐊᓯᐢᑮᕽ, ᐁᑲᐧ ᐁᑯᑕ ᒫᓇ ᐊᔭ, ᒑᐸᑳᐧᓂᓴ ᒫᓇ ᐁᑯᑕ ᐁ ᑮ ᐊᑯᑖᐟ. ᐊᔨᐢ ᐆᑭ ᐱᐦᐁᐊᐧᐠ ᑳ ᓃᒥᐦᐃᑐᒋᐠ, ᑯᓂᑕ ᒫᓇ ᐁ ᐱᒥ ᓈᐦᓇᐊᐧᑭᐢᑫᐧᓯᒧᒋᐠ, ᑳ ᐱᒥ ᓇᐊᐧᑭᐢᑫᐧᓯᒧᑖᐧᐃᐧ ᒫᓇ ᐁᑯᑕ, ᐱᒥ ᑖᐸᑳᐧᓯᐊᐧᐠ, ᐁᑯᓯ ᒫᓇ ᒥᓴᐦᑲᒥᐠ ᒫᓇ ᐁ ᑮ ᒫᐦᒥᓯ ᓂᐸᐦᐋᐧᐟ ᐱᐦᐁᐊᐧ ᐁᑯᓯ ᐃᓯ ᓅᐦᑯᑦ. ᐁᑲᐧ ᒫᓇ ᒥᐦᒉᑖᐧᐤ ᓂᑮ ᐄᐧᒉᐋᐧᐤ ᑳᓂᑕᐃᐧᓈᑕᑫᐧᒋ, ᑯᓂᑕ ᒫᓇ ᐆᑭ ᐱᐦᐁᐊᐧᐠ ᑮ ᐋᐦ ᐊᑯᒋᓇᐧᐠ – ᐁ ᑮ ᑭᒋᒪᐦᐃᐦᒋᐠ ᐋᑕ ᐁ ᓃᒥᐦᐃᑐᒋᐠ.

[23] ᐁᑲᐧ, ᐃᐢᐲ ᐁᑲᐧ ᒦᓇ ᒥᑐᓂ ᐁ ᒥᓯᑭᑎᔮᐣ, ᓂᓰᒥᓴᐠ ᐁᑲᐧ ᐄᐧᐢᑕᐋᐧᐤ ᓃᓯ, ᓈᐯᓯᓴᐠ, ᒣᑐᓂ ᐁ ᒫᐦᒥᓯᑭᑎᒋᐠ, ᓂᑭᐢᑭᓯᐣ ᒫᓇ ᓂᐹᐹ ᐁ ᑮ ᑭᐢᑭᓄᐦᐊᒫᑯᔮᕽ ᐊᔨ, ᐁ ᓂᑕᐃᐧ ᐃᐧᔭᐦᐱᒋᑫᔮᕽ, ᒥᓴᑎᒪᐧᐠ ᐆᑭ ᐁ ᐃᐧᔭᐦᐱᑖᔮᐦᑭᐠ, ᐁᑲᐧ ᒫᓇ ᐁ ᑮ ᓈᑕᐢᑯᓯᐁᐧᔮᕽ. ᐯᐢᑭᐢ ᒫᓇ ᐊᓯᒋ ᐃᔨᑯᕽ ᐁ ᑮ ᒫᓯᐦᐃᑐᔮᕽ, ᓈᑕᐢᑯᓯᐁᐧᔮᐦᑭ ᒪᐢᑯᓰᕽ. ᐁᐊᐧᑯ ᒦᓇ ᒫᓇ ᐁ ᑭᐢᑭᓯᔮᐣ ᐁ ᑮ ᒥᔦᐧᔨᐦᑕᒫᐣ ᐁ ᓈᑕᐢᑯᓯᐁᐧᔮᕽ, ᓂᐹᐹ ᐅᑌᒪ ᑕ ᐊᓴᒫᐟ.

[24] ᐯᔭᑳᐧᐤ ᐸᒪᐧᔦᐢ ᐊᔭ, ᒫᑲ ᒦᓇ ᐁ ᑮ ᒉᐢᒋᓀᒋᐠ ᐊᔭ, ᐊᔭ, ᐋᐧᐳᓴᐧᐠ, ᑫᑕᐦᑕᐁᐧ ᐁ ᑲᑳᐧᐦᔭᑫᔭᑎᒋᐠ, ᓰᐢᑳᐧᐨ ᒫᓇ ᓂᐹᐹ ᐅᐄᐧᐢᒋᐦᑳᓂᓴ ᐃᔨᓂᑐᕽ ᑮ ᐄᐧ ᑳᐦ ᑭᑖᔨᐊᐧ, ᐃᔨᑯᕽ ᒫᓇ ᐁ ᑮ ᒥᐦᒉᑎᒋᐠ ᐋᐧᐳᓴᐧᐠ. ᑫᑕᐦᑕᐁᐧ ᒦᓇ ᐁᑯᓂᐠ ᑲᐦᑭᔭᐤ ᑳ ᓇᒪᑌᒋᐠ. ᑫᔮᐱᐨ ᐆᒪ ᐊᓂᒪ ᐊᓄᐦᐨ ᑳ ᑮᓯᑲᐠ, ᒨᔭ ᐊᓂ ᒥᐦᒉᐟ ᐋᐧᐳᓴᐧᐠ ᑳ ᐋᐧᐸᒫᔮᐦᑭᐠ ᓂᔭᓈᐣ ᓂᑕᐢᑮᓈᕽ. ᐯᔭᐠ ᐱᑯ ᓂᑮ ᐋᐧᐸᒫᐤ ᒉᐢᑲᓈᕽ ᐁ ᐊᔭᐱᐟ ᐋᐧᐳᓯᐢ, ᒥᑐᓂ ᐋᑕ ᑳ ᐊᑳᐋᐧᑕᐠ ᐁᐊᐧᑯ ᐊᓇ, ᒫᑲ ᒥᑐᓂ ᒨᔭ ᐊᐦᐴ ᓂᑭᐢᑭᓯᐣ ᑖᓂᓯ ᐋᐧᐳᓯᒦᒋᒫᔨᐩ ᐁ ᐃᐢᐸᑲᐧᕽ].

XI

[25] ᐚ, ᑯᑕᐠ – ᓂᑭᐢᑭᓯᐣ ᐋᓴᐩ ᒥᓇ, ᐯᔭᐠ ᑯᑕᐠ ᑮᑿᐩ ᓂᑲ ᐋᑐᑌᐣ. ᐊᔭ, ᐊᔭ ᐆᒪ ᐁᑿ ᐁ ᑫᐦᑌ ᐊᔨᐏᔮᐣ ᓃᐢᑕ, ᓂᑮ ᐅᐦᐱᑭᐦᐋᓈᐣ ᓅᓯᓯᒥᓈᐣ ᐯᔭᐠ, ᓈᐯᓯᐢ. ᐁᑿ ᐊᔭ, ᑑᐦᑑᓵᐳᐩ ᒨᔭ ᐁ ᐅᐦᒋ ᑲᐢᑭᐦᑖᐟ ᐊᔨ ᑕ ᐚᐸᒋᐦᑖᐟ, ᐁ ᑮ ᒫᔨᐢᑳᑯᐟ ᒥᐢᑕᐦᐃ, ᐁᑿ ᒫᓇ ᐊᐘ ᓂᑭᓴᔨᓃᒼ ᒫᓇ ᐚᐳᓴᐧ ᑲᐦᒥᓯ ᓂᐸᐦᐋᒋ, ᐚᐳᓱ ᒦᒋᒫᐳᐩ ᒫᓇ ᐁ ᑮ ᐅᐦᒋ ᐅᐦᐱᑭᐦᐋᔮᕽ ᐊᐘ ᓅᓯᓯᒼ, ᐁ ᑮ ᐑᐦᑭᐢᑕᕽ ᐚᐳᓱ ᒦᒋᒫᐳᐩ. ᐘᐦᐚ, ᑫᑕᐦᑕᐍ ᐆᑌᓈᕽ ᐁ ᐃᑐᐦᑌᔮᕽ ᐊᔨ, «ᒦᒋᓱᐏᑲᒥᑯᕽ ᐊᐘ ᓂᑲ ᐃᑐᐦᑕᐦᐋᐤ,» ᐃᑗᐤ ᓂᑖᓂᐢ ᐆᐦᐃ, ᐊᓇ, ᐊᓇ ᓅᓯᓯᒥᐢ ᐊᐘ – ᒫᑲ ᐊᔭ, ᑯᑕᐠ ᓂᑖᓂᐢ ᐅᑯᓯᓴ, ᒨᔭ ᐊᐘ ᑳ ᐑ ᐃᑐᐦᑕᐦᐋᐟ ᐊᔨ, ᒦᒋᓱᐏᑲᒥᑯᕽ. ᐋ, ᐁ ᐊᔭᐱᒋᐠ ᐁᓴ ᐆᒪ ᐁᑐᑵ, ᐁ ᓂᑐᑕᐦᑭᐠ ᑮᑿᐩ ᑲ ᒦᒋᒋᐠ (ᐋ, 'Cory' ᐃᓯᔩᐦᑳᓱᐤ ᐊᐘ ᓅᓯᓯᒼ ᐊᐘ), ᐁᑿ ᐁᑐᑵ ᐊᐘ ᐃᑌᐤ ᓂᑖᓂᐢ, «Cory, ᑮᑿᐩ ᒫᑲ ᐆᒪ ᑭᔭ ᐁ ᓅᐦᑌ ᒦᒋᔭᐣ ᐆᒪ ᐆᑌ ᑳ ᐯ ᒦᒋᓱᔭᕽ.» ᐃᑌᐤ ᐁᓴ. «ᐋᐤ, ᐚᐳᓱ ᒦᒋᒫᐳᐩ ᓂᔭ ᐁ ᐑ ᒦᒋᔮᐣ,» ᑳ ᐃᑗᐟ ᐁᓴ ᓅᓯᓯᒥᐢ, ᒨᓂᔮᐏ ᒦᒋᓱᐏᑲᒥᑯᕽ ᐆᒪ ᐚᐳᓱ ᒦᒋᒫᐳᐩ ᐁ ᓂᑐᑕᕽ.

XII

[26] ᐊᐚᓯᓰᐦᑳᓇᐠ ᐆᑭ ᐊᔨ, ᒪ ᑮᑿᐩ ᐊᔨᐢ ᐑᐦᑳᐨ ᐊᐚᓯᓰᐦᑳᓇᐠ ᐁ ᐅᐦᒋ ᐊᔮᐚᔮᐦᑭᐠ ᑕ ᒣᑕᐚᑫᔮᕽ. ᐚ, ᐁᑯᐢᐲ ᐊᐘ ᐊᐘ ᑳ ᑮ ᐋᒋᒪᐠ ᐊᐘ ᐊᔭ, ᓈᐯᐤ ᐊᓇ ᑳ ᒥᔨᑯᔮᕽ ᐊᓂᐦᐃ ᓈᑎᑎᓴᐦᐃᑫᐘᓯᓇᐦᐃᑲᓇ, ᐚ, ᐁᑯᑕ ᐁᑿ ᒦᓇ ᑳ ᐏᔦᔨᐦᑕᒫᕽ ᐊᐘ ᐊᔭ, ᓂᑳᐑᐢ ᐊᓯᒋ, ᐁ ᐏᔨᓵᐧᔮᐦᑭᐠ ᐁᑿ ᐆᑭ ᐊᔭ, ᐊᐚᓯᓰᐦᑳᓇᐠ. ᑲᐦᑭᔭᐤ ᐆᑭ ᓂᐏᔨᓵᐧᓈᓇᐠ, ᓈᐯᐘᐠ, ᐃᐢᑵᐘᐠ, ᐊᐚᓯᓴᐠ. ᑕᐦᑐ ᐁ ᐃᐦᑕᑯᒋᐠ ᐆᑭ ᐊᔭ, ᐊᔨᓯᔨᓂᐘᐠ ᐊᓂᑕ ᐊᔭ, Elizabeth ᓂᑕᐢᑮᓈᕽ, ᑲᐦᑭᔭᐤ ᐁᑯᓂᐠ ᓂᑑᓰᐦᐋᓈᓇᐠ ᐁᑿ. ᐘᐦᐚ, ᐁᑿ ᒫᓇ ᐊᐢᒋᑫᐏᑲᒥᑯᕽ ᐁ ᑮ ᒣᑕᐍᔭᕽ, ᐊᓯᒋ ᐊᓇ ᓂᑳᐑᐢ. ᐚ, ᑳ ᓃᒥᐦᐃᑐᕽ ᐁᓴ ᐁᑿ, ᑲᐦᑭᔭᐤ ᐁᑿ ᐆᑭ ᐊᐚᓯᓰᐦᑳᓇᐠ ᐆᑭ ᐁ ᐯ ᓃᒥᐦᐃᑐᒋᐠ. ᐁᑿ ᒫᓇ ᐊᔭ, ᐅᑭᐢᑭᓄᐦᐊᒫᑫᐤ ᐁ ᑮ ᐊᔮᐚᔮᕽ ᐊᔨ, ᑭᓭᔨᓂᐤ (ᒣᑐᓂ ᐁᑐᑵ ᑌᐸᑯᐦᐳᒥᑕᓇᐤ ᐁ ᐃᑕᐦᑐᐱᐳᓀᐧᐟ ᐊᐘ ᑭᓭᔨᓂᐤ, ᒫᓇ ᐁ ᑮ ᑭᐢᑭᓄᐦᐊᒫᑯᔮᕽ, ᐅᓵᒼ ᑯᓂᑕ ᐃᑌ ᐆᒪ ᐁ ᑮ ᐊᔮᔭᕽ, ᒨᔭ ᒫᓇ ᐅᑭᐢᑭᓄᐦᐊᒫᑫᐘᐠ ᐅᐦᒋ ᒥᔦᐧᔨᐦᑕᒪᐧᐠ ᐁᑯᑌ ᑕ ᐊᔮᒋᐠ, ᐅᓵᒼ ᐚᐦᔭᐤ, ᓇᒪ ᑮᑿᐩ ᒦᑭ ᐆᑌᓇᐤ). ᐁᑯᓯ ᐆᒪ ᔮᐦᑭ ᐆᒪ ᑳ ᓃᒥᐦᐃᑐᕽ, ᑫᑕᐦᑕᐍ ᐊᐘ ᐊᔭ, ᐊᔭ (ᓅᐦᒑᐑᐢ ᐊᐘ, ᐁᑿ ᐊᔭ, ᐁᑿ ᓂᒫᒫ ᐏᔭ ᐊᔭ, ᐅᓰᒥᓴ ᐁᑐᑵ), ᑫᑕᐦᑕᐍ ᑳ ᐯ ᐃᑐᐦᑌᒋᐠ ᐆᑭ ᓈᐯᓯᓴᐠ, «ᐋ, ᑲ ᐑᒋ ᒣᑕᐍᒥᑎᓈᐣ,» ᓂᑎᑎᑯᓈᓇᐠ. ᐁᑯᓯ, ᒫᑲ ᐁᑿ ᐊᓂ ᐁᑿ, ᐑᐢᑕᐚᐤ ᐁᑿ ᐁ ᓃᒥᐦᐋᒋᐠ ᐆᐦᐃ ᐋᑎᐦᐟ ᐊᐚᓯᓰᐦᑳᓇ, ᐁ ᓃᓯᓂᑐᒋᐠ ᐆᑭ ᐊᐚᓯᓰᐦᑳᓇᐠ ᐁᑿ ᐁ ᓃᒥᐦᐋᔮᐦᑭᐠ ᒫᓇ. ᐘᐦᐚ, ᑫᑕᐦᑕᐍ ᐊᐘ ᓅᐦᒑᐑᐢ ᐊᐘ ᐃᑗᐤ, «ᑖᓂᒪ ᐁᓴ ᑭᔭ.» ᓂᑎᑎᐠ ᐆᐦᐃ ᐊᐚᓯᓰᐦᑳᓇ ᐆᐦᐃ, ᐁᑿ ᔮᐦᑭ ᓂᔭ ᐊᐘ ᐯᔭᐠ, ᐆᒪ ᓂᔭ ᐊᐘ ᐊᐚᓯᓰᐦᑳᐣ. ᐚ, ᐁ ᓃᐱᑌᐦᐋᔮᐦᑭᐠ ᒧᐦᒋᕽ ᐆᑭ, ᐁ ᒣᑕᐍᔮᕽ. ᐚ, ᐁᑿ, «ᑖᓂ ᐁᓴ ᐊᔭ» ('Flip' ᑮ ᐃᓯᔩᐦᑳᓱᐤ ᐊᐘ ᐅᑭᐢᑭᓄᐦᐊᒫᑫᐤ, ᑭᓭᔨᓃᐏ ᐅᑭᐢᑭᓄᐦᐊᒫᑫᐤ), «Flip ᐁᓴ, ᑖᓇ.» ᐋ, ᐁᑿ ᐊᐘ ᐑᐢᑕ

ᑭᓭᐳᓃᐃᐧ ᐅᑭᐢᑭᓄᐦᐊᒫᑫᐤ ᓂᑑᓰᐦᐋᓈᐣ, ᓃᑌ ᐄᐧᐦᑫᐧᐦᑕᑳᕽ ᐊᐱᐤ, ᑳ ᓂᑕᐃᐧ ᓈᑖᐟ ᐊᐊᐧ ᓅᐦᒉᐄᐧᐣ ᐆᐦᐃ ᐁᑲᐧ, «ᐋ, ᔮᐦᑭ ᐁᓭ ᐁ ᐄᐧᓵᒥᐣᐠ ᐁᓭ Flip,» ᓂᑎᑎᐠ. ᐋ, ᐁᑲᐧ ᐊᓂ ᐁ ᓃᒥᐦᐃᑑᐦᐋᐧᐟ ᐆᐦᐃ, ᔮᐦᑭ ᐁᑲᐧ ᐊᐊᐧ ᓂᔭ ᑭᓭᐳᓂᐤ ᐊᐊᐧ ᐁ ᐄᐧᒋᓯᒨᒪᐠ ᐊᐊᐧ ᐅᑭᐢᑭᓄᐦᐊᒫᑫᐤ, ᑳ ᐊᑎ ᐊᐧᔭᐄᐧᓯᒧᐟ ᐆᒪ ᐆᑌ ᐃᓯ ᐊᐢᒋᑫᐃᐧᑲᒥᑯᓯᕽ, «ᔮᐦᑭ ᐃᑖᑊ ᐁᓭ ᐁ ᑳᐧᓯᐦᐃᐣᐠ Flip» – ᐊᐢᐱᐟ ᐁ ᑳᐧᓯᐦᐋᐧᐟ ᓂᑕᐋᐧᓯᓰᐦᑲᓇ.

[27] ᑫᑕᐦᑕᐁᐧ ᐁᑲᐧ ᐊᐳ, ᒦᓇ ᐊᔭ ᐁ ᓂᑕᐃᐧ ᑭᐢᑭᓄᐦᐊᒫᑯᓯᔮᕽ, ᐁᑲᐧ ᒨᔭ ᓴᒫᐠ ᑳᐃᐧ ᓂᑮ ᐄᐧ ᓂᑕᐃᐧ ᒉᑕᐋᐧᓈᐣ, ᐴᑎ ᐁᓭ ᑳ ᓂᑕᐃᐧ ᐲᐦᑐᑫᐧᒋᐠ ᐆᑭ ᓈᐯᓯᓭᐠ ᐁᑯᓂᐠ ᐊᓂᑭ, ᐯᔭᑲᐧᐣ ᐁᑯᓂᐠ ᓈᐯᓯᓭᐠ, ᓅᐦᒉᐄᐧᓯᓈᓇᐠ ᐆᑭ, ᑳ ᐅᑎᓇᐦᑭᐠ ᐁᓭ ᐊᔭ, ≷ᐊᒥ≷ᐋᐧᐣ, ᐁᓭ ᐁᑯᑌ ᐁ ᐃᑐᐦᑕᑖᒋᐠ, ᑲᐦᑭᔭᐤ ᐁᓭ ᐁᑯᓂ ᐊᓂᐦᐃ ᓂᑕᐋᐧᓯᓰᐦᑳᓂᓈᓇ ᐆᒪᑐᐃᐧˣ, ᐊᔭ, on the wall ᐁᓭ ᐁᑯᑕ ᑲᐦᑭᔭᐤ ᐁ ᐸᓭᑲᐧᐦᐋᐧᒋᐠ. ᐆᐦ, ᐁ ᒥᓯᐊᐧᓈᒋᐦᐋᐧᒋᐠ, ᐁᑯᓯ ᐁᑲᐧ ᒪ ᑮᑲᐧ ᐊᐋᐧᓯᓰᐦᑲᓇᐠ ᓂᑖᔭᐋᐧᓈᓇᐠ, ᐁ ᑲᑳᐧᐦᔭᑭᐦᐃᑯᔮᐦᑭᐠ ᓈᐯᓯᓭᐠ.

XIII

[28] ᐊᔭ, ᐊᔭ ᒦᓇ ᒫᓇ, ᐁ ᑮ ᐅᓰᐦᑕᒫᓱᔮˣ ᐊᐳ, ᐊᐋᐧᓯᓰᐦᑲᓇᐠ, ᑯᓂᑕ ᒫᓇ ᐋᔮᓂᓭ ᑳ ᐱᑎᑫᐧᑭᓇᒫᐦᑭ, ᐁ ᐋᐧᐃᐧᔦ ᐱ ᑎᑫᐧᑭᓇᒫˣ, ᐁᑲᐧ ᐁᑯᑕ ᐋᐧᐱᐢᑲᐹᐃᐧᓂᐣ ᒫᓇ, ᐁ ᐁᐧᐁᐧᑭᓇᒫˣ. ᐁᑲᐧ ᐃᐧᔭ ᒫᓇ ᓂᒫᒫ ᐁ ᑮ ᒪᓯᓂᐢᑕᐦᐃᑫᐟ, ᐁᑲᐧ ᐁ ᑮ ᑭᐢᑭᓄᐦᐊᒪᐃᐧᐟ ᑕᒪᓯᓂᐢᑕᐦᐃᑫᔮᐣ, ᐁᑲᐧ ᒫᓇ ᐅᐢᑮᓯᑯᐋᐧᐊᐧ ᒫᓇ ᐁ ᑮ ᒪᓯᓂᐢᑕᐦᐊᒫˣ, ᐅᐢᑭᐊᐧᓂᐋᐧᐊᐧ ᐅᑑᓂᐋᐧᐊᐧ ᐆᑭ ᐊᐋᐧᓯᓰᐦᑲᓇᐠ. ᐁᑲᐧ ᐊᐢᑐᑎᓇ, ᐊᐢᒍᒋᓂᓭ ᒫᓇ ᐁ ᐅᓰᐦᑕᒪᐋᐧᔮᐦᑭᐠ, ᐁᑲᐧ ᒥᐢᑯᓚᑲᓭ ᒪᑲ ᐃᐧᔭ ᒫᓇ ᒪ ᑮᑲᐧ+ ᐅᐢᐱᑐᓂᐋᐧᐊᐧ ᑮᑲᐧ+, ᐋᐧᐢᐱᓰᓂᓭ ᒫᓇ ᐁ ᑮ ᐅᓰᐦᑕᒪᐋᐧᔮᐦᑭᐠ, ᐁᑲᐧ ᐁᑯᑌ ᐁ ᓵᑭᐢᑫᐧᐦᐱᑖᔭᐦᑭᐠ ᐆᑭ ᐊᐋᐧᓯᓰᐦᑲᓇᐠ, ᐁᑯᓯ ᒫᓇ ᐁ ᑮ ᒉᑕᐋᐧᑫᔮˣ. ᑲᔮᐣ ᐊᐳᐣ ᒪ ᑮᑲᐧ+, ᓲᐢᑳᐧ- ᑲᐦᑭᔭᐤ ᑮᑲᐧ+ ᒫᓇ ᐊᔭ, ᐁ ᑮ ᒥᐢᑲᒫᓱᔮˣ ᐁ ᒉᑕᐋᐧᑫᔮˣ. ᐁᑲᐧ ᒫᓇ ᐊᔭ, ᓵᑲˣ ᒫᓇ ᐁᑯᑌ ᐁ ᑮ ᐅᓰᐦᑖᔭˣ ᒉᑕᐁᐧᐃᐧᑲᒥᑳᐧ, ᑯᓂᑕ ᒥᐢᑎᑯˣ ᒫᓇ ᐁᑯᑌ ᐁ ᑮ ᓴᑲᐦᐊᒫˣ ᐊᐳ, ᐋ, ᐊᑯᒋᑲᓂᓭ, ᑯᓂᑕ ᑲᐦᑭᔭᐤ ᑮᑲᐧ+ ᒫᓇ ᐊᔭ, ᑲᔮᓯ ᐊᔭ, ᐊᓯᐊᐧᒋᑲᓇ ᒫᓇ ᐁ ᑮ ᒉᑕᐋᐧᑫᔮˣ. ᑫᑕᐦᑕᐁᐧ ᐊᐊᐧ ᓅᐦᑯᐨ ᑳᒥᐳᐟ ᐊᐳ, ᐆᐦᐃ ᐊᔭ, ᒥᓂᐦᑳᐧᒋᑲᐣ ᒫᓇ ᑳᑭᑫ ᐁ ᑮ ᐊᔮᐟ ᐁ ᒥᔮᐧᓯᓂᐳᐠ. ᑫᑕᐦᑕᐁᐧ (ᐁ ᐲᐋᐧᐱᐢᑳᐧᐳᐠ ᒫᑲ), ᑫᑕᐦᑕᐁᐧ ᐅᐦᒋᑲᐋᐧᓂᐳᐤ ᐆᒪ, ᐆᒪ ᐅᒥᓂᐦᑳᐧᒋᑲᐣ, ᐋᐧ, ᑳᒥᐳᐟ ᐆᒪ ᐁᐊᐧᑯ ᑕᒉᑖᐊᐧᑫᔮᐣ ᐆᒪ ᓂᒉᑕᐁᐧᐃᐧᑲᒥᑯˣ, ᐊᐧᐦᐋᐧ, ᐃᐳᑯˣ ᐁ ᒪᒥᐦᒋᐦᐃᑯᔮᐣ ᐆᒪ ᓂᔭ ᐊᐳ, ᓂᔭ ᐱᑯ ᐁ ᐊᔮᔮᐣ ᐆᒪ ᐊᐳ, ᐊᔭ, ᒥᓂᐦᑳᐧᒋᑲᐣ ᐁ ᒥᔮᐧᓯᐠ, ᒉᑕᐁᐧᐃᐧᑲᒥᑯˣ.

[29] ᐁᑯᓯ ᒫᓇ ᐆᑭ, ᑯᑕᑲᐠ ᒫᓇ ᐆᑭ ᐄᐧᐢᑕᐋᐧᐤ ᐃᐢᑫᐧᓯᓭᐠ ᐅᐦᐱᒉ ᐁ ᐋᐧᐦ ᐄᐧᑭᒋᐠ, ᐁᑲᐧ ᒫᓇ ᐁ ᑭᔦᑳᑐᔮˣ. ᑫᑕᐦᑕᐁᐧ ᐆᑭ ᐃᐢᑫᐧᓯᓭᐠ ᐆᑭ, Martineau ᐃᐢᑫᐧᓯᓭᐠ ᓂᐯ ᑭᔦᑳᑲᐧᐠ. ᐁᑐᑫᐧ ᐆᒪ ᓂᑕᑳᐊᐧᑕᒫᑲᐧᐠ ᐆᒪ ᓂᒥᓂᐦᑳᐧᒋᑲᐣ, ᐊᐧᐦᐋᐧ, ᑫᑕᐦᑕᐁᐧ ᓂᐊᐧᓂᐦᑖᐣ ᓂᒥᓂᐦᑳᐧᒋᑲᐣ, ᑖᓂᑌ. – ᒥᓯᐁᐧ ᓂᓇᑐᓅᐣ. «ᐊᐧᐦᐋᐧ,» ᓂᑎᑌᐳᐦᑌᐣ, «ᓂᑫᐦᒋᓈᐦᐅᐣ ᐆᑭ ᐃᐢᑫᐧᓯᓭᐠ, ᓂᑯᑖᐧᐤ ᐁ ᑭᒧᑕᒪᐃᐧᒋᐠ,» ᓂᑎᑌᐳᐦᑌᐣ ᐆᒪ ᓂᒥᓂᐦᑳᐧᒋᑲᐣ. ᐋᐧ, ᐁᑲᐧ ᐊᓂ ᐁᑲᐧ, ᑲᐦᑭᔭᐤ ᐁᑲᐧ ᑳ ᐸᐹᐧᒥ ᑭᔦᑲᐊᐧᑭᐠ ᐁᑲᐧ, ᒪᐦᑎ ᑲ ᑲᑫᐧ ᐋᐧᐸᐦᑕᒫᐣ

ᐆᒪ ᐊᐋᐧᓇ ᐁ ᑮ ᑭᒧᑕᒪᐃᐧᐟ ᓂᒥᓂᐦᑳᐧᒋᑲᐣ. ᐋᐧ, ᐃᐢᑫᐧᔮᐨ ᐆᑭ ᐁᑲᐧ Martineau ᐃᐢᑫᐧᓯᓴᐠ ᐁᑲᐧ ᐁᑯᑌ ᐁᑲᐧ, ᓂᓂᑕᐃᐧ ᑭᔪᑳᐣ. ᒫᑲ ᒌᑭ ᐁ ᐊᑎ ᐋᔮᔮᐣ, ᓂᐚᐸᒫᐤ ᐊᐊᐧ ᐯᔭᐠ ᐃᐢᑫᐧᓯᐢ ᑮᑲᐧᐩ ᐁ ᑳᒋᐁᐧᐱᓇᕽ, ᐁ ᐊᑲᐧᓇᐦᐊᓯᐟ ᐅᒪ ᐊᔭ, ᐹᐦᑳᐧᐦᐃᑳᑲᓂᐢ ᐅᐦᒋ ᑮᑲᐧᐩ. ᐁᑯᓯ, ᓂᑕᑯᐦᑖᐣ ᐁᑯᑌ ᐁᑲᐧ ᐊᔭ, ᔮᐦᑭ ᐃᑖᑊ ᐆᒪ ᑯᓂᑕ ᐁ ᒪᐢᑭᐦᑮᐋᐧᐳᐦᑫᒋᐠ, ᐁᑲᐧ ᐁ ᐄᐧᒥᓇᐦᐃᒋᐠ ᔮᐦᑭ. ᐋᐧ, ᐁ ᑮ ᑮᓯᒥᓂᐦᑫᐧᔮᐣ ᐆᒪ, ᔮᐦᑭ ᐃᑖᑊ ᒪᐢᑭᐦᑮᐋᐧᐳᐩ ᐁᑲᐧ, ᑳ ᐃᑐᐦᑌᔮᐣ ᐆᒪ ᓅᑌ ᐁᑲᐧ, ᐃᑌ ᑳ ᑮ ᑳᒋᑫᒋᐠ ᐆᒪ, ᐊᐋᐧᓇ ᐆᒪ ᑖᐯᐧ ᐁᑯᑕ ᓂᒥᓂᐦᑳᐧᒋᑲᐣ ᑮ ᐊᐢᑌᐤ, ᐃᐧᔭᐋᐧᐤ ᐁᓴ ᐁ ᑮ ᐯ ᑭᒧᑕᒪᐃᐧᒋᐠ. ᐊᐧᐦᐋᐧ, ᒣᑐᓂ ᓂᑭᓯᐋᐧᓯᐣ ᐆᒪ ᐁ ᑮ ᑭᒧᑕᒫᑲᐃᐧᔮᐣ, ᐁ ᑮ ᒪᒥᐦᒋᓯᔮᐣ ᓅᐦᑯᒼ ᐁ ᑮ ᒥᔨᐟ. «ᑕ ᑮ ᓅᐯᐃᐧᓯᔦᐠ ᐆᒪ ᐁᑯᑌ ᑳ ᐯ ᑭᒧᑎᔦᐠ, ᐁᑲᐧ ᐁ ᑮ ᑲᑫᐧᒋᒥᑕᑯᐠ, ᒨᔭ ᓂᔭᓈᐣ, ᐁ ᑮ ᐃᓯᔮᕽ.» ᐊᐧᐦᐋᐧ, ᑫᑳᐨ ᓂᐸᑲᒪᐦᐋᐧᐊᐧᐠ ᐃᔨᑯᕽ ᐁ ᑭᓯᐋᐧᐦᐃᒋᐠ. ᐋᐧ, ᑯᓂᑕ ᐁᑲᐧ ᐋᑕ ᐃᐧᔭ ᐁ ᑮᐁᐧᐦᑕᑖᔮᐣ ᓂᒥᓂᐦᑳᐧᒋᑲᐣ, ᑳᐃᐧ ᓂᒣᑕᐁᐧᐃᐧᑲᒥᑯᕽ.

XIV

[30] ᐊᐢᑭᔭ ᒫᓇ ᐊᔨ, ᐄᐊᐧᐦᐃᑲᓇᐠ ᐁ ᑮ ᐅᓰᐦᒋᑳᑫᔮᕽ. ᐁᑲᐧ ᐊᔭ, ᐋᑎᐦᐟ ᒦᓇ ᒫᓇ ᐊᔭ ᐃᐧᔮᐢ, ᐁᑲᐧ, ᑫᑕᐦᑕᐁᐧ ᒦᓇ ᐊᔭ, ᓂᑎᑐᐦᑖᓈᐣ ᐊᔭ, ᐁ ᒥᐢᑲᒫᕽ, ᓃᐱᔭ (ᑮᑲᐧᐩ ᐁᑐᑫᐧ ᒫᓇ ᐁ ᑮ ᐅᐦᐱᑭᐦᑭ ᓯᓯᓄ ᓵᑲᐦᐃᑲᓂᓯᓯᕽ, ᐋ, ᒣᐧᐦᒋ ᐊᓴᓯᓇᐧ, ᐊᐦᐴ ᐊᔭ, ᒪᐢᑭᓯᓄᑭᓇᐧ ᒫᓇ ᑖᐱᐢᑰᐨ ᐁ ᑮ ᐃᓯᓈᑲᐧᐦᑭ), ᐁᑯᓂ ᒦᓇ ᒫᓇ ᐁ ᑮ ᒥᓯᒪᓂᐱᑕᒫᕽ ᐁᑲᐧ ᔮᐦᑭ ᐃᑖᑊ ᐁ ᒪᐢᑭᓯᓂᐦᑫᐦᑳᓯᔮᕽ, ᒣᑐᓂ ᒫᓇ ᓇᓈᑐᕽ ᑳ ᐃᑌᑭᓇᒫᐦᑭ, ᐁᑲᐧ ᒫᓇ ᐁ ᑮ ᒫᐦᒫᒪᑲᐧᐦᑕᒫᕽ ᐁᑯᓂ ᐊᓂᐦᐃ ᓃᐱᔭ ᐊᓂᐦᐃ, ᐁᑲᐧ ᐆᒪ ᑳ ᑕᓴᐧᑭᓇᒫᕽ ᑖᐱᐢᑰᐨ ᐁ ᒦᑭᓯᐦᑲᐦᑌᑭ ᐁ ᐃᓯᓈᑲᐧᐦᑭ, ᐁᑲᐧ ᒫᓇ ᐁ ᑮ ᑲᐢᑭᑳᐧᑕᒫᕽ ᐁᑯᓂ ᐊᓂᐦᐃ ᐁ ᒪᐢᑭᓯᓂᐦᑫᔮᕽ ᐆᐦᐃ ᐊᔭ, ᓃᐱᔭ.

[31] ᑲᐦᑭᔭᐤ ᑮᑲᐧᐩ ᒫᓇ ᑳ ᐊᐋᐧᓯᓰᐃᐧᕽ ᐊᔨᐢ ᐆᒪ ᐊᔭ ᐊᓯᐢᑮᐃᐧ ᐸᐦᑫᐧᓯᑲᓇᐠ ᒦᓇ ᒫᓇ ᓂᑮ ᐅᓰᐦᐋᐧᓈᓇᐠ. ᐁᑲᐧ ᐊᐊᐧ ᒦᓇ ᓂᒥᐢ ᐊᐊᐧ, ᑫᑕᐦᑕᐁᐧ ᑳ ᐯ ᐃᑐᐦᑌᐟ ᓂᒣᑕᐁᐧᐃᐧᑲᒥᑯᕽ, – ᐆᐦ, ᒫᑲ ᒨᔭ ᐁ ᑭᐢᑫᔨᐦᑕᒫᐣ ᑖᓂᓯ ᐁ ᐃᓯᔩᐦᑳᑌᐠ, mustard, ᐁᑯᑐᐊᐧᕽ ᐆᒪ ᐊᔭ – «ᐁᑯᑐᐊᐧᕽ ᐁ ᑮ ᐅᓰᐦᑖᔮᐣ,» ᐃᑌᐧᐤ, ᐊᔭ, ᐸᓴᑯᐢᑭᐃᐧ ᐊᔭ – ᐸᓴᑯᐢᑭᐤ, ᑖᐱᐢᑰᐨ ᒦᑐᓯᕽ ᒫᑲ ᐁ ᐊᐧᐅᐦᒋᑲᐃᐧᐟ ᒫᓇ, ᐁᑯᑐᐊᐧᕽ ᐁᓴ ᐆᐦᐃ ᐁ ᑮ ᐸᐹᒥ ᐋᐧᐦᐅᑎᓈᐟ ᐁᑲᐧ ᐸᐦᑫᐧᓯᑲᓇ ᐊᓯᒋ ᐁᑯᑌ ᐁ ᑕᑯᓈᐟ, ᐁᑯᓯ ᒣᐧᐦᒋ ᐊᔭ, mustard ᐁ ᐅᓰᐦᑖᐟ, ᐁ ᒪᒥᐦᒋᓯᐟ ᐃᔨᑯᕽ. ᐋ, ᐁᑯᓯ ᐯᔭᑳᐧᐤ ᐁᑯᑕ ᐁ ᑮ ᐅᑕᐦᐅᐟ ᐊᔨ, ᐃᐧᔦ ᓇᐊᐧᐨ ᐁ ᑮ ᑭᐢᑫᔨᐦᑕᕽ ᑮᑲᐧᐩ ᐁ ᐃᓯ ᐅᓰᐦᑖᐟ.

8.
A Woman's Life

Glecia Bear

[GB:] matwân cî mâka ka-miyopayiw?
[FA:] ohcitaw êtikwê; mâh-maskâc [*sic; sc.* mâmaskâc] mâk ôma.
êkos êsa k-âcimonaw k--, â, anohc aw ê-wî-âcimostâkoyahk nikâwîs, nêhiyaw – *Mrs Glecia Bear, f-- Meadow Lake* ohci.
hâw, kiya, âcimo!
[GB:] êha.

I

[1] aya, aw âwa nitôsimiskwêm, *Freda*, ê-nitawêyihtahk nika-kiyâskiwina [*laughs*]. êkwa nik-âcimon, nistam ê-pê-wîc-âyâmâyâhkwâw mêkwât ninîkihikonânak, tânis ê-kî-pê-isi-kitimâkisiyâhk nik-âtotên. kayâs ayis kî-kitimâkan.

[2] ayi, iyikohk ê-kî-kakwâtakatoskêyâhk mâna kayâs, nânitaw êtikwê *thirteen* niy ê-itahtopiponêyân, sâsay nipâpâ ê-kî-wîcihak ê-pakitahwât sâkahikanihk. êkwa mân âkotê ohc êkwa kinosêwak ê-kî-pêsiwakik, *Hudson's Bay store* ôta ôma *Green Lake* ê-pê-atâwâkêyân, mîskot kistikân, kîkway mîciwinis êkota ohc ê-- ê-atâwêt nipâpâ, nîkinâhk âtiht ê-itohtatâyân, âtiht sâkahikanihk itê kâ-pakitahwât. êkwa ispî mîn êkwa, ê-kî-aya--, atoskêwin ê-kî-ayât ê-aya--, *mail* ê-pimohtatât, *Big River* ohc êkwa isko *Ile-la-Crosse* [*sic*] mân ê-kî-pimohtatât *mail*. êkw êkot[a] ânim êkwa ê-kî-sôniyâhkêt, âta mâka môy êtikwê mistahi ê-ohci-tipahamâht. mâna kâ-kî-pê-takohtêt *Big River* ohci, mîciwin mân ê-kî-pêtât, êkwa âtiht ayiwinisisa kîkway, *rubbers* êkos îsi, asikana ê-kî-atâwêstamâkoyâhk.

[3] êkwa nikî-k--, ât[a] ê-kî-omostosomisiyâhk, âta môy mihcêt mâka, nânitaw nikotwâsik mostoswak [*sic; sc.* mostoswa] ê-kî-ay-ayâwât; niyanân êkwa mân ê-oskinîkiskwêwisiyâhk, ê-kî-pamihâyâhkwâw mostoswak. kahkiyaw kîkway ê-kî-tôtamâhk,

[GB:] I wonder, though, if it [*sc.* the tape-recorder] will work right?

[FA:] I am sure it will; but it is strange sometimes.

So we will tell stories, and today my aunt *nêhiyaw* – Mrs. Glecia Bear, is going to tell us stories, she is from Meadow Lake.

Right, it is your turn, tell a story!

[GB:] Yes.

I [*Childhood*]

[1] My niece here, Freda, wants my lies [*laughs*]. I will tell a story now about the earliest times when we were living with our parents, I will tell how it was when we were poor. For life was poor in the old days.

[2] We used to work so very hard in the old days, as for me, I must have been about thirteen years old, and I was already helping my dad fishing [*sc.* by net] in the lake. And then I would haul the fish from there, coming here to Green Lake to sell them at the Hudson's Bay store, and in exchange my dad would buy oats and some food with that [*sc.* with the proceeds], and some of it I would take to our house and some to the lake where he was fishing. And later he also had a job hauling mail, he used to haul mail from Big River all the way to Ile-à-la-Crosse. And with that he made money, although he probably was not paid very much. But when he came back from Big River he would bring food, and he would buy clothes for us, rubbers and things like that, and stockings.

[3] And we also had a few cows, though not many, he used to have about six of them; and we as young girls would look after the cows. We used to do everything, we used to mud the house and the

ê-kî-asiskîhkâtamâhk wâskahikan mâna, mistatimokamik; ê-nikohtêyâhk, sakâhk ê-ohti-nikohtêyâhk, ê-kî-âwacitâpêyâhk mâna mihta, osâm nipâpâ ê-kî--, pêyakw-âya piko mistatimwa ê-kî-ayâwât, ê-sipwêhtahât.

[4] êkwa wiya nimâmâ mâna wiy ê-kî-nitaw-âya-akotât tâpakwâna, wâposwa ê-kî-nipahât ê-wî-kakwê-asamikoyâhk wiya, wiy âskaw kîkway êkos îsi ê-kî-nitawi-nipahtât ahpô mâna pihêwa ê-kî-nitawi-pâh-pâskiswât sakâhk mâna nimâmâ. êkwa ê-kî-kiskinahamâsoyâhk, iskôl nistam ê-ihtakok, sâsay anima niya nânitaw êtikwê --, aya, *nine* êtikwê ê-itahtopiponêyân, iskôl êkota kâ-pê-osîhtâhk, *log-school,* ê-kiskinahamâsoyâhk. êkwa êkotê mâna êkw ê-kî--, kâ-nîpihk mân ê-kî-sâsâkihtiyân, âta sâsay ê-oskinîkiskwêwiyân; at[i] ê-kî-sâsâkihtiyâhk mâna. kâ-kî-nîmâyâhk, nayêstaw pahkwêsikan, êkwa *tallow* mâna kî-icikâtêw pimiy, ê-- kî-maskawâw pimiy, êwakw ân[i] ânima mân âsic ê-kî-pahkwêhahk nimâmâ ê-kî-nîmâhikoyâhk. âskaw mâna sôkâs[a] ê-kî-pîwênât mâna, nipahkwêsikaninâhk.

[5] anohc kâ-kîsikâk, êkwa ômayikohk ê-miyw-âyâcik awâsisak, êy, sôskwât piko ka-kipwaskinêyik êkwa onîmâwiwatiwâw wiyawâw, ê-âtawêyihcikêcik âhci piko. kwayask ê-pohtayiwinisêcik, êkwa mîn ê-nipahikanêcik anohc awâsisak. niyanân, nama kîkway êwakw ânima, nikî-pê-kakwâtakatoskânân misakâmê, miht[a] ê-pîhtikwatâyâhk, ê-âwatôpêyâhk, nipiy ê-kwayâc-âstâyâhk nîkinâhk. anohc awâsis môy âhpô êkwa kaskihtâw mihta ka-pîhtikwatât, ka-pônahk, nama kîkway kaskihtâwak, wiy ê-môniyâw-ôhpikicik. kahkiyaw kîkway êkwa anohc, môniyâw ê-misiwanâcihtât, kayâs kâ-kî-isi-pê-pimâcihohk.

[6] êkwa kâ-kî-oyôhkomiyâhk, nôhkom, kahkiyaw kîkway ê-kî-pê-kakêskimikoyâhk ê-kî-pê-wîhtamâkoyâhk kîkway; kîkway êkâ ka-kî-tôtamâhk, kahkiyaw kîkway nikî-pê-wîhtamâkonân; êkâ ka-pîwêmâyâhkwâw kêhtê-ayak. kâ-pê-pîhtikwêt ayisiyiniw, sêmâk ka-sîkinamawâyâhk *tea,* ka-minahâyâhk, ê-- ê-kî-isi-wîhtamâkawiyâhk ê--, kêyâpic anohc kâ-kîsikâk êwakw ânima niya nipimitisahên.

horse-barn; we cut wood, we cut wood in the bush and dragged the firewood home, because my dad only had one team of horses, and he took them with him.

[4] And my mom would go and set snares, she killed rabbits and tried to feed us, and sometimes she would go out to kill things like that [*sc.* rabbits], or she would go and shoot partridges in the bush. And we would go to school, when there first was a school, I must have been about nine years old already at the time when they came and built a school, a log-school, and we went to school. And then in the summer I would go barefoot, although I was a young woman already; and we would still go barefoot. When we took lunch, there was only bannock, and the grease was called tallow, it was hard grease, and my mom would cut chunks of that and add it to our lunch. Sometimes she would sprinkle a little sugar on our bannock.

[5] Today the children are so well off, hey, their lunch boxes are full to the brim, and they are still dissatisfied. They are properly dressed, and they are incredibly lazy, the children of today. For us, there was none of that, we worked very hard all along, carrying firewood into the house and hauling water, providing sufficient water in our house. Today the children are not even able to carry firewood into the house and to make a fire, they are unable to do anything, for they are raised as Whites. Today the White-Man has entirely ruined the traditional lifestyle.

[6] And our late grandmother, my grandmother, all along she used to counsel us about everything and tell us about things; she told us about all the things we should not do; we were not to be disrespectful towards the old people. When people came in, we were to pour tea for them right away so as to give them to drink, that is what we were told, and I still follow that teaching today.

[7] êkwa ayihk, ê-kî-ohpihk-- [?*sic*] mâna nimâmâ, *gunny-sacks* mân ê-kî-ayi---kaskikwâtahk, êkota mân êkwa ê-kî-pim-âyi-- ê-kî-nitaw-âsiwatâyâhk mâna maskosiya; êwakw ân[i] ânima ê-kî-ay[a]-âspisimoyâhk, *our mattress* êwako. êkwa *canvas* êkwa mâna, êkwa tahkohc ê-kî-astâyâhk êwako, *that's our sheet* êwakw ân[i] ânima. nama kîkway wîhkâc aspiskwêsimon wiya nôhc-âpacihtânân, ê-kî-mâ--, ê-kî-misahtât mân ânima, anima kâ-mâmawokwâtahk; nânitaw êtikwê mâna niyânan ê-kî-ihtasiyâhk ê-kî-nipâyâhk anima, ê-mâmawihkwâmiyâhk mâna awâsisak. môy k-- anohc awâsis, môy kîkway kiskêyihtam êwakw ân[i] ânima, tânisi ê-kî-pê-isi-kitimâkisihk; pêyakwan anohc kihc-ôkimâwak ita kâ-wî-nipâcik, piko ka-wâpisk-ânâskâtihcik, ka-kanâtahk ita ka-nipâcik anohc awâsisak.

[8] êkwa nipâpâ, kâ-kî-minahot mâna, kî-- kâ-kî-nipahtât wiyâs, nimâmâ mân ê-kî-pânisâwêt; êkwa, anim êkwa, wiyâs anima, *fresh meat* anima mân êkwa kâ-nitawêyihtamâhk – maskêkohk mân ê-kî-- ê-kî-nitawi-wâtihkêt nipâpâ, êkotê mân êkwa nimâmâ ê-kî-asiwatât *flour-bags* anihi -- wiyâs, êkwa ispî êkwa *gunny-sack* ê-astât, êkotê mân êkwa êwakw ân[i] ânima wiyâs ê-kî-nitawi-astêk; wiy êkâ kîkway âhkwaci-- k-âhkwatihk [*sic*] ita kîkway ê-ohc-îhtakok, môy ôhci-kiskêyihtâkwan *fridge* kîkwây anima, *deep-freeze* ahpô. êkwa mâna kâ-kî-nâtamâhk êkwa sakâhk êkwa wiyâs, nimâmâ kâ-kî-wî-kîsisahk, sôskwâc *they are fresh,* sôskwâc iyikohk ê-- ê-miywâsik wiyâs, ma kîkway n-- ka-misiwanâtahk; iyikohk ê-kî-miywâsik.

[9] wâwîs cî, wayawîwikamikwa, môy kîkway ohci-kiskêyihtâkwan kîkwây êwakw ân[i] ânima, anohc êkwa ôho -- kahkiyaw kîkway k-âpatahk, ma kîkway ohc-îhtakwan kîkway êkotowa; pikw îta sôskwâ [*sic*] ê-kî-sêskisiyan, êkota ê-kî-nitawi-kihci-wayawîyan, ma kîkway ê-ohci-ihtakok. tânis êtikwê mâna, anohc êkwa mân ê-isi-- ê-itêyihtamân mâna, môy wîhkâc ê-ohci-kiskêyihtamân kîkway, kimisâhowin ka-kî-pê-âpacihtahk; êkos êtikwê piko ê-kî-isi-ma-mêyiwiciskêhk ê-kî-isi-pasikôhk.

[7] And my mom used to sew gunny-sacks together, and then we would go and put hay into them; on that we used to lie, that was our mattress. And then we would lay canvas on top, and that, that was our sheet. We never used any pillows, she used to make it big, that which she sewed together into one piece [*sc.* the mattress]; there must have been about five of us children who slept together, sleeping on one mattress. Today the children do not know anything about that, how it was to be poor; today you have to make their beds with white sheets, the same as where kings are going to sleep, it has to be clean where the children of today are to sleep.

[8] And when my dad would kill an animal, when he killed something for the meat, my mom would cut it into sheets [*sc.* for dried meat]; and that which we wanted as meat [*sc.* not as dried meat], as fresh meat – my dad would go and dig a hole in the muskeg, and over there my mom would put the chunks of meat into flour-bags, and then she put them into a gunny-sack, and then one would go over there and that meat wo uld be put there [*sc.* in the hole]; for there was no place where you could freeze it, it was not known what a fridge was, or a deep-freeze. And then when we fetched the meat from the bush, when my mom was going to cook it, it was fresh, the meat was so good, without any spoilage at all; it was so good.

[9] And as for toilets, especially, it was not known at all what that was, and today they -- all these things are in use, there was nothing of that kind; you just went into the bush, anywhere, and went and did your big business there, there were no toilets. I wonder how it was, I think about it today, I had never known anything about toilet-paper having been in use; one simply got up dirty, I guess.

II

[10] êkwa êkwa, piyis êkwa kâ-- kâ-onâpêmiyân êkwa; nipâpâ ê-kî-nitawi-pawahikêt, â, sâsay êkwa ni--, *sixteen* ê-itahto-- nikotwâsosâ--, *sixteen* ê-itahtopiponêyân, êkwa nipâpâ êkwa k-- anima kâ-nitawi-pawahikêt ôtê *Battleford,* mistatimwa ê-âpacihât. êkot[ê] êtikwê êkw êkwa kâ-nakiskawât êkwa ôho kêt--, awa kâ-kî-wîkimak nâpêw awa ('macawâsis' kî-isiyîhkâsow kâ-kî-osisiyân), êtikwê êkot[ê] êkwa awa nipâpâ kâ-mêkiskwêwêt niya. môy ôm âhpô ê-nisitawêyimak awa nâpêw, kâ-wîkihtahikawiyân. kwayas nikî-mâton ispî nimâmâ ê-wîhtamawit, "ka-- ka-wîkihtoyêk, ê-kî-isîhcikêt kipâpâ," ê-itwêt, ê-pê-takopayit nipâpâ. nêtê ka-têpwâtikawiyâhk ê-ayamihêwikîsikâk, kwayas nikî-mâton, êkâ ê-nisitawêyimak aw âwiyak kâ-miyiht niya, ka-wîkimak.

[11] êkw ân[i] êkwa kâ-wî--, k-âti--, kâ-wîki-- kâ-wîkihtoyâhk êkwa. êy, êy, nikî-nêpêwisîstawâw, mîn ânikik nis-- kâ-osikosiyân, nama kîkway nôhci-- ê-nisitawêyimakik, êkwayôc [*sic; cf.* êkwayâc] êkota ê-wâpamakwâw anima kâ-pê-takohtêcik kâ-wî-wîkihtoyâhk. môy nôhci-kaskihkihikawin [*sic; sc.* -kaskihikawin] ahpô, mîcisowinâhtikohk ka-nitawi-wîci-mîcisômak awa kâ-onâpêmiyân, iyiko-- iyikohk ê-pakwâtamân ê-- ê-mâtoyân, nêtê mistatimokamikohk êkwa ê-nitawi-ma-mâtoyân. kîtahtawê awa pêyak môniyâskwêw êkotê kâ-pê-nâsit (mâka ê-kî-kiskinahamâkêyit onâpêma kiskinahamâtowikamikohk kwâkopîwi-sâkahikanihk), ê-pê-pîkiskwâsit ka-pê-mîcisoyân; nipê-apin mîcisowinâhtikohk, mâka kisik ê-mâtoyân, môy âhpô nôhci-kaskihtân ka-mîcisoyân.

[12] môy nôhci-kaskihikawin ahpô ka-pê-kîwêyân ôtê is ôma paskwâwi-sâkahikanihk, pêyak-pîsim êkotê ê-kî-kisâtamân nîkinâhk, êkâ ê-kaskihikawiyân ka-pê-itohtêyân anima itê kâ-wîkicik. êkw âni tâh-tâpwê êkw âkotê ês êk-- ayiwâk ê-kitimâkahk ita kâ-pê-itohtêyân. tâpiskôc, anohc êkwa ôho mistatimokamikwa ê-miywâsiki ita kâ-kî-pîhtikwahikawiyân, napakikamik; misiwê sôskwâc asiskiy ê-apahkwâtêk maskosiy[a] âsici, ê-micimoskowâhtêk [?*sic*], ê-kî-capahcâsik, wâsênamâwina

II [*Marriage and Childbirth*]

[10] And then, at last, I got married; my dad had gone threshing, well, I was already sixteen then, I was sixteen years old, when my dad went threshing over there at Battleford with his horses. And there he must have met the man I married (*macawâsis* was the name of my late father-in-law), it must have been there that my dad arranged to marry me off. I did not even know the man whom it was arranged that I would marry. I bawled my eyes out when my mom told me, "You two are to be married, your dad has made the arrangements," she said, when my dad arrived home. The banns were to be announced for us that Sunday over there [*sc*. at Green Lake], and I bawled my eyes out, since I did not know this person to whom I had been given, for me to be married to him.

[11] And then we were married. Hey, hey, I was shy towards him, and also towards my mother-in-law and her family, I did not know them at all, I saw them for the first time when they arrived at our wedding [*sc*. at Green Lake]. They could not even prevail on me to eat with my husband at the table, I hated it so much and I was crying, I went and cried over there in the horse-barn. After a while a certain White woman came there to fetch me (her husband was teaching at the school in *kwâkopîwi-sâkahikanihk* [*sc*. Green Lake]), she came to talk to me so that I would come and eat; I came and sat at the table but I was crying throughout, I was not even able to eat.

[12] They could not even prevail on me to come home here to *paskwâwi-sâkahikanihk* [*sc*. Meadow Lake], I stayed at our house over there [*sc*. at Green Lake] for one month, for I could not be prevailed upon to come to where they lived. And in fact it was even poorer there where I went. The horse-barns of today seem good compared to the flat-top house into which I was brought; the roof was all of dirt and sod, held together by mud, it was low, there were two

man-- nîso ê-ihtakoki, mâka maskimotêkinwa ohci wâsênamâwina ê-kî-astêki. êkwa tâh-tâpwê nikî-kakwâhyakêyihtên êkota, kêyiwêhk niyanân kî-miywâsin it[a] ê-kî-asiwasoyâhk; âta wiya *log-house,* mâka kî-- kî-miywâsin, kwayas ê-kî-osîhcikâtêk, wâsênamâwina ê-kî-kikamoki ita kâ-kî-wîkiyâhk.

[13] êkw ân[i] êkwa, ita ka-kawisimoyâhk nipêwin anima – cah, kani tâpwê ôma, nistam êkwa, môy n-- êkâ ê-kaskihikawiyân ka-pê-itohtêyân, nipê-nâtik aw ôta *my uncle, 'Charlie Laliberté'* ê-kî-isiyîhkâsot, "piko ka-pê-kîwêyan, kikî-onâpêmin, piko ka-pê-kîwêtotawat kinâpêm, kikî-kihci-wîkimâw, piko ka-pê-kîwêyan," nititik. êkw ân[i] êkwa ka--, môy nikaskihik, piyis êkwa, *my uncle Payette* êkwa, kâ-isit êkwa nistês ostêsimâw, "ka-wîcêtinân isko ka-nakayâskawacik anikik ayisiyiniwak, êkota nika-pê-kîwânân," nititikwak. tâpwê êkwa kâ-pê-kî--, kâ-pê-wîcêwâyâhk êwakw âwa kâ-pê-nâsit êkwa. êy, êy, âyiman, ayisiyiniw êkosi (kâ-wîkihtahiht êkos îsi) êkâwiya isi kâ-nisitawêyimât, ê-nêpêwisiyân; sôskwât namôy nôhci-kiskêyihtên tânisi ka-kî-itôtamân, nayêstaw ê-kî-mâtoyân mâna.

[14] êkw ân[i] êkwa, "êkot[a] êkwa ka-kawisi--, kiyawâw ka-nipâyêk," ê-- ê-isit awa kâ-osikosiyân, êkw êkwa êkota ninitawi-nipân êkwa. êy, cîki ninâpêm kâ-wî-pê-itisihk mân ê- ê-wî-- ê-tahkiskawak ê-wîkatêwêpinak [*sic*], wiy êkâ ê-nisitawêyimak. pôt ôma mîn êwakw ân[i] ânim âspisimowin, môsopîwaya ohc ês ê-kî-osîhtâhk, aspiskwêsimona môsopîwaya ohci, mistiko-nipêwin ê-kî-osîhtâhk, êkot[a] ânima ê-kî-onipêwiniyâhk; pêyak piko akohp mîn ê-kî-- ê-kî-ihtakok, kayâs-*Hudson's-Bay-blanket* [*sic*], *green* ê-isinâkwahk nêt[ê] ê-kaskitêwasinâstêk, ê-wâpâstêk, êtikwê ê-kî-kisîpêkinikâtêk, nawat piko ê-kî-ocipwâpâwêk, êwakw ânima ê-kî-akwanaho-- akwanahon ê-kî-ayâyâhk.

[15] êy, êkwa kêtahtawê êkwa, kâ-w-- k-âyâwak êkwa, aya --, kâ-kikiskawâwasoyân êkwa (â, nama kîkway nôh-kiskêyihtên, kayâs iyikohk kêhtê-ayak ê-kî-kanawêyimiwêcik, môy wîhkâc nânitaw kôhc-îtohtân), kîtahtawê êkwa, "tânis êtik ôm ê-is-âyâyân," êkwa kâ-wîhtamawak kâ-osikosiyân, "môy ôm ê-ayâyân kîkway," nititâw,

windows, but there were sacks on the windows. And I truly despised it there, at least the place we [*sc.* my parents and I] were in had been fairly nice; although it was a log-house, it was nice and had been built properly, and there were window-panes where we lived.

[13] And then, the bed where we were to lie – oh yes, it is true, at first, when they could not prevail on me to come there [*sc.* to Meadow Lake], my uncle, Charlie Laliberté he was called, had come here [*sc.* to Green Lake] to fetch me, "You have to come home, you are married, you have to come home to your husband, you married him in church, you have to come home," he said to me. And then he could not prevail on me, and finally my uncle Payette and my oldest brother said to me, "We will go with you until you are used to these people, and then we will come home," they said to me. Then indeed we went there with the one [*sc.* Charlie Laliberté] who had come to fetch me. Hey, hey, it is difficult (when it is arranged for a person to be married like that) when she does not know anyone, I was so shy; I simply did not know what to do, I only used to cry.

[14] And then, "You two are to sleep over there," my mother-in-law said to me, and then I went and slept there. Hey, and when my husband would move closer, I would kick him and push him away, for I did not know him. And that mattress, to my surprise, was made of moose-hair, and the pillows were also made of moose-hair, and a wooden bedstead had been made, that was our bed; and there was only one blanket, an oldtime Hudson's Bay blanket, it was green in colour and had black trim over there [*sc.* at the edge], it was faded, it must have been washed and was sort of shrunk, that we had as our cover.

[15] Hey, and then, after a while, I had [*sc.* a child] -- then I was pregnant (well, I did not know anything because in those days the old people used to guard the girls so closely, you never went anywhere), and then, after a while, "I wonder what is the matter with me," and then I told my mother-in-law about it, "I have not had it,"

"ka-kî-ayâyân ôma tahto-pîsim," nititâw; "ê-kikiskawâwasoyan anima," kâ-isit êkwa.

III

[16] wahwâ, êkota êkwa, ispî êwakw âwa ê-kî-ayâwâyâhk awa, nistam iskwêsis ê-ayâwâyâhk, *Florence* awa, *'Bear'* isiyîhkâsow nitânis. êkw ân[i] êkw âyi, kâ-mâyi-kîsikâk, êy, êy, kwayas kimiwan, nisto-kîsikâw ê-kimiwahk, ê-wâsaskotêpayik, êy, êy, kwayas kî-- ê-kî-mâyi-kîsikâk; nistam ôma kâ-misi-kimiwahk anima, êy, konit ânihi ispimihk mis-- anim âyi, kâ-kî-apahkwâtêk maskosiya êkwa asiskiy, iyawis êwakw ân[i] ânihi sôskwât ê-pîhtikwêyâpâwêk asiskiy anima, êkwa, anim îyikohk êkwa ê-kimiwahk, êkwa ê-wî-kawisimoyâhk ôma, "tânis ôma k-êsi-nipâyâhk êkwa?" n-- ê-itak awa kâ-wîkimak. mîcisowinâhtik anima, ê-kî-mosc-ôsîhtâhk mîcisowinâhtik, êwakw ân[i] ânim êkwa, tahkohc nipêwinihk êkwa, êwako ê-têhtastâyâhk êwak ôma, anim âyi, *tablecloth* anima, êwakw ân[i] ânima kêyiwêhk êkota nipiy ê-sôskwakotêk; mâk êkwa, êkotê kapê-ayi ê-pitikwapiyâhk êkwa, atâmihk anima mîcisowinâhtik anima, êkotê êkwa ayi, ê-tahkonak an[a] ê--, awa iskwêsis, kayâs ayis kî-mosci-nôhâwasonâniwan, êkotê mân ê-kî-na-nôhak. â, êkwa pimic-âyihk, misiwê sôskwâc ê-manâpâwêk mîn âsiskiy, sôskwâ [*sic*] wayawîtimihk ê-itâpiyan, êkw îyikohk ê-wâsaskotêpayik!

[17] *well,* kîtahtawê êkwa kâ-itwêt awa ninâpêm, "piko ka-wîkatêhtêyahk [*sic*] ôta ohc," îtwêw. kayâs mâna ê-kî-ihtakok as-- asahtowikamik; êkwa ayi, mâk âyi, ê-kî-kiposakahikâtêk, êkot[a] êkwa kâ-nitawi-tawinahk kayâsi-wâskahikan, mâk ê-apahkwâtêk *shingles* ohc êwako, kayâsi-wâskahikan. êkot[a] êkwa kâ-isi-- kâ-itohtêyâhk êkwa ê-sâsâkihtiyâhk ôma, ma kîkway waskipicikana ê-ayâyâhk. êkot[a] êkwa ê-nitaw-îtohtêyâhk, êkotê aw âsici kâ-tahkonak aw îskwêsis. êwakw ânima k-âs-- asê-- ayi, k-âs-âyi--, *tablecloth,* êwako ê-akwanahoyân, êkotê ê-itohtêyân. êkot[ê] êkwa, môy êkwa -- miywâsin, êkotê môy kimiwan; êkotê nitayânân, mâk êkwa nama kîkway ka-mîciyâhk êkotê ê-ayâyâhk.

I said to her, "which I should have each month," I said to her; "You are pregnant, that is the reason," she said to me.

III [*Rained Out*]

[16] Oh my, it was then that we had this one, we had a girl first, this daughter of mine is called Florence, Bear. And then there was a storm, hey, hey, it rained hard, there was rain and lightning for three days, hey, hey, it was a bad storm; when first it rained hard, hey, the sod and the mud which made up the roof above us, all of that mud simply washed into the house, it rained so much, and then, when we were going to go to bed, "How will we sleep now?" I said to my husband. The table, a home-made table, we put on top of the bed, and most of the water ran off the tablecloth [*sc.* oil-cloth]; but then we sat there huddled all along, underneath that table, there I now sat holding her, the baby girl, and in the old days you simply breastfed your children, and there I would be nursing her. Well, and everywhere on the sides the mud simply came washing down so that you could look outside, and there was so much lightning!

[17] Well, after some time my husband said, "We have to get away from here," he said. In the old days there used to be a ration house; it had been nailed shut, and he went there and opened up the old house, but that old house was roofed with shingles. There we now went, barefoot, we did not have any rubbers. There we now headed, with me carrying the baby girl along there. I used that tablecloth as my cover and went there. It was nice there, it did not rain through there; there we stayed, but we did not have anything to eat there.

[18] êkotê ê-kî-takohtêyâhk, môy kinwês kotakak sâsay mîn âkota kâ-pê-takohtêcik wîstawâw. êkotê êkwa wîstawâw anima wîkiwâw pêyakwan, tâpiskô [*sic*] niyanân anima, ê-sâpohci-kimiwahk anima kahkiyaw kîkway, wîstawâw êkot[ê] êkwa, ê-- nânitaw êtikw êkwa *ten* ê-ihtasiyâhk, wîstawâw awâsis[a] âkota ê-pêsiwâcik, êkwa pêyak, pêyak awa kisêyiniw miton ê-kisêyinîwit, wîst âkota pê-takohtêw. ê-nôhtêyâpâkwêyâhk ôma, wiy ê-kim-- môy kîkway kotawânâpisk êkota pîhc-âyihk, "êskw," îtwêw ana kîsêyinîsis ana, "ka-minihkwânâwâw maskihkîwâpoy," itwêw. wahwâ, aspin ê-kî-wayawît, êcik ân[i] ê-nitawi-kîskatahahk nî-- ê-- nîpisiya, ê-ot-- tâpiskô [*sic*] mîkiwâhpis ê-isîhtât anima, ê-akwanahahk êkwa akwanahikan ohci, êkot[a] êkwa sîpâ ê-pônahk, ê-kisâkamisikêt êkwa, ana kisêyinîsis; wahwâ, nimiywêyihtênân ê-kisitêk kîkway ê-minihkwêyâhk, nikawat-- nikawacinân ayis anim îta k-âyâyâhk.

[19] êkos êkwa ayi, êkot[ê] êkwa ê-kî-ay-âstê-kimiwahk êkwa, kâ-itwêt awa ninâpêm, "mahti ka-itohtânaw êkwa kîkinâhk ka-nitawâpênikânaw," itwêw. tâpwê êkwa ninakatâw an[a] êkwa nipêpîm êkota, ninitawi-mostohtânân, nititohtânân êkotê, êy, nânitaw êtikwê pêyak-misit iyikohk nipiy, êkot[a] âsiskiy, maskosiya konita kahkiyaw kîkway êkota ê-ihtakok. "ka-kakwê-nânapâcihtânaw," kâ-itak ninâpêm êkwa; "kon--, askihk kik-âpacihânaw ôma nipiy ka-wayawî-wêpinamahk," ê-itak. "namôya," nititik, "osâm mistah-âtoskêwin, nika-pâh-pakwanêhên misiw îta, wâh-wîhkwêhtakâhk," kâ-itwêt anima, "nipiy ka-kotâwiciwan." tâpwê êkw âkosi ê-itôtahk êkwa, tâpwê kotâwiciwan kahkiyaw anima nipiy. êkos êkw îspî êkwa ninânapâcihtân êkwa niwâskahikan, mâka misiwê ê-sâpotawâk ispimihk.

[20] êkw ân[i] êkwa wiya kâ-- kâ-nâtât êkwa mistatimwa, ê--, ê-pîkopitahk – *walking-plough* anihi mân ê-pîkopitahk *squares* anih êkwa, ê-wâh-otinahk maskosiya nîkân astâw, kâw âpahkwêw asiskiy ohci, anima, sêkwâ mîn âs--, ê-ati-pimi-micimoskowâhtât [*?sic*] wâsakâ anima kâwi wâskahikan. kâw êkw âkot[a] êkwa kâ-pê-itohtêyâhk, êkot[a] êkwa ê-ayâyâhk.

[18] When we had arrived there, it was not long before others arrived also. Their houses, too, were just the same as ours, it had rained right through everything, and they, too, brought their children there, we were about ten altogether, and one old man, one very old man, came there too. We were thirsty, and there was no stove in there, "Wait," that old man said, "you shall drink tea," he said. Oh my, and with that he had gone out, evidently in order to cut willows, and he arranged them like a little lodge and covered them with canvas, and underneath that he then made a fire and boiled water for tea, that old man; oh my, we were glad to drink something hot, for we were cold in that place where we were.

[19] And then, when the rain had ceased, my husband said, "Let us go and check out our home," he said. And, indeed, I left my baby there, and we went and walked over there, hey, there was about a foot of water, mud, sod, and everything else there. "Let us try to clean it up," I said to my husband; "we will use a pail to get this water out," I said to him. "No," he said to me, "that would be too much work, I will make holes all over, in every corner," he said, "and the water will run out into the ground." And, indeed, he did that, and all that water indeed ran out into the ground. And so I fixed up my house, then, but it was open through and through, all over, up above.

[20] And then he fetched the horses, and ploughed – with a walking-plough he ploughed up squares and took these pieces of sod and put them into place first and made a new roof with sod and earth, and then beneath that he went around and mudded the house with clay again all around. Then we moved back there again, and then we lived there.

IV

[21] êkwa ma kîkway sôniyâhkêwin. ê-kî-mônahaskwêyâhk mâna, wâhyaw mân ê-kî-isi-mostohtêyâhk, ê-nahâwasoyân mâna, êkwa wiya ê-kî-tahkonahk mônahaskwâkana, pî-- wêwêpison, pîminahkwân ê-tahkonahk (pêyakwan mâna sakâhk êkw ê-kî-wêwêpisonihkêyân, ê-kî-akocihk awa êkotê nicânis êkwa ê-mônahaskwêyâhk), mâka wâsakâ mân âkota niya nikî-mônahaskwân, ê-ohci-nâkatohkêyân.

[22] ma kîkway pîsimôhkân, môy wiya kîkway *wrist-watch* êkospî. pîsimwa mân ê-kî-kitâpamât, mitoni mân ê-kî-kiskêyihtahk tânitahto-tipahikan. êkwa mân ê-kî-pê-kîwêyâhk mân êkwa, ê-kî-nitaw-âtâwâkêt anihi mînisîhkêsa, mitâtahto-pîwâpiskos pêyako-kosikwan ê-ohtisiyâhk. mîciwinis mân ê-kî-atâwêt êk-- êkota, mâk âyis êkospî kahkiyaw kîkway kî-wêhtakihtêw; miscahîs mâna kî-pêcikêsiw mâna, mîciwin ê-atâwêt. êkos ê-kî-itahkamikisiyâhk mâna, ê-kî-sôniyâhkâkêyâhk mînisîhkêsa. mâka wiya kîkway ayiwinisa ka-kî-atâwêstamâsohk, nama kîkway; têpiyâhk ka-mîcisohk.

[23] anohc êk ôma kâ-kîsikâk, kahkiyaw kîkway ê-mîcihk, kahkiyaw kîkway – ê-kî-tâpakwêt mâna, kisik ôm âkotê kâ-kî-mônahaskwêyâhk, ê-kî-tâpakwêt. wâposwa mâna kiyikaw êkotê ê-kî-nipahât; êkotê mâna nikî-pônênân ê-ma-mîcisoyâhk, wâpos ê-pakâsimâyâhk; nikî-nîmâsinân mâna, pahkwêsikan, sîwîhtâkan, *tea* ê-kî-tahkonamâhk, êkotê mâna ka-- ê-kî-ma-mîcisoyâhk mâna.

[24] mâka mân ânohc kâ-kîsikâk kâ-mâmitonêyihtamân, ê-kî-miyo-pimâcihoyâhk tâpiskôc, ê-itêyihtamân. osâm môy wîhkâc kîkway ê-ohci-masinahikêyan ohpimê; kîkway kâ-sôniyâhkêsiyan, êwako piko ê-kî-ohci-âpacihtâyan. môy tâpiskôc anohc, misiwê ê-pîkwasinahikêhk, pikw ît[a] ê-masinahikêyan anohc êkwa. mistahi pîtos anohc ispayiw.

IV [*Working for Cash*]

[21] And there was no way to earn money. We would dig seneca-root, we would walk long distances, with me carrying the baby on my back, and he would carry the diggers, and he carried a rope for a swing (I would make a swing, just the same [*sc.* as in the house] in the bush, and my little daughter would be swinging there and we dug seneca-root), but as for me, I would be digging right around there and watch her from there.

[22] There was no clock, there was no wrist-watch in those days. He would look at the sun and he would know exactly what time it was. And then we would come home, and he would go and sell that seneca-root, we got ten cents per pound for it. He would buy some food there, but in those days everything was cheap; he would bring back quite a bit when he bought food. That is what we used to do, we used to earn money with seneca-root. But as far as buying clothes for ourselves, that was impossible; just enough so one could eat.

[23] Today, you eat everything, everything – he would put up snares while we were digging seneca-root over there, he would put up snares. He would kill rabbits over there, along with the digging; we would make a fire over there and eat, boiling a rabbit; we would take things along for lunch, we carried bannock, salt and tea, and then we would eat over there.

[24] But when I think of it today, it seems we made a good life for ourselves, I think. For you never had debts anywhere else for anything; when you made some money, you only used that. Not like today, where one has debts all over, today you have debts everywhere. Things are very different today.

[25] êkwa mâna kâ-kî-- wiya wâskahikanihk, ma kîkway *electricity* ahpô cî kîkway, kîkway ôh ôho môniyâw-âpacihcikana, ê-kî-mâna-pimiy-tihkisamân [*sic*], ayiwinis mân ê-kî-pîmahamân, êwakw ân[i] ânima ê-kî-wâsaskotênikâkêyâhk, *our lamp* êwakw ân[i] ânima, ê-kî-ohci-wâsaskotawêpiyâhk. mihcêt êtikwê kêhte-ayak, ka-pêhtahkik ôma, wîstawâw êtikwê êkosi kî-pê-isi-pimâcihowak. nama kîkway wêpahikan, sakâhk mân ê-kî-nitawi-môsâhkinamân nîpisîsa, ê-kî-mâmaw--mâwasakwahpitamân, êkon ê-kî-wêpahikâkêyân. nama kîkway kisîpêkinikan, ê-kî-mosc-ôsîhiht kisîpêkinikan wiyin[wa] ôhci, *lye* ê-âpacihtâyan ê-osîhat kisîpêkinikan. kâ-kî-mân--ê-kisîpêkinikêyâhk, *'javex'* mâna kâ-kî-- wiy êtikwê kâ-kî-itamihk êwako, *ashes* mân ê-kî-pitikwahpitamâhk ni-- ayihk, ayiwinisisihk ê-kî-pakistawêhamâhk mân îta ka-- kâ-osamâhk ayiwinisa kîkwaya. ni-- tâpwê mâka mâna mêton ê-kî-kanâtahki, ê-kî--ê-kî-kanâcahciwâhtêki [*sic*]. kâ-kî-kisîpêkinihtakwêyâhk, pêyakwan êkotowa mân ê-kî-tahkopitamâhk, êkwa ê-osamâhk nipîhk, êkwa êwakw ân[i] ânima ê-kî-kisîpêkinihtakwâkêyâhk; maskosiya ê-kî-pitikwahpitamâhk, êwakw ânima mâna *scrubbing-brush* ê-kî-itâpacihtâyâhk.

[26] tâpwê mâna ê-kî-mam-- ê-kî---kî-kanâtahki mîna napakihtakwa, êkos ê-kî-itôtamihk. askiya mân ôhci ê-kî-pâhk---pâhkwahamâhk mâna, kâh-kisîpêkin--kâ-kisîpêkinihtakwêyâhk. êkwa ispî mân êkwa ê-kî-wêpahamâhk kâ-pâstêki, ê-mâwasakowêpahamâhk askiya. mitoni mân ê-kî-kanâtahk, ê-kî-wîhkimâkwahk mîna mân îyikohk ayi, wâskahikan; askiy[a] ânih îyikohk ê-kî-wîhkimâkwahki. wâsênamâna kâ-kisîpêkinaman êkoni mîna, askiy[a] ê-kî-âpacihtâhk êkosi, ê-kisîpêkinamihk wâsênamâwina.

[27] nikî-pê-wâpahtên kitimâkisiwin misakâmê, kâ-onâpêmiyân mîna iyikohk pêyakwan ê-kî-isi-kitimâkisiyân. piyis êkwa, ê-pôni-nôhâwasoyân êkwa, kâ-kî-aya---nitaw-âtoskêyân ôtênâhk, ê-nitaw-atoskêyân êkwa niya. pêyakwâpisk pêyak-kîsikâw kapê-kîsik ê-atoskêyân ê-tipahamâkawiyân, ê-kisîpêkinihtakwêyân, ê-mosci-kisîpêkinikêyân *washboard*. êkwa mân ê-kî-pê-acâwêsiyân

[25] And so far as the house was concerned, there was no electricity or any of these White-Man's appliances, I would melt down some grease and twist some rag, and that we used as our light, that was our lamp in our home. There must be many old people, when they hear this, who must have lived the same way, too. There was no broom, I would go and gather willows in the bush and tie them together in a bunch, and use them to sweep with. There was no soap, one simply made soap from fat, using lye when you made soap. When we would do the laundry, we would tie ashes in a bundle for what one might have called javex and put it into the water with the clothes and things when we boiled them. But the clothes would be very clean indeed, they would be clean from the boiling. When washing the floors, we would tie the same kind [*sc.* ashes] up in a piece of cloth and boil it in the water, and with that we would wash the floor; we would tie reeds in a bundle and use that as a scrubbing-brush.

[26] And the floor boards would be clean indeed when one did them in this way. We also would use moss to dry the floor after having washed it. And then we would sweep the moss up when it was dry, sweeping the moss together. It [*sc.* the floor] would be really clean, and the house also would smell so nice; the moss would smell so nice. When you washed the windows, one used to use moss again, in washing the windows.

[27] All along I have known poverty, and when I got married I also was just as poor. Finally, when I stopped breastfeeding the baby, that was when I went to work in town, then I for my part went to work. I was paid one dollar per day, working all day long, I was washing floors and doing the laundry with a washboard. And then I would buy a little food to

mîciwin, êkwa kâ-pê-- kâ-kîsi-tipahamâkawiyân tahto-kîsikâw, ê-kî-nitaw-âtoskawak awa môniyâskwêw. êwakw âwa kâ-kî-kiskinahamâkêt kwâkopîwi-sâkahikanihk, ôtê êkwa ê-pê-kiskinahamâkêt ôta paskwâwi-sâkahikanihk, êkot[a] êkwa niya kâ-kî-mâtatoskawak êkwa; kinwês nikî-atoskawâw. êkwa wîst êkwa ninâpêm êkwa, kâ-pîkopicikêt; nîso piko mistatimwa ê-âpacihât, *new breaking* ê-osîhtât, ê-kistikêt. êkwa tâpwê, piyis mâna ê-kî-wîcihak, âskaw; kîkway k-âtoskâtahk, iyi-- iyikohk ê-kî-kakwâtakatoskêt wîsta.

[28] mâk ê-kî-wîc-âyâmâyâhkwâw ôma nisikos ôma, êkospî môy nitipiyawêhowinân wâskahikan. kîtahtawê êkwa kâ-piskihci-wîkiyâhk, *log-house* êkwa ê-atâwêyân êkwa, ê-atâwêyahk, nikotwâsikomitanaw ê-tipahamâhk piko wâskahikan, *log-house*. ê-kî-wêpinitocik ôkik êkota kâ-kî-wîkicik, êkonik ê-atâmâyâhkwâw. êkos êkwa êkota ohc êkwa ninâpêm êkwa kâ-nitawi-pawahikêt mâna, ôta ôma ê-w-- paskwâwi-sâkahikanîhk; ê-cimacikêt, ê-otinahk mân âtoskêwin nikî-- ka-cimacikêt, nikî-wîcihâw mân ê-cimacikêyâhk. nimâci-sôniyâhkânân; nistam anim îta kâ-ispiciyâhk, môy âhpô kotawânâpisk nitayâwânân. êkotowa sêmâk atâwêw wiya, *cook-stove* atâwêw ôta ôtênâhk, *thirty-five* ê-tipahwât, miton ê-miyosit kotawânâpisk.

[29] êkos êkwa, kâ-mâc-êkwa-pâh-paskwatahamâhk êkwa, piyis ayiwâk êkw ê-ati-misâk êkwa ayi, nikistikâninân êkwa. cîkahikan ê-- ê-ohci-paskwatahamâhk ê-mâh-misikiticik mistikwak. ê-wîkatêtâpêt [*sic*] mistatimwa ohci wiya ninâpêm. êkwa ispî êkwa mân êkwa kâ-takwâkik êkwa, *cordwood* êkon ânihi mân ê-kî-mosci-kîskipotâyâhk; kayâs mâna ê-- kîskipocikana ê-ay-âpacihtâyâhk, kî-kinwâpêkanwa, *two handles* mâna *each side* kî-astêwa. êkon ânihi mân ê-kî-kîskipotâyâhk, *seventy-five cents a cord* ôtênâhk ê-ohtatâwâkêt ninâpêm; êkwa êkoni mîn êkwa ê-âwatât; ê-tâskatahahk, *bakery* ê-itohtatât ê-at-- ê-atâwâkêt. âskaw mâna nîswâw pêyak-kîsikâw ê-kî-itohtatât, *two cords* ê-kî-kîskipocikêt.

bring home, when I was paid at the end of each day, I used to work for a certain White-Woman. She was the one who had taught at *kwâkopîwi-sâkahikanihk*, then she had come over here to teach, here at *paskwâwi-sâkahikanihk*, that was when I for my part began working for her; I used to work for her for a long time. And my husband, too, he broke land; using only two horses, he was breaking new land and planting it. And finally I would indeed help him sometimes; when he worked at something, he, too, worked so terribly hard.

[28] But we used to live with my mother-in-law, at that time we did not have our own house. Then, after a time, we had a separate house, then I bought, we bought, a log-house, and we only paid sixty dollars for the house, a log-house. The people who had lived there split up, and we bought it from them. And then, from that time on, my husband would go harvesting, here at *paskwâwi-sâkahikanihk*; he would stoke, taking a contract for stoking, and I would help him with the stoking. We began to earn money; in the house to which we had first moved, we did not even have a stove. That kind he bought right away, he bought a cook-stove here in town [*sc.* Meadow Lake], paying thirty-five dollars for it, a very nice stove.

[29] So then, when we began clearing the land, finally our field was getting bigger. We cleared the land with an axe, and the trees were big. My husband pulled them away with the horses. And then, in the fall, we would cut the cordwood by hand; in those days we used to use long saws with two handles, one on each side. We would cut the cordwood, and my husband sold it in town for seventy-five cents a cord; and he would also haul it; he split it and took it to the bakery and sold it. Sometimes he would take two loads in one day, he would cut two cords.

V

[30] êkwa awâsisak âta êkwa ê-ati-ohpikihâyâhkwâw êkwa. kahkiyaw ê-kî-pê-nôhakik nicawâsimisak, pêyakosâp ê-- ê-ayâwakwâw, kahkiyaw ê-kî-nôhakwâw, môy niya nôh-tâpwêwakêyihtên ôkik kâ-- kâ-nônâcikêhâwasocik. manitow ê-kî-miyikoyahk mitôhtôsima ita ka-ohci-pimâcihâyahkik awâsisak; êwako niya nikî-pimitisahên. môy tâpiskôc anohc, ôkik êkwa kâ-- kâ-wî-- kâ-wî-nihtâwikihâcik awâsisa, âhkosîwikamikohk êkwa, nikah-- nama kîkway âhkosîwikamik niya, kahkiyaw nîkihk ê-kî-nihtâwikicik --

[*external break*]

---ayâsit [*?record*] awâsis, êwak ôhc ânohc kâ-kîsikâk, êtikwê ôkik wiyawâw, kâ-- kâ-- pâmwayês ka-nihtâwikiyit awâsisa, sâsay ê-kwayâci-nitonahkik piskihcikamikos, nipêwinis êkot[a] ê-astâcik, mîna nônâcikan, kahkiyaw kîkway môniyâwi-kîkway. kayâs kî-wa-wâspitâwak awâsisak, askiy[a] âsic ê-kîsowâspisocik, wiyawâw sôskwât ê-mosci-wêwêkinâcik, kâ-pîhcikwahâcik wîkiwâhk, êkos êkot[a] ânihi ê-pîhtikwêwêpinâcik anihi, ocawâsimisiwâw[a] ânima piskihcikamikos. kâ-mâtoyit, sâsay mosti-tôhtôsâpoy [*sic*], ê-asiwatâcik ê-mosci-miyâcik, môy tahkonâwasowak, môy kitimâkêyi--, êwak ôhc ânohc kâ-kîsikâk kâ-- iyikohk kâ-wêpinâcik ocawâsimisiwâwa. kayâs kî-tahkonâw awâsis ê-nônit, ê-wa-ocêmat, ê-ta-tahkonat, ê-ay-âpahwat; anohc môy êwakw ânima kîkway ispayiw. môy kâh-kî-- môy kâh-kî-itwêwak anikik, ôkik wiyawâw osk-âyak anohc kâ--, kâ-nihtâwikihâcik awâsisa, wiyawâw ka-ocawâsimisicik ka-itwêcik ocawâsimisiwâwa, moscoswa ê-pê-ohpikihtamâkocik anihi awâsisa; ayis mostos ana kâ-pimâcihât anihi awâsisa kâ-nihtâwikiyit.

[31] êwak ôhc anohc kâ-kîsikâk, mîna mistahi wêpinitowin k-êspayik; kayâs kî-- kiyât[a]-- îyikohk ê-pê-kitimâkisiyan, namôy wîhkâc kôhci-nakatâw kicawâsimis; kahkiyaw ê-kî-wawêyîhacik, itê kâ-itohtêyan ê-kî-itohtahacik; tâpiskô [*sic*] pâhpahâhkwânisisak ê-pimitisahoskik kicawâsimisak, âtiht ê-tahkonâwasoyan; kahkiyaw ê-sipwêhtahacik. anohc osk-âyak, nayêstaw, kotaka pikw îs

V [*Infant and Child Care*]

[30] And at the same time we were raising our children. I breastfed all of my children, I had eleven and I breastfed all of them, as for me, I did not believe in the practice of those who bottlefeed their children. God has given us breasts with which to give life to our children; as for me, I followed that. Not like today when those who are about to give birth to their children go to the hospital – there was no hospital for me, they were all born at home --

[*external break*]

-- a child, that is why today, for them at least, before the child is born, they already look for a separate room, they put a crib in it and also a bottle, all these White-Man's things. In the old days the children were swaddled in a mossbag, warmly swaddled up with the moss, but they now wrap them without anything, and when they bring them home, there they simply dump their baby into that nursery. When the baby cries, they immediately put cow's milk into a bottle and simply give that to the baby, they do not hold the child, they do not love--, that is the reason why they abandon their children so much today. In the old days the baby used to be held while suckling, you kissed it and held it and you unbundled it; today none of that happens. These young women who give birth to a child today, they could not claim to be the ones to have the child and to call it their child, the cows have raised the child for them; for the cows have given life to the child which has been born.

[31] That is the reason why today there is also a great deal of abandoning; in the old days, even though you were so poor, you would never leave your child behind; you got all of them ready and took them with you wherever you went; your little children followed you along like little chickens, while you carried some; you took all of

âyisiyiniw[a] ê-at[i]-îsi-kanawêyihtamôhâcik awâsisa, ê-- sôskwât tâpiskôt tânitahto-kîsikâw ê-nakatâcik ê-papâmi-minihkwêcik. kêhtê-aya kâ-wâpamat, sâsay ôsisima piko ka-pimi-wîcêwat; ê-wêpinamâht, kiyâm piko iyikohk kâ-kêhtê-ayiwit. tâpiskôt nîsta, nânitaw êtikwê niyânanosâp ê-pê-ohpikihakik, nôsisimak âtiht, âtiht kotakak awâsisak, wêpinikanak ê-kî-ohpikihtamâsoyân; êkwa niya pêyakosâp asic ê-ayâwakik awâsisak. kahkiyaw kîs-ôhpikiwak.

[32] êkwa nist--, nistam kâ-pê-nihtâwikit awâsis, "nâpêsis nihtâwikiw, iskwêsis nihtâwikiw," ê-kî-- kî-itwêwak mâna kêhtê-ayak kâ-pamihiskik kâ-nihtâ-- kâ-nihtâwikit awâsis. êkwa mâcik êwako mâk ê--, mayaw kâ-icahcopiponêsicik êkonik, ê-pê-nâpêwisîhiht nâpêsis, iskwêsis ê-kî-pê-iskwêwisîhiht, wiy ê-kî-nihtâwikit ê-iskwêsisiwit. anohc kâ-kîsikâk, nama kîkway êwakw ânima mîna kikî-wâpahtên, môy kinisitawêyimâw ahpô kîspin iskwêw ahpô nâpêw anohc. kahkiyaw ayisiyiniw ê-nâpêwisîhot, pêyakwan tâpiskôc nâpêw, ê-wan-- ê-wani-- ê-wanisîhot. âskaw kipisci-pîkiskwâtâw 'iskwêw' kâ-itêyimat, nâpêw kipîkiskwâtâw, wiy ê-wanisîhocik, môy kikiskêyihtên kîspin ê-nâpêwit ahpô ê-iskwêwit. kahkiyaw kîkway mistahi-pîtos kîkway anohc ispayiw.

[33] ahpô êtikwê mîna, tako mîna kiyânaw, ê-itôtamahk êkâ ê-- ê-pê-kakêskimâyahkwâw, kîkway ka-pê-wîhtamawâyahkwâw, tânis ôm ê-kî-pê-isi-- ê-kitimâkisihk, tânisi manitow k-êsi-pê-pakitiniwêt, ka-kî-isi---is-ôhpikihâwasoyahk; anohc awâsis kîkway pîhtaw mîna kâ-wî-wîhtamawat, *"oh, that's old-fashioned,"* kititikwak, ma kîkway kinitohtâkwak. kîkway kâ-kakwê-wîhtamawat, tânisi kayâs ê-kî-ispayik, kimosci-pâhpihikwak anohc kâ-kîsikâk; ê-sasîpihtahkik, ahpô âtiht kâ-onîkihikocik ê-wiyâhkwâtâcik onîkihikowâwa. môy wîhkât nôhci-pê-kiskêyihtên, ât[a] ânohc *seventy-five* ê-itahtopiponêyân, wîhkâc ka-kî-pê-naskwêwasimak nimâmâ, kâ-kî-oyôhtâwiyân; wiya nikî-pê-wîhtamâkonân nôhkominân, tânisi ka-kî-isi-pimâtisiyâhk. mistah âyamihâwin, nikî-pê-kiskinahamâkonân kâ-kî-oyôhkomiyâhk. mîna kinîkihikwak, ê-kî-wîc-âyamihâmacik pâmwayês ka-nipâyan, ê-kî-wîc-âyamihâmacik iyawis ê-kî-ayamihâcik, asici niyanân

them with you. The young people of today, all they do is to get just anyone to baby-sit the children, it seems as though they leave them for days and go about drinking. When you see an older person, she will always have her grandchildren along; they are just dumped on her, no matter how old she may be. Just like me, too, I must have raised about fifteen, some of them my grandchildren, some of them other children who had been abandoned and whom I have raised for myself; and in addition to the eleven children I had myself. They are all grown up.

[32] And when a child was newly born, they would announce it, "A little boy has been born, a little girl has been born," the old people who were your midwives when a child was born. And as soon as they were a little older, for instance, a little boy was dressed as a little boy, and a little girl was dressed as a little girl, for she was a little girl when she was born. Today, you also do not see any of that, today you cannot even distinguish between females and males. Everybody is dressed as a man, the women are dressed just as if they were men, wrongly dressed. Sometimes you accidentally speak to someone thinking she is a woman, and you have spoken to a man, for they are wrongly dressed, you do not know if it is a man or a woman. Everything is very different today.

[33] It might even be that we ourselves are also at fault for not counselling them, that we should have told them things, how life had been poor, how God had put man on this earth for us to be able to raise our children; today, of course, when you are going to tell a child anything, they tell you, "Oh, that's old-fashioned," and they do not listen to you at all. When you try to tell them something, how things used to be long ago, they simply laugh at you today; they have no obedience, even some of those who do have parents swear at them. I have never known that, although I am now seventy-five years old, that I would ever answer back to my mom and my late father; for our grandmother had told us how we should live. Our late grandmother had taught us a lot about religion. You also used to pray with your parents before you went to sleep, you used to pray

kahkiyaw ê-awâsisîwiyâhk, ê-ocihcihkwanapihikawiyâhk ê-ayamihâyâhk; ayamihêmina ê-kî-ayamihât nimâmâ, êkwa kî-- mâna nîstanân ê-kî-wîc-âyamihâmâyâhk. êwak ôhc êtikwê ahpô mistah âyisiyiniw kwayask kî-pê-isi-pimâtisiw, wiya mistahi kîkway ê-pê-kiskinahamâkêcik kayâs, kâ-onîkihikoyan.

VI

[34] anohc kahkiyaw – 'wâpiskiwiyâs' kâ-isiyîhkâsot, môniyâw, kahkiyaw misiwanâcihêw kitâyisiyinîminawa, kahkiyaw ôma môniyâwi-kîkway êkw anôhc ê-pim-- ê-otinikâtêk, ê-pê-wêpinahkwâw ôma kikayâsi-nêhiyâwininaw, tânisi kâ-kî-pê-isi-pakitinikowisiyahk ka-kî-pê-pimitisahamahk. anohc kahkiyaw kîkway minihkwêwin, kahkiyaw kîkway anohc; kayâs ma kîkway minihkwêwin ohc-îspayiw.

[35] mîna kâ-kî-kawisimoyan, kâ-kî-- kinîkihikwak kâ-wîc-âyâmacik, kikiki-kawisimon, môy wîhkât nânitaw kôhci-nîpâhtân, kikiki-waniskân kinîkihikwak, mitoni kwayask ê-pamihacik kinîkihikwak. anohc êkwa osk-âyak, nama kîkway mânacihêwak kêhtê-aya. â, pê-tako-kîskwêpêwak, êy, êy, pêtôpêwak, êkwa mîna konit êkwa kâ-kitohcikêcik, â, *T.V.* kî--, ma kîkway ka-manâ-koskoniskik ât[a] ê-kêhtê-ayiwiyan, kâ-kakwê-nipâyan, yâ! ka-tawinamwak ka-pîkiskwêwâk êkota wiyawâw. ma kîkway kayâs êwako ohci-pêhtâkwan, ma kîkway. pîhtaw ayis môy kîkway ohc-âyâniwan êkospî môniyâwi-kîkway, nanâtohk anohc ôho kahkiyaw kîkway, kâ-kitohcikêmakahki, kahkiyaw kîkway ê-ihtakok anohc.

[36] môniyâw êwako mîna kâ-kî-osîhtât minihkwêwin, mihcêt ayisiyiniwa anohc kâ-kîsikâk ê-kitimahât. kayâs môya kîkway êwakw ân[i] ânima ohc-îhtakon. oskinîkiskwêwak mihcêt anohc kâ-kîsikâk, kayâhtê piko kikiskawâwasowak minihkwêwin ohci, môniyâw-âyisiyiniw ka-minahêw, kiyâm êkâ kâ-wî-minihkwêyit, "â, pêyak kanakê minihkwê!" ka-itêw; pêyak kâ-kitâyit, "mîna pêyak." â, ispî kâ-takahkipahâcik, êkos ân[i] êkwa ê-sipwêhtahâcik ê-sipwêtâpêcik, kîkwây ânim ôhci kâ-minahâcik êkwa

with them and the whole household used to pray, all of us children included, we were made to kneel and we prayed; my mom used to say the rosary, and we, too, prayed along with her. That may even be the reason why people truly led a proper life, for they used to do a great deal of teaching in the old days, when you had parents.

VI [*The Modern Way and the Evils of Alcohol*]

[34] Today the White-Skin as he is called, the White-Man, has ruined everybody, all our people, today all the White things are chosen, and they have come to abandon our traditional Creeness, which we had been put on this earth to follow. Today everything revolves around alcohol, everything today; in the old days there had been no alcohol at all.

[35] Also when you went to bed, when you lived with your parents, you went to bed with them, you never stayed out late at night for any reason, and you got up with your parents, you very much treated your parents properly. Today the young people do not respect the old people at all. Well, they come home drunk, hey, hey, they bring liquor home, and then they also simply play the stereo, well, the T.V., there is no thought of not waking you up even though you are old, when you are trying to sleep, oh gosh! they will turn it on and they will also speak themselves. None of that used to be heard in the old days, there was none of it. For of course no one used to have this White stuff in those days, all the various music-blasters of today, all the stuff which exists today.

[36] Also by making that alcohol, the White-Man has brought misery upon many people today. In the old days there was none of that. Many young women today are prematurely pregnant because of alcohol, some White-Man will give them drink, even when they have no intention of drinking, "Well, just have one drink!" he will say to her; and when she has had one drink, "And another." Well, then, when they have made them 'feel good', then they take them away, they drive away with them, that is the reason why they gave

ê-nitawi-wayêsihâcik anima, âskaw ê-kawipahâcik. 'maci-manitowi-môtêyapisk' kâ-itamihk, mayaw kâ-tawinaman pêyak iskwêsisâpoy, âsay ê-tawinamawat êkota maci-manitow. kiminihkwân, êy, âpihtaw kâ-i-- kâ-i-- kâ-minihkwêyan, sâsay anim âkot[a] ôhci sôskwât ê-tipêyimisk maci-manitow, kisâkôcihik ayis sâsay. sôskwât -- sôskwât misiwanâcihêw kitôsk-âyiminawa, 'wâpiskiwiyâs' kâ-isiyîhkâsot.

[37] tânis êtikwê mân ê-itêyihtamân

[LD:] *– come in! –*

ôtê mwêstas, mwêstas at[i] ôtê nîkân tânisi k-êsi-kitimâkisicik awâsisak.

[EL:] ôt[a] âyâw *Freda?*

them drinks, now they go and take advantage of them, sometimes they give them booze until they pass out. 'The devil's bottle' as it is called, as soon as you open one beer, there already you open the door for the devil. You drink it, hey, and when you have drunk half of it, from that point on already the devil has you in his clutches for he has already overpowered you. He has completely ruined our young people, the White-Skin as he is called.

[37] How miserable, I tend to think,

[LD:] – Come in! –

are things yet to become later, there in the future, how miserable will the children be.

[EL:] Is Freda here?

[FA:] ᐁᑯᓯ ᐁᓴ ᑲ ᐋᒋᒧᓇᐤ, ᐊᓄᐦᐨ ᐊᐘ ᐁ ᐐ ᐋᒋᒧᐢᑖᑯᔭᕽ ᓂᑳᐑᐢ, ᓀᐦᐃᔭᐤ – Mrs Glecia Bear, Meadow Lake ᐅᐦᒋ.
ᐦᐋᐤ, ᑭᔭ, ᐋᒋᒧ.

I

[1] ᐊᔭ, ᐊᐘ ᐊᐘ ᓂᑑᓯᒥᐢᑵᑦ, Freda, ᐁ ᓂᑕᐍᔦᐦᑕᕽ ᓂᑲ ᑮᔮᐢᑭᐏᓇ. ᐁᑿ ᓂᑲ ᐋᒋᒧᑉ, ᓂᐢᑕᑦ ᐁ ᐯ ᐐᒋ ᐊᔮᒫᔮᐦᒁᐤ ᒣᒁᐨ ᓂᓃᑭᐦᐃᑯᓈᓇᐠ, ᑖᓂᓯ ᐁ ᑮ ᐯ ᐃᓯ ᑭᑎᒫᑭᓯᔮᕽ ᓂᑲ ᐋᑐᑌᑉ. ᑲᔮᐢ ᐊᔦᐢ ᑮ ᑭᑎᒫᑲᑉ.

[2] ᐊᔦ, ᐃᔦᑯᕽ ᐁ ᑮ ᑲᒁᑕᑲᑐᐢᑫᔮᕽ ᒫᓇ ᑲᔮᐢ, ᓈᓂᑕᐤ ᐁᑎᑵ thirteen ᓂᔭ ᐁ ᐃᑕᐦᑐᐱᐳᓀᔮᑉ, ᓵᓴᐩ ᓂᐹᐹ ᐁ ᑮ ᐐᒋᐦᐊᐠ ᐁ ᐸᑭᑕᐦᐚᐟ ᓵᑲᐦᐃᑲᓂᕽ. ᐁᑿ ᒫᓇ ᐁᑯᑌ ᐅᐦᒋ ᐁᑿ ᑭᓄᓴᐘᐠ ᐁ ᑮ ᐯᓯᐘᑭᐠ, Hudson's Bay Store ᐆᑕ ᐆᒪ Green Lake ᐁ ᐯ ᐊᑖᐚᑫᔮᑉ, ᒉᐢᑯᐨ ᑭᐢᑎᑳᑉ, ᑮᑿᐩ ᒦᒋᐏᓂᐢ ᐁᑯᑕ ᐅᐦᒋ ᐁ ᐊᑖᐌᐟ ᓂᐹᐹ, ᓃᑭᓈᕽ ᐋᑎᐦᐟ ᐁ ᐃᑐᐦᑕᑖᔮᑉ, ᐋᑎᐦᐟ ᓵᑲᐦᐃᑲᓂᕽ ᐃᑌ ᑳ ᐸᑭᑕᐦᐚᐟ. ᐁᑿ ᐃᐢᐲ ᒦᓇ ᐁᑿ, ᐊᑐᐢᑫᐏᑉ ᐁ ᑮ ᐊᔮᐟ mail ᐁ ᐱᒧᐦᑕᑖᐟ, Big River ᐅᐦᒋ ᐁᑿ ᐃᐢᑯ Ile-à-la-Crosse ᒫᓇ ᐁ ᑮ ᐱᒧᐦᑕᑖᐟ mail. ᐁᑿ ᐁᑯᑕ ᐊᓂᒪ ᐁᑿ ᐁ ᑮ ᓰᓂᔮᐦᑫᐟ, ᐋᑕ ᒫᑲ ᒨᔭ ᐁᑎᑵ ᒥᐢᑕᐦᐃ ᐁ ᐅᐦᒋ ᑎᐸᐦᐋᒫᐦᐟ. ᒫᓇ ᑳ ᑮ ᐯ ᑕᑯᐦᑌᐟ Big River ᐅᐦᒋ, ᒦᒋᐏᑉ ᒫᓇ ᐁ ᑮ ᐯᑖᐟ, ᐁᑿ ᐋᑎᐦᐟ ᐊᔦᐏᓂᓯᓴ ᑮᑿᐩ, rubbers ᐁᑯᓯ ᐃᓯ, ᐊᓯᑲᓇ ᐁ ᑮ ᐊᑖᐍᐢᑕᒫᑯᔮᕽ.

[3] ᐁᑿ ᐋᑕ ᐁ ᑮ ᐅᒧᐢᑐᓯᒥᓯᔮᕽ, ᐋᑕ ᒨᔭ ᒥᐦᒉᐟ ᒫᑲ, ᓈᓂᑕᐤ ᓂᑯᑤᓯᐠ ᒧᐢᑐᓴᐧ ᐁ ᑮ ᐊᔭᔮᐚᐟ, ᓂᔭᓈᑉ ᐁᑿ ᒫᓇ ᐁ ᐅᐢᑭᓃᑭᐢᑫᐏᓯᔮᕽ, ᐁ ᑮ ᐸᒥᐦᐋᔮᐦᒁᐤ ᒧᐢᑐᓴᐧᐠ. ᑲᐦᑭᔭᐤ ᑮᑿᐩ ᐁ ᑮ ᑑᑕᒫᕽ, ᐁ ᑮ ᐊᓯᐢᑮᐦᑳᑕᒫᕽ ᐚᐢᑲᐦᐃᑲᑉ ᒫᓇ, ᒥᐢᑕᑎᒧᑲᒥᐠ, ᐁ ᓂᑯᐦᑌᔮᕽ, ᓴᑳᕽ ᐁ ᐅᐦᒋ ᓂᑯᐦᑌᔮᕽ, ᐁ ᑮ ᐋᐘᒋᑖᐯᔮᕽ ᒫᓇ ᒥᐦᑕ, ᐅᓵᑦ ᓂᐹᐹ ᐯᔭᑯ ᐊᔭ ᐱᑯ ᒥᐢᑕᑎᒷ ᐁ ᑮ ᐊᔮᐚᐟ, ᐁ ᓯᐍᐦᑕᐦᐋᐟ.

[4] ᐁᑿ ᐏᔭ ᓂᒪᒫ ᒫᓇ ᐏᔭ ᐁ ᑮ ᓂᑕᐏ ᐊᑯᑖᐟ ᑖᐸᒁᓇ, ᐚᐳᓴᐧ ᐁ ᑮ ᓂᐸᐦᐋᐟ ᐁ ᐑ ᑲᑵ ᐊᓴᒥᑯᔮᕽ ᐏᔭ, ᐏᔭ ᐋᐢᑲᐤ ᑮᑿᐩ ᐁᑯᓯ ᐃᓯ ᐁ ᑮ ᓂᑕᐏ ᓂᐸᐦᑖᐟ ᐊᐦᐳ ᒫᓇ ᐱᐦᐁᐘ ᐁ ᑮ ᓂᑕᐏ ᐹᐦ ᐹᐢᑭᓵᐧᐟ ᓴᑳᕽ ᒫᓇ ᓂᒪᒫ. ᐁᑿ ᐁ ᑮ ᑭᐢᑭᓇᐦᐊᒫᓯᔮᕽ, ᐃᐢᑰ≤ ᓂᐢᑕᑦ ᐁ ᐃᐦᑕᑯᐠ, ᓵᓴᐩ ᐊᓂᒪ ᓂᔭ ᓈᓂᑕᐤ ᐁᑎᑵ nine ᐁᑎᑵ ᐁ ᐃᑕᐦᑐᐱᐳᓀᔮᑉ, ᐃᐢᑰ≤ ᐁᑯᑕ ᑳ ᐯ ᐅᓰᐦᑖᕽ, log-school, ᐁ ᑭᐢᑭᓇᐦᐊᒫᓯᔮᕽ. ᐁᑿ ᐁᑯᑌ ᒫᓇ ᐁᑿ ᑳ ᓃᐱᕽ ᒫᓇ ᐁ ᑮ ᓵᓴᑭᐦᑎᔮᑉ, ᐋᑕ ᓵᓴᐩ ᐁ ᐅᐢᑭᓃᑭᐢᑫᐏᔮᑉ, ᐊᑎ ᐁ ᑮ ᓵᓴᑭᐦᑎᔮᕽ ᒫᓇ. ᑳ ᑮ ᓃᒫᔮᕽ, ᓇᔦᐢᑕᐤ ᐸᐦᑵᓯᑲᑉ, ᐁᑿ tallow ᒫᓇ ᑮ ᐃᒋᑳᑌᐤ ᐱᒥᐩ, ᑮ ᒪᐢᑲᐚᐤ ᐱᒥᐩ, ᐁᐘᑯ ᐊᓂ ᐊᓂᒪ ᒫᓇ ᐊᓯᒋ ᐁ ᑮ ᐸᐦᑵᐦᐊᕽ ᓂᒪᒫ ᐁ ᑮ ᓃᒪᐦᐃᑯᔮᕽ. ᐋᐢᑲᐤ ᒫᓇ ᓲᑳᓴ ᐁ ᑮ ᐲᐌᓈᐟ ᒫᓇ, ᓂᐸᐦᑵᓯᑲᓂᓈᕽ.

[5] ᐊᓄᐦᐨ ᑳᑮᓯᑳᐠ, ᐁᑲᐧ ᐆᒪᔨᑯᕽ ᐁ ᒥᔪ ᐊᔮᒋᐠ ᐊᐋᐧᓯᓴᐠ, ᐁᐩ, ᓵᐢᑳᐧᐨ ᐱᑯ ᑲᑭᐸᐧᐢᑭᓄᔨᐠ ᐁᑲᐧ ᐅᓃᒫᐃᐧᐊᐧᑎᐋᐧᐤ ᐃᐧᔭᐋᐧᐤ, ᐁ ᐋᑕᐁᐧᔨᐦᒋᑫᒋᐠ ᐋᐦᒋ ᐱᑯ. ᑲᐧᔭᐢᐠ ᐁ ᐳᐦᑕᔨᐃᐧᓂᓴᒋᐠ, ᐁᑲᐧ ᒦᓇ ᐁ ᓂᐸᐦᐃᑲᓄᒋᐠ ᐊᓄᐦᐨ ᐊᐋᐧᓯᓴᐠ. ᓂᔮᓈᐣ, ᓇᒪ ᑮᑲᐧᐩ ᐁᐊᐧᑯ ᐊᓂᒪ, ᓂᑮ ᐯ ᑲᑳᐧᑕᑲᑐᐢᑳᓈᐣ ᒥᓴᑳᒣ, ᒥᐦᑕ ᐁ ᐲᐦᑎᑲᐧᑖᔮᕽ, ᐁ ᐋᐊᐧᑑᐯᔮᕽ, ᓂᐱᐩ ᐁ ᑲᐧᔮᒋ ᐊᐢᑖᔮᕽ ᓃᑭᓈᕽ. ᐊᓄᐦᐨ ᐊᐋᐧᓯᐢ ᒨᔭ ᐊᐦᐴ ᐁᑲᐧ ᑲᐢᑭᐦᑖᐤ ᒥᐦᑕ ᑲ ᐲᐦᑎᑲᐧᑖᐟ, ᑲᐴᓇᕽ, ᓇᒪ ᑮᑲᐧᐩ ᑲᐢᑭᐦᑖᐊᐧᐠ, ᐃᐧᔭ ᐁ ᒨᓂᔮᐃᐧ ᐅᐦᐱᑭᒋᐠ. ᑲᐦᑭᔭᐤ ᑮᑲᐧᐩ ᐁᑲᐧ ᐊᓄᐦᐨ, ᒨᓂᔮᐤ ᐁ ᒥᓯᐊᐧᓈᒋᐦᑖᐟ, ᑲᔮᐢ ᑳ ᑮ ᐃᓯ ᐯ ᐱᒫᒋᐦᐅᕽ.

[6] ᐁᑲᐧ ᑳ ᑮ ᐅᔫᐦᑯᒥᔮᕽ, ᓅᐦᑯᑦ, ᑲᐦᑭᔭᐤ ᑮᑲᐧᐩ ᐁ ᑮ ᐯ ᑲᑫᐢᑭᒥᑯᔮᕽ ᐁ ᑮ ᐯ ᐄᐧᐦᑕᒫᑯᔮᕽ ᑮᑲᐧᐩ, ᑮᑲᐧᐩ ᐁᑳ ᑲ ᑮ ᑑᑕᒫᕽ, ᑲᐦᑭᔭᐤ ᑮᑲᐧᐩ ᓂᑮ ᐯ ᐄᐧᐦᑕᒫᑯᓈᐣ, ᐁᑳ ᑲ ᐲᐁᐧᒫᔮᐦᑳᐧᐤ ᑫᐦᑌ ᐊᔭᐠ. ᑳ ᐯ ᐲᐦᑎᑫᐧᐟ ᐊᔨᓯᔨᓂᐤ, ᓴᒫᐠ ᑲ ᓰᑭᓇᒪᐋᐧᔮᕽ tea, ᑲᒥᓇᐦᐋᔮᕽ, ᐁ ᑮ ᐃᓯ ᐄᐧᐦᑕᒫᑲᐃᐧᔮᕽ, ᑫᔮᐱᐨ ᐊᓄᐦᐨ ᑳᑮᓯᑳᐠ ᐁᐊᐧᑯ ᐊᓂᒪ ᓂᔭ ᓂᐱᒥᑎᓴᐦᐁᐣ.

[7] ᐁᑲᐧ ᐊᔨᕽ, ᒫᓇ ᓂᒫᒫ, gunny-sacks ᒫᓇ ᐁ ᑮ ᑲᐢᑭᑳᐧᑕᕽ, ᐁᑯᑕ ᒫᓇ ᐁᑲᐧ ᐁ ᑮ ᓂᑕᐃᐧ ᐊᓯᐊᐧᑖᔮᕽ ᒫᓇ ᒪᐢᑯᓯᔭ, ᐁᐊᐧᑯ ᐊᓂ ᐊᓂᒪ ᐁ ᑮ ᐊᐢᐱᓯᒧᔮᕽ, our mattress ᐁᐊᐧᑯ. ᐁᑲᐧ canvas ᐁᑲᐧ ᒫᓇ, ᐁᑲᐧ ᑕᐦᑯᐦᐨ ᐁ ᑮ ᐊᐢᑖᔮᕽ ᐁᐊᐧᑯ, that's our sheet ᐁᐊᐧᑯ ᐊᓂ ᐊᓂᒪ. ᓇᒪ ᑮᑲᐧᐩ ᐄᐧᐦᑳᐨ ᐊᐢᐱᐢᑫᐧᓯᒧᐣ ᐃᐧᔭ ᓅᐦᒋ ᐋᐸᒋᐦᑖᓈᐣ, ᐁ ᑮ ᒥᓴᐦᑖᐟ ᒫᓇ ᐊᓂᒪ, ᐊᓂᒪ ᑲ ᒫᒪᐅᐧᑳᐧᑕᕽ, ᓈᓂᑕᐤ ᐁᑎᑫᐧ ᒫᓇ ᓂᔮᓇᐣ ᐁ ᑮ ᐃᐦᑕᓯᔮᕽ ᐁ ᑮ ᓂᐹᔮᕽ ᐊᓂᒪ, ᐁ ᒫᒪᐃᐧᐦᑳᐧᒥᔮᕽ ᒫᓇ ᐊᐋᐧᓯᓴᐠ. ᐊᓄᐦᐨ ᐊᐋᐧᓯᐢ, ᒨᔭ ᑮᑲᐧᐩ ᑭᐢᑫᔨᐦᑕᑦ ᐁᐊᐧᑯ ᐊᓂ ᐊᓂᒪ, ᑖᓂᓯ ᐁ ᑮ ᐯ ᐃᓯ ᑭᑎᒫᑭᓯᕽ, ᐯᔭᑲᐧᐣ ᐊᓄᐦᐨ ᑭᐦᒋ ᐅᑭᒫᐊᐧᐠ ᐃᑕ ᑳ ᐄᐧ ᓂᐹᒋᐠ, ᐱᑯ ᑲ ᐋᐧᐱᐢᑭ ᐊᓈᐢᑳᑎᐦᒋᐠ, ᑲ ᑲᓈᑕᕽ ᐃᑕ ᑲ ᓂᐹᒋᐠ ᐊᓄᐦᐨ ᐊᐋᐧᓯᓴᐠ.

[8] ᐁᑲᐧ ᓂᐹᐹ, ᑳ ᑮ ᒥᓇᐦᐅᐟ ᒫᓇ, ᑳ ᑮ ᓂᐸᐦᑖᐟ ᐃᐧᔮᐢ, ᓂᒫᒫ ᒫᓇ ᐁ ᑮ ᐹᓂᓵᐁᐧᐟ, ᐁᑲᐧ, ᐊᓂᒪ ᐁᑲᐧ, ᐃᐧᔮᐢ ᐊᓂᒪ, fresh meat ᐊᓂᒪ ᒫᓇ ᐁᑲᐧ ᑳ ᓂᑕᐁᐧᔨᐦᑕᒫᕽ – ᒪᐢᑫᑯᕽ ᒫᓇ ᐁ ᑮ ᓂᑕᐃᐧ ᐋᐧᑎᐦᑫᐧᐟ ᓂᐹᐹ, ᐁᑯᑌ ᒫᓇ ᐁᑲᐧ ᓂᒫᒫ ᐁ ᑮ ᐊᓯᐊᐧᑖᐟ flour-bags ᐊᓂᐦᐃ – ᐃᐧᔮᐢ, ᐁᑲᐧ ᐃᐢᐲ ᐁᑲᐧ gunny-sack ᐁ ᐊᐢᑖᐟ, ᐁᑯᑌ ᒫᓇ ᐁᑲᐧ ᐁᐊᐧᑯ ᐊᓂ ᐊᓂᒪ ᐃᐧᔮᐢ ᐁ ᑮ ᓂᑕᐃᐧ ᐊᐢᑌᐠ, ᐃᐧᔭ ᐁᑳ ᑮᑲᐧᐩ ᑳ ᐋᐦᑲᐧᑎᕽ ᐃᑕ ᑮᑲᐧᐩ ᐁ ᐅᐦᒋ ᐃᐦᑕᑯᐠ, ᒨᔭ ᐅᐦᒋ ᑭᐢᑫᔨᐦᑖᑲᐧᐣ fridge ᑮᑲᐧᐩ ᐊᓂᒪ, deep-freeze ᐊᐦᐴ. ᐁᑲᐧ ᒫᓇ ᑳ ᑮ ᓈᑕᒫᕽ ᐁᑲᐧ ᓴᑳᕽ ᐁᑲᐧ ᐃᐧᔮᐢ, ᓂᒫᒫ ᑳ ᑮ ᐄᐧ ᑮᓯᓴᕽ, ᓵᐢᑳᐧᐨ they are fresh, ᓵᐢᑳᐧᐨ ᐃᔨᑯᕽ ᐁ ᒥᔮᐧᓯᐠ ᐃᐧᔮᐢ, ᒪ ᑮᑲᐧᐩ ᑲᒥᓯᐊᐧᓈᑕᕽ, ᐃᔨᑯᕽ ᐁ ᑮ ᒥᔮᐧᓯᐠ.

[9] ᐋᐧᐄᐧᐢ ᒌ, ᐊᐧᔭᐄᐧᐃᐧᑲᒥᑲᐧ, ᒨᔭ ᑮᑲᐧᐩ ᐅᐦᒋ ᑭᐢᑫᔨᐦᑖᑲᐧᐣ ᑮᑲᐧᐩ ᐁᐊᐧᑯ ᐊᓂ ᐊᓂᒪ, ᐊᓄᐦᐨ ᐁᑲᐧ ᐆᐦᐅ ᑲᐦᑭᔭᐤ ᑮᑲᐧᐩ ᑳ ᐋᐸᑕᕽ, ᒪ ᑮᑲᐧᐩ ᐅᐦᒋ ᐃᐦᑕᑲᐧᐣ ᑮᑲᐧᐩ

ᐁᑯᑐᐘ, ᐱᑯ ᐃᑕ ᓰᐢᒁᐟ ᐁ ᑮ ᓴᐢᑭᓯᔭᐣ, ᐁᑯᑕ ᐁ ᑮ ᓂᑕᐏ ᑭᐦᒋ ᐘᔭᐑᔭᐣ, ᒪ ᑮᑿᕀ ᐁ ᐅᐦᒋ ᐃᐦᑕᑯᐠ. ᑖᓂᓯ ᐁᑎᑵ ᒫᓇ, ᐊᓅᐦᐨ ᐁᑿ ᒫᓇ ᐁ ᐃᑌᔨᐦᑕᒫᐣ ᒫᓇ, ᒨᔭ ᐑᐦᑳᐨ ᐁ ᐅᐦᒋ ᑭᐢᑫᔨᐦᑕᒫᐣ ᑮᑿᕀ, ᑭᒥᓵᐦᐅᐏᐣ ᑲ ᑮ ᐯ ᐚᐸᒋᐦᑖᕽ, ᐁᑯᓯ ᐁᑎᑵ ᐱᑯ ᐁ ᑮ ᐃᓯ ᒪ ᒣᔨᐏᒋᐢᑫᕽ ᐁ ᑮ ᐃᓯ ᐸᓯᑰᕽ.

II

[10] ᐁᑿ ᐁᑿ, ᐱᔨᐢ ᐁᑿ ᑳ ᐅᓈᐯᒥᔮᐣ ᐁᑿ, ᓂᐹᐹ ᐁ ᑮ ᓂᑕᐏ ᐸᐘᐦᐃᑫᐟ, ᐋ, ᓵᓴᕀ ᐁᑿ sixteen ᐁ ᐃᑕᐦᑐᐱᐳᓀᔮᐣ, ᐁᑿ ᓂᐹᐹ ᐁᑿ ᐊᓂᒪ ᑳ ᓂᑕᐏ ᐸᐘᐦᐃᑫᐟ ᐆᑌ Battleford, ᒥᐢᑕᑎᒷ ᐁ ᐋᐸᒋᐦᐋᐟ. ᐁᑯᑌ ᐁᑎᑵ ᐁᑿ ᐁᑿ ᑳ ᓇᑭᐢᑲᐚᐟ ᐁᑿ ᐆᐦᐅ, ᐊᐘ ᑳ ᑮ ᐑᑭᒪᐠ ᓈᐯᐤ ᐊᐘ (ᒪᒐᐚᓯᐢ ᑮ ᐃᓯᔩᐦᑳᓱᐤ ᑳ ᑮ ᐅᓯᓯᔮᐣ), ᐁᑎᑵ ᐁᑯᑌ ᐁᑿ ᐊᐘ ᓂᐹᐹ ᑳ ᒣᑭᐢᑵᐍᐟ ᓂᔭ. ᒨᔭ ᐆᒪ ᐊᐦᐴ ᐁ ᓂᓯᑕᐍᔨᒪᐠ ᐊᐘ ᓈᐯᐤ, ᑳ ᐑᑭᐦᑕᐦᐃᑲᐏᔮᐣ. ᑿᔭᐢ ᓂᑮ ᒫᑐᐣ ᐃᐢᐲ ᓂᒫᒫ ᐁ ᐑᐦᑕᒪᐏᐟ, «ᑳ ᐑᑭᐦᑐᔦᐠ, ᐁ ᑮ ᐃᔩᐦᒋᑫᐟ ᑭᐹᐹ,» ᐁ ᐃᑘᐟ, ᐁ ᐯ ᑕᑯᐸᔨᐟ ᓂᐹᐹ. ᓀᑌ ᑲ ᑌᑆᑎᑲᐏᔮᕽ ᐁ ᐊᔭᒥᐦᐁᐏᑮᓯᑳᐠ, ᑿᔭᐢ ᓂᑮ ᒫᑐᐣ, ᐁᑳ ᐁ ᓂᓯᑕᐍᔨᒪᐠ ᐊᐘ ᐊᐏᔭᐠ ᑳ ᒥᔨᐦᐟ ᓂᔭ, ᑲ ᐑᑭᒪᐠ.

[11] ᐁᑿ ᐊᓂ ᐁᑿ ᑳ ᐑᑭᐦᑐᔮᕽ ᐁᑿ. ᐁᕀ, ᐁᕀ, ᓂᑮ ᓀᐯᐏᓰᐢᑕᐚᐤ, ᒦᓇ ᐊᓂᑭᐠ ᑳ ᐅᓯᑯᓯᔮᐣ, ᓇᒪ ᑮᑿᕀ ᐁ ᓂᓯᑕᐍᔨᒪᑭᐠ, ᐁᑿᔮᐨ ᐁᑯᑕ ᐁ ᐚᐸᒪᒁᐤ ᐊᓂᒪ ᑳ ᐯ ᑕᑯᐦᑌᒋᐠ ᑳ ᐑ ᐑᑭᐦᑐᔮᕽ. ᒨᔭ ᓅᐦᒋ ᑲᐢᑭᐦᐃᑲᐏᐣ ᐊᐦᐴ, ᒦᒋᓱᐏᓈᐦᑎᑯᕽ ᑲ ᓂᑕᐏ ᐑᒋ ᒦᒋᓱᒪᐠ ᐊᐘ ᑳ ᐅᓈᐯᒥᔮᐣ, ᐃᔨᑯᕽ ᐁ ᐸᒁᑕᒫᐣ ᐁ ᒫᑐᔮᐣ, ᓀᑌ ᒥᐢᑕᑎᒧᑲᒥᑯᕽ ᐁᑿ ᐁ ᓂᑕᐏ ᒪ ᒫᑐᔮᐣ. ᑫᑕᐦᑕᐍ ᐊᐘ ᐯᔭᐠ ᒨᓂᔮᐢᑵᐤ ᐁᑯᑌ ᑳ ᐯ ᓈᓯᐟ (ᒫᑲ ᐁ ᑮ ᑭᐢᑭᓇᐦᐋᒫᑫᔨᐟ ᐅᓈᐯᒪ ᑭᐢᑭᓇᐦᐋᒫᑐᐏᑲᒥᑯᕽ ᒁᑯᐲᐏ ᓵᑲᐦᐃᑲᓂᕽ), ᐁ ᐯ ᐲᑭᐢᒁᓯᐟ ᑲ ᐯ ᒦᒋᓱᔮᐣ, ᓂᐯ ᐊᐱᐣ ᒦᒋᓱᐏᓈᐦᑎᑯᕽ, ᒫᑲ ᑭᓯᐠ ᐁ ᒫᑐᔮᐣ, ᒨᔭ ᐊᐦᐴ ᓅᐦᒋ ᑲᐢᑭᐦᑖᐣ ᑲ ᒦᒋᓱᔮᐣ.

[12] ᒨᔭ ᓅᐦᒋ ᑲᐢᑭᐦᐃᑲᐏᐣ ᐊᐦᐴ ᑲ ᐯ ᑮᐍᔮᐣ ᐆᑌ ᐃᓯ ᐆᒪ ᐸᐢᒁᐏ ᓵᑲᐦᐃᑲᓂᕽ, ᐯᔭᐠ ᐲᓯᒼ ᐁᑯᑌ ᐁ ᑮ ᑭᓵᑕᒫᐣ ᓃᑭᓈᕽ, ᐁᑳ ᐁ ᑲᐢᑭᐦᐃᑲᐏᔮᐣ ᑲ ᐯ ᐃᑐᐦᑌᔮᐣ ᐊᓂᒪ ᐃᑌ ᑳ ᐑᑭᒋᐠ. ᐁᑿ ᐊᓂ ᑖᐦ ᑖᐻ ᐁᑿ ᐁᑯᑌ ᐁᓴ ᐊᔨᐚᐠ ᐁ ᑭᑎᒫᑲᕽ ᐃᑕ ᑳ ᐯ ᐃᑐᐦᑌᔮᐣ. ᑖᐱᐢᑰᐨ, ᐊᓅᐦᐨ ᐁᑿ ᐆᐦᐅ ᒥᐢᑕᑎᒧᑲᒥᑿ ᐁ ᒥᔼᓯᑭ ᐃᑕ ᑳ ᑮ ᐲᐦᑎᑿᐦᐃᑲᐏᔮᐣ, ᓇᐸᑭᑲᒥᐠ, ᒥᓯᐍ ᓰᐢᒁᐨ ᐊᓯᐢᑭᕀ ᐁ ᐊᐸᐦᒁᑌᐠ ᒪᐢᑯᓯᔭ ᐊᓯᒋ, ᐁ ᒥᒋᒧᐢᑯᐚᐦᑌᐠ, ᐁ ᑮ ᒐᐸᐦᒑᓯᐠ, ᐚᓭᓇᒫᐏᓇ ᓃᓯ ᐁ ᐃᐦᑕᑯᑭ, ᒫᑲ ᒪᐢᑭᒧᑌᑭᓇᐧ ᐅᐦᒋ ᐚᓭᓇᒫᐏᓇ ᐁ ᑮ ᐊᐢᑌᑭ. ᐁᑿ ᑖᐦ ᑖᐻ ᓂᑮ ᑲᒁᐦᔭᑫᔨᐦᑌᐣ ᐁᑯᑕ, ᑫᔨᐍᕽ ᓂᔭᓈᐣ ᑮ ᒥᔼᓯᐣ ᐃᑕ ᐁ ᑮ ᐊᓯᐘᓱᔮᕽ, ᐋᑕ ᐏᔭ log-house, ᒫᑲ ᑮ ᒥᔼᓯᐣ, ᑿᔭᐢ ᐁ ᑮ ᐅᔩᐦᒋᑳᑌᐠ, ᐚᓭᓇᒫᐏᓇ ᐁ ᑮ ᑭᑲᒧᑭ ᐃᑕ ᑳ ᑮ ᐑᑭᔮᕽ.

[13] ᐁᑲᐧ ᐊᓂ ᐁᑲᐧ, ᐃᑕ ᑲ ᑲᐃᐧᓯᒨᔮᕽ ᓂᐯᐃᐧᐣ ᐊᓂᒪ – ᒐᐦ, ᑲᓂ ᑖᐯᐧ ᐆᒪ, ᓂᐢᑕᒼ ᐁᑲᐧ, ᒨᔭ ᐁᑳ ᐁ ᑲᐢᑭᐦᐃᑲᐃᐧᔮᐣ ᑲ ᐯ ᐃᑐᐦᑌᔮᐣ, ᓂᐯ ᓈᑎᐠ ᐊᐊᐧ ᐆᑕ my uncle, 'Charlie Laliberté' ᐁ ᑮ ᐃᓯᔩᐦᑳᓱᐟ, « ᐱᑯ ᑲ ᐯ ᑮᐁᐧᔮᐣ, ᑭᑮ ᐅᓈᐯᒥᐣ, ᐱᑯ ᑲ ᐯ ᑮᐁᐧᑐᑕᐊᐧᐟ ᑭᓈᐯᒼ, ᑭᑮ ᑭᐦᒋ ᐄᐧᑭᒫᐤ, ᐱᑯ ᑲ ᐯ ᑮᐁᐧᔭᐣ,» ᓂᑎᑎᐠ. ᐁᑲᐧ ᐊᓂ ᐁᑲᐧ, ᒨᔭ ᓂᑲᐢᑭᐦᐃᐠ, ᐱᔨᐢ ᐁᑲᐧ, my uncle Payette ᐁᑲᐧ, ᑳ ᐃᓯᐟ ᐁᑲᐧ ᓂᐢᑌᐢ ᐅᐢᑌᓯᒫᐤ, « ᑲ ᐄᐧᑫᑎᓈᐣ ᐃᐢᑯ ᑲ ᓇᑲᔮᐢᑲᐊᐧᒋᐠ ᐊᓂᑭᐠ ᐊᔨᓯᔨᓂᐊᐧᐠ, ᐁᑯᑕ ᓂᑲ ᐯ ᑮᐋᐧᓈᐣ,» ᓂᑎᑎᑲᐧᐠ. ᑖᐯᐧ ᐁᑲᐧ ᑳ ᐯ ᐄᐧᑫᐋᐧᔮᕽ ᐁᐊᐧᑯ ᐊᐊᐧ ᑳ ᐯ ᓈᓯᐟ ᐁᑲᐧ. ᐁᐩ, ᐁᐩ, ᐋᔨᒪᐣ, ᐊᔨᓯᔨᓂᐤ ᐁᑯᓯ (ᑳ ᐄᐧᑭᐦᑕᐦᐃᐦᐟ ᐁᑯᓯ ᐃᓯ) ᐁᑳᐃᐧᔭ ᐃᓯ ᑳ ᓂᓯᑕᐁᐧᔨᒫᐟ, ᐁ ᓀᐯᐃᐧᓯᔮᐣ, ᓲᐢᑳᐧᐟ ᓇᒨᔭ ᓅᐦᒋ ᑭᐢᑫᔨᐦᑌᐣ ᑖᓂᓯ ᑲ ᑮ ᐃᑑᑕᒫᐣ, ᓇᓴᐢᑕᐤ ᐁ ᑮ ᒫᑐᔮᐣ ᒫᓇ.

[14] ᐁᑲᐧ ᐊᓂ ᐁᑲᐧ, « ᐁᑯᑕ ᐁᑲᐧ ᑭᔭᐋᐧᐤ ᑲ ᓂᐹᔭᐠ,» ᐁ ᐃᓯᐟ ᐊᐊᐧ ᑳ ᐅᓯᑯᓯᔮᐣ, ᐁᑲᐧ ᐁᑲᐧ ᐁᑯᑕ ᓂᓂᑕᐃᐧ ᓂᐹᐣ ᐁᑲᐧ. ᐁᐩ, ᒦᑭ ᓂᓈᐯᒼ ᑳ ᐄᐧ ᐯ ᐃᑎᓯᕽ ᒫᓇ ᐁ ᑕᐦᑭᐢᑲᐊᐧᐠ ᐁ ᐄᐧᑲᑌᐁᐧᐱᓇᐠ, ᐃᐧᔭ ᐁᑳ ᐁ ᓂᓯᑕᐁᐧᔨᒪᐠ. ᔩᑎ ᐆᒪ ᒦᓇ ᐁᐊᐧᑯ ᐊᓂ ᐊᓂᒪ ᐊᐢᐱᓯᒧᐃᐧᐣ, ᒨᓯᐲᐊᐧᔭ ᐅᐦᒋ ᐁᓴ ᐁ ᑮ ᐅᓰᐦᑖᕽ, ᐊᐢᐱᐢᑫᐧᓯᒧᓇ ᒨᓯᐲᐊᐧᔭ ᐅᐦᒋ, ᒥᐢᑎᑯᓂᐯᐃᐧᐣ ᐁ ᑮ ᐅᓰᐦᑖᕽ, ᐁᑯᑕ ᐊᓂᒪ ᐁ ᑮ ᐅᓂᐯᐃᐧᓂᔮᕽ, ᐯᔭᐠ ᐱᑯ ᐊᑯᐦ ᒦᓇ ᐁ ᑮ ᐃᐦᑕᑯᐠ, ᑲᔮᐢ Hudson's-Bay-blanket, green ᐁ ᐃᓯᓈᑲᐧᕽ ᓀᑌ ᐁ ᑲᐢᑭᑌᐊᐧᓯᓈᐢᑌᐠ, ᐁ ᐋᐧᐹᐢᑌᐠ, ᐁᑎᑫᐧ ᐁ ᑮ ᑭᓰᐯᑭᓂᑲᑌᐠ, ᓇᐊᐧᐟ ᐱᑯ ᐁ ᑮ ᐅᒋᐹᐧᐹᐁᐧᐠ, ᐁᐊᐧᑯ ᐊᓂᒪ ᐊᑲᐧᓇᐦᐅᐣ ᐁ ᑮ ᐊᔮᔭᕽ.

[15] ᐁᐩ, ᐁᑲᐧ ᑫᑕᐦᑕᐁᐧ ᐁᑲᐧ, ᑳ ᐊᔮᐊᐧᐠ ᐁᑲᐧ, ᐊᔭ, ᑳ ᑭᑭᐢᑲᐋᐧᐊᐧᓱᔮᐣ ᐁᑲᐧ (ᐋ, ᓇᒪ ᑮᑲᐧᐩ ᓅᐦ ᑭᐢᑫᔨᐦᑌᐣ, ᑲᔮᐢ ᐃᔨᑯᕽ ᑫᐦᑌᐊᔭᐠ ᐁ ᑮ ᑲᓇᐁᐧᔨᒥᐁᐧᒋᐠ, ᒨᔭ ᐄᐧᐦᑳ-ᓈᓂᑕᐤ ᑰᐦᒋ ᐃᑐᐦᑖᐣ), ᑮᑕᐦᑕᐁᐧ ᐁᑲᐧ, « ᑖᓂᓯ ᐁᑎᑫᐧ ᐆᒪ ᐁ ᐃᓯ ᐊᔮᔮᐣ,» ᐁᑲᐧ ᑳ ᐄᐧᐦᑕᒪᐊᐧᐠ ᑳ ᐅᓯᑯᓯᔮᐣ, « ᒨᔭ ᐆᒪ ᐁ ᐊᔮᔭᐣ ᑮᑲᐧᐩ,» ᓂᑖᐤ, « ᑲ ᑮ ᐊᔮᔭᐣ ᐆᒪ ᑕᐦᑐ ᐲᓯᒼ,» ᓂᑖᐤ, « ᐁ ᑭᑭᐢᑲᐋᐧᐊᐧᓱᔭᐣ ᐊᓂᒪ,» ᑳ ᐃᓯᐟ ᐁᑲᐧ.

III

[16] ᐊᐧᐦᐋᐧ, ᐁᑯᑕ ᐁᑲᐧ, ᐃᐢᐲ ᐁᐊᐧᑯ ᐊᐊᐧ ᐁ ᑮ ᐊᔮᐋᐧᔮᕽ ᐊᐊᐧ, ᓂᐢᑕᒼ ᐃᐢᑫᐧᓯᐢ ᐁ ᐊᔮᐋᐧᔮᕽ, Florence ᐊᐊᐧ, 'Bear' ᐃᓯᔩᐦᑳᓱᐤ ᓂᑖᓂᐢ. ᐁᑲᐧ ᐊᓂ ᐁᑲᐧ ᐊᔨ, ᑳ ᒫᔨ ᑮᓯᑳᐠ, ᐁᐩ, ᐁᐩ, ᑲᐧᔭᐢ ᑭᒥᐊᐧᐣ, ᓂᐢᑐ ᑮᓯᑳᐤ ᐁ ᑭᒥᐊᐧᕽ, ᐁ ᐋᐧᓴᐢᑯᑌᐸᔨᐠ, ᐁᐩ, ᐁᐩ, ᑲᐧᔭᐢ ᐁ ᑮ ᒫᔨ ᑮᓯᑳᐠ, ᓂᐢᑕᒼ ᐆᒪ ᑳ ᒥᓯ ᑭᒥᐊᐧᕽ ᐊᓂᒪ, ᐁᐩ, ᑯᓂᑕ ᐊᓂᐦᐃ ᐃᐢᐱᒥᕽ ᐊᓂᒪ ᐊᔨ, ᑳ ᑮ ᐊᐸᐦᑳᐧᑌᐠ ᒪᐢᑯᓯᔭ ᐁᑲᐧ ᐊᓯᐢᑭᐩ, ᐃᔭᐃᐧᐢ ᐁᐊᐧᑯ ᐊᓂ ᐊᓂᐦᐃ ᓲᐢᑳᐧᐟ ᐁ ᐲᐦᑎᑫᐧᔮᐹᐁᐧᐠ ᐊᓯᐢᑭᐩ ᐊᓂᒪ, ᐁᑲᐧ, ᐊᓂᒪ ᐃᔨᑯᕽ ᐁᑲᐧ ᐁ ᑭᒥᐊᐧᕽ, ᐁᑲᐧ ᐁ ᐄᐧ ᑲᐃᐧᓯᒨᔮᕽ ᐆᒪ, « ᑖᓂᓯ ᐆᒪ ᑲ ᐃᓯ ᓂᐹᔮᕽ ᐁᑲᐧ.» ᐁ ᐃᑕᐠ ᐊᐊᐧ ᑳ ᐄᐧᑭᒪᐠ. ᒦᒋᓱᐃᐧᓈᐦᑎᐠ ᐊᓂᒪ, ᐁ ᑮ ᒧᐢᒋ ᐅᓰᐦᑖᕽ ᒦᒋᓱᐃᐧᓈᐦᑎᐠ, ᐁᐊᐧᑯ ᐊᓂ ᐊᓂᒪ ᐁᑲᐧ, ᑕᐦᑯᐦ- ᓂᐯᐃᐧᓂᕽ ᐁᑲᐧ, ᐁᐊᐧᑯ ᐁ ᑌᐦᑕᐢᑖᔮᕽ ᐁᐊᐧᑯ ᐆᒪ, ᐊᓂᒪ ᐊᔨ, tablecloth

ᐊᓂᒪ, ᐁᐊᐧᑯ ᐊᓂ ᐊᓂᒪ ᑫᔨᐁᐧᕽ ᐁᑯᑕ ᓂᐱᐩ ᐁ ᓲᐢᑲᐧᑯᑌᐠ, ᒫᑲ ᐁᑲᐧ, ᐁᑯᑌ ᑲᐯ ᐊᔨ ᐁ ᐱᑎᑲᐧᐱᔮᕽ ᐁᑲᐧ, ᐊᑖᒥᕽ ᐊᓂᒪ ᒦᒋᓱᐃᐧᓈᐦᑎᐠ ᐊᓂᒪ, ᐁᑯᑌ ᐁᑲᐧ ᐊᔨ, ᐁ ᑕᐦᑯᓇᐠ ᐊᓇ, ᐊᐊᐧ ᐃᐢᑫᐧᓯᐢ, ᑲᔮᐢ ᐊᔨᐢ ᑮ ᒧᐢᒋ ᓅᐦᐋᐊᐧᓯᓈᓂᐊᐧᐣ, ᐁᑯᑌ ᒫᓇ ᐁ ᑮ ᓇ ᓅᐦᐊᐠ. ᐋ, ᐁᑲᐧ ᐱᒥᒋ ᐊᔨᕽ, ᒥᓯᐁᐧ ᓲᐢᑳᐧᐨ ᐁ ᒪᓈᐹᐁᐧᐠ ᒦᓇ ᐊᓯᐢᑭᐩ, ᓲᐢᑳᐧᐟ ᐊᐧᔭᐄᐧᑎᒥᕽ ᐁ ᐃᑖᐱᔭᐣ, ᐁᑲᐧ ᐃᔨᑯᕽ ᐁ ᐋᐧᓴᐢᑯᑌᐸᔨᐠ.

[17] well, ᑮᑕᐦᑕᐁᐧ ᐁᑲᐧ ᑳ ᐃᑌᐧᐟ ᐊᐊᐧ ᓂᓈᐯᒼ, «ᐱᑯ ᑲ ᐄᐧᑲᑌᐦᑌᔮᕽ ᐆᑕ ᐅᐦᒋ,» ᐃᑌᐧᐤ. ᑲᔮᐢ ᒫᓇ ᐁ ᑮ ᐃᐦᑕᑯᐠ ᐊᓴᐦᑐᐃᐧᑲᒥᐠ, ᐁᑲᐧ ᐊᔨ, ᒫᑲ ᐊᔨ, ᐁ ᑮ ᑭᐳᓴᑲᐦᐄᑲᑌᐠ, ᐁᑯᑕ ᐁᑲᐧ ᑳ ᓂᑕᐃᐧ ᑕᐃᐧᓇᕽ ᑲᔮᓯ ᐋᐧᐢᑲᐦᐃᑲᐣ, ᒫᑲ ᐁ ᐊᐸᐦᑳᐧᑌᐠ shingles ᐅᐦᒋ ᐁᐊᐧᑯ, ᑲᔮᓯ ᐋᐧᐢᑲᐦᐃᑲᐣ. ᐁᑯᑕ ᐁᑲᐧ ᑳ ᐃᑐᐦᑌᔭᕽ ᐁᑲᐧ ᐁ ᓵᓴᑭᐦᑎᔮᕽ ᐆᒪ, ᒪ ᑮᑲᐧᐩ ᐊᐧᐢᑭᐱᒋᑲᓇ ᐁ ᐊᔮᔭᕽ. ᐁᑯᑕ ᐁᑲᐧ ᐁ ᓂᑕᐃᐧ ᐃᑐᐦᑌᔮᕽ, ᐁᑯᑌ ᐊᐊᐧ ᐊᓯᒋ ᑳ ᑕᐦᑯᓇᐠ ᐊᐊᐧ ᐃᐢᑫᐧᓯᐢ. ᐁᐊᐧᑯ ᐊᓂᒪ tablecloth, ᐁᐊᐧᑯ ᐁ ᐊᑲᐧᓇᐦᐅᔮᐣ, ᐁᑯᑌ ᐁ ᐃᑐᐦᑌᔮᐣ. ᐁᑯᑌ ᐁᑲᐧ, ᒨᔭ ᐁᑲᐧ – ᒥᔮᐧᓯᐣ, ᐁᑯᑌ ᒨᔭ ᑭᒥᐊᐧᐣ, ᐁᑯᑌ ᓂᑕᔮᓈᐣ, ᒫᑲ ᐁᑲᐧ ᓇᒪ ᑮᑲᐧᐩ ᑲᒦᒋᔮᕽ ᐁᑯᑌ ᐁ ᐊᔮᔭᕽ.

[18] ᐁᑯᑌ ᐁ ᑮ ᑕᑯᐦᑌᔮᕽ, ᒨᔭ ᑭᓀᐧᐢ ᑯᑕᑲᐠ ᓵᓭᐩ ᒦᓇ ᐁᑯᑕ ᑳ ᐯ ᑕᑯᐦᑌᒋᐠ ᐄᐧᐢᑕᐋᐧᐤ. ᐁᑯᑌ ᐁᑲᐧ ᐄᐧᐢᑕᐋᐧᐤ ᐊᓂᒪ ᐄᐧᑭᐋᐧᐤ ᐯᔭᑲᐧᐣ, ᑖᐱᐢᑰᐟ ᓂᔭᓈᐣ ᐊᓂᒪ, ᐁ ᓵᐳᐦᒋ ᑭᒥᐊᐧᕽ ᐊᓂᒪ ᑲᐦᑭᔭᐤ ᑮᑲᐧᐩ, ᐄᐧᐢᑕᐋᐧᐤ ᐁᑯᑌ ᐁᑲᐧ, ᓈᓂᑕᐤ ᐁᑎᑫᐧ ᐁᑲᐧ ten ᐁ ᐃᐦᑕᓯᔮᕽ, ᐄᐧᐢᑕᐋᐧᐤ ᐊᐋᐧᓯᓴ ᐁᑯᑕ ᐁ ᐯᓯᐋᐧᒋᐠ, ᐁᑲᐧ ᐯᔭᐠ, ᐯᔭᐠ ᐊᐊᐧ ᑭᓭᔨᓂᐤ ᒥᑐᓂ ᐁ ᑭᓭᔨᓃᐃᐧᐟ, ᐄᐧᐢᑕ ᐁᑯᑕ ᐯ ᑕᑯᐦᑌᐤ. ᐁ ᓅᐦᑌᔮᐹᑫᐧᔮᕽ ᐆᒪ, ᐃᐧᔭ ᒨᔭ ᑮᑲᐧᐩ ᑯᑕᐋᐧᓈᐱᐢᐠ ᐁᑯᑕ ᐲᐦᒋ ᐊᔨᕽ, «ᐁᐢᑲᐧ,» ᐃᑌᐧᐤ ᐊᓇ ᑭᓭᔨᓃᓯᐢ ᐊᓇ, «ᑲ ᒥᓂᐦᑳᐧᓈᐋᐧᐤ ᒪᐢᑭᐦᑮᐋᐧᐳᐩ,» ᐃᑌᐧᐤ. ᐊᐧᐦᐋᐧ, ᐊᐢᐱᐣ ᐁ ᑮ ᐊᐧᔭᐄᐧᐟ, ᐁᒋᑲ ᐊᓂ ᐁ ᓂᑕᐃᐧ ᑮᐢᑲᑕᐦᐊᕽ ᓃᐱᓯᔭ, ᑖᐱᐢᑰᐟ ᒦᑭᐋᐧᐦᐱᐢ ᐁ ᐃᓰᐦᑖᐟ ᐊᓂᒪ, ᐁ ᐊᑲᐧᓇᐦᐊᕽ ᐁᑲᐧ ᐊᑲᐧᓇᐦᐃᑲᐣ ᐅᐦᒋ, ᐁᑯᑕ ᐁᑲᐧ ᓰᐹ ᐁ ᐴᓇᕽ, ᐁ ᑭᓵᑲᒥᓯᑫᐟ ᐁᑲᐧ, ᐊᓇ ᑭᓭᔨᓃᓯᐢ, ᐊᐧᐦᐋᐧ, ᓂᒥᔦᐧᔨᐦᑌᓈᐣ ᐁ ᑭᓯᑌᐠ ᑮᑲᐧᐩ ᐁ ᒥᓂᐦᑫᐧᔮᕽ, ᓂᑲᐊᐧᒋᓈᐣ ᐊᔨᐢ ᐊᓂᒪ ᐃᑕ ᑳ ᐊᔮᔭᕽ.

[19] ᐁᑯᓯ ᐁᑲᐧ ᐊᔨ, ᐁᑯᑌ ᐁᑲᐧ ᐁ ᑮ ᐊᔮᐢᑌᑭᒥᐊᐧᕽ ᐁᑲᐧ, ᑳ ᐃᑌᐧᐟ ᐊᐊᐧ ᓂᓈᐯᒼ, «ᒪᐦᑎ ᑲ ᐃᑐᐦᑖᓇᐤ ᐁᑲᐧ ᑮᑭᓈᕽ ᑲ ᓂᑕᐋᐧᐯᓂᑳᓇᐤ,» ᐃᑌᐧᐤ. ᑖᐯᐧ ᐁᑲᐧ ᓂᓇᑲᑖᐤ ᐊᓇ ᐁᑲᐧ ᓂᐯᐲᒼ ᐁᑯᑕ, ᓂᓂᑕᐃᐧ ᒧᐢᑐᐦᑖᓈᐣ, ᓂᑎᑐᐦᑖᓈᐣ ᐁᑯᑌ, ᐁᐩ, ᓈᓂᑕᐤ ᐁᑎᑫᐧ ᐯᔭᐠᒥᓯᐟ ᐃᔨᑯᕽ ᓂᐱᐩ, ᐁᑯᑕ ᐊᓯᐢᑭᐩ, ᒪᐢᑯᓯᔭ ᑯᓂᑕ ᑲᐦᑭᔭᐤ ᑮᑲᐧᐩ ᐁᑯᑕ ᐁ ᐃᐦᑕᑯᐠ. «ᑲ ᑲᑫᐧ ᓈᓇᐹᒋᐦᑖᓇᐤ,» ᑳ ᐃᑕᐠ ᓂᓈᐯᒼ ᐁᑲᐧ, «ᐊᐢᑭᕽ ᑭᑲ ᐋᐸᒋᐦᐋᓇᐤ ᐆᒪ ᓂᐱᐩ ᑲ ᐊᐧᔭᐄᐧ ᐁᐧᐱᓇᒪᕽ,» ᐁ ᐃᑕᐠ. «ᓇᒨᔭ,» ᓂᑎᑎᐠ, «ᐅᓵᒼ ᒥᐢᑕᐦᐃ ᐊᑐᐢᑫᐃᐧᐣ, ᓂᑲ ᐹᐦ ᐸᑲᐧᓀᐦᐁᐣ ᒥᓯᐁᐧ ᐃᑕ, ᐋᐧᐦ ᐄᐧᐦᑫᐧᐦᑕᑳᕽ,» ᑳ ᐃᑌᐧᐟ ᐊᓂᒪ, «ᓂᐱᐩ ᑲ ᑯᑖᐃᐧᒋᐊᐧᐣ.» ᑖᐯᐧ ᐁᑲᐧ ᐁᑯᓯ ᐁ ᐃᑑᑕᕽ ᐁᑲᐧ, ᑖᐯᐧ ᑯᑖᐃᐧᒋᐊᐧᐣ ᑲᐦᑭᔭᐤ ᐊᓂᒪ ᓂᐱᐩ. ᐁᑯᓯ ᐁᑲᐧ ᐃᐢᐲ ᐁᑲᐧ ᓂᓈᓇᐹᒋᐦᑖᐣ ᐁᑲᐧ ᓂᐋᐧᐢᑲᐦᐃᑲᐣ, ᒫᑲ ᒥᓯᐁᐧ ᐁ ᓵᐳᑕᐋᐧᐠ ᐃᐢᐱᒥᕽ.

[20] ᐁᑲᐧ ᐊᓂ ᐁᑲᐧ ᐃᐧᔭ ᑳ ᓈᑖᐟ ᐁᑲᐧ ᒥᐢᑕᑎᒪᐧ, ᐁ ᐲᑯᐱᑕᕽ – walking-plough ᐊᓂᐦᐃ ᒫᓇ ᐁ ᐲᑯᐱᑕᕽ squares ᐊᓂᐦᐃ ᐁᑲᐧ, ᐁ ᐚᐦ ᐅᑎᓇᕽ ᒪᐢᑯᓯᔭ ᓃᑳᐣ ᐊᐢᑖᐤ, ᑳᐃᐧ ᐊᐸᐦᑫᐧᐤ ᐊᓯᐢᑭᕀ ᐅᐦᒋ, ᐊᓂᒪ, ᓴᑳᐧ ᒦᓇ ᐁ ᐊᑎ ᐱᒥ ᒥᒋᒧᐢᑯᐚᐦᑖᐟ ᐚᓴᑳ ᐊᓂᒪ ᑳᐃᐧ ᐚᐢᑲᐦᐃᑲᐣ. ᑳᐃᐧ ᐁᑲᐧ ᐁᑯᑕ ᐁᑲᐧ ᑳ ᐯ ᐃᑐᐦᑌᔮᕽ, ᐁᑯᑕ ᐁᑲᐧ ᐁ ᐋᔮᔮᕽ.

IV

[21] ᐁᑲᐧ ᒪ ᑮᑲᐧᕀ ᓲᓂᔮᐦᑫᐃᐧᐣ. ᐁ ᑮ ᒨᓇᐦᐊᐢᑫᐧᔮᕽ ᒫᓇ, ᐚᐦᔭᐤ ᒫᓇ ᐁ ᑮ ᐃᓯ ᒧᐢᑐᐦᑌᔮᕽ, ᐁ ᓇᐦᐋᐊᐧᓲᔭᐣ ᒫᓇ, ᐁᑲᐧ ᐃᐧᔭ ᐁ ᑮ ᑕᐦᑯᓇᕽ ᒨᓇᐦᐊᐢᑳᐧᑲᓇ, ᐁᐧᐁᐧᐱᓲᐣ, ᐲᒥᓇᐦᑳᐧᐣ ᐁ ᑕᐦᑯᓇᕽ (ᐯᔭᑲᐧᐣ ᒫᓇ ᓴᑳᕽ ᐁᑲᐧ ᐁ ᑮ ᐁᐧᐁᐧᐱᓯᓂᐦᑫᔮᐣ, ᐁ ᑮ ᐊᑯᒋᕽ ᐊᐊᐧ ᐁᑯᑌ ᓂᒫᓂᐢ ᐁᑲᐧ ᐁ ᒨᓇᐦᐊᐢᑫᐧᔮᕽ), ᒫᑲ ᐚᓴᑳ ᒫᓇ ᐁᑯᑕ ᓂᔭ ᓂᑮ ᒨᓇᐦᐊᐢᑳᐧᐣ, ᐁ ᐅᐦᒋ ᓈᑲᑐᐦᑫᔮᐣ.

[22] ᒪ ᑮᑲᐧᕀ ᐲᓯᒨᐦᑳᐣ, ᒨᔭ ᐃᐧᔭ ᑮᑲᐧᕀ wrist-watch ᐁᑯᐢᐲ. ᐲᓯᒪᐧ ᒫᓇ ᐁ ᑮ ᑭᑖᐸᒫᐟ, ᒥᑐᓂ ᒫᓇ ᐁ ᑮ ᑭᐢᑫᔨᐦᑕᕽ ᑖᓂᑕᐦᑐ ᑎᐸᐦᐃᑲᐣ. ᐁᑲᐧ ᒫᓇ ᐁ ᑮ ᐯ ᑮᐁᐧᔮᕽ ᒫᓇ ᐁᑲᐧ, ᐁ ᑮ ᓂᑕᐃᐧ ᐊᑖᐚᑫᐧᐟ ᐊᓂᐦᐃ ᒦᓂᓲᐦᑫᓴ, ᒥᑖᑕᐦᑐ ᐲᐚᐱᐢᑯᐢ ᐯᔭᑯ ᑯᓯᑲᐧᐣ ᐁ ᐅᐦᑎᓯᔮᕽ. ᒦᒋᐃᐧᓂᐢ ᒫᓇ ᐁ ᑮ ᐊᑖᐍᐟ ᐁᑯᑕ, ᒫᑲ ᐊᔨᐢ ᐁᑯᐢᐲ ᑲᐦᑭᔭᐤ ᑮᑲᐧᕀ ᑮ ᐁᐧᐦᑕᑭᐦᑌᐤ, ᒥᐢᒐᐦᐄᐢ ᒫᓇ ᑮ ᐯᒋᑫᓯᐤ ᒫᓇ, ᒦᒋᐃᐧᐣ ᐁ ᐊᑖᐍᐟ. ᐁᑯᓯ ᐁ ᑮ ᐃᑕᐦᑲᒥᑭᓯᔮᕽ ᒫᓇ, ᐁ ᑮ ᓲᓂᔮᐦᑳᑫᔮᕽ ᒦᓂᓲᐦᑫᓴ. ᒫᑲ ᐃᐧᔭ ᑮᑲᐧᕀ ᐊᔨᐃᐧᓂᓴ ᑲ ᑮ ᐊᑖᐍᐢᑕᒫᓱᕽ, ᓇᒪ ᑮᑲᐧᕀ, ᑌᐱᔮᕽ ᑲ ᒦᒋᓱᕽ.

[23] ᐊᓄᐦᐨ ᐁᑲᐧ ᐆᒪ ᑳ ᑮᓯᑳᐠ, ᑲᐦᑭᔭᐤ ᑮᑲᐧᕀ ᐁ ᒦᒋᕽ, ᑲᐦᑭᔭᐤ ᑮᑲᐧᕀ – ᐁ ᑮ ᑖᐸᑫᐧᐟ ᒫᓇ, ᑭᓯᐠ ᐆᒪ ᐁᑯᑌ ᑳ ᑮ ᒨᓇᐦᐊᐢᑫᐧᔮᕽ, ᐁ ᑮ ᑖᐸᑫᐧᐟ. ᐚᐳᓴᐧ ᒫᓇ ᑭᔨᑲᐤ ᐁᑯᑌ ᐁ ᑮ ᓂᐸᐦᐋᐟ, ᐁᑯᑌ ᒫᓇ ᓂᑮ ᐴᓀᓈᐣ ᐁ ᒪᒦᒋᓱᔮᕽ, ᐚᐳᐢ ᐁ ᐸᑳᓯᒫᔮᕽ, ᓂᑮ ᓃᒫᓯᓈᐣ ᒫᓇ, ᐸᐦᑫᐧᓯᑲᐣ, ᓰᐄᐧᐦᑖᑲᐣ, tea ᐁ ᑮ ᑕᐦᑯᓇᒫᕽ, ᐁᑯᑌ ᒫᓇ ᐁ ᑮ ᒪᒦᒋᓱᔮᕽ ᒫᓇ.

[24] ᒫᑲ ᒫᓇ ᐊᓄᐦᐨ ᑳ ᑮᓯᑳᐠ ᑳ ᒫᒥᑐᓀᔨᐦᑕᒫᐣ, ᐁ ᑮ ᒥᔪ ᐱᒫᒋᐦᐅᔮᕽ ᑖᐱᐢᑰᐨ, ᐁ ᐃᑌᔨᐦᑕᒫᐣ. ᐅᓵᒼ ᒨᔭ ᐄᐧᐦᑳᐨ ᑮᑲᐧᕀ ᐁ ᐅᐦᒋ ᒪᓯᓇᐦᐃᑫᔭᐣ ᐅᐦᐱᒣ, ᑮᑲᐧᕀ ᑲ ᓲᓂᔮᐦᑫᓯᔭᐣ, ᐁᐊᐧᑯ ᐱᑯ ᐁ ᑮ ᐅᐦᒋ ᐋᐸᒋᐦᑖᔭᐣ. ᒨᔭ ᑖᐱᐢᑰᐨ ᐊᓄᐦᐨ, ᒥᓯᐁᐧ ᐁ ᐲᑲᐧᓯᓇᐦᐃᑫᕽ, ᐱᑯ ᐃᑕ ᐁ ᒪᓯᓇᐦᐃᑫᔭᐣ ᐊᓄᐦᐨ ᐁᑲᐧ. ᒥᐢᑕᐦᐃ ᐲᑐᐢ ᐊᓄᐦᐨ ᐃᐢᐸᔨᐤ.

[25] ᐁᑲᐧ ᒫᓇ ᐃᐧᔭ ᐚᐢᑲᐦᐃᑲᓂᕽ, ᒪ ᑮᑲᐧᕀ electricity ᐊᐦᐴ ᒌ ᑮᑲᐧᕀ, ᑮᑲᐧᕀ ᐆᐦᐅ ᐆᐦᐅ ᒨᓂᔮᐃᐧ ᐚᐸᒋᐦᒋᑲᓇ, ᐁ ᑮ ᒫᓇ ᐱᒥᕀ ᑎᐦᑭᓴᒫᐣ, ᐊᔨᐃᐧᓂᐢ ᒫᓇ ᐁ ᑮ ᐲᒪᐦᐊᒫᐣ, ᐁᐊᐧᑯ ᐊᓂ ᐊᓂᒪ ᐁ ᑮ ᐚᓴᐢᑯᑌᓂᑳᑫᔮᕽ, our lamp ᐁᐊᐧᑯ ᐊᓂ ᐊᓂᒪ, ᐁ ᑮ ᐅᐦᒋ ᐚᓴᐢᑯᑕᐁᐧᐱᔮᕽ. ᒥᐦᒉᐟ ᐁᑎᑫᐧ ᑫᐦᑌ ᐊᔭᐠ, ᑲ ᐯᐦᑕᐦᑭᐠ ᐆᒪ, ᐄᐧᐢᑕᐚᐤ ᐁᑎᑫᐧ ᐁᑯᓯ ᑮ ᐯ ᐃᓯ ᐱᒫᒋᐦᐅᐊᐧᐠ. ᓇᒪ ᑮᑲᐧᕀ ᐁᐧᐸᐦᐃᑲᐣ, ᓴᑳᕽ ᒫᓇ ᐁ ᑮ ᓂᑕᐃᐧ ᒨᓴᐦᑭᓇᒫᐣ ᓃᐱᓰᓴ, ᐁ ᑮ ᒫᐊᐧᓴᑲᐧᐦᐱᑕᒫᐣ, ᐁᑯᓂ ᐁ ᑮ ᐁᐧᐸᐦᐃᑳᑫᔭᐣ. ᓇᒪ

ᑮᑲᐧᐩ ᑭᓰᐯᑭᓂᑲᐣ, ᐁ ᑮ ᒧᐢᒋ ᐅᓰᐦᐃᐦᐟ ᑭᓰᐯᑭᓂᑲᐣ ᐃᐧᔨᓇᐧ ᐅᐦᒋ, lye ᐁ ᐋᐸᒋᐦᑖᔭᐣ ᐁ ᐅᓰᐦᐊᐟ ᑭᓰᐯᑭᓂᑲᐣ. ᐁ ᑭᓰᐯᑭᓂᑫᔮᕽ, 'javex' ᒫᓇ ᐃᐧᔭ ᐁᑎᑫᐧ ᑳ ᑮ ᐃᑕᒥᕽ ᐁᐊᐧᑯ, ashes ᒫᓇ ᐁ ᑮ ᐱᑎᑲᐧᐦᐱᑕᒫᕽ ᐊᔨᕽ, ᐊᔨᐃᐧᓂᓯᓯᕽ ᐁ ᑮ ᐸᑭᐢᑕᐁᐧᐦᐊᒫᕽ ᒫᓇ ᐃᑕ ᑳ ᐅᓴᒫᕽ ᐊᔨᐃᐧᓂᓴ ᑮᑲᐧᔭ. ᑖᐯᐧ ᒫᑲ ᒫᓇ ᒣᑐᓂ ᐁ ᑮ ᑲᓈᑕᐦᑭ, ᐁ ᑮ ᑲᓈᑕᐦᒋᐚᐦᑌᑭ. ᑳ ᑮ ᑭᓰᐯᑭᓂᐦᑕᑫᐧᔮᕽ, ᐯᔭᑲᐧᐣ ᐁᑯᑐᐊᐧ ᒫᓇ ᐁ ᑮ ᑕᐦᑯᐱᑕᒫᕽ, ᐁᑲᐧ ᐁ ᐅᓴᒫᕽ ᓂᐲᕽ, ᐁᑲᐧ ᐁᐊᐧᑯ ᐊᓂ ᐊᓂᒪ ᐁ ᑮ ᑭᓰᐯᑭᓂᐦᑕᑳᐧᑫᔮᕽ, ᒪᐢᑯᓯᔭ ᐁ ᑮ ᐱᑎᑲᐧᐦᐱᑕᒫᕽ, ᐁᐊᐧᑯ ᐊᓂᒪ ᒫᓇ scrubbing-brush ᐁ ᑮ ᐃᑖᐸᒋᐦᑖᔭᕽ.

[26] ᑖᐯᐧ ᒫᓇ ᐁ ᑮ ᑲᓈᑕᐦᑭ ᒦᓇ ᓇᐸᑭᐦᑕᑲᐧ, ᐁᑯᓯ ᐁ ᑮ ᐃᑑᑕᒥᕽ. ᐊᐢᑭᔭ ᒫᓇ ᐅᐦᒋ ᐁ ᑮ ᐹᐦᑲᐧᐦᐊᒫᕽ ᒫᓇ, ᑳ ᑭᓰᐯᑭᓂᐦᑕᑫᐧᔮᕽ. ᐁᑲᐧ ᐃᐢᐲ ᒫᓇ ᐁᑲᐧ ᐁ ᑮ ᐁᐧᐸᐦᐊᒫᕽ ᑳ ᐹᐢᑌᑭ, ᐁ ᒫᐊᐧᓴᑯᐁᐧᐸᐦᐊᒫᕽ ᐊᐢᑭᔭ. ᒥᑐᓂ ᒫᓇ ᐁ ᑮ ᑲᓈᑕᕽ, ᐁ ᑮ ᐄᐧᐦᑭᒫᑲᐧᕽ ᒦᓇ ᒫᓇ ᐃᔨᑯᕽ ᐊᔨ, ᐋᐧᐢᑲᐦᐃᑲᐣ, ᐊᐢᑭᔭ ᐊᓂᐦᐃ ᐃᔨᑯᕽ ᐁ ᑮ ᐄᐧᐦᑭᒫᑲᐧᐦᑭ. ᐋᐧᓴᓇᒫᓇ ᑳ ᑭᓰᐯᑭᓇᒪᐣ ᐁᑯᓂ ᒦᓇ, ᐊᐢᑭᔭ ᐁ ᑮ ᐋᐸᒋᐦᑖᕽ ᐁᑯᓯ, ᐁ ᑭᓰᐯᑭᓇᒥᕽ ᐋᐧᓴᓇᒫᐃᐧᓇ.

[27] ᓂᑮ ᐯ ᐚᐸᐦᑌᐣ ᑭᑎᒫᑭᓯᐃᐧᐣ ᒥᓴᑳᒣ, ᑳ ᐅᓈᐯᒥᔮᐣ ᒦᓇ ᐃᔨᑯᕽ ᐯᔭᑲᐧᐣ ᐁ ᑮ ᐃᓯ ᑭᑎᒫᑭᓯᔮᐣ. ᐱᔨᐢ ᐁᑲᐧ, ᐁ ᐴᓂ ᓅᐦᐋᐊᐧᓯᔮᐣ ᐁᑲᐧ, ᑳ ᑮ ᓂᑕᐃᐧ ᐊᑐᐢᑫᔮᐣ ᐆᑌᓈᕽ, ᐁ ᓂᑕᐃᐧ ᐊᑐᐢᑫᔮᐣ ᐁᑲᐧ ᓂᔭ. ᐯᔭᑳᐧᐱᐢᐠ ᐯᔭᐠ ᑮᓯᑳᐤ ᑲᐯ ᑮᓯᐠ ᐁ ᐊᑐᐢᑫᔮᐣ ᐁ ᑎᐸᐦᐊᒫᑲᐃᐧᔮᐣ, ᐁ ᑭᓰᐯᑭᓂᐦᑕᑫᐧᔮᐣ, ᐁ ᒧᐢᒋ ᑭᓰᐯᑭᓂᑫᔮᐣ washboard. ᐁᑲᐧ ᒫᓇ ᐁ ᑮ ᐯ ᐊᒑᐁᐧᓯᔮᐣ ᒦᒋᐃᐧᐣ, ᐁᑲᐧ ᑳ ᑮᓯ ᑎᐸᐦᐊᒫᑲᐃᐧᔮᐣ ᑕᐦᑐ ᑮᓯᑳᐤ, ᐁ ᑮ ᓂᑕᐃᐧ ᐊᑐᐢᑲᐊᐧᐠ ᐊᐊᐧ ᒨᓂᔮᐢᑫᐧᐤ. ᐁᐊᐧᑯ ᐊᐊᐧ ᑳ ᑮ ᑭᐢᑭᓇᐦᐊᒫᑫᐟ ᑳᐧᑯᐲᐃᐧ ᓵᑲᐦᐃᑲᓂᕽ, ᐆᑌ ᐁᑲᐧ ᐁ ᐯ ᑭᐢᑭᓇᐦᐊᒫᑫᐟ ᐆᑕ ᐸᐢᑳᐧᐃᐧ ᓵᑲᐦᐃᑲᓂᕽ, ᐁᑯᑕ ᐁᑲᐧ ᓂᔭ ᑳ ᑮ ᒫᑕᑐᐢᑲᐊᐧᐠ ᐁᑲᐧ, ᑭᓀᐧᐢ ᓂᑮ ᐊᑐᐢᑲᐚᐤ. ᐁᑲᐧ ᐄᐧᐢᑕ ᐁᑲᐧ ᓂᓈᐯᒼ ᐁᑲᐧ, ᑳ ᐲᑯᐱᒋᑫᐟ, ᓃᓯ ᐱᑯ ᒥᐢᑕᑎᒪᐧ ᐁ ᐋᐸᒋᐦᐋᐟ, new breaking ᐁ ᐅᓰᐦᑖᐟ, ᐁ ᑭᐢᑎᑫᐟ. ᐁᑲᐧ ᑖᐯᐧ, ᐱᔨᐢ ᒫᓇ ᐁ ᑮ ᐄᐧᒋᐦᐊᐠ, ᐋᐢᑲᐤ, ᑮᑲᐧᐩ ᑳ ᐊᑐᐢᑳᑕᕽ, ᐃᔨᑯᕽ ᐁ ᑮ ᑲᑳᐧᑕᑲᑐᐢᑫᐟ ᐄᐧᐢᑕ.

[28] ᒫᑲ ᐁ ᑮ ᐄᐧᒋ ᐊᔮᒫᔭᐦᑳᐧᐤ ᐆᒪ ᓂᓯᑯᐢ ᐆᒪ, ᐁᑯᐢᐲ ᒨᔭ ᓂᑎᐱᔭᐁᐧᐦᐅᐃᐧᓈᐣ ᐋᐧᐢᑲᐦᐃᑲᐣ. ᑮᑕᐦᑕᐁᐧ ᐁᑲᐧ ᑳ ᐱᐢᑭᐦᒋ ᐄᐧᑭᔮᕽ, log-house ᐁᑲᐧ ᐁ ᐊᑖᐁᐧᔮᐣ ᐁᑲᐧ, ᐁ ᐊᑖᐁᐧᔭᕽ, ᓂᑯᑖᐧᓯᑯᒥᑕᓇᐤ ᐁ ᑎᐸᐦᐊᒫᕽ ᐱᑯ ᐋᐧᐢᑲᐦᐃᑲᐣ, log-house. ᐁ ᑮ ᐁᐧᐱᓂᑐᒋᐠ ᐆᑭᐠ ᐁᑯᑕ ᑳ ᑮ ᐄᐧᑭᒋᐠ, ᐁᑯᓂᐠ ᐁ ᐊᑖᒫᔮᐦᑳᐧᐤ. ᐁᑯᓯ ᐁᑲᐧ ᐁᑯᑕ ᐅᐦᒋ ᐁᑲᐧ ᓂᓈᐯᒼ ᐁᑲᐧ ᑳ ᓂᑕᐃᐧ ᐸᐊᐧᐦᐃᑫᐟ ᒫᓇ, ᐆᑕ ᐆᒪ ᐸᐢᑳᐧᐃᐧ ᓵᑲᐦᐃᑲᓂᕽ, ᐁ ᒋᒪᒋᑫᐟ, ᐁ ᐅᑎᓇᕽ ᒫᓇ ᐊᑐᐢᑫᐃᐧᐣ ᑲ ᒋᒪᒋᑫᐟ, ᓂᑮ ᐄᐧᒋᐦᐋᐤ ᒫᓇ ᐁ ᒋᒪᒋᑫᔮᕽ. ᓂᒫᒋ ᓲᓂᔭᐦᑳᓈᐣ, ᓂᐢᑕᒼ ᐊᓂᒪ ᐃᑕ ᑳ ᐃᐢᐱᒋᔮᕽ, ᒨᔭ ᐊᐦᐴ ᑯᑕᐚᓈᐱᐢᐠ ᓂᑕᔮᐚᓈᐣ. ᐁᑯᑐᐊᐧ ᓴᒫᐠ ᐊᑖᐁᐧᐤ ᐃᐧᔭ, cook-stove ᐊᑖᐁᐧᐤ ᐆᑕ ᐆᑌᓈᕽ, thirty-five ᐁ ᑎᐸᐦᐋᐧᐟ, ᒥᑐᓂ ᐁ ᒥᔪᓯᐟ ᑯᑕᐚᓈᐱᐢᐠ.

[29] ᐁᑯᓯ ᐁᑲᐧ, ᑳ ᒫᒋ ᐁᑲᐧ ᐹᐦᐸᐢᑲᐧᑕᐦᐊᒫᕽ ᐁᑲᐧ, ᐱᔨᐢ ᐊᔨᐚᐠ ᐁᑲᐧ ᐁ ᐊᑎᒥᓵᐠ ᐁᑲᐧ ᐊᔨ, ᓂᑭᐢᑎᑳᓂᓈᐣ ᐁᑲᐧ. ᒌᑲᐦᐃᑲᐣ ᐁ ᐅᐦᒋ ᐸᐢᑲᐧᑕᐦᐊᒫᕽ ᐁ ᒫᐦᒥᓯᑭᑎᒋᐠ ᒥᐢᑎᑲᐧᐠ. ᐁ ᐋᐧᑲᑌᑖᐯᐟ ᒥᐢᑕᑎᒪᐧ ᐅᐦᒋ ᐃᐧᔭ ᓂᓈᐯᒼ. ᐁᑲᐧ ᐃᐢᐲ ᐁᑲᐧ ᒫᓇ ᐁᑲᐧ ᑳ ᑕᑳᐧᑭᐠ ᐁᑲᐧ, cordwood ᐁᑯᓂ ᐊᓂᐦᐃ ᒫᓇ ᐁ ᑮ ᒧᐢᒋ ᑮᐢᑭᐳᑖᔭᕽ, ᑲᔮᐢ ᒫᓇ ᑮᐢᑭᐳᒋᑲᓇ ᐁ ᐋᔮᐸᒋᐦᑖᔭᕽ, ᑮ ᑭᓈᐧᐯᑲᓇᐧ, two handles ᒫᓇ each side ᑮ ᐊᐢᑌᐊᐧ. ᐁᑯᓂ ᐊᓂᐦᐃ ᒫᓇ ᐁ ᑮ ᑮᐢᑭᐳᑖᔭᕽ, seventy-five cents a cord ᐆᑌᓈᕽ ᐁ ᐅᐦᑕᑖᐋᐧᑫᐟ ᓂᓈᐯᒼ, ᐁᑲᐧ ᐁᑯᓂ ᒦᓇ ᐁᑲᐧ ᐁ ᐋᐊᐧᑖᐟ, ᐁ ᑖᐢᑲᑕᐦᐊᕽ, bakery ᐁ ᐃᑐᐦᑕᑖᐟ ᐁ ᐊᑖᐋᐧᑫᐟ. ᐋᐢᑲᐤ ᒫᓇ ᓃᓵᐧᐤ ᐯᔭᐠ ᑮᓯᑳᐤ ᐁ ᑮ ᐃᑐᐦᑕᑖᐟ, two cords ᐁ ᑮ ᑮᐢᑭᐳᒋᑫᐟ.

V

[30] ᐁᑲᐧ ᐊᐋᐧᓯᓴᐠ ᐋᑕ ᐁᑲᐧ ᐁ ᐊᑎ ᐅᐦᐱᑭᐦᐋᔮᐦᑳᐧᐤ ᐁᑲᐧ. ᑲᐦᑭᔭᐤ ᐁ ᑮ ᐯ ᓅᐦᐊᑭᐠ ᓂᒐᐋᐧᓯᒥᓴᐠ, ᐯᔭᑯᓵᑊ ᐁ ᐊᔮᐊᐧᑳᐧᐤ, ᑲᐦᑭᔭᐤ ᐁ ᑮ ᓅᐦᐊᑳᐧᐤ, ᒨᔭ ᓂᔭ ᓅᐦ ᑖᐯᐧᐊᐧᑫᔨᐦᑌᐣ ᐆᑭᐠ ᑳ ᓅᓈᒋᑫᐦᐋᐊᐧᓱᒋᐠ. ᒪᓂᑐᐤ ᐁ ᑮ ᒥᔨᑯᔭᕽ ᒥᑑᐦᑑᓯᒪ ᐃᑕ ᑲ ᐅᐦᒋ ᐱᒫᒋᐦᐋᔮᐦᑭᐠ ᐊᐋᐧᓯᓴᐠ, ᐁᐊᐧᑯ ᓂᔭ ᓂᑮ ᐱᒥᑎᓴᐦᐁᐣ. ᒨᔭ ᑖᐱᐢᑰᐨ ᐊᓄᐦᐨ, ᐆᑭᐠ ᐁᑲᐧ ᑳ ᐄᐧ ᓂᐦᑖᐃᐧᑭᐦᐋᒋᐠ ᐊᐋᐧᓯᓴ, ᐋᐦᑯᓰᐃᐧᑲᒥᑯᕽ ᐁᑲᐧ, ᓇᒪ ᑮᑲᐧᐩ ᐋᐦᑯᓰᐃᐧᑲᒥᐠ ᓂᔭ, ᑲᐦᑭᔭᐤ ᓃᑭᕽ ᐁ ᑮ ᓂᐦᑖᐃᐧᑭᒋᐠ – ᐁᐊᐧᑯ ᐅᒋ ᐊᓄᐦᐨ ᑳ ᑮᓯᑳᐠ, ᐁᑎᑫᐧ ᐆᑭᐠ ᐃᐧᔭᐋᐧᐤ, ᐹᒪᐧᓭᐢ ᑲ ᓂᐦᑖᐃᐧᑭᔨᐟ ᐊᐋᐧᓯᓴ, ᓵᓴᐩ ᐁ ᑲᐧᔮᒋ ᓂᑐᓇᐦᑭᐠ ᐱᐢᑭᐦᒋᑲᒥᑯᐢ, ᓂᐯᐃᐧᓂᐢ ᐁᑯᑕ ᐁ ᐊᐢᑖᒋᐠ, ᒦᓇ ᓅᓈᒋᑲᐣ, ᑲᐦᑭᔭᐤ ᑮᑲᐧᐩ ᒧᓂᔮᐃᐧ ᑮᑲᐧᐩ. ᑲᔮᐢ ᑮ ᐊᐧ ᐋᐧᐢᐱᑖᐊᐧᐠ ᐊᐋᐧᓯᓴᐠ, ᐊᐢᑭᔭ ᐊᓯᒋ ᐁ ᑮᓯᐋᐧᐢᐱᓱᒋᐠ, ᐃᐧᔭᐋᐧᐤ ᓲᐢᑳᐧᐟ ᐁ ᒧᐢᒋ ᐁᐧᐁᐧᑭᓈᒋᐠ, ᑳ ᐲᐦᒋᑲᐧᐦᐋᒋᐠ ᐄᐧᑭᐋᐧᕽ, ᐁᑯᓯ ᐁᑯᑕ ᐊᓂᐦᐃ ᐁ ᐲᐦᑎᑫᐧᐁᐧᐱᓈᒋᐠ ᐊᓂᐦᐃ, ᐅᒐᐋᐧᓯᒥᓯᐋᐧᐊᐧ ᐊᓂᒪ ᐱᐢᑭᐦᒋᑲᒥᑯᐢ. ᑳ ᒫᑐᔨᐟ, ᓵᓴᐩ ᒧᐢᑎ ᑑᐦᑑᓵᐳᐩ, ᐁ ᐊᓯᐊᐧᑖᒋᐠ ᐁ ᒧᐢᒋ ᒥᔮᒋᐠ, ᒨᔭ ᑕᐦᑯᓈᐊᐧᓱᐊᐧᐠ, ᒨᔭ ᑭᑎᒫᑫᔨᒣᐊᐧᐠ, ᐁᐊᐧᑯ ᐅᒋ ᐊᓄᐦᐨ ᑳ ᑮᓯᑳᐠ ᐃᔨᑯᕽ ᑳ ᐁᐧᐱᓈᒋᐠ ᐅᒐᐋᐧᓯᒥᓯᐋᐧᐊᐧ. ᑲᔮᐢ ᑮ ᑕᐦᑯᓈᐤ ᐊᐋᐧᓯᐢ ᐁ ᓅᓂᐟ, ᐁ ᐊᐧ ᐅᒣᒪᐟ, ᐁ ᑕ ᑕᐦᑯᓇᐟ, ᐁ ᐋᔮᐸᐦᐊᐧᐟ, ᐊᓄᐦᐨ ᒨᔭ ᐁᐊᐧᑯ ᐊᓂᒪ ᑮᑲᐧᐩ ᐃᐢᐸᔨᐤ. ᒨᔭ ᑳᐦ ᑮ ᐃᑌᐧᐊᐧᐠ ᐊᓂᑭᐠ, ᐆᑭᐠ ᐃᐧᔭᐋᐧᐤ ᐅᐢᑭ ᐊᔭᐠ ᐊᓄᐦᐨ, ᑳ ᓂᐦᑖᐃᐧᑭᐦᐋᒋᐠ ᐊᐋᐧᓯᓴ, ᐃᐧᔭᐋᐧᐤ ᑲ ᐅᒐᐋᐧᓯᒥᓯᒋᐠ ᑲ ᐃᑌᐧᒋᐠ ᐅᒐᐋᐧᓯᒥᓯᐋᐧᐊᐧ, ᒧᐢᒍᓴᐧ ᐁ ᐯ ᐅᐦᐱᑭᐦᑕᒫᑯᒋᐠ ᐊᓂᐦᐃ ᐊᐋᐧᓯᓴ, ᐊᔨᐢ ᒧᐢᑐᐢ ᐊᓇ ᑲ ᐱᒫᒋᐦᐋᐟ ᐊᓂᐦᐃ ᐊᐋᐧᓯᓴ ᑳ ᓂᐦᑖᐃᐧᑭᔨᐟ.

[31] ᐁᐊᐧᑯ ᐅᒋ ᐊᓄᐦᐨ ᑳ ᑮᓯᑳᐠ, ᒦᓇ ᒥᐢᑕᐦᐃ ᐁᐧᐱᓂᑐᐃᐧᐣ ᑳ ᐃᐢᐸᔨᐠ, ᑲᔮᐢ ᐋᑕ ᐃᔨᑯᕽ ᐁ ᐯ ᑭᑎᒫᑭᓯᔭᐣ, ᓇᒨᔭ ᐄᐧᐦᑳᐨ ᑰᐦᒋ ᓇᑲᑖᐤ ᑭᒐᐋᐧᓯᒥᐢ, ᑲᐦᑭᔭᐤ ᐁ ᑮ ᐊᐧᐁᐧᔩᐦᐊᒋᐠ, ᐃᑌ ᑳ ᐃᑐᐦᑌᔭᐣ ᐁ ᑮ ᐃᑐᐦᑕᐦᐊᒋᐠ, ᑖᐱᐢᑰᐟ ᐹᐦᐸᐦᐋᐦᑳᐧᓂᓯᓴᐠ ᐁ ᐱᒥᑎᓴᐦᐅᐢᑭᐠ ᑭᒐᐋᐧᓯᒥᓴᐠ, ᐋᑎᐦᐟ ᐁ ᑕᐦᑯᓈᐊᐧᓱᔭᐣ, ᑲᐦᑭᔭᐤ ᐁ ᓯᐯᐧᐦᑕᐦᐊᒋᐠ. ᐊᓄᐦᐨ ᐅᐢᑭ ᐊᔭᐠ, ᓇᓭᐢᑕᐤ, ᑯᑕᑲ ᐱᑯ ᐃᓯ ᐊᔨᓯᔨᓂᐊᐧ ᐁ ᐊᑎ ᐃᓯ ᑲᓇᐁᐧᔨᐦᑕᒨᐦᐋᒋᐠ ᐊᐋᐧᓯᓴ, ᓲᐢᑳᐧᐟ ᑖᐱᐢᑰᐟ ᑖᓂᑕᐦᑐ ᑮᓯᑳᐤ ᐁ ᓇᑲᑖᒋᐠ ᐁ ᐸᐹᒥ ᒥᓂᐦᑫᐧᒋᐠ. ᑫᐦᑌ ᐊᔭ ᑳ ᐋᐧᐸᒪᐟ, ᓵᓴᐩ ᐆᓯᓯᒪ ᐱᑯ ᑲ ᐱᒥ ᐄᐧᒣᐊᐧᐟ, ᐁ ᐁᐧᐱᓇᒫᐦᐟ, ᑭᔮᒼ ᐱᑯ ᐃᔨᑯᕽ

ᑳ ᑫᐦᑌ ᐊᔨᐃᐧᐟ. ᑖᐱᐢᑰᐟ ᓃᐢᑕ, ᓈᓂᑖᐤ ᐁᑎᑫᐧ ᓂᔮᓇᓅᓵᑊ ᐁ ᐯ ᐅᐦᐱᑭᐦᐊᑭᐠ, ᓅᓯᓯᒪᐠ ᐋᑎᐦᐟ, ᐋᑎᐦᐟ ᑯᑕᑲᐠ ᐊᐋᐧᓯᓴᐠ, ᐁᐧᐱᓂᑲᓇᐠ ᐁ ᑮ ᐅᐦᐱᑭᐦᑕᒫᓱᔮᐣ, ᐁᑲᐧ ᓂᔭ ᐯᔭᑰᓵᑊ ᐊᓯᒋ ᐁ ᐊᔮᐊᐧᑭᐠ ᐊᐋᐧᓯᓴᐠ. ᑲᐦᑭᔭᐤ ᑮᓯ ᐅᐦᐱᑭᐊᐧᐠ.

[32] ᐁᑲᐧ ᓂᐢᑕᒼ ᑳ ᐯ ᓂᐦᑖᐃᐧᑭᐟ ᐊᐋᐧᓯᐢ, «ᓈᐯᓯᐢ ᓂᐦᑖᐃᐧᑭᐤ, ᐃᐢᑫᐧᓯᐢ ᓂᐦᑖᐃᐧᑭᐤ,» ᑮ ᐃᑌᐧᐊᐧᐠ ᒫᓇ ᑫᐦᑌ ᐊᔭᐠ ᑳ ᐸᒥᐦᐃᐢᑭᐠ ᑳ ᓂᐦᑖᐃᐧᑭᐟ ᐊᐋᐧᓯᐢ. ᐁᑲᐧ ᒫᒋᑲ ᐁᐊᐧᑯ ᒫᑲ, ᒪᔭᐤ ᑳ ᐃᒐᐦᒍᐱᐳᓀᓯᒋᐠ ᐁᑯᓂᐠ, ᐁ ᐯ ᓈᐯᐃᐧᓲᐦᐃᐦᐟ ᓈᐯᓯᐢ, ᐃᐢᑫᐧᓯᐢ ᐁ ᑮ ᐯ ᐃᐢᑫᐧᐃᐧᓲᐦᐃᐦᐟ, ᐃᐧᔭ ᐁ ᑮ ᓂᐦᑖᐃᐧᑭᐟ ᐁ ᐃᐢᑫᐧᓯᓯᐃᐧᐟ. ᐊᓄᐦᐨ ᑳ ᑮᓯᑳᐠ, ᓇᒪ ᑮᑲᐧᐩ ᐁᐊᐧᑯ ᐊᓂᒪ ᒦᓇ ᑭᑮ ᐋᐧᐸᐦᑌᐣ, ᒨᔭ ᑭᓂᓯᑕᐁᐧᔨᒫᐤ ᐊᐦᐴ ᑮᐢᐱᐣ ᐃᐢᑫᐧᐤ ᐊᐦᐴ ᓈᐯᐤ ᐊᓄᐦᐨ. ᑲᐦᑭᔭᐤ ᐊᔨᓯᔨᓂᐤ ᐁ ᓈᐯᐃᐧᓲᐦᐅᐟ, ᐯᔭᑲᐧᐣ ᑖᐱᐢᑰᐨ ᓈᐯᐤ, ᐁ ᐋᐧᓂᓲᐦᐅᐟ. ᐋᐢᑲᐤ ᑭᐱᐢᒋ ᐲᑭᐢᑳᐧᑖᐤ ᐃᐢᑫᐧᐤ ᑳ ᐃᑌᔨᒪᐟ, ᓈᐯᐤ ᑭᐲᑭᐢᑳᐧᑖᐤ, ᐃᐧᔭ ᐁ ᐋᐧᓂᓲᐦᐅᒋᐠ, ᒨᔭ ᑭᑭᐢᑫᔨᐦᑌᐣ ᑮᐢᐱᐣ ᐁ ᓈᐯᐃᐧᐟ ᐊᐦᐴ ᐁ ᐃᐢᑫᐧᐃᐧᐟ. ᑲᐦᑭᔭᐤ ᑮᑲᐧᐩ ᒥᐢᑕᐦᐃ ᐲᑐᐢ ᑮᑲᐧᐩ ᐊᓄᐦᐨ ᐃᐢᐸᔨᐤ.

[33] ᐊᐦᐴ ᐁᑎᑫᐧ ᒦᓇ, ᑕᑯ ᒦᓇ ᑭᔮᓇᐤ, ᐁ ᐃᑑᑕᒪᕽ ᐁᑳ ᐁ ᐯ ᑲᑫᐢᑭᒫᔭᐦᑳᐧᐤ, ᑮᑲᐧᐩ ᑲ ᐯ ᐄᐧᐦᑕᒪᐋᐧᔭᐦᑳᐧᐤ, ᑖᓂᓯ ᐆᒪ ᐁ ᑮ ᐯ ᐃᓯ ᑭᑎᒫᑭᓯᕽ, ᑖᓂᓯ ᒪᓂᑐᐤ ᑳ ᐃᓯ ᐯ ᐸᑭᑎᓂᐁᐧᐟ, ᑲ ᑮ ᐃᓯ ᐅᐦᐱᑭᐦᐋᐊᐧᓱᔭᕽ, ᐊᓄᐦᐨ ᐊᐋᐧᓯᐢ ᑮᑲᐧᐩ ᐲᐦᑕᐤ ᒦᓇ ᑳ ᐄᐧ ᐄᐧᐦᑕᒪᐊᐧᐟ, «oh, that's old-fashioned,» ᑭᑎᑎᑲᐧᐠ, ᒪ ᑮᑲᐧᐩ ᑭᓂᑐᐦᑖᑲᐧᐠ. ᑮᑲᐧᐩ ᑳ ᑲᑫᐧ ᐄᐧᐦᑕᒪᐊᐧᐟ, ᑖᓂᓯ ᑲᔮᐢ ᐁ ᑮ ᐃᐢᐸᔨᐠ, ᑭᒧᐢᒋ ᐹᐦᐱᐦᐃᑲᐧᐠ ᐊᓄᐦᐨ ᑳ ᑮᓯᑳᐠ, ᐁ ᓵᓲᐱᐦᑕᐦᑭᐠ, ᐊᐦᐴ ᐋᑎᐦᐟ ᑳ ᐅᓃᑭᐦᐃᑯᒋᐠ ᐁ ᐃᐧᔮᐦᑳᐧᑖᒋᐠ ᐅᓃᑭᐦᐃᑯᐋᐧᐊᐧ. ᒨᔭ ᐄᐧᐦᑳᐟ ᓅᐦᒋ ᐯ ᑭᐢᑫᔨᐦᑌᐣ, ᐋᑕ ᐊᓄᐦᐨ seventy-five ᐁ ᐃᑕᐦᑐᐱᐳᓀᔮᐣ, ᐄᐧᐦᑳᐨ ᑲ ᑮ ᐯ ᓇᐢᑫᐧᐊᐧᓯᒪᐠ ᓂᒫᒫ, ᑳ ᑮ ᐅᐚᐦᑖᐃᐧᔮᐣ, ᐃᐧᔭ ᓂᑮ ᐯ ᐄᐧᐦᑕᒫᑯᓈᐣ ᓅᐦᑯᒥᓈᐣ, ᑖᓂᓯ ᑲ ᑮ ᐃᓯ ᐱᒫᑎᓯᔮᕽ. ᒥᐢᑕᐦᐃ ᐊᔭᒥᐦᐋᐃᐧᐣ, ᓂᑮ ᐯ ᑭᐢᑭᓇᐦᐊᒫᑯᓈᐣ ᑳ ᑮ ᐅᐚᐦᑯᒥᔮᕽ. ᒦᓇ ᑭᓃᑭᐦᐃᑲᐧᐠ, ᐁ ᑮ ᐄᐧᒋ ᐊᔭᒥᐦᐋᒪᒋᐠ ᐹᒪᐧᔦᐢ ᑲ ᓂᐹᔭᐣ, ᐁ ᑮ ᐄᐧᒋ ᐊᔭᒥᐦᐋᒪᒋᐠ ᐃᔭᐃᐧᐢ ᐁ ᑮ ᐊᔭᒥᐦᐋᒋᐠ, ᐊᓯᒋ ᓂᔭᓈᐣ ᑲᐦᑭᔭᐤ ᐁ ᐊᐋᐧᓯᓰᐃᐧᔮᕽ, ᐁ ᐅᒋᐦᒋᐦᑳᐧᓇᐱᐦᐃᑲᐃᐧᔮᕽ ᐁ ᐊᔭᒥᐦᐋᔮᕽ, ᐊᔭᒥᐦᐁᒥᓇ ᐁ ᑮ ᐊᔭᒥᐦᐋᐟ ᓂᒫᒫ, ᐁᑲᐧ ᒫᓇ ᓃᐢᑖᓈᐣ ᐁ ᑮ ᐄᐧᒋ ᐊᔭᒥᐦᐋᒫᔮᕽ. ᐁᐊᐧᑯ ᐅᐦᒋ ᐁᑎᑫᐧ ᐊᐦᐴ ᒥᐢᑕᐦᐃ ᐊᔨᓯᔨᓂᐤ ᑲᐧᔭᐢᐠ ᑮ ᐯ ᐃᓯ ᐱᒫᑎᓯᐤ, ᐃᐧᔭ ᒥᐢᑕᐦᐃ ᑮᑲᐧᐩ ᐁ ᐯ ᑭᐢᑭᓇᐦᐊᒫᑫᒋᐠ ᑲᔮᐢ, ᑳ ᐅᓃᑭᐦᐃᑯᔮᐣ.

VI

[34] ᐊᓄᐦᐨ ᑲᐦᑭᔭᐤ – ᐋᐧᐱᐢᑭᐃᐧᔮᐢ ᑳ ᐃᓯᔩᐦᑳᓱᐟ, ᒨᓂᔮᐤ, ᑲᐦᑭᔭᐤ ᒥᓯᐊᐧᓈᒋᐦᐁᐤ ᑭᑖᔨᓯᔨᓃᒥᓇᐊᐧ, ᑲᐦᑭᔭᐤ ᐆᒪ ᒨᓂᔮᐃᐧ ᑮᑲᐧᐩ ᐁᑲᐧ ᐊᓄᐦᐨ ᐁ ᐅᑎᓂᑳᑌᐠ, ᐁ ᐯ ᐁᐧᐱᓇᐦᑳᐧᐤ ᐆᒪ ᑭᑲᔮᓯ ᓀᐦᐃᔮᐃᐧᓂᓇᐤ, ᑖᓂᓯ ᑳ ᑮ ᐯ ᐃᓯ ᐸᑭᑎᓂᑯᐃᐧᓯᔭᕽ ᑲ ᑮ ᐯ ᐱᒥᑎᓴᐦᐊᒪᕽ. ᐊᓄᐦᐨ ᑲᐦᑭᔭᐤ ᑮᑲᐧᐩ ᒥᓂᐦᑫᐧᐃᐧᐣ, ᑲᐦᑭᔭᐤ ᑮᑲᐧᐩ ᐊᓄᐦᐨ, ᑲᔮᐢ ᒪ ᑮᑲᐧᐩ ᒥᓂᐦᑫᐧᐃᐧᐣ ᐅᐦᒋ ᐃᐢᐸᔨᐤ.

[35] ᒦᓇ ᑳ ᑮ ᑲᐃᐧᓯᒧᔭᐣ, ᑭᓃᑭᐦᐃᑲᐧᐠ ᑳ ᐄᐧᒋ ᐊᔮᒪᒋᐠ, ᑭᑭᑭ ᑲᐃᐧᓯᒧᐣ, ᒨᔭ ᐄᐧᐦᑳᐟ ᓈᓂᑕᐤ ᑑᐦᒋ ᓃᐸᐦᑖᐣ, ᑭᑭᑭ ᐊᐧᓂᐢᑳᐣ ᑭᓃᑭᐦᐃᑲᐧᐠ, ᒥᑐᓂ ᑲᐧᔭᐢᐠ ᐁ ᐸᒥᐦᐊᒋᐠ ᑭᓃᑭᐦᐃᑲᐧᐠ. ᐊᓄᐦᐨ ᐁᑲᐧ ᐅᐢᑭ ᐊᔭᐠ, ᓇᒪ ᑮᑲᐧᐩ ᒪᓈᒋᐦᐁᐊᐧᐠ ᑫᐦᑌ ᐊᔭ. ᐋ, ᐯ ᑕᑯ ᑮᐢᑫᐧᐯᐊᐧᐠ, ᐁᐩ, ᐁᐩ, ᐯᑑᐯᐊᐧᐠ, ᐁᑲᐧ ᒦᓇ ᑯᓂᑕ ᐁᑲᐧ ᑳ ᑭᑐᐦᒋᑫᒋᐠ, ᐋ, T.V., ᒪ ᑮᑲᐧᐩ ᑲ ᒪᓈ ᑯᐢᑯᓂᐢᑭᐠ ᐋᑕ ᐁ ᑫᐦᑌ ᐊᔨᐃᐧᔭᐣ, ᑳ ᑲᑫᐧ ᓂᐹᔭᐣ, ᔮ. ᑲ ᑕᐃᐧᓇᒪᐧᐠ ᑲ ᐲᑭᐢᑫᐧᐋᐧᐠ ᐁᑯᑕ ᐃᐧᔭᐋᐧᐤ. ᒪ ᑮᑲᐧᐩ ᑲᔮᐢ ᐁᐊᐧᑯ ᐅᐦᒋ ᐯᐦᑖᑲᐧᐣ, ᒪ ᑮᑲᐧᐩ. ᐲᐦᑕᐤ ᐊᔨᐢ ᒨᔭ ᑮᑲᐧᐩ ᐅᐦᒋ ᐊᔮᓂᐊᐧᐣ ᐁᑯᐢᐲ ᒨᓂᔮᐃᐧ ᑮᑲᐧᐩ, ᓇᓈᑐᕽ ᐊᓄᐦᐨ ᐆᐦᐅ ᑲᐦᑭᔭᐤ ᑮᑲᐧᐩ, ᑳ ᑭᑐᐦᒋᑫᒪᑲᐦᑭ, ᑲᐦᑭᔭᐤ ᑮᑲᐧᐩ ᐁ ᐃᐦᑕᑯᐠ ᐊᓄᐦᐨ.

[36] ᒨᓂᔮᐤ ᐁᐊᐧᑯ ᒦᓇ ᑳ ᑮ ᐅᓰᐦᑖᐟ ᒥᓂᐦᑫᐧᐃᐧᐣ, ᒥᐦᒉᐟ ᐊᔨᓯᔨᓂᐊᐧ ᐊᓄᐦᐨ ᑳ ᑮᓯᑳᐠ ᐁ ᑭᑎᒪᐦᐋᐟ. ᑲᔮᐢ ᒨᔭ ᑮᑲᐧᐩ ᐁᐊᐧᑯ ᐊᓂ ᐊᓂᒪ ᐅᐦᒋ ᐃᐦᑕᑯᐣ. ᐅᐢᑭᓃᑭᐢᑫᐧᐊᐧᐠ ᒥᐦᒉᐟ ᐊᓄᐦᐨ ᑳ ᑮᓯᑳᐠ, ᑲᔮᐦᑌ ᐱᑯ ᑭᑭᐢᑲᐋᐧᐊᐧᓯᐊᐧᐠ ᒥᓂᐦᑫᐧᐃᐧᐣ ᐅᐦᒋ, ᒨᓂᔮᐃᐧ ᐊᔨᓯᔨᓂᐤ ᑲ ᒥᓇᐦᐁᐤ, ᑭᔮᒼ ᐁᑳ ᑳ ᐄᐧ ᒥᓂᐦᑫᐧᔨᐟ, «ᐋ, ᐯᔭᐠ ᑲᓇᑫ ᒥᓂᐦᑫᐧ.» ᑲ ᐃᑌᐤ, ᐯᔭᐠ ᑳ ᑭᑖᔨᐟ, «ᒦᓇ ᐯᔭᐠ.» ᐋ, ᐃᐢᐲ ᑲ ᑕᑲᐦᑭᐸᐦᐋᒋᐠ, ᐁᑯᓯ ᐊᓂ ᐁᑲᐧ ᐁ ᓯᐯᐧᐦᑕᐦᐋᒋᐠ ᐁ ᓯᐯᐧᑖᐯᒋᐠ, ᑮᑳᐧᔭ ᐊᓂᒪ ᐅᐦᒋ ᑳ ᒥᓇᐦᐋᒋᐠ ᐁᑲᐧ ᐁ ᓂᑕᐃᐧ ᐊᐧᓭᓯᐦᐋᒋᐠ ᐊᓂᒪ, ᐋᐢᑲᐤ ᐁ ᑲᐃᐧᐸᐦᐋᒋᐠ. ᒪᒋ ᒪᓂᑐᐃᐧ ᒨᑌᔮᐱᐢᐠ ᑳ ᐃᑕᒥᕽ, ᒪᔭᐤ ᑳ ᑕᐃᐧᓇᒪᐣ ᐯᔭᐠ ᐃᐢᑫᐧᓰᓵᐳᐩ, ᐋᓴᐩ ᐁ ᑕᐃᐧᓇᒪᐋᐧᐟ ᐁᑯᑕ ᒪᒋ ᒪᓂᑐᐤ. ᑭᒥᓂᐦᑳᐧᐣ, ᐁᐩ, ᐋᐱᐦᑕᐤ ᑳ ᒥᓂᐦᑫᐧᔭᐣ, ᓵᓴᐩ ᐊᓂᒪ ᐁᑯᑕ ᐅᐦᒋ ᓰᐢᑳᐧᐟ ᐁ ᑎᐯᔨᒥᐢᐠ ᒪᒋ ᒪᓂᑐᐤ, ᑭᓵᑯᒋᐦᐃᐠ ᐊᔨᐢ ᓵᓴᐩ. ᓰᐢᑳᐧᐟ ᒥᓯᐊᐧᓈᒋᐦᐁᐤ ᑭᑑᐢᑭ ᐊᔨᒥᓇᐊᐧ, ᐋᐧᐱᐢᑭᐃᐧᔮᐢ ᑳ ᐃᓯᔩᐦᑳᓱᐟ.

[37] ᑖᓂᓯ ᐁᑎᑫᐧ ᒫᓇ ᐁ ᐃᑌᔨᐦᑕᒫᐣ ᐆᑌ ᒣᐧᐢᑕᐢ, ᒣᐧᐢᑕᐢ ᐊᑎ ᐆᑌ ᓃᑳᐣ ᑖᓂᓯ ᑲ ᐃᓯ ᑭᑎᒫᑭᓯᒋᐠ ᐊᐋᐧᓯᓴᐠ.

III
Dialogue

9.
Reminiscences of Muskeg Lake

Alpha Lafond & Rosa Longneck

Edited and translated by

Freda Ahenakew & Arok Wolvengrey

F: *'Alpha Lafond'* isiyîhkâsow awa kâ-wî-âcimostawit anohc.
ê-wî-- ê-kakwêcimak ôma, tânis
ê-kî-pê-ay-isi-pimâcihisocik ayisiyiniwak, tânis
ê-kî-pê-is-ôhpikinâwasocik, iskohk ôma wiya, tânis
ê-kî-pê-isi-pimâcihâwasot, tânis
ê-kî-pê-is-ôhpikinâwasot; êkosi.

1

A: ê-pê-isi-kiskisiyân ôm ê-ispîhcisiyân, mitoni kî-miywâsin kayâs pimâtisiwin. câh-cîk ê-kî-wâh-wîkiyâhk, wâh-wîpac miton ê-kî-wâpamâyâhkik, â, êk-- niwâhkômâkaninânak; nikâwîsak, nôhkom. mitoni mâna nikî-miywêyihtên nôhkom nit-- kâ-nitawi-kiyokawak, nanâtohk kîkway maskihkiya ê-kî-kiskêyihtahk. nikiskisin ê-awâsisîwiyân mân ê-kî-papâmipahtâyâhk misiwê, ê-papâ-manipitamâhk, nanâtohk kîkway wâpakwanîs[a] ê-kî-âpacihtât, maskihkîwina ohci.

F: *go ahead.*

A: *okay.*

F: *I'm just writing notes.*

A: *oh; okay.*

A: aya, môy wîhkât nôh-kiskêyihtên aya, tita-wawânêyihtahk nôhkom kîkwây êkwa tit-âsamikoyâhk; kâkikê kî-ayâw kîkway tit-âsamikoyâhk. êwakw âna piko ê-kî-kiskêyihtamân mâna, *'baby-sitters'* ôki k-êtihcik, nôhkom kâkikê nikî-kanawêyimikonân; âtayôhkan[a] ê-wîhtamâk-- ê-âh-âcimostâkoyâhk, nanâtohk kîkwây. ê-kî-kiskinohamâkoyâhk tit-âyamihâyâhk, ê-kî-nâh-nitihkomâtikoyâhk, ê-wâh-ocihcihkwanapiyâhk. (F: [*laughs*])

mitoni nikî-kistêyimâw nôhkom, wîpac ê-kî-wanihât nimosôma. nôhkom ê-kî-otinât, mihcêt ôsisima ê-kî-wa-ohpikihât. êkosi môy wîhkât nôh-pêhtên, nôhkom wîhkâc t-êtwêt, ê-âyimît. misatimwa kî-ayâwêw, mostoswa

F: The one who is going to tell me stories today is called Alpha Lafond.

I'm going to -- I am asking her this: how people lived, how they raised their children, and also how she made a living for her own children and raised them; alright.

1 [*Childhood Memories*]

A: As I remember back to the time when I was small, life was very good long ago. We were living close together and we saw our relatives quite often; my aunts, and my grandmother. I really used to like to go and visit my grandmother; she knew about different kinds of medicine. I remember when I was a child we used to run about everywhere picking all kinds of flowers and she would use them for medicine.

F: Go ahead.

A: Okay.

F: I'm just writing notes.

A: Oh; okay.

A: Well, I never knew my grandmother to be lost for something to feed us; she always had something to feed us. She was the only 'baby-sitter', as they are called, that I ever knew; my grandmother always took care of us. She told us sacred stories --, she would tell all kinds of stories to us. She taught us to pray and would pick out our lice while we were kneeling. (F: [*laughs*])

I thought very highly of my grandmother; my grandfather had died early. My grandmother took many of her grandchildren and raised them. But I never heard my grandmother say that she had a difficult life. She had horses, and also cows that

mîna, kî-îkinikêw. nanâtohk kîkway nikî-mîcinân, wâposwak, mîcimâpoya, sîsîpak, pihêwak – nanâtohk mînisa kî-ihtakonwa kayâs ôm ôtê iskonikanihk. pikw îta k-- kâ-sêskisiyan, (ayôskanak) kî-mihcêtinwa; aya mîna wîsakîmina, misâskwatômina. nanâ-- kî-takwahiminêw mâna nôhkom, nikî-wâpamâw, ê-pâh-pitikonahk, ê-astât tita-pâstêki. êkoni anihi ê-kî-kanawêyihcikâtêki kâ-pipohk, ê-kî-osîhtâhk kâ-pipohk, takwahiminâna. kî-pânisâwêw mîna mâna nôhkom, kâhkêwakwa. wayawîtimihk mîna mâna kî-kîsiswêw â--, pahkwêsikana, nikiskisin êwako, ê-kisâkamisikêhk wayawîtimihk. kîkway mâna nikî-môsâhkinênân, ê-kî-minihkwêhk, *from* --

– tânis ôm ê-isiyîhkâtêk anima mâna --

F: 'maskêkwâpoy'.

A: 'maskêkwâpoy' mâna kî-itamwak anihi, nikiskisin.

mihcêt kîkway nikiskisin ê-awâsisîwiyân. iyikohk ê-kî-miywêyihtamak [*sic; sc.* -miywêyihtamâhk] mâna nîc-âyisak, pikw îtê ê-papâmipahtâyâhk sakâhk. êkoni êtikw ânihi *'buffalo-trails'* mâna kâ-kî-itamihk kayâs, mêskanâsa, êkoni anihi mâna nikî-papâmitisahênân, ê-papâmipahtâyâhk.

êkwa kâ-kisîpêkinikêhk, nikî-papâ-wîcihiwânân mâna. âsay mîn êkota misiwê ê-papâ-mêtawêyâhk, nanâtohk kîkway ôma kâ--, ê-nâh-nâtwâpitamâhk *willow branches*, êkoni anihi ê-pâh-pîhtopitamâhk, êkwa ê-sâ-sisopâtamâhk, *the sap*. pêyakwan mîna kâ-nitâmisoyâhk, â, wîsakîmina, 'pikiw' mâna nikî-itânân ana, ê-mâh-manahkwatatahwâyâhk, *from* --

– tânisi -- –

minahikohk, êwakw âna mân ê-kî-misîmâyâhk.

nikiskisin mîn ê-kî-mâmawatoskêyâhk mâna, ê-nitawi-wîst-- [*sc.* -wîstihkêyâhk], â,

– *stoking* [*sic*]?

F: ê-cimacikêhk.

A: ê-kî-nitawi-cimacikêyâhk, kahkiyaw awâsisak mân ê-kî-papâmipahtâyâhk, ê-papâ-wîcihtâsoyâhk ê-cimacikêhk; kâ-papâmi-nitâmisoyâhk ê-papâmi-mâmawêyatiyâhk.

êwakw ân[i] ânima mâna mitoni nikî-kiskêyihtên ê-kî-sâki-- ê-kî-sâkihi-- ê-kî-sâkihikawiyâhk, nî-- nôhkom,

she milked. We ate all kinds of things; rabbits, soups, ducks, prairie-chickens – there were all kinds of berries over here on the Reserve long ago. Everywhere you went into the bush, the berries were plentiful, (there were raspberries) and also cranberries and saskatoons. My grandmother used to crush chokecherries; I saw her as she made them into patties and set them out to dry. These were kept for winter, and in winter the dried chokecherries were prepared for eating. My grandmother also used to cut meat into sheets, for dried meat. She also used to bake bannock outside, I remember that and how one would heat water outside. We used to pick things for drinking, from [*sc.* the muskeg] --

– what was that called?

F: 'Muskeg tea' [*sc.* Labrador tea].

A: They used to call that 'muskeg tea'; I remember.

I remember many things from when I was a child. My siblings and I were always so happy as we ran all over in the bush. I guess they were called 'buffalo-trails' long ago; we followed those trails as we ran about.

And when it was time for washing clothes, we used to go along with her [*sc.* my grandmother]. There too, we would run about all over the place playing with different things -- we would break off willow branches, and we'd peel the bark off them and lick off the sap. In the same way, when we picked, ah, cranberries; we would peel that which we used to call 'gum', from --

– what is it -- –

from the spruce tree; we used to chew that.

I also remember that we all used to work together, we went to -- ah,

– stooking?

F: Stooking [*sc.* tying sheaves].

A: When we went stooking, all the children used to run around, and we used to help with the stooking. When we went about berry-picking we would all go together.

That's what I knew then, that we were -- we were -- we were truly loved. My -- my grandmother and all of my siblings, my

êkwa kahkiyaw ôki nîc-âyisak, kahkiyaw nicâhkosak, êkwa mîna nimâmâ wiyawâw kahkiyaw, nikâwîs. tâpitaw ê-kî-papâmi-mâmawêyatiyâhk kîkway kâ-tôtamâhk, câh-cîk âyisk nikî---â---wâh-wîkinân.

– *turn it off, let me thi--*

[*external break*]

2

A: -- ôta *in thirty-- July thirty-first*, kahkiyaw maskwêkowiyiniwak [*sic; sc.* maskêkowiyiniwak] kâ-wî-wîhkômihcik ta-pê-itohtêcik ôta; ta-pê-kiyokêcik, kâwi kita-pê-wâpamâcik owâhkômâkaniwâwa, êkos îsi. êkota anim âya --

[*pause*]

F: êkosi, sôskwâc ati-pâh-pîkiskwê, (A: âha!) *it's still recording!*

A: aya, kit-âya--, ê-isi-mâmitonêyiht-- ê-isi-mâm-- ê-kî-pê-isi-kiskisiyan, kôhkominawak ê-kî-pê-isîhocik, êkosi ta-kakwê-isîhohk, êkwa mîna kayâs, aya, k-ây--, nâpêwak, êwakw ân[i] ânima niwî-ayânân, (F: âha.) aya, masinipayiwina nitayânân nôhkom ohci, êkw âsay nikakwêcihkêmon kîspin ta-kî-osîhtamâkawiyân, pîhconês (F: âha.) êkwa aya --

F: kîskasâkay?

A: âha, êkwa aya --

– *a shawl?*

F: akwanân.

A: mhm.

A: akwanân. môy wîhkât nôh-wâpamâw nôhkom *very bright colours* ta-kikiskahk, osâm piko *navy, black.*

F: êkw âpiscâpakwanîsa mân ê-kî-takahkêyihtahkik, (A: âha.) pakahkam. (A: *yes.*)

A: môy wîhkât nôhkom oskât[a] âyis nôh-wâ-- â, â, oskâta nôh-wâpahtên, kah-- ka-- pisisik kî-kinwâpêkasâkêw, ê-pê-kiskisiyân nôhkom.

F: mhm, êkosi nîsta. (A: âha.)

A: tâpitawi kî-kinwâpêkasâkêw êkwa aspascâkanis mân ôta, (F: âha.) âha. êwakw ân[i] ânima pêyak kîkway niwî-ayânân ôta. êkwa mîna niwî-kakwêcimânân *Buck Greyeyes* kîspin ta-kî-wiyahpit---wiyahpicikêt; êkwa awiyak

cousins and my mom too, and my aunt; all of them, we were always all together doing something, because we were living close together.

– Turn it off, let me thi--

[*external break*]

2 [*Plans for a Reunion I: Praying in Cree*]

A: Here on the thirty -- July 31st, all of the people of Muskeg are going to be invited to come here, to visit, to come back and see their relatives, that kind of thing. It will be there --

[*pause*]

F: Alright, just continue speaking, (A: yes!) it's still recording.

A: Ah, do you have -- as you think of -- as you remember how our grandmothers used to dress, that way people will try to dress, and also the men, how long ago -- that's what we're going to have; (F: yes.) we have pictures of my grandmother, and I have already asked if I can have a blouse made, (F: yes.) and ah --

F: a skirt?

A: Yes, and ah, --

– a shawl?

F: A shawl.

A: Mhm.

A: A shawl. I never saw my grandmother wear very bright colours, only navy and black.

F: And they used to like little flowers, (A: yes.) I think. (A: yes.)

A: And I never saw my grandmother's legs, -- as I remember my grandmother, she always wore long skirts.

F: Mhm, the same with mine, too. (A: yes.)

A: She wore long skirts all the time and usually an apron here as well, (F: yes.) yes. That is one thing we are going to have here. And we're also going to ask Buck Greyeyes if he could harness nôhtê-papâmitâpâsoci, ta-- ta-papâmitâpâsohk; (F: ôh, âha.) ta-wâpahcikâtêk êwako. (F: âha.) êkwa mîna niyâ--, êkwa mîn âya, ninitawêyimânânak âtiht, â, ta-- ta-pê---aya---mêtawêcik aya, *football,* â, *soccer*! (F: âha.) êwakw âyisk ohc ôta, aspin ohc ôta ôm ê-pê-awâsisîwiyân, êwako nayêstaw ê-kî-wâpahtamân ôt[a] ê-mêtawêhk; mitoni kî-nâh-nahîwak mân ôk ôta ayisiyiniwak, ôt[a] êwakw ân[i] ânim ê-pâkâhtowêcik.

êkwa mitoni kîkway kîspin mînisa ta-mihcêtiki, misâskwatômina, tita-kîsisikâtêki tâpiskôt kayâs, pimîhk. (F: mhm.) êkwa mîna kîspin, takwahiminâna, pahkwêsikan, êkos îsi na-- aya, iyinico-pimîs, kayâs kîkway ê-kî-pê-mîciyâhk, êkoni anihi ki-- kîspin ta-kî-kaskihtâyâhk êkospî tit-âsamâyâhkok kâ-wî-pê-takohtêcik. mêkwâc êwakw ân[i] ânima nitatoskâtênân ôta, tânisi ta-kî-isi-nahêyihtamihâyâhkok kâ-wî-pê-takohtêcik, mask-- maskwêkiyiniwak [*sic; sc.* maskêkowiyiniwak]. *We'll have Antoine Sand*, êwakw ân[a] âna *the Elder from Saskatoon district,* tit-âyamihâniwan nîkân; kîspin osâm mihcêtitwâwi, môy ânit[a] *in the church* tit-âyamihâniwan, mâka *it'll be an open-air mass*, êkwa *the--, we'll have both things, the incense* êkwa tita-- tita-miyâhkasikâniwan *th-- th-- the sweet-grass*, âha, *ya, the -- both!* êkosi nikî-isi-wâpahtên mân ôtê, *Hobbema* tahtwâw k-êtohtêyân, êkotê nôsisimak kâ-sîkahâhtâhcik. êkoni anihi nîso kîkway –°

F: âpatanwa.

A: °– âpatanwa, âha, *ya; both are --* êkoni anihi, âha, *ya.*

F: ê-miyâhkasikêhk.

A: âha! ê-miyâhkasi-- –°

F: nîswayak isi.

A: âha, nîswayak isi, môn-- môniyâw-îhtwâwin êkwa mîna nêhiyawak kâ-kî-pê-isi-miyâhkasikêcik wîstawâw, êwakw ân[i] ânima ta-- (F: mhm.)

F: ê-wî-pîhtwât; ê-wî-pîhtwâhk cî mîna, *Antoine* kâ-itwêyan?

A: *Antoine* an[a] êwakw âna, ayisk êwakw ân[a] âna kiyânaw *our Elder for the district*, êwakw ân[a] âna, âha, *ya*.

miton âya, nitâyim-- –°

a team; then if anyone wants to go for a ride -- there will be rides. (F: oh, yes.) That'll be something to see. (F: yes.) And also we -- and we also want some, ah, to come and play football, ah, soccer! (F: yes.) Because that was here, from the time I was a child, that is all I saw being played here. The people here used to be really good at playing soccer.

And if berries, saskatoons, are really plentiful, they will be cooked like long ago, in grease. (F: mhm.) And also chokecherries, in bannock; just in, ah, ordinary grease; things that we ate long ago. If we can at the time, those are the things which we'll feed those who are going to attend. That's what we are currently working on here; how we can make it feel right for the people of Muskeg who will attend. We'll have Antoine Sand, that one -- the Elder from Saskatoon district. There will be mass first, but if there are too many, mass will not be in the church, but rather it will be an open air mass, and the -- we'll have both things, the incense, and the smudging with sweet-grass, th-- the sweet-grass, yes, ya, the -- both! I have seen it done that way over at Hobbema every time I went over there, when my grandchildren were baptized. Those two things –°

F: They are used.

A: °– are used, yes, ya; both are --, those ones, yes, ya.

F: They smudge with sweet-grass.

A: Yes! Sweet-grass –°

F: Both together.

A: Yes, both together, white-- the White way and the way the Crees themselves have been smudging with sweet-grass; that too -- (F: mhm.)

F: Will he perform the pipe ceremony; will there also be a pipe ceremony, with the one you mentioned, Antoine?

A: That is Antoine, for that one is our own Elder for the district, that one, yes, ya.

We had real diffic-- –°

F: kîkisêpâ?

A: âha, têpa-- *well*, âha, têpa--

A: aya, *the only thing we found very difficult was, uh, if it's a feast,* (F: aha.) tit-âyiman êwako, (F: âha.) âha, tit-âyiman, ayisk *it's a different way of doing a feast*, mâka wiya nik-âsamânânak wiya ayisiyiniwak, pôn-âyamihâhki, *and as much Cree to be used,* tita-nêhiyawi-nakamonâniwan --

F: ayamihâhki.

A: ayamihâhki, *the 'Our-Father' will be s--* tita-nêhiyawâniwan, ayisk ôma niyanân kâ-kî-pê-kiskinohamâkosiyâhk kiskinohamâtowikamikohk, nikî-ayamihânân ê-nêhiyawêyâhk, kahkiyaw êkon ânih êtikwê ta-kâh-kiskisiwak ôki kîspin kî-wanikiskisiwak êwako; *we prayed in Cree.*

F: mhm, hm!

[*external break*]

3

F: tânitê ôma kiy ê-kî-pê-kiskinahamâkawiyan?

A: *All my educated years were in St Michael's, nineteen-thirty-four* êtikwê nânitaw êkotê niya kâ-pakitinikawiyân; *but I had, uh, I already knew English,* (F: mm!) *and I knew Cree,* ayisk -- nôhtâwiy ayisk mitoni kî-nihtâ-âkayâsîmow, (F: âha.) êkwa mîna kî-nihtâ-nêhiyawêw; (F: mhm.) *and of course I had these two* (F: âsay.) *things already with me,* âha, *ya.*

êkotê nikî-kiskinohamâkosin, *I left school in nineteen-forty-two,* kâ-nakatamân, â, (F: âha.) *school*, êkosi sêmâk nikî-mâtatoskân, nikî--, *around here* nikî--, nikî-mâc-âtoskân êkota ohc êkwa aya, *when I wanted to test my wings;* (F: âha.) êkosi nikî-ati-sipwêhtân êk ôhpimê nikî--, misiwê nikî-papâmatoskân, môniyânâhk osâm piko ayisk, êkotê --

F: êkota piko?

A: êkota piko.

A: kâ-pê-kîwêyân mâna *train* ê-kî-pê-pôsiyân, kayâs ayisk môy âwiyak sêhkêpayîsa ohc-âyâwêw. (F: mhm.) *Today it's just an hour to go to Saskatoon but in my day,* mitoni mâna nikî-pê-wâsakâmêyâpôyon, *Prince Albert* tita-pê-kîwêyân. (F: *tsk.*)

F: Early in the morning?

A: Yes, ah--, well, yes, ah --

A: Well, the only thing we found very difficult was, uh, if it's a feast, (F: yes.) that will be difficult, (F: yes.) yes, it will be difficult because it's a different way of doing a feast, but we will feed the people after mass, with as much Cree to be used, with the singing to be in Cree --

F: During mass.

A: During mass, the 'Our Father' will be s--, Cree will be spoken, because this is the way that we ourselves were taught in school; we prayed in Cree. These people will remember all of that if they have forgotten it; we prayed in Cree.

F: Mhm, hm!

[*external break*]

3 [*Working Hard and Dancing Hard*]

F: Where is it that you went to school?

A: All my educated years were in St Michael's, around 1934 I guess they let me out of there, but I had, uh, I already knew English, (F: mm!) and I knew Cree, because my father really spoke English well (F: yes.) and he also spoke Cree well, (F: mhm.) and of course I had these two (F: already.) things already with me, yes, ya.

I went to school over there; I left school in 1942, and when I left, ah, (F: yes.) school, I began to work right away, I -- around here, I began to work from then on, when I wanted to test my wings; (F: yes.) then I left and went away, I -- I went all over the place working, mainly among the Whites, over there --

F: Only there?

A: Only there.

A: When I came home, I used to ride the train, because no-one had cars long ago. (F: mhm.) Today it's just an hour to go to Saskatoon but in my day I used to come all the way around Prince Albert to get home. (F: tsk.)

ocêhtowi-kîsikâki mâna, mêtoni mâna *I looked forward* êkota ta-pê-takohtêyân, ayisk, kayâs mistahi ê-kî-- kî-miywâsin kâ-ocêhtowi-kîsikâk; pikw îtê ê-papâ-kiyokêhk, pikw îtê ê-miyo-wîcêhtohk, pikw îtê ayisiyiniwak ê-papâ-atamiskâhcik. (F: mhm.) êkwa mîna pikw îta kâ-pîhtikwêyan ê-mîcisoyan – tânitê êtikwê mân ê-kî-astâyâhk, mâka pikw îtê nikî--, (F: [laughs]) mayaw kâ-pîhtikwêhk, (F: êkosi.) êkosi nikî-mîcisonân; *everywhere*!

F: êkwa môy wîhkâc ohc-âsênikâtêw ayis.

A: *No, no,* êkosi ê-ati-nîmihitohk; k-âti-tipiskâk, êkosi ê-nîmihitohk. (F: âha.) miton ê-wî-nipahi-wâpani-môcikihtâhk! (F: [*laughs*]) êkwa kîspin nôh--, â, kâ-pônisimohk, êkwa kâ-t-- kâ-wâpani-takohtêhk, kîspin kîkway kisîpêkinikêwin, êkosi mîn ê-ati-kisîpêkinikêhk ê-at-âtoskêhk!

F: môy wiya kîkway ka-wâ--, â, kapê-kîsik ka-nâh-nipâhk.

A: *No! No, no, it,* â, kiyâm mitoni kapê-kîsik k-âtoskêyan, êkosi kâ-tipiskâk, kîspin nânitaw ê-nîmihitohk, âsay mîn êkota ê-ati-wîcihiwêyan, âsay mîna miton ê-ati-wâpanisimoyan. [*laughter*] kî-sôhkisiwak kayâs ayisiyiniwak.

F: kwayask!

F: pêyak -- pêyak-tipiskâw êkây ka-nipâyan, êk ôm êkwa mâna mitoni kiwî-nipahi-nôhtêsinin.

A: âha; nisto-kîsikâw âskaw kî-nîmihitonâniwan kâ-wîkihtohk mîna.

F: âha; môy wiya pêyak-tipiskâw piko. (A: âha)

A: aya, ayisiyiniwak kî-nihtâwikiwak wîkiwâhk, kî-wîkihtowak wîkiwâhk, (F: âha.) êkwa mîna kâ-pôni-pimâtisicik wîkiwâhk.

F: kî-nîpêpinâniwan.

A: kî-nîpinêp-- kî-nîpêpîstawâw ayisiyiniw, kîspin ê-ati-nêsowisit wîkihk. (F: ha!) môy êkw ânohc, tâpiskôc, â, *hospital*, âskaw ê-pêyakocik kêhtê-ayak, nam âwiya ê-wa-wîtapimikocik *in their final hours*. (F: âha.)

On New Year's Day, I really looked forward to arriving there, because long ago it was very nice on New Year's Day. Everywhere there was visiting, everywhere there was good will, everywhere people were being greeted. (F: mhm.) And you also ate at every place you went to – I wonder where we used to put it, but everywhere we --, (F: [*laughs*]) as soon as you entered, (F: that's right.) then we all ate; everywhere!

F: For you never turned it down.

A: No, no, and then there was dancing; when night fell then there was dancing. (F: yes.) There was really a lot of merry-making until dawn! (F: [*laughs*]) And if we -- ah, when the dancing came to an end, then when you got there [*sc.* to your place of work] at daybreak, if there was any laundry, then you simply got to work and did the laundry!

F: There was none of that sleeping through the day.

A: No! No, no, it, ah, even if you really worked all day, if there was a dance anywhere at night, again you were taking part and again you danced hard until dawn. [*laughter*] People were strong long ago.

F: Absolutely!

F: One -- now, you go without sleep for one night and you're going to be dreadfully played out.

A: Yes; sometimes there was dancing for three days when there was a wedding.

F: Yes; not only for one night. (A: yes.)

A: Ah, people were born in their homes, they were married in their homes (F: yes.) and they also died in their homes.

F: There were wakes.

A: They -- you sat up with people in their homes, when they were near death. (F: ha!) Not like today, sometimes, in, ah, the hospital, where old people are alone and nobody sits with them in their final hours. (F: yes.)

4

F: awîna mâ--, awîna mân ôta *midwife*, kâ-itihcik ôki, kâ-ôh-- –°

A: nôhkom.

F: °– aya, iskwêwa kâ-kî-nâkatohkêcik.

A: nôhkom wiy âta wiya nikiskisin *Sarah*, êwakw ân[a] âna pêyak; êwako mitoni pêyak ê-kî-kiskêyihtamân ôta iskwêwa *that* --, êkonik êtik ôk îskwêyâc ôki, kî-nihtâwikiwak ôki, aya, *Jimmy Arcand*, êkwa *Tommy. Tommy and Jimmy were born in nineteen-forty-eight*; *nineteen-forty-nine* kâ-wanihâyâhk nôhkom, (F: ôh.) *July nineteen-forty-nine*. kî-nêwiwak aniki: *June was Mrs Wolf; July was* iskwêsisak, *Rosa* ôki omâmâwâwa, êkospî kâ-kî---â---mêstihkâhtêk *the church, July, forty-nine; in August* kî-pôni-pimâtisiw wiya nôhkom; *a month after, John Arcand*, êkonik ôki *Sammy* opâpâwâwa – *four, all in -- different months*. kahkiyaw kî-pôni-pimâtisiwak, âha.

F: ha.

5

F: kîkway mâna kî-asahkâniwan ôm ê-isi-kiskisiyan kâ-wîhkohtohk, tâpiskôc, â, kâ-ocêhtowi-kîsikâk, ôma mâna kâ-kî-papâ-kiyokêhk?

A: wahwâ! pitikonikanâpoy, êwako.

F: êwakw ânima kihci.

A: êwakw ân[i] ânima, êwakw ân[i] ânima kihci, âha!

nanâtohk ayisk mînisa mâna kî-kaskâpiskahikâtêwa, *blueberries*, aya, ayôskanak, (F: âha.) êkoni [*sic*]. êkoni mâna kî-mihcêtinwa, aya mîn âya, wîsakîmina, êkoni.

manahikan mâna kî-ayâwak, ayisk piko, aniki tahto kâ-kî-ayâwâcik moscoswa, ohcitaw mâna kî-îkinikêsiwak mîna kî-ayâwak aya, manahikan, (F: mhm.) êkoni anihi.

F: mînisa ohci?

A: âha, mînisa, âha, êkotowahk anihi, (F: ha!) *ya*.

F: êkwa?

4 [*Birth and Death*]

F: Who was -- who used to be the midwife here, as they are called? Those who –°

A: My grandmother.

F: °– those who looked after women.

A: My grandmother Sarah was one that I remember, she was one of them; she was one that I knew looked after the women here. I guess, those ones were the last to be born [*sc.* at home with a midwife's aid], ah, Jimmy Arcand and Tommy. Tommy and Jimmy were born in 1948; in 1949, we lost my grandmother, (F: oh.) in July 1949. There were four of them: in June it was Mrs Wolf, in July *iskwêsisak,* Rosa and her siblings, their mother, at the time when -- the church burnt down, July '49; in August, my grandmother died; a month after, John Arcand, the father of Sammy and his siblings – four, all in -- different months. They all died, yes.

F: Ha.

5 [*Festive Foods*]

F: Do you remember what used to be put out to eat at a gathering, like, ah, when it was New Year's Day, when there was a lot of visiting?

A: Oh my! Meatball soup, for one.

F: That was the best.

A: That was the one, that one was the best, yes!

All kinds of berries used to be canned; blueberries, ah, raspberries, (F: yes.) all of them. They used to be numerous, and cranberries were too.

They used to have cream, because those who had cows always used to do their milking and then had cream, (F: mhm.) for them.

F: To go with the berries?

A: Yes, the berries, yes, for that kind, (F: ha!) ya.

F: And?

A: nôhko--, êkwa nimâmâ nikiskisin îwahikana kî-ayâwêw, (F: âha.) îwahikana.

– *I asked Isabelle, uh, if she had some; she didn't have any when I went.*

F: awîna?

A: *Isabelle Paddy.*

F: ôh!

A: "â, kitayâwâwak cî?" – "â, môya mêkwâc," nititik, *you know; I remember* îwahikanak.

F: ka-kî-kakwê-mâwacihâyâhkik ôma mêkwâc, *for* ôma kâ-wî-pê-kîw--kîwêhk.

A: îwahikanak, âha, awiyak tasi, âha, awiyak t-ôsîhtât anima. (F: âha.) *I remember those, ya; ya, currants* mâna nimâmâ kî-âpacihêw, *ya, currants and then meat, sugar,* âta wiya nikiskisin.

F: pimiy, (A: *ya.*) iyinito-pimiy êtikwê.

A: âha, *ya.*

F: êkwa êtikw--

[*external break*]

6

F: â, *Rosa Longneck* ôta mîn êkwa kipîht-- pîhtokwêw, ê-wî-pê-âcimot wîsta, ka-kâh-kiskisohtocik ê-- otâcimowiniwâwa.

[*to* R:] awa s--, awa [*sc.* cistêmâw] kiki sôniyâs (R: mhm!) ê-kîskisamâkawiyan.

R: pêskis ômâ, âha, ê-wî-aya--, ôtênâhk ê-wî-itohtêyân ici; (A: ôh.) "kî-ma-mîcisoyâni niwî-sipwêhtân," ê-itwêyân ôma mwêhci.

[*to* F:] awas, êkây anita!

F: ââ, môy nânitaw, âhkam-âcimo, wanikiskisi wiy ôhi ê-pimakotêki! môy nânitaw.

R: âha, ha! hm!

[*external break*]

R: êwako cî awa [*sc. Colleen Youngs*] kâ-kî-itâyêk ka-pê-wîcêkoyêk?

F: êwakw âna, otâkosihk kâ-kî-wî-pê-itohtêyâhk, mâk ê-mâmawôpiyâhk osâm kinwês, at-îspayin, nama mayaw.

R: *Harry James,* ana mîn ê-kî-pê-itohtêt.

A: My grandmoth--, and I remember that my mom had pounded meat; (F: yes.) pounded meat.

– I asked Isabelle, uh, if she had some; she didn't have any when I went.

F: Who?

A: Isabelle Paddy.

F: Oh!

A: "Ah, do you have any of that?" – "Not right now," she told me, you know. I remember pounded meat.

F: We should be saving this right now for those who will be coming home.

A: Pounded meat, yes, someone --, yes, someone will make that. (F: yes.) I remember those, ya; ya, my mom used to use currants, ya, currants and sugar too, with the meat, as I remember.

F: Grease, (A: ya.) ordinary grease, I guess.

A: Yes, ya.

F: And I guess --

[*external break*]

6 [*Three's Company*]

F: Ah, Rosa Longneck is here now too; she has come in to tell stories as well and they can remind each other of their stories. [*to* R:] This m--, here is tobacco for you, along with money. (R: mhm!)

R: Yes, besides, I'm going to town later; (A: oh.) I was just saying "I'm going to leave when I've finished eating." [*to* F:] Go on, don't turn that [tape-recorder] on.

F: Aah, it's alright, keep on talking, forget that these are running! It's fine.

R: Yes, ha! Hm!

[*external break*]

R: Is this the one [*sc.* Colleen Youngs] that you said was coming with you?

F: She's the one; we were going to come yesterday, but our meeting went too long and it got too late.

R: Harry James had come, too.

F: ôh, âha, wîst âyis ana masinahikan ê-osîhtât, ôm ôtê kâ-- kihci-kiskinahamâtowikamikohk kâ-kiskinahamâht.

R: katisk ôm ê-waniskâyân, môy âhpô *my glasses*.

F: tânitê? mâka mîna cî ê-kî-papâ-mêtawêyan?

R: môya. (F: môya.) ê-kihtimiyân mitoni.

F: ôh! môy ê-miyomahcihoyan?

R: kîtahtawê mâna mêtoni niskât[a] ê-nipahi-wîsakêyihtamân, *my bones, you know, and headache last night* – pîhtaw ê-wayawîyân êkos îsi konita nama kîkway. (F: hm.)

A: ê-têyistikwânêyan?

R: ââh! kêtahtawê mâna *I just* -- miton ôti.

A: miton ôma piko tita-nâh-nêhiyawêyahk, môy tita-kakwê-âkayâsîmoyahk ôma. (R: âha.)

F: âha! sôskwâc ôm ê-nêhiyawêhk. (A: âha.) (R: âha.)

7

R: kâ-nâh-nitâmisoyahk cî mîna k-âcimoyahk?

A: âsay wiy êwako nikî-âcimon, "mitoni kayâs ê-kî-mihcêtiki, pikw îtê kâ-sêskisihk, osâm piko kî-miskawâwak (R: mînisa ê-kî-astêki.) ayôskanak," nititwân, (R: ayôskanak, âha.) tâpwê wiy êwako. (R: âha.)

R: wâposwak mîna.

A: âha, pihêwak.

R: pihêwak, sîsîpak, (A: âha.) ôh, piko kîkway (F: kî-wêyôtan!) ê-kî-miywâsik! mâk êkwa mêskoc êkospî môy ê-ohc-âsamihcik ayisiyiniwak. (F: âha!) kîspin môy nânitaw tôtamwak ka-mîcisocik, êkosi <u>nama kîkway ta-mîcicik</u>.

F: <u>nôhtêhkatêwak</u>.

R: âha.

F: ha!

A: piko mitoni tâpitawi namôy ê-na-nakîhk, (R: âha.) ta-nitonikâtêk kîkway, (R: êkosi piko.) tit-â-- tit-âsamihcik awâsisak.

F: Oh, yes, because he is also working on a book, over here at -- he is going to school at the University.

R: I woke up just now, I don't even have my glasses.

F: Where? Were you going around playing [*sc.* bingo] as usual?

R: No. (F: no.) I was really lazy.

F: Oh! Are you not feeling well?

R: Once in a while my legs really hurt, my bones, you know, and I also had a headache last night – and so I just went out like this without anything. (F: hm.)

A: You had a headache?

R: Aah! Often all of a sudden I just -- really!

A: Really we must just speak Cree; we're trying not to speak English. (R: yes.)

F: Yes! It's just Cree that is being spoken. (A: yes.) (R: yes.)

7 [*Making a Living I: Cutting Posts*]

R: Are we also going to tell of the times when we used to go picking berries?

A: I have already told that, "Long ago, they were really numerous, raspberries were found more or less everywhere you went in the bush," (R: berries were there.) I said. (R: raspberries, yes.) Truly they were. (R: yes.)

R: Rabbits too.

A: Yes, prairie-chickens.

R: Prairie-chickens, ducks, (A: yes.) oh, everything (F: there was an abundance!) was good! But at that time, unlike today, the people were not fed [*sc.* welfare]. (F: yes!) If they did nothing to procure food, then they ate nothing.

F: They went hungry.

R: Yes.

F: Ha!

A: There really could be no stopping at any time, (R: yes.) in the search for something, (R: that was the only thing to do.) with which to feed the children.

R: yâyâhk, mihcêtwâw nikî-apwêsin sakâhk ê-cîkahikêyân, cimacêsa ê-cimâ-- ê-cîkahamân. ê-papâmi-pa-pêyakoyân *in the spruce* --

– mâka mîn âsay nitâkayâsîmon.

A: minahikohk.

R: minah-- minahikohk ê-papâ-pa-pêyakoyân, *you know*!

kîtahtawê kâ-sâkaskinahtâyân anihi mâna kâ-âhkwêhtawastêki mistikowata, (F: âha.) kâ-pê-takosihk aw âya, awa *'Guy'* kâ-kî-itiht, (F: âha!) kâ-pê-takosihk êwako, katisk ê-matâwisipitamân. "tânis ôh ê-wî-itôtaman, nicâhkos!" nikî-itik ayisk mâna, osâm onôtokwêma –°

A: ê-kî-itâhkômisk, âha.

R: °– ê-kî-itâhkômiyit mâna, "nicâhkos!" nikî-itik mâna. "ê-wî-atâwâkêyân ôhi, ê-wî-sipwêhtatâyân," nititâw, "sîwîhtâkani-sâkahikay-- sîwîhtâkani-sâkahikanihk," nititâw; (–

F: *Blaine Lake* cî êwako?

R: âha.

A: êwakw âha!

R: môy âyis ôm ê-ohci-kaskihtâyân nistam kîkway ahpihc, mêton ôt[i] ê-kî--, *you know,* nama kîkway ê-ohci-nisitohtamân, êtataw mitoni, *you know*?

F: k-âkayâsîmoyan cî?

R: âha, ka-pîkiskwêstamâsoyân.

F: âha.

R: aspin êkwa ôki kâ-mâci-kiskinohamâhcik awâsisak, wiyawâw êkwa ê-kiskinohamawicik ciyêkwac.

F: âha.

R: miton ôt[i] ê-kisiskâ-kiskêyihtamân, kîkwây piko ê-manêsiyân, ka-masinahikêyân, k-âyamihcikêyân; êwako piko ê-manêsiyân. –)

R: – nititâw. "niya kik-âtâmitin, nicâhkos!" nititik. "tânis ôh ê-itakihtaman?" – "môy âhpô nikiskêyihtên," nititâw, "tânis ôhi k-êtakihtamân, ê-nitawêyihtamân mâk ê-nôhtê-atâwâkêyân," nititâw, "awâsisak k-âpacihtâcik," nititâw. ay--, â, ayinânêwimitanaw kâ-pê-miyit.

– kinisitohtên 'ayinânêwimitanaw'? (F: mhm.) (A: mhm.) –

R: Really, many times I would sweat in the bush chopping, I was chopping fence-posts. I'd be going about alone in the spruce

– and I'm already speaking English again.

A: In the spruce.

R: I'd be going about alone in the spruce, you know!

At one time I was filling up the wagon-box with posts piled crosswise, (F: yes.) and this one arrived, Guy he was called, (F: yes.) he arrived just as I was pulling them out into the open. "What are you going to do with these, Sister-in-law!" he said to me, as he usually did, because his wife [*sc.* was a sister to my husband] –°

A: She was related to you in that way, yes.

R: °– as she was related to me in that way, "Sister-in-law!" he used to say to me. "I'm going to sell these, I'm taking them with me," I told him, "to *sîwîhtâkani-sâkahikanihk*," I told him; (–

F: Is that Blaine Lake?

R: Yes.

A: That's it, yes!

R: For at first I wasn't able to speak any, really I was -- you know, I didn't understand anything, next to nothing, you know?

F: For you to speak English?

R: Yes, to speak for myself.

F: Yes.

R: From the time when the children started school, then they were teaching me instead.

F: Yes.

R: I really learned quickly; the only thing I lack is to write and to read. I lack that only. –)

R: – I said to him. "I will buy them from you, Sister-in-law!" he said to me. "What are you charging for these?" – "I don't even know," I said to him, "what to charge for these, but I want to sell them," I said to him, "the children can use it," I said to him. Ah, he came and gave me eighty dollars.

– Do you understand *ayinânêwimitanaw*? (F: mhm.) (A: mhm.) –

kâ-pê-miyit; "êkosi cî ôhi kika-miyin," nititik. "âha," nititâw. môy âhpô ê-wiyakihtamân, ayis mâna wiyawâw kâ-nitaw-âtâwâkêcik, pêyak anima cimacês --

A: âha; nîso-sôniyâs.

R: nîso-sôniyâs. (A: âha!) âha, pêyak-sôniyâs, kahtap ê-kî-isi-tipahamâhcik, *you know*.

R: êkosi, mâcik êkwa nititohtân ôtênâhk êkwa, mitoni. kayâs ayis kî-wêhtakihtêw kîkway. (A: tâpwê.) mistahi ka-pêcikân, kiyâm nîstanaw-tahtwâpisk ohcit--, kayâs, *you know*.

A: tâpwê wiy êwako.

R: êkosi nititohtân, mêtoni nimisi-pêcikân. "hâ!" nititêyihtên, âsay mîn êkwa nimaci-mâmitonêyihtên. (F: âha!) ay êkwa, minahi-- minahikwak êk ôhc ânihi mâna, mênikan-- aya, --

A: kâ-kî-mênikanihkâkêcik.

R: kâ-kî-mênikanihkâkêhk, "mâka cimacêsa nik-ôsîhtân," nititêyihtên. êy, nisêskitâpâson, (F: êkoni --) (– *the old man* aw ôtê ê-ay-atoskêt wiy âya, ayamihêwikamikohk êkospî kâ-wî--, kâ-kîsitêk anima ayamihêwikamik (F: ôh.) êkwa kotak kâ-osîhtâhk.

F: *nineteen-fifty*.

A: nâh, *nineteen-forty-nine* kâ-kî-kîsitêk, omâmâwâwa êkospî kâ-nahinimiht; (R: âha, *same day*.) *and then they built it fifty-three*.

R: pêyakwan êwako ê-kîsikâk, ê-kî-wanikiskisit an[a] âya, wâsaskocênikanisa anih âyamihêwiyiniw, (A: âha, *ya*.) êkot[a] ôhc ânim ê-kî-kîsitêk, (F: ôh.) âha. –)

R: – êkosi, ê-kî-wiyahpicikêyân nisêskitâpâson. sôskwâc ê-ay-iskwâki, êkwa ôhi mênikan--, ôhi mâna apisâsinwa.

A: mênikanâh-- mênikanâhti-- mênikanâhtikwa.

R: âha.

R: sôskwâc ê-âh-iskwâki. nimatâwisipitên, mwêhci nistwâw ê-pimohtêyân, kâ-pîkonamân anihi kâ-sâpostamoki mâna. môy ê-wâpamak ôtê ê-- ê-cimasot (iskwatahikanak aniki) (A: ôh, âha!) kâ-nakâwâskwêsihk, kâ-pîkonamân anima. êkota ohci, êy, mâninakisk êkwa ninîhtinêhtay êkwa, anihi ê-nîhtinamân. nipê-kîwêpayin, (–

He came and gave me it; "You will give me all of these?" he said to me. "Yes," I told him. I did not even set a price for them, because for those who went to sell them, one fence-post was --

A: Yes; fifty cents.

R: Fifty cents. (A: yes!) Yes, twenty-five cents. They were paid different prices, you know.

R: So, then I certainly went to town. Things were cheap long ago. (A: truly.) You came away with a lot for twenty dollars, long ago, you know.

A: That's for sure.

R: So, I went and I really came away with a lot. "Ha!" I thought, for already I was thinking greedy thoughts. (F: yes!) Well, then the spruce -- then from those spruce trees, fence-- ah --

A: What they used to make fences with.

R: What one used to make fences with. "But I will make fence-posts," I thought. Hey, I drove into the bush, (F: those --) (–
the old man was working here, ah, at the church at that time -- for that church had burned down (F: oh.) and another was being built.

F: 1950.

A: No, it burnt in 1949, at the time that their mom was buried; (R: yes, the same day.) and then they built it in '53.

R: That same day, the priest had forgotten the candles, (A: yes, ya.) and it burnt because of that, (F: oh.) yes. –)

R: – So, when I had harnessed the horses, I drove into the bush. They were full length, these fence-- but they were usually small around.

A: Fence-- fence-- fence-rails.

R: Yes.

R: They were full length. I pulled them out; when I went for the third time, I broke the reaches [*i.e.,* part of the undercarriage]. I didn't see it standing there (one of those treestumps) (A: oh, yes!) and when I hit it and stopped dead, I broke that wagon. Well, from there, I proceeded to unload all of the rails; I took them off. I drove home, (–

ôta mêkwâc ê-ayâyâhk, anim îta *Emile* k-âyât, (F: âha.) aya, *Kerline* îh, anima okayâsi-wâskahikan.

A: *the old ration-house*, (R: âha.) âha, *ya*.

R: êkot[a] ôm ê-ayâyâhk k-âcimoyân; –)

R: êy, nipê-kîwêpayin êkwa.

– môy âyis ôma mâna wîhkâc ê-wawânêyihtamihikoyân kîkway, ayis kisêyiniw nikî-pê-kiskinawâpamâw tânis ê-kî-pê-tôtahk mâna. êkos ê-kî-isit mâna: "kiskinawâpamin, ôta kisiwâk nîpawi!" ê-kî-isit mîna mâna kâ-wâskahikanihkêt, *you know*, (A: mhm.) "k-- môy ôma tâpitawi k-ôsîhtamâtin kîkway," ê-kî-isit mâna, *you know*! –

êkosi; êk ôki kâ-- pasiposôsak ôki, êkotowahk êkwa k-ôtinak êkwa, êy, nipâh-pôskwahwâw êkwa, sôskwâc ê-- ayinânêwi-misit ê-iskosit awa, sôskwât nipâh-pôskwahwâw êkwa nipostamôhâw êkota, sakahikana nisâ-sâposci-sakahên êkây ka-tâskipayit – tâskipayiwak ayis mâna. (A: âha.)

êkosi, êkwa mîna nisêskitâpâson, nipê-wayaw-- nipê-wayawîpitên. êy, mâninakisk êkwa ê-kî-wayawîpitamân êkwa, *in eight* êkwa, tâsi-- ayinânêw anihi, êkos îs ê-isi-kîskipotâyân. nikî-- nawac piko mâna nikînwâhkwêhikon aya, ka-kînikatahikêyân. (A: âha.) îh, êkwa an[a] êkwa kisêyiniw ê-takosihk êkwa kâ-kînikatahikêt. miton êtokwê mitâtahtomitanaw, iyikohk ispayinwa anihi, *you know*, (A: âha.) ê-osîhtâyân.

êkosi; "âsay mîna wâpahki niwî-âwacipitên," nititâw, "mîna kika-kînikatahamawin, nika-kâh-kîskipotân," nititâw.

A: kitâcimon cî mâk ê-kî-pîkonikêyan?

R: âha.

A: ôh, kitâcimostawâw, (R: âha.) âha.

R: êkosi, "nîswâw wâpahki nika-pimohtân mîna," nititâw, "nika-pêcipitên, êkosi kika-kâh-kînikatahamawin mîna," nititâw – mitoni kâ-sâkaskinahtâyân mistikowat sâsamîna. (A: âha!) (– êkw ê-kî-nihtâ-kînikatahikêt ayisk mân âna kisêyiniw.

A: kî-nahîwak aniki okinwâpêkikwayawak (R: âha.) *in carpentry*, (F: âha.)

R: êkwa mîna kî-- piko kîkway sôskwâc.

at that time we were staying here, where Emile lives, (F: yes!) ah, at Kerline's, look, that old house of hers.

A: The old ration house, (R: yes.) yes, ya.

R: That's where we were at the time I'm telling of; –)

R: hey, I came driving home then.

– Nothing ever really stumps me, for I had observed how the old man used to fix things. He used to say this to me: "Watch me, stand near here," he would say to me when he built houses, you know. (A: mhm.) "I will not always be making things for you," he used to tell me, you know! –

So; then I took one of those reaches, and, hey, I made holes in it then, just -- this one was eight feet long, and I just made holes in it and put it on there, and I drove nails through so it wouldn't break apart – because they often break apart. (A: yes.)

So then I drove into the bush, and I came out -- I came pulling them out. Hey, just then when I had pulled them out, in eight then, -- those were eight -- I was chopping them like that. I was -- it used to be beyond me to chop the pickets to a point. (A: yes.) Look, then the old man arrived and he would chop them to a point. I guess there really were a hundred or so of those, you know, (A: yes.) that I had made.

So; "Tomorrow I am going to go pull more out again," I said to him, "and you will chop them to a point for me again, and I'll saw them into lengths," I told him.

A: But did you tell about your break-down?

R: Yes.

A: Oh, you told him about it, (R: yes.) yes.

R: Alright; "I'll go twice tomorrow," I said to him, "I'll pull them here, and you will again chop them to a point for me," I told him – when I had completely filled the wagon-box again. (A: yes!) (–

Because the old man used to be good at chopping them to a point.

A: Those Longnecks were good (R: yes.) in carpentry. (F: yes.)

R: And also -- just everything.

A: piko kîkway, *the bunks*.
F: ê-kî-osîhtâcik.
A: *bunks* ê-kî-osîhtâcik, (R: âha.) *runners*, (F: ôh.) *poles*.
R: ahpô, âha, ê-kî-osîhât mâna *the old man*. (A: âha!) pimipayîsak aniki, êkotowahk ê-kî-osîhât, êkw ânihi kâ-pimitastêki.
A: âha, *bu--, uh, bunks*. (R: âha.)
F: môya nânitaw.
R: piko kîkway.
A: *oh yes, however*, –°
F: âwaci-- ê-kî-âwacikêhk anihi mâna.
R: âha.
A: âha, *they -- they were very good*.
R: ê-kî-osîhât mâna. –)

R: êkosi. êkw ân[i] êkwa, nisipwêtâpâsonân êkwa, *Blaine Lake* êkwa, ê-nikotwâsiko-kîsikâk.
A: ê-nitaw-âtâwakêyan êkwa ôm, âha.

R: sîwîhtâkani-sakahikanihk, âha, nititohtânân; êkota pônatoskêw, *you know*, ê-niyânano-kîsikâk isko mân ê-atoskêt; nisipwêtâpâsonân. wahwâ, namwâc kinwês, yêyâpisinwak nimistikoma. wiya, "kiya," nititâw, pikw îsi, "kiya kikiskêyihtên," nititâw, "mêtoni misi-kâspatahok ôk ôpîtatowêwak!" nititâw. [*laughter*]

êkosi; wahwâ, miscahîs ispayinwa. êkosi ê-kî-otinikêyân êkwa, "hâ, pêyak-tipahôpân k-âcâwânânaw," mâka mîna. [*laughs*]
A: mâka mîna, ê-wî-- êwako nayêstaw, âha.
F: [*laughs*] êwakw ânima, iyâyaw.
A: âha, pêyak, âha!

R: êkwa nâpêsis awa *Jim* niwîcêwânân, êwakw âwa ê-pamihcikêt, ê-pamihastimwêt.

êkosi; nânitaw âpihtawanohk ê-pê-ayâyâhk, âsay namôy nipê-nisitohtâtonân. [*laughs*] (A: âha.) mitoni nîst ê-takahkipêyân,
A: âw! (R: mhm.)
R: wiy ânima, âha.
A: kiy âyis kitatoskêwin anima. (F: [*laughs*]) (R: mhm.) (A: [*laughs*])

A: Everything, the bunks.

F: They made them.

A: They made bunks, (R: yes.) runners, (F: oh.) poles.

R: Even those, yes, the old man used to make them. (A: yes!) He made those runners, and those bunks [*sc.* those which are sideways].

A: Yes, bu-- uh, bunks. (R: yes.)

F: Fine.

R: Everything.

A: Oh, yes, however –°

F: Those were used for hauling.

R: Yes.

A: Yes, they -- they were very good.

R: He used to make them. –)

R: That's it. Then we left with a team of horses for Blaine Lake, on a Saturday.

A: You went to sell that then, yes.

R: At *sîwîhtâkani-sâkahikanihk*, yes, we went there; he stopped work there, you know, he usually worked through to Friday; we left with the team of horses. Well, it wasn't long before they had appraised my wood. "You deal with it," I said to him, just this way, "you, you know how to deal with it," I said to him, "gyp these Ukrainians good and proper!" I told him. [*laughter*]

Alright; well, they came to quite a bit. So I did my shopping and then, "Ha, we'll buy ourselves a gallon," as usual. [*laughs*]

A: As usual, -- only that, yes.

F: [*laughs*] That was it, first things first.

A: Yes, one, yes!

R: And we were going with this boy of mine, Jim, who was driving the horses.

So, we had come about halfway and already we couldn't understand each other. [*laughs*] (A: yes.) I too was feeling really good from the drink.

A: Wow! (R: mhm.)

R: On account of that, yes.

A: You had earned it yourself, of course. (F: [*laughs*]) (R: mhm.) (A: [*laughs*])

R: kêkâc kâ-kwatapisimikoyâhk nikosis; sêhkêpayîs[a] ê-nakiskawât, osâm mistah ê-paskêtâpâsot, êkw âyis âsay mêskanawa kî-wâh-osîhcikâtêwa, (A: âha.) kî-miywâsinwa. ôh, tânisi mîna; îh, konit ê-pasikwâ-- ê-pasikô-kwâskohtiyân, "nik-âti-nîpawipayihon," nititêyihtên, kâ-pakamisiniyân, âsay ê-itipêyân, îh, (A: âha, *ya, ya*.) âsay ê-môcikipêyân mitoni!

konita nanâtohk kîkway ê-kî-isi-pimâcihoyâhk mâna, – aya mîn ôk âya, kâ-mihkosicik ôki minahikwak, (A: âha.) – êkonik mîna mâna, ôki kâ-ocipitamihk wâskahikana, sîpâ ayisk ahâwak.

A: *skids*.

R: êkonik, âha.

A: âha, *ya*.

F: kîkwây mâk âniki kâ-mihkosicik, *tamarack*?

R: *tamarack*, âha, *ya*.

A: âha, *ya*! *She's talking about what you put skids under; a granary* kâ-ocipicikâtêki.

R: êkotowahk mîna mân ê-kî-cîkahwâyâhkok, iyikohk ê-kî-miywakisocik, *just* pêyak ana piko, nîstanaw-tahtwâpisk ê-kî-ohtisit mâna *the old man*, ê-miyosiyit.

ôh, nanâtohk mân ê-kî-tôtamâhk, anihi mîna ayinânêwi-misit kâ-kîskatahikâtêki, êkotowahk mîna mâna.

F: *cordwood* aya?

R: âha.

F: môya --

R: aya, *eight-footers* – âh, nitâkayâsîmowân awa.

8

A: aya, mâka kikî-- kikî-mônahikân?

R: kîkwâya?

A: anihi mâna *seneca-root*?

R: âha.

A: kîkwây--

F: tânisi ê-isi-nêhiyawiyîhkâtêki kan êkoni?

R: mînisîhkês.

F: mînisîhkês. (A: âha.)

R: My son nearly turned us over; he met a car and pulled over too much; for roads were already being built then, (A: yes.) and they were good. Oh, and how it went; look, I just jumped up, "I'll stand up," I thought, but I fell down with a thud, as I was already that way with drink, see, (A: yes, ya, ya.) I was already really having fun from the drink!

We used to make a living from just all kind of things,

– and these ones too, these red spruce, (A: yes.) –

these ones too, usually, these which you used to move houses, as they were placed under them.

A: Skids.

R: Those ones, yes.

A: Yes, ya.

F: But what were these red ones, tamarack?

R: Tamarack, yes, ya.

A: Yes, ya! She's talking about what you put skids under; a granary, when it is pulled.

R: That kind we used to chop too, they were so favourably priced, the old man used to get twenty dollars for just one, the good ones.

Oh, we used to do various things; those which are cut to eight feet, we made that kind too.

F: Cordwood?

R: Yes.

F: Not --

R: Well, eight-footers – ah, I'm talking English.

8 [*Plans for a Reunion II: Implements; Dress*]

A: But did you dig?

R: What things?

A: That seneca-root?

R: Yes.

A: What --

F: How are they called in Cree?

R: *mînisîhkês*.

F: Seneca-root. (A: yes.)

R: êkoni mîna mân ôtê ê-ayâyâhk, nistam nawac kâ-pê-ispiciyâhk ôta, ôt[a] ôhci mân ê-kî-sipwêhtêyân, *all* -- kapê-kîsik mâna *in a* --, mêkwâc môy mostoswak ê-asiwasocik. oh, iyikohk mân ê-kî-mâh-miywâsiki, îh, ê-kî-na-nîmâsiyân mâna.

A: matwân cî nânitaw tâh-kî-miskikâtêwa anihi 'mônahaskwâna' mâna kî-itamwak anihi, anihi k-âpacihtâhk kâ-mônahaskwêhk.

R: osîhcikâtêwa anihi, ê-mosc-ôsîhcikâtêki, miywâs--

A: kîspin êkon ânihi ta-kî-ayâyâhk ôta, *July* ôma kâ-wî---nitomihcik kahkiyaw maskwêkowiyiniwak [*sic; sc.* maskêkowiyiniwak] ta-pê-- ta-pê-kîwêcik, êkospi, (R: âha.) *July the thirty-first.*

R: kikiskêyihtên awîna kâh-ayât? nâpêw.

A: ôh, tâh-ayâw?

F: kêyâpic cî mân ê-mônahaskwêt wiya?

R: âha, môy kayâs, *about maybe four years ago, five years ago,* kêyâpic kî-mônahikêw.

A: ôh, tâh-ayâw êtikwê ana, âha.

R: âha, ayâw êtikwê.

F: nahascikêw ayis mâna. (R: âha.)

A: êkospî kîspin -- kayâs ê-kiskisiyan kâ-kî-omâmâyan ê-kî-isîhot, kîspin miskotâkay kîkway kinôhtê-osîhtamowinihkân, ê-wî-- kâw êkos ê-wî-isîhohk. (R: ôh!) (A: âha.) (R: aya.) pîhconês --

R: âha, kî-kîskasâkêw mâna mîna. (F: â, âha.) ôta sêhkwêpitêwa ôtê [*points to waist*], ôtê mitoni kinwâwa [*gestures to leg*]. (A: âha, *ya*.) âha, êkosi kî-isîhow.

F: êkwa aspascâkanis.

R: âha.

A: âha, *ya*.

R: êkwa ôma opîhconês, (A: pîhconês, âha!) ê-kî-kakwâhyaki-nihtâwikwâtahk mâna, kî-nihtâwikwâsow ayis.

F: konita mâna, *pleats*. (R: âha.) (A: âha.)

A: êkwa ôtê mâna kâ-kî-nitaw-âyamihâhk, nanâtohk kîkway anihi kiskinawâcihowinisa mâna kî-kikamohtâw nôhkom ôta. (R: âha.) êkoni mâna ayis--, aya mîna mâna *safety-pins* êkota kî-at[i]-âkwamohtâw, môy wîhkâc ohci nôhtêpayiwak

R: Those ones too, when we lived here, about the time we first moved here, I used to leave [*sc.* to dig] from here all -- all day usually, in a --, while the cattle were not in the pasture. Oh, they used to be so good then, and I used to take a little lunch along.

A: I wonder if those could be found somewhere, they used to call them *mônahaskwâna,* those ones which were used for digging.

R: They were made, they were made by hand, good --

A: If we could have them here in July when all the people of Muskeg will be invited to come back; at that time, (R: yes.) July the 31st.

R: You know someone who has one? *nâpêw.*

A: Oh, would he have one?

F: Does he still dig?

R: Yes, not long ago, about maybe four years ago, five years ago, he was still digging.

A: Oh, I guess he would have one then, yes.

R: Yes, he has one, I guess.

F: Because he always puts things away. (R: yes.)

A: If you remember how your late mom dressed at one time long ago -- if a dress is something you want to have made, we're going to -- that's how they are going to be dressing. (R: oh!) (A: yes.) (R: well.) A blouse--

R: Yes, she used to wear a long skirt too. (F: ah, yes.) They were gathered with an elastic here [*points to waist*], and really long over here [*gestures to leg*]. (A: yes, ya.) Yes, she dressed just like that.

F: And an apron.

R: Yes.

A: Yes, ya.

R: And this blouse of hers, (A: a blouse, yes!) she used to sew them really well then, for she was a good seamstress.

F: And there used to be pleats. (R: yes.) (A: yes.)

A: And when they went to the pilgrimage here, my grandmother used to fasten on all kinds of decorative jewellry here. (A: yes.) Because those -- well, she also used to fasten safety-pins there;

êkotowahk, (R: âha.) kâkikê nôcikwêsiwak êkotowahk kî--
[... ;?*record*] ---âwak.

R: êkwa kayâs aya, *they used to be* anihi, tânisi, anihi kâ-sêkwamoki, *I don't know* --

F: *bobby-pin?*

R: môya.

F: môya, *hair-pin?*

A: *clips, clips.*

R: êkoni.

A: âha.

R: mâka nanâtohk (F: ê-isinâkwahki.), ê-kî-isi-kiskinawâcihcikâcêsiki acâhkosak, piko kîkway pîsim ahpô ê-kî-masinisihk. (A: âha.) êkwa kâ-sêkipatwâcik, ôtê isi ômis îsi kî-itamoniyiwa. (F: âha.) (A: âha.) ôtê êkwa sênapân[a] (A: sênapâna, âha.) ê-kî-kikamôhâcik wanaskoc, wêstakâwâhk.

A: êkwa pikw âwiyak ômatowahk ohci kikiskawêw, ê-kaskitêsiyit, â, –°

R: âha, nîst âniki nitayâwâwak.

A: °– *black beads, I know she has them.* (R: âha.)

F: nimâmâ nîsta, (R: âha.) nikanawêyimimâwa êkotowahk; kî-miywêyihtam ayis mâna wîst ê-wawêsît. (R: âha.)

A: âha, *ya, black beads.*

R: nîst ê-nipahi-miywêyihtamân nîsta kîkway. ât[a] êkwa mâna nimiyikwak ôki nanâtohk, *you know,* (A: âha.) ê-miyicik mâna ka-tâpiskamwak, namôy nimiywêyimâwak ôki!

F: ôki piko.

A: âha.

R: âha, ôki!

A: *ya.*

F: piko mâk êkwa kahkiyaw ka-k-- ka-kikamôhacik kipîhconêsihk ôt[a] âya.

A: ê-isi-kiskisiyan piko ta-kakwê-osîhtâyan miskotâkay, êkospî anima ta-pê-kikiskaman ôta, (R: ôh!) mâmawôpayiyâhki, êkwa mîna mâna kî-kikiskawêwak anihi aya, tâpihtêpisona. (R: âha.) êkosi *little gold ones,* (R: âha.) kî-kikiskawêwak mâna, *little gold earrings, they had those* --

they were never short of those. (R: yes.) All the old ladies carried those around with them.

R: And long ago, there used to be those -- how -- those which slip underneath, I don't know --

F: Bobby-pin?

R: No.

F: No, hair-pin?

A: Clips, clips.

R: Those.

A: Yes.

R: But different things (F: appeared.), [*sc*. on barrettes] there were images of little stars, all kinds of things, even the sun was represented. (A: yes.) And those with braids used to have them hang like this [*sc*. with a row of barrettes high on the braid]. (F: yes.) (A: yes.) And they fastened ribbons here (A: ribbons, yes.) on the ends of their hair.

A: And everyone wore this kind, these little black, ah, –°

R: Yes, I had those too.

A: °– black beads, I know she has them. (R: yes.)

F: My mom, too, (R: yes.) I keep that kind of hers; she used to like getting dressed up too. (R: yes.)

A: Yes, ya, black beads.

R: I really like those things too. They always give me these different things, you know, (A: yes.) they usually give me necklaces to wear, but I don't like them!

F: Only these.

A: Yes.

R: Yes, these!

A: Ya.

F: But now you will have to fasten all of them here on your blouse.

A: You must try to make the dress as you remember it, and then you can wear it here, (R: oh!) when we have the gathering, and also they used to wear those, ah, earrings. (R: yes.) Those little gold ones, (R: yes.) they used to wear little gold earrings, they had those --

R: nika-kakwê-pôskwahikâson (A: *pierced.*) nîhtawakâhk. (F: âha. [*laughs*])

A: niya wiya, *mine are pierced. If I can find those,* âha!

F: nîsta, môy--

R: aya; aw âwa mâna nisikos ê-nôhtê-kakwêcimak anihi, tanitê ê-kî-ohtinât mâna wîhcawakâsihk kâ-kikamoniyiki, tânis-- kayâs ayisk anik ôhc âniki (A: âha, *yes.*) kayâs; nistam mâwacêyas ê-mâtitâpihtêpisocik iskwêwak, êkonik anik âniki, (A: âha.) *copper*; nika-mosci-atahamâson. [*laughter*]

F: tânisi mâka kâ-isi-nêhiyawîhkâtâwak aniki? sôniyâwâpisk, osâwi-sôniyâwâpisk.

R: â, êtikwê, âha. âha, êkotowahk êtikwê.

R: êkwa mîna mâna âhcanisa ê-kî-osîhât, *the old man*, êkotowahk ohci. ê-kî-osîhât, ê-kî-wiyatahwât mâna, (A: âha.) ê-kî-pôskwatahwât ê-pakamahwât, (A: âha.) îh! ê-kî-tâh-takahkîsihât mâna.

A: ôh, kî-nahîwak nanâtohk kîkway.

R: âha.

A: môy ânima konita kîst êkota kâ-kî-pahkisiniyan.

R: ka-câh-cowêskihtêw ôma ê-mâh-mâmiskomâyahk. [*laughter*] awas, ê-kî-mêkihk anima niya, môy ânima ê-ohci-pakitinisoyân, êkota.

F: êkosi ma cî mân âyis kayâs?

R: âhâ!

F: ê-kî-mosci-mêkihk?

R: ê-kî-pîkonit, ê-kî-wanâhit mitoni, ahpô êtikwê --

F: awîna mâk ê-kî-itêyimoyan?

R: ahpô êtikwê miton âya ê-wâpiskistikwânêt! [*laughter*]

F: kisêyiniw êtikwê. [*laughter*]

R: mitoni nikâh-câh-cîsiskawâw, [*laughs*] (A: âha.) mêkwâc ê-oskinîkiskwêmakisiyân. [*laughs*]

A: âha.

[*pause*]

R: I'll try to pierce (A: pierced.) my ears. (F: yes. [*laughs*])

A: As for me, mine are pierced. If I can find those [earrings], yes!

F: Mine too, not--

R: Well; I want to ask this [paternal] aunt of mine where she used to get those which she wore attached to her ears, because they were from (A: yes, yes.) long ago; from the time when women first started wearing earrings, it was these ones, (A: yes.) copper; I will just pound them out for myself. [*laughter*]

F: But what are these called in Cree? *sôniyâwâpisk*, *osâwi-sôniyâwâpisk*.

R: Ah, I guess so, yes. Yes, that kind I guess.

R: And the old man also used to make rings from that material. He made them, he used to forge them, (A: yes.) he made holes in them and pounded them, (A: yes.) look! he used to make really nice ones.

A: Oh, they were good at all kinds of things.

R: Yes.

A: It's not for nothing that you fell [*sc.* for him] there.

R: His ears will be ringing, since we are talking about him. [*laughter*] Go on, I was given away, for I didn't choose to go there.

F: Wasn't it like that long ago?

R: Yes!

F: They were simply given away?

R: He had spoiled my plans, he had really distracted me, I suppose --

F: Who did you have in mind for yourself, then?

R: Maybe even a really light-haired one [*sc.* white-haired]! [*laughter*]

F: An old man, I guess. [*laughter*]

R: Maybe I could have excited him, [*laughs*] (A: yes.) while I was a young woman. [*laughs*]

A: Yes.

[*pause*]

9

A: êwakw âwa mâna nanâtohk *rugs* kâ-osîhât anihi kâ--
kâ-kaskikwâtât anihi.

F: ê-apihkâtahk?

R: â, piko kîkway, k-âpihkâtamân mâna.

F: ahpô cî anihi mîna, (R: âha.) – tânis êtikwê
kâh-isi-nêhiyawiyîhkâtên '*crochet*'?

R: môy, môy wiy êwako.

A: môy wiy êwako, môya.

R: nipakwâtên êwako. tânêhk êtikwê?

A: apihkâtêw anihi ta--

R: ê-kakwê-kiskinohamâkawiyân.

F: mosci kâ-apihkâtêk[i] (R: âha.) ânihi kotaka.

R: êkotowahk ê-kaskikwâtamân. (A: *ya*.)

R: êkotowahk, anihi mâna kâ-âh-atâmiyan.

F: âha! ê-atâmak – mihcêtwâw mâk êkwa kitatâmitin.

R: pikw âwiyak, awa mîna mâna, mitoni. kêtahtawê m--
ka-kiskisotototawinâwâw mâna, capasîs itâpiyêko, piko kîkway.

F: âha! pim-âya---tahk---tahkoskêyâhki. [*laughs*] (A: âha, *ya*.)

R: nanâtohk mân âkohpa mîna, pikw îsi ê-isikwâtamân.

A: nanâcohkikwâcêsa mîn ê-nihtâ-kaskikwâtahk.

F: âha! ê-nipahi-nihtâ-- –°

A: nipahi-nihtâwêyihtam awa, nanâtohk kîkway t-êsi-wîcihisot,
misihêwa (R: âha.) mîna kêyâpic ê-ayâwât awa.

R: âha!

F: ââha!

F: wah, mitoni mân âskaw kikoskohin mâk, îyikohk
ê-âhkamêyimoyan, môy wîhkât ê-pê-pôyoyan.

A: mitoni namôy wîhkâc ê-pôyot, âha.

R: môy wîhkâc, –°

F: môy wîhkâc ê-pê-pômêyan.

R: °– môy nikaskihtân ômis îsi k-ây-apiyân.

A: *roothouse* mîn ê-kî-osîhtât.

R: nôhtaw kâ-pômêyân, êkây ê-kî-kîsi-wâtihkâtamâhk, êkây
âwiyak, *you know*, aciyaw *the frame* ê-kî-osîhtâyân.

9 [*Leading an Active Life*]

A: This is the one who makes all kinds of rugs, which -- she sews them.

F: She braids them?

R: Ah, everything, I usually braid them.

F: Or even those too, (R: yes.) – what would you call 'crocheting' in Cree?

R: No, not that.

A: Not that, no.

R: I don't like that. I don't know why?

A: She braids those to --

R: Someone tried to teach me how.

F: Those others which are merely braided. (R: yes.)

R: I sew that kind. (A: ya.)

R: That's the kind that you usually buy from me.

F: Yes! I buy them from her; I have bought them from you many times.

R: Everybody does, and this one does too, really. Someday you will remember me, when your eye falls on all these things.

F: Yes! When we happen to step on them. [*laughs*] (A: yes, ya)

R: And all kinds of blankets too that I sew in various ways.

A: She is also good at sewing patchwork quilts.

F: Yes! She's really very good at –°

A: She is very resourceful, helping herself out with different things, like chickens, (R: yes.) and she still has them.

R: Yes!

F: Yes!!

F: Oh, you really surprise me at times by being so persistent; you never give up.

A: She really never quits, yes.

R: Never, –°

F: You have never become discouraged.

R: °– I'm not able to just sit around like this.

A: And she built a roothouse, too.

R: I did give up, when we couldn't finish digging the hole for it, none of us had finished it, you know, and I had made the frame.

F: â, wâwâc mâna wiya ê--, iyikohk ê-tahkahkinâkohtât, mênikan wâ-- wâsakâ wîkihk.

A: ê-kî-sisopêkahaman.

R: môy ânima anim êwako kîkway ê-kî-sisopêkahamân.

F: sôskwâc êkwa mîna mâ-- *porch* –°

A: pîhc-âyihk, pîhc-âyihk mîna mân ânima ê-kaskihtât *to, uh, panelling.* [*laughs*]

R: niy ânima ê-kî-osîhtâyan ayis anima [... ; *?record*] nîki –°

F: *porch* mîna ê-kî-wa-osîhtâyân (R: ââhâ!) ma cî? (A: *yes, ya.*) ê-kî-âniskôscikêt.

R: ê-kî-ânisko-- môy cêskw âhpô ê-kîsîhtâyân, êkosi mîn êwako piko ta-kakwê-kîsîhtâyân; môy âta mistah, âpisîs piko.

[*pause*]

F: tânitê kiy ê-kî-kiskinahamâkawiyan cî, ka-isi-kakâyawisîyan ê-awâsisîwiyan?

R: tânis êtikwê, mâskôc êtikwê nimâmâ ahpô ê-kî-kakâya-- kî-nipahi-kakâyawisîw ayis nimâma; (F: ôh.) êkot[ê] êtikwê ahpô ê-kî-ohtinamân, *you know*. ninipahi-pakwâtên ayis ôma wêtinâhk k-ây-apiyân, *you know*, miton ôti. êkwa mîna, kâ-ispayik ka-waniskâyân, mîna niwaniskân, kâ-itamahcihoyân, kiyâm, *you know, but* kâ-mâyamahcihoyân, ninôhtê-pimisinin.

F: êkwa ot[i] êkwa. (A: âha.) (R: âha.)

R: môy nôh-kiskêyihtên kîkwây anima "ninêstosin" kayâs; (F: âha.) *when I was eighteen-year-old, boy,* ayinânêwosâp ê-itahtopiponêyân, [*laughter*] (A: *ya.*) môy nôh-kiskêyihtên kîkwây anima nêstosiwin. (A: âha; kî-miywâsin kiyaw.) wâh-wâhyaw ê-kî-isi-sipwêhtêyân, mîna mâna mînis[a] ê-kî-nâtâwatâyân, ê-atâwâkêyân, (F: ê-kî--) ê-pâsamân, takwahiminân[a] ê-takwahamân, ê-pâsamân.

F: ê-mosci-takwahaman.

R: ê-mosci-takwahamân asiniy, kêyâpic nitayâwâw. (A: âha, *ya.*) ê-wîc-ôhcîmât ana nitânis, kâ-wiyinot ana.

F: âh, mhm. tânimatahtw-âskîwinêw êwako?

R: hâ, môy âhpô nikiskisin, tânitâhto-- ê-tahto--

F: miton êtikw âni, *older than Dolores anyway*. miton êtikwê kêkâc nêmitanaw êkwa at-îtahtopiponêw cî?

F: Ah, even then she -- she made the fence look so nice all around her house.

A: You painted it.

R: That was nothing when I painted that one.

F: And that was just-- porch –°

A: Inside, and inside she was able to do -- to, uh, do the panelling. [*laughs*]

R: I had built that too, because -- my house –°

F: °– And you had built a porch too, (R: yes!!) right? (A: yes, ya.) She had built an extension.

R: I had built an ext-- I haven't even finished that yet, I must try to finish it; there's not too much, just a little.

[*pause*]

F: Where were you taught to work so hard; when you were a child?

R: I wonder, I guess it was perhaps because my mom was very hard-working; (F: oh.) I guess I got it from there, you know. Because I really dislike this leisurely sitting around, you know, I really do. And when it's time to get up in the morning, I get up, if I am feeling well, you know, but when I'm feeling poorly I want to lie down.

F: It's only so now. (A: yes.) (R: yes.)

R: I didn't know anything about that "I'm tired" in the old days; (F: yes.) when I was an eighteen-year-old, boy, when I was eighteen years old, [*laughter*] (A: ya.) I didn't know anything about tiredness. (A: yes; your body was good.) I used to go very far for berries and I would haul them and sell them; (F: it was --) I would dry them, I would crush the chokecherries and dry them.

F: You crushed them by hand.

R: I crushed them by hand, with a stone, I still have it. (A: yes, ya.) I got it at the time my daughter was born, the one who is fat.

F: Ah, mhm. How old is that one?

R: Ha, I don't even remember, how many-- how--

F: Really, I guess, older than Dolores anyway. I guess she would be almost forty years old, no?

R: môya, tânis ôma (F: môya?) kâ-kî-isit? *thirty*; â, môy âhpô nikiskisin. (F: ha!)

A: nistomitanaw nânitaw?

F: ayiwâk wiya, mis-âyiwâk wiya. (A: âha, *ya*.)

R: maht âya, awa nikosis ostêsimâw, nîs ôki nikosisak, êkot[a] êkwa kâ-kî-wanihâyâhk ana (nistam mâwacêyas anik îskwêwak môy ê-akimakik ôk âya, omâmâwâwa (F: âha.) nôsisimak ôki) mâka *from* anita ana *Jim*, (F: âha.) êkota ohci; *Gabe* aw ê-kî-askôskâkot, anihi *deceased-Dorothy*. (F: âh.) (A: ôh, *ya*.) êkota êkwa awa, --

F: êkota cî an[a] êkwayâc êkwa wiya?

R: êkota êkwa wiya, âha.

F: miton ês âna osk-âya.

R: âha.

R: êkwa ê-osîmisit anih âna kêyâpic, 'cipwân' k-êtâyâhk, ê-osîmisit êkoni.

A: âha, *Lloyd*.

R: âha, êkot[a] ôhc âniki nâh-nâway êkwa, piyis êkwa.

A: kotakak aniki, âha. (R: âha.) (F: ha.)

F: kahkiyaw cî kîkihk ê-kî-ayâwacik awâsisak?

R: â, â, nisto piko nikî-ayâwâwak âhkosîwikamikohk.

F: ôh, iskwêyâc.

R: âha, *Barry*.

A: awîna mâka mâna kâh-kanawêyimisk, kimâmâ?

R: sôskwâc nêhiyawi-maskihkîwiskwêwak, (F: âha.) –°

A: kimâmâ?

R: '*slim*-mêriy' kâ-kî-itiht, –°

A: ha?

R: '*slim*-mêriy' kâ-kî-itiht, (A: *oh, ya. Mary Slim--*) pêyak piko nimâmâ nikî-paminik; pêyak wiy ân[a] âyis ê-kî-osîht-- ê-kî-wîcihisoyân niya, ost-- omisimâw mâmâwacêyas ê-kî-pêyakoyân.

F: ê-kî-pa-pêyakoyan?

R: ââha!

R: miton êtikw ê-kî-wa-wîcihikowisiyân, môy kika-mâyinikêyân.

êkwa êkospî nayêstaw miht[a] ê-pônamihk; (A: âha.) ê-kî-misi-pônahk aya kisêyiniw, êkwa ê-sipwêpahtât, êkwa *he had been*, -- môy, môya nikî-pêhon, *you know, you just have to.*

R: No, what was it (F: no?) she told me? Thirty; ah, I don't even remember. (F: ha!)

A: About thirty?

F: She is older, a lot older. (A: yes, ya.)

R: Let's see: my oldest son, my two sons, then the one we lost (I didn't count the oldest girls [*sc.* killed in a car accident], the mothers (F: yes.) of my grandchildren) but then Jim was next, (F: yes.) and Gabe was followed by the late Dorothy. (F: ah.) (A: oh, ya.) Then there is this one --

F: Does she only fit in at this point?

R: That's where she comes in, yes.

F: She is very young.

R: Yes.

R: And she has a younger brother still; we call him *cipwân,* that one is younger than her.

A: Yes, Lloyd.

R: Yes, this is their order, one after another, from the first to the last.

A: All of them, yes. (R: yes.) (F: ha.)

F: Did you have all of the children at your house?

R: Ah, ah, I only had three of them in the hospital.

F: Oh, the last ones.

R: Yes, Barry.

A: But who took care of you then, your mom?

R: Always Cree midwives (F: yes.) –°

A: Your mom?

R: No, she was called *slim-mêriy* –°

A: Ha?

R: She was called *slim-mêriy,* (A: oh, ya. Mary Slim--) my mom only helped me with one; for one I made -- I helped myself, for the eldest girl, I was alone.

F: You were all alone?

R: Yes!!

R: I guess really I had spiritual help so that nothing bad happened to me.

At that time, we only had wood to build a fire; (A: yes.) the old man had built a big fire and then ran off [for help], and he had been -- no, I couldn't wait, you know, you just have to.

ê-kî-pêyakoyân ana, awa mîna nikî-pêyakonân *Joey*. (A: âha.) mâka wiy êkospî kisêyiniw ana nikî-wîcihik.

A: âha.

[*pause*]

10

F: aw âw îsk-- oskinîkiskwêw [sc. *Colleen Youngs*] kâ-pê-wîcêwak, êwak ôm âya, mâk âya k-âti-kâh-kakwêcimitinâwâw ôma, pâh-pêyak ômis îsi.

R: âha.

F: ê-nôhtê-kiskêyihtahk tânisi ê-kî-isi-- na-- â--, kayâs ê-kî-isi-nahastâyêk mâna wiyâs, ka-kakwê-kanawêyihtamêk, tâpiskôc –°

R: aya, ê-pâsikâtêki piko –°

A: ê-pânisâwêhk.

R: °– ê-pânisâwêhk; (F: âha.) êkos îsi piko, êkamâ kîkway kayâs ôh âhkwatihcikana ohc-îhtakohki; âstamispî wâhyaw ôm êkwayâc ôh âhkwatihcikana k-âyâki.

F: wîhkâc cî êkwa kipânisâwân?

R: nikâ-pân-- nikâh-pânisâwân kika-aya-, *you know*, môy wîhkât mâka nitôtinên ayis, anihi mâna nitôtinên --, pêyakwâw ôma nikî-otinên anihi mâna -- kâ-kwayâci-sikwatahikâtêk anima wiyâs, (F: âha.) yôskâw (A: *minute steak*.) mâna mitoni. (F: ôh, âha.) êwako mâka mîna nitôtinên pêyakwâw, *about a year ago* êtikwê, "îwahikanak niwî-osîhâwak," nititâwak awâsisak. nitôtinên êkwa ôhi, kâ-sêkwâpiskinamân êkwa, mêtoni nikâspihkasên, *you know*; ê-kî-tahkâk êkwa aya, êkwa aya, *canvas* anihi mâna, (F: âha!)

– 'pakwânikamikwêkin' anima nik-êtwân, – êkotowahk êkwa nikî-ka-kanawêyihtên, êkot[a] êkwa k-âstâyân êkwa, êy, mâninakis êkwa ê-pakamahamân êkwa, *but* wîpat mâka –°

A: ê-sikwatahaman.

R: ° – wîpac sikopayiw, ayis sikwatahikâtêw (A: âha!) kwayâci. îh, êkw ân[i] êkwa ê-kî-tôtamân êkwa, sîkosâkanak kâ-tihkiswakik

I was alone for that one, and I was also alone for Joey, (A: yes.) but that time the old man helped me.

A: Yes.

[*pause*]

10 [*Preparing Meat*]

F: This young woman [*sc*. Colleen Youngs] who has come with me, this is [the one who has questions] --, well, I will ask each of you in turn like this.

R: Yes.

F: She wants to know how you used to put away meat in the old days, to try and preserve it, for example –°

R: Ah, it was only dried –°

A: It was cut into sheets.

R: °– it was cut into sheets; (F: yes.) that was the only way, for there were no freezers long ago; it was only much later that there were freezers.

F: Do you ever cut meat into sheets now?

R: I would -- I would cut it into sheets --, you know, but I never buy it, I always buy those --, once I bought that pre-pounded meat, (F: yes.) it's always really (A: minute steak.) tender. (F: oh, yes.) I bought that once, about a year ago, I guess, "I'm going to make pounded meat," I told my children. I bought it and put it in the oven until it was really crisp, you know; and when it had cooled, well, then, ah, that canvas, (F: yes!)

– 'tent canvas' I'll say, –

now I had kept that kind, and I put the meat there, hey, I kept pounding it then, but, soon –°

A: You pounded it into pieces.

R: °– it was soon crushed because it had been pounded (A: yes!) beforehand. Look, then when I had done this, I rendered the êkwa, êkot[a] êkwa nitahâwak êkwa [*laughs*], êkwa aya, aniki mân âtâwâkâniwan aniki sôminisak, apisîsisiwak,

A: *currants*. (F: âha.)

R: êkonik, (F: âha.) âha.

R: êkonik, êkot[a] êkwa nitahâwak. îh, "wiy ôma awâsisak," nititêyihtên, "â, môy ka-miywêyihtamwak," nititêyihtên, mêton âciyaw ê-kitâpayîhtamawicik nîwahikana. [*laughter*]

"maht êkwa mîna osîhtâ anima wiyâs mâna k-ôsîhtâyan," k-êsit ôt[a] âna nôsisim, anihi kâ-kanawêyimât pôfay. "kêtahtawê," nititâw, "kêtahtawê nik-âtâwân, mîna nik-ôsîhâwak," nititâw. ahpô ayis ôki wâposwak ê-kî-pâsohcik, ê-pânisohcik, (F: ôh!) âha. ê-pâniswat, sôskwât ê-tâh-taswêkisâwâtaman ospiconisiwâwa (F: âha, êkw ê-pâsaman.) êkwa êkos îsi ê-paskiciwêpinacik ay âkwâwânihk, akwâwâna anihi, ê-kaskâpasocik, ê-nipahi-miyosicik.

F: kêhcinâ!

A: wacaskwak.

R: wacaskwak, âha, kinosêwak mîna nikaskihon ê-pâniswakik.

F: amiskwak mâka, kikî-mowâwâwak?

R: âha.

F: âha. pêyakwan êkonik cî kikî-pânis-- –°

R: pêyakwan, –°

F: °– kikî-pâniswâwâwak?

R: °– m-- amiskwak ôki t-ôsîhacik mêtoni kwayas, piko misiwê ayisk aniki owiyihkosiwâwa k-êtwêhk, misiwê apiyiwa; (F: êkoni.) pikw îyawis t-ôtinimat êkoni. *Between the* [*gesture*], *between mea--* owiyâsiwâhk anita, oskâtiwâhk, êkwa ômatowihk, êkwa ôta [*gesture*]; piko kahkiyaw t-ôtinimat. (F: ôh!) êkwa miton êkwa ki-- kisikokahwâwak êkwa, *you know*; (F: âha.) êkos êkwa kipakâsimâwak, pitamâ, (A: mhm.) nîswâw kimêskotâpinên [*sic*] anima. (A: nipiy.) niya wiy ôti mâna, êkosi (A: âha, *ya*, âha.) ê-kî-is-ôsîhakik, âha; nîswâw nimêskotônên. miton êkwa kâ-sikwâciwasocik êkwa, êkwa nimêsciwêpahên êkwa wiyâ--, ayi, oskana anihi, *you know*. (A: âha.) êkwa aya, wîhcêkaskosiya ôhi, êkon êkwa mitoni nisikosâwâtên, papêskomina, êkw êkos îsi nisêkwâpiskinâwak, ôh, takahki – êy, –°

F: wîhkitisiw!

fat and then I put the cracklings in [*laughs*], and then, ah, those ones that are usually sold, those raisins, they are very small,

A: Currants. (F: yes.)

R: Those ones, (F: yes.) yes.

R: I put those in it. Look, "The children," I thought, "ah, they won't like it," I thought, but in a very short time they ate up all my pounded meat on me. [*laughter*]

"Please make that meat again which you made," that one grandchild of mine said to me, the one that *pôfay* takes care of. "Sometime," I told him, "sometime I'll buy it again and make it," I told him. Even rabbits were dried; they were cut up into sheets, (F: oh!) yes. You cut them into sheets, just cut their little legs into thin little sheets (F: yes, and then you dry them.) and then you throw them over the drying rack like this, and they were smoked on those drying racks, and they were really nice.

F: For sure!

A: Muskrats.

R: Muskrats, yes, and I also know how to cut fish into sheets.

F: But how about beavers, did you used to eat them?

R: Yes.

F: Yes. Did you used to cut them the same –°

R: The same –°

F: °– did you used to cut them into sheets?

R: °– to really prepare beaver properly, since their glands, as they are called, are all over them, (F: those ones.) you have to remove them entirely. Between the [*gesture*] -- their meat there, between their legs and right here and here [*gesture*]; you must remove all of them. (F: oh!) And then you cut them into really small pieces, you know, (F: yes.) and you boil them first, (A: mhm.) changing the water twice. (A: water.) At least that's the way I did it, (A: yes, ya, yes.) that's how I used to prepare them, yes; I changed the water twice. When they are done so that the meat falls off, I throw away the bones, you know. (A: yes.) And then I cut some onions up really small, add pepper, and put them in the oven like that, oh, good – hey, –°

F: Beaver tastes good!

R: °– êy, wîhkitisiwak. (F: ha.) nipahi-wîhkitisiw an[a] 'âmisk' kâ-isîyihkâsot. pêyakwan êkosi wacaskwak, kwayas k-ôsîhacik. (A: âha, *ya*.)

F: âw, kakwâhyaki-wîhkitisiwak.

R: kayâs mîna mâna miscanikwacâsak ayis ê-kî-mowihcik, –°

A: âha, miscanikwacâsak mistahi kî-wâh-wiyinowak, êwako wiya nikiskisin.

R: °– oski-napatâkwa, (A: âha.) âha.

F: nikî-takahkêyihtên mâna kâ-miyoskamik kâ-nipahâyâhkik a-- –°

A: êkota ê-kî-wiyinocik.

F: °– anikwacâsak.

A: "wâpiskatayêwak," kî-itwêwak mâna. êkonik –°

R: êkonik ê-wiyinocik.

A: °– êkonik ê-wiyinocik, âha!

R: nitayâwâwak.

A: êkwa mîna mân âya, kî-ohpahamawêwak ta--, *in the morning* ôma kâ-waniskâhk, (F: âha.) ê-nitohtamihk, "mahti tânitê pihêwak ê-nîmihitocik," kî-nihtâ-itwêwak mâna.

R: êkotowahk mîna mân ê-kî-nipahakik, pihêwak, (A: âha.) ê-kî-tâpakwêyân.

A: êkwa *traps* kî-âpacihtâwak mâna, itê ê-nîmihitocik, ayis kî-ayâwak itê ê-nîmihitocik (F: âha.) ôki pihêwak, "ê-nîmihitocik," (R: âha.) kî-itwêwak mâna, *you know*. itê ôma –°

R: ê-wa-wiyasinâkosicik aniki ka-kitâpamacik ka-- ka-nîmihitocik.

A: °– kî-wanihikêwak mân êkota. (R: mhm.)

sîsîpi-mîcimâpoy, wâcistakât! nanâtohk mîcimâpôsa; (R: âha.) wâposo-mîcimâpoy, sîsîpi-mîcimâpoy, êkwa aya --

F: paspaskiwak.

A: paspaskiwak.

R: paspaskiwak. (A: âha.) kêyâpic nimâh-mowâwak paspaskiwak. nâpêsis ana, môy kayâs nîso wâposwa kî-nipahêw. (A: mhm.)

F: nîst âniki nêtê nisto êsa nipahêwak. (R: âha!)

A: mêkwâc ôma mitoni ta-wâh-wiyinowak sîsîpak. nistam kâ-takohtêcik mâna, êkota wiyinowak, (R: êkota, âha.) âha.

R: mâka wiya wâposwak âsay pâwanîwak.

R: °– hey, they taste good. (F: ha.) The one called *amisk* tastes delicious. It's the same with muskrats, when you prepare them properly. (A: yes, ya.)

F: Ah, they're absolutely delicious.

R: And gophers also used to be eaten long ago, –°

A: Yes, gophers were really fat, for I remember that.

R: °– and new potatoes, (A: yes.) yes.

F: I used to like it when it was spring and we killed the g-- –°

A: They were fat then.

F: °– gophers.

A: "The white-bellies," they used to say. They –°

R: They were fat.

A: °– they were fat, yes.

R: I've had them.

A: And they would also set traps for them to -- in the morning when people got up, (F: yes.) and listened, "let's see where the prairie-chickens are dancing," they used to be in the habit of saying.

R: I used to kill that kind, too, prairie-chickens. (A: yes.) I trapped them.

A: And they used to set traps, where they were dancing, because the prairie-chickens had a place where they danced, (F: yes.) and they used to say, "They are dancing," (R: yes.) you know. It's where –°

R: They look funny when you see them dance.

A: °– they used to set traps there. (R: mhm.)

Duck soup, oh my! Different soups; (R: yes.) rabbit soup, duck soup, and ah, --

F: Partridges.

A: Partridges.

R: Partridges. (A: yes.) I am still eating partridges. That little boy killed two rabbits not long ago. (A: mhm.)

F: Mine too, they killed three over there. (R: yes!)

A: At this time the ducks will be really fat. Usually when they first arrive, they are fat, (R: there, yes.) yes.

R: But the rabbits are already scrawny.

A: âha; *mallards*, êy, êkonik. wahwâ, ê-nawacîhk niya, êkosi nitisi-wîhkipwâw awa sîsîp, ê-nawacîhk.

F: ê-nawacîhk.

A: ê-nawacîhk, âha.

F: kîkwây kî-- –°

A: ôki *the old*, –°

F: °– *stuffing* cî mâna kitôsîhtân?

A: môya, môya!

F: mosci-- ê-mosci-sêkwâpiskinat.

A: anik âya -- môy ôki *electric stoves*, an--, tâpiskôt mâna nawac kîkway ê-wîhkasik, ê-pê-isi-kiskisiyân ôki *wood--*, (F: *wood*.) *wood-stoves* êkota.

R: âha, mihta kâ-pônamihk, âha.

F: takahk âniki êkonik, wâwâc (R: pahkwêsikan.) mâna pahkwêsikan ê-nipahi-wîhkitisit.

A: *oh yes!*

R: pisisik nitôsîhâw pahkwêsikan. êk ôta kâ-misi-yôtik ôta, anihi kâ-kêcikwâstahki, êkosi môy cêskwa nikikamohtân.

A: *pipes*. (R: âha.)

R: pisisik nikîsiswâw êkotê, êkotê mîna mâna nipa-piminawasosin.

A: kêhtahtawê mîna mâna ta-- kâ-takohtêyân awa nitasamik ê-kî-pahkwêsikanihkêt. (R: âhâ!)

F: â, nîsta mîna mâna, nimiywêyihtên ê-kiyokawak. [*laughter*] (A: âha.)

R: wâposwa pêyakwâw, mêtoni ê-takahkâciwasomak, (F: ââha.) mîcimâpoy miton ê-misi-mîcit. (F: [*laughs*]) êk ôm êkwa, “kimwêsiskawâw wâpos,” nititâw, kâ-pê-pîhtikwêt, –°

F: tânispî kani ôma –°

R: °– tânispî ôma kâ-pê-pîhtikwêyan.

F: °– k-âyamihêwikîsikâk ôma kâ-itohtêyân. (R: âha.)

R: “kimwêsiskawâw wâpos,” nititâw.

11

F: wâh! môy kika-tâpwêhtaman, tânimatahtw êtikw âkohpa ê-pê-atâmitân.

A: Yes; and mallards, hey! Oh my, when they are roasted, I especially like the taste of roasted duck.

F: Roasted.

A: Roasted, yes.

F: What do you –°

A: Those old, –°

F: Did you used to make stuffing?

A: No, no!

F: Just-- you just put it in the oven.

A: Those ah -- not these electric stoves; it seems that things used to taste better, as I recall, in the wood-- (F: wood.) <u>wood-stoves</u>.

R: <u>Yes, when a fire is built with wood</u>, yes.

F: Those are especially good, (R: bannock.) bannock usually tastes very good.

A: Oh yes!

R: I make bannock all the time. But when it was very windy here, those [*sc*. pipes] were blown down, and I haven't put them back yet.

A: Pipes. (R: yes.)

R: I bake it there all the time, and I usually do a little cooking over there too.

A: Sometimes when I arrive, she feeds me bannock that she has made. (R: yes!!)

F: Ah, and me too. I like visiting her. [*laughter*] (A: yes.)

R: And once I had cooked rabbits really well, (F: yes!) and she ate a whole lot of soup. (F: [*laughs*]) But then, "You missed the rabbit," I told her when she came in, –°

F: When was it that –°

R: °– when was it that you came?

F: °– I went there on Sunday. (R: yes.)

R: "You missed the rabbit," I told her.

11 [*Selling Blankets*]

F: Well! You won't believe how many blankets I have bought from you.

R: wah, misahkamik!

A: êkwa niy ânihi *carpets*.

F: âha, êkoni wiy âta wiya mîna mâna.

A: misahkamik wiya nîst[a] êkoni. nitati-mêkin mân ôm âskaw, kâ-takohtêcik awâsisak, nâha mîna nêtê an[a] âya, k-âyât an[a] *in Wetaskiwin* mâna, nimiyâw an[a] âya, *Butch* anihi –°

F: kistim.

A: °– nist--, nistimihkâwin an[a] âya.

R: wâhyaw ohc âna nitihkwatim kâ-kî-pê-atâmit nîso, *Regina*.

A: awîna?

R: aya, *Brian*.

A: ôh, âha.

F: ahpô cî *Winnipeg*?

R: *Winnipeg* cî ahpô?

F: *Winnipeg* cî ana *Brian*, kîtim kâ-wîkit?

R: âha, êkotê.

A: âha, *ya*.

R: nîso nikî-pê-atâmik, *forty dollars apiece* sôskwâc ê-itisinamawit.

A: atoskêw ayisk.

R: âha. (F: âha.) (A: âha.)

F: sôskwâc awa mâna, mâka mâna nimiywêyihtên-- ê-- –°

R: "êkoni cî piko ê-ayâyan?" nititê-- k-êsit. "ayiwâk k-âyâyan, ayiwâk kâh-atâmitin," k-êsit.

A: ôh, miton êsa kâkêswân.

R: âha!

A: mâka nîso piko ê-ayâyan.

R: niyânan ê-kî-ayâyân, âsay nisto ê-atâwâkêyân. (A: ôh; ha.) ê-kî-mihtâtamân êwako.

12

F: kakwâhyaki-nihtâ--, kîspin êkoyikohk ka-kakâyawisîhk, iyikohk kâ-kakâyawisîyan, mistahi kikâh-miyw-âyâ--, (R: âha.) kâh-miywâyâwak ayisiyiniwak ôta. (R: âha.)

R: Oh, lots!

A: And I have bought all those carpets.

F: Yes, I have bought those as well.

A: I have bought a lot of those too. I give them away sometimes when the children come back; I have given some to that one over there, the one who lives in Wetaskiwin, ah, Butch, and his –°

F: Your daughter-in-law.

A: °– my daughter-in--, my common-law daughter-in-law.

R: My nephew came from far away, from Regina, to buy two.

A: Who?

R: Ah, Brian.

A: Oh, yes.

F: Or is it Winnipeg?

R: Is it Winnipeg?

F: Isn't Brian in Winnipeg, where your brother-in-law lives?

R: Yes, over there.

A: Yes, ya.

R: He came and bought two from me, he just handed me forty dollars apiece.

A: He works, of course.

R: Yes. (F: yes.) (A: yes.)

F: This one simply, but I usually –°

R: "Are these the only ones you have?" I sai-- he said to me. "If you had more, I'd buy more from you," he said to me.

A: Oh, it was really a coincidence.

R: Yes!

A: But you only had two.

R: I had had five, but I had sold three already. (A: oh; ha.) I was sorry about that.

12 [*Life with a Husband*]

F: Extremely good at -- if people were that hard-working, as hard-working as you are, we'd be really well-- (R: yes.) the people here would be well-off. (R: yes.)

R: kîspin mîna kî-pê-miskamâsoyân, sêmâk kwayask awiyak mitoni ka-wîcihit, *you know*, (F: âha.) *but* môy êkos ôhc-îs-âyâw ana kisêyiniw, ôma, ôma kî-otamihikow, âha.

A: mâk âyis kahkiyaw ôma kâ-osk-âyiwiyahk, ohcitaw kipâh-patinikânaw. (R: âha.)

F: âha. [*laughs*]

R: mitoni nikî-pê-misiwânat--

A: ê-mâh-mâ-- ê-mâh-mâyi-nawasônikêyahk, [*laughter*] âha.

R: ê-kî-mâyi-nawasônikêyân mitoni -- [*laughter*] – ê-kî-mâyahpinatiht [*sic*]. [*laughter*]

F: kikî-kitimahikawin.

R: nikî-kitimahik, môy âhpô wîhkât nôhci-pakitinik, ka-môcikihcâsiyân ohpimê. tâpitawi pikw ê-asiwacikêyân. [*laughter*] (A: *ya.*)

A: anohc mâk ôsk-âyak, mitoni cî pîtos kititêyihtên tâpiskôt kiyânaw kâ-kî-pê-is-ôhpikiyahk, (R: â, wâhyaw pîtos.) iyikohk tâpitawi kîkway ê-kî-ayâyahk t-âcoskâcasiyahk. (R: âha.) misi-pîtos anohc.

R: ôh, pîtos.

13

F: tânisi kititêyihtên ôma, tânêhk êwako k-ôh-ispayik?

R: osâm aya –°

A: sêhkêpayîs, pêyak.

R: °– osâm ê-wêhci-pimâtisicik; (A: âha.) (F: âha.) piko kîkway (F: ê-miyihcik.) wêhcasiniyiw, piko kîkway ê-miyihcik; mayaw kîkway kâ-nitawêyihtahkik, itisinamâwawak; ahpô cî --, êkâ cî sôniyâwa, *you know*, (F: êkos âna.) osâm mistahi, âha.

êkwa kâ-ispayik êkwa ka-kaskihtamâsocik êkwa, âyimêyihtamwak êkwa. pikw âyis kayâs ê-atoskêhk kîkway, sôniyâw kâ-kî-kâhcitiniht. ahpô piko mîna mân âya, *potatoes* anihi, napatâkwa (A: napatâkwa, âha.) ê-kî-kistikêhk, iyikohk êkot[a] ê-kî-wîcihiwêyân iyikohk, *you know*, ê-kî-sôniyâhkêyân.

F: piko kîkway mîna mâna pîsikiscikânisa êtikwê kî-kistikâniwan.

R: And also if I had found someone for myself, someone who would have helped me properly, you know, (F: yes.) but my old man never was like that, this [*sc.* the Bottle] was in his way, yes.

A: But, of course, when we were young, we naturally made mistakes. (R: yes.)

F: Yes. [*laughs*]

R: I was really in bad shape --

A: We-- we all chose poorly, [*laughter*] yes.

R: I had made a very poor choice -- [*laughter*]
– she was badly beaten. [*laughter*]

F: You were treated badly.

R: He was mean to me, and he never even let me have fun elsewhere. I was always pregnant. [*laughter*] (A: ya.)

A: But for today's youth, it's really different, don't you think, compared to when we grew up, (R: ah, far different.) as we had so many things to work at. (R: yes.) It's much different today.

R: Oh, quite different.

13 [*Making a Living II: Growing Vegetables; Imported Fruit*]

F: What do you think about why this has happened?

R: Because, ah –°

A: The car for one.

R: °– because they live an easy life; (A: yes.) (F: yes.) everything (F: is given to them.) is easy, they are given everything; as soon as they want something it is handed to them; even money, isn't it, you know, (F: it is.) far too much of it, yes.

And then when they need to make some money themselves, they think it is too difficult. Long ago, of course, you had to do some work when money was needed. For instance, planting potatoes, (A: potatoes, yes.) I used to go along doing so much of that, you know, and I used to make money.

F: And all kinds of vegetables were planted, I guess.

R: piko kîkway ê-kî-kistikêhk, âha, piko kîkway ê-kistikêhk ê-isi-miskwêyihtamihk.

A: âha, otisihkâna, (R: âha.) êkoni anihi mitoni mâna nikiskisin, napatâkwa, otisihkâna, oskâcâskosak, (R: mhm.) êkoni.

R: êkwa wîhcêkaskosiya.

A: êkwa wîhcêkaskosiya, âha. (R: âha.)

R: môy wiya –°

F: êkwa--, êkwa napatâkwa.

A: âha, napatâkwa, âha; aniki wiy âniki ayicîminak, awêkâ cî aniki, môy wiya, *no* –°

F: môy âkwâskam êkonik.

A: °– *no peas, no beans, no, no, no; these were four*, êkon ôhi.

F: nêwo.

A: âha, êkoni.

R: kayâs mîna mân ânik âya, tânisi kan ê-isiyîhkâsocik, misikitiwak *oran--*

F: *pe--* pumpkin?

R: êkonik, âha.

R: êkonik mîna mâna kayâs ê-kî-mâh-misi-kistikêyân, nêtê k-âyâyâhk, ê-kî-mâh-miyokicik mâna. môy êkwa --

F: tânisi mâna kikî-itâpacihâwak êkonik?

R: ê-miyosicik aniki, *pie* ê-osîhihcik, (F: âha.) êkwa mîna, *you know, fruit --*

F: kikî-âpacihtân, (R: âha.) kikî-âpa--

A: âha.

A: hâw, wîht[a] êkwa tânis ê-isiyîhkâcikâtêki [*sic*] ôhi *apple, orange, banana, pear, peach*! nê-- êkoni, wâh-wîhta êkoni tânis ê-isi-nêhiyaw-îsiyîhkâtêki!

R: m-- aya 'picikwâsak' wiy aniki.

A: *apple*.

R: âha; êkwa 'k-ôsâwisicik' aniki.

F: *banana* cî?

A: *orange*.

F: *orange*!

A: *orange*, 'k-ôsâwisicik', âha.

R: êkwa 'ka-wâkisicik'.

A: *banana*.

R: All kinds were planted, yes, everything that you could think of was planted.

A: Yes, turnips, (R: yes.) I really remember them, potatoes, turnips, carrots. (R: mhm.)

R: And onions.

A: And onions, yes. (R: yes)

R: But not –°

F: And --, and potatoes.

A: Yes, potatoes, yes; but as for peas, or even those [beans], not those ones, no –°

F: These not as much.

A: °– no peas, no beans, no, no, no; there were four of them.

F: Four.

A: Yes, those.

R: And long ago those too, ah, I've forgotten what they are called, they are big, oran--

F: Pe-- pumpkin?

R: Those, yes.

R: I used to plant a lot of those too, long ago, when we lived over there, and they used to grow well. Now they don't --

F: What did you use them for?

R: They're good when made into pie, (F: yes.) and also, you know, fruit --

F: You used them, (R: yes.) ya.

A: Yes.

A: Sure, now tell what they are called, the apple, orange, banana, pear, peach! Tell what each is called in Cree!

R: Well, *picikwâsak*.

A: Apples.

R: Yes, and *k-ôsâwisicik*.

F: Bananas?

A: Oranges.

F: Oranges!

A: Oranges, *k-ôsâwisicik*, yes.

R: And *kâ-wâkisicik*.

A: Bananas.

F: *banana*. (A: âha.) (R: mhm.)

A: *pear?*

R: *pear*, tânis ôm êtikwê ê-isiyîhkasot êwako? – 'kâ-cîposicik' pakahkam isiyîhkâtâwak (F: ôh *ya*.) êkonik, âha.

A: *peach?*

R: mwâc êkonik; mwâc ê-kiskisiyân êkonik wîhkâc ê-pa-pêhtamân ka-nêhiyawiyîhkâtihcik, *you know*. (A: âha.) kikiskêyihtên kiya?

A: mwâc.

R: mwâc?

F: môy nîsta, môy nîsta.

14

F: tân--, aya; êkwa wiyâsa ôhi, tânis âsici kî-isi--, â, tânispî ôm âspin êkwa – tâpiskôc anohc, tânis êkwa ê-isi-nahastâyan *mea--*, ka-kanawêyihtaman wiyâs?

R: sôskwâc aya, nitatâwân mân ânih âhkwacihcikanisa, *you know*. mitoni mistahi nikî-nahastân *last* -- takwâkohk. (F: âha!) mâk âyisk mâna nimihcêtinân, tâpitaw âhkwacihcikanisa anihi, âskaw mâna kwayâci ninâh-napakisên ôma, apisimôsoswa kâ-nipahâcik, *you know*; (F: mhm.) kwayâci ninâh-napakisên, êkwa êkos îsi êkwa nitâhkwatihtân.

F: kitâhkwatihtân sôskwâc; (R: âha.) piko kîkway êkwa âhkwatihcikâtêw.

R: piko kîkway êkwa âhkwatihcikâtêw, takwahiminâna ahpô mâna nitâhkwatihtân!

F: âha. kâh-takwahimin-- kâh-takwahiminêyani cî?

R: âha. kâ-- [... ; *?record*] ---kihci-kîsikâk.

A: êkos êkwa pâh-pitikonikâtêwa ê-pâsamihk anihi, êkos êkwa ê-kanawêyihtamihk, (R: âha.) kayâs êkosi anima.

F: âha, kayâhtê wiya. (A: *ya*.) (R: âha.)

F: aya mîn âya, misâskwatômina mân êkosi.

R: misâskwatômina, âha, êkoni mîna.

A: kî-pâsikâtêwa.

R: kî-pâsikâtêwa, êkwa mîn ôhi, âtiht ayis ôhi misâskwatômina kisikwahên, ta--, cîstâsêpon ohc âhpô cî anima *potato--* (A: *---masher*.) *---masher*. kisikwahên miton êkwa

F: Bananas. (A: yes.) (R: mhm.)

A: Pears?

R: Pears, I wonder what they are called – I think they are called ***kâ-cîposicik***, (F: oh ya.) yes.

A: Peaches?

R: No; I don't remember ever hearing what they are called in Cree, you know. (A: yes.) How about you?

A: No.

R: No?

F: Me neither, me neither.

14 [*Preparing Various Foods*]

F: How-- well; as for meat, with what -- when was the last time – like today, how do you put meat away now to preserve it?

R: I simply bought a little freezer, you know. I put away a lot last fall. (F: yes!) I always put it in the freezer, because there are many of us, and sometimes I cut it into chops [for frying] beforehand, when they kill a deer, you know; (F: mhm.) I cut it into chops beforehand and in that way I freeze it.

F: You simply freeze it; (R: yes.) everything is frozen now.

R: Now everything is frozen, I usually even freeze chokecherries!

F: Yes. When you'v-- when you have crushed the chokecherries?

R: Yes. When it's the [...] day.

A: In this way they are made into patties and dried and that's how they are preserved; (R: yes.) that's how it was long ago.

F: Yes, before [*sc.* freezers were used]. (A: ya.) (R: yes.)

F: And saskatoons were also kept that way.

R: Saskatoons, yes, those too.

A: They were dried.

R: They were dried, and some of those were crushed too -- with a fork or even with the potato-- (A: --masher.) ---masher. You really kinâh-napakinên, tâpiskôt takwahiminâna k-êsi-nâh-napakinaman, êkos îs ê-pâsaman. (F: ôh.)

ôtê mân ê-kî-ohtinamân, *deceased-Françoise*, (F: ôh.) mihcêt kîkway ê-kî-kiskinohamawit. ahpô môy ê-ôhci-kiskêyihtamân ka-yîkinikêyân, ê-kî-kiskinohamawit mîna mostoswa, nikî-yîkinikân mîna, (F: âha.) (A: *ya*.) mostoswak [*sic*], âha.

F: kî-- mistahi kî-- kikî-- ôm ôta, k-- â, kî-âpatisiwak ôki tâpiskôc misihêwak, êkwa mostoswak, misatimwak, kôhkôsak.

A: nanâtohk kîkway, pikw âwiyak misatimwa kî-ayâwêw.

R: aya, kîkway piko mistahi ê-kî-âpatahk ôta, mostoswak êkwa misatimwak, (A: âha, *ya*.) (F: âha.) âstamispi ôma misihêwak, *way* -- âstami-- (F: môy.) âstamita, âha.

A: wiyawâw mâka kî-wâh-wîtap---wâh-wîtapihtahêwak misihêwa, (R: âha, k-âyâwâcik.) nanâtohk kîkway --, nanâtohk kîkway kî-miyêwak, *some had goose eggs, some had turkey eggs*. (R: âha.) (F: kî-wîtapîht--) misihêwa ki--, kî-wîtapihtahêwak wiyawâw, (R: âha.) kî-âpacihêwak misihêwa.

R: ispî êkwa ê-mâc-îhtakocik êkwa misihêwak nîstanân. kêtahtawê, tâpiskôc ê-pêkopayiyân, "hâ, misihêwak nik-âtâwân," k-êtêyihtamân.

– anim ânita *Sonny* k-âyât anima nîhc-âyihk anima, sâkahi--, nipiy anima k-âstêk, êkot[ê] âyis nikî-wîkinân mîna. (F: ôh.) –

kêtahtawê k-êtêyihtamân, êy, êkw ân[i] âwâsisisôniyâs êkwa ê-takopayit, êkwa kâ-nâtitisahwakik êkwa misihêwak.

A: *family allowance*.

R: âha.

R: niyânanomitanaw ninâtitisahwâwak; *ev*--, êkospî aspin ohci mitoni *there*, –°

A: misâkamê!

R: âha.

R: mitoni ê-wîcêwicik aniki misihêwak. "tânis êtikwê nika-tôtên, môy k-âyâwakik misihêwak!" – êkosi mân ê-itakik awâsisak. kîspin êkây ôta ôma tatahkamikisiyâni, êkâya ayâyâni kîkway, nika-kaskêyihtên; (F: mhm.) tâpwê mâk êkos ê-is-âyâyân,

crush them and flatten them out, like the way you flatten chokecherries, and dry them in that way. (F: oh.)

I used to get many things over here, from the late Françoise, (F: oh.) she taught me many things. I didn't even know how to milk, but she also taught me about cows, and I did the milking as well, (F: yes.) (A: ya.) I milked the cows, yes.

F: A lot -- ah, there were many domestic animals here, such as chickens, cows, horses, and pigs.

A: All kinds of animals, and everybody had horses.

R: Well, lots were kept here, cows and horses, (A: yes, ya.) (F: yes.) and more recently also chickens, (F: no.) much later, yes.

A: But they had the chickens sit on eggs (R: yes, they had chickens.) of all kinds -- , they gave them all kinds of eggs, some had goose eggs, some had turkey eggs. (R: yes.) (F: they sat --) They had the chickens sit on the eggs, (R: yes.) they used chickens for that.

R: And when they started to be common, we also kept chickens. One day, I woke up and thought, "Ha, I'll buy chickens."

– where Sonny lives, it was down the hill from there, where that water is over there, for we lived there too. (F: oh.) –

One day I thought that and hey, when the family allowance arrived, then I ordered chickens.

A: Family allowance.

R: Yes.

R: I ordered fifty; ev-- since that time I have –°

A: All the time!

R: Yes.

R: Those chickens have really grown on me. "I don't know what I will do if I don't have chickens!" – that's what I tell the children. If I don't have things to do, if I don't have something, I will be lonesome; (F: mhm.) that truly is the way

pêyakwanohk k-âpiyân. piko tâpitawi kîkway ê-tasîhkamân êkosi piko.

A: nîkân tâpitaw ê-âti-mâmitonêyihtaman tân-- –°

R: tâpitawi.

A: âha.

R: mâcik ôma nisaskaci-wâpahtên anima kâ-kî-kikamohtâyân anima, "niwî-kîskinên," nititâwak, "êkwa aya, masinahikanêkin niwî-kikamohtân," nititâwak, (A: mhm.) "pîtos ka-isinâkwahk *inside*," nititâwak, (A: mhm.) ôm âspin êkwa.

A: pîhc-âyihk pîtos t-êsinâkwahk, (R: âha.) âha.

R: "pêyakwan kapê-ay ôsâm isinâkwan." – "wâh, *Mom*," nititikwak mâka mîna, *you know*, "*even you, you can't please yourself*." [*laughter*]

15

A: osâm piko mîna mân ê-kî-pakâhcikêhk.

R: ê-pakâhtêk, âha, kîkway mîcimâpoy.

A: ânohc êkwa mitoni kahkiyaw kîkway ê-sâsâpiskitikâtêk. (R: ôh, âha.) môy aya –°

F: êwak ôhci êtikwê mâka k-ôh-sâ-sôkâwâspinêyahk êkwa. (R: âha.)

A: ° – *boiled*, (R: âha.) awêkâ cî ê-nawacîhk.

F: ê-nawacîhk.

A: âha, *tha--*, (R: âha.) *those were the two main ways of* -- anohc êkwa mitoni wâh-wîpac ka--

R: môy nikaskihtân ka-mîciyân kîkway ê-sâsâpiskitêk. (A: âha.) êkwa tipiskohk, osîhtâw êkwa mîcimâpoy nitânis awa, sikwatahikanâpoy anima; (A: âha.) pikonita [*sic*] mitoni nanâtohk ê-is-âstât, *you know*, mitoni --

F: *vegetables* cî? (R: âha.)

A: nanâtohk kîkway (R: â, piko kîkway.) êkota macipakwa ê-kikâpôhkêt. (F: [*laughs*])

R: âha, piko kîkway.

R: wahwâ, niwî-mîcin, niwîhkistên anihi *vegetables*, mâka pimiy ê-akohtik, "wahwâ," nititâwak, "kikitimahinâwâw ôma mâna

it is when I sit still in one place. I must have something to do all of the time and that's that.

A: From the first, you're always thinking ahead how-- –°

R: All the time.

A: Yes.

R: For instance, I got tired of looking at that [*sc.* the wall-covering] which I had put up. "I'm going to cut it off," I told them, "and I'm going to put up wallpaper," I told them. (A: mhm.) "It will look different inside," (A: mhm.) I told them, and so it does.

A: For it to look different inside, (R: yes.) yes.

R: "It has looked the same too long." – "Well, Mom," they said to me, as usual, you know, "even you, you can't please yourself." [*laughter*]

15 [*Dietary Concerns*]

A: And food used to be boiled.

R: It was boiled, yes, as <u>some kind of soup</u>.

A: <u>Now today absolutely</u> everything is fried. (R: oh, yes.) Not ah –°

F: That must be why we all get diabetes now. (R: yes.)

A: °– boiled, (R: yes.) or even roasted.

F: Roasting.

A: Yes, (R: yes.) those were the two main ways of -- now today it's really so often --

R: I'm not able to eat anything that is fried. (A: yes.) Last night, my daughter made soup, hamburger soup, (A: yes.) and she put in a lot of different things, you know, really --

F: Vegetables? (R: yes.)

A: All kinds of things, (R: ah, everything.) she used herbs to make the soup. (F: [*laughs*])

R: Yes, everything.

R: Well, I was going to eat it, for I like the taste of vegetables, but it had grease floating in it, "Oh my," I said to them, "you are

pisisik kâ-kakwê-asamiyêk kîkway êkota," nititâw; (A: mhm.) "êkotowahk," nititâw. mwâc –°

F: kiya, ka-kî-otinaman ahpô anita k-âsta--, itê ê-wî-mîciyan, êkwa miskwamîs êkota aya maskimocisihk k-âhat, ka-kohtânat, êkwa kika-ocipitên (R: mhm.) anima pimiy kahkiyaw. (R: mhm.)

A: ka-manahên.

R: êkosi -- âha.

F: ka-manahên ahpô.

A: ka-manahên anima, âha.

R: êkosi nitititikwak âta, "ka-kî-otinên anim ânima *tha--*, anima pimiy," nitititikwak, *you know.* (F: âha.) aya mâna wiya nitânis ê-tôtahk nâha nêtê osîmimâs ana, *tissue* mân ê-âpacihtât, *you know.*

A: âha, tâpwê wiy âta wiya, âha.

R: ahpô kôhkôsiwiyinwa kâ-kîsiswât, *in the dish* mân (F: âha.) êkot[a] ê-astât, êkot[a] ê-ahât; micon ê-pahkosicik aniki kahkiyaw anita, pimiy anim ê-astêk wiyâkanihk, (F: âha.) âha.

16

A: kî-miywêyihtamwak kayâs, pêyakopêhikana ê-mêtawêcik.

R: â, kîkway ê-kî-miywêyihcikâtêk kayâs, micihciy kâ-mêtawêcik.

A: êwakw ânim ânima wiya, âha, nikiskisin wiy êwako.

R: ôh, kî-nîkânîmakan. (A: âha.) êkwa mâna –°

A: kisêyinîpan mâna nêtê wîsta kî-wîcihiwêw ayisk nêma nêtê, (R: âha.) *Françoise* itê –°

R: âha, kâ-kî-opâpâyan.

A: °– kâ-kî-opâpâyân pâsîl, êkonik.

R: kahkiyaw kisêyiniwak ôki, *Benjamin*, (A: âha, *ya.*) êkwa êk--, *Joe.*

A: *hand-games, that--* êwako wiya *I remember hand-games, ya*!

R: âha, *Joe*, êkonik aniki piko, nîso, mitoni ê-kî-otinikocik nistêsak.

A: cimêriy; cimêriy (R: âha.) mâna kî-nakamow, âha.

R: âha, êwako.

R: êkwa mîn âya, anim âya, *poker* ôma kâ-mêtawêhk, kâ-tipahamâtohk mâna.

A: âha.

R: ôh –°

unkind to me, always trying to feed me that stuff in the soup," I said to her. (A: mhm.) No –°

F: You could have taken it out yourself -- where you were going to eat, putting a little ice in a small bag, dunking it in and pulling out (R: mhm.) all the grease. (R: mhm.)

A: You skim it.

R: That's so, yes.

F: You skim it.

A: You skim off the grease, yes.

R: That's what they told me, "You could have taken the grease out," they told me, you know. (F: yes.) What my daughter usually does, that youngest one over there, she uses tissue, you know.

A: Yes, that's the way, yes.

R: Even when she cooks bacon, she puts it [*sc.* a paper towel] in the dish, (F: yes.) and then she puts the bacon on that; and the bacon strips dry off and the grease stays in the dish, (F: yes.) yes.

16 [*Games and Gambling*]

A: They liked playing cards long ago.

R: Ah, something that was enjoyed long ago, were hand-games.

A: Oh those, yes, I remember those.

R: Oh, they were the best. (A: yes.) And then –°

A: The old man, too, was always over there because he played (R: yes.) at Françoise's place –°

R: Yes, your late dad.

A: °– my late dad, *pâsîl*, and those others.

R: All those old men, Benjamin, (A: yes, ya.) and Joe.

A: Hand-games, I remember hand-games, ya!

R: Yes, Joe, it had really taken hold of those two brothers of mine.

A: *cimêriy; cimêriy* (R: yes.) used to sing.

R: Yes, she did.

R: And they also played poker, on Treaty Days.

A: Yes.

R: Oh –°

F: kwayask kî-mêtawâniwan.
R: ôh, kî-mêtawâniwan, âha.

R: êkwa nîst ê-kî-mêtawêyân êkota. *five* --
– mâka mîna tâpitawi ninôhtê-âkayâsimon. –
niyânanwâpisk pêyakwâw ê-isi-wêpinihcik, *you know*, (A: âha.) ê-isi-wêpiniht sôniyâw.

A: mâk êkwa anohc ayisk, kâ-tipahamâtohk mitoni nama kîkway, (R: nama kîkway.) wiya nama nânitaw ana kîkway tâpwê mistahi kîkway (R: môy âhpô.) ê-kî-atâwêyan. (R: [*laughs*]) mâka kayâs ayisk k-âtâwêhk kîkway mitoni kî-mis-ôtinikâniwan.

R: mitâtahtwâpisk ayisiyiniw pêyak kî-miyâw kayâs. (A: âha, *ya*.) nitôcihci-kiskisin ôta aya;
– tânis ôma kani ê-isiyîhkâtêk? –
'pimicaskêkâs.'

A: âtiht mâna kî-pê-kapêsiwak.

R: 'pimicaskêkâs' ôm îsiyîhkâtêw, âha, êkota.
A: âha! Leask êwako, âha, *ya*!
R: êkota;

R: anima mâna, '*Tommy Hobbs*' kâ-kî-itiht, nêma ispimihk êkotê ê-tipahamâtohk, âha.
A: ispimihk, âha! (R: âha.)

R: nikiskisin, mitâtahtwâpisk pêyak.
– êkospî ê--, ê-nîsicik aniki piko awâsisak, niyanân.
A: âha, *ya*!

17

A: êwakw ân[a] âna, sôniyâw ana nêtê, ispî k-âtâwâkêhk ôm âskiy, âskaw mâna kî-pâh-pahkwênamawâwak ayisk, ôk ôt[a] ôhci k-âkisocik ôta, (R: âha.) kî-pâh-pahkwênamawâwak anihi sôniyâwa, *so much* (R: mhm.) *that was interest* nêtê ana kâ-k--, kâ-kî-atâwâkêhk ôm âskiy ôma, kâ-kî-- aya -- (R: mhm.)
[*pause*]

A: kikî-misi-wanohtânaw êkospî, (R: ôh.) ispî k-âtâwâkêhk ôm âskiy, (F: kwayask.) mitoni, âha!
R: kî-misi-wiyakihtâwak sapiko. (A: âha, *ya*.)

F: There were serious games.

R: Oh, there were games, yes.

R: And I also played there. Five --

– as usual, I'm always wanting to speak English. –

Once five dollars was thrown in, you know, (A: yes.) money was thrown in.

A: But today, on Treaty Day, there's really nothing, (R: nothing.) for there isn't much of anything (R: not even.) that you can buy. (R: [*laughs*]) But long ago, on the other hand, when you bought things, you really came away with a lot.

R: One person got ten dollars long ago. (A: yes, ya.) I remember back to that;

– what was the place called again? –

pimicaskêkâs.

A: Some used to come to stay over-night.

R: It is called *pimicaskêkâs*, yes, there.

A: Yes! That is Leask, yes, ya!

R: There;

R: It was upstairs at Tommy Hobbs' place, Treaty was paid there.

A: Upstairs, yes! (R: yes.)

R: I remember, one was given ten dollars.

– At that time, we ourselves only had two children.

A: Yes, ya!

17 [*Selling the Land*]

A: That money, at the time when they sold the land, sometimes they used to pay out a part of it to those who were band members; (R: yes.) they used to pay out part of the money (R: mhm.) that was the interest from when the land was sold; when-- (R: mhm.)

[*pause*]

A: We really made a big mistake at that time, (R: oh.) when this land was sold, (F: right) absolutely, yes!

R: As a matter of fact, they really botched it. (A: yes, ya.)

R: kisêyinîpanak kayâs, kisêyinîpanak êkonik kâ-kî-atâwâkêcik anim âskiy; êkwa kiyâm ât[a] êkwa ta-kakwê-kâhcitinamihk, osâm misahkamik aya --

A: âha, kimihcêtinânaw êkwa, âha. (R: âha.)

R: *farmers* ot[i] ê-mihcêticik.

A: mâk êwakw âw âwa tipahamâtowi-sôniyâw awa, (R: mhm.) kîspin êkwa ta-kî-kâwi-ana-kitâpamiht ana niyânanwâpisk cî ana, (R: mhm.) anohc êkwa tânis ân[a] ê-itakisot, kâh-wêyôtisinânaw êkwa, (R: mhm.) kâwi!

R: kâwi kâh-wêyôtisinânaw.

A: *if they would look at the value of the five* –°

F: *of today's value,*

A: °– *today's value*, âha, *the-- the treaty money* ana, (R: âha.) (F: mhm.) âha, *ya*.

F: *then it would be something*. (R: mhm.)

R: kîspin –°

F: kêyâpit wiy âta wiya mân ê-kihcêyihtahkik nêhiyawak anima, *it repres-- what it represents* êtikwê.

R: °– kîspin kik-âyâyahk aya.

A: *from what I remember*, nawac kayâs mâna *there was a* --

F: kî-mihcêtinâniwan mâna; (A: âha.) (R: âha.)

A: *because everybody came*. (F: âha.)

18

R: êkwa mîna mâna, maskihkîwiyiniwak êkwa mîna wîpitiwâwa, ê-kî-wîkicik mân, ê-kî-pê-ispitahkik mân âya.

A: âha, ôta mâna kî-astêwa --

F: wâskahikanisa.

R: ôh, ê-kî-mihcêtihk.

A: kayâs nawat mihcêt kîkway ôta kikî-miyikawinânaw mâna, tâpiskôt *toothache drops*, (R: mhm.) nanâtohk kîkway; kahkiyaw êkoni mîna ê-ati-namatakohki, (R: nama kîkway.) êkwa mâna kâ-kî-astêk[i] ôta ta-- –°

R: âha.

F: k-âpatahki.

A: °– *the medicine chest, has a* –°

R: Old men long deceased, it was the old men long deceased who sold the land; and even if an attempt were made now to get it back, there's too many ah --

A: Yes, we are too many now, yes. (R: yes.)

R: There are too many farmers.

A: But the treaty-money, (R: mhm.) if you looked back on that five dollars now, (R: mhm.) and its equivalent today, we would be rich (R: mhm.) again.

R: We would be rich again.

A: If they would look at the value of the five –°

F: Today's value,

A: °– today's value, yes, the -- the treaty money; (R: yes.) (F: mhm.) yes, ya.

F: Then it would be something. (R: mhm.)

R: <u>If</u> –°

F: Although the Crees <u>still</u> think a lot of it, for what it represents, I guess.

R: °– <u>if we had it</u>.

A: <u>From what I remember</u> of the old days, there was a --

F: There were many then; (A: yes.) (R: yes.)

A: Because everybody came. (F: yes.)

18 [*Medical Practices I*]

R: And doctors and also dentists used to live here, they used to bring [trailers].

A: Yes, they were placed here.

F: Shacks.

R: Oh, <u>there were many</u>.

A: We were given <u>more</u> things <u>long ago</u>, like toothache drops, (R: mhm.) and all kinds of things; all of these things are gone now, (R: nothing.) though they used to be here to –°

R: Yes.

F: To be used.

A: °– the medicine chest has a –°

R: môya, namôy ê-pêtât ana maskihkîwiyiniw, pîtos kîkway osk-âya, êkon îyâyaw maskihkiya osk-âya, êkoni mistah ê-âpatahki. ôhi wiya kayâhtê ayisiyiniwak kâ-kî-âpacihtâcik; kîkway pikw êkwa ê-âpaciht-- - iyâyaw ê-kêcikwâpitêpitâcik ayisiyiniwa; (A: âha.) anohc êkwa wiya.

kayâs anihi maskihkiya, ahpô mân ê-kakwêtawêyihtamân anim âya, awâsisak mâna kâ-kî-sisopêkahohcik wâskikanisiwâhk, (A: âha, *ya*!)

– tânis ânim ê-isiyîhkâtêk?

A: pêyak mâna '*capsolin*' kî-itamwak, kî-nipahâhkwan mân êwako.

R: môtêyâpiskohk, môy, môcêyâpis--

A: *camphorated oil*.

R: êwako. (F: âha.) (A: *ya*.)

F: tâpwê!

R: âha, môy wîhkâc!

F: nikiskisin.

A: namôy ânim êkwa mîn êwakw ân[i] ânima ê-kî-kâhcitinamihk; mâka mîna nikî-kocihtân tânitahtwâw nêtê *Saskatoon* êkotowahk ê-papâ-kakwêcihkêmoyân. "â, nama kîkway, môy êkwa êkotowahk." nipê-takopayin anita *Blaine Lake*, anit[a] ê-pê-pîhtikwêyân pêyak anima, (R: mhm.) – awîn ôm êkota pêyak môcêyâpiskos k-âstêk; pêyak piko.

R: ây! kimiskên.

A: âha; êkos êkw ân[i] ânima nitayân êkwa. (R: âha.) mayaw ana kâ-mâc-ôscoscocasit ana nôsisim, (F: êkosi.) êkos êwakw ânima ê-sisopêkinâyâhk êkwa –°

R: êkwa ê-kisitêk.

A: °– êkwa ê-kisitêk kîkway ôt[a] ê-astamawâyahk *a -- a -- a cloth, you know.*

R: êkosi wiy ê-itakik (A: âha!) ôki nîsta, aspin ôki nîsôcêsisak oti, mêtoni ê-wî-nânâspicipayicik, iyikohk ê-ostostotahkik.

R: No, the doctor doesn't bring them, just new and different things instead; these new medicines are used a lot. The things that people used to use formerly; the only thing used now – instead, they just pull people's teeth; (A: yes.) today anyway.

Those old-time medicines, I even miss the one that used to be rubbed on the children's chests. (A: yes, ya!)

– What is that called?

A: One used to be called Capsolin, that one was powerful.

R: In a bottle, no, in a bot--

A: Camphorated oil.

R: That one. (F: yes.) (A: ya.)

F: That's right!

R: Yes, never!

F: I remember it.

A: That one can't be found now; but I've tried many times going around asking for it over there in Saskatoon. "Ah, there is nothing, not that kind." I arrived back in Blaine Lake and went into a store there, (R: mhm.) – what was that! there was one bottle there; only one.

R: Hey! You found it.

A: Yes; so I have that now. (R: yes.) As soon as my grandchild starts coughing a little (F: that's it.) we rub that oil on her chest –°

R: And a warm compress.

A: °– and put a warm compress on her, a -- a -- a cloth, you know.

R: That's what I, too, tell them, (A: yes!) since these twins really go into coughing fits, coughing so hard.

19

F: aya mâka, wîhkâc cî kiyawâw ôt[a] âya, kinosêwak kikî-tasîhkawâwâwak, tânitê ê-kî-nôcikino-- [*sc*. ê-kî-nôcikinosêwêcik] –°

R: mwâc.

A: mwâc. (F: mwâc.)

R: mwâc.

F: °– pihtâw ayis wiy ôma môy miywâsin.

R: ayis ôta kî-pakitinâwak kinosêwak, kî-nipiwak mâk âyis, môy ôhci-ohpikiwak; môy êkot--, môy êkotowahk nipiy ôta ôma k-âyâcik, *you know*. (A: âha, *ya*.)

F: ma cî mâk ôki maskêkowi-- maskêkowiyiniwak ê-kî-miyihcik nêma nêtê, ê-kî-otinahkik *Redberry Lake*, ka--, ka-nôcikinosêwêcik.

R: âha.

A: *Ya, Uncle Joe will remember that, because* êkotê mâna kî-- –°

F: kî-isi-piciwak.

A: âha, *ya, they used to--* êkotê mîna –°

R: ôtê mâna nitawi-wâh-ocipitêwak –°

A: °– *rats* mîna; –°

R: °– kinosêwa ôm âya.

A: °– *Uncle Joe will remember that, ya*!

R: ôm âya, tânis ân[a] ê-isiyîhkâsot, â, *Garand* ana pêyak.

F: *Peter*?

R: êwako, kisiwâk ayis apîstam anima –°

F: *Iroquois Lake*.

R: âha, môy wâhyaw, êkotê aniki mâna ê-nâh-nâtâcik --

F: kinosêwa.

R: kîspin –°

A: anohc wiya, âha.

R: âha, anohc wiya.

F: mâk âyis wiy ânohc ka-kî-âhkwatimâwak, (R: âha.) miyosiwak, wêhcasin êkwa cî, *eh*?

A: êwakw ân[i] ânima nêtê anima, kîspin kayâs êkotê kî-ay-itohtêwak ôk ôta ohci, êkosi mîn êwakw ân[i] ânima ê-ati-wanihtâyâhk, (R: piko kîkway.) ê-ati-wanikiskisiyâhk ôma niyanân ê-at-îs-ôhpikiyâhk êkwa ê-wanikiskisiyâhk êwakw ân[i] ânima, êkos êwakw ân[i] ânima kâw êkwa (R: âha.) môniyâw at-ôtinam.

19 [*Gone Fishing*]

F: Have either of you ever worked with fish, where they used to get fish –°

R: No.

A: No. (F: no.)

R: No.

F: Besides, this [water] is no good.

R: They released fish here but they died, they didn't grow; it's not the kind of water for them to live in, you know. (A: yes, ya.)

F: But wasn't the Muskeg Band given the lake over there, they took Redberry Lake for their fishery.

R: Yes.

A: Ya, Uncle Joe will remember that, because over there, they used to –°

F: They used to move camp there.

A: Yes, ya, they used to -- over there too –°

R: They'd usually go over there to pull the –°

A: °– muskrats also; –°

R: °– fish from it.

A: Uncle Joe will remember that, ya!

R: Now, what's his name, that Garand.

F: Peter?

R: That one, because he lives close to that –°

F: Iroquois Lake.

R: Yes, not far, they go over there to fetch --

F: Fish.

R: If –°

A: Today though, yes.

R: Yes, today though.

F: But today they can be frozen, (R: yes.) they are good, and it's easy now, isn't it?

A: That place over there, if they had gone over there long ago from here, then we are losing that too, (R: everything.) and we are forgetting that it is ours, forgetting it as we grow up, and so again (R: yes.) the White-Man takes it.

R: êkwa mîna mâna ê-k--,

– âha –

êkwa mîna mân âya, ê-kî-sipwêpayihk mâna, (F: âha.) ê-nita- ê-nitawi-pakitahwahk; (A: âha.) êkw êkotê ê-ma-mîcisohk êkwa, *you know*, kâ-ocipitihcik kinosêwak. (A: âha.)

F: ayapiyak cî? ayapiyak?

R: namôya, ê-kî-mosci-pâskiswâcik mâna âtiht aya, cîstahikana anihi, ohci cîstahikan ê-kî-cîstahwâcik.

F: ôh, aya cî ôma mâna kâ-miyoskamik –°

A: *spears?*

R: âha.

F: °– kâ-miyoskamik.

A: *spearing?*

R: mayaw k-ât--, k-âti-mâh-mâhkipakâk, (F: âha.) (A: âha.) "ê-natahipayihocik," itwâniwan mâna, "ê-natahipayihocik."

F: ôh, êkos êcik ânima ê-itwêhk, âha.

R: âha.

A: âha.

R: kâ-pimipayihocik mâna kinosêwak, anima, êwakw ânim ê-natahipayihocik.

A: *the stream*, (R: âha.) âha, *ya*.

R: êkota mân ê-kî-miywâsik, kâ-kî-- mâka nîpiya k-âstêk[i] êkwayâc, *you know*, (A: ôh, âha.) êkwêyâc êkot[a] ê-natahipayihocik.

[*pause*]

20

A: misi-kâh-kîhkîhtonâniwan mân ôm ôt[a], ê-pê-isi-kiskisiyân aspin ohci k-âpiyân ôm ôta, wiyasiwêwinihk, (R: âha.) ôm âskiy. ayisk wiya niy ê-kî-pê-isi---â--

R: ê-pê-is-ôhpikihikawiyan.

A: ê-pê-is-ôhpikihikawiyân mâna nôhtâwiy nikî-pêhtawâw, "kahkiyaw ôm ôta k-âkisot ayisiyiniw, ôm ê-tipêyihtahk ôm âskîhkân," kî-itwêw mâna. (R: âha.) mitoni -- mihcêtwâw nikiskisomâwak ôk ôta k-âpiyâhk mâna, anohc êkwa

R: And it was also --,

– yes –

and they also used to go off by team, (F: yes.) and set fishing nets; (A: yes.) then they'd eat there, you know, when the fish were pulled out. (A: yes.)

F: Nets? Nets?

R: No, some merely used to shoot them with harpoons, they'd spear them with harpoons.

F: Oh, this was in the spring –°

A: Spears?

R: Yes.

F: °– when it was spring.

A: Spearing?

R: As soon as the leaves were starting to get big, (F: yes.) (A: yes.) "They are spawning," it was said, "they are spawning."

F: Oh, that's what it was called, yes.

R: Yes.

A: Yes.

R: When the fish are migrating, that's when they're spawning.

A: The stream, (R: yes.) yes, ya.

R: It used to be nice then, only then when the leaves were out, you know, (A: oh, yes.) only then would they be spawning.

[*pause*]

20 [*Land Rights*]

A: I remember many arguments here, since I have been on the council, (R: yes.) about the land. For I --

R: That's the way you were raised.

A: In the way I was raised, I used to hear my father say, "All the people that are band members here, they all own this reserve." (R: yes.) Many times do I remind them when we sit here on

mitoni ê-kîhkîhtohk ayisk ôma, askiy ohci, (R: âha.) ê-nôhtê-tipêyihcikâtêk. (R: tâpwê.) pê-- môy ânim êkosi ta-kî-ispayik, pikw ân[i] âwiyak, ôm âskiy ôma kâ--, pikw îtê ôm âya, kâ-kistikêhk, ta-kî-kakwê-pâh-pahkwênamâht ayisiyiniw, kîkway ohc ê-ohtisicik anima, mâna mihcêtwâw êkos ê-itwêyân, mâk âyisk, anohc êkw âyisiyiniw, nanâtohk kîkway –°

R: êwakw ânima k-êtwêyân.

F: wiy ôhci piko.

A: °– ocipitamâsow wiya piko. (R: âha.) (F: mhm.)

R: êwakw ânima k-êtwêhk anima, ê-mâtinamâtohk k-êtwêhk. kahkiyaw --, pêyak ayisiyiniw, kahkiyaw pêyakwan ta-kakwê-isi-wîcihiht, pêyakwan t-êsi-pâh-pahkwênamâht kiyâm apisîs, *you know*, kayâs, *you know*; êkos ânima ka-kî-ta-tôtahkik, mâk âyisk êkwa anohc êkwa ohci-nôtinitowak!

A: âha; kâ-- nikâh-- nikâh-kisîwi-tahkiskawâwak, mâna mihcêtwâw (R: mhm.) nitisi-môsihtân; (R: mhm.) nanâtohk kîkway êkosi kâ-isi-pîkiskwâtamân, mâka, mâka kêtahtawê pôni-pimâtisiyâni, êwakw ân[i] ânima ta-mâmitonêyihtamwak (F: âha.) ê-kî-pê-itwêyân, (R: tâpwê.) kâkikê (R: âha.) ê-kî-kiskisomakik.

R: mhm, tâpwê.

A: mihcêtiwak ôm ôta, namôy wîhkâc askiy t-âyâcik. (R: âha.) (F: âha.) êkonik aniki ta-kî-mâmitonêyimihcik, ta-kî-pahkwênamâhcik.

R: kîkway k-ôh-pimâcihocik.

A: *yes*.

R: âha.

A: *ya, ya*.

F: ahpô --, ahpô môy pikw îta kikî-ati-wa-wîkin êkwa (R: môy, âha.) kiwayawîtisahokawin tâpiskôc êkây âskîhkân.

A: *ya*.

R: tâpwê.

A: *that's right*.

F: tânitahto-askiy ôm êk ôtê ê-ati-- ôh, â, tânisi ê-is-- --

A: ê-nîkânîyân.

F: ê-nîkânîyan.

council, for today there's much disagreement about the land, (R: yes.) there is a desire to own it. (R: truly.) It should not happen that way, that this land, which is being farmed all over, should be parcelled out to each individual person, with everyone getting something of it, and thus have I said many times, but people today want different things –°

R: That's what I say.

F: Only for themselves.

A: °– they pull only for themselves. (R: yes.) (F: mhm.)

R: That's what is said; they are grabbing from each other, it is said. Everyone should be helped in the same way, everyone should be given the same portion, even if it is small, you know, as in the old days, you know; that's how they should do it, because today they are fighting over it.

A: Yes; I would kick them in anger, (R: mhm.) I feel that way many times; (R: mhm.) I have spoken of it in many ways, but one day when I am dead, they will remember (F: yes.) that I have said this, (R: truly.) that I have always (R: yes.) reminded them of this.

R: Mhm, that's right.

A: There are many here who will never have land. (R: yes.) (F: yes.) They are the ones that should be considered, that should be given a share.

R: Something to make a living from.

A: Yes.

R: Yes.

A: Ya, ya.

F: Even -- you cannot even build a home just anywhere and (R: no, right.) you are sent away as if it were not a reserve.

A: Ya.

R: Truly.

A: That's right.

F: How many years is it now here that --, ah, how -

A: That I have been a leader.

F: That you have been a leader.

A: *nineteen-seventy, to the present date, continuous. but I had nineteen-fifty-eight to nineteen-sixty as Council, nineteen-sixty to sixty-two as Chief; so I will have completed twenty-four years at the end of nineteen-ninety, twenty-four years* (F: wahwâ!) *of serving the people.*

R: kinwês, âh?

F: kinwês!

21

F: êkw ân[i] êkwa ati-mêscipayin ôma, pakahkam. nîswayak ôm ê-otinamâhk kipîkiskwêwiniwâw, nâha [*sc. Colleen Youngs*] mîna.

A: wîst âna.

F: êkây âya miyo--, pêyak êkâ tâpwê miyopayiki, êkwa kotak anima nik-âpacihtân; ê-wî-masinahamân ayisk ôma kititwêwiniwâwa.

R: ê-wî-- ê-wî-pakamahaman. kikaskihon ka-pakamahaman?

F: môya, nimosci-masinahên, mitoni ê-ay-itwêyêk mâna, nikakwê-- nikakwê-itasinahên. ahpô, "aya," âh-itwêyani, êwako mîna nika-masinahên. wâh-wanitonâmoyani, êwako mîna nika-masinahên.

R: êwako mâka k-êtwêyân, mitoni ê-micimôhikoyân êwakw ân[i] ânima, aspin awâsisak kâ--, *you know*, âsay mîna, îh, âsay mîna --

F: ê-kakwê-âkayâsîmosit âsay.

R: ê-mosc-- mitoni ê-mosc-- –°

F: mêtoni mâk ânima ka-kî-pôyoyan, mitoni nayêstaw ka-nêhiyawimototawacik kitawâsimisak; kiya, ê-nisitohtahkik.

R: ahâ. môy mâk âyis --, kâ-misikiticik wiy ôki, kâ-kêhtê-ayiwicik; êkonik wiya, mâk ôki --

F: nîsta mîn êkonik, mâka, wahwâ, nitâyimihikwak nîsta, pahkaci ê-kî-isi-nitawi-kiskinahamawakik.

R: kôsisiminawak oti.

F: wâwîs cî wiya nôsisimak, môy nikaskihtân ka-kitotakik, kîst êtikwê.

A: âha, nôsisimak wiy, âha.

A: 1970, to the present date, continuous. But I had 1958-1960 as Council, 1960-62 as Chief; so I will have completed twenty-four years at the end of 1990, twenty-four years (F: my!) of serving the people.

R: A long time, eh?

F: A long time!

21 [*Language Maintenance*]

F: I think it [*sc*. the tape-recorder] is beginning to run out. We are recording your speech in two places; I and that one [*sc*. Colleen Youngs], too.

A: She, too.

F: When it doesn't -- when one is not working properly, then I will use the other one; for I'm going to write your words down.

R: You're going to type them? Are you able to type?

F: No, I simply write it down, I try to write exactly what you are saying. Even when you say, "ah," I will write that down too. When you make a mistake, I'll write that down too.

R: But that's what I said, that's what is really getting me stuck, since the children-- you know, already, look, already --

F: She is trying to speak a little English again.

R: Just -- it's really just –°

F: But you should really stop that, you should really speak nothing but Cree to your children; because yours understand it.

R: Yes. But not for -- the big ones, the older ones; but for these --

F: Mine too, but oh my, they give me a hard time too, the way I have taught them.

R: Our grandchildren, too.

F: Especially as for my grandchildren, I'm not able to speak with them; just as with you, too, I guess.

A: Yes, as for my grandchildren, yes.

R: êk ômisi nititâwak, "pêyak ôma ê-kiskinohamâkoyêk ka-nêhiyawêyêk êkotê," nititâwak. "kîkwây ôm ôma ka-nêhiyawêyêk," nititâwak, "mwât nikiskêyihtên," nititâwak, "kâ-ka-kitotitakok mâna kâ-nêhiyawêyân," nititâwak, kâ-mosci-ka-kitâpamicik mâna.

êkwa niy êkwa, pikw êkwa âskaw miton âyimanwa pîkiskwêwina, pikw êkwa *I try and* – tâpiskôc ê-kakwê-nisitohtamôhakik; nita-- nitâyimisin mâna kêtahtawê, (A: âha.) êkamâ, êkamâ ohci-kiskinohamâkawiyân (A: âha.) k-ây-- kik-âkayâsîmoyân.

F: êkây -- mâka kîsta, mêtoni sôskwâc nayêstaw ka-kî-nêhiyawimototawacik.

A: âhkamêyimo! (R: âha.)

F: êkây pakicî! (R: âha.)

A: âhkamêyimo!

F: êkây kakwê-âkayâsîmo! [*laughs*]

22

A: kayâs, kikiskisin êtikwê kîsta, mistahi kî-kakâyawisîwak nâpêwak, ayisk piko ta-cîkahikêcik, ta-pônikâtêk mihta; (R: âha.) êkwa ê-kî-âhkisîhocik, mân ê-kî-wâpamakik. (R: ôh!) môy ânohc êkw ânihi tâpiskôc anihi (R: âha.) misi-kis---kispakiwêsâkaya kâ-kikiskahkik, môy êkosi nôhci-wâpahtên, *smocks*; (R: âha.) ê-kî-âhkisîhocik ê-nitawi-cîkahikêcik. (R: âha.)

R: êkwa namôy kîkway kayâs ôhi pîswê-maskisina ôh ôhc-âyâwak; asikana, mâk ê-kî-âh-ahkwêtawêskawâcik. êkwa mîna mâna nimâmâ aya, ê-kî-osîhtamawât mâna nipâpâwa aya, apahkwâson ohci maskisina ôtê âkwâc, otâsihk mâna nimâ-- nipâpâ atâmihk ê-kî-ahât, êkwa mân ânihi ômis ê-kî-itêkinahk.

F: ê-waskicipitahk. (R: âha.) (A: âha.)

R: êkwa waskipicikana, êkos ânima miton ê-kîsowahot. (A: âha, *ya*.) mâka wiya mêskoc kî-ayâwak aniki, kâ-kinosicik aniki sôskwâc, atâmihk (A: âh.) kâ-kikiskawihcik [*sic*], êkotowahk kî-ayâwêwak mêskoc wiya kisêyiniwak, *you know*.

R: And I said to them, "Someone is teaching you to speak Cree over there," I said to them. "What are you going to say in Cree?" I said to them, "I don't understand," I said to them, "when I am speaking to you in Cree," I said to them, but they just look at me.

And now for me, sometimes words are really difficult and I try and, like, I try to make them understand me, but I have a hard time sometimes, (A: yes.) because I was not taught (A: yes.) to speak English.

F: Don't -- but you, too, should really speak nothing but Cree to them no matter what.

A: Be persistent! (R: yes.)

F: Don't let go! (R: yes.)

A: Be persistent!

F: Try not to speak English! [*laughs*]

22 [*Warm Clothes*]

A: Long ago, and I guess you remember too, the men used to work very hard for they had to chop firewood to keep the fire burning; (R: yes.) and they used to dress lightly then, as I used to see them. (R: oh!) It was not like today (R: yes.) when they wear those big, thick jackets, I didn't used to see anything like that, just smocks, really; (R: yes.) they dressed lightly when they went chopping. (R: yes.)

R: And they had nothing like these felt-liners long ago; they had socks, but they wore several of them. And also my mom would make canvas overshoes for my dad, far up over here, my dad put his pants inside them and folded the overshoes like this [*gesture*].

F: He pulled them over top. (R: yes.) (A: yes.)

R: And also rubbers, so then he was dressed really warmly. (A: yes. ya.) But instead [of heavy outer clothes] there were these long things (A: ah.) that were worn underneath, the old men had that kind instead, you know.

A: aya mîna nôhkom kî-osîhtâw aya, *rabbit-skins* ê-kaskikwâtêki, (R: âha.) '*rabbit-robe*' mâna kî-isiyîhkâtamwak anihi (F: akohpa.) akohpa, (R: âha.) âha.

F: wâposwayânakohpa.

R: wâposwayânakohpa.

A: êkotowahk, âha, *ya*.

F: pêyak nitâcimostâk nêt--,

– awîn ôm êtikwê kani k-âcimostawit mastaw ôma; – wiyawâw mâna ê-kî-- ê-kî-m-- ômis îsi,

– ôh, ana *Mrs Whitecalf* ôta kâ-pîkiskwêt; ê-kî-- ômisi mâna ê-kî-itisahkik anihi aya –°

A: wâposwayâna,

F: °– wâposwayâna, êkw êkot[a] ê-apihkêhk.

R: êkw ê-tihtipiwêpinâcik ômis îsi, êkw (A: ôh.) ê-at[i]-âpihkâtâcik, ômis îsi wiya kâh-kîskipayiwak ayisk, (A: ôh, âha.) pikw ânik ê-tihtipiwêpinihcik, *you know*, (F: âha.) tâpiskôc aya, tâpiskôc ôma pîminahkwân k-êsi-tihtipinahkik, (A: âha.) êkos îs âniki piko, êkwa ê-pim-âpihkâtâcik êkw êkota.

F: ôh, mâskôc ani kwayask kî-kîsowâwa, cî?

R: âha. (A: âha, *ya*.) kî-kîsowâwa.

F: kâ-kî-ôhkomiyân mâna nîst ânihi okisêyinîma, "sôminis," kâ-itwêskicik mân ôki cwâciy, (R: âha.) êwakw âna mâna ê-kî-akohpihkâht (R: âha.) ana nimosômipan, êkotowahk mâna wâposwayânakohpa.

A: wâposwayânakohpa nikî-ayânân, âha.

R: wâwîs kwayask ê-pîhtawêkinamihk, kwayask ê-wêwêkinamihk.

A: pêskis ê-wêwêkinamihk. (R: âha.) êkotowahk mâna pêyak nikî-ayânân nôhkom ê-kî-osîhtât. (R: âha.)

êkwa mân âya, nîsotâpânâsk mâna nikî-âpacihânân, pêyak nipâpâ ê-pamihât êkwa pêyak nîsta pêyak. (R: âha.) mân êkota ê-kî-pôsihikawiyân, nîst êkw âniki ê-ati-paminakik aniki misatimwak, *Blaine Lake*, (R: âha.) ê-nitaw-âtâwâkêyâhk mihta. (R: mhm.) *one load* nîsta; *the wood -- we'd go there and, uh, sell wood,* (R: mhm.) kâ-pê-kîwêpayiyâhk êkwa, ômis ê-âpocikwânipitiht ana *the sleigh*, (R: mhm.) nêtê êkw *in front* niyanân, ôtê aniki ê-tahkopitihcik misatimwak, êkos êkwa ê-pê-kîwêyâhk êkwa

A: And my grandmother used to make, ah, rabbit-skins that had been sewn together, (R: yes.) they used to call them rabbit-robes, those (F: blankets.) blankets, (R: yes.) yes.

F: Rabbitskin-blankets.

R: Rabbitskin-blankets.

A: That kind, yes, ya.

F: Someone told me over ther--,

– I wonder who it was that told me recently; –

they used to -- like this,

– oh, that was Mrs Whitecalf who spoke here;

they used to cut them like this, the, ah, –°

A: Rabbit-skins,

F: °– rabbit-skins, and then they were braided.

R: And then they twisted them like this and (A: oh.) braided them, because they'd break apart like so [*gesture*], (A: oh, yes.) they have to be twisted, you know, (F: yes.) twisted just like rope is twisted, (A: yes.) just like those, and then they braid them there.

F: Oh, they were probably very warm, eh?

R: Yes. (A: yes, ya.) They were warm.

F: My late grandmother also used to make them for her old man, *sôminis,* as *cwâciy* and his family always used to call him, (R: yes.) that kind of rabbitskin-blanket used to be braided (R: yes.) for my late grandfather.

A: We used to have rabbitskin-blankets, yes.

R: Especially if they are properly lined, and properly covered.

A: They also were covered. (R: yes.) We had one of those which my grandmother had made. (R: yes.)

And we used to take two sleighs, with my dad in charge of one, and I, too, in charge of one. (R: yes.) I used to be given a ride there, and I also took care of the horses when we'd go to Blaine Lake (R: yes.) to sell firewood. (R: mhm.) I, too, had one load; the wood -- we'd go there and, uh, sell wood, (R: mhm.) then when we were driving home, one sleigh was turned upside down [on the other], (R: mhm.) and we were in front; and the horses were tied on over here, and that way my dad and I came home; but I was

nipâpâ; mâk âna niya *rabbit-robe* an[a] ê-wêwêkisiniyân, (R: âha.) ê-wêwêkapiyân. (R: âha.)

F: aya mîna mân âya, opîwayakohpa, kâ-kî-- (R: âha.) (A: âha.) kêyâpic sapiko, êkwa môniyâsak (A: âha.) êkwa kahkiyaw (R: âha.) êwako, ahpô piko oskotâk-- miskotâkaya êkwa.

R: ayisk anihi tâpiskôc aya, ômis îsi; (A: âha.) êkw êkot[a] êkwa ê-asiwatâyan anih ôpîwâs[a], êkwa ê-kipokwâtaman. (A: âha.) tâpitaw êkos, îyikohk ka-têpipayiyan, êkwayâc êkwa ê-mâmawinaman êkota.

A: âha, *ya*; akohpa.

23

R: nikî-wîcihâw, nikî-wîcihâw an[a] âya, nikâwîs an[a] ê-osîhât êkotowahk, ana mân ôtê aya *Green Lake* ana, nôhcâwîs kâ-kî-ayât.

A: *you're a Gladue your mother's side; Gladue?*

R: âha. (A: âha.) (R: âha.)

R: mâka nôhcâwîs ana,

– tânis ôma kâ-isiyîhkâsot? –

êwako kâ-kî-nipahiht ana nôhcâwîs, ê-osôniyâmit ê-itêyimiht, kikî-pa-pêhtên? (A: âha.) *all this time* nîswâpisk mîna nîso-sôniyâs piko ocasiwacikanisihk ê-asiwasoyit.

A: ôh, wâcistak [*sic*]!

R: kâ-kî-miskâht. êwakw âna nikâwîs ana, matwân cî ôm ê-pa-pimâtisit, ê-itêyihtamân.

A: *Françoise* cî?

R: âha.

A: *oh no, she died; Françoise is dead, ya, she's died, ya. Frank Lafond* aniki k-êtacik.

F: ôh, êkot[a] êcik ân[i] ôhci!

R: kahkiyaw êcik ân[i] êkwa, âha.

A: kahkiyaw kî-pôni-pimâtisiwak.

R: nipâpâ wiy âyis ana –°

A: ana wiy ân[a] ê-kî-nipahiht ana tâpwê, ê-osôniyâmit (R: âha, nôhcâwîs ana.) ê-itêyimiht, *and the old lady died, too, ya, Françoise*; â, êkotê nikî-itohtân.

all wrapped up in that rabbit-robe, (R: yes.) I was sitting wrapped up. (R: yes.)

F: And also, ah, feather-blankets, (R: yes.) (A: yes.) they still have them like that actually, White-Men (A: yes.) and everybody, (R: yes.) and even jackets now.

R: For they are like this (A: yes.) and you put the down inside and sew them closed [*sc.* into squares]. (A: yes.) Always that way, until you have enough, and only then do you sew them together.

A: Yes, ya; blankets.

23 [*Family*]

R: I used to help her, I used to help my aunt when she made those, the one over here at Green Lake, where my uncle used to live.

A: You're a Gladue on your mother's side; a Gladue?

R: Yes. (A: yes.) (R: yes.)

R: But my uncle,

– what was he called? –

that uncle of mine was killed because it was thought that he had money, had you heard about that? (A: yes.) All this time he only had two dollars and fifty cents in his pocket.

A: Oh, oh my!

R: He was found. That is the aunt I mean, I've been thinking about whether she's still alive.

A: Françoise?

R: Yes.

A: Oh no, she died; Françoise is dead, ya, she's died, ya. It's Frank Lafond and his family who you're talking about.

F: Oh, that's where that one is from.

R: All of them, yes.

A: They all died.

R: My dad, that was his –°

A: That one was killed, it is true, for it was thought that he had money, (R: yes, he was my uncle.) and the old lady died, too, ya, Françoise; ah, I went there [*sc.* for the funeral].

R: nikî-nitawi-wâpamâw, nikî-nitawi-wâpamâw ôta kayâsîs [*sic; sc.* kayâsês], mêkwâc nipêpîm aw âwa osîmimâs awa, *four* êtikwê, *four or five* ê-itahtopiponwêt, nikî-nitawi-wâpamâw ana nikâwîs. tâspwâw acimosisa nikî-miyik, ê-kî-wâpiskisit ana, ê-kâh-kaskicêwasinâsosit ômis îsi, (A: âha.) ê-kî-miyât oti nipêpîma. (A: âha.)

F: tânitê ê-kî-wîkicik, *Green Lake*?

A: âha, *Green Lake*.

R: âha, êkotê aniki, êkotê.

R: kêyâpic mâna nikanawêyimâw wêwêkiscikwânêhpisonisa ê-kî-miyit.

A: *oh yes*, âha!

R: êkwa êkos ê-kî-isit, "wahwâ, tâpwê nimiywêyihtên ê-wâpamitân," ê-isit. êkota okosisa pêyak kî-wîc-âyâmêw êkospî. (A: âha.)

A: *he* [*sic*] *had two, Vital and Ernest*.

R: âha, pêyak mâk âsay ê-kî-paskêt.

F: pimâtisiwak?

A: *no*!

F: ê-isi-nîsicik?

A: *ya, they both died; Suzette* mîna kî--, *the family is all dead; Suzette* mîna --

R: *Suzette* cî mîna?

A: âha.

R: kani nîkân êwako cî?

A: âha.

A: â, kâ-wîkihtot anita *Uncle Joe's* anita kî-nîmihitonâniwan wiy êwakw âna, *I remember; I remember her wedding*.

F: awîn ân[a] êwako, otânisiwâwa?

A: otânisiwâwa, '*Suzette*' kî-itâw êwakw âna.

F: awîniwa ê-kî-wîkimât?

R: opîtatowêwa pêyak.

A: opîtatowêwa. êwakw âw âw âsic âya, ay âw âya, *Ben* anih ôsisima, *they were together* aniki *them*.

R: stâcikow aniki.

A: stâcikow êkwa, aya.

R: I had gone to see her, I had gone to see her here quite some time ago, when my baby, the youngest one, was four I guess, four or five years old, I had gone to see that aunt of mine. As a matter of fact, she gave me a puppy, a white one with black markings like this, (A: yes.) she gave it to my baby. (A: yes.)

F: Where did they live, at Green Lake?

A: Yes, at Green Lake.

R: Yes, they were over there.

R: I still keep a head scarf that she gave to me.

A: Oh yes, yes!

R: And she said to me, "Oh my, I'm really happy to see you," she said to me. She lived with one of her sons at that time. (A: yes.)

A: She had two, Vital and Ernest.

R: Yes, but one had already left.

F: Are they still living?

A: No!

F: Both of them?

A: Ya, they both died; Suzette, too, the family is all dead; Suzette, too.

R: Suzette, too?

A: Yes.

R: I forgot, she died first, didn't she?

A: Yes.

A: Ah, when she got married, there was a dance at Uncle Joe's for her, I remember; I remember her wedding.

F: Whose, their daughter's?

A: Their daughter's, she was called Suzette.

F: Who did she marry?

R: A Ukrainian.

A: A Ukrainian. And this one also, Ben's granddaughter, they were together [*sc.* at the same time].

R: The *stâcikows*.

A: The *stâcikows*, ya.

R: tânis êtikw âna kotak ê-kî-is-âspiyîhkâsot; môya wiya ê-ohc-ôsîmihtocik aniki, môya, pâh-pîtos –°

A: môya, môya, pâh-pîtos, âha.

R: °– ê-kî-pê-nitonikêcik ôta maskêko-sâkahikanihk iskwêwa ê-kî-pê-nitawêyimâcik; nîso kî-kâhcitinêwak, êkoni pêyak anihi --

A: *Marie* pêyak, â, *Ben's daughter*, (R: âha.) êkwa pêyak, â, *Suzette*. (R: âha.)

F: ôh, êkota cî an[a] ôhci *Ben*?

A: âha, *ya*, (R: âha.) *ya*.

A: aspin an[a] ê-kî-pimâtisit, nêtê mâna nikî-pê-nâh-nitawâpamik kî-pê-pâh-pîhtikwêw mâna, *when I was working at the Marigold* --

R: wâh, mâk ês âni mitoni ê-kî--, êwakw ânima k-êtwêyân; anohc êkwa ayisiyinîsisak ê-isi-tâwakisihkik, mayaw nimiywêyimik -- kâ-miywêyimocik, êkos ê-ati-kihci-wîkimâcik; êkosi ê-kî-ispayicik aniki. (A: âha, *ya*.)

F: kî-wâ-- –°

R: môya -- ê-kî-kitimahikocik mistahi. (F: ha!) êkosi ê-kî-isi-misiwanâcisicik, *they were*, môy kwayask aya, ayisiyiniwa ê-kî-wîc-âyâmâcik.

A: âha, *ya*.

24

F: tânisi ôm êkwa, mêkwâc ôma, tâpiskôc ôta kitaskînaw ôma, mistahi cî ôma mawisonâniwiw kêyâpic, êkos îsi nanâtohk?

R: mwâc.

A: mitoni wiya niya nititêyihtên, nanâtohk kîkway misiwanâcisîmakan, aspin ohci nanâtohk kîkway kâ-sisopâcikâtêk êkwa. (R: âha.)

R: mwâc sôskwât, mistah êkwa âyiman, mînisa ka-kâhcitinamihk.

A: êkw ânihi mînis[a] ânih, îyikohk ê-wî-nipah-âpisiminakâsiki anihi misâskwatômina, (R: âha.) môy êkwa ê-miywâsiki.

R: ayisk kîsisikêwak, tâpitawi kîsitêwa. mâcik ôma mâka mîna mêton ôm ê-mâh-misi-kîsitêk.

A: kâ-pâh-pasisâwêhk cî, âha. mâk êkwa mîn ânihi nanâto-- --

[*external break*]

R: I wonder what the other's last name was, for they weren't brothers, no, they were from different –°

A: No, no, different, yes.

R: °– they came looking here at ***maskêko-sâkahikanihk*** as they wanted women; they got two, and one of those --

A: Marie was one, ah, Ben's daughter, (R: yes.) and Suzette was one. (R: yes.)

F: Oh, is she from that family, Ben's?

A: Yes, ya, (R: yes.) ya.

A: When he was alive, he used to come to see me over there, he would always come in when I was working at the Marigold [*sc.* restaurant] --

R: Wow, but it's really -- as I said; today as the young people bump into something, as soon as he likes --, when they take a fancy to him, they marry him; that's what happened to these two [*sc.* Suzette and Marie]. (A: yes, ya.)

F: They –°

R: No -- they [*sc.* their husbands] were very mean to them. (F: ha!) In this way they perished, they were --, they lived with people who were not right.

A: Yes, ya.

24 [*Berry-picking*]

F: How is it nowadays, here on our Reserve, is there still much berry-picking and things like that?

R: No.

A: I really think that all the various things that are being sprayed have come to ruin it now. (R: yes.)

R: There are practically none, it's extremely difficult to get berries now.

A: And the berries one gets turn out to be such very small berries, the saskatoons (R: yes.) are no good now.

R: For they burn the fields, the fields are always burning. There is usually an awful lot of burning of fields.

A: When they set the stubble on fire, yes! But they also --

[*external break*]

25

A: -- môy êkwa tipahikâniwan ayisk, ta-nitawâpamat ana kiya *your eye-doctor in the city*. (R: ôh.) awa pik ôt[a] êkwa cîk âwa kâ-pê-itohtêt, namôy mâk êwakw ân[a] ê-nitawêyimak, ê-âtawêyimak, (R: mhm.) kâkikê awa niy ê-itohtêyân awa *this one eye-d--*, êkos êwakw ân[a] âna niwî-itohtân. (R: mhm.)

nika-kaskihon êkotê t-êtohtêyân, kâwi ta-pê-kîwêyân, –°

R: awa niya ê-kî-miyit ohi. (A: âha.)

A: °– môy wiya, niy âwa, *I have my own doctor, eh*, (F: âha.) *but they won't pay --*

F: kinakayâskawâw êwako.

A: êwakw âna ê-nakayâskawak.

R: nikotwâsomitanaw tahtwâpisk êkwa nîswâpisk ê-kî-tipahamân ôhi. (A: ha.)

F: ê-tako-tipahaman kâ--, ê--, (R: ê-tipahamân, âha.) kâ-miyi-- kâ-mêkihk wiy âyis anihi, aya.

R: tâniyikohk pikw êtikwê ê-kî-itakihtêki wiyawâw, tâniyikohk pikw êtikwê (A: âha.) [...; *?record*] êkoyikohk.

A: wah, ôta mân âstâwak. "â, êkon ôhi nikotwâw ka-kî-nawasônikân," itwêwak mâna; (R: âha.) mâka kîspin kotaka nawac ê-nitawêyihtaman ê-âhkwakihtêki, pikw êkw (R: êkoni êkwa, âha.) ânima ta-tipahaman anihi –°

F: ta-tako-tipahaman.

A: °– ta-tako-tipahaman anihi k-êtakihtêki nêhi nêtê.

R: âha, êkos ânim ê-kî-ispayiyân.

R: êkwa aya, pêyakwâw, "piko tâpitawi pêyak-askiy piko kik-âpacihtâyan, piko ka-mêskotinaman," nikî-itik ana, (A: ôh, âha.) "nêsowanwa kiskîsikwa; wâwîs ana kâ-ispâhkêpayit, aya cî ê-sôkâwâspinêyan?" nititik; (A: ôh, âha.) "âha," nititâw. "wâwîs kâ-ispâhkêpayit êwako," itwêw. (A: ôh, âha.) "mêtoni kisîhcihtân ôhi, môy kikî-wâpin," nikî-itik ana; (A: ôh, âha.) êkos ôm ê-ispayiyân âsay. (A: ôh.) *do you know* aya mâna, kâ-kisipi-kîsikâk mâna, mitoni mân ê-sîhciyân ka-wâpiyân. êkwa mitoni nika-kêcikonên ôma, môy niwâpahtên! (A: ôh.) tâpiskôc ê-kaskâpahtêk. ôh[i] ê-itôtâkoyân âsay, (A: ôh, âha.) osâm kinwês ê-- ê-âpacihtâyân êkwa. (A: âha, ha.)

25 [*Medical Services*]

A: -- for they do not pay for it now, for you to see your own eye-doctor in the city. (R: oh.) Only the one who comes around here, but I don't want that one, I reject him, (R: mhm.) as for me, I always go to this one eye-d--, so that's the one I'm going to go to. (R: mhm.)

I will be able to go there and come back home –°

R: As for me, he gave me these [*sc.* glasses]. (A: yes.)

A: °– but that one's not for me, I have my own doctor, eh, (F: yes.) but they won't pay --

F: You are used to that one.

A: That's the one I'm used to.

R: I paid sixty-two dollars for these. (A: ha.)

F: You pay extra, (R: I paid it, yes.) over and beyond those which are provided.

R: I wonder how much they had cost for them [*sc.* Indian Affairs], I wonder (A: yes.) how much of that.

A: Well, they put them here. "You can choose any of these," they usually say; (R: yes.) but if you'd rather have others, they cost more and (R: for those, yes.) you have to pay that for them –°

F: You have to pay extra.

A: °– you have to pay extra for what those over there cost.

R: Yes, that's what happened to me.

R: And once, that one told me, "It's important that you use them for only one year and then you have to change them." (A: oh, yes.) "Your eyes are weak; especially when the sugar goes up; do you have diabetes?" he said to me; (A: oh, yes.) "Yes," I said to him. "Especially when the sugar goes up," he said. (A: oh, yes.) "'You really strain your eyes and you can't see," he said to me; (A: oh, yes.) and that's what has happened to me already. (A: oh.) Do you know, at the end of the day, I really have a hard time seeing. And if I take them off, I can't see! (A: oh.) As if there is smoke. These have done this to me already, (A: oh, yes.) as I've used them too long. (A: yes, ha.)

piko mân ê-nitopahtwâyân niskîsikosa. êkosi mâka, mâka mîna nititâwak ôta, “môy wîhkâc mân ê-ohci-wâpahtamân ôma, ê-ohc-îtêyihtamân,” nititâwak, (A: t-ôhc--) “kika-mâh-mîsahamân niskîsik-- nîhkwâkanis [*sic*],” nititâwak (A: âha, tâpwê.) – ê-oskîsikohkâyân êkwa mîna.

A: mîpitihkâna nanâtohk kîkway.

R: mîpit kîkway! (A: âha.)

A: iskwê-- [*sc*. iskwêyâc] nikî-pâhpihikwak mân âwâsisak kâ-wî-sipwêhtêyân, êkon ôhi mân ê-kiskisomicik, nîpitihkâna, (R: mhm.) êk ôhi, êkwa *my wallet*; (R: mhm.) ayisk niwâh-wanikiskisin êkwa. (R: mhm.) [*laughs*].

R: tâpwê êkos ê-ispayiyân nîsta, ê-misi-môhcowiyân mitoni. [*pause*]

26

A: kîkwây ôm êkwa mîna ka-kî-âcimonânaw? nanâtohk kîkway ayisk mâna kî-wa-osîhtamâsowak wiyawâw ayisiyiniwak; (R: âha.) môy wîhkât nôh-kiskêyihtên, tâpiskôt anohc ôm êkwa atâwêwikamikohk, iyikohk nanâtohk kîkway kâ-nîhcipicikâtêk kâ-otinikêhk, (R: âha.) môy âyisk ohc-ôsôniyâm--, môy ôhc-âyiwâkipayiw sôniyâw. (R: môya.)

R: mâk êkwa mêskoc ê-kî-wêhtakihtêk kîkway.

A: âta wiy âyisk, âha. ahpô piko kâ-kisîpêkinikêcik wiyawâw. (R: âha.) mâka mîna nikî-âcimôhikawin ôtê, awâsisak ôtê ta-nitawi-kitotakik ôki kâ-kî-kiskinohamâhcik ôta. mâka mîna nanâtohk kîkway, mâka mîna nikî-- (R: mhm.) ---wawiyatêyihtên (R: mhm.) nitawâc ê-âcimoyân. (R: mhm.) ôma mêkwâc ôm êkwa, kisîpêkinikêwikamikwa ôhi k-âyâki, (R: âha.) *laundromats*, “kîstan--” –°

R: nipakwâtên!

A: °– “kîstanaw kikî-ayânaw ôta,” nititwân. ôta mâna pêyak, miton ô--, ita *your brother* kâ-kî-ayât, (R: âha.) *that big slough, eh*, (R: âha.) êkotê mâna -- (F: êkot[a] ânima.) êkotê mân ê-kî-itohtêhk, *tubs* ê-pê-pêcikâtêk[i], êkwa anihi *washboard*, êkw ê-kî-osîhiht awa *soap*; êkot[a] êkw ê-kisîpêkinikêhk êkwa, –°

R: îh, ê-kî-tâh-takahkâpâwêki, –°

I always have to search for my glasses. But that's what I say to them here, "I had never seen this, and I had never thought," I say to them, (A: from that --) "that I'd be mending my eye-- my face," I say to them (A: yes, truly.) – and now I wear glasses.

A: And false teeth, and all kinds of things.

R: Something for teeth! (A: yes.)

A: The children always laugh at me when I am about to go out; they remind me of these things, my false teeth, (R: mhm.) and the [glasses], and my wallet, (R: mhm.) for I forget them. (R: mhm.) [*laughs*]

R: That's certainly what happens to me, too, I'm really very stupid. [*pause*]

26 [*Making Soap*]

A: What else will we be able to tell about now? For the people used to make all kinds of things for themselves. (R: yes.) I had never known it to be as in a store today, when so much of everything is taken down [*sc.* by the customer; self-serve] when one buys things, (R: yes.) for no money used to -- there used to be no extra money. (R: certainly not.)

R: But instead things used to be cheap then.

A: Of course that was so, yes. Even when they had to wash their clothes themselves. (R: yes.) As usual, I had been asked to tell stories over here, to go and talk to the students at the school here. And again, I did find all kinds of things (R: mhm.) funny, (R: mhm.) in spite of everything, when I was telling stories. (R: yes.) Nowadays, those laundromats of the present time, laundromats, "We also --" –°

R: I hate them!

A: °– "We also had those here," I said. One was here, right here -- where your brother used to live, (R: yes.) at that big slough, eh, (R: yes.) over there -- (F: it was there.) they used to go over there, and tubs were brought and washboards, and soap that had been made. And there the washing was done –°

R: Look, the clothes were washed beautifully, –°

A: °– êkw ânima *laundromat* ê-kî-ayâyahk. (F: [*laughs*])

R: °– mênikanihk ê-akocikêyahk. [*laughs*]

A: âha, tâpwê; *on the wire*, âha.

F: tânisi mâk ê-kî-is-ôsîhâyêk kisîpêkinikan?

R: aya, anima mân âya, – °

A: *lye*.

R: °– *lye*, êkwa sîkosâkanak, *that's all*. kipakâsimâwak –°

F: wiyin, (R: âha.) wiyin asici.

R: °– wiyin asici sîkosâkanak (A: wiyin, âha!) kipakâsimâwak.

F: anima cî âhkwaci-pimiy mâna, ahpô cî pikw îtowahk –°.

R: sôskwât pikw îtowahk, âha, *ya, the old* –°

F: °– pikw îtowahk ê-ay-isi-mâ-- ê-ay-isi-ka-kâhci-- --

R: °– têpiyâhk êkây ê-wiyâsiwicik, *you know*, (F: âha.) wiyâs môy ê-astêk. aniki mân îyôskisiwak [*sic*] ay[a], âhkwaci-pimiy anima kâ-osîhacik, (F: âha.) pîkinipayiwak mâna mitoni, *you know*, êkonik kî-miyosiwak mâna, nikaskihon nîst ê-osîhakik aniki.

A: *and then they would let it set, and you cut it into bars*; (R: âha.) âha.

R: kipakâhtân aya, *to a dish*, *you know*; mêton îskw âniki sîkosâkanak ê-sikwâciwasocik. êkos êkwa miton ê-sikwâciwasocik, êkwa *lye* êkota kititêhên êkwa anima, mêton ôti –°

A: *you know 'lye*? (F: âha.) *they're in tins* anima, êwakw ân[i] ânima, âha.

R: °– kititêhên. êkos êkwa kinakatên êkota, pôn-ôsowak, kinakatên, *you know; after* êkw ê-kî-tahkipayicik êkwa; (A: âha.) âha.

êkw ê-nipahi-miyosicik mâmaskâc iyikohk. aya mâna niy ê-kî-itêyihtamân, "kêhtinâc ôma pimiy piko aya --, kisîpêkinikan piko ka-sîkinak," ê-kî-itêyihtamân mâna, (F: âha.) nistam mâwacêyas. (A: âha.) "wahwâ," k-êtêyihtamân, "mahti nika-kocîn."

> – ôtê ê-ayâyâhk aya, *Duck Lake* ê-ayâyâhk. (A: âha.) misahkamik sîkosâkanak ê-kî-osîhakik, pimiy[a] âyisk mâna nêtê kî-otinikâtêwa nêma kotak, *Rosthern* nêma; (A: âha.) îh, mitoni wiyinwa nimisâhcinêhên. êkw ânima mâka mîna *they* -- pêyakwâw ê-ay-apiyân êkota, ka-kâh-kisk--, nama kîkway kisîpêkinikan nitayâwâw. –

A: °– and we used to have that as our laundromat then. (F: [*laughs*])

R: °– we hung [the clothes] on the fence. [*laughs*]

A: Yes, indeed; on the wire, yes.

F: But how did you used to make soap?

R: Well, that was –°

A: Lye.

R: °– lye, and cracklings, that's all. You boil them –°

F: Fat, (R: yes.) with fat.

R: °– you boil fat and cracklings. (A: fat, yes!)

F: Was it that hard-grease [*sc.* organ or abdominal fat] then or simply any kind –°

R: Just any kind, yes, ya, the old –°

F: – any kind was obtained --

R: °– as long as they had no meat on them, you know, (F: yes.) there was no meat on them. They are generally soft, when you make that hard grease, (F: yes.) they really crumble, you know, those used to be good, and I, too, am able to make those.

A: And then they would let it set and you cut it into bars; (R: yes.) yes.

R: You boil it, ah, in a dish, you know, until those cracklings are really coming apart from boiling. Then, when they have come apart from the boiling, you stir the lye in there, you really stir it –°

A: You know what lye is? (F: yes.) It comes in tins, that's it, yes.

R: °– you stir it in. Then you leave it there, and the cracklings stop boiling, you leave it, you know; and then they used to cool down; (A: yes.) yes.

And they were very good, it's surprising how good. As for me, I used to think, "Surely it's just grease, I'll have to pour in soap," I used to think that, (F: yes.) the very first time, (A: yes.) "Oh my!" I thought, "I will try it."

– We were over here, ah, we were living at Duck Lake. (A: yes.) I had made a large amount of cracklings, for fat was obtained over there, from that other place, Rosthern; (A: yes.) oh, I bought a lot of fat. And again over there --, once I was at home -- I did not have any soap. –

"wahwâ!" nititêyihtên, "niwî-kocîn." – nimâmạ mân ê-kî-osîhât, ê-kî-wa-wâpamak ê-itôtahk, *you know*; piko kîkway ana nimâmâ ê-kî-itôtahk mâna.

A: mhm; ôh, kayâs!

R: kayâs.

A: ôh, kayâs kî-kiskêyihtamwak nanâtohk is ê-isi-wîcihisocik.

R: ê-kî-ka-kwayâ-- ê-kakwâhyaki-nihtâ-pânisâwêt mîna mâna.

A: kî-nihtâwêyihtamwak. (R: mhm.)

F: ê-kî-kakâyawâtisicik.

A: mitoni, âha.

R: êkwa mîn âya, êkos êkwa n--,

– pitamâ ôma nika-kîs-âcimon; –

êkos êkwa nitahâw ana, nipiy anima nitôsên; êkwa sîkosâkanak nipakastawêhwâwak, ninawasônâwak êkwa ê-yôskisicik, *you know*, ê-kî-tôtahk mâna. niwa-oswâwak, êkota kisêyiniw ê-pê-pîhtikwêt, "kîkwây ôma kâ-osaman?" – "sîkosâkanak." (A: âha.) "kîkway mâk ê-wî-osîhtâyan?" – "kisîpêkinikan." (A: âha.) "â, piko kîkway mâna kitôtên," k-êsit. (A: âha.)

êkosi; ê-kî-pa-pakâsocik ê-sikwâciwasocik, mâk ânihi k-âpisâsiki nitayân anihi, *you know*, "k-âhkwâpahtêk," nik-êtwân, –°

A: âha, *lye*. (R: âha.)

R: °– mâka nahiyikohk miton *a whole* -- pêyak-*a-can* [*sic*] ka-sîkinamân, *you know*, êkota iyikohk aniki mistahi, miton ê-misâk anima *dish, you know*.

êkosi; môy mîna ninôhtê-ispisîhaw mitoni, ôta nânitaw, iyikohk ka-miyo-mâh-manisoht, *you know*. (A: âha.) êkosi, nisîkinâw; wahwâ, konit ê-ohtêpayik anima, êkos âyis ispayiw mâna. (A: âha.) niyay-itêhên [*sic*], êkwa niyay-itêhên [*sic*], isko mitoni môya kîkway, *you know*, (A: âha.) nitay-itêhwâw. êkosi, nitôtinâw êkwa, ohpimê êkwa nitahâw; ayis îkamâ [*sic; sc.* êkamâ] kayâs ka-pîminamihk, ka-pa-pônamihk; (A: âha, *ya*.) kotawânâpiskohk, mihta piko, *you know*. (A: âha!) namôy ka-kî-nakinâw! nitôtinên êkwa ohpimê nitastân.

"Oh my!" I thought, "I'm going to try." – My mom had used to make it, and I had watched her do it, you know. My mom used to do everything.

A: Mhm; oh, long ago!

R: Long ago.

A: Oh, in the old days they used to know all kinds of ways of helping themselves.

R: She was good -- and she was extremely good at cutting meat into sheets.

A: They used to be innovative. (R: mhm.)

F: They used to be hard-working.

A: Really, yes.

R: And also, it was then --

– first I will finish telling the story; –

so then I put it on and boiled the water; then I put the cracklings into the water, and I picked out the soft ones, you know, as she had used to do. I was boiling them there when the old man [*sc.* my husband] entered, "What are you boiling?" – "Cracklings." (A: yes.) "But what are you going to make?" – "Soap." (A: yes.) "Ah, you are always doing everything," he said to me. (A: yes.)

So, the cracklings were boiling away, and dissolving in the boiling, but I had those small things [*sc.* crystals], you know, I'll say 'the one with the acidic fumes' –°

A: Yes, lye. (R: yes.)

R: °– but the right amount was for me to pour one whole can in, you know, there were so many cracklings, and the dish was very large, you know.

So, I also did not want to make it very high, about here [*gesture*], so it would be easy to cut, you know. (A: yes.) So I poured it; oh my, it really bubbled, for that's the way it usually goes. (A: yes.) I kept stirring it, and kept stirring it, until there were no bubbles left, you know, (A: yes.) I kept stirring it. Then I took it and put it to the side; for long ago, you couldn't turn down a wood-fire; (A: yes, ya.) it's just firewood in a stove, you know. (A: yes!) I couldn't turn it off! I took it and put it to the side.

êkos ây-apiw. "wahwâ!" nititêyihtên, "êkwa êtikwê tahkisiw." môy âyisk mîna ka-câhkinat, (A: âha, *ya*.) ka-kîsison. ê-tahkisit êkwa (êkw âni mistihkomâna mân ânihi, k-âpacihtâyâhk êkotowahk êkwa), nikapatênâw êkwa, nikwatapiwêpinâw êkwa; masinahikanêkin ê-astâyân, nikwatapiwêpinâw, kêcikopayiw, *you know*. îh, mâninakis êkwa nimaniswâhtay êkwa, mitoni misahkamik kisîpêkinikan. (A: âha.)

êkosi, kîhtwâm êkwa ê-kîsikâk êkwa, êkwa nikâh-kisîpêkinikân êkwa. îh, êkw ân[i] ê-pipohk mâk ôma êkotê k-âyâyâhk; îh, êkwa an[i] êkwa mahkahkohk ê-kî-otinamân êkwa, kôna êkwa ê-nitawi-sâkaskinahâw, apisîs nipîs nisîkinên, (A: âha.) tahkohc kotawânâpiskohk nitahâw. mêton îsko mistah ê-astêk, êkw âni êkwa nanânis êkwa kâ-sîkinak êkwa, têpiyâhk êkwa ka-têpipayiyân êkwa, (A: âha.) mâninakis êkwa kapê-kîsik. wahwâ, iyikohk ê-wâpiskinikêmakisit (A: âha, *ya*.) ana kisîpêkinikan; mâk êkwa mêskoc aya, kîspin mistahi ka-sinikonat, nawac piko kiwî-kîsison, *you know*, (A: âha.) osâm ayisk âhkohtêwisow.

A: âhkohtêwisow ana *lye*, âha.

F: pîhtaw ayis mîna mâna miyopayin kôn-- kônâpoy [*sic; sc*. kôniwâpoy] – tânisi?

A: ê-kîsohpîhkêyan.

R: kikiskêyihtên cî, nitayân anima kôniwâpoy.

F: ôh, mêkwâc.

R: âha, nîsw âniki *gallons* ê-kî-asiwatâyân. [*laughter*]

F: piko kîkway mân âwa ay-itahkamikisiw.

R: "êkay ka-misiwanâcihtâyêk ôma," nititâwak, "nipiy, niy ôma," nititâwak.

27

A: aya mîna nikî-âtotên kayâs, namôy wîhkâc ohci-pêhtâkwan, misiwêpayihcikanisa awâsisak ta-- (R: nama kîkway.) ta-miskahkik, ta-piscipo-- ta-pisc-ôtinahkik. ayisk kayâs aya, kî-osîhtâwak anima, (R: mhm.) maskihkiy; (F: âha.) kâ-osahkik. (R: âha.)

F: nanâtawâpôhkân.

A: âha, nanâtawâpôhkân, ê--; *there was <u>no such thing as overdose</u>*.

So there it sat. "Well!" I thought, "I guess it's cool by now." For you couldn't touch it, (A: yes, ya.) or you would burn. When it was cool (we used to use those big knives), I took it from the water and flipped it over; I had put some paper there, I flipped it over and it came out, you know. Look, then I kept cutting away at it, there was really a lot of soap. (A: yes.)

So, the next day, I was washing clothes again. Look, it was winter when we were living there; look, then I took a tub and went and filled it with snow, and I poured a little water in, (A: yes.) and put it on top of the stove. Until there was really a lot of water, and then I poured it into various containers, so I had just enough, (A: yes.) and so it went on all day. Oh my, that soap whitens so much; (A: yes, ya.) but in turn, if you rub it a lot, you are more or less going to burn, you know, (A: yes.) for it's too caustic.

A: That lye is caustic, yes.

F: Of course, it works well, that sno-- snow-water – how [do you say it]?

A: When you heat snow to make water.

R: Do you know, I have snow-water.

F: Oh, still?

R: Yes, I had put away two gallons. [*laughter*]

F: She does everything.

R: "Don't you ruin it for me," I said to them, "this water is mine," I said to them.

27 [*Medical Practices II*]

A: I have also said that it was unheard of long ago for children (R: not at all.) to find pills and to be poiso-- to take them accidentally. For long ago they made (R: mhm.) medicine; (F: yes.) they boiled it. (R: yes.)

F: Medicinal drinks.

A: Yes, medicinal drinks; there was no such thing as an overdose.

R: nimâmâ ê-kî-kâh-kiskinohamawit mâna maskihkiya. kêyâpic wiya nikiskêyihtên, iskwêw kâ-kawacit ka-nanâtawihak, *you know*. êkwa mîna ôh[i] ôcêpihkosa nanâtohk, êkoni mîna kêyâpit nikiskêyihtên k-ôtinamân, êkwa mîn ôhi kâ-wîhkimâkwahki mâna.

A: mâna *mint, ya*. (R: âha.)

R: ê-sisikopo--, piko ê-misîhtaman, êkonik êkwa ê-sisopâtacik awâsisak kâ-kisisocik, (A: âha.) mitoni ômatowihk ê-astamawacik, *you know*. (A: âha.) kisisopâtâwak, kisikwahtên miton ânihi. (F: âha.) êkwa kisisopâtâwak, êkwa misiwê, *you know*, (A: âha.) êkw êkota ê-kisitêk êkwa, kitastân. anim ê-otinikêmakahk (F: âha.) kâ-kisisocik, *you know*, (A: âha.) ê-otinikêmakahk anima. êkwa mîn âya, apisîs, ômatowahk *teaspoon*, apisîs ka-pahko--, nânitaw nîswâw, nistwâw wâwîs wiy ê-apisîsisicik ê-minahacik, *you know*, wayawîtisahikêmakan anima kâ-kisisocik, (A: âha.) wayawîtisahikêmakan. (A: âha.) tâpiskôc ôm âya, anima môcêyâpiskosihk mâna k-âsiwatâcik, kâ-kisisoyit awâsisa kâ-miyâcik (A: âha.) – kîkwâpoy êtikw ânima pikw êwako? (A: âha.) kîkway ê-ohc-ôsîhcikâkêcik?

F: môy kikiskêyihtênânaw, kîkwây mân ânima maskihkiy (R: ââhâ!) kâ-miyikawiyahk êkwa; ahpônâni ka-kakwêcihkêmoyahk.

R: ahpô niy âwiyak ka-kakwêcimit, kîspin cî niya, niya nimihko nikikiskên, môy nika-kaskihtân "âha," k-êtwêyân, nistwâw ayis ôm ê-miyikawiyân êkotowahk, (A: ôh.) êkwa mâna (A: ôh, âha.) ê-kî-isit kisêyiniw, "maci-manitowi-mihkw ânima, êwak ôhci kâ-mac-âyiwiyan." [*laughter*]

A: nikiskisin wiya nistês *Harry*, ê-cîkahosot ôta ôma -- (F: âha.) (R: âha.) ***not the big toe, the other one***; ê-cîkahosot, ê-pê-kîwêt, ê-kî-nitawi-nikohtêcik mâka mîna. êwakw ân[i] ânim êkwa, ê-otinikâtêk, â, ***birch-bark***, (R: mhm.) ê-pîhtopitiht ômis îsi, êkota anim ê-astâhk anima ***on the--, on that wound***. mêtoni tâpiskôc mâna ôma môniyâwi-***antiseptic***, mitoni ê-wâpiskâpâwêt ana ***the --, the skin***; (R: mhm.) ***birch-bark*** mâk ê-pîhtoniht, ê-pîhtopitiht.

R: êkwa mîna môy kâ-kî-aya--, môy kâ-kî-- –°

F: waskic cî ana? ahpô cî?

A: môya, môya.

R: ***between***.

R: My mom used to teach me about medicines. I still know how to treat a woman who has the chills [*sc.* in breastfeeding], you know. And I still know how to gather various roots, and also those aromatic ones.

A: Mint, ya. (R: yes.)

R: You have to grind-- to chew it and then you spread it on children who are feverish, (A: yes.) you apply it right here [*gesture*], you know. (A: yes.) You spread it on them, you really chew it. (F: yes.) And you spread it all over them, you know, (A: yes.) and you put a hot compress on there. It takes the fever away, (F: yes.) you know, (A: yes.) it takes it away. And you give them a little to drink, this kind of a teaspoon, about two or three times, especially when they are small, you know, and it drives the fever out, (A: yes.) it drives it out. (A: yes.) It's like the stuff which they put in little bottles, and give to children when they have a fever. (A: yes.) – I wonder what kind of liquid that is? (A: yes.) What do they make it from?

F: We don't know what that medicine is (R: yes!!) that we are given now. We never even ask!

R: Even if someone were to ask me if I have my own blood in me, I wouldn't be able to say "Yes," for I have been given that kind [*sc.* transfusions] three times, (A: oh.) and (A: oh, yes.) the old man would say to me, "It is devil's-blood, that's why you are wicked." [*laughter*]

A: I remember when my older brother Harry had injured himself with an axe, -- (F: yes.) (R: yes.) not the big toe, the other one; he had injured himself and he came home from having gone to chop wood as usual. And they took birch-bark, (R: mhm.) and peeled it like this [*gesture*] and put it there on the -- on that wound. It was very much like the White-Man's antiseptic, the -- the skin really turned white; (R: mhm.) the birch-bark was peeled, peeled off.

R: And then not able to -- it can't-- –°

F: The top? Or is it?

A: No. No.

R: Between.

F: *between.*

A: âha, *ya.*

R: ê-mâwaci-yôskisit. (F: âha.)

A: âha, pîhtopitâw ayisk ana, *you know*, (F: âha.) *then you peel it, you know*, (F: âha.) *and then you put it right on the wound there; it works as an antiseptic.*

R: mitoni ayisk âtiht iyôskisiw [*sic*] ana kâ-pîhtopitiht miton ôhci.

A: âha, *yes*, –°

F: êkos îsi.

A: °– *I've seen that; ya, ya, I saw that.*

R: êkosi mâka mîna nitay-itâwak ôta wiya kâ-osikôhoyân ôma niskât, "êy, kî-ayâwak ôma," nititâwak; êkwa nitati-miyw-âyân. (A: âha.)

A: êwakw ân[i] ânima kikî-kiskisitotâtin ôtê kâ-nitawi-nîpêpiyâhk awa *my cousin* (R: âha.) kâ-pôni-pimâtisit, *Irene, Tommy* aw ômâmâwa. niwa-wîtapimânân awa *Tony.* (R: mhm.) nitay-âcimostâkonân;

– ayis *she was diabetic* wîsta; (R: mhm.) –

"êkwa," itwêw, "ê-kî-pâpakwâtahokot ôm ômaskisin," itwêw, "êtikwê kî-omikîw ôtê, k-ât-âyât ôm âya, *gangrene*," itwêw.

R: êkotowahk êcik âna kâ-misiwanâcihikot cî?

A: môya, môya, môya; ôtê anima kâ-kî-manisoht anima, *she had that, uh, cancer.* (R: âha.)

A: "mâcik êkwa ninitawâpamâw aw," itwêw aya, *Mrs* â -- (– tânis ôma, awiyak anita *Sweet Grass* wîhêw anihi, *Doreen Pooyak* omâmâwa –°

F: ôh, *Mrs Pooyak*!

A: °– *Mrs Pooyak*, êwakw ân[a] êkwa. –)

A: "ay," îtwêw, "nêhiyawi-sîwîhtâkan." – "iyaw! kîkwây mâk êwako?" nititâw. "*salt-lake* anima *the* --" –°

R: âha, êwakw ân[i] ânima.

A: °– "pêyak ê-ispayik anima ê-kanâcihtât, anim ê-kisîpêkinahk, kî-miyw-âyâw," nititik. (R: âha.)

F: nipîhk êtikwê ê-asiw-- ê-astât --

A: môya, *you take that salt*, âha, *in water*, âha, *and then you bathe that, uh*, (R: âha. awa mân ôta.)

F: Between.

A: Yes, ya.

R: The softest. (F: yes.)

A: Yes, for that is peeled off, you know, (F: yes.) then you peel it, you know, (F: yes.) and then you put it right on the wound there; it works as an antiseptic.

R: For some of that which is peeled is really soft.

A: Yes, yes, –°

F: So it is.

A: °– I've seen that; ya, ya, I saw that.

R: And I also kept saying that to them, when I injured my leg here, "Hey, if only I had some birch-bark," I said to them; and I gradually got better. (A: yes.)

A: I remembered that about you when we went over there to my cousin's wake, (R: yes.) when Irene died, Tommy's mother. We were sitting with Tony. (R: mhm.) He was telling us stories,

– because she was diabetic too. (R: mhm.) –

"Then," he said, "she had gotten a blister from her shoe," he said, "I guess she had a sore there and she developed, ah, gangrene," he said.

R: Is that what killed her?

A: No, no, no; she was operated on over there, she had that, uh, cancer. (R: yes.)

A: "For instance, I went to see her," said, ah, Mrs, ah, -- (– what's her, someone over there at Sweet Grass gave her name, Doreen Pooyak's mother –°

F: Oh, Mrs Pooyak!

A: °– Mrs Pooyak, that's the one. –)

A: "Well," she said, "Cree-salt." – "Wow! What is that?" I said to her. "That is from a salt-lake --" –°

R: Yes, that's it.

A: °– "She cleaned it for one week, she washed it and she was well," she told me. (R: yes.)

F: I guess it's in the water –°

A: No, you take that salt, yes, in water, yes, and then you bathe that, uh, (R: yes, this one here.) --

A: "*one week*," kî-itwêw. (F: âsay.) *It was setting gangrene already*, ê-nâh-nitawâpamât ôhi *doctor* [*sic*]; *they couldn't -- that did it*; (R: âha.) "kî-miyw-âyâw," itwêw an[a] âya. misiw îtê --

R: 'okimâw' kâ-kî-itiht.

A: âha, nikiskisin wiy êwako, (R: âha.) ôta mâna kî-ayâw, (R: âha.) âha, nikiskisin wiy êwako.

R: êwakw âna mâna, ôta mâna, êwako ê-pêyako-- kâ-nîpiniyik mâna, êkota mân ê-kî-ohtinahk, ôm ôta (A: mhm.) sîwîhtâkani-sâkahikan.

F: âwin âwa?

R: êwakw ân[a] âna 'okimâw' kâ-kî-itiht, (F: ôh.) –°

A: okimâw, âha, *that's the* –°

R: °– nikisêyinîm ohcâwisâ -- (F: ôh.) (A: âha, *ya*.)

A: °– *Longnecks* êkonik; (F: âha.) kinwâpêkikwayawak êkonik, âha. *Michael and Gabe*, (F: ha.) êkonik; (R: âha.) (A: âha.) êkonik anik ôta kî-ayâwak.

R: êkos ôm ê-isiyîhkâsot ayis awa *Gabe*.

F: ââh!

A: êkoni, âha.

R: ê-okwêmêsit ê-nîsiyit omosôma. (F: hm!)

28

A: kîkwây ôma kâ-- –°

R: kîkwây kanihk ôma kâ-wî-âcimostâtân, kiwa-wanâmin.

A: kâ-wî-opêpîmihk mâka mâna kâ-kî-nât-- kâ-kî-pâsikâtêki anihi askiya cî?

R: askiya, âha, (F: ôh, *ya*.) nikî-âpacihtân anihi. an[a] âna omisimâs ana nitânis, nikî-âpacihtân anihi.

A: *moss*. (R: âha.) (F: mhm.)

F: misakâmê nimâmâ wiya êkotowahk kî-pê-âpacihtâw.

R: môy âyis anihi, pikw îta anihi kitôtinên êkoni. piko kana--, anihi mâna nawac piko kâ-mihkwâki tahkohc. mihkwâwâ mâna tahkoht nawac piko, êkon ânih ê-miywâsiki.

A: kikî-wâspitâw cî? kî-wâs-- kî-wâspitâw?

R: âha; wâspison nikî-âpacihtamôhâw.

A: "For one week," that one said. (F: already.) It was getting gangrenous already, she kept going to see that doctor; they couldn't -- that did it; (R: yes.) "She was well," that one said. All over --

R: He was called *okimâw*.

A: Yes, I remember that one, (R: yes.) he used to live here, (R: yes.) yes, I remember him.

R: He lived here, he used to live alon--, in the summer, he used to get it here (A: mhm.) from *sîwîhtâkani-sâkahikan*.

F: Who is this?

R: The one who was called *okimâw*, (F: oh.) –°

A: *okimâw*, yes, that's the –°

R: °– my old man's uncle -- (F: oh.) (A: yes, ya.)

A: °– one of the Longnecks, (F: yes.) one of the *kinwâpêkikwayawak*, yes. Michael and Gabe, (F: ha.) them; (R: yes.) (A: yes.) they lived here.

R: For that is how Gabe got his name.

F: Ah!

A: From that one, yes.

R: He is named after two of his grandfathers. (F: hm!)

28 [*Infant Care*]

A: What was it –°

R: I forgot what it was that I was going to tell you, you are distracting me.

A: When one was going to have a baby, did one used to dry moss?

R: Moss, yes, (F: oh, ya.) I used that. I used that for my oldest daughter.

A: Moss. (R: yes.) (F: mhm.)

F: My mom used that kind all along.

R: But you don't take them from just anywhere. Only the ones which are reddish on top. They are usually reddish on top, the good ones.

A: Did you lace her up [*sc.* in a moss-bag]? Was she-- was she laced up?

R: Yes; I used a moss-bag for her.

A: âha; *moss-bag, you know*.

A: ôta kâ-mâyipayiyâhk kisêyiniw, anihi kâ-kî-pêsiwât, anihi wî-- kâ-wîcêwât êkwa *Marvin*, (R: mhm.) nicâhkos an[a] ôkosisa, (R: mhm.) kâ-pîhtikwêyâhk, ka-- kî-pê-pêsiwêw pêpîsisa, mâk êkwa *zipper* êkwa. kayâs wiy âyisk ômis îsi kî-ayâ-- –°

F: âha.

R: âha.

A: âha; *but she had one*, –°

R: ayâw ana nôsisim êkotowahk.

A: °– *were you here for the funeral*; (F: âha.) *Auguste*? (F: âha.)

R: kikî-wâpahtên cî?

A: kikî-wâpamâw cî?

F: mwâc, môy nôh-wâpamâw.

A: *ya, she had that zipper, ya*; (F: ôh.) *uh, she was sitting in front of us, uh*, pêpîsis[a] ânihi, mâk êkwa, kayâs wiy âyisk ômis îsi kî-aya-- –°

R: *Donna* mân âyâw cî?

F: êkotowahk mân âna nitâniskotâpân k-âpacihtât, anihi kâh-kwêkwask, (A: âha, *ya*.) ômisi kâ-isi-tâpisahamohk.

A: *no, this one had a zipper, but it's the same* –°

F: pêyakwan, pêyakwan.

A: °– *ya, ya, she had that*.

R: *Donna* an[a] âyâw nôsisim (F: âha.) êkotowahk, opâpâwa ê-kî-miyikot, (A: ôh, âha.) ê-apisîsisit ana.

A: *I saw it*, âha!

R: âha, nicâniskocâpânis ana. (A: âha.)

A: êwako kî-kaskikwâsowak.

R: â?

A: kî-kaskikwâsowak *by hand*.

R: âha, âha. ê-mîkisistahahkik anihi, nanâtohk ê-isi-mîkisistahahkik.

F: kî-miywâsinwa, êkwa mân ômis îsi ocascocinisiwâwa.

R: âha! êkoni mîna.

A: *they made them*.

F: ê-kî-osîhtamâsocik --

A: Yes; a moss-bag, you know.

A: When we had a death here, when *kisêyiniw* [*sc.* Auguste Lafond] died, the one with whom Marvin now lives, (R: mhm.) my sister-in-law's son, (R: mhm.) she had brought one, when we came in, she had brought the baby, but it [*sc.* the bag] had a zipper. Long ago, of course, it used to be like this [*sc.* laced up] –°

F: Yes.

R: Yes.

A: Yes; but she had one, –°

R: My grandchild has one of those.

A: °– were you here for the funeral; (F: yes.) Auguste's? (F: yes.)

R: Did you see it?

A: Did you see her?

F: No, I didn't see her.

A: Ya, she had that zipper, ya; (F: oh.) uh, she was sitting in front of us, uh, with the baby, but long ago, of course, it used to be like this [*sc.* laced up] –°

R: Donna has one, hasn't she?

F: It's one of those that my great-grandchild uses, the criss-crossed kind, (A: yes, ya.) which you lace up like this [*gesture*].

A: No, this one had a zipper, but it's the same –°

F: The same, the same.

A: °– ya, ya, she had that.

R: My granddaughter, Donna, has one of those, (F: yes.) her father gave it to her, (A: oh, yes.) it's a small one.

A: I saw it, yes!

R: Yes, that little great-grandchild of mine. (A: yes.)

A: They used to sew those.

R: Eh?

A: They sewed them by hand.

R: Yes, yes. They beaded them, they put various beadwork patterns on them.

F: They were nice, and their little bonnets were the same way.

R: Yes! Those too.

A: They made them.

F: They made them for themselves --

A: êkwa ôtê ana k-âkwanâhkwêniht ômis îsi, êy, êkota mân êkwa, nanâtohk kîkway kî-isikwâtamwak –°

R: *lace*, nanâtohk, âha.

A: °– *lace, she had that* –°

F: kî-masinistahamwak êtikwê mîna.

A: °– âha; *she had that, that thing you put over*, âha; *Hobbema* ohci, *you know*. (F: âha.)

R: nanâtohk anima, askiya ôhi, êkoni anihi askiya itwâniwiw –°

A: âha, kî-pâsamwak.

R: °– êkwa mîn âyisk ôm âya, *I seen the day*, nikî-tako-- nikî-takonâw ana nîsta; kiwâpamâwak ôki mân âya, sâkahikanihk, kaskitêsiwak, ômayikohk iskosiwak – tânisi ê-isiyîhkâsocik êtikwê ka-nêhiyawêhk.

A: âha, *ya*, âha. *I know what you mean*.

F: niwanikiskisin nîst ê-isiyîhkâsocik mêkwâc.

A: *but in English* –°

R: êkoni anihi.

A: êkonik aniki --

F: *cattails*.

A: *cattails*.

R: êkoni! (F: âha.) (A: âha.)

F: *but what are th--, what are they in Cree?*

R: êkoni anih âskiya? (A: âha.) êkw êkoni ê-sikonamihk (A: âha!) êkw êkonik, ê-nipahi-kîsôsicik; –°

A: *I heard that*, âha, *ya*. (R: âha.)

R: °– ê-kîsôsicik mitoni.

F: ê-kî-wî-kakwêcimitân tânisi kani – pasânak? pasânak cî êkonik kâ-isiyîhkâsocik?

R: kêhcinâ.

F: êkosi pakahkam, pasânak.

29

F: êkwa, â, mosci wî-ay-âcimoyêko, êkwa mân ê-kî-ay-itahkamikahk, kî-isi-- nanâtohk m--, konit-âcimowinisa ahpô.

R: kayâs ayis ôm âyisiyiniwak ê-kî-miyo-wîcêhtocik.

A: And the part over there which covered the baby's face like this [*gesture*], hey, then, they also used to use various designs in sewing them –°

R: Various kinds of lacing, yes.

A: °– lace, she had that –°

F: I guess they embroidered then too.

A: °– yes; she had that, that thing you put over [the baby's face], yes; from Hobbema, you know. (F: yes.)

R: Various kinds of moss fillings, these moss fillings were said –°

A: Yes, they dried them.

R: °– for I have also seen the day, I, too, added it to the moss; you see these by the lake; they are black and this tall [*gesture*] – I wonder what they are called in Cree?

A: Yes, ya, yes. I know what you mean.

F: I also forget what they are called at the moment.

A: But in English –°

R: Those ones.

A: Those ones --

F: Cattails.

A: Cattails.

R: Those! (F: yes.) (A: yes.)

F: But what are th-- what are they in Cree?

R: Those moss fillings? (A: yes.) You crush them (A: yes!) and they are incredibly warm; –°

A: I heard that, yes, ya. (R; yes.)

R: °– they are incredibly warm.

F: I was going to ask you what, I forgot – *pasânak*? Are these called *pasânak*?

R: Certainly.

F: I think so, cattails.

29 [*Social Gatherings*]

F: Now, ah, if you will simply tell about how things used to be, perhaps some simple little stories.

R: Long ago, of course, people used to get along well.

F: êkos îs ê-itwêt awa wîsta.

R: ôh, kî-miyo-wîcêhtowak; pikw îtê, kîspin pêyak wâskahikan ka-pîhtikwêwak, kîspin nânitaw mitâtaht aw--, ayiwâk ka-ihtasicik, kâkikê waniyaw awiyak ê-kî-ayât anihi, aya --

F: ê-kitohcikêt.

A: âha, *Jeremy Lafond with his a--* –°

R: êkos ê-kî-mâci--, âha, ê-kî-mâci-nîmihitohk.

A: °– *accordion*, âha. (R: âha.) kî-pâpâ-nayâhtam mâna *in a flour-sack*, (R: âha.) kî-pâpâ-nayâhtam mân, âha.

R: êkos ê-kî-mâci-nîmihitohk. (F: [*laughs*])

A: âha, wâwîs cî kâ-wîkihtohk, (R: wâwîs cî!) katisk ê-kî-kîsi-mîcisohk, êkosi, (R: êkosi, âha.) êkos ê-mâci-wêpinikêhk.

R: tâspwâw ôtê aya, osâm mistah êwako ê-kî-âpatahk, miton ôti kwayask ê-kî-âpatahk êwako, mayaw kâ-mihcêtihk. kêtahtawê k-ât-îspayik êkwa, *five cents* êkwa –°

F: ê-âh-ahiht.

A: ê-âh-ahiht, âha;

A: ana kâ-miskwamât –°

R: °– êwako ka-nîmihitowinihkêt –°

A: êwakw ân[a] âna, âha; tâpwê.

R: °– kâ-kî-ispayik êkwa. (A: âha.)

kêtahtawê êkwa mîna k-ât-îspayik, nâpêwak ê-kî-nitomihcik k-âsiskîhkêcik, (F: âha.) ka-sisocêskiwakinikêcik, *you know*, (A: âha.) (F: âha.) êkosi êkwa mân ê-kî-nîmihihcik, êy, ê-kî-sôhkêsimohk mân ê-asahkêcik. [*laughter*]

A: *but your sister was one of the best* –°

R: ê-kî-nihtâ-asiskîhkêt, âha.

A: °– *her sister*.

F: *Josephine*.

A: wahwâ, kî-nihtâ-asiskîhkêw. wac--, ê-kî-sôhkâtisit, wâ, –°

F: kwayask mîna kotak?

A: °– kî-sôhkêwêpinam mân âsiskiy êwakw âna, *I remember that one, because she used to do ours over there, you know*. wahwâ, tâpwê mâna --

F: wîst âta wiy âwa mîna. (R: âha.) (A: âha.) nikî-pê-ay-atoskâkonân mâna, (R: âha.) kayâs aw ôhci –°

F: She, too, said that.

R: Oh, they used to get along well; if people went into a house anywhere at all, if about ten or more were there, someone always had one of these, ah --

F: Someone played a musical instrument.

A: Yes, Jeremy Lafond with his a-- –°

R: So they started --, yes, the dancing started.

A: °– accordion, yes. (R: yes.) He used to carry it around on his back in a flour-sack, (R: yes.) he used to carry it around on his back, yes.

R: So the dancing started. (F: [*laughs*])

A: Yes, especially at a wedding, (R: especially so!) the moment the meal was finished, (R: that's it, yes.) they started up.

R: As a matter of fact, there was too much of that over here, it really took off as soon as there was a crowd. At one time, it came about that five cents –°

F: was put in [a cake].

A: It was put in, yes;

A: the one who found it by biting on it –°

R: °– that one would hold the next dance –°

A: That's the one, yes; that's right.

R: °– when that happened. (A: yes.)

At one time, it also came about, that men were called in to do mudding [*sc.* of log-houses], (F: yes.) to do plaster work, you know, (A: yes.) (F: yes.) so then there was a dance for them, hey, there was serious dancing, and they put out food for everyone. [*laughter*]

A: But your sister was one of the best –°

R: She was good at mudding, yes.

A: °– her sister.

F: Josephine.

A: Oh my, she was good at mudding. She was strong, well, –°

F: Another good worker!

A: °– she used to pack the mud in hard, I remember her, because she used to do ours over there, you know. Oh my, she was truly --

F: And this one also. (R: yes.) (A: yes.) She used to come to work for us, (R: yes.) from the earliest –°

R: âha, ê-kî-ay-asiskîhkêyân mâna.
F: °– nanâtohk, ê-pê-kanâcihcikêt.
[*external break*]

30

A: êwako mâna nikiskisin, wâ, mistahi ê-kî-- mistahi kî-pimohtêw mâna wîst ôtênâhk ê-itâcihot êwakw âwa, *her sister* awa, mêkwât nêtê, *when I was raising my family*.
R: nikiskisin pêyakwâw nêtê ohci ê-pê-sipwêhtêyân;
– kîkwây kayâs kika-kîsowahohk; (A: âha.) –
nimis awa kâ-pê-naskwênak, anita mêkwâc ê-ayâcik akâmihk; (A: âha.) âsay êkwa nêtê ê-ayâyâhk niyanân, kâ-pê-naskwênak. ê-pê-pa-pimohtêyâhk ôta, nitati-nakînân kîkiwâhk, (A: âha.) *for some tea*; nawac piko niwî-kawacinân, tahkâyâw. (A: âha.) misakâmê --
– môy ka-tâpwêhtaman, ê-kî-misakâmê-mostohtêyâhk *Marcelin*, (A: *ya*.) –
konit ê-pâh-pasisêwaciyân nîsta;
– kîkwây kayâs (A: âha, *ya*.) kîsowahon, –
miton ê-pâh-pasisêwaciyân niskâta. môy mâk âyis, môy nôhc-îs-âyân ka-pômêyân, kîkway -- pahkaci kîkway kâ-kîsêyihtamân, piko ka-takosiniyân itê kâ-wî-itohtêyân, *you know*. (A: âha.) kiyâm ka-pê-nayôhcikêyân, piko ka-takosiniyân, ka-pê-takohtatamawakik awâsisak ka-mîcicik.
A: môy wiya ta-pômêyan wiya nôhtaw.
R: môya.

31

F: tân--, mâskôc êtikwê mân ê-kî-misi-kaskikwâsocik m-- kayâs mîna iskwêwak, nanâtohk ôhi, kîskasâkaya, pîhconêsa, (R: â, nanâtohk.) maskisin[a], âstisak. (A: âha.) (R: âha.)
A: nikiskisin wiya nôhkom mâna kî-maskisinihkêw.

R: Yes, I used to do mudding, too.

F: °– various things, she came to do the cleaning.

[*external break*]

30 [*Warm Clothes II*]

A: I remember her [*sc.* Josephine], oh, she used to come by a lot on her way to town, her sister, while I was raising my family over there.

R: I remember one time I was leaving from over there;

– there was nothing to dress warmly with long ago; (A: yes.) –

I picked up my older sister on the way, when they were living across there; (A: yes.) we were already living over there when I picked her up. We were walking over here and we stopped at your house (A: yes.) for some tea; we were getting cold, it was cold out. (A: yes.) All the way, --

– you wouldn't believe that we had walked all the way to Marcelin, (A: ya.) –

I, too, had some frostbite;

– there was no winter clothing long ago, (A: yes, ya.) –

I had frostbite on my legs. But of course I wasn't the type to get discouraged -- when I make up my mind about something, I have to get wherever I am going, you know. (A: yes.) Even if I'm carrying a load on my back, I have to get there with it in order for the children to eat.

A: You sure don't give up halfway.

R: No.

31 [*Sewing*]

F: Ho-- the women probably used to sew a lot in the old days, all kinds of skirts, blouses, (R: ah, all kinds.) moccasins, mitts. (A: yes.) (R: yes.)

A: I remember that my grandmother used to make moccasins.

F: pahkêkinwa.

A: pahkêkinwa, âha; 'asêsinwa' kî-isiyîhkâtam mân ânihi –°

F: *vamps*?

A: °– *vamps* aniki, âha, 'asêsinwa' kî-itwêwak. êkoni anihi mâna *porcupine quills*, ômis îsi kî-tihtipinam kî--,

– matwân cî mâna *dye*, tânis êtikwê (F: âha.) wiy êkoni ê-kî-is-ôsîhtât. –

nanâtohk mâna *colours* anihi, êkoni mâna ôta ômis îsi, ôta kî-- kî-pâh-pîhkinam anihi nôhkom; *porcupine quills*, ôh ômis îs ôta. êkot[a] êk ôta mân êkwa kî-mîkisistahikêw, ôsam piko mâna wâpakwanîsa kî-w-- kî-- kî-osîhtâw; wâpakwanîsa nikî-wâh-wâpamâw, mwêhci tâpiskôc awa mâna k-êsi--, aya; mîkis---kaskikwâsot aw âya, *Mrs*, â, aya, *Herb* ôhkom[a] âna, *Mrs*, â, tânisi kani, *Mrs Daniels*, ana soscin.

F: ôh, âha.

R: kêyâpic ê-kaskikwâsot.

A: âha, *oh yes*, *ya*.

F: kêyâpic! (A: âha.)

A: *flowers*, – °

R: môy wîhkâc êkwa nititohtân, âha.

A: °– *flowers, leaves, that--, those were the designs that I saw my granny make*. (F: âha.) asêsinwa, kî-maskisinihkêw; êkwa mâna kî-âpacihtâw anima, '*sinew*' mâna kî-isiyîhkâtêwak, (F: âha.) namôya *thread*; *sinew*, mâna tahki kî-mâmâkwamêw --

F: ômatowihk --

A: *I don't know--*, âha.

F: *on the back*, anima mâna kâ--, (A: âha.) (R: âha.)

A: êkoni anihi.

R: apisimôsosak; kimanipitên anihi êkwa ê-pâsaman.

A: âha, âha, êwakw ânihi, âha. êkwa mân êwako k-âti-kaskikwâtahk mâna, nikî-wâpamâw otônihk mâna ê-kî-ati-mâmâkwahtahk. *I don't know* -- âha, *ya*.

F: ê-kî-sâ-sôpahtahk, nôhkom mîna mâna êkosi.

A: *I-- I--, I remember, ya*, kî-maskisinihkêw mâna nôhkom, *I remember that. of course, when I got bigger, uh, there was, uh, flour-bags*, mistahi kî-miywâsinwa kayâs, *flour--*, *flour--*, kî-mâ-- (F: nanâtohk.) kî-mâwaci-sôhkanw[a] ânihi *sugar-bags*.

F: From hides.

A: From hides, yes; she used to call them *asêsinwa* –°

F: Vamps?

A: °– the vamps, yes, they used to call them *asêsinwa.* She used to roll up porcupine quills like this [*gesture*] --

– I wonder how (F: yes.) she might have made the dyes. They were in different colours, like these here, and my grandmother used to shape them; porcupine quills, like these here. And then she would also put beadwork here [*gesture*]; she usually made little flowers; I would see those little flowers, exactly like this one does-- ah; she sews, ah, Mrs, ah, well, Herb's grandmother, Mrs, what's her name, Mrs Daniels, *soscin.*

F: Oh, yes.

R: She still sews.

A: Yes, oh yes, ya.

F: Still! (A: yes.)

A: Flowers, –°

R: I never go there now, yes.

A: °– flowers, leaves, that -- those were the designs that I saw my granny make. (F: yes.) With these vamps she made moccasins; and she used to use what they used to call sinew, (F: yes.) not thread; she always used to chew sinew --

F: On here [*sc.* along the backbone] --

R: I don't know--, yes.

F: That was on the back. (A: yes.) (R: yes.)

A: Those were the ones.

R: The deer; you pull that out and dry it.

A: Yes, yes, those are the ones, yes. And when she was sewing with it, I would see it in her mouth as she was chewing it. I don't know -- yes, ya.

F: She would put it in her mouth [*sc.* to moisten it], my grandmother also did it that way.

A: I remember, ya, my grandmother used to make moccasins. I remember that. Of course when I got bigger, uh, there were, uh, flour-bags, they were very good long ago, flour-- (F: all kinds.) those sugar-bags were the strongest.

F: âha.

R: âha, êkon ânihi, âha.

A: nitay-âcimon *the other day, my m--*, kâ-kî-omâmâyân mâna kî-osîhtamawêw anihi, '*knickers*' mâna kî-isiyîhkâtêwak, kî-wâpiskisiwak *sugar-bags*, ôki kâ-mêtawêcik, ôki kâ-kî-pâkâhtowêcik, êkoni anihi mâna kî--, êkoni anihi mâna kî-- –°

F: kî-postiskawêwak.

A: âha, *ya, that's what they --*

F: *uniform* êwako.

A: °– *uniform* êwako, âha.

A: êkw ânihi *they had a -- a --, there's a soccer picture* mâna, *they have, uh, blue, uh, tops*.

R: nikiskisin mâna nîsta, mihcêtwâw nikî-atotikawin nîst êkotowahk aniki ka-nânapacihakik, *you know*, (A: âha.) *elastics* ahpô piko.

A: kî-mêtawêyiwa ayisk awa okisêyinîma.

R: âha, êkwa awa ninahâhkisim aw ômikiyiniw, êwako mîna nikî-osîhtamawâw, pêyakwâw êkotowahk anihi ê-pêtamawit, âha.

A: *there's pictures*, âha.

R: âha.

32

A: êkoni anihi mîna kîspin nôhtê--, masinipayiwina kîspin nôhtê-pêtâyani, *we'll have a place* êkota, masi--, kayâs-masinipayiwina (R: mhm.) ta-wâpahcikâtêki; (R: mhm.) êkoni anihi mîna nika-nitotênân.

R: aya, mêkwâc ôma nisipwêtisahên aya, *thirty dollars* ka-tipahamân, ôta *in Shellbrook* ê-astêki, (A: ôh.) *the old-time-pictures*, (A: âha.) *you know*; (F: âha.) êkoni anihi mêkwâc ôma ka-wayawîhtatâyân. (A: âha.)

F: takahki êsa.

A: nîsta nôhkom nitayâwâw, êkwa mîn âna ta-- kâ--, nôhkom ana *Julia*; (R: âha.) êkoni ôhi kâ-- *Isabelle* aw ân[a] ôta okosisiyiwa ayisk, kâ-kî-wîkimât aw *Is-- Isabelle Paddy* awa.

F: awîniwa?

A: *oh, my grandmother Sarah's sister's boy*; (R: âha.) (F: ôh.) êkoni awa *Isabelle* ê-kî-wîkimât, *that's where the relation --*, (F: ôh.) kâ-kî-omâmâyân anih ôcâhkosa. (F: âha.) *in Cree* ayisk (F: âha.)

F: Yes.

R: Yes, those ones, yes.

A: I was telling a story the other day, my m--, my late mom used to make those, they used to call them knickers, they were white sugar-bags, for those who played, for those who played soccer, their -- their –°

F: They used to wear them.

A: Yes, ya, that's what they –°

F: That was their uniform.

A: °– that was their uniform, yes.

A: And they had a--, there's a soccer picture, and they have, uh, blue, uh, tops.

R: I, too, remember being asked many times to mend that kind for them, you know, (A: yes.) even just the elastics.

A: Her old man, of course, used to play.

R: Yes, and my son-in-law, *omikiyiniw,* I used to make them for him, once he brought me that kind, yes.

A: There's pictures, yes.

R: Yes.

32 [*Plans for a Reunion III: Photographs; Priests*]

A: If you want to bring pictures, we'll have a place there, for old-time pictures, (R: mhm.) to be seen; (R: mhm.) we'll ask for those too.

R: Ah, I have sent them away already, and I am to pay thirty dollars for them, they are here in Shellbrook, (A: oh.) the old-time pictures, (A: yes.) you know; (F: yes.) I'm about to get them back [*sc.* from the photographer]. (A: yes.)

F: That's good, then.

A: I, too, have one of my grandmother, of her also -- my grandmother Julia; (R: yes.) she's the one whose son, of course, Isabelle married, Isabelle Paddy.

F: Whom?

A: Oh, my grandmother Sarah's sister's boy; (R: yes.) (F: oh.) that's the one Isabelle married, that's where the relation --, (F: oh.) that's my late mother's sister-in-law. (F: yes.) For in Cree, (F: yes.) it's a *it's a relation to, you know*; ê-kî-ocâhkosit anihi *Isabelle*, *that's where Isabelle comes in; ya, she was married to, uh*, --

R: nitayân anihi âtiht êkotowahk masinipayiwina, *you know*. kâ-kî-omisiyân ê-kî-miyit âniy, mihcêt (A: âw, âha.) ê-kî-miyit; *I've got three albums*, êkot[a] ê-asiwatêki *my pictures*; (A: âha.) ê-mâwacihtâyân, *collection, you know, old pictures* --

A: hâriy ôma mîna kâ-pê-- nikî-pê-pîkiskwêhik, tânis ê-isi-kiskisiyân ôma ayamihêwikamik ôma, (R: âha.) ôm ôta, ôma wâsakâm ôm ôta. "mistahi kî-miywâsin mêkwâc ôta, *Father Beaudry* k-âyât," (R: âha.) nikî-itâcimon. (R: kî-miywâsin.) ayisk ôta kî-wîkiw ana ayamihêwiyiniw, kî-nêhiyawêw, (R: âha.) kî-nisitohtawêw ayisiyiniwa, mitoni.

R: êwakw ân[a] âna ê-kî-kiskinohamâkoyâhk kâ-kî-saskamoyâhk niyanân. (A: âha, *ya*.)

A: *that's all -- that's what makes the difference*. (F: mhm.) ôt[a] ân[a] âyamihêwiyiniw, sôskwâc ôt[a] ê-kî-ayât ana, ê-kî-pa-pimâcihot wîsta, (R: êkosi nititâwak.) nanâtohk kîkway ê-kî-ohpikihtâcik. (R: âha.) êkwa mîna ê-kî-ayâwâcik aya, *chickens* êkos îsi --

R: mostoswa, (A: âha.) âha, kî-ayâwak; misatimwa, ê-kî-takahkahpicikêt mâna, *a black team* aniki, (A: âha.) ê-kî-kaskitêsicik misatimwak; *oh, gee*, ê-kî-takahkipahtâcik mâna. (A: âha.)

F: êwakw ân[a] âna
– wîsta mâna kâ-kî-oyôh---oyôhkomiyân, 'osâwisip' kî-itâw, (R: âha.) *Shem* awa nimosôm okâwiya, (R: âha.) –
êkoni, êkon ânihi mân ê-kî-pimi-kiyokâkot; êkos êtikwê ê-kî-- ê-kî-isi-sîkahâhtâht wîsta ê-awâsisîwit, (R: âha.) (A: âha.) êy, kêyâpic mâna kâkikê kî-pimi-kiyokêw ana, (R: âha.) ê-ka-kiskisiyân, (A: âha.) êwakw âna *Father Beaudry*. (R: mhm.)

R: ê-kî-miyohtwât oti, êkwa mîn âya –°

A: awa ê-kî-- awa ê-kî-nisitohtâht, âha.

R: °– *Father Paradis*.

A: êwakw âna mîna -- *ya*, êwakw ân[a] âna mîna, â --

R: êkw âna kotak ana --

F: *Menard?*

R: êwako wiy âstamispî [...; *?record*] --

F: êwako wiya nikiskisin.

relation, you know; Isabelle was her sister-in-law, that's where Isabelle comes in; ya, she was married to, uh, --

R: I have some of that kind of pictures, you know. My late older sister, âniy, gave them to me, she gave me a lot (A: oh, yes.) of them; I've got three albums, with my pictures in them; (A: yes.) I am collecting them, a collection, you know, old pictures --

A: *hâriy* also came to get me to talk about what I remembered of the church, (R: yes.) here, and all around here. "It was really good while Father Beaudry was here," (R: yes.) I declared. (R: it was good.) For that priest had his house here, and he spoke Cree, (R: yes.) <u>he really understood the people</u>.

R: <u>He's the one that</u> taught us when we took Communion. (A: yes, ya.)

A: That's all -- that's what makes the difference. (F: mhm.) That priest simply lived here, and he made his living, too, (R: that's what I said to them.) they grew various things. (R: yes.) And he also had, ah, chickens, just as --

R: And cows, (A: yes.) yes, they had cows; and horses, he used to have a good team, it was a black team, (A: yes.) the horses were black; oh gee, they used to run well. (A: yes.)

F: That's the one;

– my late great-grandmother, her name was *osâwisip,* (R: yes.) my grandfather Shem's mother, (R: yes.) –

he used to come by to visit her; so she must have been baptized [*sc.* a Roman Catholic] as a child, (R: yes.) (A: yes.) hey, he still came by to visit her all the time, (R: yes.) as I recall, (A: yes.) that Father Beaudry. (R: mhm.)

R: He was kind, <u>and also</u> –°

A: <u>He was --</u> he was understood, yes.

R: °– Father Paradis.

A: That one too -- ya, that one also, ah --

R: And that other one --

F: Menard?

R: That one <u>more recently</u> --

F: <u>I remember that one</u>.

A: êwakw ân[a] âna wiya, âha!

F: môy kayâs.

R: mâka mâna wiya kaskitêw-- kî-kaskitêsiyiwa mâna ômatowahk *truck* ê-kî-ayâwât.

– tânisi kani kâ-kî-isiyîhkâsot?

A: ôh, aya, *Father, uh, I know the -- Fortier*!

R: *Fortier*, (F: ôh, *ya*.) îh, kâ-pîhtikwêyân mân ê-kî-wêmistikosîmototawit mâna, mitoni mân ê-kî-kakwâtakâhpit, "awasitê," ê-kî-itak mâna, "kitâpihci-wanwêhkawin."

A: ayisk êkota mâna *mail* kî-pê-nâcikâtêw, *post office* anim êkot[a] ê-kî-astêk. mâna ê--, kayâs nîpâ-- ôtê mâna –°

F: *Aldina*.

A: °– âha, kayas môy, môy wîhkât nôh-wiyahpicikânân, têpiyâhk mân ê-kî-pê-mostohtêyâhk ê-pê-nâtamâhk (R: âha.) *mail*. (R: êkwa wiy êwako --) kî-nâh-nâtitisahikâniwan ayisk kayâs, *Eaton's catalogue* êkos îsi.

R: ôtênâhk mîn ôhci mân âyis *mail* ê-kî-natâmihk; *Edmond* mâna, kikiskisin kâ-kî-wa-wiyahpicikêt mâna kâ-kî-pêtâwatât *mail*. (A: *ya*.)

F: nikêhcinâhon nawac kî-cacâstapipayin êkospî aya *mail*. iyikohk wiy êkw ânohc, iyikohk nipahi-kâh-kinwês.

R: ôta 'pimicaskêkâs' ayis ôm ê-isiyîhkâtêk (F: âha.) ê-nêhiyawêhk, (A: âha.) ôta mân îsko ê-kî-pêtâhk masinahikana nanâtohk, *you know*, (F: âha.) êkot[a] ôhci wiy êkwa mâna ê-kî-mosci-nâtahk, ôt[a] ê-pêtât (A: âha.) kayâs. (A: *ya*.)

A: nawac êkos îsi, pakahkam, nawac mihcêt kî-pê-nitaw-âyamihâwak, mêkwâc ôt[a] âyamihêwiyiniw ôt[a] ê-ayât. (R: âha.) anohc êkw âw âyamihêwiyiniw, katisk ê-pê-nitaw-âyamihât, êkosi kâ-kîs-âyamihât, êkosi nam âwiyak, –°

R: nikoskwêyihtên môy ê-wî-sîkahâhtawât awâsisa.

A: °– môya, môy ê-wî-wâp--, môy êkos ê-wâpamiht.

F: môy ê-wî-sîkahâhtawât êkwa.

R: môy ê-wî-sîkahâhtawât awâsisa, ôhi mastaw ôki kâ-ihtakocik ôki awâsisak.

A: êkos îtwêwak, âha.

A: Yes, that one too!

F: Not long ago.

R: And it was a black truck, he had that kind of a truck.

– What was his name, I forget?

A: Oh, ah, Father, uh, I know the -- Fortier!

R: Fortier, (F: oh, ya.) look, he used to speak French to me when I would come in and he really used to laugh, "Go on," I used to say to him, "you have totally confused me by what you say."

A: The mail used to be picked up at the post office which was there. Then long ago we-- over here then –°

F: Aldina.

A: °– yes, long ago, we never used to harness up, we just used to come on foot to get (R: yes.) the mail. (R: and for that--) For in the old days one used to order things from Eaton's catalogue and such like.

R: And the mail was usually fetched from town; Edmond, you remember that Edmond used to harness up to bring the mail. (A: ya.)

F: I'm certain the mail was faster in those days. For it takes a very long time today.

R: All kinds of letters used to be brought from *pimicaskêkâs,* as it is called (F: yes.) in Cree, (A: yes.) you know, (F: yes.) he used to fetch them from there and bring them here (A: yes.) long ago. (A: ya.)

A: I think many more used to come to church while the priest lived here. (R: yes.) Today the priest just comes to say mass and when he is finished with the service, then there is no-one there –°

R: I was surprised he wasn't going to baptize the children.

A: °– no, he's just not to be seen.

F: He wasn't going to baptize them now.

R: He wasn't going to baptize the children, the children who were born recently.

A: So they say, yes.

F: ha!
R: tânêhk êtikwê?

F: wiyawâw êtikwê otôcikaniwâw aniki pêpîsisak, êkây kwayask kâ-- ê-itôtamiyit nîkihikomâwa!

R: môy mâka k-âtâmêyimihcik ayis pêpîsisak, anik âniki!

F: namôya, mâk êkosi ê-isinâkwahk, (R: âha.) êkos ê-isinâkwahk.

R: "mâka mîna niwî-nitawâpamâw," nititâwak ôk, "âyamihêwiyiniw; kêtahtawê kinwêsîs ayâyâni *in town*, niwî-nitawâpamâw ayamihêwiyiniw," nititâwak.

A: mâka mîna ôma –°

R: niwî-âcimostawâw piko kîkway, *you know*, ta-kî-itatoskêcik ayamihêwiyiniwak, môya *drugs* –°

A: ta-kiskisomiht, âha, *ya*.

R: °– kit-âpacihtâcik *or something like that*.

A: môya nânitaw ta-kiskisomiht wiy êwakw ân[i] ânima.

R: "môy ôm âya, kiyawâw ê-tipêyimisoyêk," niwî-itâw, *you know*; "awiyak ôm ê-tipêyimikoyêk kîstawâw," nikî-itâw [*sic*], "itwêci, êkosi piko ka-tôtamêk," niwî-itâw, *you know, I'm gonna*!

33

A: mâka mîna nikî-ka-kiskisin, pêyakwâw ê-ay-apiyân, môy kayâs ôta, (R: mhm.) ôm âya, ê-pê-isi-wâpamakik ôk ôtê, otâhk ôk ôtê, mâcika nikî-wâpamâw awa nôhkom omâmâwa; (R: mhm.) (F: ôh.) kî-kêhtê-ayiwiw ayisk ana miton âna. (R: mhm.) êwakw ân[a] ân[a], êwakw âwa nôhkom, nimâmâ, êkota niya, êkot[a] âwa kâ-kî-otânisiyân, êkot[a] âwa nôsisim, "wâcistakâc," konit ê-ay-itwêyân, "*six generations*!" (R: âha.) – wahwâ!

R: 'kisôpayîs' kâ-kî-itiht.

A: môya; â, *Sarah* –°

R: ôh, *Sarah* omâmâwa.

A: °– omâmâwa, âha, *ya*.

R: nikî-wâpamâw, *Sarah*, nikî-wâpamâw.

A: *she died abaut nineteen-thirty*, (R: âha, nikî-wâpamâw.) kî-nipahi-kêhcê-ayiwiw ana, â, --

R: yâyâhk an[i] êcikwê! êkwa mâna aya, –°

F: Ha!

R: I wonder why?

F: I guess it's those babies' fault that their parents don't live properly!

R: But the babies shouldn't be blamed, of course, not them!

F: No, but it looks that way, (R: yes.) it looks that way.

R: "I'm going to go and see the priest," I told these ones, "the next time I am in town for a while, I'm going to go and see the priest," I told them.

A: But as usual it's –°

R: I'm going to tell him everything, you know, what the priests should be doing, –°

A: To remind him, yes, ya.

R: °– [to help others] not to use drugs or something like that.

A: It's alright to remind him about that.

R: "You guys are not entirely in charge of yourselves," I will say to him, you know, "for you, too, there is One above you," I will tell him, "and what He says, that you have to do," I'm going to tell him, you know, I'm gonna!

33 [*Changing Times*]

A: One time, when I was sitting here not long ago, (R: mhm.) I was remembering how I used to see people over here in the past; for instance, I used to see my grandmother's mother; (R: mhm.) (F: oh.) of course, she was really old. (R: mhm.) There was that one, and my grandmother, and my mom, and then me, and then my late daughter and then my granddaughter. "My goodness!" I said, "six generations" (R: yes.) – Oh my!

R: She was called *kisôpayîs*.

A: No; ah, Sarah's –°

R: Oh, Sarah's mom.

A: °– her mom, yes, ya.

R: I had seen Sarah, I had seen her.

A: She died about 1930, (R: yes, I saw her.) she was extremely old, ah, --

R: She must have been, to be sure! And then –°

A: cêhcapiwinis mâna kî-ayâw anima;

– nêtê êtikwê anim âstêw. –

ê-kî-mosc-ôsîhtâhk anima cêhcapiwinis, êkota mâna kî-ay-apiw an[a] âya, *my great-great-grandmother*, âha.

F: wahwâ!

A: *ya, ya*!

R: pêyakwâw ôta aya –°

A: kî-kêhtê-ayiwiw mitoni –°

R: °– *St Lawrence* ôma mâna kâ-mâmâw-âyamihâhk.

A: °– mâk âyisk kayâs môy ôhci-kiskêyihtamwak kâ--, *what -- what was age*! (F: mhm.)

ahpô êwakw âna *Julia* ana k-âcimak ana, (R: âha.) ê-kî-tipiskahk, "pêh-pêyak ômis îsi ê-atihtêki takwahiminâna," ê-kî-itwêt mâna;

– hâw, *what month is that, you know*?

R: *August*.

A: "pêh-pêyak ômis îsi --"

F: *August*. (R: âha.) (A: *ya*.)

A: "pêh-pêyak ômis îsi ê-atihtêki takwahiminâna," ê-kî-itwêt mâna.

F: mâk âyis êk ôma, mitoni aya wîpac, êkwa mâna (A: âha.) takwahiminâna ê-at-âtihtêki; (R: piko kîkway!) piko kîkway.

A: *you see, they had a way of, you know*, –°

F: *time*, (A: âha.) *calendar*.

A: *oh yes, ya*.

R: *the last five years*, mitoni piko kîkway --, mitoni ê-âpocikwânîmakahk.

A: ê-âpoci-- ê-âpocikwânipayik kahkiyaw kîkway, (R: âha, tâpwê.) âha.

R: ê-na-nâh-nâkatohkêyân mâna. kayâs ê-kî-- aya mîna ê-kiskêyihtamihk mâtayak kâ-wî-pipohk.

A: âha, nanâtohk kîkway pîhtaw mitoni (R: piko kîkway, âha.) kî-na-nâkatohkêwak nanâtohk kîkway.

R: kwayâci kîkway ê-kî-ta-tôtamâsohk.

A: ê-kî-nipahi-nihtâ-mitihtahkik kîkway. (R: âha.) anohc êkwa ayisiyiniw kâ-pimipayit ôma sêhkêpayîsa, môy wîhkât nâkatohkêw kîkway ta-mitihtahk. (R: êkosi nititâwak.) *when we had dirt roads*, (F: âha.) *they knew exactly the track of every animal*.

A: She had a little chair;
– I guess it is over there. –
That little chair was made by hand, and she used to sit in it, ah, my great-great-grandmother, yes.
F: Oh my!
A: Ya, ya!
R: At one time here –°
A: She was very old –°
R: °– at the time of the St Lawrence pilgrimage.
A: °– but long ago, of course, they didn't know -- what was age! (F:mhm.)
Even that Julia that I have talked about, (R: yes.) she had a birthday, and she used to say, "Just like this, as one by one the chokecherries are ripening;"
– aw, what month is that, you know?
R: <u>August</u>.
A: "Just like this, as <u>one by one</u>" --
F: August. (R: yes.) (A: ya.)
A: "Just like this, as one by one the chokecherries are ripening," she used to say.
F: But it's really early now (A: yes.) that the chokecherries start to ripen; (R: everything!) everything.
A: You see, they had a way of, you know, –°
F: Time, (A: yes.) calendars.
A: Oh yes, ya.
R: The last five years, everything has really <u>been turned upside down</u>.
A: Everything is <u>turning upside down</u>, (R: yes, truly.) yes.
R: I always notice it. Long ago, ah, it was known beforehand when winter was going to start.
A: Yes, they really noticed all kinds of things. (R: everything, yes.)
R: You got things <u>ready for yourself</u>.
A: They <u>were very good at tracking</u> things. (R: yes.) Today people drive along in cars and never notice any tracks. (R: so I say to them.) When we had dirt roads, (F: yes.) they knew exactly the track of every animal.

R: ahpô kâ-nitawastimwêhk ahpô kâ-nitonâhcik misatimwak, ê-kî-mitihtihcik iskw ît[ê] ê-nîpawicik, ê-miskâhcik; (A: âha, *ya*.) ê-kî-mitihtihcik.

F: êkwa ê-kî-wî-nipahi-nahâpicik (A: âha.) (R: âha.) êkwa –°

A: *sound*.

F: °– ê-kî-nipahi-kiskisicik (A: âha.) piko kîkway. (R: âha.)

A: *they had their own computer*, (F: âha.) *and I'll take an instance like* --, *my mother*, môy wîhkâc ohci-kiskinohamawâw, *she never went to school, but she kept everything here*; (R: mhm.) (F: mhm!) *you know, everything was here*. (R: tâpwê.) pêyakwâw ta-wîhtamawat tânisi t-êsi-kaskâpiskahahk kîkway, êkosi kî-kiskêyihtam, kî-kiskisiw.

R: êkos ânim ê-is-âyâyân mwêhci nîsta.

A: *but today now with books and everything else, these kids are just* --

R: ê-kiskinawâpiyân awiyak, kotak awiyak ê-tôtahk, ê-nâ-- kayâhtê êkos ê-kî-pê-is-âyâyân, (A: *ya*.) ê-nâh-nâkatohkêyân awiyak tânis ê-tôtahk, *you know*.

F: êkosi ê-kiskêyihtaman.

A: *they kept it*, *ya*, (R: âha.) *they knew it, they* –°

F: êkos ânima, kiyânaw ê-kî-isi-kiskinahamâhcik ayisiyiniwak.

A: *that was education* (F: âha.) *at the beginning; ya, as we* –°

F: êwako. (A: *ya*, âha.)

F: *their memory was developed*, êkwa ê-kî-nipahi-nahihtahkik *and they used their eyes*; (A: *that's right*.) *all the senses*.

R: ahpô ôk êkw âya, ôki mêscacâkanisak, kâ-mêkwâ-mâyi-kîsikâk, kîspin kâ-oyoyocik, êkos ê-wî-kîsapwêk, môy êkw êkonik mîna kikî-wîhâwak, wah -- tânisi ê-wî-ispayik; (A: âha, *ya*.) pîtos ispayiw. (A: *ya*.) tâpiskôc ôtê ê-pê-pimipay-- –°

A: ê-wanihocik wîstawâw.

R: °– ê-pê-pimipayiyâhk, *Hafford* ôtâ, iskwêyâc kâ-nitawi-mêtawêyâhk êkota, ê-pê-pimipayiyâhk, mêton ê-misi-nîmihitocik, mâk ê-yôtik, (A: âha.) ê-tahkâyâk. (A: âha.) "â, ê-wî-kîsapwêk," tânisi mîna kâ-misi-mispok. [*laughter*] môy êkwa ka-kî-wîhtên, (A: âha, *ya*.) êkos âyisk kî-tôtamwak mâna, *you know* --

F: *weather-forecasting is gone down the* –°

R: Even in going after horses, even when looking for horses, their tracks were followed right up to where they stood and where they were found; (A: yes, ya.) they were tracked.

F: And they had such sharp eyes (A: yes.) (R: yes.) and –°

A: Sound.

F: °– they had a sharp memory for (A: yes.) everything. (R: yes.)

A: They had their own computer, (F: yes.) and I'll take an instance like --, my mother was never in school, she never went to school, but she kept everything here [*gesture*]; (R: mhm.) (F: mhm!) you know, everything was here [*gesture indicating head*]. (R: truly.) Once you told her how to can something [*sc.* vegetables], then she knew it and she remembered.

R: That's exactly how I am, me too.

A: But now today with books and everything else, these kids are just --

R: I observe someone, another person, doing something and learn from it, that's how I've always been, (A: ya.) I notice how someone does it, you know.

F: That's how you learn it.

A: They kept it, ya, (R: yes.) they knew it, they –°

F: As for us, that's how the people were taught.

A: That was education (F: yes.) at the beginning; ya, as we –°

F: That's it. (A: ya, yes.)

F: Their memory was developed, and their hearing was sharp and they used their eyes; (A: that's right.) all the senses.

R: Even the coyotes, if they howled in the midst of a storm, then it was going to be warm; now you can't even rely on them, as to how it's going to turn out, (A: yes, ya.) it turns out differently. (A: ya.) Like when we drove over here –°

A: They, too, are lost.

R: – when we drove here from Hafford, the last time we went to play there, as we were driving along, they [*sc.* the northern lights] were really dancing, but it was windy (A: yes.) and cold. (A: yes.) "Ah, it's going to be warm," and how it snowed! [*laughter*] You can't rely on it now, (A: yes, ya.) but that's how they used to do it, you know --

F: Weather-forecasting has gone down the –°

A: *ya, ya, it's changed, you know, we're lost in the* –°

R: tânisi mîna kâ-misi-mispok, tâpwê.

F: *even the--, even the coyotes are lost.* [*laughter*] (R: âha.)

A: wîstawâw êkwa wanihowak, âha, *ya*.

pihpihcêw ê-kitot, (R: âha, êwako mîna.) pihpihcêw, "ê-wî-kimiwahk," (R: âha.) kî-itwêw mâna nôhkom, âha; *that's the robin*, (F: âha.) pihpihcêw, âha.

R: ê-kî-mâmaskâtak mâna kisêyiniw, kâ-mêkwâ-tatahkamikisit ôma *outside* kâ-nîpihk; ê-kî-pê-pîhtikwêt mâna, "nôtokwêw, piko ka-nipâsiyân, mâka mîna wî-kimiwan," (A: âha.) ê-kî-itwêt mâna; *sure enough*, ê-kî-sîkipêstâyik *a big shower*, (A: âha, *ya*.) mitoni mân ê-kî-koskwêyimak. (A: âha.) ê-- kâ-nôhtêhkwasîpayit kâ-mêkwâ-ay-apit, "piko ka-nipâyân."

A: *they lived so close to nature, they were so observant, it was passed on to generations, but now today* –°

R: anohc êkwa môy tâpwêhtamwak –°

A: °– *it's* –°

R: °– misawâc; kiyâm ka-wîtapimikwak osk-âyak, k-ây-âcimon kayâs, aspin k-âti-pasikôcik, môy ka-nitohtâkwak! môy êkwa tâpwêwakêyihtamwak êwako, nêhiyawîhtwâwin. (A: *ya*, âha.)

A: °– *it's different now*.

R: tâpiskôc mân ê-ay-âtayôhkêyân, k-ât-ây-âcimoyân; (A: âha.) môy âwiyak nina-nitohtâk, nipa-pônwêwitên mâna. môy âyis tâpwêwakêyihtamwak, tânis ê-kî-pê-isi-pimâtisiyahk, "ahpô êtikwê awa mân ê-misi-mâh-mamihcimot," ahpô êtikwê mân êkosi nititêyimikwak. [*laughter*] (A: *ya*.)

34

A: kîkway cî mîna ta-kî-kiskisiyahk, t-âcimoyahk?

F: âta wiy âyis mîna kîhtwâm kikâh-kî-pê-âcimôhitinâwâw, (A: âha.) êkwa kika-kâh-kiskisinâwâw k-âti-- aya, ôtê k-ât-âstânâwâw, [*laughter*] âcimowin[a] âhpô. (A: âha.) mistahi kâh-miywâsinwa, ê-kî-wawiyat---wawiyasipayik kîkway ahpô.

A: Ya, ya, it's changed, you know; we're lost in the –°

R: And how much it snowed, it is true.

F: Even the coyotes are lost. [*laughter*] (R: yes.)

A: They, too, are lost now, yes, ya.

When the robin sings, (R: yes, that one too.) the robin, my grandmother used to say, "It's going to rain," (R: yes.) yes; that's the robin, (F: yes.) the robin, yes.

R: I used to marvel at the old man when he was busy outside in the summer; he used to come in and say, "I must have a little sleep, Old Lady, it's going to rain." Sure enough, it would come pouring down, a big shower, (A: yes, ya.) I really used to be surprised by him. (A: yes.) When he suddenly became sleepy in the midst of everything, he'd say, "I must sleep."

A: They lived so close to nature, they were so observant, it was passed on to generations but now today –°

R: Today they don't believe it –°

A: °– it's –°

R: °– in any case; if you sit with the young people and tell stories of long ago, they suddenly get up, they won't listen to you! They don't believe in this now, in the Cree way. (A: ya, yes.)

A: °– it's different now.

R: Like when I'm telling a sacred story, when I start telling a story, (A: yes.) nobody listens to me, so then I stop talking. Because they don't believe in how we used to live, "I guess she's even bragging about herself," or I guess that's what they think of me. [*laughter*] (A: ya.)

34 [*The One Above*]

A: Is there anything else that we should remember and tell about?

F: I suppose I could, of course, come back again to having you tell stories, (A: yes.) you could remember stories in order to put them down here, [*sc.* on the tape-recorder]. [*laughter*] (A: yes.) Such stories would be really good, or something funny.

A: ôh, ayisiyiniw, ayisiyiniw kâ-mâmawôpayit kî-pâhpiw, nanâtohk isi kîkway ê-ay-âcimocik, â --

R: nanâtohk, nânitaw ê-kî-itahkamikisihk mîna wawiyas, *you know*. (F: âha.) (A: *ya*.) macikôcicak, êkây wiy êwakw ân[i] ânima têpiwi ê-wî-âcimostâtakok!

F: âh, âwas [*sic*], êwako mîna. [*laughter*]

R: pêyak ês âya, iskwêw êtikwê awa, okisêyinîma ê-kîmôcihât, *you know*, (A: âha.) (F: âha.) awiy[a] âyâwêw awa. (F: âha.)

A: môyê-- ê-maci-môyêyihtahk.

R: aya, pêyak ê-ayâwât *beside his* [*sic*] *old man*.

A: âha, ôh!

R: âha. (A: âha.)

R: ês êkwa, êtikwê awa mac-îtêyihtam awa, wî-môyêyimêw onôtikwêma, *you know, they're middle-aged people*.

A: ê-âcimisoyan cî ôma? [*laughter*]

R: âha, ahpô êtikwê nist ê--

A: âha, êwako k-êtamân, *see, there's all a way of-- okay*, â, âcimo! konita --

R: êkosi; "maskisina osîhtamawin!" k-êtât ês âwa onôtikwêma, (F: âha.) "nîso-- nîsw-âya." – "âha!" – "osîhtamawin maskisina! niwî-mâcîn, niwî-sipwêhtân." êy, wiy âwa pâhpîmakaniyiw êtikwê ôta ocêhis ê-wî-pêyakwapit, *you know*. [*laughs*] (A: âha.)

êkosi; wâ, mwâc êsa kinwêsk kâ-kîsi-maskisinihkêt. "hâ! êkwa ana nitâs ana kâ-kîsôsit!"

– mâka *late in the fall, you know*, (A: âha) –

"nitâs ana kâ-kîsôsit, nitasikanak mîna." wâ, mwâc kinwêsk êsa kâ-kîsi-wawêyîhât; êkwa wawêyîhêw êkwa ka-mîcisosiyit kîkway. "pahkwêsikan têpiyâhk, êkwa pimiy, êkwa nihtiy; nika-nipahtamâson wiya," itwêw ês âna, *wild meat like, you know*, itwêw ês âna. "môy kinwêsk nik-âyân, kî-nîso-tipiskâki, nîswâw kî-tipiskâki nika-takosinin," itêw ês ônôtikwêma.

– mâk êtikwê *there was a cupboard* anita ômis îsi; kâ-misâk[i] îtowahk, ômis îs ê-itastêk; êkwa kotak mîna tahkohc, anihi kayâhtê *old*, (F: aha.) kayâhtê *old-time ones*, êkotowahk; êkw ês ôtê tahkohc êkwa ôma *ceiling, upstairs*

A: Oh, the people, when the people got together they laughed, they told stories of all kinds of things, ah --

R: All kinds of things, anything funny that used to be done, you know. (F: yes.) (A: ya.) For example, and don't tape this one that I'm going to tell you!

F: Ah, go on, that one too. [*laughter*]

R: There was this one woman, I guess, who was cheating on her old man, you know, (A: yes.) (F: yes.) she had someone else. (F: yes.)

A: He suspected something.

R: Ah, she had another besides her old man.

A: Yes, oh!

R: Yes. (A: yes.)

R: So, then, this one was thinking the worst, I guess, for he was getting suspicious of his old lady, you know, they're middle-aged people.

A: Are you telling this about yourself? [*laughter*]

R: Yes, I guess, even I --

A: Yes, that's what I'm saying, see, there's all a way of-- okay, ah, tell the story! Just --

R: Alright; "Make me moccasins!" he said to his old lady, (F: yes.) "Two -- two pairs." – "Yes!" – "Make me moccasins! I'm going to go hunting, I'm going to leave." Hey, her heart was laughing, I guess, that she was going to be alone, you know. [*laughs*] (A: yes.)

So; well, it wasn't long before she finished making the moccasins. "Ha! And also my warm pants!"

– For it was late in the fall, you know. (A: yes.) –

"My warm pants, and also my socks." Well, it wasn't long before she had finished getting him ready; and she had readied something for him to eat. "Just some bannock is enough, and grease and tea; for I will kill meat for myself," he said, wild meat like, you know, he said. "I won't be long, after two nights, in two nights, I'll get back," he told his old lady.

– But there was a cupboard there like this [*gesture*], I guess, the big kind which was placed like this [*gesture*]; and another was placed on top of that, those old-time, (F: yes.) the old-time ones, that kind; and there was an upstairs over there, and there in the ceiling, up above,

ê-kî-ihtakohk, êkwa âtiht piko kî-tahtinikâtêw êsa, kêyâpic anih âtiht napakihtakwa kikamonw[a] êkotê. –

êkosi; sipwêhtêw awa wîpac, (A: âha.) ê-kîkisêpâyâyik sipwêhtêw awa. êkw âw âwa, *the main one* awa, sipwêhtêw, ê-mâcît ôma. wâ, mwâc kinwês, miton êtikwê nânitaw ê-âpihtâ-kîsikâyik, ê-pôn-âpihtâ-kîsikâyik, ês âna kotak an[a] êkwa ana kâ-pê-takosihk.

A: pê-takohtêw, âha!

R: "îh, îh," k-êtât êsa, "kimiyopayinânaw! sipwêhtêw ôma nîso-tipiskâw ê-sipwêhtêt, ê-mâcît." – "â, êkosi mâk êsa nika-kîwân."

kotak[a] êsa kâ-pê-wîcêwât, nîsîw-- pê-nîsiwak êkwa, "nika-kîwân, nika-pê-itohtânân," itêw êsa. itowahk mitoni k-âyapinikêcik an[a] îskwêw, êkos ês ê-kî-is-âyât, kîmôc mâka, (A: ôh, âha.) *you know*.

A: kâ-wâstinikêt âsay kotaka, (R: âha.) âha.

R: kotaka; êkotowahk ês âna iskwêw. (F: âha.)

– kîkwây kayâs wiyawâw pîsimôhkâna, (A: âha.) pakwanaw ê-kî-kiskêyihtahkik, tâniyikohk ê-ispayiniyik, tânis ê-it--, ê-kî-wîhtahkik, (F: âha.) (A: âha.) *you know*. –

kâ-pê-takosiniyit, âsay mâk êkwa ati-tipiskâyiw kâ-pê-takosiniyit. êtikwê ay-âcimowak, kîkwây êtikwê, konita nanâtohk, *you know*, nistiwak ayisk.

êtikwê êkw ê-at-âkwâ-tipiskâk êkwa, wâ, nawac pikw âwa pêyak wî-îhkêyihtam, pasikôw êsa mâna ê-paspâpit, *you know*. (F: mhm.) "â, kîkwây ôma, kîkwây ôm ê-papâsiwihikoyan, ê-tipêyimisoyân ôm ânohc, sipwêhtêw ôma nikisêyinîm."

A: iskwêw awa? (R: âha.)

R: êkos êtikwê êkwa, tânitê êtikwê awa onipêwinis ê-astêyik, êkota ês êkwa itohtêwak ay-apiwak, *you know*, ê-mâh-mâsihitocik; môy mâka wiya âta wiya cêskwa ê-mâyi---maci-mâmitonêyihtahkik. [*laughter*] (A: âha.)

wah, kêtahtawê êsa iskwâhtêm, mêtoni, nitawi-yôhtênamawêw, okisêyinîma kâ-pê-pîhtikwêyit. (A: âha.) "âha!" k-êtikot êsa. "kîspin ani --"

– miton êsa, pêyak ana, *cupboard* anita pîhtikwêyâmow, anima ê-matwêhikâtêyik, êkwa pêyak ôtê tahkohc

some boards must have been taken off, but some of them were still in place there. –

So, he left early, (A: yes.) he left in the morning; this main one left and went hunting. Well, it wasn't long, I guess it was about noon or afternoon, when that other one arrived.

A: He arrived, yes!

R: "Look, look," she said to him, "we are in luck! He has left, he has left and gone hunting for two nights." – "Ah, in that case, I'll go home."

He had come with another man, there were two of them, "I'll go home, but we'll come back later," he said to her. That woman was the kind that is always into things, but she was sneaky, (A: oh, yes.) you know.

A: She only needed to wave, and there was another man, (R: yes.) yes.

R: Another; she was that kind of woman. (F: yes.)

– For then, there were no clocks long ago, (A: yes.) they knew instinctively what time it was, -- they could tell, (F: yes.) (A: yes.) you know. –

When they got back, it was already getting dark when they arrived. I guess they were telling stories, about what I don't know, just various things, you know, because there were three of them.

I guess it was getting quite late then, and this one, well, was getting kind of anxious, he got up and looked out of the window, you know. (F: mhm.) "Ah, what is it, what is it that's bothering you, I am my own boss today, my old man has gone away."

A: That woman? (R: yes.)

R: So then, I guess, wherever her bed was, there they went, and they were sitting there, you know, and jostling one another; although they were not yet thinking anything bad. [*laughter*] (A: yes.)

Well, all of a sudden, she ran and opened the door, and it was her old man who had returned and was coming in. (A: yes.) "Okay!" he said to her. "So now --"

– When there was a knock, the one jumped straight into that cupboard, and the other fled upstairs,

itâmow, (F: âha.) mayaw ê-matwêhikâtêyik ôma, anihi *boards* anihi, (F: âha.) kîhcêkosîw-ôhpîw êtikwê êkotê; – tânisi êsi-kîhcêkosîkwê, wiy âta wiya nânitaw êkotê isi-kihcêkosîw. –

wâ, mac-îtêyimêw. kâ-m-- îkân-- aya, ka-- kî-miyâmêw anih âyisiyiniwa êkot[a] ê-kî-ayâyit.

A: ê-pasot kîkway, âha.

R: âha, ê-pasot kîkway. (A: âha.)

R: "mâka mîna, nôtikwêw, êkos ôm ê-itahkamikisiyan," k-êtât êsa, "ê-mêkwâskâtân ôma cî?" itêw êsa. "môya! mwêhc ôm ê-wî-ka-kawisimonihkêyân, ê-pêyakohitân ôma, kisêyiniw!" itêw êsa, *you know*. "tâpwê, ôta ôm ê-ayâcik awiyakak [*sic*] ê-sêkihakik," itêw êsa, *you know*. (F: mhm.) "môya!"

"kîspin êkay wî-wîhtamawiyani," k-êtât ês âna, ê-isi-mîskwêyihtamipayit [*sic; sc.* miskw...] êtikwê, manitowa êkwa, "aw îspimihk ôtê k-âyât, kiskêyihtam kahkiyaw kîkway," –°

A: [*laughs*] *oh dear*, âha.

R: °– kâ-pê-sâkiskwêpayihot ês âna, "môy niya piko nikiskêyihtên, ana mîn âkocikanihk k-âsiwasot!" [*laughter*]

konit ês êwakw ân[a] ê-papâtinikêt ana, ociwâma êkwa ê-wayawîyâmohkêt. [*laughter*]

A: *the One above*! [*laughter*]

R: itêyihtam wiya ispimihk.

A: awa wiya ê-nanitohtahk, âha.

F: wiya, "niy ê-itikawiyân," itêyihtam.

R: "môy niya piko nikiskêyihtên, ana mîn âkocikanihk k-âsiwasot."

F: êkos ês êtikwê, mitoni kitatamihinâwâw ôma kâ-pê-âcimostawiyâhk anohc. êkosi mâka.

(F: yes.) as soon as there was a knock, he jumped up on those boards, (F: yes.) I guess – I don't know how he got up, but he got up there somehow. –

Well, he thought the worst of her. He could smell the people having been there.

A: He smelled something, yes.

R: Yes, he smelled something. (A: yes.)

R: "As usual, Old Lady, you are up to your tricks," he said to her. "I've caught you in the act, haven't I?" he said to her. "No, I was just getting ready for bed, ever faithful to you, Old Man!" she said to him, you know. "It is true, there are others here, and I have scared them," he said to her, you know. (F: mhm.) "No!"

"If you're not going to tell me about it," he said to her, and I guess it suddenly occurred to him to refer to God, "the One Above knows all things."

A: [*laughs*] Oh dear, yes.

R: In a flash, that one stuck out his head, "Not I alone know, there's also the one in the cupboard!" [*laughter*]

With a wild rush, he chased his rivals out of the house. [*laughter*]

A: The one above! [*laughter*]

R: The one above thought it was him.

A: Because he was listening, yes.

F: He thought, "It's me that is meant."

R: "Not I alone know, there's also the one in the cupboard."

F: That's it, I guess, you really did me a favour by coming to tell stories today. That's it then.

Notes

H.C. Wolfart

In the critical edition of spoken texts we rely as much as possible on the long-established principles and conventions governing the publication of documents preserved in manuscript. As outlined in the Introduction to the Texts (pp. 34–40), however, the transfer of a text from spoken performance to printed page also presents fundamental problems of its own.

The preliminary notes, immediately below, summarise the orthographic and editorial conventions used in this book. References to the text are by chapter-and-paragraph, e.g., 4-7; cross-reference within the notes is by chapter (preceded by the code N) and page, e.g., N4:443.

The notes to the individual chapters take the form of brief essays which are in all respects selective rather than exhaustive. In attempting to explicate some of the more obscure passages, in adding supplementary information about the *realia* reflected in these narratives and in exemplifying a few of the rhetorical devices employed by the narrators, the commentary is intended above all to draw the reader's attention to the linguistic and literary form of the texts.

Orthographic Representation

The first eight chapters are presented in two versions: a critical edition (in roman orthography) based directly on the audio-recording, and a reading version (in syllabic orthography) derived from it. The two orthographies are presented in some detail in Wolfart & Ahenakew 1987*a* and, from a slightly different perspective, in Wolfart 1988.

THE READING VERSION, in syllabic orthography, is heavily standardised: false starts, corrections made by the speaker, and slips of the tongue are smoothed over (along with the requisite syntactic adjustments); most asides and interventions (and all editorial notations) are omitted; fluctuations in vowel quality reflecting dialect differences and other surface variations are reduced to standard Plains Cree forms; and all the manifestations of the vowel-combination rules which appear between preverb and stem or between words are removed.

The extent of the modifications required by the conventions of syllabic orthography is best gauged in the case of preverbs, which in the syllabic version appear in a uniformly expanded form while the critical edition preserves the variation between an occasional full preverb and the reduced variants mostly heard in spoken Cree.

That the syllabic version is an idealised rendition of the text is most readily illustrated by a comparison between the critical edition of a text, e.g., Glecia Bear's 'Lost and Found' (Chapter 5), and the derived version prepared according to the conventions of syllabic orthography (but not actually converted into syllabic type), e.g., the reading version published in roman type in Bear 1991. (For examples of an intermediate level of standardisation, with fragments either removed or completed and full words restored between words but not between preverb and stem, cf. Vandall & Douquette 1987 or Ahenakew 1989.)

The biographies with which Freda Ahenakew introduces the present book (pp. 1-15) are instances of written Cree. Not only is their style distinct from that of spoken prose; even when printed in roman characters, their written form follows the rules of syllabic orthography.

THE CRITICAL EDITION, in roman orthography, is an attempt to transfer as much as possible of the spoken performance onto the printed page; while some normalisation is inevitable, there is a conscious effort to keep it to a minimum.

The presentation and exegesis of texts is the quintessential work of humanistic scholarship. Based on a cycle of transcription, identification, interpretation, and review which is repeated many times over, the critical edition of the text necessarily reflects the editors' analytical judgment.

Editorial Conventions and Abbreviations

In this book we follow the practice of other recent text editions (Vandall & Douquette 1987, Beardy 1988, Ahenakew 1989) in matching the critical edition of the text and the translation across facing pages; the reading version in syllabics is printed separately.

While the principles guiding the presentation of spoken text are outlined in the Introduction to the Texts (pp. 34–40), the present section provides a summary of those features which most clearly distinguish a critical edition from an ordinary book.

THE SPOKEN PERFORMANCE represented by the printed text is transcribed as fully as possible from audio-tape; but the extraneous sounds which are recorded along with it are documented only if they directly affect the discourse. When the speaker interrupts herself – whether in response to doorbell or telephone or in order to review, off-stage, the next topic to be discussed – and the recorder is turned off and on, this is documented in the printed text by the centred notation [*external break*], which also marks the involuntary interruption at the end of the tape. In all such cases, the recording may stop while the speaker is still in mid-sentence (or start after she has already begun to speak); as a result, the record often shows a fragmentary sentence.

Fragmentary words are mainly due to the speaker interrupting herself while searching for the *mot juste*, or catching herself in a slip of the tongue. In normal speech, however, not all slips of the tongue are corrected, and audio-recordings in any language include sentences which an author might well rewrite in revising a written text for publication; such sentences have not been modified in this edition but left as originally spoken.

THE MANUAL AND FACIAL GESTURES which are part of most narrative events are documented only at a minimal level. Where their linguistic and pragmatic traces can be recovered in the text as recorded, they are identified by the standard notation [*gesture*] and, occasionally, some further detail.

Amongst other non-linguistic features, only those audible responses which can be subsumed under the category of laughter have been included in the first eight chapters. While the notation [*laughs*] refers to the speaker, [*laughter*] marks the response of the audience (but may, of course, also include the speaker).

The dialogue text of Chapter 9 offers a much greater range of confirmatory and dissenting interventions, and a special effort has been made to document as many of these as possible. Identified by speaker, they are presented in smaller type and enclosed in parentheses.

ACOUSTIC CUES also take precedence over considerations of content matter in the establishment of paragraphs. For the most part, paragraphs are identified by such prosodic phenomena as concluding pitch and a pause followed by a distinct elevation in pitch and volume. While the paragraphs themselves are thus typographical representations of spoken sound (cf. Wolfart & Ahenakew 1987*a*:115*a*), they typically (though by no means always) coincide with narrative units.

INDENTED BLOCKS OF TEXT represent stretches which are incidental to the main text: queries and asides (enclosed in dashes where they interrupt the flow of the text), opening or concluding remarks, and any other part of the discourse which is by pitch, volume, or pause marked as subsidiary.

In Chapter 4 (and once in Chapter 5), the typographical device of block indentation is also used to represent distinct layers of text. In this particularly complex text, MF's third-person narrative alternates with long stretches of direct quotation from her late husband's original report (e.g., 4-1); a third level of indentation (4-9) marks the further shift from the perspective (and locale) of the hero and his mother to that of his grandparents.

WHEN THE SPOKEN TEXT includes occasional words or brief stretches in English, these are printed *in italics*; the same rule applies to English proper names. (In the translation, conversely, proper names or technical terms which retain their original Cree form are also printed in italics.)

Single quotation marks are used for terms being cited or defined where this fact is not obvious from the context or, in the case of English proper names, the use of capitalisation.

Summary of Typographical Conventions, Special Symbols and Abbreviations:

xxxx	[text in roman type] primary language (Cree in the text, English in the translation)
xxxx	[text in italic type] secondary language (English in the text, Cree in the translation)
(xxxx)	[text in small type enclosed in parentheses; in Chapter 9 only] interjection by another speaker
xxxx	[underlined text; in Chapter 9 only] overlapping speech
"xxxx"	[double quotation marks] quoted speech
'xxxx'	[single quotation marks] quoted speech (if embedded within quoted speech); cited word
–	[en-dash] syntactic or rhetorical break (usually sharper than those marked by comma or semicolon) within a sentence

( ) [parentheses]
parenthetical insertion (usually spoken at lower pitch or volume)

(- -) [parentheses-*cum*-dash; in Chapter 9 only]
long parenthetical insertion

-~- [wave-hyphen within the word]
fragmentary word, resumed

-~ [wave-hyphen at the end of the word]
fragmentary word

 -~ [wave-hyphen following the word (and a space)]
fragmentary sentence

-° [dash-and-circle; in Chapter 9 only]
interruption by another speaker

°- [circle-and-dash; in Chapter 9 only]
end of interruption by another speaker

[a] [roman type enclosed in square brackets]
editorially supplied word-final vowel (elided under the rules of vowel combination and restored on the basis of vocalic, prosodic, or syntactic evidence)

[*xxxx*] [italic type enclosed in square brackets]
editorial comment (including such standard comments as [*external break*], [*gesture*], [*laughs*], etc.)

[*sic*] ['indeed']
confirmation that the preceding word is correctly printed (usually in the case of an uncommon or otherwise remarkable form, e.g., minor idiosyncracies, dialect discrepancies, slips of the tongue)

[*sc.*] ['that is']
proposed emendation or completion of a fragment; explication or elaboration

[*cf.*] ['see also']
cross-reference (usually to an emended or standard form)

[*?sic*] ['really?']
caution that the identification of the preceding word remains in doubt

[...;*?record*] indication that a short stretch of speech remains unidentified

Proper Names

Cree names keep their Cree form in the English translation, just as French and English names are freely scattered through the Cree text. This principle is followed even where widely known English equivalents exist.

THE EDITORIAL TREATMENT of proper names is a thorny matter. For place-names there are long-standing conventions which allow *Firenze* or *Kebenhavn* to appear in English as *Florence* or *Copenhagen*, and *Rivière Rouge* as *Red River*, but few of the equivalencies are so straightforward and usage also changes over time.

With personal names, in particular, the practice of referring to *atâhk-akohp*, for example, as *Starblanket* was widespread in the 19th century; today, only punsters or cartoonists would translate names such as *Chrétien* or *Lévesque* (as 'Christian' or 'Bishop') – or, indeed, *Winnipeg* as 'Muddy Waters.'

The situation is not always as complex as in the case of the English name *Starblanket* which may stand, undifferentiated, for two distinct Cree names, both of them now the names of reserves in Saskatchewan: *atâhk-akohp* 'Star Blanket' and *acâhkosa-k-ôtakohpit* 'Has-Little-Stars-on-His-Blanket.'

On the other hand, many reserves and settlements have at least two names in either Cree or English: the name of the band, which is often identical with that of the chief who took treaty, and the name of the place. In the case of *atâhk-akohp*'s band, the reserve is usually referred to by a place-name in Cree and in the English of the people who live there: *yêkawiskâwikamâhk* or *Sandy Lake*; the Cree term is inflected as a locative and should literally be translated as 'at Sandy Lake.'

The convolutions of nomenclature do not end here: on the standard topographical maps, this name does not appear in any of the above forms (not even in some macaronic approximation). Instead, the official label is *Hines Lake*, after the priest who established the Anglican mission there. Similarly, *maskêko-sâkahikanihk* 'at Muskeg Lake' or *Muskeg Lake*, the site of *opitihkwahâkêw*'s reserve and often simply called *Muskeg*, appears on the standard maps as *Paddling Lake*.

BY RETAINING CREE NAMES in the English translation, we preserve the distinction made by the narrators, who in certain contexts may have a preference for one term or the other and sometimes go back and forth between them.

Proper names, moreover, are notoriously difficult to translate. Popular practice notwithstanding, many names resist morphological analysis and etymological interpretation, and even the pragmatic identification of persons and places is often far from certain. A text edition would be quite uneven if transparent and unambiguous names were translated while others remained, opaque in structure and meaning and obscure in their reference.

Location is indicated not only by place-names but, at least as often, by deictic morphemes forming part of particles or verbs, such as *ôta* 'here' or *ka-pê-itohtêyân* 'for me to go there and get there' (8-13). Spatial references of either type often remain incomprehensible to the reader without further explication.

For personal names, by contrast, pragmatic identification tends to be less critical. Unless they are the subject of linguistic or historical-genealogical studies, personal names need to be glossed only if their meaning bears on the text, as in the case of *macôhow* 'Bad-Owl' (4-9; cf. N4:444), or where they form part of a pun, as when Janet Feitz refers to herself (1-17) as *masko-nôcokwêsiw* 'Old Lady Bear.'

1 *Janet Feitz, Encounters with Bears*

Audiography

Recorded 18 January 1990 at the residence of the Northern Teacher Education Program (NORTEP) in Lac la Ronge; in the presence of Sarah Whitecalf (SW) and Freda Ahenakew (FA); recording time 26 minutes.

Biography

Janet Feitz (whose married name is sometimes spelled *Fietz* but always pronounced as if it were written *Fitz*) was born and raised at La Ronge and has lived there all her life. She is a *sakâwiskwêw,* a

'Bush Cree,' and the dialect of the Cree language which she uses is generally called Woods Cree.

Woods Cree

The most striking aspect of Woods Cree is the presence of *ð*, a sound very much like the *th* of English *they* or *either*, in such words as *aðisiðiniw* 'human being, person' or *ðîwahikanak* (plural) 'pounded meat,' which in Plains Cree have the sound *y* instead: *ayisiyiniw*, *yîwahikanak*. This correspondence is systematic: whenever a Woods Cree word with an *ð*-sound in it has a direct Plains Cree counterpart, the latter shows the sound *y* in exactly the same position; (cf. Wolfart 1988:vii–x, Wolfart & Carroll 1981:xv-xix).

The reverse, however, does not hold: some words have *y* in both Plains Cree and Woods Cree (and, in fact, in all the many dialects of the Cree language); for example, *pêyakwâw* 'once' or *ê-kiskisiyân* 'I remember.' In short, Woods Cree has either the *ð*-sound or the *y*-sound in words where Plains Cree only has a *y*-sound. Both sounds may even occur in a single Woods Cree word, e.g., *ê-wawiyatêðihtahk* 'as she considered it funny' (1-24).

The systematic correspondence between Woods Cree *ð* and Plains Cree *y* is the sharpest and most easily noticed difference between the sound systems of Woods Cree and Plains Cree.

THE CHOICE OF PLURAL MARKER in the conjunct endings of verbs is another widely recognised difference, this time in the morphological system. As the following example shows, there are two plural morphemes which appear in the conjunct, *-wâw* and *-ik*:

> ...; *êkonik nistam ê-wâpamakwâw ê-pimiðâcik*.
> '...; they were the first ones I saw fly.' (3-7).

In the Woods Cree dialect spoken by Janet Feitz, the plural is marked by *-wâw* when the preceding part of the ending happens to end in the sound *k*, and by *-ik* in all other cases. (In Plains Cree, it is *-ik* even after *k*, e.g., *ê-wâpamakik* 'as I see them.')

THE GENERAL DIFFERENCES we have discussed so far apply to all instances of a sound, or to all cases of a particular verb ending or pronoun. They do not depend on a particular word: if the general condition is met, the rule takes effect. The differences amongst the dialects of a language may, however, also be much more isolated, even idiosyncratic.

In Woods Cree, for example, the verb stem *kospi-* VAI 'go away from a body of water' ends in a short *i* while its Plains Cree counterpart ends in a long *î*; this is easy to hear in such forms as,

nikospin (Woods Cree) 'I go away from the water'
nikospîn (Plains Cree).

In other cases, the difference may affect only a single form rather than the entire verb stem. While both dialects have a long *î* in the third-person forms of the VAI stem *waðawîw* (Woods Cree), *wayawîw* (Plains Cree) 'she/he goes outside,' they follow their own, separate patterns for the first-person forms: in Woods Cree the stem vowel appears as *â*, while the final *î* of the stem remains unchanged in Plains Cree:

niwaðawân (Woods Cree) 'I go outside'
niwayawîn (Plains Cree).

Again, such isolated differences between dialects are not restricted to sounds. Comparative constructions, for example, are much the same in both dialects, but Janet Feitz uses the marker *ispî* 'than' to balance *nawac* 'more' (where *ispîhci* would be more common in Plains Cree):

..., *nawac kimaðiskâkonânaw, ispî wiða kwayask kik-êtiskâkowahk*, ...
'..., they are bad for us, instead of being good for us, ...' (3-9).

Finally, Janet Feitz's texts also contain many examples of whole words which seem to be restricted to Woods Cree (or at least not common in Plains Cree). Some of these are individual terms, such as the particle *kosa*, which is always followed by the demonstrative pronouns *awa* or *ôma* and seems to express surprise and emphasis (much as Plains Cree *pôti*); e.g.,

> *êkwân êkwa, ôta kos âw ê-ay-apit awa maskwa kapê-kîsik*, ...
> 'And so this bear sat here all day, ...' (1-11);

all twenty instances of this particle occur in the narrative prose of Chapter 1.

Sometimes the two dialects seem to have similar words but with subtle differences both in form and use; the Woods Cree particle *êkwâni* 'and then,' for instance, occurs much more frequently (no fewer than ninety times in these few pages) than the corresponding phrase *êkwa ani* does in Plains Cree.

In other cases, we see entire sets of words favoured in one of the dialects; all four of the following are from Janet Feitz's bear stories:

> *ayami-* VAl 'speak'
> *ayamiwin-* NI 'what is said, message'
> *ayamih-* VAI 'speak to s.o.'
> *ayamihito-* VA 'speak to one another, converse.'

While other stems derived from the same base, such as *ayamihâ-* VAI 'pray' or *ayamihcikê-* VAI 'read,' occur in Woods and Plains Cree alike, the stem *ayami-* itself and the others derived from it in the meaning 'speak' is characteristic of Woods Cree, the northern variant of Plains Cree used by Glecia Bear, and Swampy Cree.

Variation within Woods Cree

The distinction between the two long vowels *î* and *ê* is often obscured in Woods Cree: sometimes a speaker will use a more *ê*-like sound, and sometimes a more *î*-like sound. These sounds (which correspond *very roughly* to the vowels of English *bed* [*ê*] and bead [*î*] tend to be used interchangeably in Woods Cree.

The word for 'once,' for example, is sometimes pronounced *pêyakwâw* and sometimes *pîyakwâw*; the word for 'at last, finally' is sometimes heard as *pêðisk* and sometimes as *pîðisk*. In those variants of the Plains Cree dialect which strictly maintain the distinction between *ê* and *î*, the first example shows an *ê* and the second an *î* (which in the standard roman orthography is written without a length-mark before the *y*, as *piyisk*).

One of these variants may be more frequent than the other, but both do occur within Woods Cree and in some of the northern variants of Plains Cree, for instance in the speech of Glecia Bear; (cf. also Greensmith 1985). In our transcription of Janet Feitz's texts into roman orthography we have tried to record the fluctuation between *î* and *ê* in her speech even where we have heard the same word sometimes with one, sometimes with the other of these phonological variants. Only in the normalised version of the texts which is printed in the syllabic orthography have the manifestations of this surface variation (cf. Wolfart & Ahenakew 1987*a*:115–119) been removed.

ANOTHER VARIABLE FEATURE which may catch the eye (or ear) of those who are more familiar with Plains Cree than Woods Cree is found when verb stems of the VAI class which end in the stem vowel *o*, such as *pêyako-* VAI 'be single, be alone,' are followed by the first- or second-person endings of the conjunct order; in Plains Cree and in Woods Cree, too, so long as the stem vowel is not *o*, these endings begin with a *y*: *ê-kiskisiyân* 'as I remember,' but *ê-pêyakowân* 'as I am alone' (cf. Plains Cree *ê-pêyakoyân*); or, with the corresponding plural ending (and with stems which are more common in Woods than in Plains Cree): *ê-ayamiyâhk* 'as we spoke,' but *ê-ayamihitowâhk* 'as we conversed.' While Janet Feitz normally uses *-wân* and *-wâhk* with *o*-stems, the texts contain a few exceptions; sometimes the two variants are heard side by side:

> ... *kit-ôhci-asamâwasowahk mîna kit-ôhci-pamihoyahk* –
> '... for us to feed our children and also for us to live on –' (3-9).

A final example of sound variability within Woods Cree is provided by several instances of the VII stem *ihtakon-* 'exist'; as a set, they exemplify what appears to be a growing divergence between independent and conjunct forms: while the independent forms show the last vowel of the stem as *o*, e.g., *ohc-îhtakonwa* (3-7), conjunct forms like *ê-ohc-îhtakwahki* (3-4) let it appear as a sequence, *wa*. (Note also *pikwanita* 'in vain, without purpose' in 1-9 and the corresponding Plains Cree particle, which we write *konita*.)

VARIABILITY IS NOT, of course, restricted to the sound system: in the Woods Cree dialect spoken by Janet Feitz, the demonstrative pronouns for the proximate third-person plural and the obviative are *ôko* and *ôho* (cf. Plains Cree *ôki* and *ôhi*) but a variant *ôki* also occurs.

The Text

The first bear story told by Janet Feitz is, above all else, a factual account of her experience with a bear; but it also provides a great deal of incidental information about the pattern of life at her fishing camp. While she charters a float-plane to get there (and back to La Ronge) and uses a two-way radio (which at any one time either transmits or receives, but not both at once) to stay in touch with other trappers and the float-plane base, she has only herself to rely on once she is at her camp.

The arrival of a bear leads to an increasingly detailed description of the spatial setting, and other circumstantial details are gradually introduced as the bear's visits become more and more troublesome to her. Unable to stay but unwilling to kill the bear and see the meat go to waste, she finally chooses to leave herself. Ironically, the bear she spared is later killed by trophy hunters, and the irony is redoubled when the game wardens seem to blame her, of all people, who had protected it!

As one bear story leads into another, the irony of life gives way to self-mockery: despite the best efforts of two seasoned hunters, the bear they want fails to let itself be killed. In linking the two stories, Janet Feitz projects all these ironies to yet another level when she assumes, in mock-concern, the name *masko-nôcokwêsiw* 'Bear-Old-Woman' – or should it perhaps be translated as 'Old Lady Bear'?

Possessions and Loans

Janet Feitz's texts illustrate terms for animals which have been captured and are being held or processed as food with the possessive suffix *-im-*; e.g., *niwâposom* 'my rabbit, the rabbit I cook,' *nikinosêm* 'my fish, the fish I clean'; the same suffix appears with other intimate possessions, e.g., *nôrêtiyôm* 'my radio.'

Personal possessions are also often marked with the diminutive suffix *-is-*, as in *nicakwâwânisisihk* 'at my little drying rack,' where the diminutive tells us less about the size of the object than about the fact that it is her personal, familiar drying rack. Both patterns appear in

niwâskahikanisihk 'in my (little) cabin'
kicâpakwânisinawa 'our (little) snares'
nikinosêmisak 'my fishes, the fish I have filleted'.

AS THE UNMISTAKABLE LOAN-WORD *-orêtiyôm-* shows by its possessed stem, borrowings may be integrated almost entirely into the structure of Cree:

orêtiyow- NI 'two-way radio': *orêtiyowa* 'radios'
iskôl- NI 'school, schooling': *iskôlihk* 'in school';

in both these examples, Cree adds a vowel before an alien sound or cluster but otherwise retains it.

In other cases, English words may remain unchanged except for the addition of a Cree suffix, e.g.,

porch*ihk* 'on the porch'
German*ak* 'Germans';

or they may, as in the case of *thirty-thirty*, show no modification at all. Since, at the other extreme, some loan-words have all non-Cree sounds replaced, e.g., *tîniki* 'thank you,' we can distinguish at least four levels or degrees of integration.

Just as English words may appear in a Woods Cree text, there is also at least one clear case of interference from Plains Cree:

beside eight occurrences of *îðikohk* 'to such a degree, to such an extent,' Janet Feitz's two texts include one instance of Plains Cree *iyikohk* (1-11).

Dialect Diagnostics

The standard classification of Cree dialects is based on a single diagnostic. In reality, however, the dialect boundaries are much more complex and even the reflexes of this single diagnostic are much less straightforward than is implied in most general treatments (including the sketch which introduces the present notes).

While it may be true that all cases of Woods Cree *ð* which represent common Algonquian **l* do indeed correspond to Plains Cree *y*, there are of course also instances of Woods Cree *ð* which reflect not a single **l* but a cluster with **l* as its second member; this cluster is reflected in Plains Cree either as *y* varying with *hy*, as in *ayapiy- / ahyapiy-* NA 'fishing net,' or as *h* alone, as in *pimihâ-* VAI 'fly' (but cf. Glecia Bear's *pimiyâkan* in 2-23).

In Woods Cree, too, the cluster with **l* as its second member does not always appear as simple *ð*; while *aðapiy- or pimiðâ-*, for example, always exhibit the single voiced sonorant *ð*, other lexical items which appear to reflect the same Proto-Algonquian cluster have the sonorant preceded by a fricative, with the entire cluster indisputably voiceless in Janet Feitz's speech: *wâhðaw* IPC 'far off,' *nahahð-* VTA 'put s.o. away.'

While contemporary Saskatchewan Plains Cree rarely distinguishes between word-initial *î* and *yî*, the Woods Cree forms of Janet Feitz show that *ðîwahikan-* NA 'pounded meat' begins with the reflex of Proto-Algonquian **l* while *îkatêhtê-* VAI 'walk off to the side' does not.

Note, finally, the stem *nôskwât-* VTI 'lick s.t.' and the particle *otâskanâhk* 'behind on the path' with their *sk*-clusters (cf. Plains Cree *nohkwât-, otâhkanâhk*), which are not well represented in the modern literature.

2 *Glecia Bear, Daily Life*

Audiography

Recorded 25 November 1988 at the house of her daughter Leona Derocher on Flying Dust Reserve, Meadow Lake; in the presence of Leona Derocher and Freda Ahenakew (FA); recording time 24 minutes.

The three texts told by Glecia Bear were recorded in a single session; they are separated from one another by informal discussions which remained unrecorded. As the opening remarks suggest, Chapter 2 was recorded some time after Glecia Bear had finished telling her first text (Chapter 8).

Setting

In her introduction to the interviews she conducted for the Department of National Health and Welfare (in its abbreviated form the name is stressed as a compound and therefore written with hyphens), Glecia Bear contrasts the relative luxury of government-funded survey work with decades of heavy manual labour at minimal wages. Succinct and explicit, this résumé of her employment history is an essential part of her biography (for other aspects of which cf. N5 and N8).

Although reported in Glecia Bear's words, this text consists almost entirely of the recollections of three women much older than her. They are variously identified by locale and/or name:

at Waterhen,	*Larocque* (2-4);
[at Joseph Bighead],	*Mrs Blackbird* (2-14);
at Mudie Lake,	– (2-19);

for the second interview it seems reasonable to assume that it took place at Joseph Bighead, the second reserve mentioned by name in the introduction.

While the date of her survey is not specified, Glecia Bear stresses the advanced age of the three women she interviewed. If they were her seniors by at least one (and probably two) generations and she was born ca. 1912, they must have been adolescents by the turn of the century at the latest.

Waterhen Reserve lies due north of Meadow Lake, on Waterhen Lake, and Joseph Bighead Reserve due west from there, upstream on the Waterhen River (between Lac des Iles and Pierce Lake, and not far below Cold Lake). Mudie Lake, with a reserve (and a small 'town' of the same name) lying to the south of it, is part of the Beaver River system; it is situated due west of Meadow Lake (and just across the Alberta border from the *pakicahwânisihk* / Fishing Lake and Elizabeth Settlements; cf. N6, N7 and the map on p. 33). The terms *kîwêtinohk* 'in the north' and *north* by which Glecia Bear refers to these places are, thus, not to be taken literally, in the sense of the cardinal directions defining topographical maps, but as features of a 'mental map' with *north* as a standard label for remote regions.

Reported Speech

Except for the introductory paragraphs, all of Chapter 2 is presented in the form of reported speech. It differs from the vast majority of texts based on second-hand speech in reporting, not a narrative of events, but a long series of questions and answers.

Direct quotation is the normal manifestation of reported speech in Cree, and almost the only one in terms of text frequency; this text offers a rare example, in 2-9, of indirect speech framed by the QUOTATIVE verb *itwêw* 'so she said' but removed from the first-person perspective of the direct quotations which precede and follow it by the third-person inflexion of the verb, *ê-kî-maskatêpot* 'she used to roast things on a spit.'

AS DIRECT QUOTATIONS, both Glecia Bear's questions and the responses of the three old women she interviewed are most frequently framed by *nititâw* 'so I said to her' and *itwêw* 'so she said.' (Of the 289 instances of *itwêw* in the first eight chapters of this book, conversely, 62% occur in this text, and another 28% in Chapter 4.)

First-person accounts mediated by quotative *itwêw* are typical of narratives told on the authority of another narrator; even in very long texts, the perspective of narration at a remove is maintained throughout. In this genre, the quoted material usually takes up the larger part of the text. (Since this is the case for many of the stories in Vandall & Douquette 1987, that book has the narrative itself printed in italics; cf. the brief discussion in Ahenakew & Wolfart 1987:xiii*b*–xiv. For the present volume, which has only two chapters with a significant proportion of quoted speech, this typographical device would have been too sweeping.)

Quoted dialogue is not at all uncommon in Cree texts; in myths and factual accounts alike, the narrator is expected to report what was said. But Chapter 2 is the only text in this book to be told almost exclusively in the form of reported speech.

THE QUOTATIVE VERBS *it-* VTA 'say so to s.o.' and *itwê-* VAI 'say so' mark the end (and sometimes also the beginning) of direct quotations; they identify the speaker and, in the case of *it-*, also the person to whom the quoted speech is addressed.

This is their primary function in spoken discourse, and they do not indicate in any way whether the sentence being quoted is declarative or interrogative; this distinction is marked within the sentence itself.

Nor do these Cree verbs do double duty by serving as quotatives and performatives at once. While these functions may be combined in English written prose (where such framing verbs as *ask*, *demand*, *enquire* take their synonymic turn even in the lowliest trash novel), Cree sharply distinguishes between the quotatives and such ordinary verbs as *wîhtamaw-* VTA 'tell s.o. about (it/him)' or *kakwêcim-* VTA 'ask s.o.; ask s.o. about (it/him), make a request of s.o.'; for example:

> well, *nôhkom aw êkwa kâ-wîhtamawak êkwa, "nôhkom!" nititâw, …*
> 'Well, when I told this one old woman about it I said to her, "Grandmother!" …' (2-4);
> *êkwa mîna ni-- êkwa nikakwêcimâw, "…?" nititâw, "…" nititâw.*
> 'And then I also asked her, "…?" I said to her, "…?" I said to her.' (2-12).

(For such a constative stem to be linked to a quotation, it would have to be compounded with the preverb *isi* 'there, thus' – but even then its function and meaning would focus on the manner of declaring or asking rather than simply on the quoted stretch of speech.)

The fact that the quotative verbs are repeated over and over in spoken Cree may seem remarkable to readers used to the conventions of written English. Once the English translation is set aside, however, this difference is readily recognised as one of the stylistic patterns crucially dependent both on the structure of each language and on the mode of literary production, oral or written. Simply to apply the aesthetic yardstick of one language-and-literature universe to another would be as misguided and futile as an attempt to judge Mordecai Richler by the poetic rules of Sanskrit.

The Nature of the Evidence

While the Golden Age evoked by these three sets of reminiscences, in displaying the familiar signs of an idealised reconstruction, calls for critical analysis by historians or ethnologists, the text in which the recollections of the three old women are passed on to us includes purely linguistic features which have a direct bearing on the question of evidence.

ONE IS THE MODALITY in which the reported speech is presented. In relating events which he or she did not witness in person, a Plains Cree narrator typically indicates that fact by means of the dubitative particle *êtikwê*. While this particle is frequent in Glecia Bear's narrative texts (Chapter 5, for example, has fifteen examples even though it is shorter than the present text), it is here limited to six instances.

Only one of these occurs in a factual context, where *êtikwê* normally functions to indicate the hearsay status of what is being reported; but even this passage may well be deliberative or speculative rather than purely factual:

> "*êkosi nawac êkw êtikwê kî-nitohtâkowisinâniwan*," ...
> '"At that time, it seems, one's worship received more of a hearing,"
> ...' (2-19).

Two are found in interpretative sentences:

> *"..., êwak ôm étik ôm âkwa pimiyâkan êkwa,"* ...
> '"..., that must be the airplane of nowadays," ...' (2-23);

> *"â, anohc kâ-kîsikâk, êwak ôhc êtikwê ayisiyiniw kâ-maskawâtisit,"* ...
> '"Well, that must be the reason why people are strong today," ...' (2-15).

Both state a conclusion, in the first case drawn on the basis of a formal prophesy, in the second on an account of traditional childbirth practices.

The other three examples with their future preverbs are purely hypothetical:

> *"..., ahpô êtikwê wîstawâw ka-kakwê-âsô-kiskinawâpiwak, ..."*
> ' "..., and they may even themselves try to follow the example set for them, ..." ' (2-22).

In the following sentence, the hypothetical quality imparted by *êtikwê* is reinforced by the irrealis form of the verb:

> *"...; ahpô êtikwê piyis kâh-mâmitonêyihtamwak, ..."*
> ' "...; some day they might even think about it, ... " ' (2-24).

Only the last instance is not part of the reported speech of the three old women:

> *êy, wîpac êtikw êkwa nika-mêscitonêsinin, wâcistakâc!*
> 'Hey, soon now I will probably wear out my mouth, by golly!' (2-24);

a light-hearted aside, this remark is also clearly hypothetical even though the verb is in the simple future rather than the irrealis.

The recollections of the old women are given simply in the form of direct quotation: neither Glecia Bear nor the original speakers themselves evidently felt any need to mark their reports as being anything but first-hand, eyewitness accounts.

OTHER STYLISTIC FEATURES corroborate this conclusion. The reported speech of the old women relies heavily on the indefinite agent form of verbs, an inflexional form especially common in technical prose (cf. N3:438–440, N9:488–490) and illustrated in both verbs in the following sentence:

> *"kayâs ma kîkway ohci-pakâhtâniwan, ..., kahkiyaw kîkway ê-kî-mosci-nawacîhk, ..."*
> ' "In the old days one did not do any boiling, ..., one simply roasted everything, ..." ' (2-9).

These forms and, even more so, their English translations, which often make use of the passive, tend to create a sense of generality which English readers, especially in the context of ideological appeals to ancient purity, might easily take as a sign of vagueness.

This impression is misleading; there is nothing imprecise about indefinite agent forms except that the agent remains unspecified. If independent confirmation were required, the factual nature of the reports in Chapter 2 is indicated by the first-person perspective in which the indefinite agent forms are embedded, and stressed further by the relatively frequent use of the personal pronoun *niyanân* 'we (but not you)' (e.g., in 2-13, 2-15, 2-16) and the highly specific reference to the speaker's husband in 2-7. As full participants in the culture they describe, finally, the three old women use none of the standard formulae employed by narrators who report in their old age what they had witnessed as children.

Realia and Translations

Besides offering terms for various items of material culture, the text also includes ethnographic details of the non-terminological kind; for example, the lodge described by the old lady at Waterhen, whose name is given as Larocque, appears to be the tipi of the plains rather than the birch-bark lodge of the boreal forest. Whether stated explicitly or incidentally, even small pieces of information often turn out to be valuable as raw material. All such snippets, however, need to be analysed and interpreted rather than simply being taken at face value; even clear and forceful statements (whether about the lack of pots to cook in (2-9) or, by casual omission or in jest (8-9), the role of moss and the like before toilet-paper came into use) must be seen in their full archaeological, historical, and ethnological context.

There is great emphasis on the traditional imperative of sharing food (2-19), even after a limited kill; the issue of sharing as seen from the perspective of an immature member of the society is one of the major themes of Minnie Fraser's text (Chapter 4).

Another aspect of traditional life which is often the subject of sweeping ideological pronouncements is childbirth and the care of the newborn, but the reminiscences of Mrs Blackbird in fact include specific post-partum practices such as abdominal girding, the immediate administration of a herbal drink and the use of moss to absorb the blood in addition to the more commonly discussed lack of bed-rest. This is one of the rare instances (for another cf., N9:481–482) where childbirth is discussed from a relatively technical perspective (rather than being part of a myth or an historical narrative) without the discussion being directed by an outsider's questions.

The social rules which govern a woman's life include the injunction not to go visiting on her own and her inability (not merely due to inherent weakness or age; cf. Whitecalf 1993, Lecture IV) to take up for her children in later life: she has to stand by helplessly (2-21, 2-22) while her daughters are beaten and her grandchildren abandoned.

The identification of plants is one of the thorniest problems encountered in the preparation of a text edition. Even where the real-world experience of eating various wild plants is shared by the editors (in Freda Ahenakew's judgment, the stembase of the *pasân* is tastier than that of the *mâskosiwân*), the discrepant referential ranges of common names in both Cree and English would require detailed ethno-botanical and dialectological studies before plant-names can be fully translated. In rendering *mâskosiwân-* NI (2-11, 6-20) as 'bulrush' and *pasân-* NA (FA, 9-28, p. 384) as 'cattail' in this book, we do so without prejudging their eventual identification as *Scirpus spp.* and *Typha spp.*, respectively (or, indeed, *Phragmites spp.* and others as well; cf. also Leighton 1985).

Translation problems persist even where the taxonomic situation is simple. Since Glecia Bear uses both *môniyâw-* NA (e.g., 2-19) and *wâpiskiwiyâs-* NA (e.g., 2-23) to refer to Whites, a literary translation which would reduce them to a single term, as is normally done in the casual English usage of Cree speakers, would obliterate a distinction which she alone of the seven narrators in this volume chose to make.

Some discrimination is unavoidable when the two terms are used side by side:

> *anohc kahkiyaw – 'wâpiskiwiyâs' kâ-isiyihkâsot, môniyâw, kâhkiyaw misiwanâcihêw kitâyisiyinîminawa, kahkiyaw ôma môniyâwi-kîkway êkw ânohc ...*
> 'Today the White-Skin as he is called, the White-Man, has ruined everybody, all our people, today all the White things ...' (8-34).

Although *môniyâw* and *wâpiskiwiyâs* seem to be used interchangeably by many Cree speakers, the latter may well be slightly pejorative or at least more highly marked than the former. In compounds, which are very frequent in this book and even include such bilingual compounds as *môniyâwi-antiseptic* (AL, 9-27, p. 376), only *môniyâwi* appears as the prenoun.

3 *Janet Feitz, Then and Now*

Audiography

Recorded 12 January 1989 at the residence of the Northern Teacher Education Program (NORTEP) in Lac la Ronge; in the presence of Freda Ahenakew (FA); recording time 13 minutes.

The Scope of the Text

As a piece of expository prose rather than narrative, Chapter 3 both begins and ends with the perennial topic of lifestyles in the age of fur-trapping and in the present, post-fur world; the discussion concentrates on nutrition and its effects on health. Depicting the people of today as weak and sickly, the speaker compares them to the strong men she used to watch carrying heavy loads in freighting contests.

These comparisons frame an alternating sequence of descriptive and evaluative sections. A survey of trapping and snaring culminates in a brief but fairly technical discussion of the design and function of a rabbit snare; childhood memories contrast the uselessness of school learning (with social studies apparently taking pride of place) with the value of daily religious instruction and the Christian (here, Anglican) discipline also held high in the home. The introduction of airplanes is set against a background of travel by boat as the major mode of transport, and the self-sufficiency of the trapping life is compared to the practice of financial planning which so sharply divides White (and largely middle-class, it would appear) existence from life in the bush.

Simple and straightforward in style, this text still exhibits some classical traits of Cree rhetoric. The unrestricted validity of an assertion is expressed, for example, by the general singular, which is especially impressive in a verb meaning 'be numerous':

> *namôð ôhci-mihcêtiw môniyâw êkospî ...*
> 'At that time the White-Man was not numerous ...' (3-2);
>
> *– wîða kayâhtê, wîða nîhiðaw wîð êkâ êkos îsi ê-kî-mâwacisôniyâwêt ...*
> '– for the Cree cannot pile up money in that fashion, beforehand ...' (3-9).

When a clause is repeated, the order of elements within the clause is often reversed; (for further examples of such chiastic constructions cf. Blain 1989:199–203). In the following example, the list of items begins with the animate noun *pahkwêsikan-* 'flour' and the initial verb stem belongs to the VTA class, *nât-* 'fetch s.o.'; but as the list grows longer it is divided, and the inanimate nouns which end it are followed by the corresponding VTI verb, *nât-* 'fetch s.t.':

> ..., *ê-pî-nâtâcik pahkwêsikana,* tea, *sôkâw, pimiy êkos îsi kîkwây; wâsaskocînikanisa, êkos îsi kîkwâya mân ê-kî-pî-nâtahkwâw.*

> '..., they got flour, tea, sugar, lard, things like that; they also used to get candles and things like these.' (3-3);

(while the two stems themselves have the same shape in the above sentence, they are followed by distinct suffixes, *-âcik* and *-ahkik*).

Finally, it should not go unnoticed that the factual discussion of water travel in 3-7 ends on a rather poetic note:

> *..., êkâ ê-pimiskâcik, mêskoc ðôtinwa ê-pimohtahikocik.*
> '..., not paddling but, instead, being taken along by Wind himself.' (3-7).

The translation attempts to emulate the personification of a natural force, which in the original is left ambiguous in the form of the verb (which admits either an inanimate or an obviative agent) but made explicit by the rather unusual obviative ending of the noun *ðôtinwa* 'Wind.'

The Shape of a Word

Janet Feitz's texts are especially rich in forms of the word for 'canoe': beside the singular *ôsi* 'canoe' she uses the plural *ôsa* 'canoes' several times; Glecia Bear also has the locative form *ôsihk* 'in the canoe' (2-18).

But when the stem for 'canoe' is possessed and, therefore, preceded by a personal prefix, it appears in the form *ôt-* rather than as *ôs-*; thus, *otôtiwâw* 'their canoe' (3-8).

In demonstrating the tight linkage between personal prefix and stem, the form *nitôt* 'my canoe' (1-8, 1-10) suggests further that the personal prefix is added BEFORE the matter of the final vowel – which remains after single-syllable stems and is dropped elsewhere – is resolved: thus, *ôsi* (with the inanimate singular ending *-i*, which palatalises the preceding *t*) but *nitôt*. (Cf. also *nimihko* 'my blood' (RL, 9-27, p. 376), though in another dialect and with a short stem-vowel.)

The fact that the compound *waskway(i)-ôsa* 'birch-bark canoes' (3-8, 2-16) shows *ôsa* with the final vowel (instead of an hypothetically possible **waskway-ôt*; cf. Wolfart 1973:30*a*,

1982:396-7, Ahenakew & Wolfart 1991:31–32) suggests that the linkage between the two members of this compound is much less tight than that between personal prefix and stem.

Finally, the stem-final *t* (rather than *s*) also shows up in the diminutive, where the diminutive suffix triggers pervasive palatalisation of all *t*'s to *c*: *ôcisisa* 'little boats' (1-25).

Constructions without Agents

The texts in this anthology are rich in verb forms which leave the agent indefinite (cf. N2:443); ironic as it may seem, such forms are actually preferred in formal definitions:

> ..., 'John Hastings,' 'Abby Halkett' ***kî-itâwak aniki nîso nâpêwak,*** ...
> '..., these two men were called John Hastings and Abby Halkett, ...' (3-7);

> ..., ***namôða mîna mwâsi ohc-îhtakow*** 'engine' ***k-êtiht êkospî anima,*** ...
> '..., there were hardly any 'engines' then, as they are called, ...' (3-7);

> ***'maci-manitowi-môtêyâpisk' kâ-itamihk,*** ...
> 'The devil's bottle,' as it is called, ...' (8-36).

Although the two short texts included in this volume do not permit a general statement, Janet Feitz seems to pair the VTA stem *isiðîhkât-* 'call s.o. thus, name s.o. thus,' the 'naming' term which is most explicit about its defining role, with the stem *icikâtê-* 'be thus said of' (rather than with its VTI counterpart, *isiðîhkât-* 'call s.t. thus, name s.t. thus,' which in Plains Cree is often used in indefinite agent forms). Besides examples such as

> *('waðawîstim' nitisiðîhkâtâw mâna,* ...)
> '(I used to call him 'Outside-Dog,' ...)' (1-2),

which are typical when persons (whether human or not) are identified by name, an inanimate noun is most commonly given as a name by means of the following construction,

... ôho 'pimiðâkana' k-êcikâtêki.
'... these 'planes,' as they are called.' (3-7),

of which there are many examples throughout this text.

While the asymmetry in these sets of verbs of defining may merely reflect a stylistic preference, it may also suggest a more pervasive distinction within the system of agentless verb forms (cf. Wolfart 1991, especially p. 184).

There is no lack of indefinite agent forms of verbs belonging to the VTA paradigm, including several instances of third-person forms ending in *-âw, -âwak*, *-iht*, *-imiht*; but at the conclusion of both bear stories, we find a derived stem, *âcimikosi-*, rather than an inflexional form (such as *ê-âcimiht*), e.g.,

êkwan êkota ê-iskw-âcimikosit awa maskwa;
'And that is all there is to tell about this bear;' (1-16).

It is remarkable that the two texts of Janet Feitz do not contain a single instance of a VTI stem with the indefinite agent suffix *-amihk* (or its more recent variant *-amohk*); the preferred choice with VTI stems appears to be the derived passive in *-ikâtê-* (cf. N9:488–490). The most frequent instance of this pattern in the text is *icikâtê-*; but it is by no means the only one:

..., namôða kita-kî-wêpinikâtêki êkoni ôho ihtâwina,
kita-kî-kakwê-miciminikâtêki kahkiðaw, ...
'..., these trapping territories should not be given up, an attempt should be made to hold onto all of them, ...' (3-9).

Similarly, there is not a single VAI stem inflected with the indefinite agent suffix *-hk*, as in this Plains Cree example:

wâ, kâ-nîmihitohk ês êkwa, ...
'Well, when there was a dance, ...' (7-26);

instead, we find conjunct verb forms based on the transparently derivative suffix *-(n)âniwi-*, e.g.,

..., êkâ osâm ê-ohci-pîhtwâniwik mîn êkospî.
'..., there also was not much smoking at that time.' (3-9).

While the corresponding independent form is the normal VAI indefinite agent form in contemporary Plains Cree, the conjunct form with *-(n)âniwi-* is quite striking from the perspective of Plains Cree, where the conjunct suffix *-hk* remains the norm.

4 *Minnie Fraser, His First Moose*

Audiography
Recorded in October 1986 at the house of her daughter Catherine Shankaruk in Prince Albert; in the presence of her daughters Gertrude Pratt (GP) and Catherine Shankaruk (CS), Edward Ahenakew (EA) and Freda Ahenakew (FA); recording time 14 minutes. (The acoustic quality of this recording, made on an ordinary cassette recorder, is very low.)

In preparing the translation for this text we were able to draw on the draft of an English re-telling of the story by Anita Greyeyes.

Biography
Minnie Fraser did not live to see this book published; she died in March 1987 at the age of almost 91 years.

She was born in 1896 on *atâhk-akohp's* reserve at *yêkawiskâwikamâhk* 'at Sandy Lake,' the northernmost of the three reserves lying north of the North Saskatchewan River near Carlton House and included in the term *wâskahikaniwiyiniwak* 'House People' (cf. Ahenakew & Wolfart 1987:x–xi). She was the last to survive of the many children of Louis Ahenakew (born ca. 1870; cf. Wolfart 1990*b*:376–377); Louis's younger brother Baptiste was the father of the Rev. Canon Edward Ahenakew (cf. Faries 1938, Ahenakew 1973) and the grandfather (through his son Shem) of Freda Ahenakew's late father, Edward Ahenakew.

As Freda Ahenakew tells us in her biographical introduction, her father had used the term *osikosâhkôm-* 'call s.o. one's father's sister, mother-in-law' to refer to Minnie Fraser (who, as the daughter of his father's father's brother and, thus, his father's parallel cousin, counts as his father's sister).

Minnie and Norman Fraser, who were married in 1917, lived just outside the reserve, about a mile away from Freda Ahenakew's childhood home. Norman Fraser, who died about 1980, and her father (1910–1989) used to hunt together (the place-name *wacîhk* refers to a range of hills about twenty miles northwest of *yêkawiskâwikamâhk* 'at Sandy Lake'), and Norman Fraser remained a gifted hunter to the end.

The Text

The narrative is characterised by frequent shifts in perspective; in part at least, these may be due to the narrator's poor health and advanced age. They also reflect the fact, however, that the story is told to two audiences at once: an immediate one, who had talked about these events at some length just before the recording was made and who were of course familiar with all the people and places mentioned, and a wider audience for whom certain modifications might be required.

The influence of this wider, future audience is seen most strikingly in the narrator's attempt (4-2) to suppress the fact that Easter dinner included gophers and the protests this evokes from Gertrude Pratt and Freda Ahenakew. On another occasion, she turns specifically to her immediate audience and, especially, Edward Ahenakew to situate the events of the story in terms of a known locale: the place (4-9) where the *macôhôsis* family and Willy Dreaver used to live.

The narrative perspective shifts temporally or, perhaps, generationally (and since the immediate audience, too, represents three generations, the kin-terms have considerable scope). As the hero of the tale, her late husband appears as a boy or youth:

> when my old man was a boy (4-1);
>
> the old man *ê-nâpêsisiwit* 'my husband as a little boy' (4-2);
>
> thirteen *ôma kâ-kî-itwêt pakahkam ê-itahtopiponêt*
> 'he was thirteen, I think he had said' (4-4);

êkwa wîst êtikwê ê-oskinîkiwiyinîsiwit
'he must have been just a youngster then' (4-5);

but as a person well known to all those present, he is an adult who had died at a ripe old age almost a decade earlier.

The terms by which the hero is identified reflect some of these shifts: when his grandfather is cited speaking about him, he uses his Cree name, *môniyâs* (4-9); but the narrator's consistent use of the normal English translation of the kin-term *ninâpêm* 'my husband,' *my old man* or *the old man*, when telling about the boy of twelve or thirteen requires the audience to shift back and forth – especially since she also refers to her (then future) mother-in-law, the boy's mother, as *the old lady* (4-1) or *awa nôcikwêsiw* 'the old lady' (4-3).

The same ambiguity is found with other *dramatis personae*. The hero's oldest sister, Eliza, for example, is listed in an aside in the midst of the story (4-8) along with all the younger siblings (although, at the time of these events, she apparently had already left the household to get married); but in the opening passage (4-1) she is cited as *nicâhkosipan* 'my late sister-in-law (woman speaking).'

Just as the time of the story is set within a much broader, indeed boundless time-frame of known relationships, so the narrative perspective shifts between the hero's own telling, in first-person form (here presented in quotation marks and on the first level of indentation), and the narrator's third-person reporting thereof. A further change of perspective, or at least of scene, cross-cuts these when the narrative moves back and forth between the camp of the widow and her children (and the site where the moose is butchered) and her parents' location at *kinêpiko-maskotêhk* 'at Snake Plain.' On one occasion, Gertrude Pratt intervenes to explicate the change of scene; on others, it is obvious to a Cree-speaking audience (but made explicit in print by a second level of indentation). And, of course, there are always asides (such as the identification of the locale in 4-9) which hold at the time of the performance or, perhaps, are part of an unbounded background.

In summary, and without attention to transient shifts, the changes in perspective may be charted as follows:

(1)	narrator (third-person):	*background*	Easter observances
(2)	narrator (third-person):	*background*	Easter dinner
(3)	narrator (third-person):	*scene*	the gopher
(4)	hero (first-person):	*scene*	the prayer
(5)		*scene*	killing ducks
(6)		*scene*	killing moose
(7)		*scene*	the report; butchering
(8)		*scene*	the owl's visit
(9)		*scene*	returning for the feast
	x (third-person):	*insert*	*macôhow's* report *scene*
		scene	preparing, holding the feast
(10)	narrator (third-person):	*conclusion*	hunting observances

Whether it is the narrator's perspective or the hero's which predominates in a particular section, the other may intervene in the form of commentary or quoted speech (and, of course, in asides directed to the immediate audience or, indeed, comments by that audience). In 4-1 already, much of the background is given, not by Minnie Fraser but in the quoted report of the hero's sister, Eliza. By 4-5, with the hero's perspective firmly established, the narrator still adds background information which interrupts the quoted first-person narrative with third-person commentary; e.g., ..., *êkwa wîst êtikwê ê-oskinîkiwiyinîsiwit* – '..., he must have been just a youngster then –'.

While the emergence and recognition of a man who was blessed as a hunter is clearly the major thrust of this story, there are secondary strands which also deserve attention. The most obvious, from a non-Cree perspective, is that of the boy who is torn between the practical advantages of keeping the meat and the customary obligation of giving it away.

But the secondary motif which seems most important is the role of the owl which visits the camp while the moose is being butchered. The little girl takes fright – owls are normally taken as a bad omen in Cree society – but her mother calms her and, in fact, the owl is none other than the girl's grandfather. He, ironically, is berated by his wife for neglecting their daughter and her children even though he had long since reassured himself of their welfare. Named *macôhow* (which might be translated as 'Bad-Owl'), he has the owl as his guardian spirit.

Realia

As the widowed mother of *môniyâs* / Norman Fraser moves her camp about in search of food, she is accompanied by her four younger children (with the eldest, Eliza, apparently already married): Norman, John-George, Tommy, and Mary-Jane.

Known in English as Jane Bird (and in Cree as one of the *macôhowak*), she belonged to the family of *piyêsîs*, two of whose stories are told by Peter Vandall in the *wâskahikaniwiyiniw-âcimowina / Stories of the House People* (1987:78, 92), and was also related, as made explicit in 4-2, to Freda Ahenakew's mother, who called her *nisikos* 'my father's sister.'

Her parents, *macôhow* and his wife, lived at *kinêpiko-maskotêhk* 'at Snake Plain,' and Edward Ahenakew, to whom the aside in 4-9 is addressed, must have been familiar with the place where their son *macôhôsis* used to live.

Her own nomadic lifestyle took her not only to an area just north and east of *mistawâsis*'s reserve at *kinêpiko-maskotêhk*, as identified by the towns of Ordale and Shellbrook, but also to Stump Lake, which lies about twenty-five miles farther north (due east of the town of Debden).

Like rabbits, gophers were very much part of the diet; they were boiled whole (including the brains), gutted but unskinned, with the fur singed and scraped off. As another point of culinary preference, the report which *macôhow* gives to his wife (4-9) indicates that even when fresh meat is available, some still like the taste of dried meat better.

The *nîpiya* 'leafy branches' which are placed on the ground when an animal is to be butchered (4-7) are, ideally, those of the willow in which the leaves hold firmly to the stem rather than attaching themselves to the freshly butchered meat, which is very sticky.

Linguistic Commentary

Minnie Fraser's text includes an unusual amount of English, perhaps as a concession to future audiences – for all the people present when she told her story were fluent Cree speakers.

For the most part, Minnie Fraser's dialect of Plains Cree is indistinguishable from that used by Peter Vandall and Joe Douquette in their texts (1987). While the identification of fricatives before a stop consonant is thrown into doubt by the low acoustic quality of this recording, there seems to be some preference for *st* over *ht* in such stems as *mamistêyimo-* 'be proud of oneself' (4-5) or *âpistaw-âyihk* 'at the halfway point' (4-6).

THE TEXT ILLUSTRATES two patterns of referring to relatives who are no longer alive (cf. also N9:492–493). While using the more archaic style with the preterital noun *nicâhkosipan* 'my late sister-in-law' in 4-1, Minnie Fraser later shares in the common contemporary practice (as does Freda Ahenakew in her comment in 4-2) of using a participial verb form with *kâ* which combines the denominative stem of possession, *omâmâ-* 'have a mom, have s.o. as one's mom' (cf. *onâpêmi-* 'have a husband, have s.o. as one's husband') with the completive preverb *kî* 'used to.' (The corresponding dependent noun stem, *-mâmâ-* 'mom,' is illustrated in *nimâmâ* 'my mom,' *omâmâwa* 'her mom' and *omâmâwâwa* 'their mom'; cf. also *opâpâwa* 'his dad.')

The COMITATIVE construction which allows a singular noun to occur with a plural verb (cf. N6:460) is here illustrated with a proper name:

> – *êkot*[*a*] *ânima macôhôsis kâ-kî-ayâcik*, ...
> '– there where *macôhôsis* and his family used to live, ...' (4-9).

When two noun phrases stand in apposition, the second, which is typically an elaboration of the first, may exhibit a shift in obviation if it includes a possessive construction:

..., *kâhkêwakwa ê-miyât awa nocikwêsiw, anihi omâmâwa,*
the old man.'
..., the old lady [prox], my husband's [prox] mom [obv], gave them more dried meat to take along.' (4-9).

The fact that the apposition has a status of its own, apart from the embedding sentence, is especially obvious when the original obviation assignment continues:

– *êkwa aw îtwêw, 'macôhow' kâ-kî-itiht wîwa, ..., itêw êsa, onâpêma*, ...
'– and then she [prox] said, the wife [obv] of *macôhow*, as he was called [prox], ..., she said to her husband, ...' (4-9).

Amongst the technical terms having to do with the tracking and butchering of a moose, we find a highly specialised use of the stem *mîciso-* VAI 'eat,' which here refers to rumination as evidenced by the fact that the moose is not standing up:

..., *kî-matwê-apiw nêtê, ê-mîcisot*, ...
' ..., it was in plain view, sitting over there and chewing the cud, ...' (4-6).

One of the more remarkable uses of the preverb *nitawi* 'go and, go to' occurs in a parenthetical comment about the hero's youngest sister:

(*mîn âwa kâ-kî-nicawi-nipic awa* States, *êh*)
'(the one who later died in the States, eh)' (4-8).

Although the compound verb (with its compassionate palatalisation) might be translated 'who went and died,' the stative translation with the temporal adverb seems preferable.

5 *Glecia Bear, Lost and Found*

Audiography

Recorded 25 November 1988 at the house of her daughter Leona Derocher on Flying Dust Reserve, Meadow Lake; in the presence of Leona Derocher and Freda Ahenakew (FA); recording time 22 minutes.

In referring to Glecia Bear in the third person, Freda Ahenakew's introduction stresses the formal character of this recording; they had reviewed the story once more during the break which followed the telling of Chapter 2.

Two Published Versions

As this text will have appeared in print twice, for distinct audiences and with slight differences in form, within the space of a few months, the logical priority of the critical edition needs to be emphasised. Even though the illustrated children's book, *wanisinwak iskwêsisak / Two Little Girls Lost in the Bush* (Bear 1991), was published first, it is in fact derived from the text printed here.

The reading version published in the children's book is heavily standardised and follows the conventions of syllabic orthography (cf. N:414) even though it is printed in roman characters. Of all these modifications, the most conspicuous is the omission of false starts and the like and, correspondingly, the smoothing out of the translations; instead of the place-name *kwâkopîwi-sâkahikanihk*, for example, the translation has the English equivalent, *Green Lake*. The children's book also omits two paragraphs, 5-22 and 5-23, which represent an afterthought not essential to the plot.

Since the children's book was published before the final review of both edition and translation could be undertaken, it differs in some minor matters (such as the spelling of the variants *êtikwê* and *êtokwê*) and also does not include two substantive revisions. The translation of the opening sentence of 5-9 has been recast (cf. Bear 1991:16), and a last-minute change has been made in the orthographic representation of a phonologically indeterminate particle; while the prosodic pattern of stress on the first syllable seems to suggest a trisyllabic word (i.e., *tâsipwâw*), native speaker intuition calls for the form printed here, *tâspwâw* 'as a matter of fact' (5-2, 5-13).

The Story

The events which Glecia Bear relates in this story can be dated with some confidence to the years 1924 or 1925; she was eleven at the time (and seventy-five at the time of the recording), and the post manager, who appears in the Hudson's Bay Company Archives as J.-F. Séguin (presumably Jean-François, remarkably rendered as *Frank* in the text), is listed there as having served at Green Lake from 1924 until 1931.

More than sixty years later and with the story having no doubt gone through many re-tellings, the time of year when these events took place is more difficult to determine unambiguously (except, perhaps, through a search of local records such as the parish priest's *Codex historicus* or, ultimately, a report in one of the northern Saskatchewan newspapers). Glecia Bear gives the season as *ê-ati-takwâkik* 'as it was getting to be fall,' confirming this by *kâ-tâh-tahkâyâk ati* 'when it begins to get cold' (5-6); but she also cites her father as referring to a smudge (5-1), made to protect cattle from insects, which might seem more typical of early summer.

The introductory remarks on liturgical practice (5-2) include two points the significance of which does not become clear until later: that Glecia had gone to communion and had therefore had nothing to eat that day, and that she was still wearing her Sunday best, which included sturdy shoes (the *miscikwaskisina* 'oxfords [literally: wooden shoes]' mentioned in 5-11).

Aside from the light it throws on the behaviour of individuals and community alike at a time of crisis (and, of course, on the roles of the Hudson's Bay Company post manager and the Roman Catholic priest and even on the technical organisation of a search-and-rescue effort), this story quite incidentally illustrates an aspect of Cree social structure which seems to have attracted little notice amongst ethnologists: that property needs to be released by the owner before it may be dealt with by others. Despite the urgency of the search, the hunter who had been engaged to track the children has to go back and report, seeking the permission of the girls' father before the cow, which is beyond recovery in any case, can be destroyed:

> ..., *pê-wîhtam êsa êkwa, ... êkosi nipâpâ mêkiw, anihi mostoswa ka-pê-pâskisomiht;*
> '..., he went back over there to tell, ... So my dad gave the cow up to be shot;' (5-13).

The verb *mêki-* VAI 'give (it/him) out' is also used when a woman is given away in marriage (cf. N8:474–476).

The encounter with the owl, finally, marks the dramatic turning point. The responses of the two little girls reflect the ambiguous role of owls in Cree thought: while Gigi takes fright, Glecia welcomes the owl and accepts its guidance. The same contradictory perceptions of the owl as harbinger of evil and as bearer of benevolent influence are at work in Minnie Fraser's text (cf. also N4), where the hero's grandfather, *macôhow*, visits his daughter's camp in the shape of an owl. An expository discourse on this issue, accompanied by a third example, is offered by Whitecalf 1992, Lecture III.

Local Background

Glecia Bear was born and raised at *kwâkopîwi-sâkahikanihk*, the *Green Lake* of the fur-trade journals, where her sister Gigi and many other members of the family still live; their father, Clem Laliberté, was widely known as a storyteller. Located near the great northerly bend of the Beaver River, Green Lake had been the site of North West Company and Hudson's Bay Company posts at least since 1781, and when, almost a century later, the Red River Métis were forced to find new homes on the Saskatchewan, a number of them went on to settle at this important staging point.

Throughout the 19th century, Green Lake served as a major junction between the transportation routes of the northern rivers and the freight trails of the prairies. The overland trail from Carlton to Green Lake was still in use when Freda Ahenakew was a child at *yêkawiskâwikamâhk* 'at Sandy Lake' (where her father's father, Shem Ahenakew, had been a freighter), and in some places, for example at *kinêpiko-maskotêhk* 'at Snake Plain,' the wagon-ruts are still visible today.

Freighting remained a key occupation well into the twentieth century for those living at the margin of the colonised world, and Glecia Bear recalls her father hauling mail from Big River (on *kinokamâhk* 'at Long Lake' [officially Cowan Lake], not quite halfway from Green Lake to the Saskatchewan River) to Ile-à-la-Crosse. Kin ties, too, link the pivotal settlement at Green Lake to the Cree and Métchif-speaking populations at Ile-à-Ia-Crosse and Buffalo Narrows as well as to the Plains Cree who had eventually taken reserve north of Carlton House (cf. Ahenakew & Wolfart 1987:xi). While some of the latter became Anglican, Green Lake was and is predominantly Roman Catholic.

Amongst the languages spoken at Green Lake, Cree is in competition with Métchif (a term intended to cover the entire language continuum linking Cree to French).

In her pronunciation of proper names such as Joseph, David, Sinclair, etc., Glecia Bear unmistakably uses the stress patterns and the nasalised vowels typical of French. In addition, there are occasional intrusions from Métchif such as *maskêko-litea* 'Labrador tea' (2-13), its Cree prenoun followed by an English noun construed with a French article.

With Cree-Métchif bilingualism a salient aspect of the language situation at Green Lake, it is not surprising that, in Freda Ahenakew's judgment, some of the prosodic patterns of Glecia Bear's speech have a Métchif tinge. (Note, however, that the *r*-metathesis in such words as *lantrens*, which appears twice in 5-13, would attract little notice in contemporary Winnipeg English; an early example is cited by Blain 1989:114.)

Dialect Features

Despite its extreme position, Glecia Bear's dialect is clearly Plains Cree; in contrast to the Woods Cree of Janet Feitz's stories, it has *y* instead of *ð* in such words as *kahkiyaw* 'all,' *yôtin* 'wind,' etc.

It is obvious, at the same time, that her speech represents a northern variety of Plains Cree which is quite distinct from the southern type used by the other Plains Cree speakers in this volume.

Although the variation between *ê* and *î* is too slight and sporadic to be noted in this edition, there is a clear tendency to have *î* instead of the common Plains Cree *ê* in such words as *misakâmê* 'all the way' and *sêskisi-* VAI 'go into the bush,' and often also in the preverb *pê* and in the morpheme *-êyiht-* 'by mental action' and before *y*-initial endings of the VAI conjunct paradigm, e.g., in *ka-pê-itohtêyân* 'for me to go back there.'

Another surface variation which is not documented in the text deserves at least a brief comment here. In many verbs derived with the VTA formative *-h-*, the preceding vowel tends towards *a* instead of the common *i*; this pattern can be observed not only in unstressed position such as the penultimate syllable, following a strong stress, e.g., *kâ-pê-isi-wâpahtahikocik* 'what the others have shown them' (2-22; cf. *wâpahtih-*) or *nikî-wîcahâw* 'I used to help him' (8-28; cf. *wîcih-*), but also under primary stress, as in *ê-nitawi-wayêsahâcik* 'as they go and deceive them' (8-36; cf. *wayêsih-*), and indeed also in the particle phrase *mistaha pîtos* 'very differently' (5-2; cf. *mistahi*).

SUBTLE DIFFERENCES IN sound are less distinct in some contexts than in others. With its status before *i* or *î* patently equivocal, root-initial *y* is typical of many similar indeterminacies in Cree phonology.

To distinguish consistently between examples like *nikî-yîkinikân* 'I used to milk cows' (RL, 9-14, p. 334) and *kî-îkinikêw* 'she used to milk cows' (AL, 9-1, p. 280) is notoriously difficult, and most auditory judgments are not much more reliable even where one of the neighbouring vowels is not homorganic, e.g., *ka-yîkinikêyân* 'for me to milk cows' (RL, 9-14, p. 334). Only the structural evidence of the reduplication pattern in *ê-âh-îkinamawak* 'with me squirting her with milk' (5-4) shows beyond a doubt that Glecia Bear treats this root as beginning in *î* rather than *yî*.

In another case of the same type, the *î*-initial variant is documented, also by the structural evidence of reduplication, in Janet Feitz's compound stem *ê-kakwê-âh-îkatê-wêpahamân* 'as I was repeatedly trying to push it aside' (1-13; cf. *yîkatê*), while Glecia Bear uses a third variant of this root, with initial *wî*, e.g., *ka-wîkatêhtêyâhk* 'for us to walk away' (8-17).

But root-initial *y* is also unstable before *a* and *â*, for example in the particle *yâhki* 'like, as if,' which is most common in Mary Wells's text, or *âhki*, the variant used by Glecia Bear. Even in a verb stem, if a *y*-initial root happens to be preceded by the vowel *î*, as in *ê-kî-âhkisîhocik* 'they used to be dressed lightly' (AL, 9-22, p. 302; cf. *yâhkisihô-*), the record is inherently ambiguous. Only if the stem follows one of the personal prefixes, as in *nitahkitisahwâw* 'I drove [the cow] forward' (5-4; cf. *yahkitisahw-*), does the *t* which intervenes between the prefix and a vowel-initial stem provide clear-cut structural evidence.

SEVERAL OF THE SOUND FEATURES which characterise Glecia Bear's speech are also found in the Swampy Cree dialect of Norway House (and probably elsewhere in northern Manitoba).

Glecia Bear is the only speaker in this volume (but cf. Beardy 1988) consistently to use the variant *poht-* in such stems as *pohtisk-* VTI 'put s.t. on, don s.t.' or *pohtayiwinisê-* VAI 'put one's clothes on' instead of the general Plains Cree form of the root, *post-* (which is here documented for Freda Ahenakew, Irene Calliou, Rosa Longneck, and Mary Wells).

In the particle *anohc* 'now, today,' by contrast, and in a few other words as well (but not, for the most part, in *ohci* and *mihcêt*), Glecia Bear's speech has a cluster of palatal fricative and affricate instead of the preaspirated *c* which is written as *hc* in standard orthography; (for a particularly clear example see 5-7 and 5-9, where an instance of *sîscâskwahonis* is followed by the more common *nisîhcâskwahonis* 'my breast-cloth'). The cluster which occurs from time to time in such words might well be analysed and written as *šč*; but it seems to exhibit a substantially lower degree of friction than is heard in the many instances of diminutive palatalisation (cf. Wolfart 1973:80*b*), where clusters like *st* and *sc* are retracted to a fully palatal point of articulation. This much more general kind of palatalisation, which in Chapter 5 seems especially frequent after *o*, expresses the speaker's compassion towards the referent of the noun or verb, e.g.,

ê-koškopayit, koškomik awa wîsta nisîmis, ...
'My little sister woke up, [the owl] woke her up, too, ...' (5-10);

or the pitiable cow (mentioned three times in this form in 5-13) and her calf: *moštošwa* 'the cow,' *moščošosa* [*sic*] 'the calf.'

Another feature of Glecia Bear's speech reminiscent of Manitoba dialects is the vowel-combination rule which applies when one of the resumptive deictics based on the root *êwakw-* 'that same,' such as *êkwa* 'then,' *êkota* 'there,' *êkosi* 'thus,' *êkospî* 'at that time,' is preceded by a word ending in *a*. While in most Plains Cree dialects the word-final *a* is simply dropped and the word-initial vowel lengthened if it is not already long, in Glecia Bear's dialect the quality of the dropped vowel is reflected in the initial vowel of the following deictic, e.g., *konit âkota* 'just anywhere there' (5-23), or *awâsis*[*a*] *âkota* 'the child there' (8-18).

Although this rule applies in most cases in Glecia Bear's texts, there are a few instances such as *êkw êkota* 'then there' (8-1) or *êkw êkwa* 'and then' (8-10, 8-14) where it might have been invoked and was not. Of course, the general vowel-combination rule, too, is optional and need not be invoked at all, e.g., *êkwa êkosi* 'and thus' (5-19, 8-28).

Glecia Bear's speech also has a number of features which may well be her own or limited to Green Lake rather than being typical of a more widely spoken variety of northern Plains Cree; such questions could be decided only by a much broader survey.

In several particles which for most Plains Cree speakers end in a long vowel followed by *c* or *t*, she occasionally leaves off the dental stop; thus, *tâpiskô* or *tâpiskôc* 'seemingly; as if'; *sôskwâ* or *sôskwâc* 'simply, directly,' *môy wîhkâ* or *môy wîhkâc* 'never.' The form without the final dental occurs even before a vowel, e.g., *sôskwâ ê-kî-sêskisiyan* 'you just went into the bush' (8-9). In all three examples, the apocopated variant is less frequent, even in Glecia Bear's speech, than the one which preserves the final consonant. The only other speaker in this volume to drop final dentals after a long vowel is Janet Feitz, who three times uses *namwâ* 'not' (beside eighteen instances of *namwâc*).

As Voorhis (1981) has stressed, many variant features fail to follow the clean, idealised lines of the major dialect boundaries. The third vowel in the many stems derived from ***kiskinoh-*** / ***kiskinah-*** VTI 'point s.t. out, describe s.t.' may be either *o* or *a*; but the distribution does not follow any simple lines. The first variant is used not only by Glecia Bear but also by Alpha Lafond and Rosa Longneck (both from *maskêko-sâkahikanihk*); the second is that of Janet Feitz (from La Ronge), Freda Ahenakew, Irene Calliou, and Mary Wells.

A LEXICAL VARIANT which is sometimes attributed to more northerly varieties of Plains Cree is the completive particle *sâsay*, beside *âsay*. As Ogg has pointed out (1991:53*n*, 92*n*), both appear in the texts of *nâh-nâmiskwêkâpaw* and *kâ-kîsikâw-pîhtokwêw*, recorded at Sweet-Grass in 1925. In the present volume, however, there is only a single instance of *sâsamîna* (RL, 9-7, p. 300) outside the texts of Janet Feitz (who uses *sâsay* exclusively) and Glecia Bear, who uses both variants side by side; (5-11 provides a good example, with two instances of *âsay* followed by three of *sâsay*). It is impossible to say at this point whether the variation in frequency between Chapter 5, where *âsay* is twice as common as *sâsay* (16:8), and Chapter 8, where the ratio is 1:10, has any significance.

Chapter 5 is the only text, on the other hand, to include a more distant particle of manner built on the stem *an-* 'that' (as in *ana*, *anima*) instead of the general *ômisi* built on the stem *ôm-* 'this' (as in *ôma*), e.g.,

> [...], *otahtahkwâna ôho mân ânis îsi ê-taswêkiwêpinât awa ôhow.*
> '..., as the owl would flap its wings like that [*gesture*].' (5-10);

> *"anis îsi wâskâhtê--, ka-wâskâhtêwak ôkik nâpêwak, ... "*
> ' "Let the men go around that way [*gesture*], ..." ' (5-14).

All seven instances occur in the particle phrase *anis îsi* 'in that way, that is how it is' and are accompanied by gestures.

THE PRONOUNS USED by Glecia Bear are quite distinct from those of the other narrators. Where the other Plains Cree speakers have *ôki, ôhi,* and *aniki* (and Janet Feitz, *ôko*, *ôho*), Glecia Bear has *ôkik*, *ôho,* and *anikik*.

CONJUNCT PLURAL FORMS are marked by both *-ik* and *-wâw* in the texts told by Glecia Bear. The Woods Cree rule which governs the distribution of these two morphemes (as formulated in Voorhis 1981; cf. also Wolfart 1973:49*b*, section 5.481) is illustrated in Janet Feitz's texts: after *k*, the suffix is *-wâw*, and after *t*, it is *-ik*.

Only the second part of this rule holds for Glecia Bear's texts, with *-ik* occurring after *t*. Either *-wâw* or *-ik* may occur after *k*, with the same stem and without obvious syntactic correlates, e.g.,

> *"..., kahkiyaw kîkway môniyâwi-kîkway ê-- ê-pimitisahahkik," itwêw, ...*
> ' "..., they follow every one of the White-Man's things," she said, ...' (2-18);

> *..., itwêw, "ayis môniyâwi-kîkway ê-pimitisahahkwâw," itwêw, ...*
> '..., she said, "for they follow the White-Man's customs," she said, ...' (2-19).

Such parallel clauses may even be part of the same sentence:

> *kahkiyaw ê-kî-pê-nohakik nicawâsimisak, pêyakosâp ê-- ê-ayâwakwâw, kahkiyaw ê-kî-nôhakwâw, ...*
> 'I breastfed all my children, I had eleven and I breastfed all of them, ... (8-30).

Freda Ahenakew regards this pattern as characteristic of the Green Lake dialect and quite distinct from that of Meadow Lake, where *-ik* is reported throughout.

The distribution of these two plural suffixes may, of course, be governed by a syntactic rule which remains to be isolated; in the meantime, the evidence of Glecia Bear's texts suggests a Plains Cree pattern substantially influenced by Woods Cree.

6 *Irene Calliou, Household Chores*

Audiography

Recorded 17 July 1988 at Grouard, Alberta; in the presence of Mary Wells and Freda Ahenakew (FA); recording time 21 minutes.

Biography

Irene Calliou comes from *pakicahwânisihk*, a Métis settlement stretching from Frog Lake eastwards to the Alberta-Saskatchewan border. Since place-names such as Fishing Lake (the English counterpart of the above) are common and not always readily located, it is all the more important to record the Cree place-name and its literal English gloss (here, 'at the Little Net-Fishing Place') in addition to the English common name (which in this case is the same as the official name appearing on topographic maps).

Within a few miles, even a highway map also shows a *Little Fishing Lake* and an *Angling Lake* (with *Jackfish Lake*, farther to the east, known as *kinosêwi-sâkahikanihk* 'at Fish Lake' in Cree). The same pattern is found in the case of *amisko-sâkahikanihk* 'at Beaver Lake': the name by itself does not allow us to determine whether Irene Calliou's grandparents came from Beaver Lake with its Cree-speaking reserve (to the southeast of Lac la Biche) or from Amisk Lake (farther away to the southwest of it) or, indeed, some other lake of the same name.

While English uses a single term for two fundamentally different techniques of fishing, Cree consistently distinguishes *kwâskwêpicikê-* VAI 'fish by rod' and *pakitahwâ-* VAI 'fish by net' (a distinction which may well be reflected in such place-names as *Fishing Lake* and *Angling Lake* or *Lac des Hameçons*).

The Scope of the Text

The recollections which make up this text are broken into many short stretches; as Freda Ahenakew recounts in her biographical vignette, Irene Calliou had to be prodded time and again before she would continue her account.

The text is thus marked by frequent interruptions; when the tape-recorder is turned on again, with the next topic newly reviewed, the opening sentence may well refer back to the unrecorded portion of the discourse. This seems most obvious when the new section begins with an obviative noun (e.g., *kinosêwa* 'fish'),

> *êkwa kinosewa ôh--, wâwikaniwâhk ohc âni--,*
> *ê-kî-mêtawâkêyâhk mâna ...*
> 'And the fish, we used to play with their backbones ... ' (6-11),

instead of the more common proximate plural noun (e.g., *sîsîpak* 'ducks'),

> *êkwa sîsîpak mîna, kâh-nipahâci mâna nimosôm, ...*
> 'And then the ducks, everytime my grandfather had killed them, ... ' (6-7).

In this second example, as in many of the post-break sentences in Irene Calliou's text, a pre-posed topic phrase seems to stand apart, syntactically, from the balance of the sentence.

These start-up sentences following a break are quite distinct in their stylistic form from the earlier paragraph openings, e.g.,

> *êkwa kâ-miyoskaminiyik, ê-kî-mâh-misi-nipahât sîsîpa;*
> 'And in the spring they used to kill lots of ducks;' (6-4),

which typically specify the season by means of an impersonal background clause.

IN PLACING COMMON TERMS in narrowly delimited contexts, the text draws attention to their more specialised senses. The verb *pîkiskwê-* VAI, for example, usually means 'speak, talk' (and this is also the sense it shares with its derivative *pîkîskwât-* VTA 'speak so to s.o.,' which in 6-28 marks one mode of expressing respect for one's Elders).

But in recalling her grandfather's sweat-lodge (6-17), Irene Calliou uses the same stem *pîkiskwê-* in the technical sense, 'speak one's prayers, pray,' juxtaposing it to the more common prayer term *nanâskom-* VTA 'speak thanks to s.o.'

Religious observances may, of course, also be discussed without recourse to technical terms. Irene Calliou recalls how women used to collect *mêstan-* NA 'the cambium or soft inner bark of poplar trees' with which to sustain those participating in the Sun-Dance (6-18), and she recounts (6-25) how her grandmother used to place tobacco into the hole left by digging up seneca-root.

Style

In describing the bounty which her grandfather used to bring home from his hunting and fishing, Irene Calliou shows a clear preference for compound verb stems with the preverb *misi* and heavy reduplication, e.g.,

> *ê-kî-mâh-misi-nipahât sîsîpa*
> 'he used to kill lots of ducks' (6-4),
>
> *ê-kî-mâh-misi-pakitahwât*
> 'he used to catch lots of fish in his net' (6-2).

While these two examples differ syntactically, they have the same semantic structure: in both, the meaning of *misi* IPV 'much, greatly' extends to the referential object, whether it is the explicit noun *sîsîpa* or the implicit object of the VAI stem *pakitahwâ-* 'catch fish by net.' In such INTENSIVE-DISTRIBUTIVE COMPOUNDS, the intensive meaning of *misi* is marked as distributive by the syllable *mâh*, in which the long (and increasingly devoiced) reduplicative vowel follows the initial consonant of the stem being reduplicated.

The pattern of heavy reduplication with its intermittent, distributive meaning (cf. Ahenakew & Wolfart 1983) also appears with stems which are not part of a preverb compound, e.g.,

> *ê-âh-asawâpamâyâhk*
> 'we would [repeatedly] watch for him' (6-4).

The preverb *misi*, similarly, also occurs without reduplication, e.g.,

ê-misi-piminawasot
'cooking lots of food' (6-22).

In fact, the text exemplifies the same stem with either pattern:

… , ê-pê-misi-tahkonât mâna sîsîpa, …
'… , usually carrying back many ducks, … ' (6-4);

… ; ê-kî-miyikoyâhk mâna sîsîpa ka-tahk-—tâh-tahkonâyâhkik.
'… ; he used to give [each of us] [several] ducks to carry.' (6-4).

The combination of these two patterns is especially frequent (there are six instances in this short text) with the two stems *nipah-* VTA 'kill s.o.' and *nipahtâ-* VAI 'kill (it)':

… , ê-mâh-misi-nipahâcik wâposwa;
'…, they [each] killed lots of rabbits [on several occasions];' (6-6);

… , iyikohk mâna ê-kî-- ê-kî-mâh-misi-nipahtât kîkway, êtokwê.
' …, having killed so very many things [*sc.* animals], I guess.' (6-17).

Besides, there are also several instances of compounds such as,

… , miton ê-mâh-mis-ôsîhâcik êkotowahk, …
' …, they [each] used to make many of that kind [repeatedly], … ' (6-21),

… , nôhkom mân ê-ki-mâh-mis-âsamât wiyâs ahpô kinosêwa, …
'… , my grandmother used to give [each of them] lots of meat or fish to eat [on various occasions], … ' (6-22),

which deal with the processing and distribution of the kill.

All of the above examples illustrate a common pattern of the compound undergoing reduplication. The stem *mawiso-* VAI 'gather berries' offers a striking contrast by following the opposite pattern. Although the intensive compound *misi-mawiso-* occurs in 6-9, there is not a single instance of a parallel form which would show the preverb *misi* reduplicated. Instead, there are two instances (also in 6-9) of *misi-mâh-mawiso-*, with the preverb added to a stem which is already reduplicated.

IN FIRST-PERSON COMITATIVE constructions, the first person singular is implicit in the verb form, and the conjoint noun normally appears without any conjunction, postposition or the like:

> ... *ê-awâsisîwiyâhk nimis*, ...
> '...when my elder sister and I were children, ...' (6-3).

Irene Calliou's text includes two instances of an expanded, explicitly coordinate construction with the conjunction *êkwa* and the full pronoun *niya*:

> ... , *êkwa nimis êkwa niya mân ê-kî-nakiskawâyâhk awa nimosôm;*
> '... , and my elder sister and I used to meet my grandfather;' (6-4);

> *êkwa nimis êkwa niya mân ê-kî-mêtawêyâhk sakâhk*, ...
> 'And my elder sister and I used to play in the bush, ...' (6-12).

While the comitative construction is very common indeed (cf. also N4:445–446), the fully symmetrical use of the pronoun is rare and remarkable.

Shifting Obviatives

This text includes a number of passages where shifts in obviation seem particularly abrupt, often lacking the demonstratives or resumptive noun phrases which mark such shifts in narrative prose. (This may, of course, be a stylistic feature reflecting the high degree of hesitation and the frequent interruptions in this text.)

In the following sentence, for instance,

> ... , *êkota mân ê-ki-- ê-kî-ahât kinosêwa ka-- k-âhkwaciyit, ka-mowihcik ka-- kâ-pipohk*, ...
> '... , there he used to put the fish to freeze, to be eaten in the winter, ... ' (6-2),

the obviative noun *kinosêwa* 'fish' is construed with the obviative verb *k[a]-âhkwaciyit* 'that they would freeze' but the subsequent verb, *ka-mowihcik* 'that one might eat them,' is a proximate plural form (rather than the obviative *ka-mowimiht* which might have been expected). Although separated by a prosodic break, it is also not accompanied by a noun phrase of any kind; the context clearly suggests a proximate plural noun phrase such as *ôki kinosêwak*.

With the plural noun *sîsîpak* prominently presented as the topic, the following sentence might have included a fully cross-referenced form of the dependent noun stem *-takisiy-* NDI 'intestine' (which usually occurs in the plural), *otakisîwâwa* 'their guts':

> *êkwa sîsîpak mîna, kâh-nipahâci mâna nimosôm, otakisiya mîna mân ânih ê-kî-kanâcihtâcik, ...*
> 'And then the ducks, every time my grandfather had killed them, they used to clean out the guts, ...' (6-7).

Instead, we are left to appeal to the break and the distance between the topic clause and the possessed noun form, or we might interpret the actually occurring form *otakisiya* as referring to a general possessor (cf. Wolfart 1973:15*b*) and then to be translated as 'the guts' rather than 'their guts' (cf. the use of *miskîsikwa ohci* 'for the eyes' in 6-26 with its reference to an indefinite but human/personal possessor). All this would be more plausible if it were not for counter-examples such as the following,

> *êkwa kinosêwa ôh--, wâwikaniwâhk ohc âni--, ê-kî-mêtawâkêyâhk ...*
> 'And the fish, we used to play with their backbones, ...' (6-11),

with its fully possessive suffix referring to a third person proximate possessor (even though the antecedent noun is obviative).

Finally, there is also remarkable fluctuation between proximate plural and obviative, both expressed by full noun forms (*kinosêwak* and *kinosêwa*) in the first sentence of 6-10, and again in the second sentence, where the *êkw ânih* at the start and the *wahkway[a] ânih* at the end are obviative but the intervening material is in the proximate plural.

Some of these abrupt shifts are perhaps best interpreted as anacolouthic, e.g.,

..., êkwa mês-- mêstan an[a], ê-kî-otinâcik;
'..., and the sap, they used to get it;' (6-18);

in this sentence, the prosodic break, if such it is, is minimal indeed and, in fact, overlaid with external sandhi. A similar example begins with a correction:

..., kotaka -- kotak mîn ê-kî-asamât mâna, ka-kîwêhtatâcik.
'..., and she also used to give them more food, for them to take home.' (6-22).

Instead of the proximate plural verb form *ka-kîwêhtatâcik* 'so that they would take it home with them,' the inherently obviative direct object of *ê-kî-asamât* 'she fed them' might well have been resumed by an obviative verb form such as *ka-kîwêhtatâyit*.

7 *Mary Wells, Fun and Games*

Audiography

Recorded 17 July 1988 at Grouard, Alberta; in the presence of Irene Calliou (IC) and Freda Ahenakew (FA); recording time 40 minutes.

Biographical Background

The childhood reminiscences which Mary Wells has selected from a seemingly unending stream of stories are dominated by the figure of her grandmother. Remembered with special affection and eloquence, her maternal grandmother used the name *iskwêw* for Mary, the first-born of a sizeable family. (In another text, Mary Wells refers to her as an *ocîpwayânîwiskwêw* 'Chipewyan woman' – in the Cold Lake region there is a long tradition of Cree-Chipewyan bilingualism and marriages between Cree and Chipewyan speakers; cf. Wolfart 1990*a*:581.)

The setting for Mary Wells's stories is the newly established Elizabeth Settlement which abuts the provincial border just south of the Beaver River (and north of *pakicahwânisihk*), about halfway between Cold Lake and the North Saskatchewan River. Legal status aside (cf. the Introduction to the Texts, p. 31), the 'Métis Colonies' created by the Province of Alberta under the 'Métis Betterment Act' of 1938 cannot have differed much from the other settlements at the margin of the agricultural domain left to those who had not taken treaty.

Mary Wells's family, which she introduces by listing her parents, siblings and grandmother, and that of her mother's paternal uncle were amongst the first three to settle at Elizabeth. Log-houses are built without delay (7-2) and ultimately even a school (7-8), but it is difficult to attract teachers to such a remote location (7-26); the nearest town is Grand Centre, well over 30 kilometres to the north. There is no mention of a church or of Christian teachings except, possibly, for the causal link between transgression and punishment in (7-2) or the pride Mary and her mother take in cleanliness (7-3); but there is also no mention of Cree ceremonies.

As seems the case with early reserve life in general, Mary Wells's childhood on the Elizabeth Colony is punctuated by isolated innovations superimposed on an overwhelmingly traditional lifestyle. There are rubber overshoes and tin cups and *lamilâs* NI 'syrup' (cf. the more common form *naminâs*) to be used as glue (7-27), but the cigarettes rolled from paper bags are filled with 'red willow' scrapings, and in playing house the little girls are equally interested in making mustard and moccasins decorated with bite-mark patterns.

CHILD'S PLAY often mirrors adult behaviour, and the childhood world recalled in this text constitutes a record which is especially valuable for its inadvertence. Being told in a completely undirected manner, Mary Wells's recollections offer a rare glimpse of such personality traits as assertiveness (7-29) or competitiveness (7-31); an adult illustration of the latter may be found in Peter Vandall's story of 'The Best Dancer' (Vandall & Douquette 1987:92–96).

While the girls play with cut-out paper figures, the boys introduce the first hint of adolescence (7-26) when the doll representing Mary is danced outside, in a standard courtship ploy, by her partner – a scene perceived as funny mainly because of the extreme discrepancy in age.

The first dance to take place in her parents' house, chosen by lottery, makes a deep impression on Mary; but so does the wake held for her grandmother, an old woman of extraordinary stamina and devotion to duty who was still making bannock on the day of her death.

While the remarks on her mother's tanning and sewing are cursory (and rather less engaging than the fate of her father's favourite duck-hunting dog), the text describes in some detail the technique for catching blackbirds and, in particular, her grandmother's prowess in snaring prairie-chickens. It is, in fact, in a culinary context that the incongruity between traditional and colonial cultures is brought into focus most sharply: from a Cree perspective, the notion of ordering rabbit soup in a White restaurant (7-25) is simply hilarious.

Funny as their plots are, it is the performance above all which turns the stories told by Mary Wells into masterpieces. But even the most outrageous tales out of school, about her schemes to make cigarettes and lipstick, at the same time illustrate the charisma of a leader and the assertiveness of a strong personality.

Amongst the character traits which are most highly valued in Cree society is the ability to laugh at one's own misadventures or to tell a joke about oneself (cf. Ahenakew & Wolfart 1987:xiii). In Mary Wells's text, the virtue of self-deprecation defines the episodes dealing with thwarted attempts to steal food (7-2, 7-17) and the grandmother's caustic remark about the dressed-up child (7-11).

Second-hand Stories and Narrative Perspective

The interpretation of a text depends not only on the information contained in the text itself but also on that provided by the context in which it is told.

In her story of the moccasin mistaken for dried meat, 'A Tough Mistake,' Mary Wells begins (7-16) by reporting the words of her husband, Jim Wells, but the opening portion of this section of the text was not recorded and the original narrator is not explicitly identified. The first sentence of 7-17 maintains the ambiguity: while the patient of the stem *âcim-* VTA 'tell about s.o.' is usually the person being told about (as in 7-18: *nôhkom nik-âcimâw* 'I will tell about my grandmother'), it may also be interpreted as the teller or owner of the story. This ambiguity is echoed in the English translation, where the possessive construction whose story I am telling is here to be read subjectively rather than objectively: 'I am (re-)telling the story he told,' not 'the story told about him.'

The cast consists of Jim Wells's older sisters and his younger brother, and it is the younger of Mary Wells's two sisters-in-law who mistakes the hunter's moccasin for her mother's dried meat.

As the story shifts from direct quotation (7-16) to plain narrative (7-17), the first kin-term, *osîmisa* 'his younger sibling,' links the hunter to the original narrator, and this sibling-based perspective remains in force throughout – but with one exception: in introducing the protagonist, Mary Wells calls her *nicâhkos* 'my sister-in-law (woman speaking),' thus for a brief moment leaving the reported perspective and the realm of the four siblings.

This narrator-centred identification may be confusing to the reader who recalls the preceding episode, to which the present one is linked both by the figures of the teacher and her husband and by the kin-terms *nicâhkos* (7-17) and *nitôcâhkosin* 'I have her as my sister-in-law (woman speaking); she is my sister in-law' (7-15). The text itself does not provide the pragmatic information required to establish that the thief is not the same person as the teacher; the genealogical details which Mary Wells provided in response to later queries also confirm her use of the term *ôcâhkosi-* VAI 'have s.o. as one's sister-in-law (woman speaking)' for the wife of her husband's (younger) brother (who had also been her teacher); in Freda Ahenakew's usage, this kin-type is referred to as *niciwâmiskwêw-* NDA 'my female parallel cousin (woman speaking).'

Faithful Translation: Literal or Free?

Although no effort has been spared to keep the translations in this book faithful to the original texts, there are many occasions where a strictly literal translation would mislead the reader rather than illuminate the original meaning it attempts to express in another language.

THE LEVEL OF SPECIFICATION is the most obvious point of semantic discrepancy between any two languages, with biologically-based features offering the clearest examples of (relative) under- or over-specification. The English noun *teacher*, for instance, tells us nothing either about the sex of the referent or about the obligatory choice in grammatical gender between the pronouns *she* or *he*. (The use of 'she' in the translation of the opening sentence of 7-8 is based on a subsequent portion of the text, where two instances of *okiskinohamâkêw*- NA 'teacher' are followed by the specific noun *okiskinohamâkêwiskwêw*- NA 'female teacher' and, ultimately, the phrase *okiskinohamâkêw onâpêma* 'the teacher's husband.') The same ambiguity with respect to sex is found in the Cree kin-term *kisîmis* 'your younger sibling' (7-2); if the English translation is to be idiomatic, a choice between 'brother' and 'sister,' which requires further pragmatic knowledge, is inescapable.

Cree and English often agree, as in the focal reference of the terms *nôhkom* and *my grandmother* where neither language specifies whether it is the maternal or the paternal grandmother who is being identified. They differ in other cases: where English has only the single term *my uncle*, Cree discriminates at all times, obligatorily, between *nôhcâwîs* 'my father's brother' and *nisis* 'my mother's brother' – just as Latin does with the corresponding terms *patruus* and *avunculus*. (It is remarkable that the derivation of the Latin term *patruus* 'father's brother' from *pater* 'father' is exactly parallel to that of the Cree term *nôhcâwîs* 'my father's brother' from *nôhtâwiy* 'my father.')

Would it be due faithfulness to the original, then, to translate *nôhcâwîs* as 'my paternal uncle' in every instance where the term occurs, or would this amount to pedantic excess? The answer to this question – and to countless similar ones – cannot be given once and for all; it depends crucially both on the context constituted by the discourse and on that in which the discourse takes place. For the EXTERNAL context, it makes a difference whether the discourse is part of a casual story-telling session or of the cross-examination in a capital case. The INTERNAL context, on the other hand, is created and defined by the terms and relations which are included in the text itself (and thereby selected from the set of all things that might be said) – the nature of the relations, for example, between the narrator and her paternal uncle and also any intervening members of the family, the relative importance to the narrative of the paternal uncle (who here only figures as the unwitting supplier of some tools), or the contrast between lineal and collateral relatives (father vs uncle), between consanguineals and affinals (father's brother vs mother's sister's husband), full and step-parents or between parallel and cross-uncles (father's brother vs mother's brother).

The third sentence of Mary Wells's text offers a classical example of how, in translation, questions of 'lexical definition' interact with our pragmatic knowledge of the 'real world' and literary aesthetics. In describing the extended family group which moved to Elizabeth Colony in 1939, she lists the members of her own immediate family in four sets:

> *nipâpâ nîtisânak nôhkom êkwa nimâmâ*
> 'my dad and my brothers and sisters, my grandmother and my mom' (7-1).

It is common for Cree nouns to be conjoined, as are *nipâpâ* and *nîtisânak*, without a word meaning 'and,' and the alternative terms *nipâpâ* 'my dad' and *nimâmâ* 'my mom' are freely used alongside the more traditional terms *nôhtâwiy* 'my father' and *nikâwiy* 'my mother.' The translator's problem here lies in the term *nîtisânak*: while the technical term 'sibling', which is common in ethnological and legal discourse, fits the meaning of the Cree word reasonably well, it seems far too elevated and esoteric for such a plain, everyday account. In choosing the more ordinary English phrase 'my brothers-and-sisters,' however, we solve the stylistic problem by imputing siblings of both sexes to a speaker who may, in fact, only have brothers or sisters (or one of either or both). In any translation which goes beyond individual words, pragmatic inaccuracies and distortions of this kind need to be balanced against intelligibility and fluency.

DISCREPANCIES IN SALIENCE present the translator with even thornier problems. In the first of her tales out of school (7-8), Mary Wells relates how the inventive child she was undertook the manufacture of cigarettes and enlisted the help of another girl, who was to bring a hunting-knife to school the next day. She refers to her as *nimis*, a kin-term usually translated as 'my older sister' even though its referents include not only older daughters of the speaker's parents but also those of her father's brother (which in everyday English are called cousins while ethnologists speak of *parallel cousins*). The translation of *nimis* as 'my older sister' need not merely reflect anglocentrism; it also focusses on the close social relationship between the two and attempts to reflect the special intimacy commonly associated in English with the term 'sister.' It is the common English translation of this Cree kin-term.

In both languages, some aspects of the biological relationship are played down while attention is paid to others: in English, there is no reference to the relative age of the protagonists and no distinction is made between parallel cousins (the children of one's father's brother) and cross-cousins (those of one's mother's brother) but separate terms are used to distinguish a sibling from a collateral, *sister* vs *cousin*. In Cree, on the other hand, the term *nimis* specifies that the person referred to is older than the speaker and that she is the daughter of either the speaker's parents or her father's brother. Where it is necessary to go beyond these culturally coded selections from the biological grid, speakers of either language tend to rely on the genealogical steps, taken one by one; later in Mary Wells's text, for example, when the child Mary again enlists the help of the same girl – this time the scheme is to manufacture lipstick – she introduces her as

> *nimis, nôhcâwis otânisa*
> 'my older sister-*cum*-parallel-cousin, [i.e.,] my parallel uncle's daughter' (7-13),

thereby specifying the genealogical particulars which are ignored in the normal kin-term, *nimis*.

The referential mismatch between the Cree term *nimis* and the English terms *sister* or *cousin* may be diagrammed as follows:

	SEX		AGE		DEGREE		LINK	
	f	m	+	–	lineal	collateral	parallel	cross
nimis	*x*		*x*				*x*	
sister	*x*				*x*	–		
cousin					–	*x*		

In this diagram the essential features only are marked by an *x*, with the optional or irrelevant features left blank; the dashes indicate interpretations which are excluded. There is an obvious lack of overlap between the Cree original and the two attempts at rendering it into English.

As the present discussion shows, it is entirely feasible to analyse and explicate these discrepancies between languages dispassionately and without resorting to simplistic (and often chauvinistic) interpretations of one as simpler or more complex than the other. But such discussions take time and space and often go well beyond the scope of a normal dictionary entry. And even where a referentially explicit rendition (e.g., of *nimis* as 'my older sister, my older female parallel cousin') suitable for a glossary can be achieved, it would be unspeakably awkward in the translation of a running text.

In a relatively free translation, therefore, which aims to be literary rather than literal, the Cree term *nimis* would usually be translated as 'my older sister' – but in the two passages under discussion (7-8, 7-13), where the referent is further specified, we chose instead the English phrase 'my older cousin,' leaving it to the pronoun 'she' to express the fact that this cousin is also female.

QUESTIONS OF SEMANTIC STRUCTURE and literary style aside, the immediate reason for this choice, which adds information in one respect and omits or obscures it in another, is to be found in the related term *nôhcâwîs* 'my parallel uncle, my paternal uncle.'

This term plays a key role in Mary's instructions to her older cousin:

> *êkwa nititâw aw âya, nim-- nimis aya, "pêtâhkan itâp aya, nôhcâwîs ayi, omâcîwihkomân wâpahki."* (7-8)

As reported in direct quotation, she tells her to bring the hunting-knife belonging to *nôhcâwîs* to school the next day. The literal translation of *nôhcâwîs* 'my father's brother, my parallel uncle, my paternal uncle' would not only be clumsy; it also obscures the fact that it is **her father's** hunting-knife which the other girl is asked to bring. (The referential identity of the man whose hunting-knife is to be brought to school is not at issue; but for the shortest path leading to this point from the position of the narrator, the biological grid offers a choice: reckoning in genealogical steps, one can either move UP first (from the girls' generation to that of their parents) and then ACROSS (from one sibling [or parallel cousin] to another), or one can move ACROSS first and then UP. The Cree original reflects the first path and, thus, a speaker-centred perspective; the English translation requires the second and, thus, a perspective centred on the addressee.)

Unless the relationship between the other girl and the owner of the hunting-knife is made explicit, the story will make little sense in translation – why should 'my older sister' bring along 'my paternal uncle's' hunting-knife? Only if we translate *nimis* as 'my cousin' and then maintain the perspective appropriate to English in translating *nôhcâwîs* as 'your father' can we hope to make the events intelligible to the English-speaking reader.

In terms of the overall narrative, to be sure, this is a very minor matter. With respect to translation strategies and conventions, on the other hand, it is a matter of crucial significance: the context forces us to translate a term which means 'my paternal uncle' as 'your father' – not a minor matter under any circumstances.

In order to achieve greater transparency in the free translation, we sometimes have no alternative, it appears, but to commit and tolerate a gross mistranslation at the literal level. (Not all examples are as complex as Mary Wells's kinship reckoning: in describing the preparation of rabbits (9-10, p. 320; cf. N9:491), Rosa Longneck refers to their extremities as *ospiconisiwâwa* 'their little arms' where English usage requires the term 'legs.')

Trade-offs of this kind tend to be troubling, to speakers of the language and to philologists alike, even when they are unavoidable; going beyond questions of translation practice, they highlight fundamental differences in perspective between two languages such as Cree and English.

A final variation which further complicates the present case is, in fact, more elegantly treated under the free-translation strategy chosen here. Just as the traditional term *nôhtâwiy* 'my father' is being replaced in some contexts by *nipâpâ* 'my dad,' so the diminutive derivative *nôhcâwîs* with its specialised meaning 'my paternal uncle' is paralleled by a neologistic term *nipâpâsîs* (7-8), which refers to the same kin-type and would be awkward to distinguish in translation – except in our free translation which renders the former as 'your father' and the latter as 'your dad' in the specific context of Mary Wells's text.

8 *Glecia Bear, A Woman's Life*

Audiography

Recorded 25 November 1988 at the house of her daughter Leona Derocher on Flying Dust Reserve, Meadow Lake; in the presence of Leona Derocher (LD) and, at the end, Emile Laliberté (EL), Glecia Bear's brother, and of Freda Ahenakew (FA); recording time 39 minutes.

As the first of three told in a single session, this text has a formal introduction, with the narrator's Cree name, *nêhiyaw*, followed by its conventional counterpart in English, *Mrs Glecia Bear*.

Biography

Glecia Bear (née Laliberté) raised eleven children of her own and, by her own count (8-31), about fifteen others. Even without the back-breaking work she did both in her own household and in the wage-labour market (listed in 2-2 and detailed here, beginning in

8-21), she would not have had much time left for the children of today who, as she puts it with ironic disdain, expect to sleep like royalty (8-7).

All of her eleven children were born at home and under conditions which no one could describe more drastically than she herself.

MARRIED OFF at the age of sixteen to a man she had not seen before, she vividly recalls both the blanket under which they slept and the terror she felt at having to live amongst strangers. She gives special prominence to her mother-in-law, whose advice she had to seek (8-15) on even the most elementary aspects of a woman's life.

Her grandmother's teachings were apparently restricted to the domain of proper behaviour – not to answer back to one's parents (8-33), not to speak to a man (8-32), not to leave one's children behind (8-31):

> *...; wiya nikî-pê-wîhtamâkonân nôhkominân, tânisi ka-kî-isi-pimâtisiyâhk.*
> '...; for our grandmother had told us how we should live.' (8-33).

HOLDING STRONG VIEWS on infant care, Glecia Bear expresses them with vigour and flair. She excoriates the modern reliance on bottlefeeding,

> *manitow ê-kî-miyikoyahk mitôhtôsima ita ka-ohci-pimâcihâyahkik awâsisak; êwako niya nikî-pimitisahên.*
> 'God has given us breasts with which to give life to our children; as for me, I have followed that.' (8-30),

and in a few brief sentences proclaims a psychology of common sense:

> *kâ-mâtoyit, sâsay mosti-tôhtôsâpoy, ê-asiwatâcik ê-mosci-miyâcik, môy tahkonâwasowak, môy kitimâkêyi--, êwak ôhc ânohc kâ-kîsikâk kâ-- iyikohk kâ-wêpinâcik ocawâsimisiwâwa. kayâs kî-tahkonâw awâsis ê-nônit, ê-wa-ocêmat, ê-ta-tahkonat, ê-ay-âpahwat; anohc môy êwakw ânima kîkway ispayiw.*

'When the baby cries, they immediately put cow's milk into a bottle and simply give that to the baby, they do not hold the child, they do not love--, that is the reason why they abandon their children so much today. In the old days the baby used to be held while suckling, you kissed it and held it and you unbundled it; today none of that happens.' (8-30).

She ends with a scornful indictment:

môy kâh-kî-- môy kâh-kî-itwêwak anikik, ôkik wiyawâw osk-âyak anohc kâ--, kâ-nihtâwikihâcik awâsisa, wiyawâw ka-ocawâsimisicik ka-itwêcik ocawâsimisiwâwa, moscoswa ê-pê-ohpikihtamâkocik anihi awâsisa; ayis mostos ana kâ-pimâcihât anihi awâsisa kâ-nihtâwikiyit.

'These young women who give birth to a child today, they could not claim to be the ones to have the child and to call it their child, the cows have raised the child for them; for the cows have given life to the child which has been born.' (8-30).

Kin Terms

In addressing Freda Ahenakew as *nitôsimiskwêm* 'my niece' (8-1), Glecia Bear acknowledges the term *nikâwîs* 'my aunt' by which she had been introduced.

These two terms illustrate another dialect discrepancy between Green Lake, where *nitôsimiskwêm* 'my parallel niece' is matched by the reciprocal term *nitôsis* 'my parallel/maternal aunt,' and ordinary Plains Cree, where the corresponding terms are *nikâwîs* and *nitânis*. (In fact, Freda Ahenakew recalls a recent occasion when, during a visit to *maskêko-sâkahikanihk*, Glecia Bear addressed her as *nitânis*.)

In common Plains Cree, the children of a woman's sister are terminologically equivalent to her own, and the same is true reciprocally for one's mother's sister for whom the diminutive term *nikâwîs* (cf. *nikâwiy* 'my mother') is used. The distinct and specific terms used by Glecia Bear are also reported in some of the early sources and for modern Red Earth (on the Carrot River, roughly halfway between Fort à la Corne and the Pas; cf. Meyer 1985).

In generational distance, the Cree kin terms correspond directly to their English counterparts; in Cree, however, the pair of sisters on which these terms are based is not restricted (as it is in English) to the first ascending generation. Glecia Bear's mother was the younger sister of Marie-Rose Morin, the mother of Freda Ahenakew's mother; the sisters' father was the *nâcowêw* / Pierre Morin whom Glecia Bear mentions in 5-22.

With Glecia Bear addressed as *nikâwîs*, Freda Ahenakew uses the term *nisîmis* 'my younger sibling' for Leona Derocher, Glecia Bear's daughter.

In using the English phrase *my uncle* (5-13) for both her parallel/paternal uncle Charlie and her cross/maternal uncle Payette, Glecia Bear replicates in English a pattern which is also prominent in Métchif of combining kin terms with personal names when collapsing a distinction fundamental to the kinship system of Cree. (This pattern is richly illustrated in texts collected at Ile-à-la-Crosse and Buffalo Narrows; cf. Hogman 1981.)

Even though he apparently lived at Meadow Lake, *my uncle, Charlie Laliberté* was her father's brother (cf. Plains Cree *nôhcâwîs*), while *my uncle Payette* refers to her mother's brother (cf. Plains Cree *nisis*), Payette Morin, who lived at Green Lake.

Marriage

The text reverberates with the anguish of a girl being given over to a stranger and his family:

> *môy ôm âhpô ê-nisitawêyimak awa nâpêw, kâ-wîkihtahikawiyân.*
> 'I did not even know the man whom it was arranged that I would marry.' (8-10)

Unwilling but obedient like so many of her generation, Glecia Bear evidently had no say in the matter.

A CREE WOMAN'S MARRIAGE was traditionally arranged by her father or, failing that, her (older) brother. The normal term for this arrangement, *mêki-* VAI 'give (it/him) out,' reflects the father's perspective.

This term is freely used for all manner of goods which might be given away, e.g.,

> ..., Hudson's Bay *wiy ôhci sôskwâ mîciwin ê-mêkihk.*
> '..., for the food had simply been given out by the Hudson's Bay.' (5-15);

> ...; *êkwa mân îsk-- iskwêwak mâna ê-kî-mêkicik, ...*
> '...; and the women used to give it [*sc.* dried moss] out as a gift, ... ' (6-15);

> ..., *kâ-miyi-- kâ-mêkihk wiy âyis anihi, aya.*
> '..., when those [*sc.* glasses], of course, are provided free [*sc.* by Health-and-Welfare].' (FA, 9-25, p. 364).

This is also the term used for the modern give-away ritual (an earlier form of which is described in Mandelbaum 1940:275–276).

Whether it shows a personal agent like 'I' or 'they' or takes the indefinite agent form (as in the first and last example above), the VAI stem *mêki-* is construed with a LOOSELY LINKED patient noun phrase which may be expressed by a full noun (e.g., *mîciwin* 'food' in the first example above) or pronominally (e.g., *anihi* 'those' in the last example above and *kahkiyaw kîkway* 'everything' in the first below), but which may also be left implicit (as in the second example above).

Very commonly, the VAI stem *mêki-* 'give (it/him) away' is used alongside the VTA stem *miy-* 'give (it/him) to s.o.'; note the word fragment in the preceding example and the fully developed parallel in the following:

> *kahkiyaw kîkway kikî-pê-miyikonaw, ..., kahkiyaw ... kîkway ê-kî-pê-mêkit.*
> 'He [*sc.* God] has given us everything, ..., He has been giving out everything.' (2-16).

In its semantic range, finally, *mêki-* seems to correspond primarily to possession; but Glecia Bear herself provides a classic example (cf. N5:449) which shows that it may also focus on control and the release of control.

This is the stem which serves as the standard technical term for an arranged marriage. Besides the basic stem *mêki-* there are derived stems with the medial formative *-iskwêw-* 'woman' (followed by the verb-formative *-ê-*) and correspondingly more specific meanings, e.g., *mêkiskwêwê-* VAI 'give a woman away, arrange marriage for a woman' or *mêkiskwêwêm-* VTA 'give a woman to s.o. in marriage' (as in *ê-kî-mêkiskwêwêmikawiyân* 'I was given a woman to marry,' a salient phrase once again reflecting a man's perspective).

While differing slightly in specificity, *mêki-* and *mêkiskwêwê-* are entirely parallel in scope and syntax, e.g.,

> *awas, ê-kî-mêkihk anima niya, ...*
> 'Go on, in fact I was given away, ... ' (RL, 9-8, p. 266);
>
> *..., êtikwê êkot[ê] êkwa awa nipâpâ kâ-mêkiskwêwêt niya.*
> ' ..., it must have been there that my dad arranged to marry me off.' (8-10).

In both examples, the patient noun phrase which stands in loose linkage with the VAI stem is the personal pronoun *niya* 'I, me'. These two examples are all the more remarkable as they include fully expressed noun phrases for both agent and patient.

They are paralleled by an equally remarkable sentence with the VTA stem *miy-*:

> *... , êkâ ê-nisitawêyimak aw âwiyak kâ-miyiht niya, ka-wîkimak.*
> ' ... , since I did not know this person to whom I had been given, for me to be married to him.' (8-10).

While the patient or recipient of the indefinite agent form *kâ-miyiht* is specified by the noun phrase *aw âwiyak* 'this one, this someone,' the stem *miy-* also permits the gift itself to be expressed by a noun phrase standing in LOOSE linkage, and again it is the pronoun *niya*; TIGHT linkage is resumed in the concluding verb *ka-wîkimak* with its first-person agent and third-person patient.

THE QUESTION OF CONTROL is brought to a point in an autobiographical aside (in Chapter 9), arising quite incidentally from a discussion of personal adornment. When a remark about her husband's accomplishments as a craftsman leads to some gentle banter amongst the three women, Rosa Longneck responds forcefully:

> *awas, ê-kî-mêkihk anima niya, môy ânima ê-ohci-pakitinisoyân, êkota.*
> 'Go on, the fact is that I was given away, the fact is that I did not have a choice in the matter.' (9-8, p. 310).

Her statement consists of two factive clauses, and their declamatory effect is heightened by the use of the particle *anima* instead of *ôma* (cf. Ahenakew 1987:153–159).

In her confirmatory question, Freda Ahenakew returns to the key issue of control:

> *ê-kî-mosci-mêkihk ?*
> 'You were simply given away?' (9-8, p. 310).

The use of 'you' in the English translation is an attempt to replicate the ambivalence of the original. With the agent indefinite (a construction often rendered into English as passive) in either case, the question may echo the personal patient (i.e., Rosa Longneck) of the previous sentence; in the alternative interpretation (i.e., 'one was simply given away') it would refer to women in general.

ALTHOUGH A YOUNG WOMAN'S freedom of choice seems to have been severely restricted, textual accounts of courtship behaviour suggest that traditional Cree life must also have allowed some scope for personal preferences. The same is implied by the reflexive stem *pakitiniso-* VAI 'allow (it) for oneself' in the previous example, or in Freda Ahenakew's next question:

> *awîna mâk ê-kî-itêyimoyan?*
> 'Who did you have in mind, then?' (9-8, p. 310).

Instead of the explicitly transitive stem *itêyim-* VTA 'think so of s.o.,' she chose the stem *itêyimo-* VAI 'think so with respect to oneself, think so in one's own interest,' derived by the middle suffix *-o-* 'by oneself, for oneself' (cf. Wolfart 1973:73*a*).

A stronger sense of self-determination is conveyed by a remark reported by Glecia Bear:

kâ-miskamâsoyan awiyak, nâpêw, ka-wîkimat, ...
'When you found someone, a man for yourself to marry, ... ' (2-20).

The stem *miskamâso-* VAI 'find (it/him) for oneself, which has the same specialised meaning in the example below, focusses on the result rather than on the process. (Alpha Lafond, by contrast, in her comments (9-12, p. 328) employs terms like *patinikê-* VAI 'miss things, make a mistake' and *nawasônikê-* VAI 'pick things, make a selection'; cf. also 9-25, p. 364.) Looking back wistfully at what might have been,

kîspin mîna kî-pê-miskamâsoyân, ...
'And also if I had found someone for myself, ... ' (9-12, p. 328),

Rosa Longneck uses this stem in the grammatical form of an unfulfilled past condition.

9 *Alpha Lafond & Rosa Longneck, Reminiscences of Muskeg Lake*

Audiography

Recorded 13 April 1988 at the band office on *opitihkwahâkêw's* reserve at *maskêko-sâkahikanihk*; in the presence of Freda Ahenakew (FA) and Colleen Youngs (who, not speaking Cree, restricted herself to the role of a silent observer); recording time ca. 140 minutes.

Biography

Born and raised at *maskêko-sâkahikanihk* 'at Muskeg Lake,' Alpha Lafond (née Venne) spent a number of years at St Michael's, the

Roman Catholic residential school at Duck Lake, and then for a time worked off the reserve before returning home.

Rosa Longneck (née Lafond) also was born and raised at *maskêko-sâkahikanihk* and has lived there for her entire life. (Her father's brother, Andrew Lafond, was the father of Auguste Lafond, Alpha Lafond's father-in-law.) She did not speak any English until her school-age children began to teach it to her.

Freda Ahenakew was born and raised on *atâhk-akohp*'s reserve at *yêkawiskâwikamâhk* 'at Sandy Lake' but lived at *maskêko-sâkahikanihk* for much of her adult life.

IN PRINTING THEIR DIALOGUE, we have tried to keep the space set aside for editorial matters to a minimum; the three speakers are therefore identified only by the initials of their first names:

A: Alpha Lafond
R: Rosa Longneck
F: Freda Ahenakew

Editorial Conventions

This text is, above all, a dialogue. While there are some narrative and declamatory passages, they are embedded in a constantly shifting exchange of queries, remarks, comments, asides, etc.; for the most part, it seems, the dialogue takes the form of questions (real or rhetorical) and answers. Fragmentary sentences and overlapping speech are typical features of such a DIALOGUE TEXT.

Where the speakers interrupt one another in the heat of the discussion, or when two sentences (full or fragmentary) are uttered simultaneously and with roughly equal force, it may be difficult to determine whether one of the speakers dominates the discourse, with the other(s) constituting the audience, or whether their roles are best treated as equivalent.

More commonly, however, one of the speakers clearly takes the lead and the others acknowledge the fact by offering confirmatory comments which range from single particles to brief sentences.

The editorial and typographical presentation of the text is based on a fundamental distinction between stretches of discourse where the speaker's flow is INTERRUPTED and others where it CONTINUES, largely unaffected by comments or attempts at intervention. (The examples discussed below are from the first two pages of 9-7; it should hardly require mention that the distinctions outlined, although clear enough in principle, are by no means always sharply and unambiguously recoverable in the actual text.)

WHERE THE DOMINANT SPEAKER continues, the interjections, comments, and attempted interventions are printed as part of the continuous discourse, but set apart typographically by smaller type and by being enclosed in parentheses (and preceded by a speaker code). In A's opening sentence (p. 294), R's comments illustrate three distinct types; first a full sentence, then a single-word phrase (followed by a confirmatory particle) and, finally, a confirmatory particle by itself.

Where speakers simply take turns, no special symbols (beyond the appearance of the speaker code on a new line) are required. The first two sentences by R and A which follow A's opening sentence are full-fledged parts of the dialogue but the same pattern also appears in the indented asides. Overlapping speech is awkward to present graphically (and also often difficult to identify and interpret). While simultaneously produced utterances might be vertically aligned, like voices in a musical score, this form of visual presentation could easily give the impression of adding yet further levels of indentation; instead, as the above example shows, we have chosen the expedient of underscoring the simultaneous stretches of speech.

WHERE THE SPEAKER (whether dominant or as one amongst equals) is interrupted, the fragmentary nature of the sentence is indicated by a dash or by parentheses.

The simple dash, –, is used to mark a syntactic or rhetorical break which differs prosodically from those marked by a comma or semicolon while still falling clearly within the sentence. An insertion is marked by parentheses, (xxxx); if it is long, the parentheses are combined with dashes, (– xxxx xxxx xxxx –) ; as the first few pages of

9-7 illustrate, insertions may range from a single word or phrase to a lengthy discussion (including interventions by the other speakers) of background material.

When the speaker interrupts herself, the fragmentary word or sentence is identified as such by a wave-hyphen, ~. The same symbol also marks external interruptions which occur most commonly when the audio-recorder is switched off; it re-appears, correspondingly, when a sentence begins before the recorder has started to record.

The interruption by an interlocutor which is typical of dialogue is marked by a dash followed by a raised circle, -°; where the original sentence is resumed after the interruption, the same symbol re-appears at the beginning of the resumed speech. In the example in the middle section of p. 296, R herself begins to elaborate on the metaphorical use of *nicâhkos* in the question addressed to her but then awaits the completion of A's intervention before proceeding.

THE TRANSLATION REFLECTS the casual style, corresponding to its overall form and content, of this dialogue text. It is less formal, and much closer to the vernacular, than the translations in Parts I and II, and also less literal.

The initial translation of this text was prepared by Dolores Sand.

The Scope of the Dialogue

In recalling the incidents of life as it used to be at the edge of the northern plains, the speakers roam over a wide range of topics – from arranged marriages and abusive treatment of women to technical terms for elevated blood-sugar levels and the interplay of traditional and school medicine. Most aspects of the text require fuller treatment than is possible here; in particular, no attempt is made to deal with such realia as the construction of wagons and sleighs or the genealogies evoked by a host of proper names and kin-terms; in neither case could the structural complexities be presented without appeal to elaborate technical drawings.

Many topics are discussed more than once in the course of the dialogue text, and the section headings will at least serve as a general guide. The subject of childbirth, for example, is touched upon in

9-4 and mentioned incidentally in 9-12 and 9-28 and in the briefest of autobiographical passages which appears at the end of 9-8; at the same time, the technical terms, casually used in a natural setting, are most valuable additions to those elicited for Atimoyoo et al. 1987 (cf. also Wolfart & Ahenakew 1987*b* and Wolfart 1989).

There is a clear distinction in context and register, for instance, between the indefinite agent phrase *kâ-wî-opêpîmihk*, which seems a perfect match for the rather neutral English expression 'during pregnancy', and the much more personal plaint, *tâpitawi pikw ê-asiwacikêyân* 'with me always being pregnant' with its idiomatic use of the stem *asiwacikê-* VAI 'put things in'.

Note also the standard midwifery terms: if a woman is not 'attended' (*pamin-* VTA), 'looked after' (*kanawêyim-* VTA) or 'assisted' (*wîcih-* VTA) at childbirth by a midwife (often her mother or maternal aunt) or her husband, she will 'help herself' (*wîcihiso-* VAI), counting on also 'being helped by the Powers' (*wîcihikowisi-* VAI); remarkably, not one of these terms is restricted to the context of childbirth.

ANY SERIOUS ATTEMPT to understand the traditional patterns of Cree life has to be based on linguistic and cultural approaches at once.

The dialogue text abounds in terms for commercial transactions (to be discussed elsewhere) and in culinary terminology embedded in uncommonly detailed descriptions of how various foodstuffs have traditionally been prepared.

The most common method of preserving meat is by drying, and for that purpose it is cut into thin sheets; the verb stems,

pânisw- VTA 'cut s.o. (e.g., a moose) into sheets'
pânis- VTI 'cut s.t. (e.g., meat) into sheets'
pânisâwê- VAI 'prepare meat cut into sheets',

occur throughout the volume, notably with reference to a moose in Chapter 4, but only here (9-10) is it made explicit that the same technique is applied to rabbits and other small animals (and even to fish) as well.

The ambiguity of contemporary Cree life, precariously balanced between bush and city, is splendidly symbolised in the step-by-step instructions (9-10) for preparing and boiling a beaver to be served, whether as stew or in the form of a terrine, with onions and pepper. It is less obvious in dishes such as *pitikonikanâpoy-* NI 'meatball soup' or *sikwatahikanâpoy-* NI 'minced-meat soup' and in terms such as *sikwatah-* VTI 'pound s.t.,' which refers both to the age-old method of pounding meat into small bits and to the commercially processed 'minute steak.'

Instead of the common term *pimîhkân-* NI 'processed grease, pemmican,' which does not appear in this text, A and R alike use the term for 'pounded meat,' *îwahikan-* NA both for the crumbs into which the sheets of dried meat are pounded and for the finished product of pounded meat mixed with grease and berries or, nowadays, raisins.

Many of the food processing terms in the dialogue are based on the root *sikw-* 'reduce to small bits':

sikwaht- VTI 'chew s.t. until small'
sikon- VTI 'crush s.t. (by hand) until small'
sikwah- VTI 'crush s.t. by tool until small'
sikwatah- VTI 'pound s.t. (by tool with handle) until small'
  sikwatahikâtê- VII 'be pounded until small'
  sikwatahikanâpoy- NI 'minced-meat soup'
sikokahw- VTA 'chop s.o. (e.g., a beaver) small'
sikosâwât- VII 'slice s.t. (e.g., an onion) small'
sikopayi- VII 'be reduced to small bits'
sikwâciwaso- VAI 'be boiled so as to fall into small bits'.

Except for the compound *kwayâci-sikwahikâtê-* VII 'be pre-pounded' (with a neologistic meaning 'pounded [but not reduced to small bits)' which may well reflect interference from English), the above set is semantically straightforward.

A much more complex set is made up of the various terms for fat and grease in which the primary distinction appears to be that of processing:

wiyinw- NI [sg. or pl.] 'fat, piece of fat' [unprocessed]
pimiy- NI [usually sg.] 'grease' [rendered].

With such recent meanings as 'gasoline' and 'petroleum' left aside, the latter may be further specified:

âhkwaci-pimiy- NI 'hard grease'
[congealing when cold, found in association with the internal organs]
iyinito-pimiy- NI 'ordinary grease'
often in the diminutive: *iyinico-pimîs-*
[less easily congealed, found elsewhere (especially in association with muscle tissue) and including bone-marrow or 'marrow-fat']
sîkosâkan- NA [usually pl.] 'cracklings, greaves'
[incompletely rendered pieces of fat or the solids remaining at the end of the process of rendering].

The subordinate status which this hierarchy assigns to *sîkosâkan-* remains tentative, and there is some fluctuation even with respect to the primary dimension of the semantic field.

The terminology of the cooking process itself is very rich but the primary techniques of traditional cookery, as is made quite plain in 9-15, are boiling (e.g., *pakâsim-* VTA 'boil s.o. in water') and roasting (e.g., *nawacî-* VAI 'make a roast').

The dialogue contains many examples of more specialised terms:

sikwâciwaso- VAI 'be boiled so as to fall into small bits'
sêkwâpiskin- VTA 'place s.o. in the ashes, in the oven'
sêkwâpiskin- VTI 'place s.t. in the ashes, in the oven'
kâspihkas- VTI 'heat s.t. until crisp';

and, in particular, for dealing with liquids:

pakastawêhw- VTA 'place s.o. in a liquid'
kohtân- VTA 'immerse s.o. (e.g., a piece of ice) in liquid'
manah- VTI 'skim s.t. (e.g., grease, cream) off a liquid'

mêskotâpin- VTI 'change s.t. (e.g., the water) in boiling'
mêskotôn- VTI 'exchange s.t.'.

But two key terms have the most comprehensive range of stems illustrated in the text:

pakâsim- VTA 'boil s.o. (e.g., a beaver) in water'
pakâhtâ- VAI 'boil (it) in water'
pakâhcikê- VAI 'boil things in water'
pakâso- VAI 'be boiled in water'
pakâhtê- VII 'be boiled in water';
osw- VTA 'keep s.o. (e.g., cracklings) at the boil'
os- VTI 'keep s.t. (e.g., water) at the boil'
oso- VAI 'be at the boil (e.g., cracklings)'
ohtêpayi- VII 'be at the boil (e.g., water), bubble'.

While the semantic differentiation between the two sets is by no means simple, the first has a solid immersed in water (which need not even be hot or in a pot; cf. *pakâsimo-* VAI 'immerse oneself in water, swim'); the element defining the second set appears to be an actively bubbling liquid. This analysis finds support in the second element of the derived stem *ohtêpayi-*, the form *niwa-oswâwak* 'I was keeping them at the boil' with its light reduplication (cf. Ahenakew & Wolfart 1983), and the compound *pôn-ôsowak* 'they stopped boiling' which suggests a much more abrupt cessation of the process than the stem *pakâso-* would seem to imply.

Cooking terms occur throughout this book but they are especially thick in 9-10 and 9-15. Similar sets of technical terms and word families of various kinds can be found for many other topics in a discourse ranging from traditional wisdom and personal grief to funny stories and technical descriptions – and none more specific than Rosa Longneck's splendid account (9-26) of soap-making.

WHILE THE NEED TO COMBINE linguistic and ethnographic approaches is obvious in matters of technology, reliance on both taken together is no less important in the analysis of social patterns. In a brief but striking example, F seeks to place a visitor mentioned by A (9-11) in the kinship network as *kistim* 'your daughter-in-law,' but A corrects her and identifies the visitor as *nistimihkâwin* 'my daughter-in-*common*-law.'

The derivational suffix is more elaborate than the *-ihkân-* found in nouns such as *askîhkân-* NI 'reserve,' *pîsimohkân-* NA 'clock' or *-îpitihkân-* NDI [usually plural] 'false teeth' and the corresponding verbal suffix *-ihkê-*, as in *pahkwêsikanihkê-* VAI 'make bannock' or *nîmihitowinihkê-* VAI 'hold a dance' (or in such further derivatives as *wâtihkât-* VTA 'dig a hole for s.t.,' *mênikanihkâkê* VAI 'use (it) to make a fence' or *oskîsikohkâ-* VAI 'have an apparatus for one's eyes, wear glasses'); but it is clearly the same element *-ihkê/â-* which appears in all of these, characterising an arrangement or contrivance.

The measurement of time is a complex matter which is especially well illustrated in Rosa Longneck's contributions to the dialogue. In recalling the year in which the treaty payment came to $10 instead of the normal amount of $5, she specifies it as follows:

> – *êkospî ê--, ê-nîsicik aniki piko awâsisak, niyanân.*
> '– at that time, we only had the two children.' (9-16, p. 340).

The same principle of expressing time by reference to one's children is employed to fix the date of a visit:

> *nikî-nitawi-wâpamâw ôta kayâsîs (mêkwâc nipêpîm aw âwa osîmimâs awa,* four *êtikwê,* four or five *ê-itahtopiponwêt), nikî-nitawi-wâpamâw ana nikâwîs.*
> 'I had gone to see her quite some time ago (my baby, the youngest, must have been four, four or five years old at the time), I had gone to see that aunt of mine.' (9-23, p. 360).

In the most elaborate example (9-9), Rosa Longneck lists those of her children who survived infancy in serial order: two daughters lost in a car accident, Jim, Gabe, the late Dorothy, Virginia, and Lloyd (and omitting three more too young to be relevant to the count). The entire calculation was undertaken, in response to a direct question, in order to establish the age and relative position of *ana nitânis, kâ-wiyinot ana* 'that daughter of mine, the fat one,' who in turn had been introduced merely as a means of dating the acquisition of a crushing-stone: the Cree phrase *ê-wîc-ôhcîmat ana nitânis* and its literal translation, 'that daughter of mine hails from the same time as it' exhibit a perspective which differs radically from that of the free translation required for English: 'I got it at the time that daughter of mine was born.'

AS THE ABOVE EXAMPLES show, live texts offer a great deal of cultural information which is rarely obtained by elicitation; at the same time, this information is not always readily recognised by the casual reader. After Rosa Longneck arrives for the dialogue recording and is introduced, Freda Ahenakew addresses her as follows:

> *awa s--, awa kiki sôniyâs ê-kîskisamâkawiyan.* (9-6, p. 292).

That the second instance of the demonstrative pronoun *awa* refers to tobacco, ritually presented to someone whose favour is being sought, is confirmed by the verb stem *kîskisamaw-* VTA 'cut (it/him) off for s.o.,' which is the standard term for the presentation of tobacco. Instead of the literal translation,

> *'This m--, this along with some money is being cut off for you.'*

this sentence calls for a free translation which is culturally appropriate,

> *'Here is the tobacco for you, and also some money.'*

Only rarely are the formal transactions which are required at the beginning and end of a story-telling session recorded on tape and included in the published edition of the text.

With respect to the related issue of informed consent, the text preserves Freda Ahenakew's declaration of intent:

> *...; ê-wî-masinahamân ayisk ôma kititwêwiniwâwa. ..., mitoni ê-ay-itwêyêk mâna, nikakwê-- nikakwê-itasinahên.*

ahpô "aya" âh-itwêyani, êwako mîna nika-masinahên.
wâh-wanitonâmoyani, êwako mîna nika-masinahên.

'...; for I am going to write your words down. ..., I try to write them down very much as you are saying them. Every time you even say "ah", I will write that down, too. Every time you launch into a slip of the tongue, I will write that down, too.' (9-21, p. 352).

With this explanation, in a culturally appropriate form, of what she intends to do with the text being recorded, Freda Ahenakew's dialogue text provides another rare document of proper fieldwork practice.

Style

It is in the nature of an informal dialogue held in a familiar setting that the proportion of fragmentary sentences is exceptionally high. It is no more surprising that there are also frequent lapses into English, many of them accompanied by comments about the difficulty – typical of any bilingual context – of not slipping into the other language. Where the stylistic features of this dialogue text differ from those of formal literary texts, the discrepancy seems to reflect, above all, the subject matter and the social setting.

IN DISCUSSING TECHNIQUES for preparing meat, making clothes, or gathering and processing plant stuffs, all three speakers show an overwhelming preference for verb forms in which the person performing the action is left unspecified. Where technical prose in English is characterised by pronouns like *one* (or, less formally, *you*) and the massive use of the passive, Cree relies primarily on the INDEFINITE ACTOR form of the verb:

..., êkos ê-ati-nîmihitohk;
'..., so one went on to dance;' (9-3, p. 248);

âha; nisto-kîsikâw âskaw kî-nîmihitonâniwan kâ-wîkihtohk mîna.
'Yes; sometimes one also danced for three days when one got married.' (9-3, p. 248)

[with the two instances of 'one' not necessarily co-referential];

êkwa môy wîhkâc ohc-âsenikâtêw ayis.
'For then one never turned it down.' (9-3, p. 248);

êkos êkwa pâh-pitikonikâtêwa ê-pâsamihk anihi, ...
'In this way, then, they are made into patties and one dries these, ...' (9-14, p. 286).

These examples illustrate both the inflexional endings of the VAI and VTI conjunct paradigms, *-hk* and *-amihk*, and the suppletive forms of the independent order, which are derived by *-nâniwan-* and *-ikâtê-* and inflected as VII stems. (The paradigmatic status of these inflexional and derivational forms is outlined in Wolfart 1973 and reviewed most recently in Wolfart 1991 (and discussed further in N2:433, N3: 438–439); the competition between the ending *-amihk* and the *-ikâtê*-based conjunct forms of the VTI paradigm is explored, with copious examples from this dialogue text, by Wolvengrey 1991.)

With respect to the style of the dialogue text, these sentences also illustrate some of the choices which present themselves for the translation of such constructions into idiomatic English – for the literal translations above are merely the raw material for free translations employing various nominal, impersonal, and passive constructions:

'With that the dance began.'
'Yes; at a wedding, sometimes, the dancing also went on for three days.'
'And, of course, it was never turned down.'
'In this way, then, are they made into patties and dried, ...'

While cross-linguistic morpho-syntactic consistency will always remain an elusive goal, this text deserves close syntactic and semantic study for its wealth of agentless constructions, including many parallel clauses and remarkable shifts between patterns.

In Cree as in English, the use of agentless constructions is by no means restricted to technical prose (of which Rosa Longneck's account of soap-making is the prize example). It is the most common function of a non-transitive verb in the indefinite actor form to serve as the background clause to another with a definite agent, e.g.,

> *êkwa kâ-kisîpêkinikêhk, nikî-papâ-wîcihiwânân mâna.*
> 'Then, at laundry-time, we used to go along and be all about.' (9-1, p. 242).

But the dialogue also contains long stretches of agentless verb forms. In recalling the joys of Christmases past, for example, Alpha Lafond (in 9-3, following her account of travel via Prince Albert) begins with a series of three indefinite actor forms and then slips into two second-person forms reminiscent of the general *you* of English; following a rhetorical break and two first-person verbs, with the background again given in an indefinite actor form (and a parallel comment by F), A concludes this passage with a series of seven indefinite actor verbs.

ANOTHER OF THE DERIVATIONAL FORMS manifesting themselves at the margins of the inflexional paradigm (cf. Wolfart 1973:59*b*) seems unusually frequent in this text, although it would be premature to attribute this to the genre, whether technical or dialogue.

Many VAI stems give rise to derived VII stems in *-makan-* (before which the stem vowel is lengthened if not already long), e.g.,

> *ôh, kî-nîkânîmakan.*
> 'Oh, it used to take precedence.' (9-16, p. 388);

> *..., nanâtohk kîkway misiwanâcisîmakan, ...*
> '..., all kinds of things are ruined, ...' (9-24, p. 364).

Inanimate actor stems in *-makan-* are also derived from explicitly secondary stems in *-kê-*:

..., *wayawîtisahikêmakan anima kâ-kisisocik,* ...
'..., that drives it out when they have fever, ... (9-27, p. 374).

While the above pattern is unexceptional, the corresponding stems derived by means of a VAI suffix *-makisi-* are remarkable; e.g.,

wahwâ, iyikohk ê-wâpiskinikêmakisit ana kisîpêkinikan;
'Oh my, that soap made things so white;' (9-26, p. 372).

If these secondarily derived *-makisi-* stems serve to indicate a reduction in the power of human agency, such an hypothesis would hardly fit the next example or its context:

..., *mêkwâc ê-oskinîkiskwêmakisiyân.*
'..., while I was still a young woman.' (9-8, p. 310).

Instead, the *-makisi-* form may have to be interpreted as adding distance, as marking a more general state or quality.

TRANSLATION PROBLEMS may simply reflect a poor match between the structures of two languages, but they often have further implications.

Even an individual word of unambiguous reference may not permit direct translation. In discussing the preparation of rabbits (9-10), Rosa Longneck refers to their extremities as *ospiconisiwâwa*, literally 'their little arms,' while English usage requires this term to be translated as 'their little legs' (or, at most, 'fore-legs and hind-legs').

A more pervasive problem is the mismatch between the gender categories of Cree and English and the difficult choice of rendering pronominal reference to an animate noun as either 'she/he' or 'it'. This is relatively inconsequential – except in aesthetic terms – in the case of bears and other large animals who in many ways behave like humans and may, thus, be treated anthropomorphically; but even though it attempts to echo the animacy of Cree nouns and verbs, a phrase like 'and then I boiled him' remains awkward in English. In most cases, the problem can of course be side-stepped somehow, but rarely without a deplorable increase in blandness – if, for instance, 'him who' were replaced by 'that one' in

nipahi-wîhkitisiw an[a] 'âmisk' kâ-isiyîhkâsot.
'I simply love the taste of him who is called 'Beaver.'' (9-10, p. 322)

(and 'I simply love the taste of him' by 'that one tastes awfully good').

The cultural background is illuminated to a degree that can rarely be attained through elicitation when the referential ambiguity of a kin-term like *-câhkos-* NDA 'a woman's female cross-cousin; a woman's sister-in-law' is pragmatically resolved. In 9-7, where the applicability of this term is specifically discussed, ***nicâhkos*** is clearly affinal and translated as 'my sister-in law'; but when Alpha Lafond recalls the family circle of long ago (at the end of 9-1), she contrasts ***nicâhkosak*** 'my female cross-cousins' with ***nîc-âyisak*** 'my siblings-and-parallel-cousins' in a context which leaves no doubt that all the referents are children.

Finally, the informal (and occasionally macaronic) discourse of the dialogue text offers a wider range than most narratives of illustrations for another system of nomenclature which is as important culturally as it is linguistically: the several patterns of referring to deceased members of one's family. Although the unmarked kin-term may occur occasionally (even in this text), there is a clear preference for one of two special forms.

The *-pan-* suffix which animate nouns share with one of the verbal preterites (cf. Wolfart 1973:31*a*, 44*b*) occurs both in the kin-term ***nimosômipan*** 'my late grandfather' and in ***kisêyinîpanak*** 'old men no longer alive.' It is significantly less common, however, than the periphrastic construction built on a VAI verb of possession with the preverbs ***kâ*** and ***kî***: ***kâ-kî-omisiyân*** 'my late elder sister,' ***kâ-kî-otânisiyân*** 'my late daughter.' Literally, such a form might be paraphrased in English as 'the one whom I used to have as my elder sister,' with ***kî*** clearly indicating a state which does not continue into the present.

Where the underlying dependent stem begins in a vowel, the verb of possession is usually derived with *oy-* (homophonous with light reduplication) rather than *ot-*, e.g., ***kâ-kî-oyôhkomiyân*** 'my late grandmother'; but it also seems to occur, without the *oy-*, simply as *kâ-kî-ôhkomiyân*; (the speaker is F, in both cases).

The corresponding terms for one's parents are almost always built on the stems *-mâmâ-* and *-pâpâ-* (cf. N4:445): *kâ-kî-omâmâyân* 'my late mom', *kâ-kî-opâpâyan* 'your late dad'.

Deceased relatives are not normally mentioned by name but only by an appropriately marked kin-term; the Christian names which do occur may be given a prefix which is marked as such both syntactically and prosodically:

> …; Gabe *âw ê-kî-askôskâkot, anihi* deceased-Dorothy.
> ' …; Gabe here was followed by that late Dorothy.' (9-9, p. 316);
>
> *ôtê mân ê-kî-ohtinamân,* deceased-Françoise, *mihcêt kîkway ê-kî-kiskinohamawit.*
> 'I used to learn things from over there, from the late Françoise, she used to teach me many things.' (9-14, p. 334).

In the dialect of English here exemplified, the prefix *deceased-* is functionally equivalent in all respects to the Cree suffix *-pan-*.

Whether or not the use of English *deceased-* (and sometimes also *late-*) as a bound prefix may have been reinforced (or even triggered in its syntactic manifestation) by French usage, where the preposed variant remains uninflected in *feu sa mère, sa défunte mère*, etc., the pattern is strong enough to surface in the English of Cree speakers (and to carry over to printed lists of contributors in books published by the Saskatchewan Indian Cultural College).

Details aside, it is remarkable indeed how persistently the cultural pattern of speaking respectfully of the dead is matched by the linguistic device of affixation.

References

Ahenakew, Edward. 1973. *Voices of the Plains Cree*. Edited by Ruth M. Buck. Toronto: McClelland & Stewart.

Ahenakew, Freda. 1987. *Cree Language Structures: A Cree Approach*. Winnipeg: Pemmican Publications.

——. 1989. *kiskinahamawâkan-âcimowinisa / Student Stories*. Written by Cree-speaking Students; edited, translated, and with a glossary by Freda Ahenakew. Second edition. Algonquian and Iroquoian Linguistics, Memoir 2. Winnipeg / Saskatoon: Saskatchewan Indian Cultural Centre.

Ahenakew, Freda, & H.C. Wolfart. 1983. Productive Reduplication in Plains Cree. *Actes du Quatorzième Congrès des Algonquinistes [Québec, 1983]*, ed. William Cowan, 369–377. Ottawa: Carleton University.

——. 1987. The Story-tellers and their Stories. *wâskahikaniwiyiniw-âcimowina / Stories of the House People, Told by Peter Vandall and Joe Douquette*, ed. Freda Ahenakew, x–xiv. Winnipeg: University of Manitoba Press.

——. 1991. The Reality of Morpheme-boundary Rules. *Algonquian and Iroquoian Linguistics* 16:27–32.

Atimoyoo, Rose, et al. 1987. *A Preliminary Check-list of Plains Cree Medical Terms*. Edited by Freda Ahenakew. Saskatoon: Saskatchewan Indian Languages Institute.

Bear, Glecia / Nêhiyaw. 1991. *wanisinwak iskwêsisak: awâsisasinahikanis / Two Little Girls Lost in the Bush: A Cree Story for Children, Told by Glecia Bear*. Edited and translated by Freda Ahenakew & H.C. Wolfart, illustrated by Jerry Whitehead. Saskatoon: Fifth House Publishers.

Beardy, L. 1988. *pisiskiwak kâ-pîkiskwêcik / Talking Animals, Told by L. Beardy*. Edited and translated by H.C. Wolfart. Algonquian and Iroquoian Linguistics, Memoir 5. Winnipeg.

Blain, Eleanor M. 1989. *The Bungee Language of the Red River Settlement*. M.A. thesis, University of Manitoba, Winnipeg.

Faries, Richard, ed. 1938. *A Dictionary of the Cree Language, as spoken by the Indians in the Provinces of Quebec, Ontario, Manitoba, Saskatchewan and Alberta*. Revised by [...] Edward Ahenakew [...]. Toronto: Church of England in Canada.

Greensmith, Jennifer M. 1985. *Phonological Variants in Pukatawagan Woods Cree*. M.A. thesis, University of Manitoba, Winnipeg.

Hogman, Wesley L. 1981. Agreement for Animacy and Gender in the Buffalo Narrows Dialect of French/Cree. *MASA: Journal of the University of Manitoba Anthropology Students' Association* 7:81–94.

Leighton, Anna L. 1985. *Wild Plant Use by the Woods Cree (Nihîthawak) of East-Central Saskatchewan*. Canadian Ethnology Service Paper 101, National Museum of Man Mercury Series. Ottawa.

Mandelbaum, David G. 1940. *The Plains Cree*. Anthropological Papers of the American Museum of Natural History, vol. 37, pt. 2. New York.

Meyer, David. 1985. *The Red Earth Crees, 1860–1960*. Canadian Ethnology Service Paper 100, National Museum of Man Mercury Series. Ottawa.

Ogg, Arden C. 1991. *Connective Particles and Temporal Cohesion in Plains Cree Narrative*. M.A. thesis, University of Manitoba, Winnipeg.

Vandall, Peter, and Joe Douquette. 1987. *wâskahikaniwiyiniw-âcimowina / Stories of the House People, Told by Peter Vandall and Joe Douquette*. Edited, translated, and with a glossary by Freda Ahenakew. Publications of the Algonquian Text Society / Collection de la Société d'édition de textes algonquiens. Winnipeg: University of Manitoba Press.

Voorhis, Paul H. 1981. Varieties of Cree Speech in Manitoba. Linguistics Colloquium, University of Manitoba. [abstract in *Algonquian and Iroquoian Linguistics* 6:26]

Whitecalf, Sarah. 1993. *kinêhiyâwiwininaw nêhiyawêwin / The Cree Language Is Our Identity: The La Ronge Lectures of Sarah Whitecalf*. Edited and translated by H.C. Wolfart & Freda Ahenakew. Publications of the Algonquian Text Society / Collection de la Société d'édition de textes algonquiens. Winnipeg: University of Manitoba Press.

Wolfart, H.C. 1973. *Plains Cree: A Grammatical Study*. Transactions of the American Philosophical Society, new series, vol. 63, pt. 5. Philadelphia.

——. 1982. Historical Linguistics and Metaphilology. *Papers from the Fifth International Conference on Historical Linguistics* [*Galway, 1981*], ed. Anders Ahlqvist, 394–403. Amsterdam: John Benjamins.

——. 1988. Introduction. *pisiskiwak kâ-pîkiskwêcik / Talking Animals, Told by L. Beardy*, ed. & tr. H.C. Wolfart, vii–xxiii. Algonquian and Iroquoian Linguistics, Memoir 5. Winnipeg.

——. 1989. Cree Midwifery: Linguistic and Literary Observations. *Actes du Vingtième Congrès des Algonquinistes [Hull, Québec, 1988]*, ed. William Cowan, 326–342. Ottawa: Carleton University.
——. 1990*a*. The Supplement to Petitot's Dieu-Lunaire Text. *International Journal of American Linguistics* 56:580–586.
——. 1990*b*. 1001 Nights: The Orient and the Far Northwest. *Papers of the Twenty-first Algonquian Conference [St John's, 1989]*, ed. William Cowan, 370–395. Ottawa: Carleton University.
——. 1991. Passives with and without Agents. *Linguistic Studies Presented to John L. Finlay*, ed. H.C. Wolfart, 171–190. Algonquian and Iroquoian Linguistics, Memoir 8. Winnipeg.
Wolfart, H.C., & Freda Ahenakew. 1987*a*. Notes on the Orthography and the Glossary. *wâskahikaniwiyiniw-âcimowina / Stories of the House People, Told by Peter Vandall and Joe Douquette*, ed. Freda Ahenakew, 113–126. Winnipeg: University of Manitoba Press.
——. 1987*b*. Preparing a Medical Glossary. *Our Languages, Our Survival: Proceedings of the Seventh Native American Languages Issues Institute*, ed. Freda Ahenakew & Shirley Fredeen, 207–225. Saskatoon: Saskatchewan Indian Languages Institute.
Wolfart, H.C., & Janet F. Carroll. 1981. *Meet Cree: A Guide to the Cree Language*. Second edition. Edmonton: University of Alberta Press / Lincoln & London: University of Nebraska Press.
Wolvengrey, Arok. 1991. Paradigmatic Shift within the Plains Cree VTI Indefinite Actor. Paper presented to the Twenty-third Algonquian Conference, London, Ontario.

ABOUT THE SERIES

Our Own Words

University of Regina Press's book series, *Our Own Words*, publishes the personal stories of members from the Indigenous Nations of the Great Plains in their Indigenous language.

The books in the series provide longer, more extensive Indigenous texts for both the intermediate and advanced learners of the Indigenous language, and are presented, where appropriate, in Syllabics, Standard Roman Orthography, and English translation.

Series Editor

AROK WOLVENGREY

A linguist noted for his work with Indigenous Languages of the Americas, Arok Wolvengrey is a professor of Algonquian Languages and Linguistics in the Indigenous Languages Program at the First Nations University of Canada in Regina, Saskatchewan, located on Treaty 4 territory.

For more information about publishing in the series, please contact:

Karen May Clark, Senior Acquisitions Editor
University of Regina Press
3737 Wascana Parkway
Regina, Saskatchewan S4S 0A2 Canada
karen.clark@uregina.ca
www.uofrpress.ca